CORNERSTONE
BIBLICAL
COMMENTARY

1-2 Kings
William H. Barnes

GENERAL EDITOR
Philip W. Comfort

featuring the text of the
NEW LIVING TRANSLATION

TYNDALE HOUSE PUBLISHERS, INC. CAROL STREAM, ILLINOIS

Cornerstone Biblical Commentary, Volume 4b

Visit Tyndale online at www.tyndale.com.

1–2 Kings copyright © 2012 by William H. Barnes. All rights reserved.

Designed by Luke Daab and Timothy R. Botts.

Library of Congress Cataloging-in-Publication Data

Cornerstone biblical commentary.
   p. cm.
  Includes bibliographical references and index.
  ISBN 978-1-4143-2206-3 (hc : alk. paper)
    1. Bible—Commentaries. I. Barnes, William H.
BS491.3.C67 2006
220.7´7—dc22   2005026928

Printed in the United States of America

18 17 16 15 14 13 12
7   6   5   4   3   2   1

CONTENTS

VOLUME 4b:1–2 Kings

William H. Barnes

BA, University of Wisconsin–Milwaukee;
MA, Trinity Evangelical Divinity School;
ThD, Harvard Divinity School.

GENERAL EDITOR'S PREFACE

The *Cornerstone Biblical Commentary* is based on the second edition of the New Living Translation (2013). Nearly 100 scholars from various church backgrounds and from several countries (United States, Canada, England, and Australia) participated in the creation of the NLT. Many of these same scholars are contributors to this commentary series. All the commentators, whether participants in the NLT or not, believe that the Bible is God's inspired word and have a desire to make God's word clear and accessible to his people.

This Bible commentary is the natural extension of our vision for the New Living Translation, which we believe is both exegetically accurate and idiomatically powerful. The NLT attempts to communicate God's inspired word in a lucid English translation of the original languages so that English readers can understand and appreciate the thought of the original writers. In the same way, the *Cornerstone Biblical Commentary* aims at helping teachers, pastors, students, and laypeople understand every thought contained in the Bible. As such, the commentary focuses first on the words of Scripture, then on the theological truths of Scripture—inasmuch as the words express the truths.

The commentary itself has been structured in such a way as to help readers get at the meaning of Scripture, passage by passage, through the entire Bible. Each Bible book is prefaced by a substantial book introduction that gives general historical background important for understanding. Then the reader is taken through the Bible text, passage by passage, starting with the New Living Translation text printed in full. This is followed by a section called "Notes," wherein the commentator helps the reader understand the Hebrew or Greek behind the English of the NLT, interacts with other scholars on important interpretive issues, and points the reader to significant textual and contextual matters. The "Notes" are followed by the "Commentary," wherein each scholar presents a lucid interpretation of the passage, giving special attention to context and major theological themes.

The commentators represent a wide spectrum of theological positions within the evangelical community. We believe this is good because it reflects the rich variety in Christ's church. All the commentators uphold the authority of God's word and believe it is essential to heed the old adage: "Wholly apply yourself to the Scriptures and apply them wholly to you." May this commentary help you know the truths of Scripture, and may this knowledge help you "grow in your knowledge of God and Jesus our Lord" (2 Pet 1:2, NLT).

PHILIP W. COMFORT
GENERAL EDITOR

ABBREVIATIONS

GENERAL ABBREVIATIONS

b.	Babylonian Gemara	ibid.	*ibidem,* in the same	OL	Old Latin
bar.	baraita		place	OS	Old Syriac
c.	*circa,* around,	i.e.	*id est,* that is	OT	Old Testament
	approximately	in loc.	*in loco,* in the place	p., pp.	page, pages
cf.	*confer,* compare		cited	pl.	plural
ch, chs	chapter, chapters	lit.	literally	Q	Quelle ("Sayings"
contra	in contrast to	LXX	Septuagint		as Gospel source)
DSS	Dead Sea Scrolls	M	Majority Text	rev.	revision
ed.	edition, editor	*m.*	Mishnah	sg.	singular
e.g.	*exempli gratia,* for	masc.	masculine	sv.	*sub verbo,* under
	example	mg	margin		the word
et al.	*et alii,* and others	ms	manuscript	*t.*	Tosefta
fem.	feminine	mss	manuscripts	TR	Textus Receptus
ff	following (verses,	MT	Masoretic Text	v., vv.	verse, verses
	pages)	n.d.	no date	vid.	*videtur,* it seems
fl.	flourished	neut.	neuter	viz.	*videlicet,* namely
Gr.	Greek	no.	number	vol.	volume
Heb.	Hebrew	NT	New Testament	*y.*	Jerusalem Gemara

ABBREVIATIONS FOR BIBLE TRANSLATIONS

ASV	American Standard	NAB	New American Bible	NKJV	New King James
	Version	NASB	New American		Version
CEV	Contemporary		Standard Bible	NRSV	New Revised
	English Version	NCV	New Century Version		Standard Version
ESV	English Standard	NEB	New English Bible	NLT	New Living
	Version	NET	The NET Bible		Translation
GW	God's Word	NIV	New International	REB	Revised English
HCSB	Holman Christian		Version (1984)		Bible
	Standard Bible	NIrV	New International	RSV	Revised Standard
JB	Jerusalem Bible		Reader's Version		Version
JPS	Jewish Publication	NJB	New Jerusalem Bible	TEV	Today's English
	Society Translation	NJPS	The New Jewish		Version
	(*Tanakh*)		Publication Society	TLB	The Living Bible
KJV	King James Version		Translation (*Tanakh*)		

ABBREVIATIONS FOR DICTIONARIES, LEXICONS, COLLECTIONS OF TEXTS, ORIGINAL LANGUAGE EDITIONS

ABD *Anchor Bible Dictionary* (6 vols., Freedman) [1992]

ANEP *The Ancient Near East in Pictures* (Pritchard) [1965]

ANET *Ancient Near Eastern Texts Relating to the Old Testament* (Pritchard) [1969]

BAGD *Greek-English Lexicon of the New Testament and Other Early Christian Literature,* 2nd ed. (Bauer, Arndt, Gingrich, Danker) [1979]

BDAG *Greek-English Lexicon of the New Testament and Other Early Christian Literature,* 3rd ed. (Bauer, Danker, Arndt, Gingrich) [2000]

BDB *A Hebrew and English Lexicon of the Old Testament* (Brown, Driver, Briggs) [1907]

BDF *A Greek Grammar of the New Testament and Other Early Christian Literature* (Blass, Debrunner, Funk) [1961]

BHS *Biblia Hebraica Stuttgartensia* (Elliger and Rudolph) [1983]

CAD *Assyrian Dictionary of the Oriental Institute of the University of Chicago* [1956]

COS *The Context of Scripture* (3 vols., Hallo and Younger) [1997–2002]

DBI *Dictionary of Biblical Imagery* (Ryken, Wilhoit, Longman) [1998]

DBT *Dictionary of Biblical Theology* (2nd ed., Leon-Dufour) [1972]

DCH *Dictionary of Classical Hebrew* (7 vols., D. Clines) [2000]

DLNTD *Dictionary of the Later New Testament and Its Development* (R. Martin, P. Davids) [1997]

DJD *Discoveries in the Judean Desert* [1955–]

DJG *Dictionary of Jesus and the Gospels* (Green, McKnight, Marshall) [1992]

DOTP *Dictionary of the Old Testament: Pentateuch* (T. Alexander, D.W. Baker) [2003]

DPL *Dictionary of Paul and His Letters* (Hawthorne, Martin, Reid) [1993]

DTIB *Dictionary for Theological Interpretation of the Bible* (Vanhoozer) [2005]

EDNT *Exegetical Dictionary of the New Testament* (3 vols., H. Balz, G. Schneider. ET) [1990–1993]

GKC *Gesenius' Hebrew Grammar* (Gesenius, Kautzsch, trans. Cowley) [1910]

HALOT *The Hebrew and Aramaic Lexicon of the Old Testament* (L. Koehler, W. Baumgartner, J. Stamm; trans. M. Richardson) [1994–1999]

IBD *Illustrated Bible Dictionary* (3 vols., Douglas, Wiseman) [1980]

IDB *The Interpreter's Dictionary of the Bible* (4 vols., Buttrick) [1962]

ISBE *International Standard Bible Encyclopedia* (4 vols., Bromiley) [1979–1988]

KBL *Lexicon in Veteris Testamenti libros* (Koehler, Baumgartner) [1958]

LCL Loeb Classical Library

L&N *Greek-English Lexicon of the New Testament: Based on Semantic Domains* (Louw and Nida) [1989]

LSJ *A Greek-English Lexicon* (9th ed., Liddell, Scott, Jones) [1996]

MM *The Vocabulary of the Greek New Testament* (Moulton and Milligan) [1930; 1997]

NA[26] *Novum Testamentum Graece* (26th ed., Nestle-Aland) [1979]

NA[27] *Novum Testamentum Graece* (27th ed., Nestle-Aland) [1993]

NBD *New Bible Dictionary* (2nd ed., Douglas, Hillyer) [1982]

NIDB *New International Dictionary of the Bible* (Douglas, Tenney) [1987]

NIDBA *New International Dictionary of Biblical Archaeology* (Blaiklock and Harrison) [1983]

NIDNTT *New International Dictionary of New Testament Theology* (4 vols., C. Brown) [1975–1985]

NIDOTTE *New International Dictionary of Old Testament Theology and Exegesis* (5 vols., W. A. VanGemeren) [1997]

PG *Patrologia Graecae* (J. P. Migne) [1857–1886]

PGM *Papyri graecae magicae: Die griechischen Zauberpapyri.* (Preisendanz) [1928]

TBD *Tyndale Bible Dictionary* (Elwell, Comfort) [2001]

TDNT *Theological Dictionary of the New Testament* (10 vols., Kittel, Friedrich; trans. Bromiley) [1964–1976]

TDOT *Theological Dictionary of the Old Testament* (15 vols., Botterweck, Ringgren; trans. Willis, Bromiley, Green) [1974–]

TLNT *Theological Lexicon of the New Testament* (3 vols., C. Spicq) [1994]

TLOT *Theological Lexicon of the Old Testament* (3 vols., E. Jenni) [1997]

TWOT *Theological Wordbook of the Old Testament* (2 vols., Harris, Archer) [1980]

UBS[3] *United Bible Societies' Greek New Testament* (3rd ed., Metzger et al.) [1975]

UBS[4] *United Bible Societies' Greek New Testament* (4th corrected ed., Metzger et al.) [1993]

WH *The New Testament in the Original Greek* (Westcott and Hort) [1882]

ABBREVIATIONS FOR BOOKS OF THE BIBLE

Old Testament

Gen	Genesis	Deut	Deuteronomy	1 Sam	1 Samuel
Exod	Exodus	Josh	Joshua	2 Sam	2 Samuel
Lev	Leviticus	Judg	Judges	1 Kgs	1 Kings
Num	Numbers	Ruth	Ruth	2 Kgs	2 Kings

1 Chr	1 Chronicles	Song	Song of Songs	Obad	Obadiah
2 Chr	2 Chronicles	Isa	Isaiah	Jonah	Jonah
Ezra	Ezra	Jer	Jeremiah	Mic	Micah
Neh	Nehemiah	Lam	Lamentations	Nah	Nahum
Esth	Esther	Ezek	Ezekiel	Hab	Habakkuk
Job	Job	Dan	Daniel	Zeph	Zephaniah
Ps, Pss	Psalm, Psalms	Hos	Hosea	Hag	Haggai
Prov	Proverbs	Joel	Joel	Zech	Zechariah
Eccl	Ecclesiastes	Amos	Amos	Mal	Malachi

New Testament

Matt	Matthew	Eph	Ephesians	Heb	Hebrews
Mark	Mark	Phil	Philippians	Jas	James
Luke	Luke	Col	Colossians	1 Pet	1 Peter
John	John	1 Thess	1 Thessalonians	2 Pet	2 Peter
Acts	Acts	2 Thess	2 Thessalonians	1 John	1 John
Rom	Romans	1 Tim	1 Timothy	2 John	2 John
1 Cor	1 Corinthians	2 Tim	2 Timothy	3 John	3 John
2 Cor	2 Corinthians	Titus	Titus	Jude	Jude
Gal	Galatians	Phlm	Philemon	Rev	Revelation

Deuterocanonical

Bar	Baruch	1–2 Esdr	1–2 Esdras	Ps 151	Psalm 151
Add Dan	Additions to Daniel	Add Esth	Additions to Esther	Sir	Sirach
Pr Azar	Prayer of Azariah	Ep Jer	Epistle of Jeremiah	Tob	Tobit
Bel	Bel and the Dragon	Jdt	Judith	Wis	Wisdom of Solomon
Sg Three	Song of the Three Children	1–2 Macc	1–2 Maccabees		
		3–4 Macc	3–4 Maccabees		
Sus	Susanna	Pr Man	Prayer of Manasseh		

MANUSCRIPTS AND LITERATURE FROM QUMRAN

Initial numerals followed by "Q" indicate particular caves at Qumran. For example, the notation 4Q267 indicates text 267 from cave 4 at Qumran. Further, 1QS 4:9-10 indicates column 4, lines 9-10 of the *Rule of the Community*; and 4Q166 1 ii 2 indicates fragment 1, column ii, line 2 of text 166 from cave 4. More examples of common abbreviations are listed below.

CD	Cairo Geniza copy of the *Damascus Document*	1QIsa[b]	Isaiah copy [b]	4QLam[?]	Lamentations
		1QM	*War Scroll*	11QPs[a]	Psalms
1QH	*Thanksgiving Hymns*	1QpHab	*Pesher Habakkuk*	11QTemple[a,b]	*Temple Scroll*
1QIsa[a]	Isaiah copy [a]	1QS	*Rule of the Community*	11QtgJob	*Targum of Job*

IMPORTANT NEW TESTAMENT MANUSCRIPTS

(all dates given are AD; ordinal numbers refer to centuries)

Significant Papyri (𝔓 = Papyrus)

𝔓1 Matt 1; early 3rd
𝔓4+𝔓64+𝔓67 Matt 3, 5, 26; Luke 1–6; late 2nd
𝔓5 John 1, 16, 20; early 3rd
𝔓13 Heb 2–5, 10–12; early 3rd
𝔓15+𝔓16 (probably part of same codex) 1 Cor 7–8, Phil 3–4; late 3rd
𝔓20 Jas 2–3; 3rd
𝔓22 John 15–16; mid 3rd
𝔓23 Jas 1; c. 200
𝔓27 Rom 8–9; 3rd
𝔓30 1 Thess 4–5; 2 Thess 1; early 3rd
𝔓32 Titus 1–2; late 2nd
𝔓37 Matt 26; late 3rd
𝔓39 John 8; first half of 3rd
𝔓40 Rom 1–4, 6, 9; 3rd

𝔓45 Gospels and Acts; early 3rd
𝔓46 Paul's Major Epistles (less Pastorals); late 2nd
𝔓47 Rev 9–17; 3rd
𝔓49+𝔓65 Eph 4–5; 1 Thess 1–2; 3rd
𝔓52 John 18; c. 125
𝔓53 Matt 26, Acts 9–10; middle 3rd

𝔓66 John; late 2nd
𝔓70 Matt 2–3, 11–12, 24; 3rd
𝔓72 1–2 Peter, Jude; c. 300
𝔓74 Acts, General Epistles; 7th
𝔓75 Luke and John; c. 200
𝔓77+𝔓103 (probably part of same codex) Matt 13–14, 23; late 2nd
𝔓87 Philemon; late 2nd

𝔓90 John 18–19; late 2nd
𝔓91 Acts 2–3; 3rd
𝔓92 Eph 1, 2 Thess 1; c. 300
𝔓98 Rev 1:13-20; late 2nd
𝔓100 Jas 3–5; c. 300
𝔓101 Matt 3–4; 3rd
𝔓104 Matt 21; 2nd
𝔓106 John 1; 3rd
𝔓115 Rev 2–3, 5–6, 8–15; 3rd

Significant Uncials

א (Sinaiticus) most of NT; 4th
A (Alexandrinus) most of NT; 5th
B (Vaticanus) most of NT; 4th
C (Ephraemi Rescriptus) most of NT with many lacunae; 5th
D (Bezae) Gospels, Acts; 5th
D (Claromontanus), Paul's Epistles; 6th (different MS than Bezae)
E (Laudianus 35) Acts; 6th
F (Augensis) Paul's Epistles; 9th
G (Boernerianus) Paul's Epistles; 9th

H (Coislinianus) Paul's Epistles; 6th
I (Freerianus or Washington) Paul's Epistles; 5th
L (Regius) Gospels; 8th
P (Porphyrianus) Acts—Revelation; 9th
Q (Guelferbytanus B) Luke, John; 5th
T (Borgianus) Luke, John; 5th
W (Washingtonianus or the Freer Gospels) Gospels; 5th
Z (Dublinensis) Matthew; 6th
037 (Δ; Sangallensis) Gospels; 9th

038 (Θ; Koridethi) Gospels; 9th
040 (Ξ; Zacynthius) Luke; 6th
043 (Φ; Beratinus) Matthew, Mark; 6th
044 (Ψ; Athous Laurae) Gospels, Acts, Paul's Epistles; 9th
048 Acts, Paul's Epistles, General Epistles; 5th
0171 Matt 10, Luke 22; c. 300
0189 Acts 5; c. 200

Significant Minuscules

1 Gospels, Acts, Paul's Epistles; 12th
33 All NT except Rev; 9th
81 Acts, Paul's Epistles, General Epistles; 1044
565 Gospels; 9th
700 Gospels; 11th

1424 (or Family 1424—a group of 29 manuscripts sharing nearly the same text) most of NT; 9th-10th
1739 Acts, Paul's Epistles; 10th
2053 Rev; 13th
2344 Rev; 11th

f¹ (a family of manuscripts including 1, 118, 131, 209) Gospels; 12th-14th
f¹³ (a family of manuscripts including 13, 69, 124, 174, 230, 346, 543, 788, 826, 828, 983, 1689, 1709—known as the Ferrar group) Gospels; 11th-15th

Significant Ancient Versions

SYRIAC (SYR)
syrᶜ (Syriac Curetonian) Gospels; 5th
syrˢ (Syriac Sinaiticus) Gospels; 4th
syrʰ (Syriac Harklensis) Entire NT; 616

OLD LATIN (IT)
itᵃ (Vercellenis) Gospels; 4th
itᵇ (Veronensis) Gospels; 5th
itᵈ (Cantabrigiensis—the Latin text of Bezae) Gospels, Acts, 3 John; 5th
itᵉ (Palantinus) Gospels; 5th
itᵏ (Bobiensis) Matthew, Mark; c. 400

COPTIC (COP)
copᵇᵒ (Boharic—north Egypt)
copᶠᵃʸ (Fayyumic—central Egypt)
copˢᵃ (Sahidic—southern Egypt)

OTHER VERSIONS
arm (Armenian)
eth (Ethiopic)
geo (Georgian)

TRANSLITERATION AND NUMBERING SYSTEM

Note: For words and roots from nonbiblical languages (e.g., Arabic, Ugaritic), only approximate transliterations are given.

HEBREW/ARAMAIC

Consonants

א	aleph	= '	מ, ם	mem	= m
בּ, ב	beth	= b	נ, ן	nun	= n
גּ, ג	gimel	= g	ס	samekh	= s
דּ, ד	daleth	= d	ע	ayin	= '
ה	he	= h	פּ, פ, ף	pe	= p
ו	waw	= w	צ, ץ	tsadhe	= ts
ז	zayin	= z	ק	qoph	= q
ח	heth	= kh	ר	resh	= r
ט	teth	= t	שׁ	shin	= sh
י	yodh	= y	שׂ	sin	= s
כּ, כ, ך	kaph	= k	תּ, ת	taw	= t, th (spirant)
ל	lamedh	= l			

Vowels

ַ	patakh	= a		qamets khatuf	= o
֡	furtive patakh	= a		holem	= o
ָ	qamets	= a	וֹ	full holem	= o
ָה	final qamets he	= ah		short qibbuts	= u
ֶ	segol	= e		long qibbuts	= u
ֵ	tsere	= e	וּ	shureq	= u
ֵי	tsere yod	= e		khatef patakh	= a
ִ	short hireq	= i		khatef qamets	= o
ִ	long hireq	= i		vocalic shewa	= e
ִי	hireq yod	= i	ִי	patakh yodh	= a

GREEK

α	alpha	= a	ι	iota	= i
β	beta	= b	κ	kappa	= k
γ	gamma	= g, n (before γ, κ, ξ, χ)	λ	lamda	= l
			μ	mu	= m
δ	delta	= d	ν	nu	= n
ε	epsilon	= e	ξ	ksi	= x
ζ	zeta	= z	ο	omicron	= o
η	eta	= ē	π	pi	= p
θ	theta	= th	ρ	rho	= r (ῥ = rh)

σ, ς	sigma	= s	ψ	psi	= ps
τ	tau	= t	ω	omega	= ō
υ	upsilon	= u	ʽ	rough	= h (with
φ	phi	= ph		breathing	vowel or
χ	chi	= ch		mark	diphthong)

THE TYNDALE-STRONG'S NUMBERING SYSTEM

The Cornerstone Biblical Commentary series uses a word-study numbering system to give both newer and more advanced Bible students alike quicker, more convenient access to helpful original-language tools (e.g., concordances, lexicons, and theological dictionaries). Those who are unfamiliar with the ancient Hebrew, Aramaic, and Greek alphabets can quickly find information on a given word by looking up the appropriate index number. Advanced students will find the system helpful because it allows them to quickly find the lexical form of obscure conjugations and inflections.

There are two main numbering systems used for biblical words today. The one familiar to most people is the Strong's numbering system (made popular by the *Strong's Exhaustive Concordance to the Bible*). Although the original Strong's system is still quite useful, the most up-to-date research has shed new light on the biblical languages and allows for more precision than is found in the original Strong's system. The Cornerstone Biblical Commentary series, therefore, features a newly revised version of the Strong's system, the Tyndale-Strong's numbering system. The Tyndale-Strong's system brings together the familiarity of the Strong's system and the best of modern scholarship. In most cases, the original Strong's numbers are preserved. In places where new research dictates, new or related numbers have been added.[1]

The second major numbering system today is the Goodrick-Kohlenberger system used in a number of study tools published by Zondervan. In order to give students broad access to a number of helpful tools, the Commentary provides index numbers for the Zondervan system as well.

The different index systems are designated as follows:

TG	Tyndale-Strong's Greek number	ZH	Zondervan Hebrew number
ZG	Zondervan Greek number	TA/ZA	Tyndale/Zondervan Aramaic number
TH	Tyndale-Strong's Hebrew number	S	Strong's Aramaic number

So in the example, "love" *agapē* [TG26, ZG27], the first number is the one to use with Greek tools keyed to the Tyndale-Strong's system, and the second applies to tools that use the Zondervan system.

The indexing of Aramaic terms differs slightly from that of Greek and Hebrew. Strong's original system mixed the Aramaic terms in with the Hebrew, but the Tyndale-Strong's system indexes Aramaic with a new set of numbers starting at 10,000. Since Tyndale's system for Aramaic diverges completely from original Strong's, the original Strong's number is listed separately so that those using tools keyed to Strong's can locate the information. This number is designated with an S, as in the example, "son" *bar* [TA/ZA10120, S1247].

1. Generally, one may simply use the original four-digit Strong's number to identify words in tools using Strong's system. If a Tyndale-Strong's number is followed by a capital letter (e.g., TG1692A), it generally indicates an added subdivision of meaning for the given term. Whenever a Tyndale-Strong's number has a number following a decimal point (e.g., TG2013.1), it reflects an instance where new research has yielded a separate, new classification of use for a biblical word. Forthcoming tools from Tyndale House Publishers will include these entries, which were not part of the original Strong's system.

1–2 Kings

WILLIAM H. BARNES

INTRODUCTION TO
1–2 Kings

"IN THOSE DAYS Israel had no king; all the people did whatever seemed right in their own eyes." This is what the last verse in the book of Judges tells us (Judg 21:25; cf. Judg 17:6). In what is usually considered to be the second appendix to that book (the two appendices are usually delineated as Judg 17–18, 19–21), Judges gives us some grotesque examples of such lawlessness—idolatry, kidnapping, rape and dismemberment, tribal warfare—unforgettably reminding us of how horrible things were before the institution of the monarchy was established in the land of Israel. No question about it, times were terrible before there were kings in the land, but when we turn to the books of 1–2 Kings, we soon learn that times were often terrible when there *were* kings in the land, too. For that is what the books of Kings are about—kings. Some 19 of them in the northern kingdom of Israel after the division of the united monarchy following the death of Solomon (see 1 Kgs 12), and some 19 of them after Solomon (plus Queen Athaliah) in the southern kingdom of Judah. Kings—good, bad, and ugly; we are sometimes spared some of the details, but we are rarely spared honest, harsh, even brutal theological evaluations. Fifteen of the northern kings explicitly "did what was evil in the LORD's sight,"[1] as did eight or nine of the southerners.[2] Indeed, it was the sins of the people, including the sins of the kings, which eventually led to the exile of the northern kingdom in 722 BC (see the lengthy editorial in 2 Kgs 17:5-23 concerning this subject), as well as the later exile of the southern kingdom in 586 BC (see 2 Kgs 24:20; 25:21). In essence, even when there were kings in the land, they and the people *still* "did whatever seemed right in their own eyes."[3]

The books of Kings are about prophets, as well. In fact, in the Hebrew tradition, the books of 1–2 Kings (reckoned as one book in the Hebrew Bible) are labeled "Former Prophets" (as are the books of Joshua, Judges, and 1–2 Samuel). The interplay of prophet against prophet, and especially prophet against king, is a major feature of the books of Kings. (For example, 2 Kgs 24:2 tells us that Yahweh[4] "sent bands of Babylonian, Aramean, Moabite, and Ammonite raiders against Judah to destroy it, just as [Yahweh] had promised through his prophets.") Among them were the major, writing prophets Isaiah and Jeremiah, and indeed, significant sections of 2 Kings are found in Isaiah 36–39 and in Jeremiah 39 and 52. The prophet Ezekiel should probably be added as well. Among the minor prophets, Hosea, Amos, Micah, and Zephaniah also come to mind. And who can forget the earlier northern prophets Elijah and Elisha? Major portions of 1–2 Kings are dedicated to their unforgettable exploits; indeed this is the only place where their narratives are to be found in the entire Old Testament.[5]

Priests and Levites are also found in 1–2 Kings, although references to these cultic officials[6] are relatively sparse. For example, in sharp contrast to their prominent status in 1–2 Chronicles, we find only two specific references to the Levites throughout the entirety of 1–2 Kings.[7] Individual priests of note include the rivals Abiathar and Zadok in the days of David and Solomon (1 Kgs 1–2), Jehoiada in the days of Joash (2 Kgs 11-12), Uriah in the days of Ahaz (2 Kgs 16), and Hilkiah in the days of Josiah (2 Kgs 22–23). The only other priests mentioned by name in 1–2 Kings are Seraiah and Zephaniah (2 Kgs 25:18), prisoners of the Babylonians during the fall of Jerusalem. (Nevertheless, as will be noted at length in the commentary proper, there is intermittent but significant focus on the Temple, its personnel, and its furnishings found throughout 1–2 Kings.)

But the books of Kings are, in the end, mostly about kings—their many failings, their occasional successes, and the eventual, seemingly inevitable demise of their dynasties. These books, like the book of Judges, end on a dismal note, with the fall of the city of Jerusalem and the destruction of Solomon's Temple ringing in the ears of the hearer. (I mention "hearer" because all ancient books were read aloud, even when the reader was alone.) Yet, in contrast to Judges, the book of 2 Kings concludes with a "note of modest hope" in 2 Kings 25:27-30 (see Barnes 1991:146-149). The exiled King Jehoiachin, in his 37th year of exile (he had been on the throne of Judah only three months before being deposed and exiled by Nebuchadnezzar), was released from prison and given "a higher place than all the other exiled kings in Babylon." He dined in the presence of the Babylonian king "for the rest of his life." Hardly a testimony of ringing triumph, but a testimony of modest hope. Contrary to the era of the judges (and the book of Judges), the era of the kings (and the books of Kings) ended on an optimistic note. Yes, the Davidic hope was still alive. Descendants of that line would still exist and still make a difference. And for the Christian believer, who follows Jesus the Christ, "son of David, king of the Jews," this makes *all* the difference in the world.

AUTHOR

As is the case with many of the books of the Old Testament, the author (or authors) of the books of 1–2 Kings is unknown (hereafter, the term "author" or "editor," used in the singular, can be construed to be in the plural as well, when appropriate). The title "Kings" (Heb., *melakim* [TH4428, ZH4889]) clearly has to do with the contents of Kings, not with the identity of the author. (This is also the case, for example, with 1–2 Samuel, in which Samuel the prophet himself is last mentioned in 1 Sam 28, when he is already dead and called up from the grave!) The anonymity of these biblical writers, however, is not necessarily typical of historical works elsewhere in the ancient world: The authors of classical works of history are sometimes quite well known. Two examples that immediately come to mind are Herodotus and Josephus, both unmistakable in identity even though they both heavily redacted earlier oral and written traditions. Regarding the books of Kings, evangelical scholars tend to speak of anonymous compilations of sources (Harrison 1969:723), and nonevangelical scholars usually resort to so-called Deuteronomists compiling earlier written and oral traditions before and during the Judahite exile in the mid-sixth century BC (ABD 2.160-167).[8] (The Deuteronomists are thought to have shaped Joshua—Kings, which constitute the "Deuteronomistic History"; see the judicious comments of Howard [1993:179-182], an evangelical scholar, about this.) The Talmud (*b. Bava Batra*, 15a), however, was not so circumspect concerning the identity of the author of Kings, maintaining that it was the prophet Jeremiah who wrote the book that bears his name, the book of Kings (our 1–2 Kings), and the book of Lamentations. There is, I would submit, much wisdom in this suggestion, as we soon will see.

In general, specific authorship of lengthy and heavily edited Old Testament books often remains problematic. Whether it be the Pentateuch or the canonical book of Isaiah, scholarship often differs on putative authorship, although such differences often hearken back more to prior theological assumptions or biases than to the actual historical data. In the case of the Pentateuch (the "Books of Moses"), for example, it is still hotly debated whether Moses is in some sense the "author" of each of these five books. In my own view, for example, the actual language of the present book of Deuteronomy seems more comfortably placed in the monarchic period of Israel rather than in the time of Moses, but the theology and authority of the book is unquestionably Mosaic. Why else, after all, would it have been accepted as Scripture? In any case, Moses remains the clear focus of the entire book, and his unique authority (the greatest of the prophets, whom Yahweh knew "face to face," as Deut 34:10 affirms) pervades the text from beginning to end. To a major degree this can also be said of Joshua in the book of Joshua, and to a lesser degree of Samuel in 1–2 Samuel. But this is certainly *not* the case for the books of Kings. The focus is not on the author(s) but on the kings themselves; and as I will develop below, focus should be seen as being placed on *all* the kings of *both* kingdoms of the divided monarchy of Israel. But kings did not write the books of Kings.

Friedman (1997:146-149) suggests that Baruch son of Neriah (the famous scribe of Jeremiah) was the author of Kings (and indeed author/editor of the Deuteronomistic History in general). He accepts the suggestion of Frank Moore Cross Jr. that there were two editions of Kings (see below), and that the second, exilic edition was a lightly retouched reworking of the earlier, Josianic edition. So Friedman naturally would posit that there probably was one and the same author for both editions, and Baruch could well have been that author. I confess that I myself am attracted to this position.

Baruch lived in the mid- to late seventh century BC, and he survived up to and beyond the Judahite exile in the early sixth century, after the fall of Jerusalem to the Babylonians in 586 BC (Barnes 1991:158). Walter Brueggemann has identified a "Baruch Document" comprising chapters 36–45 of the present book of Jeremiah (1998:413-414), and Baruch's influence on the Jeremiah traditions can be felt throughout Jeremiah. Baruch's existence is not in dispute, for two bullae (clay seal impressions) have been found in excavations in Israel (see Friedman 1997:147-149, especially the photograph on p. 148; cf. Lundbom 1999:876-877). The fact that the final chapter of 2 Kings finds an almost exactly parallel text in Jeremiah 52 only strengthens the case. (Of course, many would use this very fact to diminish the likelihood of Jeremiah or Baruch being the writer of the text, since both presumably ended up in exile in Egypt, and the writer of 2 Kgs 25, or at least the last part of this chapter, presumably ended up in exile in Babylon.)[9] The fact that Jeremiah himself was quite clearly estranged from the later Judahite kings also appears problematic, but Jeremiah's seeming estrangement worked both ways—he clearly and repeatedly denounced the actions of both Jehoiakim (Jer 22:13-23; cf. Jer 26) and Zedekiah (Jer 34; cf. Jer 37-38), but on the other hand, he was obviously on speaking terms with at least Zedekiah (Jer 37:3-10; 38:14-28; cf. Leuchter 2006:172). And where Jeremiah was, presumably so was Baruch.

In the final analysis, the wisest course at present (and the tendency in both evangelical and nonevangelical scholarship) is to counsel hesitation in identifying the author of 1–2 Kings. But I suspect there is more evidence for Baruch as author (or at least significant editor) of much of 1–2 Kings than present scholars tend to acknowledge.[10] Yet, ultimately, the issue of authorship is secondary. The focus of any sympathetic reader of 1–2 Kings must be on its theology—what its retelling of the monarchical villains and heroes of the Old Testament faith conveyed to its original readers, and what it means for people of faith today.

DATE AND OCCASION OF WRITING

On the one hand, the related issues of date and occasion are easier subjects to address than that of authorship, since we are told the precise date of the last event described in the books (the releasing of the long-exiled Jehoiachin from prison in 561 BC), and we hear *nothing* about the next major event in Judahite history—Cyrus's arrival on the world scene some 22 years later. Arguments from silence (that is, arguments supported by what is *not* found in a text) are usually quite weak, but I submit that we find here a clear exception—for the stark absence of reference to Cyrus's takeover of Babylon (539 BC) or to his edict for the exiled Jews to return to their homeland and rebuild the Temple stands in sharp contrast to both 2 Chronicles 36:22-23 and Ezra 1, which deal with the same general time period. So we are left with a remarkably small chronological window to date the final editing of 1–2 Kings (between 561 and 539 BC) with the likelihood of an earlier rather than a later date in this period. (The book of Lamentations, filled with "lament poetry" from an eyewitness of the destruction of the first Temple, would also date roughly to this period of time.)

However, the issue of the *unity* of these books of Kings is much more convoluted, as we will see below. In the strict sense, the "occasion" of the writing of Kings should probably be considered the "occasions" for its several layers of editing. But the *final* editing, or if you wish, its *canonical* editing, is relatively straightforward and will be addressed presently.

The books of Kings are again just that, books about kings. More specifically, they are about the kings who reigned between David (around 1000 BC) and the Judahite exile (586 BC)—and that means all of them, the good, the bad, and the ugly. The format of the books is relentlessly chronological, with brief (or not so brief) accession notices, theological evaluations, representative stories or summaries of events, occasional references to written sources containing more information for the motivated reader, and finally, burial notices for each and every king. Also, and most importantly, *all* the kings from *both* the northern and the southern kingdoms are included. This is a feature notably absent in the otherwise largely parallel accounts found in 1–2 Chronicles, whose focus and concern largely rest upon the southern Davidic dynasty.

First Kings focuses on King Solomon (as 1–2 Samuel focuses on Saul and even more, David), and significant sections of 1–2 Kings include lengthy narratives concerning prophets, most notably Elijah and Elisha, but also Micaiah (1 Kgs 22), two unnamed prophets (1 Kgs 13; the end of 1 Kgs 20), and an unnamed disciple of Elisha, sent to Jehu (2 Kgs 9). (Other significant prophetic accounts include those of Ahijah concerning Jeroboam I and his family [1 Kgs 11:29-39; 14:1-18], the brief but significant word of Shemaiah [1 Kgs 12:21-24], and the judgment oracle of Jehu [1 Kgs 16:1-7]. And let us not forget the prophet Jonah son of Amittai mentioned briefly in 2 Kgs 14:25.) After the northern kingdom of Israel falls in 722 BC (see 2 Kgs 17 with its lengthy editorial comments on why the north fell), attention naturally falls only on the southern kingdom and its Davidic pedigree. But both the north and the south matter to our authors—a feature generally downplayed in scholarly treatments of this issue—and both the north and the south represent kingdoms still under the sovereignty of Yahweh.[11] I will emphasize that the final editing of the books of Kings points to the southern or Judahite kingdom as particularly embracing Yahweh's blessing of his people and the nations; but at this juncture, it must be emphasized that 1–2 Kings includes kings from both kingdoms, and God's saving activity among his people takes place repeatedly in both kingdoms.

To summarize: The date of final composition of 1–2 Kings falls sometime between 561–539 BC,[12] and its occasion, the releasing of King Jehoiachin from prison in the first year of Evil-merodach of Babylon (2 Kgs 25:27), gives cause for the "note of modest hope" that concludes the book (Barnes 1991:146-149). This status of Jehoiachin represented no trivial occasion in the eyes of the writer(s) of Kings, for this king continued the Davidic covenant memorably described in 2 Samuel 7 (which in the words of Kaiser 1974:315; cf. 1978:152-155 contains nothing less than the "charter for humanity" [i.e., akin to the blessing of all the families on earth connected with the Abrahamic covenant in Gen 12:3], as reflected in 2 Sam 7:19; cf. Vannoy 2009:305-306; cf. also Leithart 2006:22-23). I will have occasion to return to the importance of the chronological marker of the "37th year of exile" later; suffice it for now to indicate that the focus of the final editor of Kings is on a *king*—a Davidic king, in whom the whole world is to place its hope. (It must be acknowledged that we Christians have here an example of *sensus plenior*, a "deeper meaning" to the text that would not be fully realized until the New Testament era when Jesus the Christ came into the world as "son of David, king of the Jews.")

Earlier Editions of Kings? All scholars will agree that prominent sections of 1–2 Kings, such as the Elijah and the Elisha cycles (usually specified as 1 Kgs 17—2 Kgs 2, and 2 Kgs 2–9, 13, respectively), existed separately from the other material in the book and were inserted in Kings relatively unchanged from their original forms. But there is debate about the other portions. As already noted, scholars of all theological persuasions generally recognize the complicated nature of the editing of the books of Kings. Frank Moore Cross Jr. has suggested (1973:274-289) that there were two major editions of Kings (or of the entire Deuteronomistic History, i.e., most or all of the books of Deuteronomy, Joshua, Judges, 1–2 Samuel, as well as 1–2 Kings), with the first edition intended to support King Josiah's reforms and the second adding to it to deal with issues raised by the fall of Jerusalem and the Exile. This has, in my opinion, been a clear step forward in the debate. (For a brief, accessible description of Cross's theory and his scholarly antecedents, see ABD 4.72-73; for skepticism concerning the existence of the "Deuteronomists," see Harrison 1969:730-732.) Even if such a proposal is not accepted, the primacy of King Josiah of Judah in the Kings account (see 2 Kgs 22–23; cf. 1 Kgs 13:1-2), as well as the brevity of the accounts of the kings after him, reminds the reader of the influential nature of his reforms, and the optimism of the writers concerning his status before Yahweh. And it is to that topic that we must turn.

The books of Kings include stark evaluations of nearly all the kings of both kingdoms, usually in formulaic terms.[13] The majority of the kings are evaluated negatively—this is nearly always the case for the northern kings, and about half the number of the southern kings must be included here as well. But a number of the southern kings are evaluated quite positively (eight of the southern kings "did what was pleasing in the LORD's sight," although, in the case of Amaziah, this is quali- fied by the additional statement "but not like his ancestor David"). And two of the southern kings are given exalted status, the "best in show," so to speak.

Which king of Israel or Judah is the "best of all"? Contemporary evangelical Christians often focus on David, of course, since we are reminded in Acts 13:22 that David was a "man after [God's] own heart" (a clear reference to 1 Sam 13:14). No other king of either kingdom is spoken of in such exalted terms. But the books of Kings do feature two other kings who also may merit the title of "best of all." Both King Hezekiah of Judah and his great-grandson King Josiah are given remarkably high praise by the authors of Kings. In 2 Kings 18:5 we are told that "Hezekiah trusted in the LORD, the God of Israel. There was no one like him among all the kings of Judah, either before or after his time." In 2 Kings 23:25, however, we are a bit surprised to read, "Never before had there been a king like Josiah, who turned to the LORD with all his heart and soul and strength, obeying all the laws of Moses. And there has never been a king like him since."

Some time ago, scholars such as Nicholson (1967:113-118; cf. Barnes 1991:140 n. 12) suggested that already by the time of King Hezekiah (late eighth century BC) scribes of the Deuteronomistic school were compiling a comprehensive history of the two kingdoms, which included northern royal and prophetic traditions along with their southern, Davidic counterparts (and with no small measure of critique of them). The careful study of Halpern and Vanderhooft seems to confirm this Hezekiah stratum in 1–2 Kings (1991:182-183, and passim) in light of changes in the death and burial formulas for the Judahite kings, as well as the references to the queen mothers (and to a lesser degree, the regnal evaluation formulas and the source notes). In any case, as even the Isaianic parallels to 1–2 Kings (Isa 36–39) attest, King Hezekiah was a remarkable king, and entirely worthy of an edition of Kings lending support to his radical reform efforts.

Be that as it may, a significant number of scholars have more conventionally divided the books of Kings into two major editions, a Josianic edition ("Dtr1") from the late seventh century BC (Josiah was on the throne c. 640–609), and an exilic edition ("Dtr2"), published after the year 561 in light of the last chronological datum found in the book (2 Kgs 25:27-30). That King Josiah was a very important king for the so-called "Deuteronomists," the putative writers of the books of Kings, seems entirely plausible. Both Kings and Chronicles wax eloquent on the remarkable revival Josiah brought about in the 18th year of his reign (see 2 Kgs 22:1–23:30, and especially 23:21-25; cf. 2 Chr 34–35). The prophet Zephaniah may well have provided clear impetus for the revival (Sweeney 2001:185-197). Many scholars would see the youthful Jeremiah also as being significantly influenced by its effects (e.g., Rowley 1963:205-208; and recently, Leuchter 2006:50-86; cf. the reference in 2 Chr 35:25 to Jeremiah composing laments over the death of Josiah). But the extant book of 2 Kings ends on a note of modest hope at best. The tone of the present edition of 1–2 Kings, with its heavy foreshadowing of exile in Solomon's prayer of dedication for the Temple (1 Kgs 8:23-53; cf. Yahweh's response in 1 Kgs 9:3-9) and its repeated insistence that it was the wickedness of King Manasseh which ensured that the Exile must take place (2 Kgs 21:10-15; 23:26-27; 24:2-4; cf. Jer 15:4), seems far away from any optimistic program of support for Josiah's reform efforts. Scholars have long noticed this, of course. Some remain unconvinced that there was any separate Josianic recension of the books of Kings.[14] But a close reading of the recurring regnal formulas throughout 1–2 Kings does lend support for multiple editions of the book (Halpern and Vanderhooft [1991:179-244] argue for not only two, but three layers of editing), and scholars such as Friedman (cf. my citations above; also note his "From Egypt to Egypt: Dtr1 and Dtr2," 1981:167-192) have strengthened Cross's original hypothesis of two editions of the Deuteronomistic work.

Thus, we can explain how King Josiah could be called the best king of all, one "who turned to the LORD with all his heart and soul and strength, obeying all the laws of Moses" (2 Kgs 23:25; cf. Deut 6:5). We can assume that this was the evaluation of the earlier, Josianic edition of Kings left largely intact by the later editor. Yet we soon find out that the land fell into exile relatively soon after Josiah's death, and that was the fault of the evil King Manasseh (as repeatedly asserted by the present, exilic edition of Kings). Was Manasseh really the main reason for an apparently inevitable exile? And if even good King Josiah seemingly proved insufficient, how can there be any hope for the future? These are the questions that the present edition of 1–2 Kings posed to its exilic readers and poses to us today.

AUDIENCE

In light of the above discussion, we might want to specify "audiences" for the two or more putative editions of the books of Kings. But once again, what matters for the person of faith today must be, above all, the canonical books of Kings, the books we actually have today (see "Canonicity and Textual History," below). And the "audience" for the canonical work is rather easily specified, at least more so than for other Old Testament works such as 1–2 Samuel, or Joshua and Judges (which, if the "Deuteronomistic Edition" theory be embraced, may prove to be quite similar to the audience of Kings). The audience for the final form of 1–2 Kings is necessarily exilic—Jews living in exile in Babylon (and perhaps elsewhere, such as Egypt).[15] The books of Kings address an audience that has no kings, at least no Jewish ones. The Davidic dynasty had apparently lasted some 424 years or so (assuming David ascended the throne in 1010 BC). Of course, chronological precision eludes us for the early period of the Davidic dynasty. (The "40 years" of both David and Solomon may be round numbers, or they may include a brief coregency.) In any case, this is an amazingly long dynasty, and again, according to 2 Samuel 7, an exceedingly important one as well. But by the end of 2 Kings, this dynasty has tragically come to an end! The Davidic hope is no more. Rather like the poets who wrote the book of Lamentations, the readers/hearers of Kings must have been in shock. How could Yahweh be so unfaithful to his people and to his "eternal" covenant (see 2 Sam 7:11b-16; cf. the discussion of the "lamp of David" below)? Had Yahweh utterly rejected his people (Lam 5:22)? To be sure, the classic prophets had warned, time and again, that this very thing could happen (cf. the "blessings and curses" of Deut 27–28; Solomon's prayer in 1 Kgs 8). But, as the prophet Jeremiah lamented in his "Temple sermon" (Jer 7:1–8:3), the people of Judah continually refused to listen to such doomsday talk. But by the end of the events described in 2 Kings 25:1-26, the intended audience of the author of Kings sadly knew better. Just as Haggai's audience (520 BC), for once, actually *listened* to their prophet (see Hag 1:12), the nearly contemporaneous audience of the final edition of 1–2 Kings finally had "ears to hear" its message.

And what was that message? Though much more will be said below concerning this topic, at the outset I would submit that the message of 1–2 Kings is that (1) Yahweh was not yet done with his people (Israel *and* Judah), and (2) Yahweh was still not done with the institution of the Davidic monarchy (or at least its personnel). For the book of 2 Kings does end with, as already mentioned, an obscure notice that King Jehoiachin, grandson of the great King Josiah, had been released from Babylonian prison in the 37th year of his exile (561 BC), and that he had been given a seat of honor higher than all the other exiled kings in Babylon, as well as a regular food allowance "as long as he lived" (2 Kgs 25:27-30; the parallel text in Jer 52:31-34 adds the phrase, "until the day of his death"). Not much to hope for in concrete terms, perhaps, but still "hope is alive." Gerhard von Rad's instincts were sound when he stated:

> We can attribute a special theological significance to the final sentences of the Deuteronomist's work, the notice about the release of Jehoiachin from prison. . . .

> To be sure, nothing is expressed in theological terms here, but something is just hinted at, and with great reserve. But for all that, a happening is mentioned which had the significance of an omen for the Deuteronomist, a fact from which Jahweh can start again, if it be his will. At all events, the passage must be interpreted by every reader as an indication that the line of David has not yet come to an irrevocable end. (von Rad 1953:90-91)[16]

CANONICITY AND TEXTUAL HISTORY

Like the books of Samuel, the canonicity of the books of Kings is firmly established. The Talmudic tractate *b. Bava Batra* asserts that Jeremiah was their author. The books of Kings are reckoned as one book in the Hebrew Bible or Masoretic Text (MT). The present division of the book into two nearly equal halves dates to the translation of the Septuagint (third or second century BC). In Codex Leningradensis, 1 Kings takes up just over 110 columns and 2 Kings 107 columns. By contrast, the book of Jeremiah, the longest of the Latter Prophets in the Hebrew tradition, takes up 185 columns. The tradition of two books of Kings (like that of Samuel and Chronicles), although early, is *not* editorially significant—it merely represents a physical convenience to the reader of the scroll or later codex.

The textual tradition of Kings (like that of Samuel) is complicated, with the Greek version, the Septuagint (LXX), containing an early, somewhat independent version of these books (known as 3–4 Reigns; Gr., *Basileiōn* [TG933, ZG994]). The Masoretic Text and the Septuagint versions of most of the books of the Old Testament correspond quite closely. Naturally, there are hundreds of minor textual variants between the two texts, but few of these are of more than orthographic significance. But such is not the case for Samuel, and it is definitely not the case for 1 Kings either. (Second Kings LXX is closer to the Hebrew in most of the extant manuscripts.) The Septuagint (e.g., Codex Vaticanus) of Kings represents a mixed text-type (see Tetley 2005:14-29, and especially pp. 19-21; cf. Cross 1964:292-297; Shenkel 1968:5-21), with significant additions and seeming relocations.[17] The earliest translation to Greek is referred to as the Old Greek, and the Septuagint of Kings as we now have it (especially in Codex Vaticanus) seems to reflect this from 1 Kings 2:12–21:29. Reference to the Septuagint within that section generally refers to the Old Greek as represented by Codex Vaticanus (see notes at 2:12 and 22:1). Later Septuagintal manuscripts tend to correct toward the Masoretic Text, with the so-called "Kaige" tradition a prime example of this; in Codex Vaticanus, the "Kaige" tradition is found in 2 Samuel 10:1—1 Kings 2:11, and in 1 Kings 22:1—2 Kings 25:30 (cf. Tetley 2005:19-20; Shenkel 1968:18). The varying textual traditions behind the Greek and the Hebrew texts of Kings (especially 1 Kings) will receive notes/discussion throughout the commentary. (For a discussion about the later Greek versions—Aquila, Symmachus, and Theodotion—as well as the Aramaic Targums, the Syriac Peshitta, the Old Latin, and the Vulgate, see the still invaluable textual notes found in Montgomery 1951:11-16, and passim; cf. Sweeney 2007:34-40.)

LITERARY STYLE

As befits an edited tradition, the literary style of Kings varies from chapter to chapter, even from verse to verse. But the overall tenor of the Hebrew text (apart from the brief poetic sections discussed below) is that of standard-prose Hebrew,[18] with characteristic perfect-tense verbs introducing each narrative unit, followed by the characteristic "Waw-consecutive imperfect" verbs, sometimes in long sequences (Lambdin 1971:162-163). The effect to the English ear may be monotonous, but to the classic Hebrew listener/reader, quite pleasing: "This happened . . . then that . . . then that . . . however, this also is noteworthy" (the last clause introduced by a Hebrew disjunction that may be entitled "Waw plus nonverb"; cf. Waltke and O'Connor 1990:650-654). As is the case in preexilic and exilic Hebrew prose, the overall effect is subtle, but unmistakable. The later Hebrew of Chronicles, Ezra, and Nehemiah contains more participles and fewer of the classic perfect plus Waw-consecutive imperfect constructions.[19]

In contrast to 1–2 Samuel, the books of Kings contain no "appendices" and, apart from the Elijah-Elisha cycles and other prophetic discourses, few digressions of any length. (The six "appendices" of Samuel are found, probably in chiastic format, in 2 Sam 21–24; see Vannoy 2009:14ff.) This relative lack of digressions does not, however, mean that 1–2 Kings flows as a uniform narrative. The traditions of King Ahab of Israel will illustrate the point. Ahab is roundly condemned in the Elijah traditions (see 1 Kgs 17–19, 21 [MT]), and also (probably) in the Micaiah narrative (1 Kgs 22:1-38) and in an anonymous prophetic pericope (1 Kgs 20:35-43). But the positive Ahab tradition of 1 Kings 20:1-34 (MT) stands in sharp juxtaposition with the negative traditions just listed. The effect is a bit jarring, but in the end not displeasing. Ahab of Israel was clearly an "evil" king (see the standard evaluation formula in 1 Kgs 16:30), but the king was not without some redeeming qualities. Even the Micaiah tradition of 1 Kings 22 presents Ahab as obtuse and headstrong, but heroic in battle. (In any case, one should note the alternate editing of these texts as attested in the LXX, with its juxtaposition of 1 Kgs 20 and 21.) The subtleties of such examples of sophisticated editing may well be missed by readers or hearers of short sections of text.[20]

There is poetry in 1–2 Kings, just as there is poetry in most of the "nonpoetic" books of the Old Testament. For example, in 1 Kings 12:16, the Israelite retort to Rehoboam and the house of David is poetry. The victory oracle of Isaiah provides a more extended example (see 2 Kgs 19:21-34 and its parallel in Isa 37:22-35), written in the poetic style of the classic Hebrew prophets and including many instances of tight synonymous parallelism. (The majority of commentators see the editor of Isaiah excerpting most of 2 Kgs 18:13–20:21 in what is now Isa 36–39, although the reverse has occasionally been argued; in any case, Hezekiah's poem of praise, Isa 38:9-20, finds no counterpart in Kings.)[21] A particular virtue of modern translations of the Hebrew Bible is the attempt to isolate poetic sections and set them apart from their prose counterparts. The New Living Translation (NLT) generally does well at this, although not in every place.

Lists are found in 1–2 Kings as well; they are set off nicely in the NLT with characteristic typography (see, e.g., 1 Kgs 4:1-6, 8-19; 7:41-45, 48-50). Messages and prayers are often set off typographically in the NLT, as seen in the correspondence of Solomon and Hiram in 1 Kings 5, Solomon's lengthy prayer of dedication of the Temple in 1 Kings 8, Asa's message to Ben-hadad in 1 Kings 15:19, and the sarcastic, propagandistic "warning" given by the Assyrian king's chief of staff to the besieged Judahites sitting on the city wall, found in 2 Kings 18:19-25.

The NLT also italicizes the source citations as one would italicize a book title (e.g., 1 Kgs 11:41, NLT, reads, "The rest of the events . . . are recorded in *The Book of the Acts of Solomon*"). This occurs 32 times with relatively even distribution among the kings of the north (*The Book of the History of the Kings of Israel*) and the south (*The Book of the History of the Kings of Judah*).[22] Of course, these "books" are no longer extant, but the NLT's italicizing of the citations effectively conveys that they were apparently readily available at the time. Two quick conclusions come from this: (1) As most scholars emphasize on other grounds, the writer or writers of Kings were probably professional scribes, familiar with court archives, and (2) these writers certainly did not perceive that they were "going against the grain" of their sources. Their citations from the annals, their excerpts from informal, or at times formal, regnal tradition, and even their own theological evaluations of the kings, represent some sort of general consensus that the motivated hearer/reader was urged to personally "check out" by consulting the sources listed (Childs 1979:289). Even in biblical times, it was good to document your sources!

The feature of the text of 1–2 Kings that deserves note as distinguishing and virtually unique is the appearance of regnal formulas found throughout the entire text. (Such notices appear in 1 Sam 13:1; 2 Sam 2:10; 5:4-5; but they are not integral to the structure of that book as they are in Kings.) These formulas typically include accession formulas, stereotypical statements of evaluation, synchronisms with the currently reigning king of the other kingdom (north or south—only rarely found in reference to non-Israelite kings), and concluding burial formulas (for a helpful overview of all these formulas, see Wiseman 1993:46-50). Often, as noted above, we find references to written sources where the reader can go to obtain more information. Sometimes we find a "supplemental notice" inserted between the source citation and the burial notice (e.g., 1 Kgs 15:7, "There was constant war between Abijam and Jeroboam"). (Death and burial formulas, as well as evaluation formulas, references to queen mothers, etc., have been carefully studied by Halpern and Vanderhooft [1991:179-244].) As is commonly recognized, these regnal formulas, particularly the accession formulas ("X son of Y began to rule over Israel/Judah in . . .; he reigned . . . years"), provide the backbone for all of Kings. Some years ago, Shoshana R. Bin-Nun looked closely at the accession formulas (1968:414-432; for a summary see Barnes 1991:138-140), and her literary conclusions merit direct quotation here:

> A summary of the information contained in the Book of Kings [= our 1–2 Kings] gives but a vague picture of the history of Israel and of Judah from the division of the kingdom until their destruction. Many important political events are not even mentioned. On the other hand, the unbroken lines of the kings of both states form a surprising contrast with the author's fragmentary reports. Not a single king is left out, neither usurpers nor even Atalia [Athaliah], although, not being regarded a legitimate ruler, she has no formulas. (Bin-Nun 1968:423)

Perhaps her most important conclusion, however, is the clear delineation between the accession formulas of the northern over against the southern kings. Despite their editorial locations (in other words, despite whether they are found in Halpern and Vanderhooft's DtrH [Hezekian], Dtr1 [Josianic], or Dtr2 [exilic] editions), the formulas remain remarkably consistent (to be sure, "northern" formulas do not appear after the time of Hezekiah, but the consistency of the southern formulas is still noteworthy). Bin-Nun saw these characteristic enumerations of kings with the length of their reigns as what one would expect in ancient Near Eastern "king-lists," and so she looked for similar examples elsewhere in the Hebrew Scriptures. For example, the "king-list" phenomenon could be found in Genesis 36:31-43, where the later descendants of Esau (Edom) who "ruled" from various cities in the region are listed. Closer parallels, however, to the accession formulas in Kings are to be found in the books of Judges and 1–2 Samuel. Delineation of the details of the typical southern formula over against the two characteristic northern formulas is not necessary here,[23] but the overall contrast between the northern and the southern formulas must be stressed: "There is not a single ruler among the kings of Judah, whose regnal years are recorded at the end of the [accession] formula as with the kings of Israel. Nor is there any king of Israel whose formula begins with the length of his reign" (Bin-Nun 1968:420).

In my opinion, the importance of the identification of these separate formulas for the editing style of 1–2 Kings can hardly be overstated. Richard Nelson's (1981:30-31) overly quick dismissal of Bin-Nun's conclusions in his otherwise fine study misses the mark. Nonetheless, I agree with his comments that king-lists were probably compiled all at once or at intervals unrelated to an individual king's accession (Nelson 1981:31; and note 15 on p. 135; Bin-Nun had suggested otherwise). As has already been repeatedly emphasized, the books of Kings are about the *kings*. The editing style is predictable, perhaps monotonous for our tastes, but nonetheless, in its own way, quite effective. All these kings had to be listed in strict chronological order, and compared synchronistically whenever possible. These comparisons lend themselves not infrequently to complications, as the apt title of Edwin R. Thiele's famous work attests (*The Mysterious Numbers of the Hebrew Kings*, 1983). Aside from such chronological considerations (which will be explored in the commentary notes), the overall import of this phenomenon should be evident. Chronology trumps even theology (which is the opposite of the nonchronological sequencing of the Hezekiah narratives of 2 Kings 18–20, and their parallels in the Isaiah traditions).[24] For good or ill (often the latter), kings (and once, a queen) were *always* on the throne, up to virtually the end of the era. Yahweh was faithful, even when the kings were not.

Excursus on Chronology. This is a particularly vexed issue in any discussion of the editing of the books of Kings, as already described above. I wrote my doctoral dissertation on the topic, so I have significant experience in this area—and I sometimes feel as confused as ever! The following, perhaps sardonic, slogan, said to have been posted outside the mathematics reading room at Tromsø University, Norway, says it best:

> *We have not succeeded in answering all our problems. The answers we have found only serve to raise a whole set of new questions. In some ways we feel we are as confused as ever, but we believe we are confused on a higher level, and about more important things.*

How true this is in the area of chronology. There are, to be sure, external synchronisms that can be used as pegs on which to hang the biblical chronology (or, chronologies) found in 1–2 Kings, and they will be included in the notes throughout the commentary (cf. Wiseman 1993:32-35 for a helpful listing). And there are the biblical regnal totals that often, but not always, align with these external synchronisms. And finally, there are the *internal* synchronisms that introduce nearly every accession notice for the northern and the southern monarchs (and occasionally are found elsewhere in the text). But these sometimes do not align with the other data. And that is the problem—mysterious numbers, indeed! (Once again, Thiele's very influential monograph, *The Mysterious Numbers of the Hebrew Kings*, is indeed aptly named; for an extended critique, see Barnes 1991:12-27.)

For the purposes of the present work, I will merely summarize the most radical proposal I arrived at in the 1980s when I completed my dissertation: If one antedates (that is, counts the first, partial year of reign of any given monarch as a full year), and if one notes the regnal totals for the Davidic kings as found in the Masoretic Text, the total comes to exactly 480 years—that is, if one counts from the first year of David down to the famous reference at the end of 2 Kings of the 37th year of Jehoiachin (see Barnes 1991:145-149). This, of course, is a significant number indeed (famously in 1 Kgs 6:1, exactly 480 years after the Israelites had been delivered from Egypt under Moses, the Temple of Solomon was founded).[25] Few have accepted my admittedly tentative conclusion (cf., however, Howard 1993:178 n. 26), and, to be sure, the actual historical interlude between these two dates must be significantly less than the round number of 480 (I had calculated 449 actual years, depending, of course, on the precise lengths of the reigns of David and Solomon, which are reckoned as 40 years each in Samuel—Kings).

The procedure of antedating was not the currently accepted chronological procedure in Babylon (although it was in Egypt; cf. Kitchen 1996:74-75; Tadmor 1979:48-49), and the regnal totals would have been understood as not reflecting any coregencies (overlapping reigns of a king and his crown prince), although at least a few coregencies must have actually taken place (see the commentary below for details). But I still suspect the number 480 is not a mere coincidence. Time will tell whether this observation will hold up—and in the end it is probably not all that important, for the text makes no overt mention of this or any particular number. Still, if there be king-lists, and if the Judahite king-list did add up to this very significant number in 561 BC, the 37th year of exile of King Jehoiachin, would this not mean something to the writer who ended 1–2 Kings with the "note of modest hope"? As I concluded my monograph:

> It is hoped . . . [that this discussion will lead to] a deeper appreciation of that anonymous final redactor we call Dtr 2, who saw in what was probably only a fleeting gesture of generosity by an obscure Babylonian monarch in his accession year reason enough to update and edit the Israelite and Judahite history which has long since eclipsed in fame and influence any other such historiographic work from ancient times. (Barnes 1991:149)

MAJOR THEMES

One Place of Worship. According to scholars who hold to a Deuteronomistic writer(s) for the books of Kings,[26] one of the hallmarks of this tradition is the push for "cult centralization" (Childs 1979:290-292; Noth 1981:92-97). Already in Deuteronomy 12, Moses was insisting that in the future there would be one centralized place of worship for Yahweh's chosen people ("Be careful not to sacrifice your burnt offerings just anywhere you like. You may do so only at the place [Yahweh] will choose within one of your tribal territories. There you must offer your burnt offerings and do everything I command you" [Deut 12:13-14]; cf. Deut 12:8-11). This is one of the hallmarks of the book of Deuteronomy, with, for example, the Deuteronomic tithe meant to ensure that the worshipers will be able to make the journey to that designated place of worship comfortably and with gladness of heart (see Deut 14:22-27; 26:1-11).

Whether or not Deuteronomists wrote or edited 1–2 Kings, there is no question that one of the major criteria for evaluating the kings in Kings is their adherence to this crucial theological tenet. Even Solomon, who gets special consideration for his importance in founding the Temple, is not altogether exempt: "At that time the people of Israel sacrificed their offerings at local places of worship, for a temple honoring the name of [Yahweh] had not yet been built. Solomon loved [Yahweh] and followed all the decrees of his father, David, except that Solomon, too, offered sacrifices and burned incense at the local places of worship" (1 Kgs 3:2-3). And nearly all of the later kings of both kingdoms are invariably judged by this standard: The infamous Jeroboam I, founder of the northern kingdom of Israel after Solomon's death, set up two shrines in Bethel and Dan—"at either end of his kingdom" (1 Kgs 12:29)—at the advice of his counselors. He told the people, "It is too much trouble for you to worship in Jerusalem," so he set up two golden calves, and announced, "Look, Israel, these are the gods who brought you out of Egypt!" (1 Kgs 12:28). Although this "became a great sin" (1 Kgs 12:30), it probably was not perceived as such at the time, since the Ark of the Covenant had wandered from place to place during the period of the judges, and since the newfangled Temple of Solomon also featured Phoenician-style innovations (see the commentary below on 1 Kgs 6:14-38). In any case, the "sin of Jeroboam" became the negative criterion by which most of the subsequent kings of the north and a number from the south were evaluated.[27] It was not until King Josiah of Judah that cult-centralization was effected (but cf. 2 Kgs 18:22 for credit given also to Hezekiah), and this, as noted above, is one of the chief hallmarks of Josiah's greatness, according to the author of Kings.

The "Lamp" of David. A major theme of 1–2 Kings is the primacy of the Davidic covenant. The classic text for this theme is 2 Samuel 7, where David's "house" (or dynasty) will stand for eternity (see especially 2 Sam 7:19). Obviously, this has not been fulfilled literally, "eternity" having come to an end with the demise of King Zedekiah in 586 BC. So, much of the burden on the writer of 1–2 Kings is to explain why David's "house" had to come to an end. Most, if not all, prophecies are dependent on the response of God's leaders and God's people,[28] but there was still a need to explain how the "eternal" house of David came to such an ignominious end. How can one ever forget the pitiful spectacle described in 2 Kings 25:6-7 (with parallels in Jer 39:5-7; 52:9-11) of the fleeing King Zedekiah caught by the invading Babylonians and brought to Nebuchadnezzar in Riblah in the land of Hamath (Syria), where judgment was given: Zedekiah's sons killed before his very eyes, then his own eyes gouged out. So much, seemingly, for the Davidic hope! (But the books of Kings do end with the gentle reminder that the Davidic Jehoiachin still lives, albeit in exile.[29])

One curious aspect of this theme of the primacy of the Davidic dynasty is the recurring term "lamp of David" (*nir ledawid* [TH5216/1732, ZH5775/1858]). Found three times in the books of Kings (1 Kgs 11:36; 15:4; 2 Kgs 8:19; cf. 2 Chr 21:7), it is traditionally translated "a light" (KJV)[30] or "a lamp" (NIV), but in the NLT, a more paraphrastic phrase is used: "shining like a lamp." Some time ago, Hanson argued for the Hebrew term *nir* to be translated as "yoke" or "dominion" or the like (1968:311-320), rather than the traditional translation "lamp." *Nir* as "yoke" is well attested in cognate Semitic languages such as Old Akkadian (as well as Aramaic, Syriac, and Arabic), and the Assyrian Annals attest that the term is used often as a metaphor for the king's dominion over his subjects. Recently, this translation has been adopted by Sweeney in his recent *Kings* commentary (2007:158), and there is much to commend it (e.g., the Aramaic Targums seem to support it, as well as the medieval commentator Rashi [Hanson 1968:317-320]). But a number of Hanson's arguments have been effectively countered by Cogan and Tadmor in their Anchor Bible Commentary on 2 Kings (1988:95); they take the Assyrian parallels as negative in connotation ("yoke" as imposition of a vassal relationship upon the king's subjects), quite different from the positive import of the Davidic references. Also, the imagery of a "lamp" (*ner* [TH5216A, ZH5944]) as a sign of life and hope appears in 2 Samuel 21:17 when David's fighting men adjure him: "You are not going out to battle with us again! Why risk snuffing out the light [*ner*] of Israel?" (cf. Ps 132:17). Cogan and Tadmor also cite the similar imagery found in 2 Samuel 14:7, "They want to extinguish the only coal I have left, and my husband's name and family will disappear from the face of the earth," along with its counterpart in Akkadian, "[so and so] whose brazier has gone out." I would add the references found in 2 Samuel 22:29 (// Ps 18:28) to Yahweh as David's "lamp" (*ner*) and the one who "lights up my darkness." In any case, I suspect that we should retain the traditional rendering of "a light" or "a lamp" for the phrase "*nir* of David."

In conclusion, it should be noted that Childs (1979:292-293), following the suggestions of von Rad, has made a strong case for the "promise to David" being a major theme of the books of 1–2 Kings—this theme even remaining in effect despite the national catastrophe of the Exile. As Childs points out, in 1–2 Samuel the Davidic traditions were given redactional shape in 2 Samuel 7, as well as the appendices found in 2 Samuel 21–24, which envision David as the "ideal, righteous king." So also, in 1–2 Kings we find the following parallels:[31]

David as the "righteous one"	2 Sam 22:21	1 Kgs 9:4
David "whole, or blameless" before God	2 Sam 22:24	1 Kgs 9:4
David obeying the "decrees and regulations"	2 Sam 22:23	1 Kgs 9:4; 11:38
David "keeping the Lord's ways"	2 Sam 22:22	1 Kgs 11:33
Yahweh shows his "unfailing love to his anointed"	2 Sam 22:51	1 Kgs 8:23; Ps 89:1, 28
Yahweh promises him an "eternal covenant"	2 Sam 23:5	Ps 89:3

In light of the above discussion concerning the *nir* of David, I would also add the following:

David as the "light of Israel"	2 Sam 21:17	1 Kgs 11:36; 15:4; 2 Kgs 8:19; cf. Ps 132:17

In this regard, Childs concludes: "the stereotyped portrayal of David by the author of Kings as the model of the righteous king is not to be regarded as an idiosyncratic idealization of one [exilic] author, but rather reflects a common canonical stance which was grounded in a particular understanding of Israel's sacred literature and which was testified to in its shaping" (1979:293).

The "Sins of Manasseh." One final major theme of Kings must be addressed. The overwhelming catastrophe of the Exile—with the destruction of the Temple, the takeover of the Land of Promise, and the seeming termination of the Davidic monarchy—represents the proverbial "elephant in the room." All of the "cult-centralization" focus, as well as the "lamp of David" refrain, means nothing in light of the seeming finality of the takeover by Nebuchadnezzar of the land of Judah and his destruction of the city of Jerusalem. Words of confident hope as are seen in Jeremiah (e.g., Jer 30–31 as delineated by Sweeney 2001:225-233; cf. endnote 10), and later in Chronicles and Ezra-Nehemiah, are not to be found in 1–2 Kings. As noted, the modest note of hope at the end of 2 Kings is the best we can find. Maybe more than this is beyond what would be expected by the audience of Kings. But surely they would expect some reasoning as to why the Exile had to take place. And this, of course, *is* clearly addressed in the books of Kings—indeed, if you wish, in one word: Manasseh. Or more traditionally, the *sins* of Manasseh.

King Manasseh of Judah, son of good king Hezekiah, did much evil. In the commentary I will note the oppressive Assyrian pressure he felt throughout much of his remarkably long reign, which undoubtedly contributed to this "evil." I will also cite the intriguing tradition found in Chronicles (2 Chr 33) of Manasseh's repentance and gracious restoration by Yahweh. And I will point out that there is absolutely *no* mention of this remarkable repentance anywhere in 1–2 Kings! In short, for the author of Kings, Manasseh is entirely evil. Yet beyond this, he was apparently *uniquely* evil. Even a casual reader of 1–2 Kings will note quite a number of evil kings, especially in the north, but even some in the south. Manasseh is one of many in this category. But for Kings, at least for the final part of the book (in 2 Kgs 21–25), we are reminded of the results of his great sin three separate times (cf. 2 Kgs 21:10-15; 23:26-27; 24:3-4). Manasseh truly was uniquely evil—in fact, the "sins of Manasseh" (2 Kgs 24:3) are said to be the reason for the Exile!

Scholars usually speak of "Deuteronomistic retribution theology" with Manasseh being the parade example.[32] There is some truth to this, of course. But already, in both versions of the Ten Commandments, we are told, "I [Yahweh] lay the sins of the parents upon their children . . . even children in the third and fourth generations of those who reject me" (Exod 20:5b; cf. Deut 5:9b), and this stern threat is connected specifically with those who make graven images and bow down and worship them. Manasseh did all of that and more (see 2 Kgs 21:2-9, 16). I would submit that although there is "Deuteronomistic retribution theology," it was nothing new. Yahweh famously is a "jealous God" (Exod 20:5; 34:14; Deut 4:24; 5:9a; 6:15), and he never (at least since the days of Moses) would tolerate idolatry. Manasseh's sins inevitably would lead to disaster *unless* the people repented and obeyed God. This is where I (and others such as Wolff and Childs) would rather place the emphasis—"*unless*." Notice even in 2 Kings 21:8-9, in the middle of the Manasseh material, there is a note of hope coupled with the sad historical summary:

> *"If the Israelites will be careful to obey my commands—all the laws my servant Moses gave them—I will not send them into exile from this land that I gave their ancestors." But the people refused to listen, and Manasseh led them to do even more evil than the pagan nations that the LORD had destroyed when the people of Israel entered the land.*

So, here at least, it was the sin of the people that sealed their fate—Manasseh was very culpable in connection with that sin, of course, but the people sealed their own fate as well and, alas, also the fate of the next several generations (cf. the verse that follows the high praise of King Josiah: "Even so, the LORD was very angry with Judah because of all the wicked things Manasseh had done to provoke him" [2 Kgs 23:26; cf. 2 Kgs 24:3-4]).

As already noted, Wolff has argued strongly that there is a positive "kerygma" in the Deuteronomistic work, and it is nothing less than the possibility of repentance, of "turning back" (*shub* [TH7725, ZH8740]), no matter how dire the situation may be. This is what he concludes:

> *In all of this one cannot say that DtrH [the Deuteronomistic historian] combined his idea of return with any specific hope. Considering his open-ended view of history, concretes and predictables would be absurd. As in the days of the judges and the kings one should, rather, count on completely new arrangements by Yahweh. . . .*
>
> *Perhaps one of the wholly new arrangements is to be the office of witness which the people of God will occupy in the midst of the nations, just as Jehoiachin remains in a distant land, eating at the royal table as long as he lives, enjoying a strange pre-eminence above the other kings. . . .*
>
> *This revealed word now contains the summons to return (in the text of Deuteronomy [30:1-10] that summons follows immediately). To return means that Israel will listen with her whole heart to the voice of her God alone and expect every good from him alone in order that she may become God's agent in the midst of all nations. This is, if I understand it correctly, the peculiar interest of this first comprehensive history not only of the Old Testament but of world literature. (Wolff 1975:99-100)*

This is the hope that even the horrible results of the sins of Manasseh (or of any national or international figurehead or potentate of any time) can never negate.

So, in conclusion—the books of Kings are indeed about kings. Kings of the united monarchy, kings of the divided monarchy. Kings of the north and kings of the south. Good kings and bad kings. Strong, decisive kings, and weak, vacillating kings. But, as Wolff has just noted, the outlook of the books of 1–2 Kings is decidedly toward a time when there may well be no kings at all. Just as Jeremiah the priest and prophet could well predict a time when there would be no Ark (and no one will notice or care about its absence! [see Jer 3:16-18]), so the anonymous royal scribal compilers of the books of Kings may well envision a time when there will be *no* kings, at least no Davidic ones; and again, that may in the end not matter much at all. Yahweh still has *not* given up on his people, perhaps only on the institution of the monarchy.[33]

OUTLINE

The following outline generally includes the helpful subdivisions of the text found in the NLT headings, with the overall divisions informed by the comments of Childs (1979:288). As Childs notes, the first two sections conclude with an appropriate summary by the editor (see 1 Kgs 11; 2 Kgs 17:5-41). The final section describes the destruction and exile of Judah, along with the additional note on the release of King Jehoiachin from prison.

I. King Solomon (1 Kgs 1:1-11:43)
    A. Conclusion of the "Throne Succession Narrative" (1 Kgs 1:1-2:46)
        1. David in his old age (1:1-4)
        2. Adonijah claims the throne (1:5-27)
        3. David makes Solomon king (1:28-53)
        4. David's final instructions to Solomon (2:1-12)
        5. Solomon establishes his rule (2:13-46)
    B. Solomon's Proper Priorities (1 Kgs 3:1-4:34 [3:1-5:14])
        1. Solomon asks for wisdom (3:1-15)
        2. Solomon judges wisely (3:16-28)
        3. Solomon's officials and governors (4:1-19)
        4. Solomon's prosperity and wisdom (4:20-34 [4:20-5:14])
    C. Temple and Palace Building (1 Kgs 5:1-8:66 [5:15-8:66])
        1. Preparations for building the Temple (5:1-18 [5:15-32])
        2. Solomon builds the Temple (6:1-13)
        3. The Temple's interior (6:14-38)
        4. Solomon builds his palace (7:1-12)
        5. Furnishings for the Temple (7:13-51)
        6. The Ark brought to the Temple (8:1-11)
        7. Solomon praises the LORD (8:12-21)
        8. Solomon's prayer of dedication (8:22-53)
        9. The dedication of the Temple (8:54-66)
    D. Solomon in All His Glory: Mixed Results (1 Kgs 9:1-10:29)
        1. The LORD's response to Solomon (9:1-9)
        2. Solomon's agreement with Hiram (9:10-14)
        3. Solomon's many achievements (9:15-28)
        4. Visit of the queen of Sheba (10:1-13)
        5. Solomon's wealth and splendor (10:14-29)
    E. Solomon's Improper Priorities and Their Aftermath (1 Kgs 11:1-43)
        1. Solomon's many wives (11:1-13)
        2. Solomon's adversaries (11:14-25)
        3. Jeroboam rebels against Solomon (11:26-40)
        4. Summary of Solomon's reign (11:41-43)
II. History of the Kings of Israel and Judah until the Destruction of the Northern Kingdom (1 Kgs 12:1-2 Kgs 17:41)

A. Division of Solomon's Kingdom (1 Kgs 12:1–14:20)
   1. The northern tribes revolt (12:1-20)
   2. Shemaiah's prophecy (12:21-24)
   3. Jeroboam makes gold calves (12:25-33)
   4. A prophet denounces Jeroboam (13:1-34)
   5. Ahijah's prophecy against Jeroboam (14:1-20)
B. Synchronistic History of the Early Divided Monarchy
   (1 Kgs 14:21–16:34)
   1. Rehoboam rules in Judah (14:21-31)
   2. Abijam rules in Judah (15:1-8)
   3. Asa rules in Judah (15:9-24)
   4. Nadab rules in Israel (15:25-31)
   5. Baasha rules in Israel (15:32–16:7)
   6. Elah rules in Israel (16:8-14)
   7. Zimri rules in Israel (16:15-20)
   8. Omri rules in Israel (16:21-28)
   9. Ahab rules in Israel (16:29-34)
C. Prophetic Stories from the Elijah Cycle
   (1 Kgs 17:1–19:21)
   1. Elijah fed by ravens (17:1-7)
   2. The widow of Zarephath (17:8-24)
   3. The contest on Mount Carmel (18:1-40)
   4. Elijah prays for rain (18:41-46)
   5. Elijah flees to Sinai (19:1-9a)
   6. The LORD speaks to Elijah (19:9b-18)
   7. The call of Elisha (19:19-21)
D. Prophetic Stories about the Syro-Israelite Wars
   (1 Kgs 20:1–22:40)
   1. Ben-hadad attacks Samaria (20:1-12)
   2. Ahab's victory over Ben-hadad (20:13-22)
   3. Ben-hadad's second attack (20:23-34)
   4. A prophet condemns Ahab (20:35-43)
   5. Naboth's vineyard (21:1-29)
   6. Jehoshaphat and Ahab (22:1-9)
   7. Micaiah prophesies against Ahab (22:10-28)
   8. The death of Ahab (22:29-40)
E. Synchronistic History of the Divided Monarchy, Resumed
   (1 Kgs 22:41-53 [22:41-54])
   1. Jehoshaphat rules in Judah (22:41-50 [22:41-51])
   2. Ahaziah rules in Israel (22:51-53 [22:52-54])
F. Another Prophetic Story from the Elijah Cycle: Elijah Confronts
   King Ahaziah (2 Kgs 1:1-18)

G. Stories from the Elisha Cycle (2 Kgs 2:1–8:15)
   1. Elijah taken into heaven (2:1-18)
   2. Elisha's first miracles (2:19-25)
   3. War between Israel and Moab (3:1-27)
   4. Elisha helps a poor widow (4:1-7)
   5. Elisha and the woman from Shunem (4:8-37)
   6. Miracles during a famine (4:38-44)
   7. The healing of Naaman (5:1-19)
   8. The greed of Gehazi (5:20-27)
   9. The floating ax head (6:1-7)
   10. Elisha traps the Arameans (6:8-23)
   11. Ben-hadad besieges Samaria (6:24–7:2)
   12. Lepers visit the enemy camp (7:3-11)
   13. Israel plunders the camp (7:12-20)
   14. The woman from Shunem returns home (8:1-6)
   15. Hazael murders Ben-hadad (8:7-15)
H. Synchronistic History of the Divided Monarchy, Resumed
   (2 Kgs 8:16-29)
   1. Jehoram rules in Judah (8:16-24)
   2. Ahaziah rules in Judah (8:25-29)
I. Prophetic Stories about the Coup of Jehu (2 Kgs 9:1–10:36)
   1. Jehu anointed king of Israel (9:1-13)
   2. Jehu kills Joram and Ahaziah (9:14-29)
   3. The death of Jezebel (9:30-37)
   4. Jehu kills Ahab's family (10:1-17)
   5. Jehu kills the priests of Baal (10:18-31)
   6. The death of Jehu (10:32-36)
J. Synchronistic History of the Late Divided Monarchy
   (2 Kgs 11:1–13:13)
   1. Queen Athaliah rules in Judah (11:1-3)
   2. Revolt against Athaliah (11:4-12)
   3. The death of Athaliah (11:13-16)
   4. Jehoiada's religious reforms (11:17-21 [11:17–12:1])
   5. Joash repairs the Temple (12:1-16 [12:2-17])
   6. The end of Joash's reign (12:17-21 [12:18-22])
   7. Jehoahaz rules in Israel (13:1-9)
   8. Jehoash rules in Israel (13:10-13)
K. A Prophetic Story from the Elisha Cycle: Elisha's Final Prophecy
   (2 Kgs 13:14-25)
L. Synchronistic History of the Late Divided Monarchy, Concluded
   (2 Kgs 14:1–17:41)
   1. Amaziah rules in Judah (14:1-22)

2. Jeroboam II rules in Israel (14:23-29)
3. Uzziah rules in Judah (15:1-7)
4. Zechariah rules in Israel (15:8-12)
5. Shallum rules in Israel (15:13-15)
6. Menahem rules in Israel (15:16-22)
7. Pekahiah rules in Israel (15:23-26)
8. Pekah rules in Israel (15:27-31)
9. Jotham rules in Judah (15:32-38)
10. Ahaz rules in Judah (16:1-20)
11. Hoshea rules in Israel (17:1-4)
12. Samaria falls to Assyria (17:5-23)
13. Foreigners settle in Israel (17:24-41)
III. History of the Kings of Judah up to the Exile
(2 Kgs 18:1–25:30)
A. Hezekiah: Good, Successful King of Judah
(2 Kgs 18:1–20:21)
1. Hezekiah rules in Judah (18:1-12)
2. Assyria invades Judah (18:13-18)
3. Sennacherib threatens Jerusalem (18:19-37)
4. Hezekiah seeks the LORD's help (19:1-19)
5. Isaiah predicts Judah's deliverance (19:20-37)
6. Hezekiah's sickness and recovery (20:1-11)
7. Envoys from Babylon (20:12-21)
B. Manasseh and Amon: Evil Kings of Judah (2 Kgs 21:1-26)
1. Manasseh rules in Judah (21:1-18)
2. Amon rules in Judah (21:19-26)
C. Josiah: Good Reformer King of Judah (2 Kgs 22:1–23:30)
1. Josiah rules in Judah (22:1-7)
2. Hilkiah discovers God's law (22:8-20)
3. Josiah's religious reforms (23:1-20)
4. Josiah celebrates Passover (23:21-30)
D. Four Evil Successors to Josiah (2 Kgs 23:31–24:20a)
1. Jehoahaz rules in Judah (23:31-33)
2. Jehoiakim rules in Judah (23:34–24:7)
3. Jehoiachin rules in Judah (24:8-17)
4. Zedekiah rules in Judah (24:18-20a)
E. The Fall of Jerusalem and Its Aftermath
(2 Kgs 24:20b–25:30)
1. The fall of Jerusalem (24:20b–25:7)
2. The Temple destroyed (25:8-21)
3. Gedaliah governs in Judah (25:22-26)
4. Hope for Israel's royal line (25:27-30)

ENDNOTES

1. First Kings 15:26 (Nadab); 15:34 (Baasha); 16:19 (Zimri); 16:25 (Omri); 16:30 (Ahab); 22:52 [53] (Ahaziah); 2 Kgs 3:2 (Joram, with some mitigation in the condemnation); 10:31 (Jehu, but only in an indirect sense; contrast 10:30); 13:2 (Jehoahaz); 13:11 (Jehoash); 14:24 (Jeroboam II); 15:9 (Zechariah); 15:18 (Menahem); 15:24 (Pekahiah); 15:28 (Pekah); and finally 17:2 (Hoshea, but again with some mitigation in his condemnation: "He did what was evil in the LORD's sight, but not to the same extent as the kings of Israel who ruled before him"). Indeed, 16 of the 19 northern kings are condemned in some formulaic way (see Halpern and Vanderhooft 1991:199-203). Of the three kings not so condemned, Jeroboam I (see 1 Kgs 12:20–14:20) and to a lesser extent Elah (see 1 Kgs 16:8-14) are still pictured in very negative terms overall. Only Shallum, who reigned but one month (2 Kgs 15:10-15), and who brought an end to the Jehu dynasty in the fourth generation as had been prophesied, is given no clear evaluation at all (but he was soon assassinated by Menahem anyway).

2. Second Kings 8:18 (Jehoram); 8:27 (Ahaziah); 21:2 (Manasseh); 21:20 (Amon); 23:32 (Jehoahaz); 23:37 (Jehoiakim); 24:9 (Jehoiachin); 24:19 (Zedekiah); cf. 1 Kgs 14:22, LXX (Rehoboam; but MT reads "the people of Judah did what was evil in the LORD's sight"). But eight of the southern kings "did what was pleasing in the LORD's sight": Asa (1 Kgs 15:11); Jehoshaphat (1 Kgs 22:43); Joash (2 Kgs 12:2 [12:3]); Amaziah (2 Kgs 14:3); Uzziah (2 Kgs 15:3); Jotham (2 Kgs 15:34); Hezekiah (2 Kgs 18:3); and Josiah (2 Kgs 22:2). The only southern kings not accounted for here are Abijam, who "committed the same sins as his father [Rehoboam] before him" (1 Kgs 15:3, which goes on to contrast him with his ancestor David), and Ahaz, who "did not do what was pleasing in the sight of the LORD his God, as his ancestor David had done" (2 Kgs 16:2; cf. virtually the same criticism found for Solomon in 1 Kgs 11:33).

3. See note 33 below.

4. "Yahweh" is the commonly accepted vocalization of the so-called Tetragrammaton, YHWH (*yhwh* [TH3068, ZH3378]), the most common name of the God of Israel found in the OT. Most English translations, including the NLT, render this name by the phrase "the LORD," in all but a few exceptional instances (e.g., Exod 3:15, NLT). (For further discussion of this translational choice, see the Introduction to the New Living Translation under the section entitled *The Rendering of Divine Names* [found in the introductory material of any NLT Bible].) I will generally use "Yahweh" except when quoting directly from the NLT, since I think the proper name better conveys the sense of the original Hebrew.

5. Second Chronicles 21:12-15 does contain an independent Elijah tradition about a prophetic letter of condemnation sent to King Jehoram of Judah, but apart from this, the only reference outside of 1–2 Kings to the prophet Elijah is at the end of the Minor Prophets scroll (see Mal 4:5-6). There is no mention of Elisha anywhere else in the OT besides the books of Kings.

6. Scholars use the term *cultic* in its original Latin sense of referring to "a system of religious worship or ritual"; the corresponding noun is "cult" or, more traditionally, "cultus." There is *no* negative connotation whatsoever meant to be connected to these terms as used in the scholarly literature.

7. First Kings 8:4; 12:31. And in the Old Greek of 8:4 (regarded as identical with the LXX in this verse), any reference to the Levites is lacking—the editor of BHS takes the MT here as a gloss (a later addition). In contrast, the books of 1–2 Chronicles mention the Levites over 100 times.

8. The noted conservative author Gleason Archer (1974:289), on the other hand, speaks approvingly of the prophet Jeremiah as the possible author of 1–2 Kings (in light of the Talmudic evidence), with the exception of the last chapter of 2 Kings compiled by someone dwelling in Babylonian exile (since Jeremiah went into exile in Egypt). An intriguing argument from silence for this suggestion is that there is no mention whatsoever of Jeremiah himself in the chapters dealing with King Josiah and his

successors—something hard to account for in the light of Jeremiah's prominence as prophet and his unquestionable literary ability, unless it be from modesty on the part of the prophet. (Of course if Baruch, Jeremiah's scribe, is the author, this too might account for Jeremiah's absence from the text.) Friedman also suggested at one time that Jeremiah was the Deuteronomistic author of Kings (1997:147), but he now thinks it was Baruch, Jeremiah's scribe. For a recent, intriguing study of the relationship of Jeremiah to King Josiah's reform efforts (c. 622 BC), see Leuchter (2006).

9. This objection, in my opinion, is not fatal. Biblical texts are famous for their inter-polations, additions, and (going by what we find in otherwise parallel texts) omissions (e.g., even the famous Ps 51, apparently an individual lament by the psalmist David, has as its final stanza a communal lament clearly datable much later to the Judahite exile (see Ps 51:18-19 [51:20-21]). Although I see the author of 2 Kgs 25:27-30 (i.e., the end of the book) as having a significant impact on the chronological notices found throughout 1–2 Kings, the author need not have been Baruch or Jeremiah. In any case, positing an Egyptian origin for the present, longer book of Jeremiah (as found in the MT; LXX is significantly shorter) makes the addition of the final chapter in both the Hebrew and the Greek traditions (Jer 52 // 2 Kgs 25) more problematic for the asser-tion of Jeremiah or Baruch as author.

10. Jack R. Lundbom (1986:99-104), following S. Mowinckel, has made a strong case that Baruch was the major compiler of the present book of Jeremiah, and that the "expand-ed colophon" found in Jer 45, MT (Jer 51:31-35, LXX) indicates as much (he takes the LXX ordering as more original, so this "colophon" essentially ends the book, since Jer 52 in both traditions undoubtedly comes from 2 Kings). But another "expanded colophon" is to be found in Jer 51:59-64, MT (cf. Jer 28:59-64, LXX) where Jeremiah conveys a personal word to Seraiah, Baruch's brother, which in the MT concludes Jer-emiah (again, Jer 52 being a later addition). Indeed, this text concludes with the state-ment, "This is the end of Jeremiah's messages." Lundbom then points out that Seraiah, although not termed a scribe in Jer 51:59 (NLT translates, "a staff officer"; Lundbom suggests the term "quartermaster"), probably had some such professional competence, since he presumably belonged to a scribal family. (Dearman [1990:403-421] has recently explored this topic at length; cf. Lipinski 1988:157-164.) I have toyed with the feasibility of Seraiah as the one adding the concluding passage of 2 Kings about Jehoi-achin's release from prison (and the one possibly behind the exilic king-list phenom-enon with its 480-year total [see "Excursus on Chronology," under "Literary Style," below]), since we know for certain that he (unlike his brother Baruch) *did* make it to Babylon at least once in his career (cf. Jer 51:59-64, where Seraiah is said to have accompanied King Zedekiah to Babylon in the king's fourth year of reign; it was at this time he threw into the Euphrates River a scroll listing all the terrible disasters Jeremiah had predicted Babylon would soon face). But this idea that Seraiah was the author of the conclusion of 2 Kings remains conjectural.

11. Both the late preexilic prophets Jeremiah and Ezekiel and the early postexilic prophet Zechariah seem to hold out much hope for the future restoration of the northern and southern kingdoms (Jer 30–31; Ezek 37:15-28; 48:1-35; Zech 8:13; 9–11). Many schol-ars would see this as anachronistic, but Sweeney (2001:225-233) has recently argued strongly for a Josianic date for much of Jer 30–31. He maintains that Jeremiah had allied himself with Josiah's reform efforts, and that the Benjamite prophet felt espe-cially led to reach out to the former northern kingdom and urge them to rejoin the Jerusalem Temple and the house of David. Indeed, "the seeds for a message of restora-tion . . . are evident in the *earliest preaching* of Jeremiah" (2001:233; emphasis added). And so-called "Deutero-Zechariah" (Zech 9–14) may include at least one preexilic passage; cf. the suggested preexilic interpretations to Zech 9:1-6 found in Meyers and Meyers (1993:91, although the Meyerses themselves prefer a postexilic date for this text). Baldwin (1972:63-64) also has listed a number of scholars who preferred a pre-exilic date for the entirety of Zech 9–11 (she herself seemed to prefer a Hellenistic date

and origin for the chapters). For the suggestion that (postexilic) "Deuteronomists" helped edit Deutero-Zechariah, see Person (1993).

12. R. K. Harrison (1969:731-732) suggests the dating should be around 550 BC; Cate (1994:81) prefers c. 560 BC (cf. Lundbom 1999:101, citing D. N. Freedman [e.g., see 1997:151]). However, scholars such as Linville (1997:21-42) remain quite skeptical concerning any such close "exilic" dating, preferring to see 1–2 Kings as more likely a Persian or Hellenistic work of the Diaspora: "In my view, the 'completion date' of Kings is very much an open question and studies of Persian and even Hellenistic thought should include consideration of Kings" (Linville 1997:38-39). As A. G. Auld points out, "The fact that Kings ends with the fate of Judah's last king tells us no more about the date of composition . . . than the fact that the Pentateuch ends with the death of Moses" (cited in Person 1993:43). For the suggestion that the reference to the release from prison of the Davidic Jehoiachin fits better in the early postexilic era when the Davidic Zerubbabel served as governor, see Person 2002:119-120.

13. See notes 1 and 2 for the specific references.

14. For example, M. Noth emphasized the unity of the editing of 1–2 Kings (a part of a Deuteronomistic work comprising the books of Deuteronomy, Joshua, Judges, 1–2 Samuel, and 1–2 Kings), which took a decidedly pessimistic approach to the monarchy and its ever-intensifying decline until the Exile; he did see Josiah's reign as a "golden age" in which the law was revered, but Josiah was only an "isolated" representative (1981:79-83; cf. Cogan and Tadmor 1988:330; also Cogan 2001:99-100; Long 1991:288-289). G. von Rad, however, was more optimistic; although emphasizing the terrible severity of the exilic judgment of Yahweh, he still held to Yahweh's promises to the Davidic dynasty as being an important part of the Dtr work, seeing, for example, the closing note about the release of Jehoiachin from prison as one of special theological significance (von Rad 1953:89-91; cf. von Rad 1962:344-347; also cf. the helpful summary of Childs 1979:292-294). On the overall relatively positive "kerygma" of the Dtr work, see Wolff (1975:83-100; cf. note 28 below).

15. This point is well stressed in Friedman (1981:189-191): "Egypt is plainly fundamental to the perspective of Dtr1; and so, in the full Dtr2 edition, Egypt becomes a constant and ominous presence, the setting of the last and worst of the Deuteronomistic curses. . . . [This] raises the possibility that Dtr2 is even a product of the Egyptian community, a possibility that is enhanced by the extreme similarity of style and interest between the Deuteronomistic History and the book of Jeremiah, summoning to mind the Rabbinic claim of Jeremiah's authorship of the books of Kings. . . . Whatever the situation with regard to authorship, the Deuteronomistic History, in its final form, tells the story of Israel *from Egypt to Egypt*" (1981:191, emphasis added).

16. Contrast I. B. Gottlieb, as cited in James Linville (1997:26 n. 11), who simply equated this concluding optimistic note to the English phrase "happily ever after." Linville himself called the Jehoiachin note a common stylistic device in the OT, "a closure created by reference to a chronological cycle." I myself expect there is a lot more truth in this "closure" comment than might first meet the eye (or ear) of the casual reader.

17. Cf. the additions of the so-called Solomonic "miscellanies" found in the LXX at 3 Reigns 2:35a-o (the versification is Rahlfs's [1935], located after 1 Kgs 2:35, MT); also 2:46a-l (cf. Gooding 1976 for a careful study of both of these texts). Another brief but valuable text is 3 Reigns 8:53a; cf. Swete (1914:247-248), who says it is "of the highest interest," and must be a translation from a Hebrew original. Finally, note the varying order of the narratives concerning King Ahab in 1 Kgs 20–21, MT (see Gooding 1964:269-280), as well as the additional material (or at least the varying traditions) concerning the rise of Jeroboam I to power, 3 Reigns 11:26–12:24 and 12:24a-z (see Cogan 2001:355-356; Gooding 1967b:173-189). (For other minor variations in the ordering of the texts, cf. Swete 1914:232 as well as the helpful chart found in DeVries 1985:lx-lxiv.) More controversially, Shenkel (1968) has argued strongly for a differing, and possibly more accurate, chronology of the Omride kings attested in the Old Greek (see note on 1 Kgs 16:28; cf. my comments in Barnes 1991:23-25, 154-155).

18. Recently, Rendsburg has, with some success, isolated a northern Hebrew dialect (or set of dialects) to be found in parts of the books of Kings (2002:17-26). He termed this dialect "Israelian," and he suggested that it characterizes the Elijah-Elisha narratives, as well as most of the portions of 1–2 Kings dealing with the northern monarchs (also cf. Friedman 1998:358-359, and the references cited there, for recent discussions of the linguistic evidence concerning preexilic vs. postexilic Hebrew).

19. As conveniently summarized in Smith (1991:27-33); he, however, argues that these trends can be seen as already taking place in the spoken language of the preexilic period.

20. For example, probably the most vivid case of such sophisticated editing in the books of Samuel would be the sequence of "pro-" and "antimonarchical" texts in 1 Sam 8–12, where 1 Sam 8 and 12 contain strong indictments against the institution of monarchy in Israel, whereas most or all of 1 Sam 9:1–10:16 as well as 1 Sam 11 present much more positive material concerning the kingship of Saul (but 1 Sam 10:17-26 [MT] attests an antimonarchical viewpoint). Thus, anti, pro, anti, pro, anti. Therefore, are we to conclude that 1 Samuel is for or against the institution of monarchy? The answer, as I tell my students, is "yes"! More seriously, unless one reads or hears the text of 1 Sam 8–12 in its entirety, one will not get a balanced understanding of the message of the book concerning this central topic. Childs (1979:277-278) has an excellent discussion of this phenomenon.

21. The poem was probably added to the account "at a late stage in its development," according to Williamson (1996:47-52), who concurs with Cogan and Tadmor (1988:257) that the Kings version of these Hezekiah traditions must predate those found in the book of Isaiah.

22. For the north: 1 Kgs 14:19; 15:31; 16:5, 14, 20, 27; 22:39; 2 Kgs 1:18; 10:34; 13:8, 12 [= 14:15]; 14:28; 15:11, 15, 21, 26, 31 (thus a total of 17 different kings). For the south: [Solomon's unique source already mentioned, 1 Kgs 11:41] 1 Kgs 14:29; 15:7, 23; 22:45 [22:46, MT; cf. 16:28c, LXX]; 2 Kgs 8:23; 12:19 [12:20]; 14:18; 15:6, 36; 16:19; 20:20; 21:17, 25; 23:28; 24:5 (a total of 15 kings, not counting Solomon). The source citations often include some brief "additional elements" such as a reference to the "prowess" of the king (see 1 Kgs 15:23; 16:5, 27; 22:45 [22:46]; 2 Kgs 13:8, 12; 14:15, 28; 20:20; and cf. 2 Kgs 10:34—these references are translated in the NLT, "[and] the extent of his power"). Again, all of the various elements of these source citations are carefully categorized in Halpern and Vanderhooft (1991:216-221); and these two scholars again find evidence here of the three redactional levels for Dtr, especially in the variations found in the "additional elements" material.

23. See Barnes 1991:138-140 for a summary of the Israelite versus the Judahite formulas (but note that footnote 7 on p. 139 should read only "12," not 13 examples of the "short Israelite" formula, with 2 Kgs 10:36 *not* belonging in this category). With that correction (the error was mine, not Bin-Nun's), we find a total of 17 examples out of the 19 northern kings fitting into Bin-Nun's two northern categories (Jeroboam and Jehu being the exceptions; cf. 1 Kgs 14:20 and the aforementioned 2 Kgs 10:36); and (being a bit less strict than Bin-Nun herself) all 12 southern kings from Rehoboam to Hezekiah fall into the one southern category (cf. Barnes 1991:139 n. 9; Bin-Nun would not include Rehoboam, Jeroboam [MT], or Jehoash). And I would add that the final 7 southern kings (from Manasseh to Zedekiah) all have the expected southern accession formulas, but without the opening synchronisms, of course.

24. As already noted, there is a close correspondence between most of 2 Kgs 18:13–20:19 and Isa 36–39. More precisely, in each of these books we find the apparently non-chronological arrangement of three major sections of the Hezekiah tradition, which may be entitled "Victory over Assyria" (2 Kgs 18:13–19:37 // Isa 36–37), "Victory over impending death" (2 Kgs 20:1-11 // Isa 38), and "Future defeat by Babylon" (2 Kgs 20:12-19 // Isa 39). I say "nonchronological," inasmuch as we find Isaiah's prophetic response to King Hezekiah's impassioned prayer asking for longer life (2 Kgs 20:2-3 // Isa 38:2-3) including the references that Yahweh has heard his prayer, and that he will

add 15 years to Hezekiah's life *and deliver the city from the Assyrian king.* This is found in 2 Kgs 20:6 (// Isa 38:6), in a text that directly *follows* the passage that had just described dramatically the city's miraculous deliverance from the Assyrians and the eventual assassination of the Assyrian king. Also note how Hezekiah showed off his wealth to the visiting Babylonian envoys in 2 Kgs 20:13 [// Isa 39:2], although we have been told previously that he had to empty the Temple and palace treasuries and even strip the gold from the doorposts of the Temple to pay off the Assyrian king (2 Kgs 18:13-16, but here there is no parallel in Isaiah). Thus, the editorial sequencing in these Hezekiah stories is evidently not chronological, but I certainly do not think it is at all haphazard. Rather, theology trumped chronology in the organization of the passage. (For more detailed discussions of these sections, and the possibility of two Assyrian invasions, see the commentary below.)

25. Noth (1981:18-25) was fixated on this number, maintaining that the Deuteronomistic historian "did not see 480 as a fabrication; it is founded on the copious information about dates which he found in his sources and used in his work, and on a series of dates—the 40 year periods—which he himself inserted but which spring from the traditional view of the course of history. . . . This, then, is another proof—and the reason for our detailed consideration of chronology—that Dtr's history is a planned self-contained unity and that Dt. manifestly organized the broad outline and the chronological framework before working out the details" (the quote is from p. 25, near the end of an entire chapter discussing the chronological framework of Dtr). For other attempts at chronological schematization, see Barnes (1991:147 n. 24).

26. Concerning the Deuteronomists, see "Author" in the Introduction. The eminent German scholar Martin Noth (cf. the English translation, 1981:1-153; the German edition of his work entitled *Überlieferungsgeschichtliche Studien* was first published in 1943) still deserves pride of place in connection with the theory that Joshua through Kings was put into present form by the same group of exilic editors.

27. The best study of this phenomenon is that by Halpern and Vanderhooft (1991:179-244; especially pp. 199-212). As noted in endnote 1 above, all but one of the 19 northern kings are given negative evaluations, or are at least pictured in very negative terms (in fact, 15 out of the 19 northern kings are condemned particularly for "continuing" or "refusing to turn from" the sins of Jeroboam). Of the 8 southern kings condemned by the editor of Kings (see endnote 2 above, and putting aside Rehoboam), 2 specifically "followed the example of the kings of Israel/King Ahab's family" while 5 "followed the practices of the pagan nations/example of his father" or "did what was evil . . . just as his ancestors/father had done" (Zedekiah did evil, "just as Jehoiakim had done").

28. The classic text in my opinion remains Jer 18:1-12, the "potter's house sermon," where, in what is usually considered Deuteronomistic style, the author takes pains to emphasize the *conditionality* of prophecy, indeed of "the very word of Yahweh." To put it most boldly: I think most, if not all, of Yahweh's prophecies of judgment are given through the prophets, not so they may come to pass, but so they *might not* come to pass. Yahweh wishes desperately that his people might still somehow repent, might "turn away" (*shub* [TH7725, ZH8740]) from their sin (cf., especially, Jer 18:7-8), so that the threatened disaster does not have to take place. I also suspect Wolff (1975:83-100) is correct to point to this emphasis on turning back to Yahweh, as perhaps nothing less than the main message of the Deuteronomists (cf. also von Rad 1962:346).

29. A similar phenomenon may perhaps be seen in 1 Sam 2:30 concerning the previously promised "eternal" nature of Eli's priesthood.

30. In 1 Kgs 15:4, KJV, *nir* [TH5216, ZH5775] is translated "a lamp"; in all four passages, RSV also translates *nir* as "a lamp" (cf. NRSV); JPS does the same. The more common Hebrew term, *ner* [TH5216A, ZH5944], is usually translated "a lamp" (BDB 632d); cf. 2 Sam 21:17; Ps 132:17 for interesting usages of *ner* in reference to King David or to the Davidic line (the NLT translates these two references as "light").

31. Both Pss 89 and 132 are important royal Davidic psalms, and therefore one would expect that they would also share phraseology typical of the Davidic tradition. Cross

(1973:94-97) dates Ps 132 quite early ("an old hymn of the royal cult"), where there is allusion to a procession of the Ark when Yahweh first took up his abode on Mount Zion in the time of David himself. (On the unity and integrity of Ps 89, see Clifford 1980:35-47.)

32. Noth (1981:89-99); cf. Eichrodt (1961:243, 469); Friedman (1981:167-192); Gray (1970:9-10); von Rad (1962:334-347); also note the intriguing discussion found in Hobbs 1985:xxxiii-xxxviii.

33. In the books of Kings as we now have them, there is *no* completely successful king depicted as such. Evil kings are in abundance; good kings are fewer. But even King David himself, as far as 1 Kings is concerned, is pictured ambivalently at best (see, especially, 1 Kgs 1:4, 6; 2:5-9). King Solomon is rich, wise, and militarily at peace, yet the last words concerning him (1 Kgs 11, especially v. 33) are remarkably negative. No king of the northern kingdom is "good," although, as we have seen, some of the judgmental language is occasionally leavened with concessions (2 Kgs 3:2; 17:2). A number of southern kings were categorized as "good" (see endnote 2 for details), but even these have critical comments appended to their regnal accounts (usually formulaic references to the pagan shrines not being removed; see 1 Kgs 15:14; 22:43b [22:44]; 2 Kgs 12:3 [12:4]; 14:4; 15:4, 35). And even the accounts of the "best" kings of all, namely Hezekiah and Josiah (cf. the above discussion, "Earlier Editions of Kings?"), include negative comments—I take the final significant story about Hezekiah showing off his wealth to the Babylonian emissaries as judgmental in tone ("at least there will be peace and security during my lifetime," 2 Kgs 20:19); and King Josiah, he of the powerful Passover, the relentless purifier of the cult, and clearly the "hero" of the books of 1–2 Kings, can only postpone the Exile to after his own generation (2 Kgs 22:20; cf. 23:25-27). No wonder Noth was so negative about the books of Kings—seemingly, there is no hope. (Of course, I have at length cited the responses of Childs and Wolff in reply to his view.) Perhaps Noth is largely correct: The message of Kings is that *kings are not the answer*. Not even David, Solomon, Hezekiah, or even Josiah could forestall the inevitable. Yahweh and his people are probably better off without kings (even Davidic kings) on the throne at all!

COMMENTARY ON
1 Kings

♦ I. King Solomon (1 Kgs 1:1–11:43)
  A. Conclusion of the "Throne Succession Narrative" (1 Kgs 1:1–2:46)
  1. David in his old age (1:1-4)

King David was now very old, and no matter how many blankets covered him, he could not keep warm. ²So his advisers told him, "Let us find a young virgin to wait on you and look after you, my lord. She will lie in your arms and keep you warm."

³So they searched throughout the land of Israel for a beautiful girl, and they found Abishag from Shunem and brought her to the king. ⁴The girl was very beautiful, and she looked after the king and took care of him. But the king had no sexual relations with her.

NOTES

1:1 *King David was now very old.* As noted in the commentary below, many see this verse as continuing a lengthy story from 2 Samuel. Be that as it may, the verse now begins a new book, and the NLT correctly conveys the flavor of the Hebrew disjunction. The story begins where David's life ends.

blankets. Lit., "clothes," but the accompanying verb "to cover" would imply the ancient equivalent to today's blankets.

he could not keep warm. DeVries (1985:12) suggests that David's condition was advanced arteriosclerosis. The Hebrew verb "to keep warm" could imply sexual passion, but that is probably not the main import of the present text.

1:2 *a young virgin.* This is the literal translation of the phrase *na'arah bethulah* [TH5291/1330, ZH5855/1435], but the sense of the phrase is to indicate a young, unmarried woman. Again, the sexual connotation of the term "virgin" in contemporary English is not a major feature of the text (although, to be sure, it is not entirely absent from the text either).

look after you. The NLT here reflects the noun *sokeneth* [TH5532C, ZH6125], "housekeeper," i.e., manager of a household (Cogan 2001:156; Seow [1999:14] notes that the masculine form of the term denotes a position of power and responsibility). Abishag was more than a pretty face.

lie in your arms. Seow (1999:14) points out that this expression recalls Nathan's parable in 2 Sam 12:1-4, where the little lamb also "used to cuddle in the arms" of the poor man (who in the parable represented Bathsheba's husband, Uriah the Hittite, whom David later arranged to have killed in battle).

1:3 *Abishag from Shunem.* This was a town in the territory of Issachar (cf. Josh 19:18; 2 Kgs 4:8). Sweeney (2007:53) notes its ties to the house of Saul. The "Shulammite" heroine of Song 6:13 has often been connected with this Abishag "the Shunammite" by the rabbis (the Hebrew letters "n" and "l" are sometimes interchanged), but Cogan (2001:156) terms this merely "unfounded romantic speculation." The name Abishag probably means "my father is (was) a wanderer" (BDB 4d).

1:4 *very beautiful.* This could be translated "extremely beautiful" (*yapah* [TH3303, ZH3637] *'ad-me'od*), lit., "beautiful up to abundance"; the last two words denote an "absolute superlative" (Waltke and O'Connor 1990:268). Physical attractiveness is clearly meant.

But the king had no sexual relations with her. Lit., "but the king did not know her"— where the metaphor "to know" (*yada'* [TH3045, ZH3359]) can connote sexual intercourse, as in "Adam knew Eve his wife" (Gen 4:1, KJV) (cf. Leithart 2006:30). Much speculation has attended this statement. The question is whether David's sexual impotence (for that is what is surely implied here) is a major feature of the narrative, which progresses directly to Adonijah's bold rebellion against his father's expressed wishes (cf. 1:29-30) that Solomon succeed him to the throne. The understated nature of the details of the narrative, coupled with the author's unquestioned mastery of the art of storytelling, would probably imply that the answer to this question should be "yes." David appears remarkably impotent, literally and figuratively (see ABD 1.24 for details), throughout much of the rest of the chapter. This stands in stark contrast to the original Bathsheba narrative back in 2 Sam 11:1–12:25.

COMMENTARY

What a way to start off a book! David, the hero of much of 1–2 Samuel, has grown old, apparently in more ways than one. In contrast to modern Hollywood fare, any implications of sexual intrigue are delicately expressed by the narrator here—as is often the case in Hebrew storytelling (the verbs "to keep warm" and "to lie with" can certainly convey subtle sexual nuances). But sexuality is not the main focus of the text here. David couldn't get warm! The warmhearted if impetuous warrior of 1–2 Samuel, the charismatic hero who had often had an eye for an attractive woman (cf. 1 Sam 25:3; 2 Sam 11:2), is here literally impotent. Crisis is in the air.

Many commentators understand the first two chapters of 1 Kings as the ending of the so-called Throne Succession Narrative (see DeVries 1985:8-11; McCarter 1984:9-13; cf. Cogan 2001:165-167; Wiseman [1993:67] suggests, I think correctly, that Nathan the prophet may well have been the author of this "narrative"). As we now find these two chapters, however, they directly follow the six Davidic appendices of 2 Samuel 21–24, and thus stand alone as an effective introduction to the Solomon stories. How is it that Solomon, son of Bathsheba, was able to succeed his father David to the throne? What was the will of God in this transfer of power—the first successful transfer of monarchical power in the history of Israel, no less? These will be the questions we will ponder throughout the next several sections of the present narrative. One thing is certain: David himself was clearly in no condition to effect the transfer. And let us not forget that this was no ordinary petty kingdom in the Fertile Crescent of the ancient Near East, for salvific blessings on all humankind, then and in the future, had been promised to flow from the Davidic dynasty (see 2 Sam 7, especially v. 19, as noted above in the "Date and Occasion of Writing" section of the Introduction). Then, as now, God's ways are most mysterious.

◆ ## 2. Adonijah claims the throne (1:5-27)

5About that time David's son Adonijah, whose mother was Haggith, began boasting, "I will make myself king." So he provided himself with chariots and charioteers and recruited fifty men to run in front of him. 6Now his father, King David, had never disciplined him at any time, even by asking, "Why are you doing that?" Adonijah had been born next after Absalom, and he was very handsome.

7Adonijah took Joab son of Zeruiah and Abiathar the priest into his confidence, and they agreed to help him become king. 8But Zadok the priest, Benaiah son of Jehoiada, Nathan the prophet, Shimei, Rei, and David's personal bodyguard refused to support Adonijah.

9Adonijah went to the Stone of Zoheleth* near the spring of En-rogel, where he sacrificed sheep, cattle, and fattened calves. He invited all his brothers—the other sons of King David—and all the royal officials of Judah. 10But he did not invite Nathan the prophet or Benaiah or the king's bodyguard or his brother Solomon.

11Then Nathan went to Bathsheba, Solomon's mother, and asked her, "Haven't you heard that Haggith's son, Adonijah, has made himself king, and our lord David doesn't even know about it? 12If you want to save your own life and the life of your son Solomon, follow my advice. 13Go at once to King David and say to him, 'My lord the king, didn't you make a vow and say to me, "Your son Solomon will surely be the next king and will sit on my throne"? Why then has Adonijah become king?' 14And while you are still talking with him, I will come and confirm everything you have said."

15So Bathsheba went into the king's bedroom. (He was very old now, and Abi-shag was taking care of him.) 16Bathsheba bowed down before the king.

"What can I do for you?" he asked her.

17She replied, "My lord, you made a vow before the LORD your God when you said to me, 'Your son Solomon will surely be the next king and will sit on my throne.' 18But instead, Adonijah has made himself king, and my lord the king does not even know about it. 19He has sacrificed many cattle, fattened calves, and sheep, and he has invited all the king's sons to attend the celebration. He also invited Abiathar the priest and Joab, the commander of the army. But he did not invite your servant Solomon. 20And now, my lord the king, all Israel is waiting for you to announce who will become king after you. 21If you do not act, my son Solomon and I will be treated as criminals as soon as my lord the king has died."

22While she was still speaking with the king, Nathan the prophet arrived. 23The king's officials told him, "Nathan the prophet is here to see you."

Nathan went in and bowed before the king with his face to the ground. 24Nathan asked, "My lord the king, have you decided that Adonijah will be the next king and that he will sit on your throne? 25Today he has sacrificed many cattle, fattened calves, and sheep, and he has invited all the king's sons to attend the celebration. He also invited the commanders of the army and Abiathar the priest. They are feasting and drinking with him and shouting, 'Long live King Adonijah!' 26But he did not invite me or Zadok the priest or Benaiah or your servant Solomon. 27Has my lord the king really done this without letting any of his officials know who should be the next king?"

1:9 Or to the Serpent's Stone; Greek version supports reading Zoheleth as a proper name.

NOTES

1:5 *chariots and charioteers . . . fifty men to run in front of him.* This is similar to the royal escort Absalom had procured (2 Sam 15:1; cf. 1 Sam 8:11). Other parallels to Absalom include being described as "very handsome" (1:6b; cf. 2 Sam 14:25-26) and having an indulgent father (1:6a; cf. 2 Sam 13:21, LXX [see NLT mg there]; and Joab's comments in 2 Sam 19:5-8). As Seow (1999:17-18) notes, Nathan's prediction that trouble would arise from within David's own household (2 Sam 12:11-12) had, sadly, once again, come to pass.

1:7 Joab son of Zeruiah and Abiathar the priest. Joab was David's nephew and veteran commander of the army (2 Sam 2:18; 8:16; 1 Chr 2:16); he was the one who had killed Absalom against David's expressed wish (2 Sam 18:14-17). Abiathar was a son of the priest Ahimelech (cf. 1 Sam 22:20-23; 23:6) and a brave supporter of David in his struggles with Saul. Seow (1999:18; also cf. Cogan 2001:168) describes these individuals as representing the "old guard," conservative elements dating back to David's days in Hebron (2 Sam 2).

1:8 Zadok the priest. He was the ancestor of a very important priestly family in Israel, and one of two priests on David's palace staff (2 Sam 8:17; cf. 2 Sam 20:25). Often considered Jebusite in origin, thus not Israelite (the Jebusites were the original Canaanite inhabitants of Jerusalem [2 Sam 5:6; cf. DeVries 1985:14 for references]), he was possibly also from Hebron (see Cogan 2001:158; Cross 1973:207-215). In any case, he likely would have been a natural rival of Abiathar.

Benaiah son of Jehoiada. He was one of David's "Thirty Mighty Men" (see 2 Sam 23:20-23), captain of David's bodyguard (see 1:38).

Shimei, Rei, and David's personal bodyguard. Shimei and Rei are otherwise unknown and oddly, their fathers' names are not given. "Shimei" is not the Benjamite Shimei son of Gera mentioned in 2 Sam 16:5-14 (cf. 1 Kgs 2:8-9). Some, however, do equate the present Shimei with the "Shimei son of Ela" of 4:18. "Rei," in fact, may be a corruption of the similar term for "friend" (for possible emendations of this difficult text, see DeVries 1985:14). The "personal bodyguard" is made up of David's "mighty men" (*haggibborim* [TH1368A, ZH1475]), probably remnants of the famous "Three" and the "Thirty" listed in 2 Sam 23:8-39. Seow (1999:18) plausibly suggests that David's fragile coalition of old guards from Hebron (see note on 1:7) and new personnel from various locations connected with Jerusalem was apparently breaking down (cf. Jones 1984:91-92).

1:9 Stone of Zoheleth near the spring of En-rogel. Cogan (2001:159) connects this with the major spring called Bir Ayyub ("Job's well") some 500 meters south of the "City of David" (see note on 3:1), where the Kidron and the Hinnom valleys meet; he also discusses the possible rendering "Serpent's Stone" (cf. NLT mg). This location, on the boundary between the tribal territories of Benjamin and Judah (cf. Josh 15:7; 18:16), would have been well known (cf. 2 Sam 17:17), and the open area around the spring could easily accommodate the crowd commemorating the hasty coronation.

sacrificed sheep, cattle, and fattened calves. Adonijah and his confederates were ready for a public celebration, costly but savory to the smell. Modern Western culture often forgets how delightful such a "barbecue" would have been to the average Israelite, who would probably eat meat only three times a year (during the pilgrim feasts of Passover, etc.). It was not only Yahweh who would enjoy the "pleasing aroma" of the sacrifices placed on the altar. Cogan (2001:158) makes the important observation that all the action through the end of this chapter takes place on a single day—and what a momentous day it was.

1:10 did not invite Nathan . . . Benaiah . . . king's bodyguard . . . Solomon. The invited crowd, though large, was exclusive, as the narrator takes pains to note. Solomon in particular, who was born later in Jerusalem (cf. the separate lists found in 2 Sam 3:2-5; 5:13-16; cf. 1 Chr 3:1-9), could not be trusted. Not inviting "Nathan the prophet," however, would soon prove to be a tactical error (even though inviting him would probably have precluded any later hostile action against him and his interests, under the laws of Middle Eastern hospitality; cf. Wiseman 1993:70).

1:12 *follow my advice.* What follows is a carefully choreographed procedure, designed to awaken even the most uninvolved monarch. Nathan quickly made plans to bring about, as it were, the promised succession he himself seemingly prophesied back in 2 Sam 7. Believers in any age stand amazed at the remarkably contingent nature of God's will being accomplished. Note that Nathan scarcely exaggerates when he states that both Solomon's and Bathsheba's lives hang in the balance.

1:13 *didn't you make a vow . . . "Your son Solomon will surely be the next king"?* We have no previous record of this vow (but see below on 1:29-30 for apparent confirmation). We were told back in 2 Sam 12:24-25 that "[Yahweh] loved the child [named Solomon]," and that Nathan the prophet declared that David and Bathsheba name him Jedidiah, which meant "beloved of [Yahweh]." Cogan (2001:167) makes much of biblical storytelling describing "the wily ways of heroes" (here Nathan and Bathsheba) and how they, against all odds, outsmart the competition (cf. Seow 1999:19). Certainly such is the case in Genesis, especially in the stories about Jacob (see Gen 25–33; also the commentary on 1:28-53). But I suspect that what is particularly celebrated in the present passage is Nathan's quick thinking—his ability to turn a sudden crisis into a remarkable opportunity to wake up a king (the aged David), who was now sadly immune even to the charms of an extraordinarily beautiful woman (Abishag). Surely David had already given some thought to who would succeed him to the throne and brought up the subject in Bathsheba's presence. Walsh (1996:11) points out the hidden irony in Bathsheba's question about the vow inasmuch as her name probably means "Daughter of an Oath." However, Harvey (IDB 1.366) prefers the etymology "Daughter of Abundance."

1:14 *I will come and confirm everything.* In classical biblical style, Nathan's actual speech (1:24-27) "confirms" something quite different, seemingly asking the very aged King David (see the way the hearer/reader is reminded of this once again in 1:15) if he had peradventure authorized Adonijah's coronation without letting his officials in on the decision. A clever stratagem indeed!

1:15 *the king's bedroom.* This was surely a bittersweet location for Solomon's mother to enter. "Bathsheba, who had been desired by David even though she was in the bosom of another man, now speaks to the old king in front of the young and beautiful Abishag, who was brought to lie in his bosom" (Seow 1999:18).

1:20 *all Israel is waiting for you to announce who will become king after you.* Surely one of the most basic decisions any king would make is who will succeed him on the throne. David recognized (or at least once did recognize) the court intrigue such a decision (or the postponing of such a decision) could lead to. But again, for the hearer/reader of 1–2 Kings, this is not just another petty kingdom in the ancient Near East—rather, this is the vehicle of salvation for all humanity (see 2 Sam 7, especially David's own words of praise in 2 Sam 7:18-19).

1:21 *treated as criminals.* This is scarcely hyperbolic in the present context (see note on 1:12). As will be amply illustrated in the next chapter (2:1-12), the penalty for being on the losing side of this royal contest could well be sudden death, or at least banishment. Apart from such measures, the "losers" would represent a clear and abiding potential for usurpation, and at this time in history there had never been a successful transfer of power from father to son in Israel.

1:24 *have you decided that Adonijah will be the next king?* As noted above, Nathan took an independent tack in his speech to the king. He got to the gist of the matter: Had David really decided that Adonijah would sit on his throne? If David had avoided this decision in the past, he could avoid it no longer.

1:25 Long live King Adonijah! This is standard rhetoric for the occasion. The Hebrew reads, "May King Adonijah live!"—that is, "May Adonijah prosper." For the same statement concerning Solomon, see 1:34. (For Saul, this acclamation was given in 1 Sam 10:24; and for Joash, see 2 Kgs 11:12.) Bathsheba will soon use an even stronger expression (see 1:31).

1:27 Has my lord the king really done this without letting any of his officials know who should be the next king? This is a powerful conclusion to Nathan's speech (see note on 1:14). Here we see that "Nathan takes up the guise of the offended loyal servant" (Cogan 2001:160).

C O M M E N T A R Y

In this section we see Adonijah claiming to be king (1:5). He was David's fourth son (cf. 2 Sam 3:3-4); his name means "Yah(weh) is my Lord." Absalom, David's third son, had previously killed Amnon, David's first son, for raping Tamar (see 2 Sam 13; Tamar was Absalom's full sister and Amnon's half sister). Absalom had been killed for fomenting rebellion against his own father. The fate of the second son, Kileab/Daniel (see NLT mg at 2 Sam 3:3), is unknown; he perhaps died in childhood. Therefore, Adonijah presumably was the oldest surviving heir to the throne; he would naturally expect to inherit the throne by primogeniture (cf. 2:15). As for his mother, Haggith (whose name probably means "born on a feast day"; cf. the name "Haggai"), nothing further is known about her. Cogan (2001:157) cautions against interpreting the repeated references to her name in the present chapter as indicating a rivalry between her and Bathsheba, Solomon's mother.

Nathan went to Bathsheba to tell her that Adonijah had proclaimed himself king. He was the brave prophetic critic of David's adultery with Bathsheba and subsequent arrangement for the murder of her husband, Uriah the Hittite (2 Sam 11). He also was the prophet who announced Yahweh's blessing on David's dynasty (2 Sam 7:5-16), with repercussions both international and eternal. I think a remarkable amount of focus should be placed on Nathan the prophet at this juncture in the narrative. As Cogan has noted (see note on 1:9), all these actions and reactions occurred on a single day—and Nathan was equal to the task of "crisis management." The same prophet who gave David a message clearly *out of* God's will back in 2 Samuel 7:3 (although probably unintentionally so) and bravely *in* God's will in 2 Samuel 12:1-12, addressed the current crisis with masterful strategy and probing questions. Some time ago, Halpern (1981:59-96) studied the relationship between prophet and king in the early monarchical period, and his conclusions are germane here. Following his (and my) mentor, Frank Moore Cross Jr., he developed Cross's observation that "the institution of prophecy arose and declined with monarchy" (1981:83). It was the prophet who appointed the *nagid* [TH5057, ZH5592] (Hebrew for "designee for kingship" according to Halpern—the term is traditionally translated "prince" or "leader"), the candidate for king, and anointed him as designated king (e.g., Saul in 1 Sam 10:1, and David in 1 Sam 16:13). It was the prophet who denounced the king's excesses, and it was the prophet who initiated holy war. As Halpern (1981:83) concludes,

> *Thus the prophet in the monarchy imposed a sacral restraint—in theory—on the king's secular power. Such an office represents precisely the concession one would expect the priestly establishment to extract from the [tribal] assembly in return for the erection of a monarchy.*

Concerning the issue of "holy war," we will have much to say below (see especially ch 22). But my point here is more basic: It is the *prophet* who takes the initiative, who indeed is *expected to take the initiative* in reference to things monarchical. And Nathan certainly did not shrink from the challenge. Nathan was unafraid of confronting the king—speaking truth to power—that we already know (see 2 Sam 12). That is the bravery of *reaction*. He addressed a crisis others had caused. But here Nathan does more than react—he is proactive. Yes, he reacted to Adonijah's coronation party, but he also "pro-acted" to force David to react to the crisis. This will not be the last time that a godly prophet acts decisively to save the monarchy. (Some commentators, perhaps of a more cynical bent, suggest that Nathan fabricated the story of David's oath concerning Solomon as chosen successor, preying on the aged king's mental frailty. But I doubt that such a blatant falsehood could have successfully stood the test of time—not to mention the clear will of God [cf. 2 Sam 12:24-25; but note that God can effect division and strife, too; cf. 2 Sam 12:11-12; 1 Kgs 12:23-24].)

◆   ### 3. David makes Solomon king (1:28-53)

28King David responded, "Call Bathsheba!" So she came back in and stood before the king. 29And the king repeated his vow: "As surely as the LORD lives, who has rescued me from every danger, 30your son Solomon will be the next king and will sit on my throne this very day, just as I vowed to you before the LORD, the God of Israel."

31Then Bathsheba bowed down with her face to the ground before the king and exclaimed, "May my lord King David live forever!"

32Then King David ordered, "Call Zadok the priest, Nathan the prophet, and Benaiah son of Jehoiada." When they came into the king's presence, 33the king said to them, "Take Solomon and my officials down to Gihon Spring. Solomon is to ride on my own mule. 34There Zadok the priest and Nathan the prophet are to anoint him king over Israel. Blow the ram's horn and shout, 'Long live King Solomon!' 35Then escort him back here, and he will sit on my throne. He will succeed me as king, for I have appointed him to be ruler over Israel and Judah."

36"Amen!" Benaiah son of Jehoiada replied. "May the LORD, the God of my lord the king, decree that it happen. 37And may the LORD be with Solomon as he has been

with you, my lord the king, and may he make Solomon's reign even greater than yours!"

38So Zadok the priest, Nathan the prophet, Benaiah son of Jehoiada, and the king's bodyguard* took Solomon down to Gihon Spring, with Solomon riding on King David's own mule. 39There Zadok the priest took the flask of olive oil from the sacred tent and anointed Solomon with the oil. Then they sounded the ram's horn and all the people shouted, "Long live King Solomon!" 40And all the people followed Solomon into Jerusalem, playing flutes and shouting for joy. The celebration was so joyous and noisy that the earth shook with the sound.

41Adonijah and his guests heard the celebrating and shouting just as they were finishing their banquet. When Joab heard the sound of the ram's horn, he asked, "What's going on? Why is the city in such an uproar?"

42And while he was still speaking, Jonathan son of Abiathar the priest arrived. "Come in," Adonijah said to him, "for you are a good man. You must have good news."

43"Not at all!" Jonathan replied. "Our lord King David has just declared Solomon king! ⁴⁴The king sent him down to Gihon Spring with Zadok the priest, Nathan the prophet, and Benaiah son of Jehoiada, protected by the king's bodyguard. They had him ride on the king's own mule, ⁴⁵and Zadok and Nathan have anointed him at Gihon Spring as the new king. They have just returned, and the whole city is celebrating and rejoicing. That's what all the noise is about. ⁴⁶What's more, Solomon is now sitting on the royal throne as king. ⁴⁷And all the royal officials have gone to King David and congratulated him, saying, 'May your God make Solomon's fame even greater than your own, and may Solomon's reign be even greater than yours!' Then the king bowed his head in worship as he lay in his bed, ⁴⁸and he said, 'Praise the LORD, the God of Israel, who today has chosen a successor to sit on my throne while I am still alive to see it.'"

⁴⁹Then all of Adonijah's guests jumped up in panic from the banquet table and quickly scattered. ⁵⁰Adonijah was afraid of Solomon, so he rushed to the sacred tent and grabbed on to the horns of the altar. ⁵¹Word soon reached Solomon that Adonijah had seized the horns of the altar in fear, and that he was pleading, "Let King Solomon swear today that he will not kill me!"

⁵²Solomon replied, "If he proves himself to be loyal, not a hair on his head will be touched. But if he makes trouble, he will die." ⁵³So King Solomon summoned Adonijah, and they brought him down from the altar. He came and bowed respectfully before King Solomon, who dismissed him, saying, "Go on home."

1:38 Hebrew *the Kerethites and Pelethites;* also in 1:44.

NOTES

1:29 *the king repeated his vow.* We have already discussed the issue of how novel this vow was (see note on 1:13). Though I suspect the vow (or at least its content) had already been declared in the past, the NLT's translation in 1:29, "and the king repeated his vow," is too interpretive for the Hebrew, *wayyishaba'* [TH7650, ZH8678] (and he vowed).

1:31 *May my lord King David live forever!* As noted at 1:25, this is a stronger sentiment than the usual sentiment, "long live the king." DeVries (1985:16) suggests that Bathsheba did not indulge in wishful thinking (the immediate context is David's impending death, after all), but rather expressed the desire that David's "life-power" continue in his posterity. I would suggest more directly that the wish was for his dynasty to be eternal in duration—still a standard wish to be expressed for any good king, but in the present context all the more appropriate in light of 2 Sam 7 and its prophecy of David's dynasty lasting till the end of time (Seow 1999:19).

1:33 *Gihon Spring.* In the Kidron valley, this is the standard water source for the city of Jerusalem, also known as the Siloam Spring, or the Virgin's Spring. The term "Gihon" denotes "gushing," and its waters indeed gush from an underground karstic (eroded limestone) cave (Cogan 2001:161). The site would afford maximum publicity to the anointing of Solomon. Sweeney (2007:58) notes that Solomon's anointing would take place in full view of the entire city of Jerusalem, whereas Adonijah's would have been visible from the city, but at a greater distance. Some scholars take the last verse of Ps 110, an ancient Davidic psalm, as referring to a royal ritual in which the king ceremonially drank from this spring, a symbolic action enduing the new Davidic king with power (Anderson 1972:772; cf. Allen 1983:87), but this last point is conjectural.

ride on my own mule. Heb., *pirdah* [TH6506, ZH7235] (female mule), a hybrid animal, favored by the upper class (Cogan 2001:161; cf. 2 Sam 13:29; 18:9). Commoners would ride on a donkey (*khamor* [TH2543, ZH2789]).

1:34 *anoint him king over Israel.* As noted in the commentary on 1:5-27, both Saul and David were anointed as "king-designate" by the prophet Samuel. But this is a public anointing, unlike the earlier two events; here both priest and prophet participated in the anointing.

Blow the ram's horn. Blowing the shofar, or ram's horn, is a common Hebrew custom that can indicate celebration (as here), or alarm. DeVries (1985:17) suggests there was no mention of this in regard to Adonijah's ceremony so as to preserve stealth.

Long live King Solomon! See note on 1:25.

1:35 *ruler.* Heb., *nagid* [TH5057, ZH5592], possibly "king-designate" or the like (see discussion in the commentary on 1:5-27). Some scholars see a four-year coregency between David and Solomon (cf. 6:1); the term *nagid* here would lend support to that view. But Cogan (2001:161-162) notes it may be used of a king's rule, as well.

over Israel and Judah. This is the common way to refer to the entirety of David's realm (see 4:20; 2 Sam 5:5; 24:9). Cogan (2001:162) describes these entities as the "two constituent political components" of David's kingdom. These separate entities will reemerge forcefully in ch 12.

1:36 *Amen!* The English transliterates the Heb. *'amen* [TH543, ZH589], meaning "so be it."

1:38 *the king's bodyguard.* Lit., "the Kerethites and Pelethites" (see NLT mg). As noted above (1:8), Benaiah was their commander (2 Sam 20:23; cf. 2 Sam 20:7b, NLT mg). Apparently foreign mercenaries, they are often linked to the Cretans and the Philistines, respectively (Cogan 2001:162; but see Sweeney 2007:58). Apparently even foreign mercenaries appropriately celebrated Solomon's accession.

1:39 *from the sacred tent.* Heb., *min-ha'ohel* [TH168, ZH185], "from the tent." On the identity of this tent, see the note on 1:50.

1:40 *all the people . . . playing flutes and shouting for joy.* Again in contrast to Adonijah's exclusive ceremony, Solomon's ceremony was open to the public—and all the people celebrated with great joy, the noisy fanfare inevitably echoing down the valley. Parallels to David's famous dancing before the Ark (2 Sam 6:14-15) also come to mind.

1:41 *What's going on?* This is Joab's predictable question when he and Adonijah's party heard the celebration at the Gihon Spring. Secrecy can work both ways!

1:42 *You must have good news.* With consummate artistry, the narrator tells the tale. Jonathan son of Abiathar will soon disabuse them of such notions. This Jonathan had also been a bearer of news from the city during Absalom's rebellion (see 2 Sam 15:27-28, 36; 17:17-21).

1:43 *Not at all!* Hebrew narrators love to retell their tales with subtle variations. Here Jonathan's words "tumble out and pile up" as he fervently "adds one detail after another to his report" (Cogan 2001:163, citing Long 1984:39). Sweeney (2007:59) notes that Jonathan's report particularly emphasized the faithful compliance of Zadok, Nathan, and Benaiah with David's commands.

1:47 *fame even greater . . . reign be even greater.* Cf. Benaiah's wish back in 1:37. "Fame" is lit. "name," referring to one's fame and reputation; "reign" is lit. "throne" (*kisse'* [TH3678, ZH4058]), referring to extended rule and dominion (Cogan 2001:163). For the editor of 1–2 Kings, David's name and David's dominion still remain the hallmarks of greatness (14:8; 15:3-5, 11; 2 Kgs 14:3; 16:2; 18:3; 22:2).

bowed his head in worship as he lay in his bed. There are definite echoes of the aged patriarch Jacob here (see Gen 47:31, MT; cf. NLT mg there), who after a similarly tumultuous life, was likewise able to experience Yahweh's faithful transfer of authority to the next generation. Cogan (2001:164) appropriately cites Speiser (1964:356-357) who notes that in the Genesis text, MT is to be preferred: "The term 'to bow low' need not signify here anything more than a gesture of mute appreciation on the part of a bedridden man on the point of death. The bow or nod would come naturally from the head of the bed." (The identical verb, *wayyishtakhu* [TH7812A, ZH2556], is found in both texts.)

1:48 *Praise the LORD, the God of Israel, who today has chosen a successor to sit on my throne while I am still alive to see it.* David praised Yahweh for this great blessing. Scholars who posit a coregency between David and Solomon (see note on 1:35) naturally read this verse quite literally (DeVries 1985:19). On the other hand, biblical narrators love to put such set speeches in the mouths of their protagonists (e.g., Josh 23; 1 Sam 12; and much of 1 Kgs 8 [cf. Noth 1981:5-6]). (I am not suggesting that David did not utter such words, only that there is a stereotypical tendency in biblical narrative to formalize such utterances.)

1:49 *jumped up in panic.* One should not take literally that Adonijah's guests or even Jonathan himself for that matter (Sweeney 2007:163) actually heard the bedridden David's speech. In any event, news of Solomon's kingship reached them.

1:50 *rushed to the sacred tent.* The MT reads, "he arose and went." Some Lucianic LXX manuscripts do include a reference "to the tent of the LORD" here, but DeVries (1985:19) takes this as a later addition inspired by 2:28. David had previously erected some sort of tent to protect the Ark of God when it was brought into Jerusalem (see 2 Sam 6:17), and it is this tent that is mentioned here. This was presumably not identical to the Tabernacle erected in the wilderness in the days of Moses (Anderson 1989:106), where the brazen altar was naturally placed outside in the courtyard in front of the actual tent housing the golden altar of incense.

grabbed on to the horns of the altar. Both the brazen altar and the altar of incense in the days of Moses had "horns" on each of the four upper corners (Exod 27:2; 30:2). These particular altars have been lost to history (I expect even before the days of David), but other examples of Israelite altars with horns have been excavated (see Cogan 2001:164 for references). As Cogan notes, the significance of the horns is nowhere stated, "but it seems that, since the blood of sacrifices was daubed on the horns (e.g., Lev 4:7, 25), the horns were considered the most significant area of the altar." DeVries (1985:19), who sees this altar as being within the tent, comments, "To seek refuge in a sanctuary, protected from summary execution, was widely practiced in the ancient world, so much so that the Romans had to abolish it (Tacitus *Annals* III, lx-lxiii)." A similar sentiment seems to be expressed in the legal material found in Exod 21:14 (see the excellent discussion found in Propp 2006:208-210).

1:52 *proves himself to be loyal.* Heb., *yihyeh leben-khayil* (will become a son of valor). Ironically, the term *khayil* [TH2428, ZH2657] (which is also used of Jonathan, "a good man," in 1:42) more often than not refers to prowess in battle (DeVries 1985:20); but in the present situation, bravery (which one must admit Adonijah did possess in some measure) was not the issue—honor and loyalty were.

1:53 *King Solomon.* The full title is used here; perhaps he should be reckoned as full coregent with his father David at this point (see note on 1:35).

COMMENTARY

We now see the "old" David, the one who acts decisively and "saves the day." David called in Bathsheba and confirmed that Solomon was his choice as heir apparent. For all intents and purposes, Solomon's accession to the throne was secure and his royal prerogatives uncontested. This was the first time that such a transfer of royal power had taken place successfully in Israel or Judah. Saul's son Ishbosheth did rule briefly in Israel after his father's death, as the regnal accession formula states in 2 Samuel 2:10a, but since his "capital" was in Mahanaim in Transjordan, this hardly proves to be a real exception, as the very next verses (2 Sam 2:10b-11) emphasize.

Isaiah 55:8-9 reminds us that God's ways are far higher than our ways. The book of Genesis repeatedly emphasizes this fact particularly in regard to father-and-son transitions. We see this with (1) Abraham and Isaac, where Abraham says to God, "May Ishmael live under your special blessing!" (Gen 17:18); (2) Isaac and Jacob, where Esau asks his father Isaac, "What about me? Bless me, too!" (Gen 27:34-36); (3) Jacob and his sons, Joseph, Judah and the others, where Jacob on his deathbed said to Judah, "All your relatives will bow before you" (Gen 49:8, in clear contrast to Joseph's dreams back in Gen 37:5-11, which, to be sure, were fulfilled in Gen 42:6; 43:26; and probably also 47:31); and (4) Joseph and his sons, Ephraim and Manasseh, where it is said the "younger brother will become even greater" (Gen 48:17-20). Certainly, the ancient custom of primogeniture is no guarantee of status when it comes to the Bible and the God of the Bible.

That God of the Bible reigns sovereign, even in 1 Kings 1. Whether it be prophet over king (a favorite theme throughout the books of Samuel and Kings), David over Saul, or here, Solomon over Adonijah, God's ways will win out in the end. In the next chapter, both Adonijah and Solomon publicly attest to this (cf. 2:15b, 24a). Human machinations can and will accomplish the will of God! But this is *no* guarantee that the apparent victors are themselves *in* the will of God. The reader of the final redaction of 1–2 Kings knows well how the whole story will turn out: Solomon will *not* transcend his father David in status (see first note on 1:47), and for that matter, neither will the kingdom of David even survive his son intact (see ch 12). The Davidic dynasty would long endure, but not eternally as such (contrast 2 Sam 7, which is understood as a reference to a literal, earthly throne). There would come a day, however, when another son of David, whose kingdom is not of this world (John 18:36), would transcend all others by becoming the lowest of servants (cf. Phil 2:6-8). No prophet, such as Nathan, had to take initiative to raise Jesus from his earthly status; it was God himself who raised him up from the dead, literally to ascend into heaven, from which his kingdom will one day become evident to all (Phil 2:9-11).

◆   ## 4. David's final instructions to Solomon (2:1-12)

As the time of King David's death approached, he gave this charge to his son Solomon:

2"I am going where everyone on earth must someday go. Take courage and be a man. 3Observe the requirements of the LORD your God, and follow all his ways. Keep the decrees, commands, regulations, and laws written in the Law of Moses so that you will be successful in all you do and wherever you go. 4If you do this, then the LORD will keep the promise he made to me. He told me, 'If your descendants live as they should and follow me faithfully with all their heart and soul, one of them will always sit on the throne of Israel.'

5"And there is something else. You know what Joab son of Zeruiah did to me when he murdered my two army commanders, Abner son of Ner and Amasa son of Jether. He pretended that it was an act of war, but it was done in a time of peace,* staining his belt and sandals with innocent blood.* ⁶Do with him what you think best, but don't let him grow old and go to his grave in peace.*

⁷"Be kind to the sons of Barzillai of Gilead. Make them permanent guests at your table, for they took care of me when I fled from your brother Absalom.

⁸"And remember Shimei son of Gera, the man from Bahurim in Benjamin. He cursed me with a terrible curse as I was fleeing to Mahanaim. When he came down to meet me at the Jordan River, I swore by the LORD that I would not kill him. ⁹But that oath does not make him innocent. You are a wise man, and you will know how to arrange a bloody death for him.*"

¹⁰Then David died and was buried with his ancestors in the City of David. ¹¹David had reigned over Israel for forty years, seven of them in Hebron and thirty-three in Jerusalem. ¹²Solomon became king and sat on the throne of David his father, and his kingdom was firmly established.

2:5a Or *He murdered them during a time of peace as revenge for deaths they had caused in time of war.* **2:5b** As in some Greek and Old Latin manuscripts; Hebrew reads *with the blood of war.* **2:6** Hebrew *don't let his white head go down to Sheol in peace.* **2:9** Hebrew *how to bring his white head down to Sheol in blood.*

NOTES

2:1 *As the time of King David's death approached.* For the possibility of a coregency between David and Solomon, see note on 1:35.

2:2 *I am going where everyone on earth must someday go.* Joshua said much the same thing as he was facing imminent death (see Josh 23:14). In OT times, rarely was any distinction made between what we would refer to as heaven and hell—all people (with the rare exceptions of special saints such as Enoch or Elijah) were reckoned as going to Sheol (probably best understood as the personified grave; cf. Johnston 2005) when they died. We should remember David's own words in 2 Sam 12:23 concerning the sad death of his and Bathsheba's first child: "Can I bring him back again? I will go to him one day, but he cannot return to me." Concerning the Hebrew conception of the afterlife, and its notable reticence concerning details, see Segal 2006:65-68. (This reticence stands in sharp contrast to what the peoples of Egypt and Mesopotamia wrote.) Most OT texts suggest a kind of sleepy quasi existence, where, notably, the dead cannot praise or worship Yahweh as the living do (cf. Pss 30:9 [10]; 88:10-12 [11-13]; Isa 38:18-19). There are, however, some more optimistic references (mostly in the later texts) to the possibility of resurrection, or at least a positive conscious existence with God for the righteous (cf. Ps 115:16-18; Ezek 37:1-14; Dan 12:2-3.)

Take courage and be a man. This section finds close Deuteronomic and Deuteronomistic parallels, especially with Moses and Joshua (cf. Deut 31:7-8; Josh 1:6-9; on Deuteronomistic literature, see the Introduction, "Date and Occasion of Writing").

2:3 *Observe the requirements. . . . Keep the decrees . . . written in the Law of Moses so that you will be successful.* Classically understood as an example of Deuteronomistic retribution theology (cf. endnote 32 of the Introduction), we certainly find close parallels here to Deuteronomy (both spoken in the plural for the people, and in the singular for the leader—see, e.g., Deut 31:5-6, 7-8, respectively).

2:4 *If your descendants live as they should.* Some (e.g., Cross 1973:219-273) have contrasted conditional statements such as this (also cf. Ps 132:11-12) with the unconditional language found in 2 Sam 7 (especially 2 Sam 7:11b-16, where the Davidic covenant is said to remain in effect *no matter* how faithless a Davidic ruler might prove to be), as probably earlier and later theological formulations of the Davidic covenant, respectively. I am quite sympathetic to such reasoning (understanding, as Cross [1973:264-265] does, that the present text is part of the earlier, more traditional covenantal ideology—the covenant will *only* stand *if* the stipulations are kept), but I must point out that later prophetic statements such as the famous "potter's house sermon" found in Jer 18:1-12 (see endnote 28 in the Introduction) caution us against minimizing the "if . . . then" statements found here and elsewhere in the Hebrew Bible. To be sure, Cross himself (1973:265) argues that this earlier covenantal ideology does survive along with the later, triumphalistic ideology up to and beyond the Exile; in fact, the sins of Jeroboam in the north and Manasseh in the south irrevocably void Yahweh's covenant with king and people (cf. Introduction, endnote 29).

with all their heart and soul. This is again the language of Deuteronomy (see Deut 4:29; 6:5; 10:12; 11:13; 13:3 [4 MT]; 26:16; 30:2, 6, 10); it is also notably the language used to praise the incomparability of King Josiah (2 Kgs 23:3, 25; cf. the discussion of the greatness of Josiah in the Introduction, under "Earlier Editions of Kings?"). King Hezekiah, although also "incomparable" (2 Kgs 18:5), is not described with these terms. (On the meaning of the terms "heart" and "soul" in Hebrew, see the third note on 2 Kgs 23:3.)

2:5 He pretended that it was an act of war, but it was done in a time of peace. Lit., "he assigned (*wayyasem* [TH7760, ZH8492]) the bloodshed of war in peacetime" (so Cogan 2001:173); the NLT mg note on 2:5a tries to explicate the contrast here between "blood of war" and "peacetime."

staining . . . with innocent blood. The Hebrew (MT) reads lit., "and he put (*wayyitten* [TH5414, ZH5989]) the bloodshed of war . . . ." Cogan (2001:173) takes this phrase as explicating the previous one ("he assigned the bloodshed of war in peacetime"), which admittedly is quite terse as it stands. Codex Vaticanus omits this second reference to the "bloodshed of war" entirely, but that is probably due to an error by a scribe (cf. DeVries 1985:26). The essence here is that the blood of Joab's victims was indelibly spattered on his garments, and such a stain (at least metaphorically) could never be removed. The Bible is very clear that the shedding of innocent blood must be accounted for (cf. Gen 4:10-12; Deut 19:10; Jer 26:15). The Lucianic Greek tradition and the Old Latin communicate by a change of pronouns that it was *David's* "belt and sandals" that were stained with blood— i.e., David was guilty in these affairs because Joab was understood to be following David's orders (cf. Cogan 2001:173; DeVries 1985:36). The changes between "his" and "my" in Hebrew involve a shift in (or the loss of) only one consonant. The phrase "innocent blood" (following Greek and Old Latin witnesses) probably is a later explanatory gloss on the MT's second reference to "blood of war" (cf. NLT's mg note at 2:5b), which in turn had contributed to the haplography in Codex Vaticanus. The textual variant that is more difficult and that can best explain other textual variants is to be preferred, and here, that appears to be the tradition behind the MT.

2:6 go to his grave in peace. A very similar phrase is found in 2:9. The word "grave" signifies the term *she'ol* [TH7585, ZH8619] ("realm of the dead"; cf. note on 2:2).

2:7 Be kind to the sons of Barzillai of Gilead. Perhaps being "permanent guests" at the king's table should be taken as a dubious honor since such guests might then be kept more effectively under royal surveillance (see Seow 1999:28). But in light of the present ending of 1–2 Kings, in which the exiled King Jehoiachin is given a place of honor, "din[ing] in the king's presence for the rest of his life" (2 Kgs 25:29b; cf. the Introduction), I suspect the present command (as in 2 Sam 9:7) is authentically meant to be generous. On the occasion of David being taken care of when he had to flee from Absalom, see 2 Sam 17:27-29; cf. 2 Sam 19:31-39. (Concerning the Barzillai interests in the nascent iron industry, see Seow 1999:28. "Barzillai" is derived from *barzel* [TH1270, ZH1366], "iron.")

Be kind. Lit., "show loving-kindness" (*khesed* [TH2617, ZH2876]); see note on 3:6 concerning this very rich expression in the Hebrew.

2:8-9 *remember Shimei son of Gera. . . . that oath does not make him innocent.* In contrast to the possible ambiguity of the suggested treatment of the sons of Barzillai, David's present command is straightforwardly condemnatory.

2:9 *You are a wise man.* This is an ironic foreshadowing of the major criterion for Solomon's suitability to succeed David as king (see ch 3). Solomon's "wisdom" (*khokmah* [TH2451, ZH2683]; in the present verse the adjective "wise" *khakam* [TH2450, ZH2682] is found) is clearly of a practical, not theoretical bent (as will soon be illustrated in the account of the two prostitutes and the contested infant in 3:16-28). Scott (1965:xvii) has helpfully described *khokmah* as "expertness of a particular kind" that is a combination of special, innate gifts coupled with training and experience. Such is evidently the case here where Solomon's wisdom will supersede any timidity or inappropriate tenderheartedness he might have toward Shimei and his extended family. In my opinion (contrast Cross 1998:93), the unforgettable image of the aged King David as coldhearted and bent on revenge bespeaks authenticity here—a later apologist for the Solomonic tradition would be unlikely to make up such a cynical comment about Solomon's wisdom or to paint such an unflattering picture of David. If David was suffering from the onset of senility, or perhaps what is now known as Alzheimer's disease, such uncharacteristic aggressiveness and paranoia would be symptomatic of the progression of the disease (cf. the incidents described in ch 1).

2:10 *was buried with his ancestors in the City of David.* This is a formulaic death notice (for details, see "Literary Style" in the Introduction). Concerning the exact location of David's tomb (still known in Peter's day according to Acts 2:29), see DeVries 1985:36-37, where he suggests the south slope of the Ophel (but see Cogan 2001:175). In any case, it is probably not the "tourist" tomb of David on the western hill known today as "Mount Zion."

2:11 *David had reigned over Israel for forty years.* This chronological summary is also found in 2 Sam 5:4-5, although it probably is a secondary expansion there (McCarter 1984:130-131, 133). Bin-Nun (1968:422) categorizes the style of this summary as from the northern tradition (cf. the extended discussion in the Introduction, "Literary Style").

2:12 Here the LXX (see especially Codex Vaticanus) begins to reflect the Old Greek. On this, see "Canonicity and Textual History" in the Introduction.

COMMENTARY

This section begins with David's final words to Solomon, wherein he first tells him to follow the law of Moses (Heb., *torath mosheh* [TH8451, ZH9368], "Torah of Moses"). Jewish scholars have long noted that the term Torah is better translated "teachings" than the familiar "law," inasmuch as the verbal root behind "Torah" denotes "to direct, or teach," and the Western idea of "law" does not correspond well to the breadth of tradition found in Torah. Torah represents God's word to his people and of course includes "laws," the Ten Commandments being the best known, but there is so much more—stories of heroes and villains (God often seeming to bless the latter), genealogies, etiologies, jokes, tragedies, and so forth. To label the Old Testament as "law" (with the NT often contrasted as "grace") does a disservice to both Testaments.

The scene soon shifts from seemingly pious platitudes (2:1-4) to *realpolitik* (2:5-9). David's mostly distressing comments are (1) hard to forget—David's "final words" (at least from an editorial point of view) are mostly cruel and petty; and (2) hard to justify in light of the eternal Davidic covenant of 2 Samuel 7 and the generally very generous personality we have come to identify with David, a "man after [God's] own heart" (1 Sam 13:14). (See my comments in the Introduction, "Earlier Editions of Kings?")

David asked Solomon to deal with Joab, son of Zeruiah (2:5-6). Joab was David's veteran commander of the army (2 Sam 8:16), and he had killed Abner and Amasa. The "murder" of Abner is narrated in 2 Samuel 3:26-27 (pictured there as a revenge killing [2 Sam 3:27b, 30]). Abner had killed Asahel, a relative of Joab's, in combat between the forces of Saul's house and David's men (2 Sam 2:18-23). But shortly before he was killed, Abner had sided with David, moving to undermine the house of Saul (2 Sam 3:6-21). As for Amasa, the Throne Succession Narrative on two separate occasions describes him in essence as acting traitorously against David—on one occasion siding first with Absalom before being enticed to side with David (2 Sam 17:25; 19:11-14), and later delaying in responding to the Sheba rebellion (2 Sam 20:4-13). In sum, Joab's actions in both cases were harsh, vengeful, and underhanded, but somewhat defendable. Some commentators suspect that David's real (but unexpressed) complaint against Joab was for his murder of Absalom (2 Sam 18:9-17) as well as his subsequent remonstrance of David's indulgent mourning of Absalom's death (2 Sam 19:1-14; cf. Sweeney 2007:60).

David then asked Solomon to be kind to the sons of Barzillai (see note on 2:7) and to deal with Shimei, son of Gera (2:8). Shimei, a member of Saul's clan (2 Sam 16:5-13), had cursed David during Absalom's revolt, but had later recanted (2 Sam 19:15-23). David had conspicuously vowed an oath that his life would be spared. As Sweeney (2007:60) notes, Shimei had shown *no* sign of disloyalty after that point. David's vengeful attitude here (2:8), in direct violation of his formal vow in 2 Samuel 19:23, is, in my opinion, nothing less than despicable—and it brings into uneasy consciousness the "oath" that Yahweh swore (2 Sam 7) never to give up on the Davidic dynasty for the sake of all people (see "Date and Occasion of Writing" in the Introduction). Simon DeVries (1985:42) makes the salient point that David and Solomon's turn against Shimei, probably motivated by the desire to suppress unrest among the northern tribes, may well have had the opposite effect, leading to the division of the kingdom under Jeroboam and Rehoboam (see 1 Kgs 12).

What a combination of sincere piety and hardened cynicism we find in this section! I take the view that David historically did convey something like the Deuteronomic sentiments we find here in 2:2-4, and I do assume that David did indeed command his son to exact bloodthirsty revenge on his foes. But what does the narrator think of all this? Here we again confront the genius of Hebrew narrative, as well as its sometimes frustrating nature—its reticence to editorialize on what it reports. The David whose death we should mourn (2:10) was a realistic, if quite unheroic figure, one who was as at ease in Middle Eastern court intrigues as his son Solomon would be. Simple, pious moralism is missing here, as it so often is in the real world. But surely our narrator has a viewpoint concerning such a curious mixture of Deuteronomic posturing and Machiavellian maneuvering! At least, as current historical political figures remind us time and again, pious public posturings are no guarantee of deep ethical soundness. Our narrator here is far from naive concerning these matters, and he or she wishes us to be so, too. But what about the Davidic promise of 2 Samuel 7? The eerie disclaimer of verse 2:4b of the present text may be more germane than a quick reading suggests. If God's people consistently fail to respond to his word, all bets are off (cf. endnote 28 in the Introduction), and the attentive reader of this Solomonic Throne Succession Narrative can only tremble when he or she confronts the all-too-real protagonists we read about here.

◆ ### 5. Solomon establishes his rule (2:13-46)

¹³One day Adonijah, whose mother was Haggith, came to see Bathsheba, Solomon's mother. "Have you come with peaceful intentions?" she asked him.

"Yes," he said, "I come in peace. ¹⁴In fact, I have a favor to ask of you."

"What is it?" she asked.

¹⁵He replied, "As you know, the kingdom was rightfully mine; all Israel wanted me to be the next king. But the tables were turned, and the kingdom went to my brother instead; for that is the way the LORD wanted it. ¹⁶So now I have just one favor to ask of you. Please don't turn me down."

"What is it?" she asked.

¹⁷He replied, "Speak to King Solomon on my behalf, for I know he will do anything you request. Ask him to let me marry Abishag, the girl from Shunem."

¹⁸"All right," Bathsheba replied. "I will speak to the king for you."

¹⁹So Bathsheba went to King Solomon to speak on Adonijah's behalf. The king rose from his throne to meet her, and he bowed down before her. When he sat down on his throne again, the king ordered that a throne be brought for his mother, and she sat at his right hand.

²⁰"I have one small request to make of you," she said. "I hope you won't turn me down."

"What is it, my mother?" he asked. "You know I won't refuse you."

²¹"Then let your brother Adonijah marry Abishag, the girl from Shunem," she replied.

²²"How can you possibly ask me to give Abishag to Adonijah?" King Solomon demanded. "You might as well ask me to

give him the kingdom! You know that he is my older brother, and that he has Abiathar the priest and Joab son of Zeruiah on his side."

²³Then King Solomon made a vow before the LORD: "May God strike me and even kill me if Adonijah has not sealed his fate with this request. ²⁴The LORD has confirmed me and placed me on the throne of my father, David; he has established my dynasty as he promised. So as surely as the LORD lives, Adonijah will die this very day!" ²⁵So King Solomon ordered Benaiah son of Jehoiada to execute him, and Adonijah was put to death.

²⁶Then the king said to Abiathar the priest, "Go back to your home in Anathoth. You deserve to die, but I will not kill you now, because you carried the Ark of the Sovereign LORD for David my father and you shared all his hardships." ²⁷So Solomon deposed Abiathar from his position as priest of the LORD, thereby fulfilling the prophecy the LORD had given at Shiloh concerning the descendants of Eli.

²⁸Joab had not joined Absalom's earlier rebellion, but he had joined Adonijah's rebellion. So when Joab heard about Adonijah's death, he ran to the sacred tent of the LORD and grabbed on to the horns of the altar. ²⁹When this was reported to King Solomon, he sent Benaiah son of Jehoiada to execute him.

³⁰Benaiah went to the sacred tent of the LORD and said to Joab, "The king orders you to come out!"

But Joab answered, "No, I will die here."

So Benaiah returned to the king and told him what Joab had said.

³¹"Do as he said," the king replied. "Kill

him there beside the altar and bury him. This will remove the guilt of Joab's senseless murders from me and from my father's family. ³²The LORD will repay him* for the murders of two men who were more righteous and better than he. For my father knew nothing about the deaths of Abner son of Ner, commander of the army of Israel, and of Amasa son of Jether, commander of the army of Judah. ³³May their blood be on Joab and his descendants forever, and may the LORD grant peace forever to David, his descendants, his dynasty, and his throne."

³⁴So Benaiah son of Jehoiada returned to the sacred tent and killed Joab, and he was buried at his home in the wilderness. ³⁵Then the king appointed Benaiah to command the army in place of Joab, and he installed Zadok the priest to take the place of Abiathar.

³⁶The king then sent for Shimei and told him, "Build a house here in Jerusalem and live there. But don't step outside the city to go anywhere else. ³⁷On the day you so much as cross the Kidron Valley, you will surely die; and your blood will be on your own head."

³⁸Shimei replied, "Your sentence is fair; I will do whatever my lord the king commands." So Shimei lived in Jerusalem for a long time.

³⁹But three years later two of Shimei's slaves ran away to King Achish son of Maacah of Gath. When Shimei learned where they were, ⁴⁰he saddled his donkey and went to Gath to search for them. When he found them, he brought them back to Jerusalem.

⁴¹Solomon heard that Shimei had left Jerusalem and had gone to Gath and returned. ⁴²So the king sent for Shimei and demanded, "Didn't I make you swear by the LORD and warn you not to go anywhere else or you would surely die? And you replied, 'The sentence is fair; I will do as you say.' ⁴³Then why haven't you kept your oath to the LORD and obeyed my command?"

⁴⁴The king also said to Shimei, "You certainly remember all the wicked things you did to my father, David. May the LORD now bring that evil on your own head. ⁴⁵But may I, King Solomon, receive the LORD's blessings, and may one of David's descendants always sit on this throne in the presence of the LORD." ⁴⁶Then, at the king's command, Benaiah son of Jehoiada took Shimei outside and killed him.

So the kingdom was now firmly in Solomon's grip.

2:32 Hebrew *will return his blood on his own head.*

NOTES

2:13 One day. The Hebrew simply reads *wayyabo'* [TH935, ZH995] (and he came), a "Waw-consecutive imperfect" (concerning this terminology, see "Literary Style" in the Introduction), thus indicating a return to the main narrative. For the identity of Adonijah son of Haggith, see note on 1:5.

Have you come with peaceful intentions? This was a very appropriate query in light of Adonijah's prior actions (1:5-10, 41-53); in essence, he had tried to usurp the throne. "Peaceful intentions" (*shalom* [TH7965, ZH8934]) conveys the concept of "completeness," including prosperity, success, and especially one's "welfare" (in the sense of personal safety and state of health; cf. HALOT 1507-1508). The word *shalom* has already appeared twice in 2:5-6, and it is notably used some nine times as a literary refrain in the Jehu narrative (2 Kgs 9:1-37; cf. commentary on 2 Kgs 9:14-29). Cogan (2001:175) suggests plausibly that the conversation recorded here took place soon after Solomon's accession to the throne.

2:15 As you know, the kingdom was rightfully mine. Adonijah took the direct approach, probably to put Bathsheba on the defensive. This, however, would prove to be disastrous, as commentators point out that Bathsheba's apparent agreement to Adonijah's request may actually have set him up for future disaster (Cogan [2001:176] terms Bathsheba's actions here and throughout the chapter as "artfully ambiguous," just as they were in the previous chapter).

But the tables were turned . . . for that is the way the LORD wanted it. Cf. the commentary on 1:28-53. "The tables were turned" is lit. "the kingship has turned away" (*wattissob* [TH5437, ZH6015] *hammelukah*); the NLT nicely conveys the impersonal sense of the construction—implying, but not asserting, divine causality.

2:17 Abishag. See 1:1-4. She may now be reckoned as one of David's concubines.

2:19 The king rose from his throne to meet her, and he bowed down before her. Solomon knew he owed his throne largely to his mother. Those who understandably complain about the "double standard" of male domination over females in traditional cultures, such as was and is still found in the Near East, sometimes fail to acknowledge the significant existence of the "power behind the throne" (cf. Laffey 1989:298). In this case, Bathsheba, the queen mother, was far more than an object of David's passing fancy (see next note).

a throne be brought. A rather literal depiction of the importance of the queen mother, and perhaps illustrative of what R. K. Harrison (1970:187-189) has termed "the matriarchate," where the ancestral inheritance can be reckoned through the female line (as it was, at times, in Egypt). Note also that the Judahite regnal formulas in Kings prominently feature the names of the queen mothers as well (see "Literary Style" in the Introduction).

2:22 How can you possibly ask me to give Abishag to Adonijah? Up to then Solomon had been most solicitous of his mother, but that certainly changed here! Many have seen marriage with Abishag here as akin to Absalom's notorious cohabitation with David's concubines back in 2 Sam 16:21-22. Both attest a public, rebellious stance against the crown. As Cross (1998:94) notes, asking for Abishag at this point would indeed qualify Adonijah for execution—"for stupidity."

2:23 May God strike me and even kill me. It is notoriously difficult to translate Hebrew oath formulas into English (cf. NIV, "May God deal with me, be it ever so severely"). The concept is that if the speaker does not make good on the oath, may God do that and more to the speaker (Waltke and O'Connor [1990:679 n. 18], citing Joüon, term this a "self-curse or imprecation formula"); cf. 2 Kgs 6:31.

2:24 as surely as the LORD lives. In essence, this is another oath formula (Lambdin 1971:172). Waltke and O'Connor (1990:679) note that *khay* [TH2416, ZH2644] (life) + a name (here, "the LORD"), followed by a clause with *ki* [TH3588, ZH3954] (that), indicates the positive action (here, "Adonijah will die this very day") sanctioned by the oath.

2:25 Benaiah. This was the trusted captain of David's bodyguard (see notes on 1:8, 38), by now surely quite advanced in age. This is the last chapter where he is mentioned, apart from the list of Solomon's officials found in 4:4. Benaiah acts as Solomon's executioner here and in 2:34, 46.

2:26 Abiathar the priest. See note on 1:7. He will be mentioned in the list of Solomon's officials (4:4).

Anathoth. This was a Levitical city within the territory of Benjamin, not far from Jerusalem (Josh 21:18; cf. Cogan 2001:177 for possible locations). The prophet Jeremiah came from this town (Jer 1:1; cf. Jer 11:18-23). He was probably a priestly descendant of Abiathar (Thompson 1980:140), which would help explain his strong dissatisfaction with the priestly and royal hierarchy in Jerusalem.

2:27 So Solomon deposed Abiathar . . . thereby fulfilling the prophecy the LORD had given at Shiloh concerning the descendants of Eli. Concerning this prophecy, see 1 Sam 2:30-36. As DeVries (1985:39) has pointed out, "it is evident that kings had final authority over priests, not priests over kings" (which, by the way, stands in stark contrast to the limitations prophets placed on kings, as delineated in the commentary on 1:5-27).

2:28 Joab. See note on 1:7, and especially Seow's comment that he and Abiathar represented David's "old guard." Be that as it may, what a sad ending we find here for this crusty, effective, blunt, but generally loyal leader.

sacred tent of the LORD. See the first note on 1:50.

grabbed on to the horns of the altar. Just like Adonijah did in the previous chapter—the literary parallelism is quite exact. (See the second note on 1:50, concerning the sanctuary this would afford.)

2:32 The LORD will repay him. As Wiseman (1993:79-80) points out, "[Joab's] death was to be a divine retribution through judicial punishment." Concerning the so-called Deuteronomistic retribution theology presupposed here, see "The 'Sins of Manasseh'" under "Major Themes" in the Introduction. There I argue that already in the Ten Commandments, a retribution theology is to be found (as well as a focus on potential redemption for the offender over against mechanistic retribution for the offense).

2:33 blood. See second note on 2:5.

2:35 Benaiah . . . Zadok. For Benaiah, see note on 2:25, and the references cited there; for Zadok the priest, see first note on 1:8. On the lengthy Greek interpolation after this verse, usually termed a *miscellany*, see endnote 17 of the Introduction, and especially Gooding (1976), who sees the material as a midrashic arrangement of Solomonic material attesting his great wisdom, here especially in his building projects. (In the second miscellany inserted after 2:46, Gooding sees emphasis on Solomon's wisdom in governmental administration and palace provisions.)

2:36 Shimei. On his identity, see the third note on 1:8; on David's ignominious condemnation, see the note on 2:8-9. Once again, Shimei seems largely to be in the right here (cf. his acquiescence to Solomon's harsh command in 2:38). Yet, in Solomon's defense, he has so far acted more leniently than his aged father had wished back in 2:8-9.

2:39 three years later. The compressed chronology here should be noted; the author wanted to deal with the fate of each individual comprehensively without discussing events that occurred in the meantime.

King Achish son of Maacah of Gath. This was possibly the same Achish under whom David had sought refuge back in 1 Sam 21:10-15 (cf. 1 Sam 27:2), although he would have been quite elderly by this time. See Cogan (2001:179), who notes D. N. Freedman's suggestion that the custom of *papponymy* (naming a grandchild after his grandfather) is at work here and this is the grandson of David's Philistine patron. Cogan also cites parallels for the retrieval of runaway slaves from foreign countries; as he notes, sometimes provisions for such actions were included in state treaties. (On the probable location of Gath, Tell es-Safi, see second note on 2 Kgs 12:17 [18].)

2:41 Solomon heard that Shimei had left Jerusalem. Wiseman (1993:80-81) has plausibly argued that the narrator here implies that Shimei did indeed bring judgment upon himself by reneging on his earlier promise (2:38; cf. 2:42), but this last narrative fragment wrapping up the fates of those on David's hit list nonetheless leaves a bitter taste in the reader's mouth (see commentary below).

2:46 *So the kingdom was now firmly in Solomon's grip.* This is quite likely the conclusion to the Throne Succession Narrative (see commentary below). Once again we find a miscellany of Solomonic material in the Greek text—see the references in the note on 2:35 for further study.

COMMENTARY

"Just the facts, ma'am," was the comment police sergeant Jack Webb of *Dragnet* would give to the women he was interviewing concerning a crime. This was meant to cut off any extended extraneous or editorial comments by the interviewee. But, as scholars have been increasingly recognizing, "facts" are elusive things, and are rarely able to be understood apart from their contexts. Such is the case here. Accepting the "facts" of what we have just read in 1 Kings 2, how are we to understand them? Solomon, clearly promising to be an effective king from the outset of his rule, evidently began in nearly the exact way his aged father had counseled him. That much is clear. But what is the opinion of the narrator in regard to all this? Concerning this crucial question, scholars differ.

Recently, Friedman (1998) has suggested that there is a "hidden book in the Bible" (i.e., in the OT), and it consists largely of the "J" source in the Pentateuch ("J" is usually understood as the earliest of some four hypothetical sources underlying the first five books of the OT), various narratives in the books of Joshua, Judges, 1–2 Samuel, and especially the so-called Throne Succession Narrative of 2 Samuel that is traditionally understood to have concluded at this point in 1 Kings. The thesis is bold, sweeping, and, of course, open to criticism; but I think there is something to it, especially in Friedman's sensitivity to the parallel traditions and the use of paronomasia (wordplay) found throughout these narratives. In any case, I think he is correct to see a major ending of biblical tradition signaled by the concluding words: "So the kingdom was now firmly in Solomon's grip" (2:46). In my interpretation of Friedman's thesis, I would note the audacious delight in God's inscrutable ways found in narratives commonly assigned to J (see the commentary on 1:28-53 for examples), and the clear focus on the incredibly heroic and charismatic David in the narratives often designated "the History of David's Rise" (roughly 1 Sam 16—2 Sam 5). But the Throne Succession Narrative (2 Sam 9–20; 1 Kgs 1–2) is a different matter. In this narrative, King David was already acting in clearly ineffectual ways, riven by doubt and indecision, and notoriously guilty of adultery and murder by proxy in the Bathsheba affair. This David was hardly heroic! And, to the point, neither was his son Solomon. I would understand the present narratives of 1–2 Kings as a subtle, but effective critique of these two personages, sadly affirming, among other things, Lord Acton's dictum that "power tends to corrupt, and absolute power corrupts absolutely" (cf. also Seow 1999:35-36). This is precisely the sort of critique an Israelite prophet would make of a monarch or set of monarchs who exceeded the bounds of limited kingship as defined by the prophetic movement (see commentary on 1:5-27, and especially the work of Halpern cited there). Solomon sat on an uncontested throne, but there was no guarantee that Yahweh would allow him or his children to remain there indefinitely. (Could it not be that Tamar [see 2 Sam 13:1-22], the tragic daughter of David, was the author of the Throne Succession Narrative? This is rank speculation to be sure, but she would have been an educated noblewoman in David's court with time on her hands [cf. 2 Sam 13:20b], and a very motivated and most effective eyewitness to all the shenanigans that took place there!)

As for Solomon's new administration, he has three individuals killed: Adonijah, Joab, and Shimei. Solomon sadly acted in a manner similar to what one expects his father David would have advised (see 2:5). Adonijah's fate (2:25) corresponds most closely with that of his notorious elder half brother Absalom (2 Sam 15–18). (On Adonijah's "stupidity," see note on 2:22.) Joab was killed "beside the altar" (2:31, 34). As Cogan (2001:178-179) points out, the altar offered no sanctuary for the willful murderer (cf. Exod 21:12-14). Seow (1999:33) thinks Joab "dared" Solomon and his "hatchet man" Benaiah to kill him there ("if anyone wants to kill him, it will have to be there, right by the altar in the sanctuary!"). In any case, Cogan notes that Joab was given the honor of being buried on his estate, in the family grave in Bethlehem (cf. 2 Sam 2:32). Shimei was also killed in a ruthless manner (2:46).

Solomon was to be reckoned as king both *de jure* and *de facto* (by legal right, and in actual matter-of-fact). Nonetheless, his insecurity in relation to the Benjamite house of Shimei (2:44-45) could not be ignored. Thus, we come to the conclusion that Solomon proved to be as ruthless as his aged father could have wished. And that, at least for the time being, qualified him uniquely as king on David's throne "in the presence of the LORD" (2:45b).

◆   B. Solomon's Proper Priorities (1 Kgs 3:1–4:34 [3:1–5:14])
       1. Solomon asks for wisdom (3:1-15)

Solomon made an alliance with Pharaoh, the king of Egypt, and married one of his daughters. He brought her to live in the City of David until he could finish building his palace and the Temple of the LORD and the wall around the city. ²At that time the people of Israel sacrificed their offerings at local places of worship, for a temple honoring the name of the LORD had not yet been built.

³Solomon loved the LORD and followed all the decrees of his father, David, except that Solomon, too, offered sacrifices and burned incense at the local places of worship. ⁴The most important of these places of worship was at Gibeon, so the king went there and sacrificed 1,000 burnt offerings. ⁵That night the LORD appeared to Solomon in a dream, and God said, "What do you want? Ask, and I will give it to you!"

⁶Solomon replied, "You showed great and faithful love to your servant my father, David, because he was honest and true and faithful to you. And you have continued to show this great and faithful love to him today by giving him a son to sit on his throne.

⁷"Now, O LORD my God, you have made me king instead of my father, David, but I am like a little child who doesn't know his way around. ⁸And here I am in the midst of your own chosen people, a nation so great and numerous they cannot be counted! ⁹Give me an understanding heart so that I can govern your people well and know the difference between right and wrong. For who by himself is able to govern this great people of yours?"

¹⁰The Lord was pleased that Solomon had asked for wisdom. ¹¹So God replied, "Because you have asked for wisdom in governing my people with justice and have not asked for a long life or wealth or the death of your enemies—¹²I will give you what you asked for! I will give you a wise and understanding heart such as no one else has had or ever will have! ¹³And

I will also give you what you did not ask for—riches and fame! No other king in all the world will be compared to you for the rest of your life! ¹⁴And if you follow me and obey my decrees and my commands as your father, David, did, I will give you a long life."

¹⁵Then Solomon woke up and realized it had been a dream. He returned to Jerusalem and stood before the Ark of the Lord's Covenant, where he sacrificed burnt offerings and peace offerings. Then he invited all his officials to a great banquet.

NOTES

3:1 *Solomon made an alliance with Pharaoh.* Wiseman (1993:82) suggests that Siamūn (978–959 BC) or his successor Psusenes II (959–945 BC) of the 21st Dynasty was the pharaoh in question. Cf. Kitchen (1996:280-283, 465), who notes that such a marriage of an Egyptian princess to a foreign potentate would have been unthinkable in the New Kingdom or Empire period a few centuries earlier, but these were "humbler days."

City of David. Heb., *'ir dawid* [TH5892/1732, ZH6551/1858]. It sat on the eastern hill of Jerusalem, directly south of the modern Dome of the Rock and walled Old City (cf. note on David's tomb in 2:10). I had the privilege of digging there in 1982 under Yigal Shiloh. This hill, still heavily populated, stretched south of the Ophel, down to the Hinnom valley (see the map in Meyers 1998:254).

3:2 *At that time the people of Israel sacrificed their offerings at local places of worship.* This is a sore point with the editor of Kings, who will evaluate both the kings of the north and the south concerning the issue of the "high places" (see "One Place of Worship" under "Major Themes" in the Introduction). On the term *bamoth,* for "local places of worship," see next note.

3:3 *except that Solomon, too, offered sacrifices and burned incense at the local places of worship.* The Kings editor in essence makes a concession here (using *raq* [TH7535, ZH8370], "only") in reference to offerings given at the local shrines. This is the one exception to Solomon's "love" for Yahweh, as indicated by his otherwise faithful obedience to David's decrees. In both 3:2 and 3:3, the NLT's periphrastic reference to the "local places of worship" is a translation of the term *bamoth* [TH1116, ZH1195], the so-called "high places." However, Cogan (2001:184) prefers the more neutral translation "shrines," noting that some of the *bamoth* were located in valleys (cf. Jer 32:35) or in cities (cf. 2 Kgs 23:8). See the helpful excursus found in Wiseman (1993:82-83).

3:4 *Gibeon.* This is probably the modern village of el-Jib, some 6 miles (10 km) northwest of Jerusalem; some have suggested that Gibeon had been King Saul's capital (Cogan 2001:185). The Gibeonites had tricked Joshua into making a covenant of protection with them (Josh 9). Saul, however, had tried to wipe them out, and David had to sanction royal vengeance against Saul's family to put an end to a famine sent by Yahweh (2 Sam 21:1-14).

3:5 *the LORD appeared to Solomon in a dream.* Dreams and night visions are a valid method of divine revelation in the OT (cf. the list found in Cogan 2001:186), as they were generally in the ancient Near East (Seow 1999:39). While Jeremiah condemned the dreams of the false prophets (Jer 23:25), and Num 12:6-8 contrasts the dreams and visions of prophets with the direct word given "face to face" to Moses, we have no reason to doubt the veracity of the present dream of Solomon. See the ironic confirmation found in 9:2 in a prophecy of condemnation specified as the "second time" Yahweh appeared to Solomon (the first time having taken place in Gibeon). Concerning the uniqueness of Yahweh speaking directly to a king, see the note on 9:2.

What do you want? Ask, and I will give it to you! This is a folkloristic (i.e., popular storytelling) touch (a feature also observed in ch 20), very appropriate for this outsized personality known for great wisdom, achievements, and appetites (cf. note on 3:10). By identifying folkloristic elements, we are not questioning the historicity of the narrative but recognizing that the narrator employs literary motifs, exaggerative touches, and entertaining tropes as he draws his audience into his account of their history.

3:6 You showed great and faithful love to your servant my father, David. Twice, the rich term *khesed* [TH2617, ZH2876] is found in this verse, with both occurrences amplified by the term *gadol* [TH1419, ZH1524] (great). The term *khesed* is hard to define succinctly, with the traditional "loving-kindness" or "mercy" as too vague in meaning, and the more focused renderings of "covenantal loyalty" or "joint obligation" too constricting (cf. HALOT 336-337). The NLT phrase "faithful love," used for both occurrences of *khesed* in this verse, conveys accurately both nuances typical of the term: love and mercy on the one hand, and faithfulness and loyalty (to a covenantal relationship) on the other.

3:7 I am like a little child who doesn't know his way around. Lit., "I am a little child, I do not know how to go out or come in." The latter phrase is a common expression referring to lack of experience in military leadership (cf. Cogan 2001:1986). Probably the rationale for the choice of *nagid* [TH5057, ZH5592] or "king-designate" (see commentary on 1:5-27) up to this point was prior success in military leadership, and Solomon was indeed as a "little child" in this area. His humility here appears genuine, and his alternative proposal of seeking to demonstrate success in juridical "wisdom" to govern the people (cf. 3:9) is an appropriate substitute (3:10).

3:9 an understanding heart. Lit., "a listening heart" (*leb shomea'* [TH3820/8085, ZH4213/9048]). Practical wisdom is the key (see note on 2:9).

3:10 The LORD was pleased that Solomon had asked for wisdom. Whatever Solomon's faults, hubris was not one of them (at least at the outset of his reign). Imagine yourself in Solomon's place, where you could apparently ask for anything (except for multiple wishes, of course). This is not the last time we will find Solomon involved with such extravagant opportunities (see next note).

3:11 death of your enemies. This stands in stark contrast to David's last words back in 2:5-9, a juxtaposition that the narrator surely wishes the hearer/reader to notice. David's vengefulness, although sadly understandable in light of Middle Eastern court intrigues, nonetheless left a bad taste in the reader's mouth, and one is glad to be rid of such petty vendettas (and rid of Solomon's relentless machinations to bring them about, as well).

3:13 No other king in all the world. This extravagant claim may well have been literally true for a while, for Solomon's reign in the latter half of the tenth century BC largely took place during a time of both Mesopotamian and Egyptian weakness (cf. Bright 1981:212-214; Meyers 1998:245-246).

3:14 And if . . . I will give you a long life. The conditional nature of this last promise is striking, leading Wiseman (1993:86) to conclude that it did not come to pass (Sweeney 2007:80). As Cogan (2001:188) points out, "Length of days is not a gift given lightly; unlike riches, it is the reward for following YHWH's commands" (cf. Deut 6:2; 11:9). Solomon's proverbial 40-year reign (11:42), probably a round number, is surely meant to reassure the reader of his relatively long and generally successful life and reign.

3:15 a dream. The repetition of the term "dream" here is neither meant to diminish the veracity nor the applicability of the vision just described, but rather it acts as an *inclusio* with 3:5 above (an *inclusio* is a narrative device to signal by some sort of repetition the beginning and the end of a prose or poetic unit).

stood before the Ark of the Lord's Covenant. As Cogan (2001:188) points out, this verse
is probably an attempt to correct any misunderstanding that Solomon was acting as a
syncretist or worse (cf. 3:3). Presumably the Ark is in the tent David had previously erected
in Jerusalem (cf. the first note on 1:50). In 8:1, below, we will read that the priests later
removed the Ark from this location (in the "City of David" or "Zion") and brought it into
the newly constructed Temple.

COMMENTARY

The proverbial comment "be careful what you ask for" has a happy resolution here,
as the next section will unforgettably illustrate. Solomon here is pictured as large-
minded and truly concerned for the needs of his people. Maybe his insecurity (3:7)
had something to do with it. Solomon recognized his lack of military experience for
what it was—a clear deficiency, but by God's grace not as crucial for governmental
success as it was for his predecessors Saul and David. Solomon properly asked for
discernment to govern the people, and Yahweh threw in wealth, fame, and a chance
for long life as well. (For the mixed blessing such "wisdom" can bestow, however,
see the commentary on the next section.)

King Solomon was a man of gargantuan appetites (cf. the 1,000 burnt offerings
back in 3:4!), and despite all the wasteful extravagance this entailed, at least he was
beyond the personal, small-minded agendas that asking for "long life" or "wealth"
or the "death of your enemies" would represent. The king was called to be a servant or shepherd to the people, as the 18th-century Babylonian king Hammurapi
famously proclaimed about himself in the prologue and epilogue to his well-known
law code: "Hammurapi . . . the Shepherd . . . who causes justice to appear . . . that the
strong might not oppress the weak, to guide properly the orphan and the widow"
(ABD 3.40).

◆   2. Solomon judges wisely (3:16-28)

[16]Some time later two prostitutes came to
the king to have an argument settled.
[17]"Please, my lord," one of them began,
"this woman and I live in the same house.
I gave birth to a baby while she was with
me in the house. [18]Three days later this
woman also had a baby. We were alone;
there were only two of us in the house.

[19]"But her baby died during the night
when she rolled over on it. [20]Then she got
up in the night and took my son from beside me while I was asleep. She laid her
dead child in my arms and took mine to
sleep beside her. [21]And in the morning
when I tried to nurse my son, he was
dead! But when I looked more closely in
the morning light, I saw that it wasn't my
son at all."

[22]Then the other woman interrupted,
"It certainly was your son, and the living
child is mine."

"No," the first woman said, "the living
child is mine, and the dead one is yours."
And so they argued back and forth before
the king.

[23]Then the king said, "Let's get the facts
straight. Both of you claim the living child
is yours, and each says that the dead one
belongs to the other. [24]All right, bring me a
sword." So a sword was brought to the king.

[25]Then he said, "Cut the living child in
two, and give half to one woman and half
to the other!"

[26]Then the woman who was the real
mother of the living child, and who loved
him very much, cried out, "Oh no, my

lord! Give her the child—please do not kill him!"

But the other woman said, "All right, he will be neither yours nor mine; divide him between us!"

²⁷Then the king said, "Do not kill the child, but give him to the woman who wants him to live, for she is his mother!"

²⁸When all Israel heard the king's decision, the people were in awe of the king, for they saw the wisdom God had given him for rendering justice.

NOTES

3:16 *Some time later.* As in the previous chapter (see 2:39), time is compressed to emphasize a literary or theological point. The Hebrew simply reads *'az* [TH227, ZH255] (then), followed by an imperfect verb, which Sweeney (2007:81, citing a study by Isaac Rabinowitz) suggests is an editorial attempt "to correlate a past event with the preceding material concerning Solomon's dream." Therefore, the NLT translation here, although a bit lengthy, has much to commend it.

two prostitutes. Heb., *shettayim nashim zonoth* ("two women, prostitutes"). The final word could conceivably be translated "innkeepers" (Wiseman 1993:88, comparing Rahab the *zonah* [TH2181B, ZH2390] in Josh 2:1), but the NLT's "prostitutes" is best retained (cf. Cogan 2001:193). In any case, the neutral term "woman" is used throughout the rest of the story.

have an argument settled. This is, of course, an acid test of the king's wisdom. Easy decisions could be settled by designated assistant leaders (cf. Jethro's suggestion in Exod 18:17-23 that Moses should delegate easier cases to others, saving the most difficult for himself), but a complicated case like the present one warranted personal attention by the king. Absalom, seeking his father David's throne, offered to intercede on behalf of complainants seeking justice (2 Sam 15:2-4; also cf. 2 Kgs 8:3 for an example of a king being called upon to enforce inheritance rights).

3:17 *live in the same house.* This lends support to their identification as prostitutes (see second note on 3:16); also note the apparent lack of any identifiable fathers for the children in 3:18.

3:22 *And so they argued back and forth before the king.* A sense of urgency as well as frustration is conveyed by the verb (*wattedabbernah* [TH1696, ZH1819], "and they continued to speak").

3:23 *Let's get the facts straight.* The NLT is very periphrastic here. Still, the gist of the pedantic Hebrew (lit. "this one is saying this is my living son and your son the dead one, and that one is saying, not thus, your son the dead one and my son the living one" [a virtual repetition of the previous verse]) is aptly conveyed by the idiomatic NLT translation. The chiastic (or "a-b-b-a") pattern in the Hebrew lends itself nicely to such rhetorical touches as "Both of you claim . . . and each says."

3:24 *All right, bring me a sword.* This cuts through the rhetoric! Godly leadership sometimes requires discretion, sometimes radical decisiveness. Some commentators, however, see Solomon's brusque command as meant to be understood negatively (see commentary below).

3:26 *please do not kill him!* The Hebrew construction (infinitive absolute plus imperfect verb) is very emphatic.

3:28 *When all Israel heard the king's decision, the people were in awe.* Just like in the days of Saul (1 Sam 11:12-15), the people recognized Yahweh's clear blessing on their newly designated monarch. But note that here "wisdom" is the hallmark of such blessing, not military prowess.

COMMENTARY

The writer used what probably was a well-known story of non-Israelite provenance. DeVries (1985:58) says, "The exact wording of the anecdote may be Israelite, but the story itself comes out of international culture" (he goes on to note numerous parallels from the folklore of various cultures, including a particularly apt one from India). Yet, as is generally the case in such parallels, we have no compelling reason to doubt the historicity of the present narrative. The writer here effectively set a new agenda for confirmation of God's choice as king. As with Saul and David, God had not stinted either on human ability or divine favor in his choice of a political leader, nor had he mechanistically set this leader up for eventual failure (as, for example, the later narratives about King Saul are often mistakenly interpreted). Solomon truly excelled in the area in which he needed to excel, in the ability to render justice for the enormous and variegated group of people he had been set over. As Seow (1999:43-46) has argued, "Whatever its provenance, the story must now be read in the aftermath of Solomon's receipt of the gift of wisdom and its ancillary benefits." Seow goes on to point out quite powerfully that there are both benefits and *limitations* inherent in this gift of wisdom. Modifying Seow's argument slightly, I would say the issue here is the nature of the "gift"—its positive and its negative features. And as Seow rightly emphasizes, one key sequence in the story, its monotonous "back-and-forth" yammering of the two women (3:22-23) with its resultant impasse, was finally "cut off" by the king's startling response: "All right, bring me a sword" (3:24a). As Seow (1999:44) notes:

> *Unfortunately, the judgment of the just king is questionable. He never interrogates the two women. He accepts at face value the complainant's claim that there were no other witnesses. He does not point to the obvious gaps in her version of events and the purely circumstantial nature of her charge. He does not notice that she claimed to have been so sound asleep that she did not know that her infant had been taken from her and another placed in her bosom, and yet she is able to report on all that was happening that night. . . . Neither woman is required to take an oath or undergo some kind of test, as the law stipulates for disputes involving no witnesses (see Exod 22:10-11; Deut 19:15-18; Num 5:11-15). He does not visit the site of the crime, nor does he send investigators to look for possible clues that may have been overlooked. Instead, he threatens the life of an innocent child, expecting the horrendous threat to provoke the responses he expects from his own stereotypes of the good mother and the deceptive woman.*

Seow goes on to cite Josephus's surprisingly independent retelling of the story in *Antiquities* 8.2.2.32, where the people secretly made fun of Solomon "as of a boy." Seow also cites censorious midrashic and rabbinic commentary such as: "If I had been there, I would put a rope around Solomon's neck, for one dead child was apparently not enough for him—no, he had to command that the second be divided in two" (Rabbi Judah ben Ilai). Finally, Seow cites Walter Brueggemann's understanding of the narrative here as providing a stern warning: The story shows no indication of the king's compassion at all, and should remind the hearer/reader of the danger that public power and cool objectivity in the practice of justice can become very close to cold cynicism. As Seow himself concludes, "the wisdom of

Solomon, its divine origin and its much-vaunted fame notwithstanding, is finally limited. Wisdom, even if divinely imbued, can take one only so far. Solomon's gifts and successes are limited after all."

My own conclusion here will be brief: Divine empowerment of wisdom, no less than divine empowerment for military success, represents the proverbial "two-edged sword." We tend to glorify war and its results, at least in our retelling of the biblical stories, and likewise, we tend to glorify Solomon's wisdom as something universally brilliant and desirable. But neither is actually the case. The wars of Saul and David, many sadly necessary, were nasty and brutal. And the "wisdom of Solomon," coldly calculating as it was, probably proved to be much the same: brilliantly intuitive, beyond any need for hesitation or careful inquiry—but also standing beyond any effective appeal. No wonder the people stood "in awe of the king" (3:28). Such a monarch stands beyond any rational critique or censure. No other than God had put him there! But the narrator is not God (although fully inspired by God); the narrator tells the story as he or she is led to do—with ambiguities remaining and disturbing details intact. Solomon's gift of wisdom was indeed from God, but Solomon was not God, and even Solomon must face God's verdict regarding any arrogance or other failings. And as the hearer/reader of the final text knows quite well, this sadly *will* ensue.

◆   3. Solomon's officials and governors (4:1-19)

King Solomon now ruled over all Israel, ²and these were his high officials:

Azariah son of Zadok was the priest.
³Elihoreph and Ahijah, the sons of Shisha, were court secretaries. Jehoshaphat son of Ahilud was the royal historian.
⁴Benaiah son of Jehoiada was commander of the army. Zadok and Abiathar were priests.
⁵Azariah son of Nathan was in charge of the district governors. Zabud son of Nathan, a priest, was a trusted adviser to the king.
⁶Ahishar was manager of the palace property. Adoniram son of Abda was in charge of forced labor.

⁷Solomon also had twelve district governors who were over all Israel. They were responsible for providing food for the king's household. Each of them arranged provisions for one month of the year. ⁸These are the names of the twelve governors:

Ben-hur, in the hill country of Ephraim.
⁹Ben-deker, in Makaz, Shaalbim, Beth-shemesh, and Elon-bethhanan.
¹⁰Ben-hesed, in Arubboth, including Socoh and all the land of Hepher.
¹¹Ben-abinadab, in all of Naphoth-dor.* (He was married to Taphath, one of Solomon's daughters.)
¹²Baana son of Ahilud, in Taanach and Megiddo, all of Beth-shan* near Zarethan below Jezreel, and all the territory from Beth-shan to Abel-meholah and over to Jokmeam.
¹³Ben-geber, in Ramoth-gilead, including the Towns of Jair (named for Jair of the tribe of Manasseh*) in Gilead, and in the Argob region of Bashan, including sixty large fortified towns with bronze bars on their gates.
¹⁴Ahinadab son of Iddo, in Mahanaim.
¹⁵Ahimaaz, in Naphtali. (He was married to Basemath, another of Solomon's daughters.)
¹⁶Baana son of Hushai, in Asher and in Aloth.

¹⁷ Jehoshaphat son of Paruah, in Issachar.
¹⁸ Shimei son of Ela, in Benjamin.
¹⁹ Geber son of Uri, in the land of
    Gilead,* including the territories of

King Sihon of the Amorites and
King Og of Bashan.
There was also one governor over the
land of Judah.*

4:11 Hebrew *Naphath-dor*, a variant spelling of Naphoth-dor.   4:12 Hebrew *Beth-shean*, a variant spelling of Beth-shan; also in 4:12b.   4:13 Hebrew *Jair son of Manasseh;* compare 1 Chr 2:22.   4:19a Greek version reads *of Gad;* compare 4:13.   4:19b As in some Greek manuscripts; Hebrew lacks *of Judah*. The meaning of the Hebrew is uncertain.

NOTES

4:2 *these were his high officials.* The Hebrew term used here for "high officials" is *sarim* [TH8269, ZH8569], meaning "princes," "leaders," or the like. Cogan (2001:200) prefers the general context of "appointed civil officers" for the term in this context.

Azariah son of Zadok was the priest. The high priest in Jerusalem probably is what is meant here. Cogan (2001:200-202) notes that even though a priest heads the list of administrators, one cannot assume that he necessarily ranked that high in Solomon's court.

4:3 *court secretaries.* Heb., *soperim* [TH5608A, ZH6221], traditionally rendered "scribes" or "secretaries." Wiseman (1993:89) plausibly suggests that the existence of two of these officials in Solomon's court may indicate that one covered foreign affairs and one home affairs, or that each used a different method or language when keeping records, as was the case in Assyria.

the royal historian. Heb., *hammazkir* [TH2142C, ZH4654], meaning "the recorder," perhaps a "chief of protocol" or the like (Wiseman 1993:89), maybe even someone akin to the "secretary of state" (so NEB; cf. Cogan [2001:202], who, however, also cites the Targum's paraphrase, "archivist").

4:4 *Zadok and Abiathar were priests.* Cogan (2001:202) is surely correct to cite ancient scribal practice where contradictions in lists and traditions (cf. 4:2, which lists Azariah) are retained without further comment or harmonization; in the present case there is historic interest in listing the priests who had served only a short time at the start of Solomon's reign (cf. 2:26, 35).

4:5 *in charge of the district governors.* Heb., *'al-hannitsabim* [TH5324, ZH5893], meaning "over the supervisors"; the 12 "district governors" are listed in the following section, 4:7-19a.

Zabud son of Nathan, a priest . . . adviser. The term "priest" (*kohen* [TH3548, ZH3913], the usual term for the office) is found here, resulting in an unexpected double title in the MT (which the NLT follows) for Zabud son of Nathan. Various recensions of the Greek text (cf. Cogan 2001:202) omit the reference to "priest," but that is the easier reading, and therefore probably secondary. "Nathan" need not be the famous prophet of that name, but rather a son of David (2 Sam 5:14) or possibly someone else entirely (the name was quite common). If it was David's son, he may well have also been a "priest"; cf. the anomalous text found to that effect in 2 Sam 8:18b, "David's sons served as priestly leaders."

trusted adviser to the king. Lit., "the king's friend" (*re'eh* [TH7463, ZH8291] *hammelek*). Wiseman (1993:89) suggests the translation "personal adviser to the king," and notes a parallel in the Amarna (early Canaanite) texts (see also Cogan 2001:203 for details).

4:6 *manager of the palace property.* Lit., "over the house" (*'al-habbayith* [TH1004, ZH1074]). Wiseman (1993:89) defines it as "controller of the (royal) household," and notes the office increased in prestige eventually to that of a prime minister (cf. 16:9; 18:3; 2 Kgs 10:5; 15:5; 18:18-37).

forced labor. Heb., *'al-hammas* [TH4522, ZH4989], "over the levy" (i.e., the corvée). Later on, this will become a major bone of contention, with Solomon and his administration depicted as a veritable pharaoh of forced labor over the house of Joseph (see 11:28; also cf. 12:1-20, especially v. 18), the protestations of 9:15-23 notwithstanding. References to the "levy" may also be found in 5:13-18 [27-32].

4:7 *Solomon also had twelve district governors who were over all Israel.* As is commonly noted, these 12 districts do not correspond to the ancestral tribal boundaries of the 10 northern tribes (Judah and Simeon being excluded as southerners, and Levi being excluded since they inherited cities throughout all Israel, not contiguous territory like the other tribes). As Sweeney (2007:88-95) argues, Solomon thus treated the northern territory differently than he did his ancestral land of Judah. Whether it be the "levy" on the Israelites only (see previous note), or the district boundaries themselves, Judah's privileged status was starkly evident. As Sweeney aptly points out, "Whereas [Solomon] apparently ruled Judah directly as his home tribe, he ruled Israel through administrators much as one would rule a foreign or subject state." Sweeney goes on to delineate carefully the locations of the 12 districts, noting, for example, that the boundaries were meant to weaken or contain major elements within the northern regions, especially the two central Joseph tribes, Ephraim and Manasseh.

Each of them arranged provisions for one month of the year. This is the stated rationale for a 12-part division of the northern lands of Israel (see 4:27-28). Each district would thus have to be a viable economic unit (Cogan 2001:205), another reason ostensibly justifying the abandonment of the old tribal divisions. Apparently excluding Judah altogether from this economic arrangement again elevates her public status as Solomon's home tribe. Cogan (2001:205-211) examines each of the names of the governors and pertinent geographic references in the 12 territories in careful detail; see also Sweeney (2007:88-95).

4:11 *Naphoth-dor.* Sweeney (2007:91) suggests this means "the heights of Dor" (i.e., the forested hills overlooking Dor on the Mediterranean seacoast). In any case, this was probably a particularly wealthy district inasmuch as Taphath, a daughter of Solomon, is connected with it (cf. 4:15). (Concerning the variation "Naphath-dor" found in the mg note, cf. Josh 12:23; the only difference in meaning is substituting the plural form ["heights"], as in Josh 11:2, for the singular ["height"] in the MT.)

4:13 *Jair of the tribe of Manasseh.* The NLT mg aptly cites the independent tradition found in 1 Chr 2:22 concerning one Segub, father of Jair, who ruled 23 towns in Gilead. The term "son" (*ben* [TH1121, ZH1201]) often means "descendant of," or perhaps as here, "of the tribe of."

4:15 *Basemath, another of Solomon's daughters.* Cf. note on 4:11, above. Once again, this must have been an important district (Cogan [2001:209] notes that the major royal fortress at Hazor [cf. 1 Kgs 9:15] was part of this district).

4:19 *land of Gilead.* As the NLT mg note points out, the Greek versions attest reading "Gad" for "Gilead." Gilead has seemingly already been dealt with back in 4:13. The textual issues are complicated here (cf. next note and the excellent discussion in Cogan 2001:210-211); but the first part of the present verse may be a textual variant of 4:13a, with its references to "son of Geber," "Gilead," and later on, the reference to "Bashan." (The familiar traditions about Kings Sihon and Og are to be found in the Pentateuch [Num 21:21-35; Deut 2:26–3:11], and these traditions could be linked geographically both to Gad and to Gilead.)

There was also one governor over the land of Judah. Cogan (2001:211) suggests this sentence is actually a remnant of the entry originally delineating the 12th district, not, as usually understood, part of a separate note concerning Solomon's home tribe, as in the NRSV and NLT texts. (For details concerning the privileged place of Judah in the Solomonic empire, see the first note on 4:7.) The NIV combines all of 4:19 as part of Geber's "Gilead" district, but this translation also is quite problematic, especially with the absence of any footnote alerting the reader as to its tendentious nature.

COMMENTARY

It is beyond the scope of the present commentary to examine each and every name found in this section of 1 Kings. The reader is urged particularly to consult the uniformly excellent notes found in Cogan 2001:199-220 for such details. Lists such as these, although often seen as tedious by the casual reader, represent nothing less than a treasure trove for the Hebraist and the historian.

DeVries (1985:66) sees most of this section and the next as from *The Book of the Acts of Solomon* (cf. 11:41; on the use of italics for this title in the NLT, see the "Literary Style" section of the Introduction). The following is a slightly modified version of his analysis:

> List of Solomon's high officials (4:1-6), taken from the *The Book of the Acts of Solomon*
> List of his district governors (4:7-19a), from the *Acts*
> *Expansion: Laudatory interpolation, 4:19b-20*
> Solomon's empire (4:21 [5:1]), from the *Acts*
> Solomon's commissary arrangements (4:22-23, 26-28 [5:2-3, 6-8]), from the *Acts*
> *Expansion: Solomon's ideal reign, 4:24-25 [5:4-5]*
> *Expansion: Laudatory interpolation, 4:29-34 [5:9-14]*

Drawing theological conclusions from lists of names often requires ingenuity on the part of the commentator, but surprisingly enough, that is not the case here. Taking into account the textual irregularities as delineated above, the overall conclusion is surely evident—Solomon treated the northern tribes of Israel differently than he did his own tribe of Judah (which historically included remnants of the tribe of Simeon as well). Solomon's choices of court leadership included both old-timers and new arrivals, but it is the list of the 12 districts that surprises the reader—the time-honored tribal divisions of the proverbial 12 sons of Israel are largely gone, and the land of Judah is clearly positioned as preeminent, particularly over the tribes of Joseph. (See Ps 78:65-68 and passim for a northern perspective on this situation; also see the old tribal poem found in Gen 49:1-28.) Solomon sought to eradicate rival tribal allegiances as surely as he had previously sought to eradicate rival priestly houses (cf. 2:26-27), but as chapter 12 will show, after Solomon's death the old tribal allegiances reemerged as strongly as ever. And no son of Solomon, still less any court-appointed leader of his "levy," would be able to withstand their fury.

◆   ## 4. Solomon's prosperity and wisdom (4:20-34 [4:20–5:14])

20The people of Judah and Israel were as numerous as the sand on the seashore. They were very contented, with plenty to eat and drink. 21*Solomon ruled over all the kingdoms from the Euphrates River* in the north to the land of the Philistines and the border of Egypt in the south. The conquered peoples of those lands sent tribute money to Solomon and continued to serve him throughout his lifetime.

22 The daily food requirements for Solomon's palace were 150 bushels of choice flour and 300 bushels of meal*; 23also 10 oxen from the fattening pens, 20 pasture-fed cattle, 100 sheep or goats,

as well as deer, gazelles, roe deer, and choice poultry.*

²⁴Solomon's dominion extended over all the kingdoms west of the Euphrates River, from Tiphsah to Gaza. And there was peace on all his borders. ²⁵During the lifetime of Solomon, all of Judah and Israel lived in peace and safety. And from Dan in the north to Beersheba in the south, each family had its own home and garden.*

²⁶Solomon had 4,000* stalls for his chariot horses, and he had 12,000 horses.*

²⁷The district governors faithfully provided food for King Solomon and his court; each made sure nothing was lacking during the month assigned to him. ²⁸They also brought the necessary barley and straw for the royal horses in the stables.

²⁹God gave Solomon very great wisdom and understanding, and knowledge as vast as the sands of the seashore. ³⁰In fact, his wisdom exceeded that of all the wise men of the East and the wise men of Egypt. ³¹He was wiser than anyone else, including Ethan the Ezrahite and the sons of Mahol—Heman, Calcol, and Darda. His fame spread throughout all the surrounding nations. ³²He composed some 3,000 proverbs and wrote 1,005 songs. ³³He could speak with authority about all kinds of plants, from the great cedar of Lebanon to the tiny hyssop that grows from cracks in a wall. He could also speak about animals, birds, small creatures, and fish. ³⁴And kings from every nation sent their ambassadors to listen to the wisdom of Solomon.

4:21a Verses 4:21-34 are numbered 5:1-14 in Hebrew text.   4:21b Hebrew *the river;* also in 4:24.
4:22 Hebrew *30 cors* [5.5 kiloliters] *of choice flour and 60 cors* [11 kiloliters] *of meal.*   4:23 Or *and fattened geese.*   4:25 Hebrew *each family lived under its own grapevine and under its own fig tree.*   4:26a As in some Greek manuscripts (see also 2 Chr 9:25); Hebrew reads *40,000.*   4:26b Or *12,000 charioteers.*

NOTES

4:20 *Judah and Israel.* The separate categories these two territories represent have already been discussed; see first note on 4:7. The twofold delineation of "Judah and Israel" (or vice versa) occurs quite frequently in the MT; in Samuel—Kings alone we find this expression nine times (1:35; here in 4:20; 4:25 [5:5]; 1 Sam 18:16; 2 Sam 3:10; 5:5; 11:11; 24:1; 2 Kgs 17:13). (Concerning the various Greek additions to these archival texts, see Cogan 2001:212 and the sources cited there, especially Gooding 1976:40-49.)

4:21 [5:1] *border of Egypt.* Probably the Brook (or Wadi) of Egypt (cf. 8:65), usually identified as the Wadi el-Arish (cf. Cogan and Tadmor 1988:307). Solomon's overall territory, as described in this verse, is simply immense by ancient standards! And so, apparently, was the tribute sent to him from these foreign domains.

4:22-23 [5:2-3] *daily food requirements.* Naturally, estimates vary concerning the precise quantities listed here, but most would agree these provisions would satisfy thousands, if not tens of thousands, of people (cf. Cogan 2001:212 for references). The 10 stall-fed oxen (4:23) would in particular represent gastronomical luxury—akin to the famous fattened calf in the parable of the Prodigal Son (Luke 15:23). As for the "choice poultry" at the end of 4:23 [5:3], the rare term *barbur* [TH1257, ZH1350] (used only here in the MT) might mean "capons," "swans," or even "cuckoos" (Cogan 2001:213).

4:24 [5:4] *from Tiphsah to Gaza.* An alternative designation of Solomon's borders (cf. DeVries's analysis of this section as "ideal"; see the commentary on 4:1-19, above). The place-name "Tiphsah," however, remains problematic; presumably it is on or near the Euphrates River (Cogan 2001:213; compare the "Tiphsah" of 2 Kgs 15:16 MT [cf. NLT mg]). In contrast, "Gaza," the southernmost city of the Philistine pentapolis (see 1 Sam 6:17), clearly corresponds with the city that still bears that name today.

4:25 [5:5] *Dan . . . Beersheba.* The proverbial, ideal north–south boundaries of the land of Israel, proper (see references to this in 2 Sam 3:10; 17:11).

home and garden. A good paraphrase of the literal "grapevine . . . fig tree" cited in the NLT mg. Again, the imagery here is meant to be "ideal" (see note on 4:24). Cogan (2001:213) helpfully compares Mic 4:4 and Zech 3:10, as well as the ironic use of this same image by the Assyrian king's chief of staff (the Rabshakeh) in 2 Kgs 18:31.

4:26 [5:6] *4,000 stalls for his chariot horses.* This material begins another excerpt from the *Acts* (see the commentary on 4:1-19). Chariotry at this time usually consisted of 2 to 4 horses for each chariot (Sweeney 2007:100), hence Solomon's 1,400 chariots mentioned in 10:26 would easily necessitate this number of horses. As the NLT mg note indicates, the Hebrew (i.e., the MT) reads 40,000 stalls, a very high number (but note the 12,000 horses cited in 10:26). Some commentators would see cavalry horses as being included in the MT total, but any use of cavalry (horsemen mounted on saddled horses) remains problematic for this early period. Wiseman (1993:95) prefers the term "team-yokes" for the term *'urwoth* [TH220, ZH774], "stalls"; this translation gains plausibility in light of the 12,000 horses/horsemen found at the end of this verse.

12,000 horses. As Wiseman (1993:95) points out, the term *parashim* [TH6571, ZH7304] can refer either to horses or to their drivers (or both), hence the NLT mg note. (Concerning the famous archaeological references to the so-called chariot cities of Solomon, see note on 10:26.)

4:27 [5:7] *the month assigned to him.* See second note on 4:7.

4:29 [5:9] *sands of the seashore.* For the same simile, see 4:20; also part of secondary material representing a later expansion of the archival *Acts of Solomon* traditions (see further the commentary on 4:1-19). Although the Hebrew varies slightly in the MT, the parallel references in these two verses were probably meant to reinforce each other (cf. Sweeney 2007:98)—Solomon's "wisdom" (cf. the note on 2:9) is to be understood to be as vast and as blessed as the peoples he ruled, indeed to be spoken of properly in terms reminiscent of the divine promises given to no less than the patriarchs Abraham, Isaac, and Jacob (Gen 22:17; 32:12).

4:30 [5:10] *the wise men of the East and the wise men of Egypt.* Wiseman, who has written extensively on this topic, notes (1993:95) that the "East" would refer to Mesopotamia, not Arabia (contrast Sweeney 2007:100-101, who opts for the more traditional identification); thus, even the greatest examples of the wisdom movement in the ancient Near East are clearly found wanting in comparison to Solomon. Unfortunately, the specific examples given here ("Ethan," and the three named "sons of Mahol") are unattested outside of this verse (Cogan 2001:222); although presumably they were non-Israelites, we do find later echoes of these names in two Psalm titles (Pss 88, 89), and in two of the lists found in 1 Chronicles (1 Chr 2:6; 15:17, 19).

4:32 [5:12] *3,000 proverbs . . . 1,005 songs.* Here are two major categories of ancient poetic composition (Cogan 2001:222): a "proverb" (*mashal* [TH4912, ZH5442], etymologically a "likeness" or "comparison") and a "song" (*shir* [TH7892, ZH8877]); these would point to the short bicolons typical of Prov 10–29, and the longer poetic compositions such as Prov 1–9, 30–31, respectively (the latter category would also include the two "Solomonic" psalms, Pss 72 and 127). Some would see the Solomonic authorship of the Song of Songs perhaps in view here as well, but consider the wise comments of Longman (2006:341), who points out that Solomon may have written some of the poems in the book, but it is quite unlikely that he wrote them all (cf. Song 8:11-12).

4:33 [5:13] *speak with authority.* As this verse goes on to illustrate at length, "wisdom" comprised close observation of the natural world, as a cursory overview of the book of Proverbs demonstrates: ants (Prov 6:6-8), pigs (Prov 11:22), bears (Prov 17:12), lions (Prov 19:12; 22:13; 26:13), birds (Prov 26:2), dogs (Prov 26:11). Also note the schematized lists of animals found in Prov 30: leeches (Prov 30:15), ravens and vultures (Prov 30:17), eagles and snakes (Prov 30:19); ants, hyraxes, locusts, lizards (Prov 30:25-28), and lions, roosters, and goats (Prov 30:30-31).

4:34 [5:14] *ambassadors.* This actual term is not found in the Hebrew, although the MT's phrasing is difficult: "[sent?] from/by all the kings of the earth who had heard of [Solomon's] wisdom"). Something seems to be missing (which the later versions supply; cf. Cogan 2001:223). Perhaps "emissaries" or the like would be a less specific translation; in any case, the queen of Sheba (see 10:1-13) is the most famous example of such a royal visitation.

COMMENTARY

In this final section of chapter 4, we return to the topic of Solomon's wisdom and its effect on the people, as well as their concomitant peace and prosperity. As already pointed out (see note on 3:13), such extravagant praise of Solomon and his felicitous times probably had a significant basis in reality, and the author of this section (probably building upon the archival *Acts of Solomon*) meant little or no irony in such extravagant praise. Cogan (2001:214) cites Provan's suggestion (1995:60) that the "fantastic number" found in the Hebrew text ("40,000" in 4:26) was meant to depict Solomon as a "multiplier of horses," which was sharply warned against in the "law of the king" in Deuteronomy 17:16. But apart from this somewhat unlikely example, the commendation of Solomon here seems remarkably thorough, well attested, and genuinely heartfelt. Indeed, the present passage ends with an arresting international note: "kings from every nation" sent "ambassadors" (or "emissaries"; see note on 4:34) to listen to Solomon's wisdom—probably a sharp, intentional reminder that the Israelite covenants made with Abraham (Gen 12:3, etc.) and with David (2 Sam 7:19; cf. NLT mg note) would result in such rich international blessings. The Solomon depicted here is nothing short of heroic—nothing less than a world-changing personality—but the positive depiction we find here is not the last word we will read or hear either about Solomon himself or about his fabled wisdom.

◆   **C. Temple and Palace Building (1 Kgs 5:1–8:66 [5:15–8:66])**
          1. Preparations for building the Temple (5:1-18 [5:15-32])

¹*King Hiram of Tyre had always been a loyal friend of David. When Hiram learned that David's son Solomon was the new king of Israel, he sent ambassadors to congratulate him.

²Then Solomon sent this message back to Hiram:

³"You know that my father, David, was not able to build a Temple to honor the name of the LORD his God because of the many wars waged against him by surrounding nations. He could not build until the LORD gave him victory over all his enemies. ⁴But now the LORD my God has given me peace on every side; I have no enemies, and all is well. ⁵So I am planning to build a Temple to honor the name of the LORD

my God, just as he had instructed my father, David. For the LORD told him, 'Your son, whom I will place on your throne, will build the Temple to honor my name.'

6"Therefore, please command that cedars from Lebanon be cut for me. Let my men work alongside yours, and I will pay your men whatever wages you ask. As you know, there is no one among us who can cut timber like you Sidonians!"

7 When Hiram received Solomon's message, he was very pleased and said, "Praise the LORD today for giving David a wise son to be king of the great nation of Israel." 8Then he sent this reply to Solomon:

"I have received your message, and I will supply all the cedar and cypress timber you need. 9My servants will bring the logs from the Lebanon mountains to the Mediterranean Sea* and make them into rafts and float them along the coast to whatever place you choose. Then we will break the rafts apart so you can carry the logs away. You can pay me by

supplying me with food for my household."

10So Hiram supplied as much cedar and cypress timber as Solomon desired. 11In return, Solomon sent him an annual payment of 100,000 bushels* of wheat for his household and 110,000 gallons* of pure olive oil. 12So the LORD gave wisdom to Solomon, just as he had promised. And Hiram and Solomon made a formal alliance of peace.

13Then King Solomon conscripted a labor force of 30,000 men from all Israel. 14He sent them to Lebanon in shifts, 10,000 every month, so that each man would be one month in Lebanon and two months at home. Adoniram was in charge of this labor force. 15Solomon also had 70,000 common laborers, 80,000 quarry workers in the hill country, 16and 3,600* foremen to supervise the work. 17At the king's command, they quarried large blocks of high-quality stone and shaped them to make the foundation of the Temple. 18Men from the city of Gebal helped Solomon's and Hiram's builders prepare the timber and stone for the Temple.

5:1 Verses 5:1-18 are numbered 5:15-32 in Hebrew text.   5:9 Hebrew *the sea.*   5:11a Hebrew *20,000 cors* [3,640 kiloliters].   5:11b As in Greek version, which reads *20,000 baths* [420 kiloliters] (see also 2 Chr 2:10); Hebrew reads *20 cors,* about 800 gallons or 3.6 kiloliters in volume.   5:16 As in some Greek manuscripts (see also 2 Chr 2:2, 18); Hebrew reads *3,300.*

NOTES

5:1 [15] *King Hiram of Tyre.* In my article on "Tyre" in the fifth volume of the *New Interpreter's Dictionary of the Bible* (Barnes 2009:693-694), I demonstrate the importance both of this island city-state throughout much of the first millennium BC, as well as the particular significance of King Hiram's relationship both to David and to Solomon (see also Cogan 2001:232-233). Hiram I (Ahiram I), who first came to the throne in c. 980 BC (Barnes 1991:53; Katzenstein [1997:82, 349] prefers c. 970), built no less than three lavish temples according to Josephus (*Antiquities* 8.5.3.146-147). He would naturally be the one Solomon would consult, both to continue the peaceful relations between these two kingdoms (cf. 9:10-14), as well as to arrange a shipment of cedar timber for the Temple (and in general to draw upon Phoenician architectural expertise suitable for royal temple construction). Indeed, a later Assyrian bas-relief from Khorsabad depicting the flight of King Luli of Tyre shows a great temple (probably the temple of Melqart, as described in Herodotus *History* 2.44) in the island city, including two freestanding pillars flanking the main entrance akin to those found in front of Solomon's Temple (see 7:15-22; a drawing of the Khorsabad relief, which is now lost, may be found in Aubet 1993:34).

5:3 [17] *was not able to build a Temple.* See the gentle demurral found in 2 Sam 7:5-7; elsewhere David is categorized more directly as unfit to build the Temple since he had "shed so much blood" (1 Chr 22:8). Japhet (1993:396-398) sees this as "David's paradoxical and tragic flaw."

5:4 [18] *I have no enemies.* Lit., "there is no adversary." The term for "adversary" is *satan* [TH7854, ZH8477]; cf. 11:14, 23, 25 for such human "satans." Only later, as in 1 Chr 21:1, does the term become a proper name designating the devil, the supreme adversary of God's people.

5:5 [19] *honor the name of the LORD my God.* See the comments on "One Place of Worship" under "Major Themes" in the Introduction for this "name theology." Moses asserted that when the Temple was built, there would be only *one place* in the land where Yahweh's name would be so honored (cf. Deut 12:5, 11, 21).

5:6 [20] *cedars from Lebanon.* Wiseman (1993:100) points out that such cedars grow to a height of 100 feet (30 m), and that they typically were used for such purposes by Egyptian, Assyrian, and Babylonian kings to span large temple ceilings.

Sidonians. Both Tyre and Sidon were coastal cities in southern Lebanon. Prior to this time, Tyre served as a satellite city of Sidon to the north; but by the second half of the tenth century BC, Sidon's power (as well as that of Gebal [Byblos] yet further north) was clearly waning and that of Tyre waxing (see Aubet 1993:26-27). The use of the general term "Sidonians," presumably for the Tyrians here, may well have been an appropriate and common one, given the role of Sidon prior to this time.

5:8 [22] *cedar and cypress timber.* Concerning "cedar," see note on 5:6. Cogan (2001:228) prefers translating "cypress" as "juniper" (*Juniperus excelsa*), a fir tree that is also found in the Lebanon/Taurus hills. Possibly several varieties of fir trees are in view (so Zohary [1982:106-107], as cited by Cogan).

5:9 [23] *make them into rafts.* Such transportation by sea was the only practicable method of movement to the Israelite region; 2 Chr 2:16 further specifies that the rafts would be broken apart at the seaport of Joppa. An Assyrian bas-relief from the palace of Sargon in Khorsabad (c. 710 BC) depicting such rafts is now in the Louvre Museum in Paris (see the picture in Aubet 1993:33, figure 9; this is a different relief from that mentioned in the note on 5:1).

5:11 [25] *an annual payment.* For further information concerning some apparently later financial arrangements between Solomon and Hiram of Tyre, see 9:10-14, where the tenor of the text is that Hiram was quite dissatisfied with Solomon's transfer of land to make good on his debts. In any case, the quantities cited here are huge (cf. Solomon's overall provisions for his palace, as cited in 4:22-23). Wiseman (1993:100) suggests that the totals listed in the present chapter represent only a quarter less than the totals found in the previous chapter; he disagrees with those who insist that Hiram profited greatly from Solomon's largess (cf. Cogan 2001:228-229), but acknowledges that these payments helped contribute to the later impoverishment of his kingdom.

110,000 gallons of pure olive oil. As the NLT mg indicates, the NLT follows the Greek text and the generally parallel text found in 2 Chr 2:10 (cf. NIV). The term "thousand" has apparently dropped out of the MT here. "Pure olive oil" refers here to "beaten oil" (*shemen kathith* [TH8081/3795, ZH9043/4184]), which indicates the process used to obtain fine olive oil by carefully pounding small amounts of olives (so as not to crush the bitter pits), and then boiling the resultant mash, with the "fine oil" rising to the top (see Cogan [2001:229], who concludes, "the cooled oil is of exceptional quality"). The huge size of the annual commodity payments listed here beggars belief, and that surely is the point of the text.

5:12 [26] *formal alliance of peace.* Probably more than the present arrangement of payments is in view, "amicable commercial arrangements" being in the interests of both kingdoms (see Cogan [2001:229], who cites the references to Solomon's nautical efforts found in 9:26-28; 10:11, 22). Here, the term for "peace" is the familiar word *shalom* [TH7965, ZH8934], whose root idea is that of "completeness" or "wholeness."

5:13 [27] *conscripted a labor force.* See the second note on 4:6. Sweeney (2007:103-104) notes that the imposition of the levy or corvée was "prudently conceived to provide the labor necessary for acquiring the wood and stones necessary for building the Temple without overly burdening the Israelite population." This then is *not* to be identified with the later reference in 11:28, which notes that Jeroboam was put in charge of the levy on the "house of Joseph" (i.e., northern Israelites) only.

5:14 [28] *Adoniram.* See the second note on 4:6, where Solomon's depiction as a veritable "pharaoh of forced labor" is discussed.

5:16 [30] *3,600 foremen.* The MT reads 3,300. As indicated in the NLT mg, it follows the reading found in some LXX manuscripts and also the parallels in 2 Chr 2:2, 18. These other witnesses, and hence the NLT, represent something more than mere harmonization, because the difference between the two totals in unpointed Hebrew was only a single consonant ("three" being *sh-l-sh* [TH7969, ZH8993] and "six" being *sh-sh* [TH8337, ZH9252]). Normally, the more difficult reading is to be preferred (which would be MT; cf. NIV, NRSV), but a simple scribal error could well have led to the MT's anomalous reading.

5:18 [32] *Gebal.* Otherwise known as Byblos; cf. second note on 5:6.

C O M M E N T A R Y

We now turn to the subject of the Temple. Solomon's kingdom is properly established, and so, like David before him (see 2 Sam 7:1-17), Solomon naturally turns to the task of building an impressive house for his God, as well as a proper house for himself (7:1-12). Kings tend to fight wars or build buildings, it seems; as David was the successful fighter, Solomon will prove to be the successful builder.

Some time ago, R. K. Harrison (1970:206) argued that Solomon's Temple was originally meant to be a royal chapel (see commentary on 6:1-2) built in Phoenician style (similar structures built between 1200 and 900 BC have been unearthed in northern Syria). Within a short period of time, however, this Temple grew to "[eclipse] all other religious shrines among the Hebrew people." The cosmopolitan, international cachet of this Temple will immediately be evident even to the casual reader of the next several chapters of 1 Kings. Its potential contribution to Solomon's syncretistic tendencies, so decried in chapter 11, will soon become apparent as well. Indeed, the Assyrian relief of Tyre cited in the note on 5:1, with the prominent position of the great temple of Melqart flanked by two freestanding pillars, looks remarkably similar to the standard depictions of Solomon's Temple—except for its waterfront location!

In any case, we are now far from the provincial perspectives of the period of the judges, and even from those of the early monarchical period of Saul and David. Solomon is a major player on the world stage (cf. his marriage to Pharaoh's

daughter, as discussed in the first note on 3:1). Both his burgeoning court bureaucracy and his bold redrawing of traditional tribal boundaries reflect a Middle Eastern monarch second to none in his day (see notes and commentary on 4:1-19).
So the building of a temple (and a palace) of first-rate international status was
only to be expected. Yahweh, Solomon's God, would seemingly desire no less!
(But see 9:1-9.)

That Solomon was a veritable "pharaoh of forced labor," akin to the Egyptian
tyrants described in the book of Exodus, is not the major point of the present passage (but see note on 5:14); rather, the main point is that it required an international coalition of Tyrian (including the "Sidonians" as well as the men of Gebal),
northern Israelite, and native Judahite laborers working together to construct this
magnificent "royal chapel." Detailed comparisons and contrasts with the Mosaic
Tabernacle constructed centuries earlier in the wilderness will be found in the
notes below; the main point here is that Solomon's Temple was nothing less than
"state of the art" in temple design and construction. No one need be ashamed to
look upon this Temple, but more than one person might be confused as to which
God it truly honored.

We today, of course, face similar opportunities and similar pressures. Whether it
be the awe-inspiring Gothic cathedrals of northern France, or the magnificent mega-
churches of North America, we all desire to build the best structures we can for the
glory of God. Nothing less than the finest of present-day materials and construction techniques should be utilized, if possible. But we too can get caught up in the
seemingly inevitable compromises such plans can produce. Let us not shrink from
utilizing such an international assemblage of workers and materials if we have the
wherewithal, but let us not lose sight of the price we might have to pay to bring
about such magnificence. Even the proverbial wealth of a King Solomon might, in
the end, not prove to be sufficient for the task.

◆   ## 2. Solomon builds the Temple (6:1-13)

It was in midspring, in the month of Ziv,* during the fourth year of Solomon's reign, that he began to construct the Temple of the LORD. This was 480 years after the people of Israel were rescued from their slavery in the land of Egypt.

[2] The Temple that King Solomon built for the LORD was 90 feet long, 30 feet wide, and 45 feet high.* [3] The entry room at the front of the Temple was 30 feet* wide, running across the entire width of the Temple. It projected outward 15 feet* from the front of the Temple. [4] Solomon also made narrow recessed windows throughout the Temple.

[5] He built a complex of rooms against the outer walls of the Temple, all the way around the sides and rear of the building. [6] The complex was three stories high, the bottom floor being 7½ feet wide, the second floor 9 feet wide, and the top floor 10½ feet wide.* The rooms were connected to the walls of the Temple by beams resting on ledges built out from the wall. So the beams were not inserted into the walls themselves.

[7] The stones used in the construction of the Temple were finished at the quarry, so there was no sound of hammer, ax, or any other iron tool at the building site.

⁸The entrance to the bottom floor* was on the south side of the Temple. There were winding stairs going up to the second floor, and another flight of stairs between the second and third floors. ⁹After completing the Temple structure, Solomon put in a ceiling made of cedar beams and planks. ¹⁰As already stated, he built a complex of rooms along the sides of the building, attached to the Temple walls by cedar timbers. Each story of the complex was 7½ feet* high.

¹¹Then the LORD gave this message to Solomon: ¹²"Concerning this Temple you are building, if you keep all my decrees and regulations and obey all my commands, I will fulfill through you the promise I made to your father, David. ¹³I will live among the Israelites and will never abandon my people Israel."

6:1 Hebrew *It was in the month of Ziv, which is the second month.* This month of the ancient Hebrew lunar calendar usually occurs within the months of April and May.   6:2 Hebrew *60 cubits* [27.6 meters] *long, 20 cubits* [9.2 meters] *wide, and 30 cubits* [13.8 meters] *high.*   6:3a Hebrew *20 cubits* [9.2 meters]; also in 6:16, 20.   6:3b Hebrew *10 cubits* [4.6 meters].   6:6 Hebrew *the bottom floor being 5 cubits* [2.3 meters] *wide, the second floor 6 cubits* [2.8 meters] *wide, and the top floor 7 cubits* [3.2 meters] *wide.*   6:8 As in Greek version; Hebrew reads *middle floor.*   6:10 Hebrew *5 cubits* [2.3 meters].

NOTES

6:1 *It was in midspring, in the month of Ziv, during the fourth year of Solomon's reign.* The later (and current) Hebrew names for the months of the year are Babylonian in origin; only occasionally do we find the earlier (Canaanite or Phoenician) names as is the case here (see also the references to the months of "Bul" in 6:38 and "Ethanim" in 8:2). The Hebrew calendar, like most ancient calendars, was based on lunar months, always starting with the new moon, with the full moon always occurring on the 14th day of the month (cf. the beginning of Passover on the 14th day of the 1st month, Exod 12:6). The term "Ziv" probably means "bloom" or "blossom" (HALOT 265-266). Solomon's "fourth year" is understood by some scholars as the first year of his sole reign after the death of his father David (see the first note on 1:35), although this was probably not understood as such by the editor of Kings (see next note). Cross (1972:17 n. 11) has calculated the actual date of the founding of Solomon's Temple as 968 BC (see, conveniently, Barnes 1991:29-55 for details).

he began to construct the Temple of the LORD. Wiseman (1993:101-102), following Noth, has categorized the following architectural details of the Temple as arising probably from an archival report, or drawn from memory of an observer, or derived from oral instruction given to craftsmen. In any case, they are described "in insufficient detail for any sure reconstruction to be made." For the differences between the MT and the LXX, some of which are quite significant both in content and in editorial arrangement, see the excellent discussion found in Gooding 1967a:143-172.

This was 480 years after the people of Israel were rescued from their slavery in the land of Egypt. This reference, as well as the reference to "300 years" found in Judg 11:26, provide significant support for the so-called "early date" of c. 1450 BC for the exodus from Egypt. But most scholars see this 480-year synchronism as a round number based on a calculation of twelve generations of 40 years each (LXX reads "440 years," presumably reckoning eleven generations of 40 years; cf. Cogan 2001:236; Wiseman 1993:104). Kitchen (1966:72-75) is particularly helpful concerning the secondary nature of synchronistic calculations such as this; he posits about 300 years from the Exodus to Solomon (corresponding with the so-called "late date" for the Exodus of c. 1280 BC). In any case, many scholars including myself (see the "Excursus on Chronology" in the Introduction for details) consider this 480-year period as *editorially* very significant for the writer/editor of Kings. Furthermore, I would point to a second 480-year period of time as reckoned by the exilic compiler of

Kings, derived from the Judahite regnal totals from the accession of David to the throne to the release of Jehoiachin from prison in his 37th year of exile—but this would necessitate positing *no* overlapping of any reign, hence no coregencies—at least as calculated by the final compiler(s) of Kings.

6:2 *90 feet long, 30 feet wide, and 45 feet high.* This is essentially double the size of the Mosaic Tabernacle (Wiseman 1993:102). The NLT mg gives the original dimensions in Hebrew cubits. A "cubit" is traditionally the distance between the elbow and the tip of the middle finger; it is the most basic measure of length in the ancient world (Sweeney 2007:110). The NLT mg note represents the standard equivalence of 18 inches (46 cm) to a cubit (cf. Powell in ABD 6.899-900), though a "long" or "royal" cubit may have been employed occasionally. Powell himself (ABD 6.900) remains largely skeptical of the alleged evidence for this; the correspondence of 50 cm (plus or minus 5 percent [or more!]) for a cubit seems, in his opinion, to fit the archaeological evidence the best.

6:4 *narrow recessed windows.* This is a traditional and quite possible translation, although far from certain. Wiseman (1993:105) notes that windows such as these are not yet attested archaeologically for this time, and he prefers understanding the references here to indicate features found in a typical Syrian-Assyrian portico built in front of a main building, with side rooms, columns, lintels and doorposts.

6:5 *a complex of rooms.* Again, the details are somewhat obscure. Possibly a structure similar to Wiseman's suggested interpretation of the previous verse is in view here (see note on 6:4). Kitchen, in a helpful article (1989:110) replete with comparisons with temple complexes throughout the ancient Near East, notes that the storage area of Solomon's Temple was probably twice that of the worship area in the Temple proper—and that this ratio was not at all anomalous as some have argued. Ancient cults required significant storage space for a great variety of ritual paraphernalia, much of it made of precious metals; votive gifts required secure spaces for safekeeping; and Temple revenues such as grain, wine, oil, etc., also required enormous storage capacity.

6:6 *connected . . . by beams.* The upper floors of these storage areas are usually understood as resting on offset ledges built in the Temple walls as they diminish in thickness at higher levels (generally a three-tiered structure is envisioned). Alternatively, as in the NLT, the beams rested on "ledges built out from the wall." In any case, any such "beams" (no such term appears in the Hebrew here) were *not* inserted into the wall proper (cf. the next verse, where there was no sound from any masonry tools permitted at the site).

6:7 *there was no sound.* Although the stone used for the Temple was "finished" or "dressed" (i.e., "rough-hewn" from the quarry [so Cogan 2001:239-240]), no further work was done on site. Cogan thus sees here a clear reflection of the ancient requirement that Israelite altars were to be built of natural, unworked stone (Exod 20:25). Sweeney (2007:112) adds that this prohibition may have served to preserve "the pristine quality of the Temple as the center of YHWH's creation." Despite significant differences between the Tabernacle and the Temple, a number of which have been and will continue to be cited below, the strong continuities between the two cult sanctuaries should also be emphasized.

6:8 *entrance to the bottom floor.* Most commentators support the suggested emendation from "middle" to "bottom" as found in the NLT text (cf. mg note). The change in the Hebrew is slight, and the versional support is strong; but see Sweeney (2007:112) for a stirring defense of the MT here.

winding stairs. The Hebrew term *lullim* [TH3883, ZH4294] is a *hapax legomenon* (Greek for "said only once"), meaning it is only found here in the Hebrew Bible. The ancient versions understood the term as a "winding stairway," and Cogan (2001:240) links it possibly to the term *lule'oth* [TH3924, ZH4339], "loops" on the edges of the Tabernacle curtains (Exod 26:4), or else possibly akin to a "passageway" or "trapdoor" leading to the Holy of Holies in the Herodian Temple. Kitchen (1989:108), citing parallels from Egypt, plausibly suggests a staircase progressing upward with 90° turns, hence a "spiral stair."

6:10 *As already stated.* This phrase is not found in the original, but it does helpfully sum up the otherwise bewildering discussion. Such resumptive references are typical of Semitic exposition, with its preference for *inclusios* and refrains. (For the meaning of *inclusio*, see the first note on 3:15.)

6:12 *Concerning this Temple.* This demurral anticipates the extended discussion found in 9:1-9. The writer wisely reminds the reader that despite the extended discussion concerning the architectural minutiae of this grand Temple and its accoutrements, *no* building, no matter how grand, can stand in place of fundamental loyalty to the Davidic covenant (a favorite theme of 1–2 Kings; cf. "The 'Lamp' of David" section in the Introduction).

COMMENTARY

For the exilic reader of this passage (like the present readers), this Temple is no more. Whether it was indeed a spiral staircase (see note on 6:8) that stood in the "complex of rooms" (6:5; see note) adjoining the Temple, whether it was the first floor or the second floor where the entrance was on the south side of that complex (note on 6:8), and whether there indeed were narrow recessed windows (6:4) in the Temple proper cannot be determined. Solomon's Temple was eventually destroyed. This impermanence is suggested in 6:11-12. Only God is permanent. The reader is encouraged to maintain a good relationship with him above a connection to *any* temple.

The Temple was a small structure, and only a small part of Solomon's overall building program. It was probably meant to serve as a royal chapel, with other places of worship of Yahweh (and, sadly, of other gods also) available to the people elsewhere.[1] But it eventually became a national cathedral. The eminent historian John Bright (1981:218) wrote the following about Solomon's Temple: "The Temple served a dual purpose. It was a dynastic shrine, or royal chapel, its chief priest an appointee of the king and a member of his cabinet; it was also, as the presence of the Ark indicates, intended as the national shrine of the Israelite people." Under King Josiah (and possibly earlier), it became the *only* place where Yahweh might properly be worshiped (see "One Place of Worship" in the Introduction). But eventually even this one place of worship would be no more. And again, the Kings text here already anticipates that very point, at least to some degree.

I have emphasized at some length the role of the Temple as a royal chapel, perhaps neglecting the other stated purpose of the Temple as the repository for the Ark. (The notes and commentary on 8:1-11 will have much to say about this.) Let us recall how the people had rejoiced greatly when the Ark was first brought into the City of David (2 Sam 6), with King David blessing the people in the name of Yahweh (2 Sam 6:18) and giving them choice gifts of food in celebration (2 Sam 6:19). It is evident that all the people shared in the same joy as their dynastic ruler. This is also true in the present passage. The people shared in the nationalistic delight of seeing the Temple being built. Architectural details mattered less to them than to the priests and palace officials, but the overall effect remained grand, if not grandiose. As in Jeremiah's day (see, especially, the so-called "Temple sermon" of Jer 7), the presence of such a grand Temple already bespoke a grand deity, and, yes, a grand Davidic dynasty. Such an effect is understandable, and, if properly understood, more than acceptable. But such an effect can become nothing less than idolatrous—as noted in Jeremiah 7:4, 8 (the NLT has a particularly effective translation for both these verses). Grand storerooms surrounding a grander Temple structure were something to be proud of. But pride can certainly lead to destruction (Prov 16:18), and that is true for the people as well as for their king. Yes, the king—the one who must remain particularly close to Yahweh if there is to be any hope of permanent safety and blessing for his people (see 6:13), Temple or no Temple. For no temple can protect a people whose political/ spiritual leader is bankrupt. Thus, even the present passage, with all its fascinating and obscure architectural detail, explicitly reminds its audience of their covenantal responsibilities (6:11-13) (Seow 1999:62-63).

E N D N O T E
1. By all appearances, Solomon did not recognize his actions as implementing the ideal of one place of worship seen in Deuteronomy, a Mosaic tradition that in his day was more carefully preserved in the north (in prophetic circles) than in the south. The more basic issue of polytheism was the problem for Solomon's reign.

◆   ## 3. The Temple's interior (6:14-38)

[14]So Solomon finished building the Temple. [15]The entire inside, from floor to ceiling, was paneled with wood. He paneled the walls and ceilings with cedar, and he used planks of cypress for the floors. [16]He partitioned off an inner sanctuary— the Most Holy Place—at the far end of the Temple. It was 30 feet deep and was paneled with cedar from floor to ceiling. [17]The main room of the Temple, outside the Most Holy Place, was 60 feet* long. [18]Cedar paneling completely covered the stone walls throughout the Temple, and the paneling was decorated with carvings of gourds and open flowers.

[19]He prepared the inner sanctuary at the far end of the Temple, where the Ark of the LORD's Covenant would be placed. [20]This inner sanctuary was 30 feet long, 30 feet wide, and 30 feet high. He overlaid the inside with solid gold. He also overlaid the altar made of cedar.* [21]Then Solomon overlaid the rest of the Temple's interior with solid gold, and he made gold chains to protect the entrance* to the Most Holy Place. [22]So he finished overlaying the entire Temple with gold, including the altar that belonged to the Most Holy Place.

[23]He made two cherubim of wild olive* wood, each 15 feet* tall, and placed them in the inner sanctuary. [24]The wingspan of each of the cherubim was 15 feet, each wing being 7½ feet* long. [25]The two cherubim were identical in shape and size, [26]each was 15 feet tall. [27]He placed them side by side in the inner sanctuary of the Temple. Their outspread wings reached from wall to wall, while their inner wings touched at the center of the room. [28]He overlaid the two cherubim with gold.

[29]He decorated all the walls of the inner sanctuary and the main room with carvings of cherubim, palm trees, and open flowers. [30]He overlaid the floor in both rooms with gold.

[31]For the entrance to the inner sanctuary, he made double doors of wild olive wood with five-sided doorposts.* [32]These double doors were decorated with carvings

of cherubim, palm trees, and open flowers. The doors, including the decorations of cherubim and palm trees, were overlaid with gold.

³³Then he made four-sided doorposts of wild olive wood for the entrance to the Temple. ³⁴There were two folding doors of cypress wood, and each door was hinged to fold back upon itself. ³⁵These doors were decorated with carvings of cherubim, palm trees, and open flowers—all overlaid evenly with gold.

³⁶The walls of the inner courtyard were built so that there was one layer of cedar beams between every three layers of finished stone.

³⁷The foundation of the LORD's Temple was laid in midspring, in the month of Ziv,* during the fourth year of Solomon's reign. ³⁸The entire building was completed in every detail by midautumn, in the month of Bul,* during the eleventh year of his reign. So it took seven years to build the Temple.

6:17 Hebrew 40 cubits [18.4 meters].   6:20 Or overlaid the altar with cedar. The meaning of the Hebrew is uncertain.   6:21 Or to draw curtains across. The meaning of the Hebrew is uncertain.   6:23a Or pine; Hebrew reads oil tree; also in 6:31, 33.   6:23b Hebrew 10 cubits [4.6 meters]; also in 6:24, 25.   6:24 Hebrew 5 cubits [2.3 meters].   6:31 The meaning of the Hebrew is uncertain.   6:37 Hebrew was laid in the month of Ziv. This month of the ancient Hebrew lunar calendar usually occurs within the months of April and May.   6:38 Hebrew by the month of Bul, which is the eighth month. This month of the ancient Hebrew lunar calendar usually occurs within the months of October and November.

NOTES

6:14 So Solomon finished building the Temple. This is probably another resumptive reference (see note on 6:10).

6:16 the Most Holy Place. Lit., "the Holy of Holies"; this kind of phrase in Hebrew connotes the superlative, the best of all (as in the "Song of Songs" or the "Lord of Lords"). This sacred space, a cube of 20 cubits, corresponded with the "Most Holy Place" in the Tabernacle (see Exod 26:31-34; that place was probably a cube). Both "rooms" served, in their respective time periods, primarily to house the Ark (cf. 6:19). Parallel references to cedar paneling in 6:15 and 6:18 (yet another example of *inclusio*) further accentuate the importance of this text.

paneled with cedar from floor to ceiling. Such lavish use of cedar paneling is also mentioned in 6:18; the point is that no stonework at all was to be seen from the inside. One can also vividly imagine the delightful fragrance this lavish use of cedar would provide.

6:18 with carvings of gourds and open flowers. A likely translation of the Hebrew; some see these symbols as representing fertility (Jones 1984:168-169), but Wiseman (1993:109) simply characterizes them (in essence "wild fruits and rosettes") as well-known decorative motifs in wide use at this time.

6:20 He also overlaid the altar made of cedar. As the NLT mg note indicates, the Hebrew here is uncertain (is the altar made of cedar, overlaid with gold, or vice versa?). Cogan (2001:243) prefers the former, and equates it with the altar of incense (cf. Exod 30:1-3, where the altar there is made of acacia wood, overlaid with gold).

6:20-22 with solid gold . . . with solid gold . . . with gold. Commentaries vary on the details, especially in regard to the "gold chains" of 6:21, but the repeated references to such lavish gilding, although seemingly quite unrealistic to the present-day reader, do find rather close parallels elsewhere in the ancient world (Kitchen 1977:103). In addition, in 10:21 we are reminded that all of Solomon's drinking vessels were solid gold; they were not made of silver, "for silver was considered worthless in Solomon's day!"

6:23 two cherubim. "Cherubim" (the plural of *kerub* [TH3742, ZH4131], "a winged creature") are well known from extrabiblical as well as biblical contexts. Most likely Akkadian in derivation (i.e., the language of Assyria and Babylonia), the term "cherub" probably originally meant "tutelary spirit; sculpted mythical gatekeeper" or the like (HALOT 497; but contrast Cogan [2001:244], who doubts this etymology). Mentioned as early as Gen 3:24 as guardians of the tree of life in the Garden of Eden, cherubim are also featured in several of the great theophanies found in Ezekiel (implied in Ezek 1–2 with the winged beasts bearing the throne of God, each with four wings and four faces; specified as such in Ezek 9:3 and throughout Ezek 10). Yahweh also rides on the wings of a cherub in Ps 18:10 (cf. 2 Sam 22:11). But the most famous cherubim are the two figures that flanked the "atonement cover" in the Holy of Holies of the Mosaic Tabernacle (see Exod 25:18-22; 37:7-9). Those surely are the direct antecedents of the cherubim described in the present passage. Presumably their forms were winged sphinxes (sphinxes have the head of a human and the body of a lion, or the like), in line with Akkadian parallels rather than the later, modified versions described in Ezek 1 and 10. Two distinguishing characteristics of cherubim are their remarkable mobility and their intimate presence with the divine (ABD 1.900; Wiseman 1993:110). One final note: The "cherubs" of the OT and the ancient Near East are large, fearsome creatures and nothing like the cute, angelic baby "cherubs" found in Renaissance art and on modern valentines!

wild olive wood. Heb., *'atse-shamen* [TH6086/8081, ZH6770/9043] (lit., "trees of oil"; cf. NLT mg note on 6:23a). The translations differ on how to render this term, but Cogan (2001:244) makes a strong case for "pinewood" (i.e., wood taken from the *Pinus halepensis* or Aleppo pine, from which resinous pitch and oil can easily be extracted) as best fitting the requirements both of location and of magnitude (i.e., appropriate for carving large figures).

6:29, 32 *with carvings of cherubim, palm trees, and open flowers.* These are decorative motifs akin to the gourds and open flowers mentioned in 6:18 (cf. the note on that verse; and concerning the "cherubim," see the first note on 6:23). Wiseman (1993:110) points out that if the present motifs are meant to be symbolic, they may evoke images of the garden of God or Garden of Eden (see also Sweeney 2007:115). Cogan (2001:245) notes that the Hebrew term used here for "palm trees" (*timoroth* [TH8561, ZH9474]) may also denote a column style specifically found in Israelite buildings at this time (cf. the work of Yigal Shiloh [1977:39-52]); these so-called "proto-Aeolic" capitals look like stylized palm trees.

6:31 *double doors . . . with five-sided doorposts.* As the NLT mg note indicates, the Hebrew here is uncertain in meaning (that is to say, uncertain for us, surely not uncertain for the original audience). This is also the case in 6:33, where the NLT has the translation "four-sided doorposts." Cogan (2001:246), following Millard (1989:134-139), has argued that the Hebrew should be understood as stating that the doorjamb and the doorposts were "a fifth" (of the wall), and "a fourth" (of the wall), respectively.

6:33 *four-sided doorposts.* See previous note.

6:36 *one layer of cedar beams between every three layers of finished stones.* This is the common construction used for masonry walls in earthquake-prone regions (Cogan 2001:247); similar construction for the walls of the great courtyard is mentioned in 7:12. Cf. Ezra 5:8; 6:4 for the same type of construction used in the postexilic Temple. Such construction fares better than straight masonry, which remains brittle and inflexible (cf. Baldwin 1972:41); in recent days, one thinks of the problem of cracks in the (brittle?) Washington Monument in Washington, DC.

6:38 *month of Bul.* Concerning the use of this ancient Phoenician name for the eighth month of the Hebrew calendar, see the first note on 6:1. The term "Bul" (*bul* [TH945, ZH1004]) possibly was a short form for *yebul*, the month of harvesting (HALOT 115, 382; Sweeney 2007:116). Interestingly, the actual period of some 7 years and 6 months was rounded down to an even 7 years (a similar procedure obtained for my reckoning of the 480-year regnal period underlying the era of the Davidic monarchy—see the third note on 6:1 for details). Alternatively, perhaps Cogan (2001:248) is more on target to note simply that the "seven years" here represents an ideal number.

COMMENTARY

Having completed one chapter concerning architectural and decorative details for the Solomonic Temple, we turn again to Bright's statements (1981:218) about this Temple (see the commentary on 6:1-13 for more of his statement):

> Since [the construction of the Temple] followed Phoenician models, much of its symbolism inevitably reflected a pagan background. For example, the bronze sea (1 Kings 7:23-26) probably symbolized the underground fresh-water ocean, the source of life and fertility, while the altar of burnt offering (cf. Ezek. 43:13-17) seems originally to have suggested the mountain of the gods. This undeniably posed the danger that pagan concepts would insinuate themselves into Israel's official religion. We may, however, take it as certain that, at least in official circles, these features were given a Yahwistic rationale and made to serve as symbols of Yahweh's cosmic domain. The Temple cult, whatever it borrowed, remained essentially Israelite in character.

We have been pursuing both comparisons and contrasts between Solomon's Temple and the Mosaic Tabernacle. Here it is appropriate to emphasize some of the contrasts, many of which are international in character—for that is surely what the cedar paneling, the lavish use of gold, the decorations of gourds, "open flowers," palm trees, the large cherubim sculptures (6:23), and the sizable auxiliary buildings all represent. The Temple was very international in scope and design. This is not at all condemned in the text. Solomon's paradigmatic sin will be that of syncretism, of religious compromise—yes, of internationalism of a sort (see ch 11). But not all internationalism is evil, nor is every kind of internationalism condemned by the biblical writer. Yahweh is uniquely God, and he must be worshiped, uniquely, above all possible rivals. But Yahweh may be worshiped with Egyptian, Phoenician (Canaanite!), and even Mesopotamian motifs. That was true then, and that is true today. As Paul put it, "I try to find common ground with everyone, doing everything I can to save some. I do everything to spread the Good News and share in its blessings" (1 Cor 9:22-23).

The cherubim call for special notice. In both the Tabernacle and in the Temple, the sacred "beast" was not the bull but the cherub. This stands in stark contrast to the pagan references found in the golden-calf incident of Exodus 32–34, and the bull ("calf," NLT) iconography of Jeroboam I as described in 1 Kings 12. Some scholars consider bull imagery to be Egyptian in origin, but what is of more pressing importance here is that the bull iconography (with its patent fertility imagery) is typical of the Canaanite god Baal, a hometown deity. Yahweh, apparently from the very beginning, preferred cherub imagery—mysterious, Mesopotamian, but less likely to be connected with fertility religion. Whereas Baal rides on a bullock (Smith 1990:51), Yahweh rides on a cherub (see the first note on 6:23), easily "soaring on the wings of the wind" (Ps 18:10).

While some international imagery is permissible, some is not! Similarly, today, we must be discriminating when translating the gospel into cultures that may or may not have suitable imagery to appropriate. One quick, obvious example: The Christian cross is something quite different in appearance than the electric chair (although both represent places of capital punishment), but it is closer to the electric chair in significance than it is to the Egyptian ankh symbol (a kind of looped cross, a symbol for life), or, at least since the rise and fall of Nazism, to the swastika. Though the electric chair looks nothing like a Christian cross, and though both the ankh and the swastika are rather similar in appearance to the cross, simple intercultural awareness will lead us to suitable parallels. So it was with the bull and the cherub iconography. Yahweh did, does, and will appropriate apt symbols to further the gospel, but not just any parallel will do.

◆   ## 4. Solomon builds his palace (7:1-12)

Solomon also built a palace for himself, and it took him thirteen years to complete the construction.

2 One of Solomon's buildings was called the Palace of the Forest of Lebanon. It was 150 feet long, 75 feet wide, and 45 feet high.* There were four rows of cedar pillars, and great cedar beams rested on the pillars. 3 The hall had a cedar roof. Above the beams on the pillars were forty-five side rooms,* arranged in three tiers of fifteen each. 4 On each end of the long hall were three rows of windows facing each other. 5 All the doorways and doorposts* had rectangular frames and were arranged in sets of three, facing each other.

6 Solomon also built the Hall of Pillars, which was 75 feet long and 45 feet wide.* There was a porch in front, along with a canopy supported by pillars.

7 Solomon also built the throne room, known as the Hall of Justice, where he sat to hear legal matters. It was paneled with cedar from floor to ceiling.* 8 Solomon's living quarters surrounded a courtyard behind this hall, and they were constructed the same way. He also built similar living quarters for Pharaoh's daughter, whom he had married.

9 From foundation to eaves, all these buildings were built from huge blocks of high-quality stone, cut with saws and trimmed to exact measure on all sides. 10 Some of the huge foundation stones were 15 feet long, and some were 12 feet* long. 11 The blocks of high-quality stone used in the walls were also cut to measure, and cedar beams were also used. 12 The walls of the great courtyard were built so that there was one layer of cedar beams between every three layers of finished stone, just like the walls of the inner courtyard of the LORD's Temple with its entry room.

7:2 Hebrew 100 cubits [46 meters] long, 50 cubits [23 meters] wide, and 30 cubits [13.5 meters] high.   7:3 Or 45 rafters, or 45 beams, or 45 pillars. The architectural details in 7:2-6 can be interpreted in many different ways.   7:5 Greek version reads windows.   7:6 Hebrew 50 cubits [23 meters] long and 30 cubits [13.8 meters] wide.   7:7 As in Syriac version and Latin Vulgate; Hebrew reads from floor to floor.   7:10 Hebrew 10 cubits [4.6 meters] . . . 8 cubits [3.7 meters].

NOTES

7:1 *and it took him thirteen years to complete the construction.* As is commonly pointed out (Seow [1999:67] is particularly eloquent here; cf. Provan 1995:69), there is quite a contrast between these 13 years and the 7 years that the construction of the Temple required (also cf. 9:10); Solomon's priorities concerning the relative importance of those buildings were clearly not those of the Deuteronomic narrator. The palace complex was also considerably larger than the Temple proper, and it was located to the south, between the Temple and the old city of David. As Sweeney (2007:116) points out, "the proximity of the Temple and royal palace reflects the intimate association between the Davidic king and YHWH, who is consistently portrayed with royal imagery in the ideology of the Judean state."

7:2 *the Palace of the Forest of Lebanon.* Probably the official reception hall (Cogan 2001:254), it was so named due to the large number of cedar columns holding up the roof. It also served as a state treasury (Wiseman 1993:111). For further information concerning cedars from Lebanon, see the first note on 5:6.

7:6 *the Hall of Pillars.* This is possibly more of a portico or foyer (Sweeney 2007:117; Wiseman 1993:112); it may have served as a waiting area for those seeking an audience with the king.

7:7 *the throne room, known as the Hall of Justice.* Whether the "Hall of Pillars" served as a porch to this place or to the palace mentioned in 7:2 is uncertain, but the latter is more likely. Indeed, the present "Hall of Justice" may have been part of that palace as well, since no additional dimensions are given here (Wiseman 1993:112). Solomon's actual throne is described at length in 10:18-20.

from floor to ceiling. This is a common emendation; as the NLT mg note indicates, the Hebrew reads "from floor to floor" (which Wiseman [1993:112] suggests may mean "from one floor to another," i.e., stretching all the way through the throne room to the pillared hall beyond).

7:8 *similar living quarters for Pharaoh's daughter.* See the first note on 3:1 for details concerning this eminent princess. "The queen's quarters (and harem?) were not necessarily of separate or Egyptian design" (Wiseman 1993:112).

7:12 *the great courtyard.* Evidently an outer court surrounding the entire Temple complex is in view here (so Cogan 2001:256).

one layer of cedar beams between every three layers of finished stone. See the note on 6:36 concerning the nature of this type of construction.

COMMENTARY

Rather provocatively, Seow (1999:67) has characterized the entirety of the present chapter of 1 Kings as "mainly an intrusion" into the overall Temple narrative:

> *The preceding chapter ends with the completion of the Temple. The next chapter will give an account of its dedication. In between the two stands this odd chapter highlighting Solomon's construction of his own palace and the emphasis that the building is the work of Hiram [NLT, "Huram"], the Tyrian artisan, and Solomon. It was they who made it; it was they who completed it. . . . The digression is, perhaps, not accidental. In any case . . . [it] is theologically important. It serves at once as a postscript to the account of the completion of the Temple and a preface to the account of the Temple's dedication.*

There is much wisdom in Seow's comments, especially in regard to the theological import of these "digressions" in the text. Just as 6:11-12 shapes the initial Temple discussion in theologically subtle ways (see the commentary on 6:1-12), I would submit that 7:12 does the same. Solomon's Temple, although great and grand, was only a relatively small part of the palace complex, and not particularly different in its level of construction than (seemingly) any other part. As Seow goes on to say (1999:67), "Most important, the passage also stresses the Temple and its furnishings as human handiwork, just as the palace complex is. This is the perspective of the martyr Stephen: 'It was Solomon who built a house for [God]. Yet the Most High does not dwell in houses made with human hands' (Acts 7:47-48 NRSV)." Solomon himself will say much the same thing in his prayer of dedication (see 8:27—"even the highest heavens cannot contain [God.] How much less this Temple I have built"). But chapter after chapter, verse after verse, detail after detail—the extensive elaboration of the glories and the grandeur of the Temple and of its furnishings could serve to obscure this vital theological truth.

◆   ## 5. Furnishings for the Temple (7:13-51)

13 King Solomon then asked for a man named Huram* to come from Tyre. 14 He was half Israelite, since his mother was a widow from the tribe of Naphtali, and his father had been a craftsman in bronze from Tyre. Huram was extremely skillful and talented in any work in bronze, and he came to do all the metal work for King Solomon.

15 Huram cast two bronze pillars, each 27 feet tall and 18 feet in circumference.* 16 For the tops of the pillars he cast bronze capitals, each 7½ feet* tall. 17 Each capital was decorated with seven sets of latticework and interwoven chains. 18 He also encircled the latticework with two rows of pomegranates to decorate the capitals over the pillars. 19 The capitals on the columns inside the entry room were shaped like water lilies, and they were six feet* tall. 20 The capitals on the two pillars had 200 pomegranates in two rows around them, beside the rounded surface next to the latticework. 21 Huram set the pillars at the entrance of the Temple, one toward the south and one toward the north. He named the one on the south Jakin, and the one on the north Boaz.* 22 The capitals on the pillars were shaped like water lilies. And so the work on the pillars was finished.

23 Then Huram cast a great round basin, 15 feet across from rim to rim, called the Sea. It was 7½ feet deep and about 45 feet in circumference.* 24 It was encircled just below its rim by two rows of decorative gourds. There were about six gourds per foot* all the way around, and they were cast as part of the basin.

25 The Sea was placed on a base of twelve bronze oxen,* all facing outward. Three faced north, three faced west, three faced south, and three faced east, and the Sea rested on them. 26 The walls of the Sea were about three inches* thick, and its rim flared out like a cup and resembled a water lily blossom. It could hold about 11,000 gallons* of water.

27 Huram also made ten bronze water carts, each 6 feet long, 6 feet wide, and 4½ feet tall.* 28 They were constructed with side panels braced with crossbars. 29 Both the panels and the crossbars were decorated with carved lions, oxen, and cherubim. Above and below the lions and oxen were wreath decorations. 30 Each of these carts had four bronze wheels and bronze axles. There were supporting posts for the bronze basins at the corners of the carts; these supports were decorated on each side with carvings of wreaths. 31 The top of each cart had a rounded frame for the basin. It projected 1½ feet* above the cart's top like a round pedestal, and its opening was 2¼ feet* across; it was decorated on the outside with carvings of wreaths. The panels of the carts were square, not round. 32 Under the panels were four wheels that were connected to axles that had been cast as one unit with the cart. The wheels were 2¼ feet in diameter 33 and were similar to chariot wheels. The axles, spokes, rims, and hubs were all cast from molten bronze.

34 There were handles at each of the four corners of the carts, and these, too, were

cast as one unit with the cart. ³⁵Around the top of each cart was a rim nine inches wide.* The corner supports and side panels were cast as one unit with the cart. ³⁶Carvings of cherubim, lions, and palm trees decorated the panels and corner supports wherever there was room, and there were wreaths all around. ³⁷All ten water carts were the same size and were made alike, for each was cast from the same mold.

³⁸Huram also made ten smaller bronze basins, one for each cart. Each basin was six feet across and could hold 220 gallons* of water. ³⁹He set five water carts on the south side of the Temple and five on the north side. The great bronze basin called the Sea was placed near the southeast corner of the Temple. ⁴⁰He also made the necessary washbasins, shovels, and bowls.

So at last Huram completed everything King Solomon had assigned him to make for the Temple of the LORD:

⁴¹ the two pillars;
the two bowl-shaped capitals on
    top of the pillars;
the two networks of interwoven chains
    that decorated the capitals;
⁴² the 400 pomegranates that hung from
    the chains on the capitals (two rows
    of pomegranates for each of the
    chain networks that decorated the
    capitals on top of the pillars);
⁴³ the ten water carts holding the
    ten basins;
⁴⁴ the Sea and the twelve oxen under it;
⁴⁵ the ash buckets, the shovels, and the
    bowls.

Huram made all these things of burnished bronze for the Temple of the LORD, just as King Solomon had directed. ⁴⁶The king had them cast in clay molds in the Jordan Valley between Succoth and Zarethan. ⁴⁷Solomon did not weigh all these things because there were so many; the weight of the bronze could not be measured.

⁴⁸Solomon also made all the furnishings of the Temple of the LORD:

the gold altar;
the gold table for the Bread of the
    Presence;
⁴⁹ the lampstands of solid gold,
    five on the south and five on the
    north, in front of the Most Holy
    Place;
the flower decorations, lamps, and
    tongs—all of gold;
⁵⁰ the small bowls, lamp snuffers, bowls,
    ladles, and incense burners—all of
    solid gold;
the doors for the entrances to the
    Most Holy Place and the main room
    of the Temple, with their fronts
    overlaid with gold.

⁵¹So King Solomon finished all his work on the Temple of the LORD. Then he brought all the gifts his father, David, had dedicated—the silver, the gold, and the various articles—and he stored them in the treasuries of the LORD's Temple.

7:13 Hebrew *Hiram* (also in 7:40, 45); compare 2 Chr 2:13. This is not the same person mentioned in 5:1. 7:15 Hebrew *18 cubits* [8.3 meters] *tall and 12 cubits* [5.5 meters] *in circumference.* 7:16 Hebrew *5 cubits* [2.3 meters]. 7:19 Hebrew *4 cubits* [1.8 meters]; also in 7:38. 7:21 *Jakin* probably means "he establishes"; *Boaz* probably means "in him is strength." 7:23 Hebrew *10 cubits* [4.6 meters] *across. . . . 5 cubits* [2.3 meters] *deep and 30 cubits* [13.8 meters] *in circumference.* 7:24 Or *20 gourds per meter;* Hebrew reads *10 per cubit.* 7:25 Hebrew *12 oxen;* compare 2 Kgs 16:17, which specifies *bronze oxen.* 7:26a Hebrew *a handbreadth* [8 centimeters]. 7:26b Hebrew *2,000 baths* [42 kiloliters]. 7:27 Hebrew *4 cubits* [1.8 meters] *long, 4 cubits wide, and 3 cubits* [1.4 meters] *high.* 7:31a Hebrew *a cubit* [46 centimeters]. 7:31b Hebrew *1½ cubits* [69 centimeters]; also in 7:32. 7:35 Hebrew *half a cubit wide* [23 centimeters]. 7:38 Hebrew *40 baths* [840 liters].

NOTES

7:13 Huram. This individual (*khiram* [TH2438A, ZH2671], "Hiram"; cf. NLT mg note) should not be confused with the important Tyrian king of the same name (see note on 5:1). This Hiram was half-Israelite and, interestingly, by orthodox Jewish tradition, would be reckoned as ethnically Jewish (if one's mother is ethnically Jewish, no matter the ethnic

background of the father, one is reckoned to be Jewish; see the second note on 2:19).
Seow (1999:67) aptly points out that Solomon had "received" (*laqakh* [TH3947, ZH4374])
the daughter of Pharaoh in 7:8 (cf. 3:1-3); here he "receives" Huram from Tyre (hence the
emphasis on his foreignness, also the importance of his father in his becoming "extremely
skillful and talented in any work in bronze"). Once again, the international provenance of
the building of Solomon's Temple and its furnishings comes to the fore.

7:15 *two bronze pillars.* Probably freestanding, as was the case in a number of Phoenician
temples (see the commentary on 5:1) and other examples (Wiseman 1993:114). (Let the
reader note that many so-called "depictions" of Solomon's Temple do not include freestanding pillars.)

7:18 *pomegranates.* This was a common decorative motif (cf. the pomegranates embroi-
dered on the hem of the high priest's ephod in Exod 28:33-34; 39:24-26). The pomegranates, with their many seeds, were probably symbols of fertility (Jones 1984:181).

7:21 *Jakin . . . Boaz.* Many different suggestions have been offered as to the meaning
and significance of these names. The term *yakin* [TH3199A, ZH3521] means "he will/may he
establish" (NLT mg, "he establishes," is also possible); *bo'az* [TH1162A, ZH1245] probably
means "in him is strength" (cf. NLT mg note). Sweeney (2007:122) prefers "in strength"
(*be'oz* [TH871.2/5797, ZH928/6437]), and suggests that the columns symbolize the foundation
of the earth and the stability of creation. Scholars differ on whether the names are to be
read together, and whether they are complete names or only catchwords for longer titles
(in Mesopotamia, doors and gates bore festive names imploring the gods for blessing and
protection; cf. Cogan 2001:264).

7:23 *called the Sea.* A simply immense vat or reservoir, which served to hold water to
purify the priests prior to their service at the Temple (cf. Exod 30:17-21) and also to supply water to the bronze water carts to wash the entrails of sacrificial animals (Sweeney
2007:122). Symbolically, the Sea depicted the chaotic waters from which creation emerged
(Gen 1:1-2:3; Ps 24:1-2), as well as perhaps the sea through which Israel passed during the
Exodus (Exod 14-15; cf. Ps 114). (Also note Bright's comments concerning the primeval
"underground freshwater ocean," quoted above in the commentary on 6:14-38.)

7:25 *a base of twelve bronze oxen.* Oxen were the main work animals in ancient times,
and thus symbols of strength (Cogan 2001:264); the fact that there were "twelve" perhaps
symbolized the twelve tribes of Israel or the twelve months of the year (signs of the zodiac).

7:26 *The walls of the Sea were about three inches thick.* Lit., a "palm" or "handbreadth"
(*tepakh* [TH2947 ZH3256]); cf. NLT mg note. A "handbreadth," probably the width of the four
fingers at their base (ABD 6.899-900), was reckoned as one third of a "span" (the width of
the open hand from the tip of the thumb to the tip of the little finger), which in turn was
reckoned as half of a cubit (see note on 6:2 concerning the cubit). Some have seen in the
measurements found in 7:23-26 an ancient computation of the ratio of pi that stands quite
close to the modern value (Zuidhof 1982:181-184).

about 11,000 gallons of water. As the NLT mg note indicates, the Hebrew reads "2,000 baths."
Cogan (2001:265) cites archaeological evidence that a bath contained about 22 liters (5.8 gallons), so 2,000 baths would be 11,600 gallons, a huge amount of water by any estimation.

7:27 *ten bronze water carts.* A number of the details remain obscure, including how truly
mobile these water carts were. Most commentators suggest that the weight of the carts,
including their "bronze basins" filled with water, precluded any kind of practical mobility
(cf. their placement in 7:39).

7:29 *carved lions, oxen, and cherubim.* Lions were known in Palestine until modern times
(ABD 6.1143); they represent the fiercest of carnivores (1 Sam 17:36; Ps 7:2). "The lion of

Judah" became an apt metaphor for the regal house of David (cf. Gen 49:9; Rev 5:5). Concerning "oxen," see the note on 7:25; and concerning "cherubim," see notes on 6:23, 29, 32.

wreath decorations. Cf. the "carvings of wreaths" in 7:30-31 (also the "wreaths all around" of 7:36). The term *loyoth* [TH3914, ZH4324] may come from the root *l-w-h*, which in cognate languages means "to encircle, twist"; Cogan (2001:265) translates it with "spirals."

7:36 *cherubim, lions, and palm trees.* Concerning "cherubim" and "palm trees," see the notes on 6:23, 29, 32. Concerning "lions," see the first note on 7:29.

7:40 *He also made the necessary washbasins, shovels, and bowls.* The list found in 7:45 is similar to this list, except the term *kiyyoroth* [TH3595, ZH3963] (basins, washbasins) is replaced by *siroth* [TH5518, ZH6105] (pots, ash buckets). Many scholars (cf. Cogan 2001:267) therefore emend the MT's *kiyyoroth* to *siroth* (the change is very minor in Hebrew), a variant attested in some Hebrew manuscripts, as well as in the ancient versions. With the emendation, the implements now accord precisely with their counterparts found in Exod 27:3; 38:3.

7:46 *cast in clay molds.* Wiseman (1993:116) describes the process as follows: "The manufacture of all these articles by the *cire perdue* or lost wax process was done east of Jordan . . . where excavation shows much copper slag and the clay is suitable for digging moulds . . . and there was ample water nearby. The firing of large wax shaped cores and filling them with molten metal was a technique long employed in Egypt and Mesopotamia but required great skill to effect."

7:51 *Then he brought all the gifts his father, David, had dedicated.* Note the spoils of war mentioned in 2 Sam 8:10b-12.

COMMENTARY

There is much to think about in the welter of detail concerning the Temple implements in this lengthy textual "digression" (Seow's term, see commentary on 7:1-12). Certainly, one could remain critical of those who take undue delight in matters detailed and technical. Such untoward interest can become idolatrous. But that has been argued above. Here, instead, I want to suggest some positive thoughts about the subject of arts and crafts being devoted to God. The gold and especially the bronze work described in the last 39 verses of chapter 7 must have been simply stunning in size, quantity, and outward appearance. As Wiseman (1993:114) points out concerning the casting of the bronze Sea, "this huge basin or reservoir was one of the great Hebrew technical works, corresponding in modern metallurgy to the casting of the largest church bell." Surely, one can reflect positively about such efforts for the glory of God.

The "Teacher" reminds us in Ecclesiastes, "Whatever you do, do well. For when you go to the grave, there will be no work or planning or knowledge or wisdom" (Eccl 9:10). As we know, there is no place for mediocrity in the mind of God or in any efforts to bring honor to his name. Famously, God himself evaluated carefully his own work of creation: "Then God looked over all he had made, and he saw that it was very good!" (Gen 1:31a). We, likewise, as much as it is in our power and ability, should check out our own works of creation, to ascertain if they are likewise "very good." Of course, we are not to become unduly prideful in our efforts, still less to minimize the grace of God represented even in the very talents and treasures we can expend on those efforts; but surely our God deserves the very best we can offer. And we are permitted to describe our efforts (as well as the efforts of those, Christian and non-Christian, whom we solicit to help us) in detailed, glowing terms. And all this, too, can redound to the glory of God (cf. Ps 8). Extravagance may be entirely appropriate in these endeavors.

One of the most powerful pericopes in the Gospels is the anointing of Jesus at Bethany by an unnamed woman (see Matt 26:6-13, and parallels). She came in with a beautiful alabaster jar of expensive perfume, and poured it over Jesus' head. The disciples, perhaps like good Christian penny-pinchers of today, were indignant: "What a waste!" Jesus had a different view: "Why criticize this woman for doing such a good thing to me. . . . I tell you the truth, wherever the Good News is preached throughout the world, this woman's deed will be remembered and discussed." Sometimes, extreme extravagance may be just the right thing in the eyes of God—as long as it is for his glory.

◆   ## 6. The Ark brought to the Temple (8:1-11)

Solomon then summoned to Jerusalem the elders of Israel and all the heads of the tribes—the leaders of the ancestral families of the Israelites. They were to bring the Ark of the LORD's Covenant to the Temple from its location in the City of David, also known as Zion. ²So all the men of Israel assembled before King Solomon at the annual Festival of Shelters, which is held in early autumn in the month of Ethanim.*

³When all the elders of Israel arrived, the priests picked up the Ark. ⁴The priests and Levites brought up the Ark of the LORD along with the special tent* and all the sacred items that had been in it. ⁵There, before the Ark, King Solomon and the entire community of Israel sacrificed so many sheep, goats, and cattle that no one could keep count!

⁶Then the priests carried the Ark of the LORD's Covenant into the inner sanctuary of the Temple—the Most Holy Place—and placed it beneath the wings of the cherubim. ⁷The cherubim spread their wings over the Ark, forming a canopy over the Ark and its carrying poles. ⁸These poles were so long that their ends could be seen from the Holy Place, which is in front of the Most Holy Place, but not from the outside. They are still there to this day. ⁹Nothing was in the Ark except the two stone tablets that Moses had placed in it at Mount Sinai,* where the LORD made a covenant with the people of Israel when they left the land of Egypt.

¹⁰When the priests came out of the Holy Place, a thick cloud filled the Temple of the LORD. ¹¹The priests could not continue their service because of the cloud, for the glorious presence of the LORD filled the Temple of the LORD.

8:2 Hebrew *at the festival in the month Ethanim, which is the seventh month.* The Festival of Shelters began on the fifteenth day of the seventh month of the ancient Hebrew lunar calendar. This day occurred in late September, October, or early November.   **8:4** Hebrew *the Tent of Meeting;* i.e., the tent mentioned in 2 Sam 6:17 and 1 Chr 16:1.   **8:9** Hebrew *at Horeb,* another name for Sinai.

NOTES

8:1 *bring the Ark of the LORD's Covenant.* This Ark had quite a journey from the wilderness in the days of Moses to the Promised Land in the days of Joshua, followed by travels with the portable sanctuary during the period of the judges, and an extended side trip into the land of the Philistines (see 1 Sam 4–6). It was David who eventually brought the Ark into Jerusalem, his new capital (see 2 Sam 6; but even this journey included the tragic death of Uzzah, who had reached out to steady the Ark when the oxen had stumbled).

At this time, the Ark was placed in a "special tent" that David had erected (see 2 Sam 6:17; cf. the first note on 1:50). That is presumably the same "location in the City of David" mentioned in the present verse.

8:2 *at the annual Festival of Shelters.* Lit., "at the [unnamed] feast." Undoubtedly, the "Feast of Tabernacles" (NLT, "Festival of Shelters") is in view (cf. Lev 23:34-36, 39-43; Num 29:12-34). As Seow (1999:69) notes, this was also traditionally the time that the covenant would be renewed (Deut 31:9-13).

month of Ethanim. This was the 7th month, using the name from the old Canaanite/ Phoenician calendar (cf. NLT mg; also the comments found in the first note on 6:1). The term "Ethanim" may mean "everflowings" or the like, since by this time of the year only the perennial streams (*'ethanim* [TH388, ZH923]) had water left in them (cf. HALOT 44). Apparently there was an 11-month delay in the scheduling of the Temple's dedicatory celebration (the Temple was completed in the 8th month according to 6:38; see mg note), perhaps so that it could coincide with the celebration of the "Festival of Shelters" (see previous note). (Some suggest that the 11-month delay could also reflect the time needed to cast the bronze articles mentioned in 7:13-51.)

8:4 *the special tent.* See the note on 8:1.

8:7 *cherubim.* See the first note on 6:23.

8:8 *They are still there to this day.* Such statements as this lend strong credence for at least one preexilic edition of the books of Kings (see my comments under "Earlier Editions of Kings?" in the Introduction). Concerning the directive that the carrying poles were not to be removed from the Ark, see Exod 25:15.

8:9 *Nothing was in the Ark except the two stone tablets.* Contrast Heb 9:4, which relates that in the days of Moses a gold jar containing manna and Aaron's staff that had sprouted leaves were also put into the Ark. Presumably these items had been lost before or during the Ark's various vicissitudes in the days of Eli and Samuel (see the note on 8:1; also Wiseman 1993:118).

8:10 *a thick cloud.* In Exod 40:34-38, the "cloud of the LORD" hovered over the Tabernacle by day, and at night fire within the cloud could be seen (cf. also Exod 20:21; Num 10:34; 16:42). The parallels (at least in the pentateuchal texts) between Yahweh's "traveling" cloud and his original theophanic cloud on Mt. Sinai (Exod 19) will be immediately evident (see also the commentary below).

COMMENTARY

As Seow (1999:68) has pointed out, this chapter begins with the assembling of the people in 8:1, and ends with their dismissal in 8:66. Thus, the entire chapter is a single literary unit, and may be analyzed symmetrically as the following palistrophe (or A-B-C-B-A structure) demonstrates:

> A. Commencement of the ceremony (8:1-11)
> > B. Solomon's preliminary remarks (8:12-21)
> > > C. Solomon's prayer (8:22-53)
> > B'. Solomon's closing remarks (8:54-61)
> A'. Conclusion of the festival (8:62-66)

In the first part of this chapter, we see that the Ark of the Covenant has finally come to its "rest" (cf. 2 Sam 7:11a, where Yahweh grants "rest" for David and his subsequent dynasty). Up to now, the Ark has wandered, as it were, from place to place (cf. 2 Sam 7:6-7; also the note on 8:1), leading scholars to posit an "Ark Narrative" encompassing 1 Samuel 4-6 and 2 Samuel 6. Any such Ark Narrative also probably could encompass the present chapter (or more exactly, the present verses of the present chapter, plus perhaps 8:20-21). The Ark is something of a mysterious object of attention in the Old Testament, being both a throne for Yahweh's presence as well as a repository for the "covenant document," the second set of the Ten Commandments (Cogan 2001:280; Weinfeld 1972:208-209). But from a prophetic tradition (Jer 3:16-17; cf. Jer 23:24; also Isa 66:1), the Ark and its location, permanent or temporary, really will not matter all that much ("you will no longer wish for 'the good old days' when you possessed the Ark. . . . You will not miss those days or even remember them . . . there will be no need to rebuild the Ark" [Jer 3:16]). Already in the present chapter, of course, Solomon himself recognizes that Yahweh does not "live" in any earthly temple, nor is he enthroned, as it were, upon the Ark (8:27). Still, the contrast of Yahweh providing "rest" for the Israelites and their leadership back in 2 Samuel 7 with the present focus of providing a permanent resting place for the Ark is not to be missed. (Present speculations on where the Ark ended up, and if it still exists, are only that—idle speculations—despite some claims to the contrary!)

The most important reference to God's presence in the present passage is the "thick cloud," which interrupts the priestly activities (8:11-12) and which also leads to the unforgettable introduction to Solomon's prayer in the next section (8:12-13). Though clearly reminiscent of the cloud that accompanied the Israelites on their wilderness wanderings (see the references in the note on 8:10), the most vivid parallel to the present passage must remain the analogous interruption of the divine cloud of Moses's ministrations in the Tabernacle in Exodus 40:34-35. Often, in the church, we perceive the powerful presence of God when the worship leaders are *unable* to conduct business as usual, or the preachers "throw away their notes," as it were, and preach a message they had not previously prepared. Here is the biblical precedent for that—neither Moses in the Tabernacle nor the priests in Solomon's Temple could continue their liturgical duties and procedures, not because such duties or procedures were necessarily out of God's will, but because, at this special time, such actions were insufficient for the magnitude and significance of this unique occasion. Only once would the Tabernacle be dedicated, and only once the Temple; and in the providence of God both would call for special divine intervention signified by the presence of the dark, obscuring cloud of Yahweh. (Concerning the distinguishing features of the four-winged "cherubim" found here in the Temple [and elsewhere], see the discussion in the first note on 6:23. Concerning the significance of the Temple location for these earthly images of the heavenly host that represent the seat and residence of the deity, see the helpful comments of Haran and Greenberg, as cited at some length in the commentary on 8:22-53.)

◆　　　7. Solomon praises the LORD (8:12-21)

¹²Then Solomon prayed, "O LORD, you have said that you would live in a thick cloud of darkness. ¹³Now I have built a glorious Temple for you, a place where you can live forever!*"

¹⁴Then the king turned around to the

entire community of Israel standing before him and gave this blessing: [15]"Praise the LORD, the God of Israel, who has kept the promise he made to my father, David. For he told my father, [16]'From the day I brought my people Israel out of Egypt, I have never chosen a city among any of the tribes of Israel as the place where a Temple should be built to honor my name. But I have chosen David to be king over my people Israel.' "

[17]Then Solomon said, "My father, David, wanted to build this Temple to honor the name of the LORD, the God of Israel. [18]But the LORD told him, 'You wanted to build the Temple to honor my name. Your intention is good, [19]but you are not the one to do it. One of your own sons will build the Temple to honor me.'

[20]"And now the LORD has fulfilled the promise he made, for I have become king in my father's place, and now I sit on the throne of Israel, just as the LORD promised. I have built this Temple to honor the name of the LORD, the God of Israel. [21]And I have prepared a place there for the Ark, which contains the covenant that the LORD made with our ancestors when he brought them out of Egypt."

8:13 Some Greek texts add the line *Is this not written in the Book of Jashar?*

NOTES

8:12 *a thick cloud of darkness.* See note on 8:10.

8:13 *live forever!* The NLT mg makes reference to the longer Greek text connected with this verse (which in Codex Vaticanus [the Old Greek] is located later in the chapter, in 8:53a [following the versification of Rahlfs 1935], the entirety of 8:12-13 being omitted in the Old Greek). More to the point, at 8:53a in the Greek text, there seems to be a garbled allusion to the "Book of Jashar" (cf. Josh 10:13 and 2 Sam 1:18), which a number of scholars have suggested was also in the original Kings text (cf. Cogan 2001:281). Of further interest to scholars trying to reconstruct the original, the Greek text found in 8:53a also includes a longer half line or *stich* to go with the brief statement found in the MT of 8:12 about Yahweh living in "a thick cloud of darkness"; the fuller Greek text reads, "The Lord made known the sun in heaven/ but he said he would dwell in deep darkness." The RSV (but not the NRSV) included this half line in its translation of 8:12, and, as Cogan (2001:281) notes, a number of scholars have argued for its authenticity. But as Cogan himself further points out, the loss of this stich in the MT would then be hard to explain.

8:16 *I have never chosen a city. . . . But I have chosen David.* This is a very succinct summary of the classic Davidic covenant chapter—2 Sam 7 (cf. "The 'Lamp' of David" under "Major Themes" in the Introduction). The traditional text where Yahweh says he will choose a single location "to honor my name" is found in Deut 12.

8:18 *Your intention is good.* See note on 5:3.

8:21 *a place there for the Ark.* See the discussion in the commentary on 8:1-11.

COMMENTARY

If, as suggested in the commentary on 8:1-11, the "Ark Narrative" finds its culmination in the first part of the present chapter of 1 Kings, then we find here a similar situation in regard to the promises mentioned in 2 Samuel 7, the great Davidic covenant chapter. What Yahweh in essence told David at that time is succinctly summarized here in 8:18b-19a. David had good intentions to want to build a house for God, but it would be his son who would carry out the task. God saw to it that his people first found a home in Israel before a home was found for him. Such are the priorities of the Scriptures, both here and elsewhere: first a place for God's people and their leadership, then a place for God himself (cf. Hag 1:3-11; though their house building was intended to precede his, God did not expect the returned exiles to take some 18 years to start rebuilding his Temple!). Whether it be merely a historical reminiscence, or (as I expect) a hint at something theologically paradigmatic, what a wonderful pattern of priorities for God and for God's people! Our God is indeed a "jealous God" (see Exod 20:5-6; 34:14), and he certainly will not tolerate divided loyalties from his people (as the negative example of Solomon and his many foreign wives will illustrate). But he is also a compassionate, patient God, not seeking immediate glory for himself via earthly symbols of power and authority. (The fact that, of all things, it was the cross that became the symbol par excellence of Christianity puts to rest most contrary arguments.)

In this section we see Solomon praising Yahweh. We cannot help but note that the prevailing issue throughout many of the preexilic passages of the Hebrew Bible is not so much *how* to worship, but *whom* to worship. Yahweh, and Yahweh alone, must be our first priority—no other gods before him! Where and how to worship him are important issues (especially by the time of King Josiah in the late seventh century BC), but the main concern must be Yahweh and Yahweh alone. To Yahweh must our prayers be directed, wherever we find ourselves—whether or not we are near this Temple or any possible successor. (With respect to the second Temple, Jesus said, "The Scriptures [Isa 56:7] declare, 'My Temple will be called a house of prayer for all nations'" [Mark 11:17]). It is Yahweh's "promise" and the fulfillment of that promise which is properly the focus of chapter 8. Whatever Solomon had accomplished (for a discussion of the ancient Near Eastern parallels to such an "accomplishment," see the commentary on 8:54-66), it really represented Yahweh's accomplishment of his gracious promises.

◆   ## 8. Solomon's prayer of dedication (8:22-53)

22Then Solomon stood before the altar of the LORD in front of the entire community of Israel. He lifted his hands toward heaven, 23and he prayed,

"O LORD, God of Israel, there is no God like you in all of heaven above or on the earth below. You keep your covenant and show unfailing love to all who walk before you in wholehearted devotion. 24You have kept your promise to your servant David, my father. You made that promise with your own mouth, and with your own hands you have fulfilled it today.

25"And now, O LORD, God of Israel, carry out the additional promise you made to your servant David, my father. For you said to him, 'If your descendants guard their behavior and faithfully follow me as you have done, one of them will always sit on the throne of Israel.' 26Now, O God of Israel, fulfill this promise to your servant David, my father.

27"But will God really live on earth? Why, even the highest heavens cannot contain you. How much less this Temple I have built! 28Nevertheless, listen to my prayer and my plea, O LORD my God. Hear the cry and the prayer that your servant is making to you today. 29May you watch over this Temple night and day, this place where you have said, 'My name will be there.' May you always hear the prayers I make toward this place. 30May you hear the humble and earnest requests from me and your people Israel when we pray toward this place. Yes, hear us from heaven where you live, and when you hear, forgive.

³¹"If someone wrongs another person and is required to take an oath of innocence in front of your altar in this Temple, ³²then hear from heaven and judge between your servants—the accuser and the accused. Punish the guilty as they deserve. Acquit the innocent because of their innocence.

³³"If your people Israel are defeated by their enemies because they have sinned against you, and if they turn to you and acknowledge your name and pray to you here in this Temple, ³⁴then hear from heaven and forgive the sin of your people Israel and return them to this land you gave their ancestors.

³⁵"If the skies are shut up and there is no rain because your people have sinned against you, and if they pray toward this Temple and acknowledge your name and turn from their sins because you have punished them, ³⁶then hear from heaven and forgive the sins of your servants, your people Israel. Teach them to follow the right path, and send rain on your land that you have given to your people as their special possession.

³⁷"If there is a famine in the land or a plague or crop disease or attacks of locusts or caterpillars, or if your people's enemies are in the land besieging their towns—whatever disaster or disease there is—³⁸and if your people Israel pray about their troubles, raising their hands toward this Temple, ³⁹then hear from heaven where you live, and forgive. Give your people what their actions deserve, for you alone know each human heart. ⁴⁰Then they will fear you as long as they live in the land you gave to our ancestors.

⁴¹"In the future, foreigners who do not belong to your people Israel will hear of you. They will come from distant lands because of your name, ⁴²for they will hear of your great name and your strong hand and your powerful arm. And when they pray toward this Temple, ⁴³then hear from heaven where you live, and grant what they ask of you. In this way, all the people of the earth will come to know and fear you, just as your own people Israel do. They, too, will know that this Temple I have built honors your name.

⁴⁴"If your people go out where you send them to fight their enemies, and if they pray to the LORD by turning toward this city you have chosen and toward this Temple I have built to honor your name, ⁴⁵then hear their prayers from heaven and uphold their cause.

⁴⁶"If they sin against you—and who has never sinned?—you might become angry with them and let their enemies conquer them and take them captive to their land far away or near. ⁴⁷But in that land of exile, they might turn to you in repentance and pray, 'We have sinned, done evil, and acted wickedly.' ⁴⁸If they turn to you with their whole heart and soul in the land of their enemies and pray toward the land you gave to their ancestors—toward this city you have chosen, and toward this Temple I have built to honor your name—⁴⁹then hear their prayers and their petition from heaven where you live, and uphold their cause. ⁵⁰Forgive your people who have sinned against you. Forgive all the offenses they have committed against you. Make their captors merciful to them, ⁵¹for they are your people—your special possession—whom you brought out of the iron-smelting furnace of Egypt.

⁵²"May your eyes be open to my requests and to the requests of your people Israel. May you hear and answer them whenever they cry out to you. ⁵³For when you brought our ancestors out of Egypt, O Sovereign LORD, you told your servant Moses that you had set Israel apart from all the nations of the earth to be your own special possession."

NOTES

8:22 He lifted his hands toward heaven. Lit., "he spread (out) his palms heavenward" (see also 8:38, 54 for the same expression). Cogan (2001:283) describes this as "a gesture expressive of need and help that takes on the sense of prayer and supplication."

8:23 in all of heaven above or on the earth below. This familiar dichotomy encompasses all reality (cf. Gen 1:1; 2:1, 4, etc.). In Ugaritic (and sometimes in Hebrew; cf. Dahood 1970:27-28, 305, 313-314), the term "earth" (*'erets* [TH776, ZH824]) can signify the "nether world," giving pause to us humans who currently are residing precariously just above (or on the "top edge," so to speak) of that gloomy place!

8:24 with your own mouth . . . with your own hands. See the commentary on 8:1-11, with its summary of this fulfillment of the Davidic promises found in 2 Sam 7.

8:25 one of them will always sit on the throne of Israel. See the first note on 2:4.

8:27 But will God really live on earth? The answer is, of course, "no." This topic is discussed at some length in the commentary below.

8:29 May you watch over this Temple. This is the real importance of Solomon's Temple: its status as a special place for God's attention (see next note).

8:30 Yes, hear us from heaven where you live, and when you hear, forgive. This is the theme of the seven petitions in the next 21 verses. The Temple is not God's actual place of dwelling, but it is the place of his special attention.

8:31-32 The first petition: asking for justice in difficult cases. May the truly innocent be publicly exonerated and the guilty publicly punished.

8:33-34 The second petition: asking for forgiveness and restoration for Israel if they have sinned, been defeated in battle, and then repented of their sin. This, as well as the last of the remaining petitions, fits the exilic situation particularly well.

8:35-36 The third petition: asking for alleviation of drought conditions due to the people's sin.

8:36 Teach them to follow the right path. This is a remarkable admission of the reasons for such drought conditions in the first place. The term "teach" here is a verbal form of the familiar Hebrew word Torah (*torah* [TH8451, ZH9368]), often imprecisely translated as "law," but better translated as "teachings" or "(authoritative) instructions." The people's sin, although more than the result of simple ignorance of God's instruction, stems in part from such ignorance.

8:37-40 The fourth petition: asking likewise for forgiveness for the sin that has brought about famine, plague or crop disease, attacks of locusts or caterpillars, or even the condition of being under siege from human enemies.

8:38 raising their hands toward this Temple. See the note on 8:22.

8:39 Give your people what their actions deserve. Solomon once again (cf. the comment on 8:36) does not seek to ignore or gloss over the need to address sin forthrightly. Still, the overall accent is appropriately on forgiveness.

8:41-43 The fifth petition: asking that even foreigners who offer prayers in, or directed towards, the Temple will be heard. The book of Deuteronomy, in particular, is greatly concerned about the status of the foreigner or "stranger" (*nokri* [TH5237A, ZH5799])—this is true as well for the "resident alien" (*ger* [TH1616, ZH1731]). Therefore, such concern is not to be restricted to Hebrew teachings from the postexilic era as some scholars would argue (see Sweeney [2007:135], who also points out that "such concern builds the case that Yahweh is sovereign over all creation, and that the Temple symbolizes that sovereignty").

8:44-45 The sixth petition: asking for military success wherever Yahweh sends the people to fight. Once again, a preexilic setting is here presupposed.

8:45 uphold their cause. Lit., "act justly toward them" ('asitha mishpatam [TH4941, ZH5477], "do or perform compassionate justice for them"). The same expression appears in 8:49, and a similar expression in 8:59. The NLT translation correctly indicates the just nature of their "cause" (Cogan 2001:286). We must seek the Lord, both to forgive our sins and also to bring about justice in our world.

8:46-51 The seventh and final petition: asking mercy for the people who are (deservedly, yet tragically) in exile. Some extend this petition to 8:53, but, as already noted above, I prefer to see 8:52-53 as a general conclusion to all the petitions (cf. Cogan 2001:292).

8:46 and who has never sinned? Cf. Eccl 7:20; 1 John 1:8. Both Testaments of the Bible are very clear about this point.

8:47 We have sinned, done evil, and acted wickedly. Three significant Hebrew terms are used here for sin: khata' [TH2398, ZH2627], "to sin, to miss the mark or goal"; 'awah [TH5753, ZH6390], "to do evil, to act perversely, in a bent or twisted way"; and rasha' [TH7561, ZH8399], "to act wickedly, act against the accepted, right way"—cf. Wiseman (1993:122), who also adds a reference to "committing offenses" (from pasha' [TH6586, ZH7321], "to rebel against God"), found in 8:50.

8:48 toward the land . . . toward this city . . . toward this Temple. Here, an exilic setting seems to be presupposed, but the text itself need not be dated to the exilic or postexilic era (cf. the blessings and curses found in Deut 28, especially Deut 28:63-68).

8:50 Make their captors merciful to them. The rich Hebrew root r-kh-m is used twice in this verse, first as a noun (rakhamim [TH7356, ZH8171]) and then as a verb (rakham [TH7355, ZH8163]). It conveys the idea of a rich compassion, as a mother would have for the offspring of her womb (rekhem [TH7358, ZH8167]). Jeremiah 29:7 conveys much the same message for the exilic community: "Work for the peace and prosperity of the city where I sent you into exile. Pray to the LORD for it, for its welfare will determine your welfare." (This is the context for the well-known text of Jer 29:11, "I know the plans I have for you. . . . plans . . . to give you a future and a hope.") We should always pray blessings on our unbelieving community—it is even in our own self-interest to do so!

8:52 whenever they cry out to you. Once again, a summarizing perspective—both preexilic and exilic settings are included.

8:53 special possession. Lit., "you have separated (hibdil [TH914, ZH976]) them [Israel] for yourself from all the (other) peoples of the earth as an inheritance" (nakhalah [TH5159, ZH5709]). Parallel uses of the verb "to separate" may be found in Lev 20:24, 26; and the idea of Israel as God's "special possession" may be found in 1 Sam 10:1 (and, in a tragic sense, also in 2 Kgs 21:14). The comment that "you told your servant Moses," found earlier in the present verse, probably presupposes the foundational statement of Exod 19:5, "you will be my own special treasure (segullah [TH5459, ZH6035], "personal treasure of a king," or the like) from among all the peoples on earth." (For issues related to the text of this verse, see note on 8:13.)

COMMENTARY

The present section of the chapter is organized into several introductory paragraphs (8:23-30), plus seven petitions from Solomon to Yahweh for him to "hear from heaven" and respond graciously to the specifics of the petition being offered (8:31-51). It is particularly noteworthy that Yahweh's chief location for such a positive response is said repeatedly to be *in heaven*, not in or near the Temple of Solomon. "Each petition is formulated casuistically ["if . . . then" statements], much like standard forms of case law, so that the circumstances of the petition are followed by a statement of the recommended course of action" (Sweeney 2007:134; cf. Wiseman 1993:120). Finally, 8:52-53 is a brief summary conclusion for this lengthy prayer, ending on an emphasis of the uniqueness of Israel as God's special people.

In this section, the question that comes to mind is: Where does God really dwell? In heaven, or in the Temple, or in both? The answer is, in a sense, "both." God does (or did) "live" in a real sense in the Holy of Holies in deep darkness in the Tabernacle/Temple. But he really lives in heaven. Greenberg, in the first volume of his Ezekiel commentary (1983:196-197), has explored this apparent conundrum at length:

> The difficulty [of sorting out the various locations of the cherubim in and near Jeru-salem in Ezekiel chs 8–11] seems related to the paradoxical notion shared by all ancient religions that the deity is at once localized in its temple and "in heaven" (or ubiquitous). The image in the pagan temple is literally the seat and residence of the deity; through their images, Marduk dwells in his temple in Babylon and Sin in Haran. Analogously, the cherub statues in Jerusalem's holy of holies (like their antecedents in the tabernacle) were the throne on which YHWH sat, shrouded in darkness. At the same time the pagan god dwells in heaven or on the mountain of the gods (the two may not be sharply differentiated), and moves freely about the universe. . . . Similarly, YHWH dwells in heaven, his majesty covers the heavens and fills the earth, and he rides the clouds or a cherub on his travels. M. Haran puts it well: "We must emphasize the fact that although the cherubs of the ark-cover and the ark symbolize a throne and a footstool respectively, the Bible does not bind the deity to them or for a moment suppose that he is located (as it were) only there . . . God's chief place is conceived to be in heaven and there too is the place of his throne. His heavenly throne is supported by living cherubs; as a reflection of those heavenly cherubs the Israelites fashion cherub statues in the holy of holies of the tabernacle. The throne behind its curtain is only a miniature and a replica of the celestial throne: the heavenly cherubs are 'living creatures' as Ezekiel calls them." (Greenberg 1983:196-197; cf. Haran 1978:256-257)

There is much wisdom in these comments. When Jonah prayed in the belly of a great fish, his earnest prayer went out to God in his holy Temple (Jonah 2:7). His prayer was surely directed more toward heaven than toward any earthly location. Jonah, as a northern prophet (2 Kgs 14:25), would at least have been very reluctant to consider Solomon's Temple in the southern kingdom of Judah as God's holy Temple. He rejoiced that God heard his prayer. Solomon similarly acknowledges God's transcendence clearly in the present passage (see 8:30b, 32, 34, 36, 39, 43, 45, 49). How sweetly ironic it is that the great builder of the first Temple acknowledged forthrightly and repeatedly that God did not really and ultimately live there. What a comfort for the later exilic audience of 1–2 Kings (who sadly knew that Solomon's Temple was forever gone) that its very founder emphasized that *anyone* (8:41-43) *anywhere* (8:47-51) can raise their hands toward heaven (8:22, 54) to be heard and to be blessed and healed by the God of the universe. Thus, even this prayer in chapter 8, while very specific in setting and focus, remains remarkably universal in overall intent and effect. We today, part of the "new Israel" (Rom 11), can and must do the same as both the original and the exilic audience of 1–2 Kings: We should lift our hands toward heaven and beseech our God to forgive our sin and "uphold [our] cause" (8:45, 49).

◆   9. The dedication of the Temple (8:54-66)

⁵⁴When Solomon finished making these prayers and petitions to the LORD, he stood up in front of the altar of the LORD, where he had been kneeling with his hands raised toward heaven. ⁵⁵He stood and in a loud voice blessed the entire congregation of Israel:

⁵⁶"Praise the LORD who has given rest to his people Israel, just as he promised. Not one word has failed of all the wonderful promises he gave through his servant Moses. ⁵⁷May the LORD our God be with us as he was with our ancestors; may he never leave us or abandon us. ⁵⁸May he give us the desire to do his will in everything and to obey all the commands, decrees, and regulations that he gave our ancestors. ⁵⁹And may these words that I have prayed in the presence of the LORD be before him constantly, day and night, so that the LORD our God may give justice to me and to his people Israel, according to each day's needs. ⁶⁰Then people all over the earth will know that the LORD alone is God and there is no other. ⁶¹And may you be completely faithful to the LORD our God. May you always obey his decrees and commands, just as you are doing today."

⁶²Then the king and all Israel with him offered sacrifices to the LORD. ⁶³Solomon offered to the LORD a peace offering of 22,000 cattle and 120,000 sheep and goats. And so the king and all the people of Israel dedicated the Temple of the LORD.

⁶⁴That same day the king consecrated the central area of the courtyard in front of the LORD's Temple. He offered burnt offerings, grain offerings, and the fat of peace offerings there, because the bronze altar in the LORD's presence was too small to hold all the burnt offerings, grain offerings, and the fat of the peace offerings.

⁶⁵Then Solomon and all Israel celebrated the Festival of Shelters* in the presence of the LORD our God. A large congregation had gathered from as far away as Lebo-hamath in the north and the Brook of Egypt in the south. The celebration went on for fourteen days in all—seven days for the dedication of the altar and seven days for the Festival of Shelters.* ⁶⁶After the festival was over,* Solomon sent the people home. They blessed the king and went to their homes joyful and glad because the LORD had been good to his servant David and to his people Israel.

8:65a Hebrew *the festival;* see note on 8:2.   8:65b Hebrew *seven days and seven days, fourteen days;* compare parallel text at 2 Chr 7:8-10.   8:66 Hebrew *On the eighth day,* probably referring to the day following the seven-day Festival of Shelters; compare parallel text at 2 Chr 7:9-10.

NOTES

8:54 *prayers and petitions.* Heb., *tepillah* [TH8605, ZH9525], "prayer, supplication," and *tekhinnah* [TH8467, ZH9382], "pleading for compassionate attention"; essentially synonyms.

kneeling. The emphasis of the posture of "kneeling" is on demonstrating humility and obeisance to one's superiors. Cogan (2001:287-288) notes that this and Solomon's prior upright position (8:22) represent different moments in prayer, typical of the OT and the ancient Near East.

his hands raised toward heaven. See note on 8:22.

8:55 *blessed the entire congregation.* This is an echo of 8:14.

8:56 *given rest.* This is implied in the great Davidic covenant chapter, 2 Sam 7 (see especially 2 Sam 7:10-11); but the reference to "Moses" here focuses more on statements such as Deut 12:9 and Josh 21:43-45.

8:59 *constantly, day and night.* Cf. 8:29, where the traditional order of the Hebrew day ("night and day") is found in the MT.

each day's needs. Cogan (2001:288) notes that this idiom later signifies the "daily allowance" for the exiled King Jehoiachin in 2 Kgs 25:30. We should pray in a similar way, "Give us today the food we need" (Matt 6:11, in the Lord's Prayer; cf. also Prov 30:7-9). Too much, as well as too little, may prove fatal.

8:63 *a peace offering.* This is the traditional translation for the Heb. *zebakh shelamim* [TH2077/8002, ZH2285/8968] (cf. Lev 3). Sweeney (2007:136) emphasizes the celebratory nature of this offering. Concerning the lavish size of Solomon's offerings listed here, Wiseman (1993:123-124) cites similar reports of large numbers of sacrifices in Assyrian reports of ceremonies commemorating the opening of new buildings (cf. also Hurowitz 1992:276).

dedicated the Temple of the LORD. The verb for "dedicated" (*khanak* [TH2596, ZH2852]) underlies the term "Hanukkah," or the Festival of Dedication (cf. John 10:22). This relatively rare term is also used of educating the young and is found in Prov 22:6, "Direct your children onto the right path, and when they are older they will not leave it."

8:64 *the bronze altar.* Curiously, this altar was not described anywhere back in ch 7, although it is mentioned in 2 Chr 4:1 as one of the items fashioned by Huram. As Cogan (2001:289) points out, it is probably the same altar later mentioned in 9:25. Probably a haplography (scribal textual omission) in the MT of 7:22-23 would best explain its puzzling omission in that chapter (thus Cogan, following a personal communication from D. N. Freedman; also cf. Japhet 1993:564).

8:65 *Lebo-hamath . . . Brook of Egypt.* These are the classic northern and southern borders of the Solomonic kingdom (contrast the different sets of borders mentioned back in 4:21, 24, 25, and the notes found there). "Lebo-hamath" probably corresponds with Assyrian *Laba'u* (modern Labweh) in the Beqaa valley in eastern Lebanon; and the "Brook of Egypt" corresponds with Assyrian *Nahal-Musri* (modern Wadi el-'Arish) in the Sinai peninsula, southwest of the Egyptian border with the present Gaza Strip (Wiseman 1993:124).

fourteen days. Lit., "seven days and seven days, fourteen days" (so NLT mg). The LXX lacks the last two phrases, "and seven days, fourteen days." The longer text in the MT could be a gloss (scribal addition) taken from 2 Chr 7:9, where we read of a seven-day festival dedicating the altar, as well as the seven-day celebration of the Festival of Shelters. Chronicles also describes a similar fourteen-day festival celebrated during the time of King Hezekiah (see 2 Chr 30:23-27, and especially 30:26, where there is an explicit comparison to the time of Solomon). There is no counterpart in 2 Kings for the tradition found in 2 Chr 30.

COMMENTARY

As we have already seen, a key theme throughout this entire chapter is the *insufficiency* of Solomon's Temple. So it is in these final verses of the chapter. *Yahweh* is sufficient (8:56); Solomon hopes that the *leadership* and the *people* are sufficient (8:58-61), but the accoutrements of the Temple prove to be entirely insufficient (especially the bronze altar, 8:64). Of course, the altar is "insufficient" due to the immense number of sacrifices, not due to some flaw in its design! Still, the point is made. What is needed is the obedience of the people (8:61) more than the grandeur of their Temple. And if there would be such obedience, then "people all over the earth will know that [Yahweh] alone is God and there is no other" (8:60; cf. 2 Sam 7:19, especially understood as a "charter for humanity"; on this, see "Date and Occasion of Writing" in the Introduction). All peoples on earth will be blessed if (and only if) Israel stays faithful to the covenant. This is the message of the book of Exodus (cf. Exod 32:12, where Moses argues that the Egyptians will misunderstand the nature of Yahweh if he destroys his own people); of Numbers (cf. Num 14:13-16, again Moses arguing that the Egyptians will misinterpret Yahweh's judgmental actions against his own sinful people); in Deuteronomy (Deut 4:5-8 urges obedience to the Torah so that the surrounding nations will take notice); as well as in 2 Samuel 7; and here in chapter 8. Truly, this is the way Abraham's "seed" can be a blessing to all the earth (Gen 12:3; 22:18; 26:4).

The present chapter (indeed, much of chs 5–8) parallels cuneiform building accounts in Mesopotamian royal inscriptions (Cogan 2001:250, 291, citing Hurowitz 1992). More particularly, the beginning (8:1-11) and the ending (8:62-66) of the present chapter find direct Mesopotamian counterparts (see, particularly, Hurowitz 1992:271-277). But that is not the case for much of Solomon's central prayer, and especially its introduction in 8:23-27 (Hurowitz 1992:298-299). Assyrian and Babylonian parallels are almost to be expected in ancient Near Eastern temple dedications, biblical or otherwise, but the differences here speak volumes as well. Yahweh, unlike his Mesopotamian counterparts, does *not* live in the Temple, still less stand indebted to any king who builds it. In clear contrast to the pagan parallels, Yahweh is indebted to no one. "Unlike the Assyrian and Babylonian kings who can expect their prayers to be answered when Assur, Anu and Adad, or Shamash enter their new abodes, Solomon must rely on God's promise that his name will be in his temple. . . . The votive [an offering in fulfillment of a vow] dimension in the extra-biblical prayers has been cancelled and replaced by reliance on the word of God" (Hurowitz 1992:299).

This is the genius of the biblical writers and editors over against their ancient Near Eastern counterparts: following the form and the function of the cultural traditions of the day, but being led by the Spirit and adding their unique perspective that the true God cannot be contained by any earthly structure. This God is graciously asked to attend to the prayers of the people and their leaders. And that remains our hope even today: God is asked to answer our prayers, according to each day's needs. "Then people all over the earth will know that the LORD alone is God and there is no other" (8:59-60). To him be all the glory.

◆   D. Solomon in All His Glory: Mixed Results (1 Kgs 9:1–10:29)
         1. The LORD's response to Solomon (9:1-9)

So Solomon finished building the Temple of the LORD, as well as the royal palace. He completed everything he had planned to do. ²Then the LORD appeared to Solomon a second time, as he had done before at Gibeon. ³The LORD said to him,

"I have heard your prayer and your petition. I have set this Temple apart to be holy—this place you have built where my name will be honored forever. I will always watch over it, for it is dear to my heart.

⁴"As for you, if you will follow me with integrity and godliness, as David your father did, obeying all my commands, decrees, and regulations, ⁵then I will establish the throne of your dynasty over Israel forever. For I made this promise to your father, David: 'One of your descendants will always sit on the throne of Israel.'

⁶"But if you or your descendants abandon me and disobey the commands and decrees I have given you, and if you serve and worship other gods, ⁷then I will uproot Israel from this land that I have given them. I will reject this Temple that I have made holy to honor my name. I will make Israel an object of mockery and ridicule among the nations. ⁸And though this Temple is impressive now, all who pass by will be appalled and will gasp in horror. They will ask, 'Why did the LORD do such terrible things to this land and to this Temple?'

⁹"And the answer will be, 'Because his people abandoned the LORD their God, who brought their ancestors out of Egypt, and they worshiped other gods instead and bowed down to them. That is why the LORD has brought all these disasters on them.'"

NOTES

9:1 Although Wiseman (1993:97) has made a strong case for linking 9:1-9 with the unit entitled "Temple and Palace Building" (5:1–8:66), I have instead designated ch 9 as part of the "mixed results" of Solomon's legacy discussed in chs 9–10. (The note might be regarded as part of both sections, but the negative elements seem to predominate, thus joining it to the rest of chs 9–10.)

finished building the Temple . . . the royal palace. These are the main building projects described in chs 5–7. Primary focus, naturally, remains on these two symmetrical building projects (see note on 7:1).

everything he had planned to do. This is probably an oblique reference to his other building projects, such as his store-cities (see note on 9:19).

9:2 *the LORD appeared to Solomon a second time.* Solomon appears to be the only king of either kingdom so honored by such divine visitations (see first note on 3:5). Normally a prophet served as an intermediary between Yahweh and the king (see the suggestions of Halpern as described in the commentary on 1:5-27). Sadly, Solomon's experience of two theophanies only renders him even more guilty and deserving of punishment for his heinous sins of syncretism (see 11:9).

Gibeon. See note on 3:4.

9:3 *I have set this Temple apart to be holy.* Usually such "consecration" (Hiphil of *qadash* [TH6942, ZH7727]) is connected with human agency (cf. Cogan 2001:295), but as Wiseman (1993:124) aptly notes, "only God can make a person or place holy."

I will always watch over it, for it is dear to my heart. This is a paraphrastic translation; the Hebrew reads, "my eyes and my heart will be there all the days." As Cogan (2001:295) notes, a negative counterpart to the phrase "eyes and heart" may be found in Num 15:39 (NIV): "and not prostitute yourselves by going after the lusts of your own hearts and eyes."

9:4 *As for you.* See "The 'Lamp' of David" under "Major Themes" in the Introduction for an extended discussion of the positive appraisal of Solomon's father, David, throughout the books of Kings.

9:5 *this promise.* This promise was made in the great Davidic covenant chapter, 2 Sam 7 (cf. the first note on 2:4 on the extent of this promise).

9:6 *abandon . . . disobey . . . serve and worship other gods.* This is the classic description of apostasy; the Hebrew expression for "abandon" here (*shob teshubun* [TH7725, ZH8740]) is emphatic for "turn (aside)." Once again, the emphasis is on the people's obedience and loyalty, not on the presence or absence of any temple building (cf. note on 6:12).

9:7 *uproot Israel . . . reject this Temple.* Exile (in a prophetic, future sense) is surely in mind (see the note on 8:48). Sweeney (2007:139) makes a strong case for "Israel" here to be understood not as the entire people of God but as possibly a reference to the later northern kingdom or its territory (cf. the reference to "Judah and Israel" of 4:20; contrast 4:1). In any case, the specific reference to the Temple implies that Judah as well as the northern kingdom would be subject to such future devastation.

9:8 *And though this Temple is impressive now.* This follows the MT but understands the imperfect verb "will be" (*yihyeh*) as incipient or the like. Many commentators, however, emend *'elyon* [TH5945, ZH6609] (exalted, impressive) to *le'iyyin* [TH3807.1/5856, ZH4200/6505] ([will be] as in ruins), following the Old Latin and the Syriac. Cogan (2001:296) suggests that the Aramaic Targum's translation, "and this house that was high shall be a ruin," preserves a double reading, attesting both terms in its Hebrew Vorlage). Sweeney (2007:137-138) may well be correct in suggesting "the [Masoretic] Heb. text expunges a statement that would compromise the temple's sanctity."

all who pass by will be appalled and will gasp in horror. What a gloomy end to what had started out as such a positive prophecy! Either extravagant blessing or extreme curse (cf. Deut 29:22-28), with no middle ground. Cogan (2001:296) gives an Assyrian parallel from an inscription of Ashurbanipal concerning their victory over Arabia, the destruction of which occasions wonder to all who observe it (cf. also the repeated references in Jeremiah [Jer 18:16; 19:8—referring to Judah and Jerusalem; Jer 49:17—to Edom; Jer 50:13—to Babylon]; also Zeph 2:15—to Nineveh; Ezek 27:36—to Tyre; Lam 2:15—to Jerusalem).

gasp in horror. Lit., "will whistle"; the Hebrew idiom probably conveys "a sharp expelling of the breath, indicative of the terror which the sight inspires, [which] will issue as a kind of whistling" (Cogan 2001:296, citing Greenberg).

9:9 *That is why.* Lit., "therefore" (*'al-ken* [TH5921/3651A, ZH6584/4027]). The emphasis is again on the experiences of the people. Even in judgment, alas, the focus is properly on the people more than their land or their buildings.

COMMENTARY

Either one extreme or the other—isn't that the way of the Christian in a non-Christian world? The world watches us, for better or for worse! If we slip up, the world will be quick to remind us (using what often seems to be a double standard—see 1 Pet 4:17), but if we do what is good, the world will again often take notice (see 1 Pet 3:16-17). Our actions will often preach the cause of Christ more effectively than any of our words could. As St. Francis of Assisi said, "Preach the gospel at all times—if necessary, use words."

So it is with Solomon. So it is with God's people in Solomon's day, and so it is with their actions and their prayers. If they stayed faithful, extravagant blessing would be theirs, and the world would take note. But if they messed up, the result would be a notorious curse, so bad that the world could not help but take notice. Thus they (and we) preach the justice and the goodness of God, whether by cooperation with his will, or, if sadly necessary, by bringing about necessary judgment by our noncooperation with his will. May it be that the nations will not have to "gasp in horror" (9:8) at the disastrous sight of God's judging the actions of his people in present days. And to conclude with what must by now be painfully obvious: No temple, cathedral, or any such fine edifice will make a bit of difference in the matter. Even Solomon's fine Temple only served eventually to provide a powerful example of God having to judge his wayward people and bring devastation to their beautiful land and place of worship (see Lam 2:1-2, 15-17).

◆   ## 2. Solomon's agreement with Hiram (9:10-14)

¹⁰It took Solomon twenty years to build the LORD's Temple and his own royal palace. At the end of that time, ¹¹he gave twenty towns in the land of Galilee to King Hiram of Tyre. (Hiram had previously provided all the cedar and cypress timber and gold that Solomon had requested.) ¹²But when Hiram came from Tyre to see the towns Solomon had given him, he was not at all pleased with them. ¹³"What kind of towns are these, my brother?" he asked. So Hiram called that area Cabul (which means "worthless"), as it is still known today. ¹⁴Nevertheless, Hiram paid* Solomon 9,000 pounds* of gold.

9:14a Or For Hiram had paid.   9:14b Hebrew 120 talents [4,000 kilograms].

NOTES

9:10 Perhaps the present section (9:10-14) should be closely linked with the next section, as, for example, Wiseman (1993:125-126) does: "Solomon's work outside Jerusalem required additional resources. These he now sought by (i) a further agreement with Hiram (vv. 10-14), (ii) the extended use of forced labor (vv. 15-25), and (iii) the profits from maritime expeditions." But for the sake of consistency, the NLT divisions of the text will be retained here.

twenty years. Probably the 7 years to build the Temple (6:38), plus the 13 years to build the palace (7.1) are in view. Nevertheless, most commentators do not see the present passage as necessarily related to Solomon's previous payments for Hiram's supplies of cedar, cypress, and gold for the Temple and palace (as recalled in 9:11; cf. the first note on 5:11). In any case, there is almost certainly a new sense of economic desperation to be found in the present passage.

9:11 *twenty towns.* This is a good translation for the term *'ir* [TH5892, ZH6551], usually translated "city/cities," but actually indicating any type of settlement from a hamlet to a metropolis. This region would correspond generally to Solomon's ninth administrative district (see 4:16), as pointed out by Sweeney (2007:143-144), who also notes negatively that by this action, Solomon effectually ceded some of the ancestral Promised Land back to Hiram, who was a Phoenician/Canaanite monarch.

King Hiram of Tyre. See note on 5:1.

9:12 *not at all pleased with them.* This is a surprising reaction because the land ceded to Hiram was both generous in size and quite fertile (Cogan 2001:307). Perhaps, paradoxically, comments such as these were meant to downplay for later Judean generations the seriousness of Solomon's giving away portions of Israel's Promised Land to non-Israelites (in 2 Chr 8:2, the brief reference to Hiram giving Solomon some towns seems to be further elaboration on the present passage).

9:13 *my brother.* This is a common, neutral term for "diplomatic ally"; still, the relationship denoted here between Solomon and Hiram the Phoenician (i.e., Canaanite) may well be intended to be somewhat jarring to the later Israelite or Judean reading or hearing the text.

Cabul. Heb., *kabul*, possibly meaning "as (*ka-*) worthless (*bal/bul*)" (see Cogan 2001:300) concerning this and other possibilities).

9:14 *Nevertheless, Hiram paid.* Most commentators would read the Hebrew something like this: Hiram made a considerable payment in gold for the cities (hence, the put-down here is perhaps merely a bargaining ploy). Thus, the gold here is an *additional* payment made by Hiram to a cash-starved Solomon. More likely, however, is the view of Cogan (2001:300) for interpreting the Hebrew akin to the suggestion given in the NLT mg note, "for Hiram had [already] paid," which represents a reference back to 9:11b (which cites Hiram's previous provisions of wood for the Temple, first mentioned in 5:7-10 [21-24]).

9,000 pounds of gold. Lit., "120 talents of gold." Concerning the likely size of the Hebrew talent, see ABD 6.905-908. With the talent representing 3,000 shekels (and probably the typical maximum load one person could carry), and with the Palestinian shekel calculated at 11.4 g (0.40 oz), each talent would weigh a little over 75 lbs (34.2 kg), hence the NLT total given here in pounds is just about on target. Recently, Dever (2001:221-228) has argued that the Israelite archaeological evidence shows that the Judahite shekel was standardized around the reign of Hezekiah at about 11.33 g, with an average deviation of only 3 percent (and among the more common 1 to 8 shekel weights, of only 0.5 percent!). Such remarkable standardization represents one of the practical results of the Hezekiah revival (as well as the later reforms of Josiah), according to Dever (2001:224-226, utilizing the careful results of Kletter [1991, 1998]).

COMMENTARY

As Wiseman (1993:126) has pointed out, Solomon seems to have gone into considerable debt after the earlier commercial contract with Hiram expired (see 5:1-12). Once the Temple and the palace were finished, the narrator informs us that things seemed to go downhill rather rapidly. Solomon's lengthy 40-year reign, even if it's only a round number, almost certainly encompassed times both good and bad; and now, it seems, we move relentlessly into the latter category. How else are we to interpret the text telling us about Solomon's need to give up part of the Promised Land to—or, in a sense, *back* to—the hands of pagan Canaanites? (Cf. the comment of Sweeney cited in the first note on 9:11.)

Now, somewhat programmatically, the writer of Kings wants us to consider Solomon as the antithesis of Joshua, the leader who brought into Israelite control much of the Promised Land. "In contrast to Joshua, Solomon spurns the land of Israel granted by YHWH by giving it back to the Canaanites" (Sweeney 2007:143-144). Taking 9:15 as part of the present section, Sweeney goes on to state, "Solomon's imposition of the *mas* [TH4522, ZH4989] indicates that Solomon can only build up the land with foreign support." (Regarding the *mas*, or "forced labor," see the second note on 4:6.) Thus, the conclusion here seems inevitable: The "great" King Solomon, indeed a veritable pharaoh in fame and power, can only succeed, or even stay fiscally solvent, by means of an influx of foreign money and foreign labor. And to this end, he actually "sells off" a significant section of the Promised Land.

As this section of the commentary is being written, there is much in the news concerning contemporary economic retrenchments—harsh fiscal realities being no stranger to ancient or modern times. But to sell off parts of Yahweh's "land grant" to satisfy one's debts, and to enslave foreigners (and apparently Israelites as well; cf. 11:28) to build up one's domain, neither serves God or God's people well. The wisest king of all should certainly know that much!

◆   ## 3. Solomon's many achievements (9:15-28)

15 This is the account of the forced labor that King Solomon conscripted to build the LORD's Temple, the royal palace, the supporting terraces,* the wall of Jerusalem, and the cities of Hazor, Megiddo, and Gezer. 16 (Pharaoh, the king of Egypt, had attacked and captured Gezer, killing the Canaanite population and burning it down. He gave the city to his daughter as a wedding gift when she married Solomon. 17 So Solomon rebuilt the city of Gezer.) He also built up the towns of Lower Beth-horon, 18 Baalath, and Tamar* in the wilderness within his land. 19 He built towns as supply centers and constructed towns where his chariots and horses* could be stationed. He built everything he desired in Jerusalem and Lebanon and throughout his entire realm.

20 There were still some people living in the land who were not Israelites, including Amorites, Hittites, Perizzites, Hivites, and Jebusites. 21 These were descendants of the nations whom the people of Israel had not completely destroyed.* So Solomon conscripted them as slaves, and they serve as forced laborers to this day.

22 But Solomon did not conscript any of the Israelites for forced labor. Instead, he assigned them to serve as fighting men, government officials, officers and captains in his army, commanders of his chariots, and charioteers. 23 Solomon appointed 550 of them to supervise the people working on his various projects.

24 Solomon moved his wife, Pharaoh's daughter, from the City of David to the new palace he had built for her. Then he constructed the supporting terraces.

25 Three times each year Solomon presented burnt offerings and peace offerings on the altar he had built for the LORD. He also burned incense to the LORD. And so he finished the work of building the Temple.

26 King Solomon also built a fleet of ships at Ezion-geber, a port near Elath* in the land of Edom, along the shore of the Red Sea.* 27 Hiram sent experienced crews of sailors to sail the ships with Solomon's men. 28 They sailed to Ophir and brought back to Solomon some sixteen tons* of gold.

9:15 Hebrew *the millo;* also in 9:24. The meaning of the Hebrew is uncertain.   9:18 An alternate reading in the Masoretic Text reads *Tadmor.*   9:19 Or *and charioteers.*   9:21 The Hebrew term used here refers to the complete consecration of things or people to the LORD, either by destroying them or by giving them as an offering.   9:26a As in Greek version (see also 2 Kgs 14:22; 16:6); Hebrew reads *Eloth,* a variant spelling of Elath.   9:26b Hebrew *sea of reeds.*   9:28 Hebrew *420 talents* [14 metric tons].

NOTES

9:15 *forced labor.* Heb., *mas* [TH4522, ZH4989]; see second note on 4:6; also see the commentary below for an extended theological analysis of this phenomenon.

the supporting terraces. Heb., *hammillo'* [TH4407, ZH4864] (cf. NLT mg), probably to be translated as "the filling" (the root *m-l-'* [TH4390, ZH4848] means "to be full, fill"); and presumably signifying a "filled-in" terraced area in the ancient city of Jerusalem. The "Millo" is now usually linked to the Area G "stepped-stone structure" or massive set of stone-covered terraces built on the northern part of the eastern flank of the hill where the City of David was located (see the second note on 3:1 concerning this location; for a photograph of this impressive "stepped-stone structure," see ABD 2.56). Cogan (2001:301) notes that this "Millo" would have to be shored up periodically (11:27; 2 Sam 5:9).

9:16 *Pharaoh . . . had attacked and captured Gezer.* The Egyptian evidence is sketchy, but it seems to indicate that this pharaoh was probably Siamūn, the next to last pharaoh of the 21st Dynasty (cf. the first note on 3:1, above; also cf. Cogan 2001:301; as well as ch 3 of my chronology monograph [Barnes 1991], especially pp. 61-63; and for the historicity of this reference, see note 12 on p. 62). Gezer was a major city in the western foothills of Israel, just north of the border of the later divided monarchy of Judah. Its location, just west of the Aijalon valley, was most strategic, as it controlled the most convenient route for inland traffic from the seacoast to the hill country.

daughter. See the first note on 3:1. Once again, this indicates the relative importance of Solomon vis-à-vis the Egyptian court. Sweeney (2007:144) notes the irony of a pharaoh here giving (restoring?) part of the Promised Land to an Israelite king.

9:18 *Tamar.* Or "Tadmor," with the Qere of the MT (cf. 2 Chr 8:4). Cogan (2001:302), however, argues strongly for retaining the place-name "Tamar" here.

9:19 *supply centers.* Or "garrison cities." Cogan (2001:303) notes that the ancient versions suggest that these cities were centers for storing supplies. Concerning Solomon's stationing his chariots and horses (or charioteers) in these locations, see both notes on 4:26.

9:20 *who were not Israelites.* This is yet another candid comment on the international flavor of the Solomonic realm (see next note).

9:21 *had not completely destroyed.* This has been a theme of the writers of Joshua and Judges (often regarded as Deuteronomists; see "Author" in the Introduction). "Destroyed" renders a verbal form of the term *kherem* [TH2764, ZH3051], a word as hard to define as it is important in the Hebrew tradition. Indeed linked to the Arabic term underlying our familiar word "harem," the Hebrew root *kh-r-m* [TH2763, ZH3049] denotes "dedicating, or putting 'under the ban'; and thus devoting to destruction, rather than to redemption" (HALOT 353-354). This is particularly true of the spoils of war (as infamously illustrated by the disaster brought about by Achan stealing some of the "dedicated things"; Josh 7), but cattle, male inhabitants, and entire cities, including all inhabitants, may also be put "under the ban." The fact that a number of the Canaanites were left in the land is a major motif in both the books of Joshua and Judges (see Josh 13:1-7; 15:63; 16:10 [of particular interest concerning its reference to Gezer]; 17:12-13; Judg 1:19-36; 2:1-4, 20-23; 3:1-6).

9:21-22 *conscripted . . . did not conscript.* For these differing categories, see the commentary below, where it is pointed out that some of the subtle distinctions displayed carefully in these two verses (undoubtedly taken directly from some sort of annalistic source) were not always carefully preserved in the overall editorial perspective of the Deuteronomist.

9:24 *the supporting terraces.* See the discussion in the second note on 9:15.

9:25 *Three times each year.* These were presumably the three pilgrimage festivals (Exod 23:14-17; Deut 16:1-17). Sweeney (2007:146) notes the irony of the Canaanites, who are supposed to have been removed from the Promised Land, aiding Solomon in offering these sacrifices by their role in completing his secular building projects (also cf. the Gibeonites in the days of Joshua, as discussed in the commentary below). It should be noted that in the period of Saul, David, and now Solomon, there seems to be little reluctance to present the kings (and/or their sons; cf. 2 Sam 8:18) as personally presiding over the offerings in a priestly fashion (see Armerding 1975:75-86).

9:26 *a fleet of ships.* See 10:11-12. Cogan (2001:305, citing Gray) discusses the issue of the scarcity of wood in this southern region, noting that until the Turks deforested the region, the nearby highlands of Edom were "tolerably well-wooded."

9:27 *Hiram.* This was the king of Tyre (see 9:11). Sweeney (2007:146) is probably correct to see the reference here as further evidence that this entire section is basically about Hiram and his pressure on Solomon to increase their mutual wealth. (Both the cooperation with the Phoenicians, as well as the desire to accumulate wealth, were matters of great unease to the Deuteronomistic writers; cf. Deut 7:1-6; 17:14-20.)

9:28 *Ophir.* This was a famous place-name, usually connected (as here) with gold (cf. 10:11, 22; 22:48); in fact, the term "Ophir" itself gained the secondary meaning of fine-quality gold (Job 22:24 [see NIV]; Isa 13:12; cf. Cogan 2001:306). The precise geographical location of Ophir, however, remains uncertain, with an African, Arabian, or south-Asian (Indian) locale all being suggested, since the seaport on the Gulf of Aqabah would most naturally be used for travels to such places.

some sixteen tons. Lit., "420 talents"; see the second note on 9:14 concerning the weight of the talent.

COMMENTARY

As already mentioned several times in the notes and comments above, King Solomon is pictured in Kings as nothing less than a veritable pharaoh of forced labor, akin indeed to the tyrannical pharaohs of Egypt who enslaved the Israelites in the days of Moses. This is obviously a very negative image for the Israelites to entertain about their rich and powerful king. But such an image can hardly be resisted here. Sweeney (2007:140-147), in particular, argues forcefully for this continued negative identification.

As noted above, there is much focus in the present section once again on the *mas* [TH4522, ZH4989], the "forced labor," or corvée. Although mentioned before in general terms, it is here that we find some subtle distinctions being made between the various Israelite and non-Israelite laborers (the former including Judahites as well as northern Israelites—cf. the note on 5:13 [27]; the latter primarily, but not exclusively, consisting of the Canaanites who had not been "completely destroyed" [see the references to this listed in the note on 9:21]. But beyond these apparent distinctions, much confusion still attends the various references in 1 Kings to the forced labor in the days of Solomon (as well as beyond; cf. the end of 9:21). In fact, despite various attempts to distinguish between the various labor groups, Cogan (2001:229-230) despairs of any clear solution to the problem. But Sweeney (2007:145) does indicate effectively that the present passage seems to distinguish between Israelite (including Judahite) and non-Israelite labor, with the former performing the labor on the Temple (5:13-18 [27-32]; cf. the note on 5:13 [27]) and the latter here performing work on "secular" projects (such as those mentioned in 9:15). Again, such an effort apparently was still in effect "to this day" (9:21b). I would add that the compiler of Joshua was also interested in such matters: The infamous lapse of Joshua and the Israelite leadership in neglecting to consult Yahweh in the matter of the Gibeonites' deception (see Josh 9:14-15, 18-21) led to their becoming "woodcutters and water carriers" for the community of Israel and for the altar of Yahweh "to this day" (Josh 9:27).

A general discussion on such *de facto* slavery is in order at this point. Critics of the Bible notoriously comment on the apparent biblical toleration of slavery in both the Old and New Testaments. Of course, the Bible tolerates slavery—to do otherwise would have been unthinkable in the ancient world (but see 1 Cor 7:20-24, directed to slaves: "If you get a chance to be free, take it"). And it is a modern tragedy that there is still slavery in the world, despite repeated attempts (often by Christians) to eradicate it once and for all. But I expect that such efforts would have received a surprisingly positive response from the ancient writer(s) of the Kings text, for even in the present passage, filled with realistic notices of enslavement of foreign (and, in essence, also domestic) peoples, the writer or compiler dares to hint that the great King Solomon is to be understood as not much more than a despotic pharaoh, indeed akin to those notorious villains of the Exodus story.

To be sure, the Deuteronomic ideal for the Israelite takeover of the land of Canaan included nothing less than the outright extermination of the various Canaanite ethnic groups (see the note on 9:21), so the enslavement of those peoples was already a mitigation of their otherwise doomed status (cf. Josh 9:24-25). Yet in the present section of 1 Kings, with its consistently negative portrayal of Solomon as a despotic pharaoh, such enslavement, while for the moment tolerated (contrast ch 12), is certainly not to be idealized, much less commended. Ancient life was certainly nasty, brutish, and short for most people (just ask an inhabitant of the city of Gezer, whose cruel fate was briefly noted in 9:16), and the biblical writer was (and had to be) quite realistic about this. But he or she presented a clear and independent perspective on the protagonists, and not always a positive one. Such is the case here: powerful King Solomon = wicked king of Egypt. Solomon's mighty exploits, as listed here = a cash-strapped monarch under the power of the pagan King Hiram of Tyre. Solomon as Davidic regent of the Promised Land = relinquisher of choice portions of that same Promised Land to that same pagan potentate. (Add to this, a pagan pharaoh of Egypt of all people being the one who grants or restores the choice region of Gezer to Solomon as a wedding present for his daughter!) Editors always "get the last word," and the last word in the present passage is not all that positive concerning King Solomon and his royal activities. We, therefore, will not be all that surprised when Yahweh eventually condemns Solomon in chapter 11, for the editor (i.e., writer) of 1 Kings has subtly paved the way for the appropriateness of such strong condemnation in texts such as these.

Returning to the issue of forced labor, such was regularly practiced, and such were the expectations of the times—kings either fought battles or built structures, and both sadly seemed to require a form of *de facto* slavery (i.e., the military draft and the civilian corvée) to accomplish their intended results. But the ancient biblical writer did not have to endorse such practices uncritically, and the contemporary biblical reader need not do so either.

◆   ## 4. Visit of the queen of Sheba (10:1-13)

When the queen of Sheba heard of Solomon's fame, which brought honor to the name of the LORD,* she came to test him with hard questions. ²She arrived in Jerusalem with a large group of attendants and a great caravan of camels loaded with spices, large quantities of gold, and precious jewels. When she met with Solomon, she talked with him about everything she had on her mind. ³Solomon had answers for all her questions; nothing was too hard for the king to explain to her. ⁴When the queen of Sheba realized how very wise Solomon was, and when she saw the palace he had built, ⁵she was overwhelmed. She was also amazed at the food on his tables, the organization of his officials and their splendid clothing, the cup-bearers, and the burnt offerings Solomon made at the Temple of the LORD.

⁶She exclaimed to the king, "Everything I heard in my country about your achievements* and wisdom is true! ⁷I didn't believe what was said until I arrived here and saw it with my own eyes. In fact, I had not heard the half of it! Your wisdom and prosperity are far beyond what I was told. ⁸How happy your people* must be! What a privilege for your officials to stand here day after day, listening to your wisdom!

⁹Praise the LORD your God, who delights in you and has placed you on the throne of Israel. Because of the LORD's eternal love for Israel, he has made you king so you can rule with justice and righteousness."

¹⁰Then she gave the king a gift of 9,000 pounds* of gold, great quantities of spices, and precious jewels. Never again were so many spices brought in as those the queen of Sheba gave to King Solomon.

¹¹(In addition, Hiram's ships brought gold from Ophir, and they also brought rich cargoes of red sandalwood* and precious jewels. ¹²The king used the sandalwood to make railings for the Temple of the LORD and the royal palace, and to construct lyres and harps for the musicians. Never before or since has there been such a supply of sandalwood.)

¹³King Solomon gave the queen of Sheba whatever she asked for, besides all the customary gifts he had so generously given. Then she and all her attendants returned to their own land.

10:1 Or *which was due to the name of the LORD.* The meaning of the Hebrew is uncertain.   10:6 Hebrew *your words.*   10:8 Greek and Syriac versions and Latin Vulgate read *your wives.*   10:10 Hebrew *120 talents* [4,000 kilograms].   10:11 Hebrew *almug wood;* also in 10:12.

NOTES

10:1 the queen of Sheba. Even though many scholars suggest plausibly that the queen's actual visit was largely a trade mission (Kitchen 1997:138; Wiseman 1993:129), in the biblical account she simply serves to signify "riches and glory" (DeVries 1985:139). As Sweeney (2007:149-150) points out, scholars are still uncertain concerning both the identity of this queen as well as the location of her realm. The primary candidates for her kingdom remain Ethiopia in east Africa and "Saba" in south Arabia (modern Yemen), with contemporary scholarship leaning more and more to the latter location (e.g., Kitchen 1997:126-153). As to the queen's identity, she is known in the NT only as the "queen of the south" in Matt 12:42 and Luke 11:31 (cf. NLT mg), and she is sometimes compared to "the Kandake" in the story about the Ethiopian eunuch in Acts 8:26-40 (see Ullendorff 1963:489-491). She is mentioned only once in the Talmud (*b. Bava Batra* 15b), and she is apparently equated with the notorious female demon "Lilith" in the Targum [Aramaic paraphrase] of Job 1:15. In Ethiopian tradition she is famously depicted as a most noble queen who ended up being seduced by Solomon, and giving birth to a son Menelik, the founder of the Ethiopian dynasty (Ullendorff 1963:496-500).

brought honor to the name of the LORD. As the NLT mg indicates, the meaning of this phrase (*leshem yhwh* [ᵀᴴ3068, ᶻᴴ3378], "to or for the name of Yahweh") is uncertain. Lacking in the Chronicles parallel (2 Chr 9:1), but present in the LXX Kings text, some scholars have dismissed the phrase as a later scribal addition. Certainly, the preceding Hebrew text with its repetition of Shin, Mem, Lamedh, and He ("sh," "m," "l," and "h" consonants) could lend itself to such confusion. If the Hebrew phrase is retained, the NLT translation

"brought honor" does convey well its meaning. Seow (1999:86-87) notes how theologically crucial this brief Deuteronomistic phrase is: "it is Solomon's conduct as regards the
name of the Lord that is in question."

hard questions. Heb., *khidoth* [TH2420, ZH2648], "riddles or enigmas" (BDB 295c). Thus, Solomon's fabled "wisdom," even more than his fabulous wealth, makes all the difference.
(Cf. 3:10-15, where wisdom and wealth, again both largely overlapping, are ranked as here.)

10:5 *burnt offerings Solomon made.* Concerning Solomon personally presiding over the
offerings in a priestly fashion, see the note on 9:25.

10:6 *your achievements.* As the NLT mg indicates, the Hebrew term is *debareyka* (your
words), but the term *dabar* [TH1697, ZH1821] can often signify "a deed or action," as well as
a literal "word" (BDB 183, but see 182 I.1.c, "the report was true").

10:8 *your people.* As pointed out in the NLT mg, a reference to Solomon's "wives" is attested in the LXX and Syriac (in Hebrew, the term "wives" varies from the term "people" by the
omission of only an initial Aleph). Nevertheless, the MT should probably be retained, as in
the NLT (cf. Cogan 2001:312-313).

10:9 *Praise the LORD your God.* As already noted, here in the Kings account it is nothing less
than Yahweh's reputation that underlies all these Solomonic blessings (Seow 1999:87; cf. his
comment as cited in the second note on 10:1). Solomon's role, as it were, is clearly to rule
"with justice and righteousness" (cf. Ps 72, not coincidentally entitled "a psalm of Solomon").

10:10 *9,000 pounds.* See the second note on 9:14 concerning the likely weight of the
Hebrew talent. Wiseman (1993:131) sees this immense gift as indicative of the successful
implementation of a commercial or even vassal treaty between the two kingdoms.

10:11 *red sandalwood.* Identification of the actual type of wood is problematic (Cogan
2001:313); the Hebrew reads "almug wood" (cf. NLT mg), whereas the Chronicles parallel
attests the variant spelling "algum wood" (2 Chr 9:10; also cf. 2 Chr 2:8 [7], cf. the NLT mg
found there).

COMMENTARY

Surely the visit of the queen of Sheba remains one of the most famous stories in the
lengthy Solomonic tradition. As Jesus later reminded his skeptical Pharisaic audience,
she will be one of the non-Israelites who will stand up on Judgment Day to condemn
his generation's lack of faith, "for she came from a distant land to hear the wisdom of
Solomon. Now someone greater than Solomon is here—but you refuse to listen" (Matt
12:42; Luke 11:31). We cannot be certain that the queen was sexually involved with
Solomon or bore him a child (see note on 10:1), and we can be still less certain that
she brought home the Ark of the Covenant (even though these are two well-known
Ethiopian traditions), but we can be certain that both her proverbial wisdom and
her fabulous wealth, while presumably measuring less than Solomon's (cf. 10:6-7),
gave her adequate experience to evaluate Solomon and his realm as truly blessed by
Yahweh (10:8-9). That, too, surely is the narrator's own perspective, as found here (cf.
10:23). Yet, an alien note is allowed to intrude here—the reference to King Hiram of
Tyre found in 10:11-12, which serves to remind us of the negative comments found
in the preceding chapter (not least the fact that Hiram "paid" the exact same amount
of gold to Solomon [120 talents; cf. 9:14] as the queen gave him here in 10:10—cf.
the commentary on 9:10-14 concerning the nature of this payment).

Recently, Kitchen (1997:137-139) has argued for an intentional "interleaved" editorial format of the present section (that includes its larger context as found in 9:26–10:22), with its alternating references to maritime trade with King Hiram of Tyre and the land-caravan with the queen of Sheba, as follows:

> Trade abroad (Ophir), part I (9:26-28), Solomon builds a fleet, in a common venture with Hiram; gold is the commodity imported
>
> Queen of Sheba, part I (10:1-10), visit by camel-caravan, with rich gifts (spices, gold, gems) for a friendly "summit meeting"
>
> Trade abroad (Ophir), part II (10:11-12), an "insertion" referring to the return of Hiram's ships with gold from Ophir, plus "almug" wood and gems; focus particularly on the use of this exotic wood
>
> Queen of Sheba, part II (10:13), the queen returns home, laden with gifts
>
> Regular revenues and conspicuous consumption (10:14-21), brief notice of annual gold-revenue, and fleeting reference to other regular trade (e.g., from the kings of Arabia)
>
> Trade abroad, part III (10:22), Ophir *not* mentioned. Two fleets (one for each king) mentioned, operating on a three-year cycle, importing gold, silver, ivory, etc.

As Kitchen notes, the Hebrew editor, by utilizing a method of editorial sequencing quite different than what we moderns might expect, had his own clear conclusion: He juxtaposed the generosity of a visiting female ruler with Solomon's own independent sources of wealth from similar environs (namely, King Hiram—a continuing relationship that entailed problems; see notes and commentary on 9:10-14). The queen of Sheba visited once, whereas the maritime ventures with Hiram remained ongoing.

Seen in this light, this narrative's format makes good sense: Levantine (eastern Mediterranean) economic entry into western Arabia (close to a southwest Arabian trade route) sparks off a southwest Arabian visit to the Levant. The solidity of the sea trade at that time could not be altered, so a *modus vivendi* (heavy stuff by sea; light stuff overland) could be implied as having been reached between southwest Arabia and the Levantine partners (who proceeded to trade still further away).

I remain less optimistic than Kitchen concerning the narrator's attitude concerning Solomon's ties with Hiram (see the commentary on 9:10 14), but otherwise I would concur that Kitchen's analysis makes excellent sense of an otherwise quite bewildering sequencing of texts. In conclusion: Both Solomon himself, as well as his trading partners, Hiram, king of Tyre, and the unnamed queen of Sheba, profited much from Yahweh's blessing of Solomon's kingdom (also see 10:23-25). As the queen herself told Solomon: "Praise the LORD your God, who delights in you and has placed you on the throne of Israel" (10:9). Yahweh's leaders always and ever bring about blessings both near and far, for God's own people and for outsiders alike. This concurs with what Jesus said, "He sends rain on the just and the unjust alike" (Matt 5:45).

◆ ## 5. Solomon's wealth and splendor (10:14-29)

[14] Each year Solomon received about 25 tons* of gold. [15] This did not include the additional revenue he received from merchants and traders, all the kings of Arabia, and the governors of the land.

[16] King Solomon made 200 large shields

of hammered gold, each weighing more than fifteen pounds.* ¹⁷He also made 300 smaller shields of hammered gold, each weighing nearly four pounds.* The king placed these shields in the Palace of the Forest of Lebanon.

¹⁸Then the king made a huge throne, decorated with ivory and overlaid with fine gold. ¹⁹The throne had six steps and a rounded back. There were armrests on both sides of the seat, and the figure of a lion stood on each side of the throne. ²⁰There were also twelve other lions, one standing on each end of the six steps. No other throne in all the world could be compared with it!

²¹All of King Solomon's drinking cups were solid gold, as were all the utensils in the Palace of the Forest of Lebanon. They were not made of silver, for silver was considered worthless in Solomon's day!

²²The king had a fleet of trading ships of Tarshish that sailed with Hiram's fleet. Once every three years the ships returned, loaded with gold, silver, ivory, apes, and peacocks.*

²³So King Solomon became richer and wiser than any other king on earth. ²⁴People from every nation came to consult him and to hear the wisdom God had given him. ²⁵Year after year everyone who visited brought him gifts of silver and gold, clothing, weapons, spices, horses, and mules.

²⁶Solomon built up a huge force of chariots and horses.* He had 1,400 chariots and 12,000 horses. He stationed some of them in the chariot cities and some near him in Jerusalem. ²⁷The king made silver as plentiful in Jerusalem as stone. And valuable cedar timber was as common as the sycamore-fig trees that grow in the foothills of Judah.* ²⁸Solomon's horses were imported from Egypt* and from Cilicia*; the king's traders acquired them from Cilicia at the standard price. ²⁹At that time chariots from Egypt could be purchased for 600 pieces of silver,* and horses for 150 pieces of silver.* They were then exported to the kings of the Hittites and the kings of Aram.

10:14 Hebrew *666 talents* [23 metric tons].   10:16 Hebrew *600 [shekels] of gold* [6.8 kilograms].   10:17 Hebrew *3 minas* [1.8 kilograms].   10:22 Or *and baboons*.   10:26 Or *charioteers*; also in 10:26b.   10:27 Hebrew *the Shephelah*.   10:28a Possibly *Muzur*, a district near Cilicia; also in 10:29.   10:28b Hebrew *Kue*, probably another name for Cilicia.   10:29a Hebrew *600 [shekels] of silver*, about 15 pounds or 6.8 kilograms in weight.   10:29b Hebrew *150 [shekels]*, about 3.8 pounds or 1.7 kilograms in weight.

NOTES

10:14 *25 tons of gold.* Lit., 666 talents of gold. (There is no eschatological significance to be attached here to this otherwise infamous number!) Concerning the modern equivalent to the weight of the Hebrew talent, see the second note on 9:14. For a recent, positive defense of the plausibility of the huge quantities of gold listed in the Solomonic traditions, see Millard 1997:38-41.

10:16-17 *200 large shields . . . 300 smaller shields.* Both these categories are familiar ones from ancient Israelite warfare. The large shield (*tsinnah* [TH6793A, ZH7558]) is of body length; the smaller one (*magen* [TH4043, ZH4482], "buckler") is small, round, and handheld (Cogan 2001:317-318; Sweeney 2007:151). The particular shields described here were for ceremonial use, thickly gilded with "hammered gold." Sadly, they were captured by Pharaoh Shishak just a few years after Solomon's death (see 14:26).

10:16 *more than fifteen pounds.* Lit., "600 (shekels)," with the term "shekels" not actually appearing in the text, as is commonly the case with amounts in the Bible. The second note on 9:14 gives the modern-day equivalences for the Hebrew shekel.

10:17 *nearly four pounds.* Lit., "three minas"; a "mina" is usually understood as the equivalent of 50 shekels (although Powell, in ABD 6.906, argues for the equivalence of 60 shekels to one mina).

Palace of the Forest of Lebanon. The official reception hall; cf. the note on 7:2.

10:18 *a huge throne.* The description of this throne is analogous to those from Egypt and Phoenicia (Sweeney 2007:151); cf. particularly the throne of the tenth-century King Ahiram of Byblos, as depicted on his sarcophagus (ANEP, pictures 456, 458).

10:19 *a rounded back.* Or, "rounded head" (*ro'sh 'agol* [TH7218/5696, ZH8031/6318]); cf. the throne of Ahiram mentioned in the preceding note. Some prefer to emend the Hebrew to read "a calf's head" (*ro'sh 'egel* [TH7218/5695, ZH8031/6319]; cf. Seow 1999:87), following the LXX. But the MT should probably be retained (cf. Cogan 2001:318).

figure of a lion. A 12th-century Canaanite lion throne is depicted on an ivory panel from Megiddo (see Dever 2001:150-153).

10:21 *silver was considered worthless.* This is an amazing comment (cf. 10:27), and not without irony in the present editing of these texts (see the commentary for the Deutero-nomic prohibition against an Israelite king multiplying gold and silver for himself).

10:22 *fleet of trading ships of Tarshish.* Tarshish is probably the name of a faraway seaport (in Spain? or in Sardinia? or in Anatolia?)—see Cogan 2001:319 for a strong argument for Tarsus in Anatolia. The gist of the present reference is that these ships are oceangoing; after all, they are presumably going to Africa, as the list of commodities seems to indicate.

peacocks. Heb., *tukkiyyim* [TH8500, ZH9415], a term used only here and in the Chronicles parallel (2 Chr 9:21). The Targum and Syriac support this translation (which Cogan [2001:320], following C. Rabin, understands as a loanword from Tamil, hence indicating trade with India). As the NLT mg indicates, a common alternative suggestion is "baboons" or the like, from the Egyptian *ky* with prefixed feminine *t*.

10:23 *So King Solomon.* Just before this verse, the LXX inserts a lengthy secondary passage that corresponds quite closely with much of the text of 9:15-22 MT (which, in turn, is entirely lacking in the LXX at that point). Probably, as Gooding (1965b:325-335) argues, this move was to help justify Solomon's accumulation of so much wealth. For other examples of significant differences between the MT and the Old Greek in the Solomonic traditions, see the notes on 2:35 and 4:20.

10:26 *horses.* See the discussion of Solomon's chariots and horses in the notes on 4:26.

chariot cities. A number of these were mentioned in passing in 9:15-19, with Hazor, Megiddo, and Gezer traditionally being the most prominent. Some years ago, archaeologists thought that they had uncovered clear Solomonic evidence for these "store cities" or "chariot cities," with their distinctive gate-houses and "horse stables," but more recent excavations have brought these discoveries into question. (This is also the case with the alleged Solomonic copper-smelting works at Tell el-Kheleifeh.) For a recent, brief overview on this topic, see Hamilton 2009:318-319; for more detail, see Davies 1986:85-94 and Knoppers 1997:19-44. For a recent, positive appraisal of the Solomonic provenance of the Gezer city gate, see Dever 2001:131-135.

10:28 *Egypt . . . Cilicia.* The MT vocalizes the Hebrew consonants *m-ts-r-y-m* as the common place-name *mitsrayim* [TH4714A, ZH5213] (Egypt), but a strong case could be made for reading the consonants as *mutsri* ("Musri"; cf. NLT mg, "Muzur"), a place near Que or Cilicia in Anatolia (hence the second NLT mg note). As Cogan (2001:321) has pointed out, both of these locations are well-known horse-rearing areas (unlike Egypt). Retaining "Egypt," however, gives more force to the implied condemnation of Solomon's multiplying horses, and going back to *Egypt* to obtain them.

10:29 *pieces of silver.* Presumably "shekels of silver"; the term "shekel" is omitted as is customary in Hebrew (cf. note on 10:16).

COMMENTARY

In this section we continue to encounter what appear to be randomly arranged notices focusing mostly on Solomon's immense wealth. (See the preceding commentary section for Kitchen's helpful organization of much of the present passage in light of the preceding queen of Sheba material.) Whether haphazard or not, the present editing of these brief Solomonic traditions is surely meant to dazzle the reader with Solomon's greatness and, by implication, with the greatness of Solomon's God.

One major feature of this section and the preceding one is the repeated reference to "gold," indeed, to large amounts of gold. Modern readers might find this overwhelming after awhile, especially if they try to calculate the costs of these caches in modern currencies! And being "overwhelmed" is surely the point here—we are dealing with major monarchs and palace households, far and above any typical human experience. But such a basic observation as this can itself be misleading—if it is understood as being unique to Solomon—for it was rather typical of Middle Eastern monarchs to brag about their deposits of gold, and indeed about their lavish gifts in general. I was first alerted to this phenomenon during a lecture given by my esteemed Akkadian professor, the late William L. Moran of Harvard, and in particular by his repeated references to the 14th-century-BC Amarna letters. Subsequently, Moran published what probably remains the definitive study of this corpus of over 380 tablets found in the el-Amarna plain in upper Egypt (see Moran 1992). A few examples from these cuneiform texts suffice to illustrate the point:

"Send the gold . . . Once I have finished the work what need will I have of gold? Then you could send me 3,000 talents of gold [here, a wildly extravagant amount], and I would not accept it" (el-Amarna 4).

"Send me much gold . . . Whatever you want from my country, write me so that it may be taken to you" (el-Amarna 9).

"Gold in your country [Egypt] is dirt; one simply gathers it up . . . Send me as much gold as is needed for [my new palace's] adornment . . . When my ancestor wrote to Egypt, 20 talents of gold were sent to him [etc.]" (el-Amarna 16).

"May my brother [i.e., foreign diplomatic partner] send me in very great quantities gold that has not been worked, and may my brother send me much more gold than he did to my father" (el-Amarna 19).

"He showed much additional gold, which was beyond measure and which he was sending to me" (el-Amarna 27).

Sizable gifts of copper and silver are often mentioned as well, as well as lapis lazuli, chariots and horses, and their accoutrements. As Moran (1992:xxiv-xxv) concluded in his book: "Acknowledgement of gifts received, praise of the gifts or even a frank expression of disappointment, expression of the motivation behind the exchange of gifts, petition of countergifts to respond to the gifts now being dispatched—these and related topics dominate the international correspondence." Previously in his Harvard lecture, Moran baldly asserted: "only the mighty can beg for gold"; there must have been a tremendous obligation for the recipient of the letter to return something grand to the royal petitioner.

The present Solomonic texts include no such actual begging for gold (but cf. the curious "Cabul" passage back in 9:10-14, and especially Hiram's negative reaction to the "gift" in 9:13). Still, the international flavor of the "gold" texts both there and here, plus their striking intimacy, favor the comparison. Solomon may have been king par excellence, but he was not king sui generis (in a class of his own).

The curious conclusion of the present set of texts in chapter 10 is also to be noted. Why such comments on horses and their prices? Again, they indicate Solomon's wealthy status both as a horse trader and a worthy king among his peers; but they also rest uneasily for the readers of the larger Deuteronomic texts (see the commentary on 4:20-34, especially concerning the "law of the king" in Deut 17:14-20). There are three things that the godly king is *not* to do: multiply horses (and especially go back to Egypt to get them), multiply wives, and amass large amounts of silver and gold! As Sweeney (2007:152) has recently pointed out, placement of the notice here about the horse trade with Egypt deliberately raises questions about the godliness of King Solomon, immediately prior to the infamous account of his love of many foreign women (11:1-13), and his support of their gods.

◆   **E. Solomon's Improper Priorities and Their Aftermath (1 Kgs 11:1-43)**
         1. Solomon's many wives (11:1-13)

Now King Solomon loved many foreign women. Besides Pharaoh's daughter, he married women from Moab, Ammon, Edom, Sidon, and from among the Hittites. ²The LORD had clearly instructed the people of Israel, "You must not marry them, because they will turn your hearts to their gods." Yet Solomon insisted on loving them anyway. ³He had 700 wives of royal birth and 300 concubines. And in fact, they did turn his heart away from the LORD.

⁴In Solomon's old age, they turned his heart to worship other gods instead of being completely faithful to the LORD his God, as his father, David, had been. ⁵Solomon worshiped Ashtoreth, the goddess of the Sidonians, and Molech,* the detestable god of the Ammonites. ⁶In this way, Solomon did what was evil in the LORD's sight; he refused to follow the LORD completely, as his father, David, had done. ⁷On the Mount of Olives, east of Jerusalem,* he even built a pagan shrine for Che-

mosh, the detestable god of Moab, and another for Molech, the detestable god of the Ammonites. ⁸Solomon built such shrines for all his foreign wives to use for burning incense and sacrificing to their gods.

⁹The LORD was very angry with Solomon, for his heart had turned away from the LORD, the God of Israel, who had appeared to him twice. ¹⁰He had warned Solomon specifically about worshiping other gods, but Solomon did not listen to the LORD's command. ¹¹So now the LORD said to him, "Since you have not kept my covenant and have disobeyed my decrees, I will surely tear the kingdom away from you and give it to one of your servants. ¹²But for the sake of your father, David, I will not do this while you are still alive. I will take the kingdom away from your son. ¹³And even so, I will not take away the entire kingdom; I will let him be king of one tribe, for the sake of my servant David and for the sake of Jerusalem, my chosen city."

11:5 Hebrew *Milcom*, a variant spelling of Molech; also in 11:33.   11:7 Hebrew *On the mountain east of Jerusalem.*

NOTES
11:1 Pharaoh's daughter. See the first note on 3:1.

11:2 Intermarriage with foreigners was strictly forbidden (Deut 7:1-4), for they would lead the Israelites away from the exclusive worship of Yahweh that the Torah insists upon (Exod 20:3; Deut 5:7; 6:4-9). Even more to the point here, in the "law of the king" (see Deut 17:17a), there is a clear limitation placed on the size of the king's harem for the same reason.

11:3 700 wives . . . 300 concubines. Presumably round numbers; obviously very large in size (and perhaps grandiose or even grotesque), but certainly not meant to be understood as totally beyond the realm of possibility (cf. Montgomery 1951:234-235 and Wiseman 1993:135 for Egyptian and Persian parallels).

11:5 Ashtoreth . . . Molech. Ashtoreth (Astarte, Babylonian Ishtar) was one of the consorts of Baal, the Canaanite storm god, possibly vocalized here to rhyme with the Hebrew word for "shame" (*bosheth* [TH1322, ZH1425]); "Molech" here is literally "Milcom" (cf. NLT mg), but the name Molech does appear in 11:7, where it probably stands for "Milcom," the Ammonite deity. Cogan and Tadmor (1988:287-288), however, argue that the term "Molech" in 2 Kgs 23:10 is to be distinguished from the Ammonite deity Milcom (1 Kgs 11:33). "Molech" (= "king" [Semitic root, *m-l-k*]?) would then be understood in more general terms as the deity to whom child sacrifice was to be offered.

11:7 Chemosh. This was the chief god of the Moabites, attested on the ninth-century Mesha Inscription (also known as the Moabite Stone).

11:9 who had appeared to him twice. See the first note on 9:2.

11:13 for the sake of my servant David and for the sake of Jerusalem, my chosen city. This softens the punishment somewhat, despite Solomon's reprehensible promotion of the cults of these false gods. As noted in the "Major Themes" section of the Introduction, there is repeated, positive emphasis throughout 1–2 Kings both on the "one place of worship" and on the "lamp of David" as eternal aspects of God's covenant with Israel and Judah. Even Solomon's sins did not entirely void that covenant (cf. 2 Sam 7:12-16).

COMMENTARY
First horses, then wives and concubines (a concubine is basically a secondary wife, often a slave-wife). Thousands of each! (I exaggerate, but apparently only modestly, concerning the quantity of the wives and concubines.) Solomon did everything to excess, and that certainly was the case for the number of his wives. In the commentary on 7:13-51, I argue that at times extravagant excess may be appropriate for the people of God, but Solomon's huge harem does not fit into that category. Egyptian and Persian kings also had large harems, but surely Solomon tried to outdo them all.

Paul reminds us that we are not to be unequally yoked with unbelievers (2 Cor 6:14), and that is very often and very rightly applied to our choice of marriage partners. Solomon, ironically, had less freedom in this regard than we do today, since his wives often represented the result of ongoing diplomatic alliances (especially the daughter of the pharaoh); but still, his clear choices and priorities in this area, while understandable to ancient Near Eastern culture, were far from what the Torah had commanded. And that, above all else, led to Solomon's downfall, and nearly to the downfall of the entire land of Israel. This was not necessarily outright apostasy (a conscious forsaking of the faith), but still it was syncretism or religious compromise.

In 11:4 he is designated as not being "completely faithful to the LORD his God," and in 11:6, he is described as refusing "to follow the LORD completely, as his father, David, had done." Modern readers of these ancient texts will surely recognize that many formerly strong believers have walked down this path: a little compromise here, a little there, satisfying cultural expectations, glorying in God-given wealth and privilege, but ending up dooming themselves, and, alas, dooming many others as well. Even the wise King Solomon was not exempt from this sad fate; how much less any of us today?

◆   ## 2. Solomon's adversaries (11:14-25)

¹⁴Then the LORD raised up Hadad the Edomite, a member of Edom's royal family, to be Solomon's adversary. ¹⁵Years before, David had defeated Edom. Joab, his army commander, had stayed to bury some of the Israelite soldiers who had died in battle. While there, they killed every male in Edom. ¹⁶Joab and the army of Israel had stayed there for six months, killing them.

¹⁷But Hadad and a few of his father's royal officials escaped and headed for Egypt. (Hadad was just a boy at the time.) ¹⁸They set out from Midian and went to Paran, where others joined them. Then they traveled to Egypt and went to Pharaoh, who gave them a home, food, and some land. ¹⁹Pharaoh grew very fond of Hadad, and he gave him his wife's sister in marriage—the sister of Queen Tahpenes. ²⁰She bore him a son named Genubath. Tahpenes raised him* in Pharaoh's palace among Pharaoh's own sons.

²¹When the news reached Hadad in Egypt that David and his commander Joab were both dead, he said to Pharaoh, "Let me return to my own country."

²²"Why?" Pharaoh asked him. "What do you lack here that makes you want to go home?"

"Nothing," he replied. "But even so, please let me return home."

²³God also raised up Rezon son of Eliada as Solomon's adversary. Rezon had fled from his master, King Hadadezer of Zobah, ²⁴and had become the leader of a gang of rebels. After David conquered Hadadezer, Rezon and his men fled to Damascus, where he became king. ²⁵Rezon was Israel's bitter adversary for the rest of Solomon's reign, and he made trouble, just as Hadad did. Rezon hated Israel intensely and continued to reign in Aram.

11:20 As in Greek version; Hebrew reads *weaned him.*

NOTES

11:14 *Hadad the Edomite.* Second Samuel 8:13-14 speaks of enmity between Israel and Edom in the days of David (reading "Edom" for "Aram" in 2 Sam 8:13 [see NLT mg], as is usually done).

Solomon's adversary. Lit., "a *satan* [TH7854, ZH8477] for Solomon" (the term is also found in 11:23 and 11:25 for Rezon son of Eliada). In 5:4 Solomon boasts to King Hiram that he has no enemies (lit., no "satan"), but circumstances have changed. A "satan" is one who hinders or opposes, and Solomon faces no less than three such "adversaries" in this chapter. In late biblical Hebrew, the term "satan" developed the more technical meaning "the prosecutor" (Zech 3:1-2, NLT, "Accuser"); at the same time, it became the actual name for the supernatural being who incites people to sinful actions (1 Chr 21:1; cf. Cogan 2001:330).

11:15 *Joab . . . killed every male in Edom.* See the second note on 2:5. Joab's infamous ruthlessness in military matters is once again apparent.

11:17 *headed for Egypt.* In fact, two of these three "adversaries" of Solomon would seek sanctuary there (cf. 11:40). Ironically, as Sweeney (2007:157) has pointed out, we find motifs from the Exodus story here, with Hadad resembling Moses, and Solomon once again playing the role of the evil pharaoh (see the commentary on 9:15-28).

11:18 *went to Pharaoh.* Cogan (2001:332) suggests the pharaoh here was Amenemope of the 21st Dynasty (see also Kitchen 1996:273-275); he dates this event to c. 990 BC.

11:19 *the sister of Queen Tahpenes.* This may also be translated as "the sister of the Tahpenes (that is, the queen mother)," as argued both by Cogan and Kitchen (see previous note for references). The term "Tahpenes" is therefore an Egyptian title, not a proper name. Concerning the "queen mother" (*gebirah* [TH1377, ZH1485]), see the note on 2:19.

11:20 *Genubath.* This was possibly an Egyptian or even an Edomite name (Cogan 2001:332).

raised him. This presupposes the verb *gadal* [TH1431, ZH1540] (so also LXX) instead of MT's *gamal* [TH1580, ZH1694] ("to wean"; cf. NLT mg). Most modern commentators, however, prefer MT. Kitchen (1996:274) suggests that both in Egypt and among the Hebrews "weaning" would take place around the age of three. Sweeney (2007:157) cites parallels with the Joseph story in Genesis, once again with Hadad as the hero and Solomon as the presumed villain.

11:21 *were both dead.* Again, there is ironic symmetry with the similar reason for the termination of Jeroboam's Egyptian sojourn as noted in 11:40.

11:23 *Rezon son of Eliada as Solomon's adversary.* The second of the three "adversaries" (see the second note on 11:14). In the LXX, this is already found in 11:14, probably as a secondary insertion, linking the first two explicitly entitled "satans" (adversaries).

11:25 *reign in Aram.* As already alluded to in the first note on 11:14, the place names "Aram" and "Edom" are written almost identically in consonantal Hebrew, and are therefore sometimes confused by later copyists. But that is certainly not the case here, for Damascus was (and still is) the capital of Aram (or Syria, as it is now called). Thus, Solomon faced two different "satans" (adversaries), so to speak, one to the southeast and the other to the northeast of his kingdom.

COMMENTARY

The aftermath to Solomon's improper priorities, seen in his excess regarding horses and wives, begins to unfold with the veritable "satans" (see note on 11:14) he faces. Two of the three "satans" (adversaries) are mentioned in this section of the Solomonic story, while the third and perhaps most far-reaching adversary (although never explicitly termed "a satan"), Jeroboam son of Nebat, is reserved for the next section.

Although God often demonstrates his wrath or judgment by, as it were, doing nothing (as seen when God abandons the wicked to the rightful results of their wayward actions; see Rom 1:24, 26, 28), this is clearly not the case in the present text. The text does not wrestle with the theological conundrum of the origin of evil that seems implicit in God raising up these two "satans" (11:14, 23) against Solomon and Israel. The text simply speaks in shorthand: An enemy appears— that is the will of God. An enemy triumphs—again this is God's doing. Solomon's two adversaries in this passage are Hadad the Edomite and Rezon son of Eliada. Both enemies are (1) international (which is ironic, since a major reason for Solomon's many marriages was to secure international peace), and (2) associated with the results of David's military activities (see especially 11:15-16, 24). If God wills otherwise, peace cannot be guaranteed, whether by diplomatic alliances or by military activity. Solomon, whose very name means "peace" (cf. 1 Chr 22:9), and who was promised peace earlier in his reign (3:11-14; also cf. 5:3-4), will *not* leave a lasting legacy of peace, for his heart did not remain truly devoted to his Lord. What a sobering reminder to us today, who still long for the return of the Prince of Peace, until which time we will continue to have "wars and threats of wars" (see Matt 24:6).

◆   ### 3. Jeroboam rebels against Solomon (11:26-40)

26Another rebel leader was Jeroboam son of Nebat, one of Solomon's own officials. He came from the town of Zeredah in Ephraim, and his mother was Zeruah, a widow.

27This is the story behind his rebellion. Solomon was rebuilding the supporting terraces* and repairing the walls of the city of his father, David. 28Jeroboam was a very capable young man, and when Solomon saw how industrious he was, he put him in charge of the labor force from the tribes of Ephraim and Manasseh, the descendants of Joseph.

29One day as Jeroboam was leaving Jerusalem, the prophet Ahijah from Shiloh met him along the way. Ahijah was wearing a new cloak. The two of them were alone in a field, 30and Ahijah took hold of the new cloak he was wearing and tore it into twelve pieces. 31Then he said to Jeroboam, "Take ten of these pieces, for this is what the LORD, the God of Israel, says: 'I am about to tear the kingdom from the hand of Solomon, and I will give ten of the tribes to you! 32But I will leave him one tribe for the sake of my servant David and for the sake of Jerusalem, which I have chosen out of all the tribes of Israel. 33For Solomon has* abandoned me and worshiped Ashtoreth, the goddess of the Sidonians; Chemosh, the god of Moab;

and Molech, the god of the Ammonites. He has not followed my ways and done what is pleasing in my sight. He has not obeyed my decrees and regulations as David his father did.

34'But I will not take the entire kingdom from Solomon at this time. For the sake of my servant David, the one whom I chose and who obeyed my commands and decrees, I will keep Solomon as leader for the rest of his life. 35But I will take the kingdom away from his son and give ten of the tribes to you. 36His son will have one tribe so that the descendants of David my servant will continue to reign, shining like a lamp in Jerusalem, the city I have chosen to be the place for my name. 37And I will place you on the throne of Israel, and you will rule over all that your heart desires. 38If you listen to what I tell you and follow my ways and do whatever I consider to be right, and if you obey my decrees and commands, as my servant David did, then I will always be with you. I will establish an enduring dynasty for you as I did for David, and I will give Israel to you. 39Because of Solomon's sin I will punish the descendants of David—though not forever.' "

40Solomon tried to kill Jeroboam, but he fled to King Shishak of Egypt and stayed there until Solomon died.

11:27 Hebrew *the millo.* The meaning of the Hebrew is uncertain.   11:33 As in Greek, Syriac, and Latin Vulgate; Hebrew reads *For they have.*

NOTES

11:26 *Jeroboam son of Nebat.* Cogan (2001:337), following Noth and Speiser, suggests that "Jeroboam" means "may the kin increase" (*yarob* [TH7298, ZH8189; cf. TH7235, ZH8049], "may he/it increase" + *'am* [TH5971A, ZH6639], "kin"). Probably not entirely coincidentally, Jeroboam's southern rival, Rehoboam, also bespeaks a blessing on the "kin" (see note on 11:43).

Ephraim. This is the more important Joseph tribe (cf. the second note on 11:28). Twice in Judges, a non-Ephraimite judge (or military leader) had to deal with hostility emanating from this prideful tribe (with mixed success; cf. Judg 8:1-3; 12:1-7).

11:27 *supporting terraces.* Heb., *hammillo'* [TH4407, ZH4864]; see the second note on 9:15 for details.

11:28 *a very capable young man.* Heb., *gibbor khayil* [TH1368/2428, ZH1475/2657]; lit., "a hero of valor" (concerning the term *khayil*, see the note on 1:52). Later on (but probably not here), this phrase denotes a person who owns substantial property (Cogan 2001:339).

Ephraim and Manasseh. The two major northern tribes, termed in the Hebrew "the house of Joseph" (cf. the first note on 4:7; also the note on 5:13 [27], where the present levy or corvée is to be distinguished from the general corvée of that chapter). It was the unfair treatment of these Joseph tribes under Solomon that led to the permanent division of his kingdom after his death (see ch 12).

11:29 *the prophet Ahijah.* Here we find the first example of the important intervention of a *nabi'* [TH5030, ZH5566] or "prophet" in 1–2 Kings (apart from the repeated references to "Nathan the prophet" in ch 1; cf. the commentary on 1:15-27 for details concerning this most important position in Israel). Prophecy is a phenomenon widely repeated throughout the rest of 1–2 Kings, and it will soon become quite evident why 1–2 Kings is part of the (Former) Prophets in the threefold division of the Hebrew Bible (= Torah, Prophets, and Writings).

a new cloak. Heb., *salmah khadashah* [TH8008/2319, ZH8515/2543], "a new robe (or outer garment)." The *newness* of the cloak is the important feature (as noted in the next verse). Contrary to the NLT rendering, Cogan (2001:339) makes a strong case for *Jeroboam* as the one who was wearing the cloak. The MT could be read either way, but the LXX clearly specifies that Ahijah is wearing the cloak. Cogan notes that Ahijah "took hold of or grabbed" (*tapas* [TH8610, ZH9530]) the garment—an action inappropriate for one's own garment, but very understandable for the garment of the other person (cf. Gen 39:12; also 1 Sam 15:27-28, where Saul took hold of Samuel's garment). Jeroboam will soon be a new king, with a new dynastic succession.

11:31-32 *ten . . . one.* There are not 11, but 12 tribes of Israel as there were 12 sons of Jacob/Israel. In fact, there are 13 tribes if one counts the tribes of Joseph, Manasseh and Ephraim, as 2 separate tribes—they did have separate territories; but then, Levi was never reckoned as a tribe with contiguous landholdings, reducing the number once again to 12. To arrive at 11, most commentators see Benjamin as the "missing" tribe here (cf. 12:18-24 and note that 12:20 is omitted in the Chronicles parallel, 2 Chr 10:18–11:4); others note Levi's lack of territory and count Joseph as only one tribe; but I have long suspected that the "missing" tribe is Simeon in the south, whose land seems to have been subsumed by Judah from an early period (cf. D. N. Freedman's comment to this effect, as cited in Cogan 2001:340). (To be sure, Benjamin is sometimes reckoned as southern [see, e.g., the note on 12:21], but to consider Simeon then as northern—with its clearly southern location—remains most problematic.)

11:33 *Solomon has abandoned me.* The NLT has followed the singular verbs found in the versions listed in the mg (correctly in my opinion; cf. Cogan 2001:340 for the secondary nature of the MT).

11:34 *leader.* Heb., *nasi'* [TH5387, ZH5954], usually translated "prince," "chief," or the like, and often understood as a somewhat derogatory title for Solomon. However, since this is the only place the term is used of a Davidic ruler in 1–2 Kings, and since the LXX seems to read a different vocalization of a similar consonantal text, not much weight should be placed on the presence of the term here (cf. Cogan 2001:341).

11:36 *shining like a lamp.* See "The 'Lamp' of David" under "Major Themes" in the Introduction for this very important catchphrase, found several times in 1–2 Kings.

11:37 *all that your heart desires.* Identical language is used for David in 2 Sam 3:21. Thus, here Jeroboam is characterized as nothing less than a northern David, founder of a new, divinely authorized dynasty over most of what was David's kingdom.

11:38 *an enduring dynasty.* This language closely parallels the great Davidic covenant, especially 2 Sam 7:16 (cf. next note). (Concerning the covenantal chapter, 2 Sam 7, and its importance for 1–2 Kings, see my comments in the Introduction, under "Date and Occasion of Writing.")

11:39 *though not forever.* This is perhaps a secondary expansion; the entire verse, plus the end of 11:38, are lacking in the LXX. In any case, it softens the otherwise incredible statement found in 11:37-38—Jeroboam as a new David, nothing less!

11:40 *King Shishak of Egypt.* This is an important chronological datum, for this "Shishak" is none other than the famous Shoshenq I, the founder of the 22nd (Libyan) Dynasty of Egypt (cf. Kitchen 1996:287-302; also Barnes 1991:57-71).

COMMENTARY

The editor of Kings saved the best enemy (or for Solomon, the worst) until the end—Jeroboam son of Nebat. And as is so often the case, the most potent enemy comes from one's own household. Jeroboam had been put in charge of the corvée for the house of Joseph (11:28); he was a very capable young man, and he was one of Solomon's own officials. But he was confronted by a prophet, who ripped someone's cloak (I think it was Jeroboam's cloak; see the second note on 11:29) into 12 pieces, giving Jeroboam 10 of them! And history was irrevocably changed as a result.

We have also seen that Jeroboam—due to Solomon's sin—had the opportunity to become nothing less than a second David, as it were (cf. the notes on 11:37, 38, 39). Solomon had "blown it," so to speak, and Jeroboam ended up having most of the Davidic kingdom in his hands—10 out of the 12 pieces—at least metaphorically. Although the emphasis in the previous commentary section has been on God raising up "adversaries" for Solomon to chasten him and his posterity for his sin of syncretism, we should not think of Jeroboam (or, for that matter, the other two "satans") merely as puppet figures, devoid of free will, only employed to accomplish the judgmental will of God. Jeroboam could truly have succeeded in making the best of his glorious opportunity for kingship—of that I remain convinced. The fact that he didn't, the fact that his name became the second-most notorious name of any king in 1–2 Kings (only Manasseh was worse), was largely in his own hands. History shows that the sins of Jeroboam (see "One Place of Worship" under "Major Themes" in the Introduction) came to characterize the rest of the various kings and dynasties of the northern kingdom of Israel, but history also shows that such sins were not necessarily predestined to take place. It will be our sorry task to examine the nature and the extent of these sins in the next several chapters of 1–2 Kings; but at the outset, let us be reminded (just as with David and Solomon) that there was ample advance warning against such sins. Jeroboam was a great choice for king, as was Solomon himself (along with both Saul and David), but like Solomon, his potential for greatness was not matched by later reality. Once again, we find here a cautionary tale for us all: "How the mighty have fallen!"

◆   ## 4. Summary of Solomon's reign (11:41-43)

⁴¹The rest of the events in Solomon's reign, including all his deeds and his wisdom, are recorded in *The Book of the Acts of Solomon.* ⁴²Solomon ruled in Jerusalem over all Israel for forty years. ⁴³When he died, he was buried in the City of David, named for his father. Then his son Rehoboam became the next king.

NOTES

11:41 *The rest of the events.* For this typical summary statement, see "Literary Style" in the Introduction. For the specific reference here to *The Book of the Acts of Solomon,* see the commentary on 4:1-19.

11:42 *forty years.* This is usually understood as a round number (cf. the notes on 2:11 and 3:14). Perhaps both David and Solomon are considered as reigning one "full generation" each, which would then be reckoned as a round number of 40 years in each case. See Kitchen (2003:307-309) concerning the reckoning of exactly 480 years (12 generations?) stretching from the Exodus to the founding of Solomon's Temple (6:1). It should be noted, however, that for both David and Solomon, Kitchen takes these 40-year figures quite literally, and with virtually no overlap or coregency between them (2003:82-83). For the possibility of a 4-year coregency between these two kings, see the first note on 6:1.

11:43 *When he died, he was buried.* For a brief discussion of the characteristics and importance of these Judahite death and burial formulas, see "Earlier Editions of Kings?" in the Introduction.

Rehoboam. The name here, akin to "Jeroboam" (see the first note on 11:26), probably means "the kin has expanded" (*rakhab* [TH7337, ZH8143], "become wide, expand" + *'am* [TH5971A, ZH6639], "kin"). As Cogan (2001:343) points out, probably both names express the spirit of national well-being typical of the Solomonic age.

COMMENTARY

Here ends the lengthy discussion of the reign of Solomon, both the good and the bad. Like his father, David, Solomon was a compelling figure, unforgettable even when he was far from the will of God. There will not be such a king (of either of the kingdoms of the divided monarchy) until the time of Hezekiah, or even Josiah. With Solomon's death, the golden age of the united monarchy of Israel came abruptly and irretrievably to an end.

◆   ## II. History of the Kings of Israel and Judah until the Destruction of the Northern Kingdom (1 Kgs 12:1–2 Kgs 17:41)
A. Division of Solomon's Kingdom (1 Kgs 12:1–14:20)
1. The northern tribes revolt (12:1-20)

Rehoboam went to Shechem, where all Israel had gathered to make him king. ²When Jeroboam son of Nebat heard of this, he returned from Egypt,* for he had fled to Egypt to escape from King Solomon. ³The leaders of Israel summoned him, and Jeroboam and the whole assembly of Israel went to speak with Rehoboam. ⁴"Your father was a hard master," they said. "Lighten the harsh labor demands and heavy taxes that your father imposed on us. Then we will be your loyal subjects."

⁵Rehoboam replied, "Give me three days to think this over. Then come back for my answer." So the people went away.

⁶Then King Rehoboam discussed the matter with the older men who had counseled his father, Solomon. "What is your advice?" he asked. "How should I answer these people?"

⁷The older counselors replied, "If you are willing to be a servant to these people today and give them a favorable answer, they will always be your loyal subjects."

⁸But Rehoboam rejected the advice of the older men and instead asked the opinion of the young men who had grown up with him and were now his advisers. ⁹"What is your advice?" he asked them. "How should I answer these people who want me to lighten the burdens imposed by my father?"

¹⁰The young men replied, "This is what you should tell those complainers who want a lighter burden: 'My little finger is thicker than my father's waist! ¹¹Yes, my father laid heavy burdens on you, but I'm going to make them even heavier! My father beat you with whips, but I will beat you with scorpions!' "

¹²Three days later Jeroboam and all the people returned to hear Rehoboam's decision, just as the king had ordered. ¹³But Rehoboam spoke harshly to the people, for he rejected the advice of the older counselors ¹⁴and followed the counsel of his younger advisers. He told the people, "My father laid heavy burdens on you, but I'm going to make them even heavier! My father beat you with whips, but I will beat you with scorpions!"

¹⁵So the king paid no attention to the people. This turn of events was the will of the LORD, for it fulfilled the LORD's message to Jeroboam son of Nebat through the prophet Ahijah from Shiloh.

¹⁶When all Israel realized that the king had refused to listen to them, they responded,

"Down with the dynasty of David!
    We have no interest in the son
        of Jesse.
Back to your homes, O Israel!
    Look out for your own house,
        O David!"

So the people of Israel returned home. ¹⁷But Rehoboam continued to rule over the Israelites who lived in the towns of Judah.

¹⁸King Rehoboam sent Adoniram,* who was in charge of forced labor, to restore order, but the people of Israel stoned him to death. When this news reached King Rehoboam, he quickly jumped into his chariot and fled to Jerusalem. ¹⁹And to this day the northern tribes of Israel have refused to be ruled by a descendant of David.

²⁰When the people of Israel learned of Jeroboam's return from Egypt, they called an assembly and made him king over all Israel. So only the tribe of Judah remained loyal to the family of David.

12:2 As in Greek version and Latin Vulgate (see also 2 Chr 10:2); Hebrew reads *he lived in Egypt.*   12:18 As in some Greek manuscripts and Syriac version (see also 4:6; 5:14); Hebrew reads *Adoram.*

NOTES

12:1 *Shechem.* This was a very significant Ephraimite town near present-day Nablus, on a saddle of land between Mount Ebal and Mount Gerizim (cf. Deut 27; also Josh 8:30-35). In the last chapter of Joshua, this prominent site sees the aged Joshua renew the covenant with the third generation of Israelites (see Josh 24:1-28). Years ago, Harrison (1969:643-647) argued convincingly that it was Shechem, not Jerusalem, which was the original place Moses had in mind as "the place the LORD your God chooses for his name to be honored" (Deut 12:11, 21). In any case, Shechem remained a very strategic place, both geographically and historically, at least for the Joseph tribes (Joseph himself was buried there; see Josh 24:32).

12:2 *he returned from Egypt.* The MT reads "remained in Egypt" (cf. NLT mg). "Returned" represents a change of one letter in the consonantal text, and the revocalization of the associated verb. Most agree with this emendation (cf. Cogan 2001:346-347; also see Japhet's comments [1993:652] on the superiority of the Chronicles text here). But the variation in Kings and Chronicles concerning when Jeroboam returned home is probably symptomatic of a larger issue of the extent of the role of Jeroboam in the northerners' rebellion (see Cogan 2001:346-347; Gooding 1967b:180-185; cf. the comments in the note on 12:24 concerning the lengthy additional text in the Old Greek concerning Jeroboam). The Kings text, therefore, may reflect an earlier understanding of that role.

12:4 *Your father was a hard master.* Lit., "your father made our yoke heavy"; the term "yoke" frequently refers to burdens and service imposed by a superior. In Mesopotamia, "yoke" is the common term signifying dominion and rule (Cogan 2001:347).

12:10 *My little finger is thicker than my father's waist!* This is the talk of mental adolescents (Sweeney 2007:170); the term "little finger" (*qatonni* [TH6995, ZH7782]) actually signifies "penis" (cf. Cogan [2001:348-349], citing the medieval sage David Qimhi). It was probably a popular proverb of the day (Wiseman 1993:141), and particularly apt in light of Solomon's proverbial harem. But, like adolescent sayings of any age, it lacked in cogency and focus what it may have contained in ribald humor. (On the childishness of Rehoboam and his younger advisors, see the commentary below.)

12:11 *whips . . . scorpions.* This is more to the point: Rehoboam will be even tougher than Solomon was. The Near Eastern scorpion's sting is exceedingly painful, as I can personally attest! Here, of course, the term "scorpion" refers to a particularly painful whip, a nail-barbed scourge, as opposed to the common whip.

12:15 *the will of the LORD.* For the seemingly inscrutable will of God as revealed here, see the commentary on 11:14-25.

12:16 *Down with the dynasty of David!* Lit., "What share do we have with [the dynasty of] David?" The fact that Yahweh seems substantially to agree with both the timing and the content of this rebellious statement (cf. 12:15, 22-24), despite all the positive references to the eternal importance of David's dynasty in Samuel and Kings, is incredibly ironic. The NLT correctly renders this retort in poetic format (two bicolons, or two-line parallel units, with tight "synonymous parallelism," i.e., "A is so, and what's more, B"; see Kugel 1981:1-12).

12:18 *Adoniram.* As the NLT mg indicates, the MT reads '*adoram* [TH151, ZH164] (so also in 2 Sam 20:24); probably this is a variant for the more familiar "Adoniram" mentioned in the same role twice previously (4:6; 5:14). But if this is the same person Solomon appointed, he would surely be quite old by this time. In any case, the results of Rehoboam's attempt to quell the uprising were, not surprisingly, disastrous. (Concerning the nature of this "forced labor" or corvée, see the second note on 4:6.)

12:19 *And to this day.* This is a secondary, yet significant, preexilic comment confirming the truthfulness of the tradition (see Childs 1963:279-292; see note on 8:8). A recent, excellent overview of the "to this day" references throughout the Deuteronomistic books may be found in Geoghegan 2010:109-118, 194-197; he concludes that the circle of Levitical priests, originally from the north, are largely the source of these references (as well as much of the overall material in the Deuteronomistic work).

COMMENTARY

As Sweeney (2007:170) aptly points out, the advice that Rehoboam act as a "servant" to the northerners (12:7) would hardly provide a lasting basis for any Near Eastern king of that era. He would be perceived as a very weak ruler, and political power would then shift markedly to the north. But Rehoboam was in a particularly weak position at this time, and the older advisers knew that. Rehoboam himself, however, apparently did not (or did not care); his actions were provocative and immature. I used to toy with the idea that the elders were suggesting hypocrisy—pretending to care for the plight of the people—and the younger advisers, brutal honesty, telling it like it is. But as I have gotten older, I have come to see the text differently. The elders embraced reality, and finessed the issue as best they could. The youngsters were less aware of reality, or less concerned about it (either option very blameworthy), and thus they counseled abrasive frankness. And thus, they helped ensure the division—or redivision—of the kingdom. Frankness, at times, can be devastating.

Sweeney (2007:168) appropriately characterizes this kingdom as more of a coalition, not of 12 individual tribes, but in essence a two-part "federation" of north and south—hence the need for Rehoboam to travel north to visit Shechem in the first place. David, for example, was crowned king of Judah in Hebron seven years and six months before he was crowned king of "all Israel and Judah," again in Hebron, but this time with the elders of *all* the tribes in attendance (2 Sam 2:1-11; 5:1-5; cf. 2 Sam 19:8b-14 for a similar differentiation between "all Israel" and the tribe of Judah). Solomon, as we have seen, also treated the north differently from his native Judah. (See the first note on 4:7, as well as "Audience" in the Introduction, concerning Yahweh's and the editor's interest in both Israel and Judah as making up the people of God.) But Rehoboam obviously did not have the political acumen of either his father or his grandfather, so the divisions between "Israel" and "Judah" once again became evident—and, by this time, irreconcilable.

◆   2. Shemaiah's prophecy (12:21–24)

²¹When Rehoboam arrived at Jerusalem, he mobilized the men of Judah and the tribe of Benjamin—180,000 select troops—to fight against the men of Israel and to restore the kingdom to himself.

²²But God said to Shemaiah, the man of God, ²³"Say to Rehoboam son of Solomon, king of Judah, and to all the people of Judah and Benjamin, and to the rest of the people, ²⁴'This is what the LORD says: Do not fight against your relatives, the Israelites. Go back home, for what has happened is my doing!' " So they obeyed the message of the LORD and went home, as the LORD had commanded.

NOTES

12:21 Judah . . . Benjamin. These were the two southernmost tribes (if Simeon is excluded); see the note on 11:31-32.

12:22 Shemaiah, the man of God. For the similarities and the differences between the expression "man [or woman] of God" and "prophet," see the notes on 13:1, 11. For our purposes, the two expressions will be taken as essentially indicating the same exalted role as a "spokesperson" for God.

12:24 what has happened is my doing! God's will is paramount and not amenable to alteration by any human (cf. 12:15 and note). As already indicated (see note on 12:2), the strongest witnesses to the LXX insert a lengthy section on Jeroboam after this verse (enumerated as 12:24a-z in Rahlfs [1935]), with the result that Jeroboam's personal role in the northerners' rebellion against Rehoboam is emphasized in quite a negative way. Cogan (2001:355-356, following Talshir), in his helpful excursus on the subject, has argued force-fully for the secondary nature of this addition (cf. also Gooding 1967b:173-189). Wallace (1986:24-29), however, does argue for some early and independent traditions underlying this LXX text. Nevertheless, the MT tradition of the hostility of the north against the Solo-monic south should be retained, and Jeroboam's own vendetta against Solomon should be understood as of only secondary historical import.

COMMENTARY
Previously, in the commentary on 11:14-25, the vexing topic of the apparent will of God to raise up "satans" against Solomon was explored. I would submit that there are too many biblical examples of Yahweh asserting his will in history, often for immediate harm (but of course for eventual good), for this bald assertion to be denied. Such was clearly the case with the accession of Jeroboam son of Nebat to the throne, as we have seen, and such is apparently the current corollary here of the prophet Shemaiah insisting that Rehoboam son of Solomon not resist that epochal event. Just as it may be God's will, in a sense, to raise up different denominations of the church in reference to human sin and historical vicissitudes (good Christians can certainly differ in their opinions on particular examples of this!), it was clearly the case (due largely to Solomon's syncretistic tendencies) that God raised up *both* kingdoms of the divided monarchy. It was also certainly God's will to send both major and minor prophets to minister to each of the kingdoms. The Deuteronomistic editors of 1–2 Kings do tend to side with the south in matters of major theological import, but their very interleaving of both northern and southern narratives throughout the next chapters bespeaks their sincere interest in God's workings in *both* kingdoms (cf. Wallace 1986:36-40). And preliminary warfare between the two kingdoms, as was contemplated here by Rehoboam, could only serve to defeat God's larger purposes. At least here, both the people and the leadership of the south were willing to recognize this, once they received the prophetic word. Would that we today might be as open as they were to the prophetic leading of God's Spirit in such emotionally charged situations.

◆   3. Jeroboam makes gold calves (12:25-33)

25 Jeroboam then built up the city of She-chem in the hill country of Ephraim, and it became his capital. Later he went and built up the town of Peniel.*

26 Jeroboam thought to himself, "Unless I am careful, the kingdom will return to the dynasty of David. 27 When these people go to Jerusalem to offer sacrifices at the Temple of the LORD, they will again give their allegiance to King Rehoboam of Judah. They will kill me and make him their king instead."

28 So on the advice of his counselors, the king made two gold calves. He said to the people,* "It is too much trouble for you to worship in Jerusalem. Look, Israel, these are the gods who brought you out of Egypt!"

29 He placed these calf idols in Bethel and in Dan—at either end of his kingdom. 30 But this became a great sin, for the people worshiped the idols, traveling as far north as Dan to worship the one there.

31 Jeroboam also erected buildings at the pagan shrines and ordained priests from the common people—those who

were not from the priestly tribe of Levi. ³²And Jeroboam instituted a religious festival in Bethel, held on the fifteenth day of the eighth month,* in imitation of the annual Festival of Shelters in Judah. There at Bethel he himself offered sacrifices to the calves he had made, and he appointed priests for the pagan shrines he had made. ³³So on the fifteenth day of the eighth month, a day that he himself had designated, Jeroboam offered sacrifices on the altar at Bethel. He instituted a religious festival for Israel, and he went up to the altar to burn incense.

12:25 Hebrew *Penuel*, a variant spelling of Peniel.   12:28 Hebrew *to them*.   12:32 This day of the ancient Hebrew lunar calendar occurred in late October or early November, exactly one month after the annual Festival of Shelters in Judah (see Lev 23:34).

NOTES

12:25 Shechem. Concerning this important city, see the note on 12:1.

Peniel. Or "Penuel" (NLT mg); either spelling probably means "face of El [God]." Both spellings of this important Transjordanian town are also found in the Jacob narrative of Gen 32:30-31. This reference seems to indicate the substantial extent of Jeroboam's kingdom.

12:28 on the advice of his counselors. Ironically, the same verb (Niphal of *ya'ats* [TH3289, ZH3619]) found here was used in 12:6, 8 in regard to Rehoboam (cf. Cogan 2001:358). Jeroboam did nothing rash here (in contrast to Rehoboam), but the results would be equally disastrous in the long run.

two gold calves . . . these are the gods who brought you out of Egypt! Perhaps "young bulls" would be a better translation (cf. Ps 106:19-20, where *'egel* [TH5695, ZH6319] or "calf" is paralleled with the term *shor* [TH7794, ZH8802] or "bull"; see Cogan 2001:358). This represents the traditional iconography (imagery) for the seat or pedestal of God (whether El, Baal, or even Yahweh!), as Aaron infamously acknowledged in the golden calf incident in Exod 32:1-29. Both Aaron and Jeroboam recognized the intrinsic appeal of this traditional image. (It was the "newfangled" cherubim in the Jerusalem Temple that probably seemed to break tradition; cf. the note on 6:23, as well as the commentary on 6:14-38.) Again, in close parallel with the Aaron tradition in Exod 32:4, 8, Jeroboam proclaims "these [plural] are the gods [*'elohim* [TH430, ZH466], which can be construed either as singular or plural] who brought [a plural verb] you out of Egypt!" Both there and here, however, commentators often suggest that the plural reference suggests plural places of worship of a singular deity (cf. NIV footnote to Exod 32:4, "This is your god"); so the theological issue here is more that of idolatry (worshiping an image) rather than polytheism per se. As in Exod 32:5, the deity in question was probably Yahweh (cf. Wiseman 1993:143).

12:29 in Bethel and in Dan. This marks the considerable extent of Jeroboam's kingdom. Bethel (usually identified with Tell Beitin) lay on the important north-south road running along the watershed ridge of the hills of Judah and Ephraim from Hebron to Shechem; it was located on the border between the tribal territories of Benjamin and Ephraim 12 miles (19 km) north of Jerusalem. Dan (Tell el Qadi) lay far to the north, near Mt. Hermon and one of the major sources of the Jordan River; in fact, it marked the northern boundary of the traditional land of Israel (see the first note on 4:25). There have been some exciting discoveries in the recent archaeological excavations at Dan (see, e.g., Sweeney 2007:177-178), including the controversial Tel Dan inscription, which attests the claim of a ninth-century Aramean king (Hazael?) to have defeated both Israel and the "house of David" (i.e., Judah).

12:30 this became a great sin. Heb., *wayehi . . . lekhatta'th* [TH2403A, ZH2633] ("and it became . . . a sin"; cf. 13:34, where virtually the same expression is used). Although the term "great" is found in neither location in the Hebrew, the NLT text certainly conveys the idea of the original. Probably Cogan (2001:359) is correct to see these statements as linked to the golden calf polemic of Exod 32 by similar wording: The calf literally "goes before" (i.e., leads) the people (as in Exod 32:1), and here, the people (lit.) "go before" the calf (i.e., lead it) all the way to Dan (cf. Wiseman 1993:144). Compare the second note on 12:28. For a discussion of the prototypical "sin of Jeroboam," see "One Place of Worship" under "Major Themes" in the Introduction.

12:31 *priests from the common people.* Although there remains some ambiguity concerning the priestly role of the king in the early monarchy (see the note on 9:25 concerning David's sons as priestly leaders), the dynastic nature of the priestly families themselves probably precluded much "wiggle room" in this area (but see Sweeney [2007:178], who argues for an earlier stratum of Israelite tradition as indicating the consecration of the first-born to serve as priests, as with Samuel in the Shiloh temple).

12:32 *fifteenth day of the eighth month.* As the NLT mg clearly indicates, this is a delay of one (lunar) month in the celebration of the Festival of Shelters (or Sukkoth; often termed the Feast of Tabernacles). Scholars have argued that the agricultural year in the northern kingdom may well have lagged a month or so behind its southern counterpart (Barnes 1991:152 n. 2), thus explaining the shift in calendar. Still, this is another major shift in the procedure for observing the holidays, with far-reaching implications.

COMMENTARY

As we have seen, Solomon got in much trouble due to his syncretism—his religious compromise. He allowed the worship of other gods to take place in and near the capital city of Jerusalem. There were good political reasons for this, of course, such as all those foreign women living there and the diplomatic alliances many of them represented; but issues of politics must always be subsumed under the rulership of Yahweh, a self-styled "jealous God" (Exod 34:14; cf. Exod 20:5; Deut 5:9), who would not tolerate any such religious laxness. Now Jeroboam, Solomon's northern successor, was in deep trouble as well—again syncretism, and again with good political reasons. But this was worse than Solomon's syncretism! Jeroboam's categories of syncretism—if not outright apostasy—included (1) matters of geography, (2) matters of genealogy, and (3) matters of chronology. The text does not say which of these three categories is the worst, but they all were serious in nature. (Wiseman [1993:144-145] lists seven areas of transgression, but they can all be subsumed under my three categories.)

One thing Jeroboam was probably not guilty of was the actual sin of polytheism (see the second note on 12:28). Surely the golden calves (or golden bulls) represented the seat or pedestal of Israel's God, Yahweh, not gods themselves, just as the golden cherubim did in the Jerusalem Temple. But there is a clear difference here—and I am not talking here about the species of the "animal" so depicted in gold. Solomon's cherubim, like their antecedents in the Mosaic Tabernacle, were mostly hidden, as was the God who resided upon (or between) them (see the commentary on 8:22-53 for the details). But Jeroboam's golden calves, like Aaron's golden calf in the wilderness, were very much public. Cogan (2001:358) provocatively points out that in the Aaron story, "the calf was meant to attract YHWH to a new resting place within the camp, luring the deity back after the long absence of Moses, which broke off communication between YHWH and Israel," and that such a tradition may well have been told and retold in northern Israelite circles in a positive form. Be that as it may, the calf/bull imagery was boldly public in form, and this probably contributed much to its denigration by the Deuteronomistic editors. Later, Jeremiah argued that even the Solomonic cherubim, hidden as they were and therefore less blatant in appearance, would eventually be absent from the Jerusalem Temple (at least the Ark would be), and would not be missed (Jer 3:16; see commentary on 8:1-11).

As was already discussed in brief (see commentary on 6:14-38), the calf/bull iconography prevalent in Israel is probably not to be linked to Egypt but rather to the Baal fertility cult of Canaan (whence its old-time flavor). Cogan (2001:358; cf. p. 361 for his helpful photograph of the bronze bull found in Samaria) cites Fleming's work concerning the association of the head of the pantheon (the god El, in Canaan) with the adult bull and the second-generation deity (the god Baal, in Canaan) with the calf. In any case, the bovine images were surely meant to evoke male fecundity (DeVries 1985:162), probably the last thing orthodox Yahwists would wish for in a land that would soon be brimming with Baalism.

Scholars often comment on the *aniconic* (anti-icon) nature of Israel's God and of his commands in the Torah: God refuses to allow anyone, ever, to make an image of the deity. This is most clearly taught in the Ten Commandments, where any image at all (whether in the heavens, or on the earth, or in the sea) is forbidden to be made (Exod 20:4; Deut 5:8; in both places we find these comments just before the "jealous God" references). In the ultimate sense, this was perhaps the most radical teaching in the entire Old Testament, for all other religions at that time expected that images would be made to represent their deities. T. N. D. Mettinger (1995), however, has contributed significantly regarding the aniconic nature of the "standing stone" shrines in the Levant, where no image of the deity would generally be found (see T. Lewis 1998:52-53 for a discussion of this important work). Although such aniconic parallels do predate even the time of Moses, and thus represent precursors to Israelite aniconism, we have as of yet no clear indication of such being an important *programmatic* feature of their theology. As Mettinger (1995:196) himself concludes: "We may thus say that in Israel aniconism developed to its very extreme: a programmatic anti-iconic attitude. Among ancient Semitic peoples there is hardly anything of similar dimensions. Whether or not this is due to the vicissitudes of archaeological discovery, we do not know of any express veto on images among other Semitic peoples of the ancient world." Such programmatic iconoclasm still remains unique to Mosaic and Israelite theology, and it probably represents something even more radical than the idea of monotheism itself. *Thou shalt never, ever make an image of thy God*—who ever heard of such a thing? But such a sharp prohibition has since taken hold in all three of the world's great Abrahamic faiths: certainly in Judaism, very much so also in Islam, and (perhaps ironically) only to some degree in Christianity. No idols, no images at all—and therefore no inappropriate adoration or abuse of them. Probably in the larger context of the present Jeroboam tradition, as well as its antecedent in the golden calf story in Exodus 32, this is the most important lesson for us to learn: The true God will tolerate no rivals, and the true God will tolerate no images. And that is the one and only God, whom we must worship "in spirit and in truth" (John 4:24).

◆   4. A prophet denounces Jeroboam (13:1-34)

At the LORD's command, a man of God from Judah went to Bethel, arriving there just as Jeroboam was approaching the altar to burn incense. ²Then at the LORD's command, he shouted, "O altar, altar! This is what the LORD says: A child named Josiah will be born into the dynasty of David. On you he will sacrifice the priests from the pagan shrines who come here to burn incense, and human bones will be burned on you." ³That same day the man of God gave a sign to prove his message. He said, "The LORD has promised to give this sign: This altar will split apart, and its ashes will be poured out on the ground."

⁴When King Jeroboam heard the man of God speaking against the altar at Bethel, he pointed at him and shouted, "Seize that man!" But instantly the king's hand became paralyzed in that position, and he couldn't pull it back. ⁵At the same time a wide crack appeared in the altar, and the ashes poured out, just as the man of God had predicted in his message from the LORD.

⁶The king cried out to the man of God, "Please ask the LORD your God to restore my hand again!" So the man of God prayed to the LORD, and the king's hand was restored and he could move it again.

⁷Then the king said to the man of God, "Come to the palace with me and have something to eat, and I will give you a gift."

⁸But the man of God said to the king, "Even if you gave me half of everything you own, I would not go with you. I would not eat or drink anything in this place. ⁹For the LORD gave me this command: 'You must not eat or drink anything while you are there, and do not return to Judah by the same way you came.' " ¹⁰So he left Bethel and went home another way.

¹¹As it happened, there was an old prophet living in Bethel, and his sons* came home and told him what the man of God had done in Bethel that day. They also told their father what the man had said to the king. ¹²The old prophet asked them, "Which way did he go?" So they showed their father* which road the man of God had taken. ¹³"Quick, saddle the donkey," the old man said. So they saddled the donkey for him, and he mounted it.

¹⁴Then he rode after the man of God and found him sitting under a great tree. The old prophet asked him, "Are you the man of God who came from Judah?"

"Yes, I am," he replied.

¹⁵Then he said to the man of God, "Come home with me and eat some food."

¹⁶"No, I cannot," he replied. "I am not allowed to eat or drink anything here in this place. ¹⁷For the LORD gave me this command: 'You must not eat or drink anything while you are there, and do not return to Judah by the same way you came.' "

¹⁸But the old prophet answered, "I am a prophet, too, just as you are. And an angel gave me this command from the LORD: 'Bring him home with you so he can have something to eat and drink.' " But the old man was lying to him. ¹⁹So they went back together, and the man of God ate and drank at the prophet's home.

²⁰Then while they were sitting at the table, a command from the LORD came to the old prophet. ²¹He cried out to the man of God from Judah, "This is what the LORD says: You have defied the word of the LORD and have disobeyed the command the LORD your God gave you. ²²You came back to this place and ate and drank where he told you not to eat or drink. Because of this, your body will not be buried in the grave of your ancestors."

²³After the man of God had finished eating and drinking, the old prophet saddled his own donkey for him, ²⁴and the man of God started off again. But as he was traveling along, a lion came out and killed him. His body lay there on the road, with the donkey and the lion standing beside it. ²⁵People who passed by saw the body lying in the road and the lion

standing beside it, and they went and reported it in Bethel, where the old prophet lived.

²⁶When the prophet heard the report, he said, "It is the man of God who disobeyed the LORD's command. The LORD has fulfilled his word by causing the lion to attack and kill him."

²⁷Then the prophet said to his sons, "Saddle a donkey for me." So they saddled a donkey, ²⁸and he went out and found the body lying in the road. The donkey and lion were still standing there beside it, for the lion had not eaten the body nor attacked the donkey. ²⁹So the prophet laid the body of the man of God on the donkey and took it back to the town to mourn over him and bury him. ³⁰He laid the body in his own grave, crying out in grief, "Oh, my brother!"

³¹Afterward the prophet said to his sons, "When I die, bury me in the grave where the man of God is buried. Lay my bones beside his bones. ³²For the message the LORD told him to proclaim against the altar in Bethel and against the pagan shrines in the towns of Samaria will certainly come true."

³³But even after this, Jeroboam did not turn from his evil ways. He continued to choose priests from the common people. He appointed anyone who wanted to become a priest for the pagan shrines. ³⁴This became a great sin and resulted in the utter destruction of Jeroboam's dynasty from the face of the earth.

13:11 As in Greek version; Hebrew reads *son*.   13:12 As in Greek version; Hebrew reads *They had seen*.

NOTES

13:1 *man of God*. Generally, this expression serves as a synonym for the more typical term "prophet" (*nabi'* [TH5030, ZH5566]; see note on 13:11). In Deut 33:1 Moses was called a "man of God" (and in Deut 34:10, he was categorized in essence as the greatest of the prophets). Both the prophets Elijah (17:18; etc.) and Elisha (2 Kgs 4:7; etc.) were also repeatedly called "men of God." (For a helpful study on the usage of this phrase throughout the Bible, see Wiseman 1993:142-143.) Here, the Judahite prophet is invariably termed "the man of God" and the old Bethelite "the prophet."

13:2 *A child named Josiah*. This is a reference to the godly seventh-century Judahite king who is the hero of what many have categorized as a major edition of 1–2 Kings (see "Earlier Editions of Kings?" in the Introduction). The fulfillment of this Josiah prophecy is detailed at some length in 2 Kgs 23:15-18 (for the overall extent of Josiah's radical reformation, see 2 Kgs 23:1-25). Many scholars would see the reference here to a king who reigned over 300 years later as a so-called prophecy *ex eventu* (after the event), indeed as *the* classical reference to Josiah's heroic status, seemingly foretold many years before the event but in actuality inserted by a scribe or editor during (or soon before, or even after?) his actual reign. Generally, an interpreter's a priori theological assumptions will tend to be the guide in regard to any acceptance or rejection of the possibility of such long-term prophecies, but the incidental nature of the reference here, along with its corresponding conclusion in 13:32, inspires confidence in its veracity. In any case, the "short-term" prediction confirming the man of God's credentials and the overall truthfulness of his message becomes the major focus of the text in the next verse.

13:3 *a sign to prove his message*. One of the famous tests of a true prophet (Deut 18:15-22) refers to the accuracy of a future prediction of the would-be prophet as a confidence-inspiring test of his or her orthodoxy. I have come to refer to this phenomenon as "the test of short-term prediction," since such a test would work best in the *short-term* future. This is the case in the present verse: Jeroboam's altar will split apart and its ashes will be poured out—a prediction that comes to pass that very same day (see 13:5).

13:6 *Please ask the LORD your God to restore my hand again!* The relative powerlessness of the king vis-à-vis the prophet is rarely represented more effectively than here (concerning the intended relationship between prophet and king, see the commentary on 1:5-27).

13:7 *Come to the palace with me.* The king was still seeking some sort of "withdrawal of judgment" from the man of God, "to link himself in fellowship with him as a form of insurance" (Wiseman 1993:146, citing Robinson and Noth).

13:9 *You must not eat or drink . . . and do not return to Judah by the same way you came.* Seemingly arbitrary prohibitions, these are seen by Cogan (2001:369) as drawing attention to God's total rejection of Bethel and its king; they were crucial in ascertaining the true extent of the obedience and devotion of the Judahite man of God to his God, as we soon shall see.

13:11 *an old prophet.* The word for "prophet" (*nabi'* [TH5030, ZH5566]) probably meant "one called out," or "one designated" (as a spokesperson for God). It was evidently derived from a foreign term, probably a passive participle from the Akkadian verb *nabû*, "to call" (see Blenkinsopp 1983:36-37; ABD 5.482). There is evidence that the term was perceived somewhat negatively in Israel in early times (cf. Num 12:6-8; Amos 7:14; also cf. Blenkinsopp 1983:20; ABD 5.487). A more neutral historical reminiscence, however, is in 1 Sam 9:9: "For prophets (*nabi'* [TH5030, ZH5566]) used to be called seers (*ro'eh* [TH7200A, ZH8014])." This is a reminder that the term "seer" or "visionary" of the early days would implicitly emphasize the phenomenon of supernatural dreams or visions (cf. Deut 13:1-5 [2-6]), whereas in later times, those men and women of God would focus more on the phenomenon of "hearing," and then "speaking forth" the word of Yahweh ("thus says the LORD"). I suspect the negative nuance of the term "prophet" in the early period is subtly meant to be noticed in the present passage, as well, in contrast with the transparently positive parallel expression "man of God" (but see the Bethelite's comment in 13:18 about his Judahite counterpart!).

sons. The MT reads the singular "son" for the first part of 13:11b and then reads plurals for the final section; as the NLT mg indicates, the LXX reads plurals throughout. Evidently, the MT envisions one son giving the preliminary information and then all the sons joining the conversation (cf. Cogan 2001:369).

13:12 *they showed their father.* The LXX (and the other versions) translates a causative verb (Hiphil), "they showed [their father]," where the MT reflects the simple transitive (Qal), "they had seen" (there would probably have been no difference in the consonantal text). The versions are probably to be preferred, as the NLT text reads.

13:18 *And an angel.* Note Paul's apparent reference to this story in Gal 1:8, "Let God's curse fall on anyone, including us or even an angel from heaven, who preaches a different kind of Good News than the one we preached to you" (see the commentary below).

But the old man was lying to him. This is a narrative aside to help the reader—after all, whom are we to trust, the "man of God," or the "prophet"?

13:24 *a lion.* Lions roamed throughout Palestine until modern times (see the first note on 7:29, above; also cf. Wenham 1994:476). With the interplay of Bethel versus Judah here, commentators have found here an ironic echo of the familiar "lion of Judah" imagery found elsewhere in the OT (see Gen 49:8-9; and cf. Joel 3:16 [4:16]; Amos 1:2; 3:8; and in the NT, Rev 5:5). That it is particularly a lion that kills the Judahite "man of God" cannot, therefore, be entirely coincidental.

13:30 *Oh, my brother!* Heb., *hoy* [TH1945, ZH2098] *'akhi*, a typical funeral lament (see Cogan 2001:372). Ironically, only after helping cause the death of the Judahite does the Bethelite indicate his prophetic solidarity. But it is true solidarity since he instructs his sons to be sure that, after he dies, they should lay his bones with the Judahite's bones (13:31). Cogan goes on to comment: "In this manner it would be impossible to distinguish bone from bone." (For more on the burial practices of the ancient Israelites, see the commentary below.)

13:33 But even after this. In the commentary on 12:25-33, I noted that Jeroboam's "sins" fall into three different areas: (1) matters of geography, (2) matters of genealogy, and (3) matters of chronology. Here, "matters of genealogy" alone are cited (see note on 12:31). Later on, however, "matters of geography" will predominate, usually in the vague sense of Jeroboam's calf-idols in Bethel and Dan still remaining as snares for the people. In contrast, "matters of chronology" will never specifically be mentioned again. Perhaps the immediate message of 13:33-34, however, is the fact that inasmuch as Jeroboam saw fit to promote just anyone into the priesthood, Yahweh could do the very same for the monarchy. "Man proposes but God disposes" (cf. Prov 16:9).

COMMENTARY

"Prophet against prophet"—this is how DeVries (1978:59-61) entitles his helpful study of the prophetic narratives found in 1–2 Kings, and it certainly also serves as an apt title for the present chapter of 1 Kings. In his later commentary on 1 Kings (1985:171-174), DeVries expands upon his work in a way that has challenged me for years. The excerpts given below for the reader's benefit offer a brief exposure to this challenge:

> Very clearly and emphatically, the Judahite man of God has been instructed [by Yahweh in 13:16-17] what not to do. . . . If the Judahite actually does die for his disobedience, the Bethel prophet will know that he did indeed have authority to denounce the holy altar at Bethel. And so it is: the lion kills him; the old prophet buries him. And the old prophet tenderly places his body in his own tomb, instructing his sons to bury him alongside himself, for truly this was a holy man, a man in whom was the very word of God. Had the prophecy not come true and the man of God come safely home to Judah, the message of the Bethel prophet would have been proven false, but not it alone. Most important, nonfulfillment would have proven the man of God false, a presumptuous liar who pretended to obey the word of God when he had received no true word from God.

> In every age there are those who presume to speak for God. . . . How will the people know to whom to listen, which prophet to fear? . . . Scripture offers many different tests, but 1 Kgs 13, once properly interpreted, offers the clearest test of all. That test is radical obedience [emphasis added]. The preacher-prophet must be so committed to the transcendent truth of what he proclaims that his own life is affected by it.

> The Judahite man of God had to believe in his own stern word of denunciation against the Bethel altar so intensely that his whole behavior would be determined by it. It was not enough to demonstrate his spiritual power by restoring the shrunken arm of a king; it had to be demonstrated by a tenacity in such "little things" as not eating, not drinking, not returning by the same road.

> Did the man of God understand the reasons for these strange prohibitions? Undoubtedly not. They seemed trivial, and in the case of refusing the king's hospitality he refused them out of a naive obedience that had not yet been put to the

sorest test. Somehow, his obedience was not carried out simply because Yahweh had said so. So what if Yahweh should speak through a colleague, some other man of the Spirit, to set these rules aside? Would it not make more sense to follow this new word than to adhere stubbornly to a set of arbitrary and aimless rules? Being of such a mind, the Judahite man of God was bound to fall for the Bethelite's trick. So he failed, and failing he perished. But let us observe that, though he failed, God's word did not fail. . . . Thus today we look for radical obedience in the way of life to which God's servants commit themselves. If they stumble—and stumble they will—their very weakness may confirm the word of God which they preach. (DeVries 1985:173-174)

For years, I stumbled over my apprehensions concerning the ethics of the Bethelite prophet—how unfair it was that he would trick the Judahite into losing his very life, and only then show him honor. But the scandal of the present text lies in this very point. The Bethelite's livelihood lay in that altar, and it would take a tremendous sign from God to change his mind and the mind of his family concerning its sanctity. That test, indeed, would have to encompass something like DeVries's call to "radical obedience"—a call that we in the ministry must embrace (and, of course, *any* committed Christian is in a real sense "in the ministry"). We must be willing to give our very life, if necessary, for that call. Not surprisingly, DeVries ends his homily with a reference to Jesus: "He too was doomed to die, but for the sins of others rather than for sins of his own. In his grave he sanctified the death of many others—of all those who call him not just 'man of God' but 'Son of God.'" This paradox is even greater than the one presented by 1 Kings 13:1-34.

To turn from this sublime truth to a more prosaic topic, an awareness of Israelite burial practices is essential for understanding the old prophet's reference in 13:29-32. Recently, McCane summarized our understanding of Iron Age burial practices as follows:

The prevailing custom in the ancient Near East, going back to the Middle Bronze Age (2000–1500 BCE), was burial in caves by extended family groups. Secondary burial—i.e., reburial of human bones after the flesh of the body has decayed—was common. Later, during the Iron Age, the Israelite "bench" tomb emerged as the most common form of tomb architecture. In these square (or slightly rectangular) underground chambers, typically about 8 ft. [2.5 m] on a side, a waist-high bench ran along three sides of the tomb. The side in which the entrance was situated usually did not have a bench. At the time of death, bodies were laid on the benches, and after decomposition was complete, the bones were gathered into a repository hollowed out beneath one of the benches. Over time, this repository came to hold all the bones of family members long dead, and when an individual's bones were placed therein, that individual was dissolved into the collective ancestral heap. The familiar biblical expression, "to sleep and to be gathered to one's fathers" (2 Kgs 22:20, et al.) vividly captures the contours of this Israelite custom. (McCane 2006:509-510)

Among other clarifications, this analysis affords insight into Ruth's famous declaration of undying devotion to her mother-in-law (Ruth 1:16-17), "Wherever you go, I will go; wherever you live, I will live. Your people will be my people, and your God will be my God. Wherever you die, I will die, and there I will be buried. May the LORD punish me severely if I allow anything [including] death to separate us!" (so the NLT text, with one alteration in the last clause, following Campbell 1975:74-75). Although Naomi urged her to go home, Ruth stubbornly wished to remain united with Naomi's family and clan forever—in fact, even in death. Her bones were to be buried with Naomi's bones. (And, of course, because of her faith and her faithfulness to her new extended family, Ruth's name will forever also be linked to the famous descendant of Naomi's family, the Messiah, the Son of David [see Matt 1:5].)

Finally, what about that "angel" reference back in 13:18? As I have noted above, I think the apostle Paul makes clear reference to this text in his "angel from heaven" comment in Galatians 1:8 (I have not seen any such parallel noted in any of the Galatians commentaries I have consulted, but I still suspect that it is there, and that Paul's Jewish audience would have immediately recognized it as such). In any case, "radical obedience" remains the key for Paul in Galatians (how ironic for the Judaizers there!), just as it is for the narrator of 1 Kings 13. "Let God's curse fall on anyone" who preaches another gospel or alleged message from God. Let us forever remain as faithful as Ruth and Paul in wherever God leads us, and in whatever he calls us to say or do—for the continued glory of God and for the continued growth of his Kingdom.

◆   ## 5. Ahijah's prophecy against Jeroboam (14:1-20)

At that time Jeroboam's son Abijah became very sick. ²So Jeroboam told his wife, "Disguise yourself so that no one will recognize you as my wife. Then go to the prophet Ahijah at Shiloh—the man who told me I would become king. ³Take him a gift of ten loaves of bread, some cakes, and a jar of honey, and ask him what will happen to the boy."

⁴So Jeroboam's wife went to Ahijah's home at Shiloh. He was an old man now and could no longer see. ⁵But the LORD had told Ahijah, "Jeroboam's wife will come here, pretending to be someone else. She will ask you about her son, for he is very sick. Give her the answer I give you."

⁶So when Ahijah heard her footsteps at the door, he called out, "Come in, wife of Jeroboam! Why are you pretending to be someone else?" Then he told her, "I have bad news for you. ⁷Give your husband, Jeroboam, this message from the LORD, the God of Israel: 'I promoted you from the ranks of the common people and made you ruler over my people Israel. ⁸I ripped the kingdom away from the family of David and gave it to you. But you have not been like my servant David, who obeyed my commands and followed me with all his heart and always did whatever I wanted. ⁹You have done more evil than all who lived before you. You have made other gods for yourself and have made me furious with your gold calves. And since you have turned your back on me, ¹⁰I will bring disaster on your dynasty and will destroy every one of your male descendants, slave and free alike, anywhere in Israel. I will burn up your royal dynasty as one burns up trash until it is all gone. ¹¹The members of Jeroboam's family who die in the city will be eaten by dogs, and those who die in the field will be eaten by vultures. I, the LORD, have spoken.' "

¹²Then Ahijah said to Jeroboam's wife, "Go on home, and when you enter the city, the child will die. ¹³All Israel will mourn for him and bury him. He is the only

member of your family who will have a proper burial, for this child is the only good thing that the LORD, the God of Israel, sees in the entire family of Jeroboam.

¹⁴"In addition, the LORD will raise up a king over Israel who will destroy the family of Jeroboam. This will happen today, even now! ¹⁵Then the LORD will shake Israel like a reed whipped about in a stream. He will uproot the people of Israel from this good land that he gave their ancestors and will scatter them beyond the Euphrates River,* for they have angered the LORD with the Asherah poles they have set up for worship. ¹⁶He will abandon Is-

rael because Jeroboam sinned and made Israel sin along with him."

¹⁷So Jeroboam's wife returned to Tirzah, and the child died just as she walked through the door of her home. ¹⁸And all Israel buried him and mourned for him, as the LORD had promised through the prophet Ahijah.

¹⁹The rest of the events in Jeroboam's reign, including all his wars and how he ruled, are recorded in *The Book of the History of the Kings of Israel.* ²⁰Jeroboam reigned in Israel twenty-two years. When Jeroboam died, his son Nadab became the next king.

14:15 Hebrew *the river.*

NOTES

14:1 *Abijah.* This person is not to be confused with the Judahite king "Abijah" or "Abijam," son of Rehoboam (cf. 14:31). The name Abijah means "My [divine] Father is Yah(weh)."

14:2 *Disguise yourself.* As Wiseman (1993:148) has pointed out, this action, even if motivated by understandable and proper motives (i.e., the desire for an unbiased response, as well as minimizing rebellion if it were known that the heir to the throne was ill), always leads to disastrous results in the OT (cf. Saul [1 Sam 28:8], Ahab [1 Kgs 22:30], or even good king Josiah [2 Chr 35:22]). One can never successfully prevent God's will from being accomplished by employing such stratagems.

Ahijah. This is the prophet already mentioned in 11:29-39. The "ten loaves" may be a literary (or literal?) reference to the ten pieces of the cloak given to Jeroboam earlier by that prophet. Wiseman (1993:148-149) sees the gift items mentioned here as those typical of an "audience-gift" (i.e., seeking an audience) from a common person.

Shiloh. This is present-day Khirbet Seilun, which is 10 miles (16 km) north of Bethel (see note on 12:29), just east of the main north-south road between Bethel and Shechem in the hill country of Ephraim. The Tabernacle and the Ark were located at Shiloh during the time of Eli the priest (1 Sam 1:3; 2:14), until the Israelites decided to bring the Ark into battle against the Philistines (cf. 1 Sam 4:3-4; Ps 78:60; Jer 7:12-15; 26:6-9). Presumably Shiloh was still a significant religious location, although it probably had been eclipsed in significance by Bethel to the south (Cogan 2001:383).

14:4 *could no longer see.* Like Ahijah, Balaam may also have been a blind prophet, depending on how one translates Num 24:3, 15, whether as "opened eye" (cf. the Peshitta), "perfect eye" (i.e., "true, clear, clairvoyant," cf. Albright 1944:216), or "closed eye" (cf. the Vulgate). In Greek mythology, Tiresias of Thebes was a blind seer who was never wrong in his pronouncements. Thus, physically blind prophets can still see quite clearly if God enables them (after all, a prophet used to be called a "seer"; see 1 Sam 9:9, and the first note on 13:11). Seow (1999:112) notes the irony in the present text: Since the prophet was now physically blind, the disguise of Jeroboam's wife proved to be unnecessary (although, to be sure, any such arrival by the queen dressed as such would not have gone unnoticed by the bystanders).

14:9 *furious with your gold calves.* In contrast to 13:33-34 (see the note on 13:33 and the commentary on 13:1-34), from now on the repeated condemnations of the sin of Jeroboam son of Nebat will invariably focus on this feature of Jeroboam's religious innovations, seen both as polytheistic and idolatrous (although they originally were meant to be neither; see commentary on 12:25-33). In the present verse, the term "furious" is a Hiphil (causative) infinitive (*lehak'iseni* [TH3707, ZH4087]), "to provoke me to anger"; the same term is used in 14:15 (and also in 15:30; 16:2, 7, 13, 26, 33; 21:22; 22:53[54]; 2 Kgs 17:11, 17; 21:6, 15; 22:17; 23:19, 26). Yahweh takes it quite personally when we are heterodox in our worship.

14:10 *every one of your male descendants.* Lit., "him who urinates against a wall" (*mashtin beqir* [TH8366/7023, ZH8874/7815]); cf. KJV. Sweeney (2007:185-186) sees an "element of contempt" in the usage of the phrase here and elsewhere (cf. 16:11; 21:21; 1 Sam 25:22, 34; 2 Kgs 9:8); in every case a reference to the extermination of an entire family or dynasty is found.

slave and free alike. Lit., "restrained and released" (*'atsur we'azub* [TH6113/5800, ZH6806/6440]), a phrase found in Deut 32:36 and four times in 1–2 Kings (14:10; 21:21; 2 Kgs 9:8; 14:26). The phrase is notoriously difficult to translate precisely (although the general import seems clear—all classes of people are to be included). Possibilities include "married and single," "minors and elderly," "unborn and born"; also the more anomalous "helpless and abandoned" (DeVries 1985:179, following Saydon), which DeVries categorizes as "an alliterative phrase of utter loathing" (hence, not to be understood as a *merism* [an all-inclusive phrase] like the earlier options listed). For yet a different interpretation, "ruler and helper," (two active participles forming a *hendiadys* [two words expressing one concept]), see Christensen (2002:818-819), following Tigay (1996:312, 405).

as one burns up trash. Lit., "as one burns, or sweeps away dung" (Piel of *ba'ar* [TH1197, ZH1277]); BDB 129b reads "to burn"; but Koehler and Baumgartner (HALOT 146) prefer "to sweep away" (*ba'ar* II [TH1197A, ZH1278], listed as #3 under Piel). Interestingly, Sweeney (2007:183) translates, "as dung burns," taking *haggalal* [TH1557, ZH1672] ([ball of] dung) as the subject of the sentence. (Animal dung was sometimes used for fuel; see Ezek 4:12 and Cogan 2001:380, citing Greenberg 1983:107.)

14:11 *dogs . . . vultures.* Dogs (*kelabim* [TH3611, ZH3978]) were usually thought of only as opportunistic scavengers in the ancient Near East (cf. Cogan 2001:380), whereas the "vultures" (lit., "birds of the air") "cleared the open fields of unwanted corpses" (Cogan 2001:380; cf. Wallace 1986:35-36; both cite similar curses from the vassal treaties of Esarhaddon).

14:13 *only good thing.* Sadly, there are a number of parallels to this in the 1–2 Samuel text: Eli the priest had evil children (see 1 Sam 2:12-36); Samuel the prophet, priest (?), and judge had evil children (1 Sam 8:1-3); David the king had a number of evil, or at least very difficult, children (2 Sam 13–19); whereas Saul the king had good children (at least Jonathan could certainly be put in that category; see 1 Sam 14:1-51; 18:1-4; 20). The present situation fits the Samuel—Kings text very well (for that matter, Rehoboam seems hardly a model child to succeed Solomon, his father; see 12:1-20; 14:21-31).

14:14 *This will happen today, even now!* The Hebrew reads, somewhat oddly, "this very day; and what? Even now!" Cogan (2001:380) suggests the possibility that the final several words in this verse might introduce the threat of the "shaking" of the nation, which directly follows (see 14:15a).

14:15 *Asherah poles.* These were infamous religious icons, probably stylized poles or trees (Ackerman 2006:297-298), representing the mother goddess of that same name. Curiously,

Asherah is apparently connected with lions in the 10th-century terra-cotta stand found at Taanach, which also contains cherubs, possibly in reference to Yahweh. Ackerman also argues that the thousands of terra cotta fertility figurines of the pillar-base type found at virtually every ancient Israelite archaeological site are images of Asherah. Although some scholars disagree, many would suggest that in the popular religion of the day, Asherah was understood to be the consort of Yahweh (as she was the consort of El at Ugarit). Of course, in official circles, such belief was repeatedly condemned. The Judahite kings Asa (15:13), Hezekiah (2 Kgs 18:4), and Josiah (2 Kgs 23:6, 14-15) are singled out for praise because they removed Asherah poles from various cultic locations (including the Jerusalem Temple itself, in Josiah's case!).

14:19 *are recorded in* **The Book of the History of the Kings of Israel.** See "Literary Style" in the Introduction. Incidentally, the LXX omits all of 14:1-20 (cf. the commentary below).

14:20 *Nadab.* See note on 15:25.

COMMENTARY

This tragic narrative is reminiscent of Nathan's message to David after his sin with Bathsheba: Their child was doomed to die, and there was nothing the father could do about it (cf. 2 Sam 12:15-23). Also, the prophetic pronouncement there is along the lines of what we read in the present text: "I promoted you. . . . I ripped the kingdom away from . . . and gave it to you. . . . But you have not been like my servant David. . . . I will [therefore] bring disaster on your dynasty" (14:7-11, cf. 2 Sam 12:7-12; there are naturally close parallels in the Kings text with the prophet Ahijah's earlier speech to Jeroboam in 11:31-39). All devoted parents, "good" or "evil," dearly love their children, and Jeroboam and his wife were evidently no exception. Presumably Abijah is the firstborn, although we are never told that explicitly. Another son, Nadab, does ascend to Jeroboam's throne; he reigns for two years before being assassinated, as Jeroboam's dynasty comes to an end (15:25-31). To be sure, the firstborn son of a king is particularly significant, but any child clearly merits deep parental love and concern. Scholars tend to dismiss the present narrative as merely an old prophetic story with heavy Deuteronomistic editorial additions, but I would submit that the story itself should be read more sympathetically in light of David's similar experience of the death of his firstborn child with Bathsheba, and that it gains much by such a comparison. It is God's inscrutable will that the sins of the parents may be visited upon the children and the grandchildren, to the third and fourth generation "of those who reject me" (Exod 20:5b; Deut 5:9b; cf. "The 'Sins of Manasseh'" under "Major Themes" in the Introduction), and that appears to be the melancholy situation here in 1 Kings, just as it self-evidently was the case back in 2 Samuel 12 (see especially 2 Sam 12:14). Surely, the Deuteronomist did not seek to draw attention away from their parental love and devotion; if anything, the sad fate of Jeroboam's child lends powerful support for the Deuteronomistic editor's overall message that Yahweh is not to be trifled with, lest heartaching tragedy ensue. Exile "beyond [the river]" (14:15 of the present text; see NLT mg) will fall particularly hard on the innocent children and grandchildren of the people of Israel, and the Deuteronomistic editor surely does not want that message ever to be forgotten (see 2 Kgs 17:5-41). Still, I do not want to minimize the contempt the Deuteronomistic editor had for Jeroboam son of Nebat, since his "sin" was the paradigmatic sin that eventually doomed the northern kingdom (see the repeated refrain in 13:34; 14:16; 15:30, 34; 16:2, 7, 19, 26, 31; 22:52 [53]; 2 Kgs 3:3; 10:29, 31; 13:2, 6, 11; 14:24; 15:9, 18, 24, 28; 17:21-23; cf. 2 Kgs 23:15), and nearly doomed the south (2 Kgs 17:19; cf. 2 Kgs 8:18, 27; 16:3).

The present passage (14:1-20) is entirely lacking in the earliest Septuagint tradition, the Old Greek. A shortened and altered version of this story is, however, to be found in the additional material located after 12:24 (cf. the note and commentary on that verse, as well as the important references there to Cogan and Gooding). Sweeney (2007:184) is probably correct to characterize the Old Greek tradition there as secondary, placing Ahijah's condemnation of the house of Jeroboam *prior* to the dynastic oracle (where the garment is ripped up, and Jeroboam is given 10 of the 12 pieces). The Greek version thus signals that Jeroboam's dynasty was doomed before he even had occasion to become king in the first place (and note that the Greek tradition has Shemaiah, not Ahijah, as the prophet who rips up the garment).

◆　　 B. Synchronistic History of the Early Divided Monarchy
　　　　 (1 Kgs 14:21–16:34)
　　　　 1. Rehoboam rules in Judah (14:21–31)

[21]Meanwhile, Rehoboam son of Solomon was king in Judah. He was forty-one years old when he became king, and he reigned seventeen years in Jerusalem, the city the LORD had chosen from among all the tribes of Israel as the place to honor his name. Rehoboam's mother was Naamah, an Ammonite woman.

[22]During Rehoboam's reign, the people of Judah did what was evil in the LORD's sight, provoking his anger with their sin, for it was even worse than that of their ancestors. [23]For they also built for themselves pagan shrines and set up sacred pillars and Asherah poles on every high hill and under every green tree. [24]There were even male and female shrine prostitutes throughout the land. The people imitated the detestable practices of the pagan nations the LORD had driven from the land ahead of the Israelites.

[25]In the fifth year of King Rehoboam's reign, King Shishak of Egypt came up and attacked Jerusalem. [26]He ransacked the treasuries of the LORD's Temple and the royal palace; he stole everything, including all the gold shields Solomon had made. [27]King Rehoboam later replaced them with bronze shields as substitutes, and he entrusted them to the care of the commanders of the guard who protected the entrance to the royal palace. [28]Whenever the king went to the Temple of the LORD, the guards would also take the shields and then return them to the guardroom.

[29]The rest of the events in Rehoboam's reign and everything he did are recorded in *The Book of the History of the Kings of Judah*. [30]There was constant war between Rehoboam and Jeroboam. [31]When Rehoboam died, he was buried among his ancestors in the City of David. His mother was Naamah, an Ammonite woman. Then his son Abijam* became the next king.

14:31 Also known as *Abijah*.

NOTES

14:21 *Rehoboam.* See the second note on 11:43 concerning the probable meaning of this name. Concerning the typical Judahite accession formula found here, with its inclusion of the king's age at accession and the name of the queen mother, see "Literary Style" in the Introduction.

Naamah, an Ammonite woman. See the first note on 14:31.

14:23 *sacred pillars and Asherah poles.* The "sacred pillars" (*matseboth* [TH4676, ZH5167]) were made of stone (Cogan 2001:386-387; cf. Pritchard 1969: pictures 871, 872); they were features of the Canaanite cult as were the Asherah poles (cf. Deut 12:3), but they were not phallic symbols as some have maintained. (Concerning the Asherah poles, see the note on 14:15.) Hence, both stone and wood images are featured here.

14:24 *male and female shrine prostitutes.* The NLT has a full, and in my opinion, entirely accurate translation here for the single word *qadesh* [TH6945, ZH7728] "sacred (one[s])," though in some contexts the word may refer simply to cultic personnel. Both masculine and feminine forms of this term are found in Deut 23:17 [18] in reference to temple prostitutes. Wiseman (1993:152) notes that in the Kings text here, the term is used for both sexes, and it is "taken to be a reference back to Canaanite ritual prostitution."

detestable practices. Heb., *to'aboth* [TH8441, ZH9359], a strongly negative term, traditionally translated as "abominations" or the like (cf. KJV). What was being condemned here was (heterosexual) fertility religion, not any sort of homosexual activity as many older translations have implied.

14:25 *fifth year.* This is an unusually precise chronological datum, probably from a royal or Temple chronicle (Cogan 2001:387-388; both Cogan and I [Barnes 1991:57-67] have concluded that the absolute date is c. 925 BC, or a bit higher, and that we cannot be certain that this campaign took place within a year or so of Shishak's death).

King Shishak of Egypt. See the note on 11:40 concerning this important pharaoh. An excellent summary of the biblical and extrabiblical evidence may be found in Cogan 2001:390-391. As Wiseman (1993:152) points out, Shishak exacted tribute from the fortified areas of Judah, and he set up a stele in Megiddo (see Cogan 2001, figure 5 for a drawing of the surviving top corner of the originally 10-foot-tall stele [cf. Kitchen 1996:299]), thus indicating at least some significant pressure was placed on Jeroboam's realm as well.

14:26 *all the gold shields Solomon had made.* See the note on 10:16-17 for details on these extravagant furnishings. This expensive attempt to buy off Shishak may have been at least partially successful: There is no record of Shishak claiming capture of Jerusalem, and it appears that Shishak himself died a year later (Wiseman 1993:152; following Kitchen 1996:293-300; 432-447; 575-576; but see the first note on 14:25).

14:29 *are recorded in* **The Book of the History of the Kings of Judah.** See "Literary Style" in the Introduction.

14:30 *constant war.* This is sadly a repeated refrain during the early period of the divided monarchy (see 15:6, 7b, 16, 32; cf. 14:19a). The peace asked for back in 12:21-24 did not last all that long. (For further discussion of this refrain, see commentary on 15:1-8.)

14:31 *His mother was Naamah.* This is a curious repetition with the accession formula in 14:21b. Cogan (2001:388) takes this as an erroneous duplication, but I wonder if there is more to this notice than that. I have argued that the curious duplications of regnal formulas found in 2 Chr 21:5, 20 for Jehoram; 2 Chr 27:1, 8 for Jotham; and the familiar dual notice concerning Josiah's 18th year (2 Kgs 22:3; 23:23, paralleled in 2 Chr 34:8; 35:19) signify in Chronicles every fifth monarch after Solomon in the Davidic king-list (see Barnes 1991:142-144). In short, repetitions are often intentional, and that may be the case here. Concerning the foreign origin of Naamah the Ammonite, cf. Cogan (2001:386), who follows Malamat in suggesting that David arranged this marriage for his son Solomon while the latter was still a prince at his father's court (also see Sweeney 2007:188).

Abijam. Or "Abijah"; see note on 15:1.

COMMENTARY

We now move into several chapters featuring the "leapfrog" treatment of the northern and southern kings, with their order of presentation apparently based solely on chronological factors. For further discussion concerning these regnal accession notices, evaluations, discussions, and concluding summaries, see "Literary Style" in the Introduction.

The section begins with Rehoboam, who was certainly no Solomon (see commentary on 12:1-20). Rehoboam was, however, still in the Davidic line, and therefore the transmitter of the Davidic blessing for all nations (see, particularly, my comments on 2 Sam 7 under "Date and Occasion of Writing" in the Introduction). Two main observations are made about Rehoboam's time as king: The people sadly grew even more heterodox in their worship (14:22-25); and King Shishak attacked Jerusalem early in Rehoboam's reign, ransacking the treasuries of palace and Temple, and, in particular, removing Solomon's ceremonial gold shields from the palace (14:25-28; cf. 10:16-17). We are clearly no longer in either Davidic or Solomonic times, for such things would not have taken place then. But we are probably seeing here the results of some of the later actions of David (cf. 2 Sam 11–20) and especially Solomon (1 Kgs 11), with resultant unrest within the realm and a successful attack from outsiders. All the Deuteronomistic commentator can do here is reflect on the necessity of bronze substitutes for the gold shields (literally a tarnishing of the memories of Solomon's fabulous wealth), and note with careful restraint the sad measures Rehoboam must undertake to guard those replacement shields. Israel's golden age was over.

Pharaoh Shishak represents a new, but soon to be all-too-familiar result of the end of the Davidic and Solomonic ages: foreign oppression. There seems, as well, to have been intermittent warfare between the northern and southern kingdoms (see commentary on 15:1-8). Suffice it to say that when one is hard-pressed from without, one particularly should seek peace from within; and although Rehoboam surely did not consider Jeroboam's realm as in the category of "within," it nonetheless was exactly that, for in 12:24, the Israelites are called the Judahites' "relatives" ('akhekem [TH251, ZH278]). Sometimes, we fight needlessly those whom we should consider to be on our side (or at least as neutral). That was true then, and that is so often still the case in the church today.

◆   2. Abijam rules in Judah (15:1-8)

Abijam* began to rule over Judah in the eighteenth year of Jeroboam's reign in Israel. ²He reigned in Jerusalem three years. His mother was Maacah, the granddaughter of Absalom.*

³He committed the same sins as his father before him, and he was not faithful to the LORD his God, as his ancestor David had been. ⁴But for David's sake, the LORD his God allowed his descendants to con-

tinue ruling, shining like a lamp, and he gave Abijam a son to rule after him in Jerusalem. ⁵For David had done what was pleasing in the LORD's sight and had obeyed the LORD's commands throughout his life, except in the affair concerning Uriah the Hittite.

⁶There was war between Abijam and Jeroboam* throughout Abijam's reign. ⁷The rest of the events in Abijam's reign

and everything he did are recorded in *The Book of the History of the Kings of Judah.* There was constant war between Abijam and Jeroboam. [8]When Abijam died, he was buried in the City of David. Then his son Asa became the next king.

15:1 Also known as *Abijah.*   15:2 Hebrew *Abishalom* (also in 15:10), a variant spelling of Absalom; compare 2 Chr 11:20.   15:6 As in a few Hebrew and Greek manuscripts; most Hebrew manuscripts read *between Rehoboam and Jeroboam.*

NOTES

15:1 *Abijam.* Or "Abijah" as in 2 Chr 13:1; cf. NLT mg. This is a different Abijah than Jeroboam's son (14:1; see the note there for the meaning of the name). The meaning of the name Abijam is disputed: it possibly means "My [divine] Father is Yam," with "Yam" either being a by-form of "Yahweh," or, more controversially, a reference to the Canaanite sea-god "Yamm" (see ABD 1.18-19 for details; also Japhet 1993:683-684).

15:2 *Maacah, the granddaughter of Absalom.* The NLT's "granddaughter" is a legitimate rendering of the Hebrew *bat* [TH1323, ZH1426] (lit., "daughter") and is presumably what is meant here (Cogan 2001:392-393; Japhet 1993:670-671). In any case, this Absalom is probably none other than the infamous son of David, who rebelled against his father, and whose untimely death David greatly mourned (2 Sam 3:3; 13:1–19:10; interestingly, Absalom's mother was also named Maacah).

15:4 *shining like a lamp.* See "The 'Lamp' of David" section in "Major Themes" in the Introduction for this very important catchphrase found several times in 1–2 Kings. Often, the southern kings are evaluated in reference to their ancestor David (see 9:4-5; 11:4-6, 38-39; 14:8; 15:11; 2 Kgs 14:3; 16:2; 18:3; 22:2).

15:5 *except in the affair concerning Uriah the Hittite.* This is the only place in 1–2 Kings where such a caveat is to be found in reference to David (the specific reference here is to David's adultery with Bathsheba and the commissioning of the murder of her husband Uriah; see 2 Sam 11:1–12:25). Since this comment is not in the LXX, some think it is a later gloss (Cogan 2001:393).

15:6 *Abijam and Jeroboam.* Possibly some sort of dittography (writing twice what should have been written once; cf. 14:30 and 15:7) is to be found here. As the NLT mg indicates, the MT reads "Rehoboam" instead of "Abijam." The verse is altogether lacking in the LXX; hence it may well be secondary.

15:7 *are recorded in* The Book of the History of the Kings of Judah. See "Literary Style" in the Introduction.

constant war. Cogan (2001:391) notes that the repeated clashes cited in these early chapters of the divided monarchy probably represented efforts to defend Jerusalem, Judah's capital, from attacks from the territory of Benjamin, only some 3 miles (5 km) to the north.

COMMENTARY

Besides the general reference to the "lamp" of David (15:4-5), and the repeated references to "war" and "constant war" between the north and the south (15:6-7), there is little new in this section (which will often be the case in the chronological leapfrog treatment of every northern and southern king in 1–2 Kings, from now on). As here, stereotypical repetitions of faithfulness-of-David or unfaithfulness-of-Jeroboam evaluations will often sharply color otherwise brief, bland recitations of a few historical minutiae. The editor's overall agenda is clear in all this: List each king of either kingdom in strict chronological order (usually synchronizing with the corresponding king of the rival kingdom), perhaps include some concise historical notices, give a clear theological evaluation of the king, and then quickly move on. Such is the case in the present passage, and for the next seven kings up to King Ahab in 16:29-34, about whom discussion continues off and on throughout the final six chapters of 1 Kings.

Constant warfare is the repeated refrain characterizing the early period of the divided monarchy (see 15:6, 7b, 16, 32; also cf. 14:19a, 30). The peace between north and south brought about by the prophet Shemaiah back in 12:21-24 was lost, and it would not be until the reigns of Ahab of Israel and Jehoshaphat of Judah (according to the MT) that peace was finally restored between the two kingdoms at Jehoshaphat's initiative (see 22:44 [45]). The references to warfare have so far been brief but insistent (indeed, they will grow even more compelling in the Asa section). Coupled with the Davidic references in the present passage, they might evoke the reminder that David himself was a man of war (5:3; cf. 1 Chr 22:7-10; 28:3), but that is at best only an implied comparison. No, the multiplied references here are surely meant to be understood quite negatively, reminding the reader that the seemingly constant skirmishing between the two kingdoms (both representing significant numbers of God's people) could, and indeed would, lead to disasters in the future. What a melancholy reminder of how God's people often fight with each other, rather than with their common foes. We will sadly have to return to this topic in more detail in the next section.

◆   3. Asa rules in Judah (15:9-24)

⁹Asa began to rule over Judah in the twentieth year of Jeroboam's reign in Israel. ¹⁰He reigned in Jerusalem forty-one years. His grandmother* was Maacah, the granddaughter of Absalom.

¹¹Asa did what was pleasing in the LORD's sight, as his ancestor David had done. ¹²He banished the male and female shrine prostitutes from the land and got rid of all the idols* his ancestors had made. ¹³He even deposed his grandmother Maacah from her position as queen mother because she had made an obscene Asherah pole. He cut down her obscene pole and burned it in the Kidron Valley. ¹⁴Although the pagan shrines were not removed, Asa's heart remained completely faithful to the LORD throughout his life. ¹⁵He brought into the Temple of the LORD the silver and gold and the various items that he and his father had dedicated.

¹⁶There was constant war between King Asa of Judah and King Baasha of Israel. ¹⁷King Baasha of Israel invaded Judah and fortified Ramah in order to prevent anyone from entering or leaving King Asa's territory in Judah.

¹⁸Asa responded by removing all the silver and gold that was left in the treasuries of the Temple of the LORD and the royal palace. He sent it with some of his officials to Ben-hadad son of Tabrimmon, son of Hezion, the king of Aram, who was ruling in Damascus, along with this message:

¹⁹"Let there be a treaty* between you and me like the one between your father and my father. See, I am sending you a gift of silver and gold. Break your treaty with King Baasha of Israel so that he will leave me alone."

²⁰Ben-hadad agreed to King Asa's request and sent the commanders of his army to attack the towns of Israel. They conquered the towns of Ijon, Dan, Abel-beth-maacah, and all Kinnereth, and all the land of Naphtali. ²¹As soon as Baasha

of Israel heard what was happening, he abandoned his project of fortifying Ramah and withdrew to Tirzah. ²²Then King Asa sent an order throughout Judah, requiring that everyone, without exception, help to carry away the building stones and timbers that Baasha had been using to fortify Ramah. Asa used these materials to fortify the town of Geba in Benjamin and the town of Mizpah.

²³The rest of the events in Asa's reign—the extent of his power, everything he did, and the names of the cities he built—are recorded in *The Book of the History of the Kings of Judah*. In his old age his feet became diseased. ²⁴When Asa died, he was buried with his ancestors in the City of David.

Then Jehoshaphat, Asa's son, became the next king.

15:10 Or *The queen mother;* Hebrew reads *His mother* (also in 15:13); compare 15:2.   15:12 The Hebrew term (literally *round things*) probably alludes to dung.   15:19 As in Greek version; Hebrew reads *There is a treaty.*

NOTES

15:9 *Asa.* Heb., *'asa'* [TH609, ZH654] (which may mean "healer"); he is a prominent king in both the books of Kings and Chronicles. His 41-year reign is longer than either David's or Solomon's; it is surpassed only by those of Uzziah (52 years) and Manasseh (55 years).

15:10 *grandmother.* Lit., "mother" (see NLT mg); some have understood Abijam and Asa to be brothers, but the NLT text is preferable. Concerning the position of the "queen mother" (15:13), see notes on 2:19.

15:11 *what was pleasing.* See note on 15:4.

15:12 *male and female shrine prostitutes.* See note on 14:24.

idols. Heb., *gillulim* [TH1544, ZH1658], lit., "round(ed) items" or the like (traditionally taken as "dung"; hence the NLT mg). For a similar term, see the third note on 14:10. Both Cogan (2001:397) and Koehler and Baumgartner (HALOT 192), however, suggest plausible alternative etymologies ("stones" and "venerable things," respectively) for this relatively common term.

15:13 *obscene Asherah pole.* See the note on 14:15 concerning the "Asherah pole" itself. The adjective "obscene" used here is a debatable translation for the strong term *mipletseth* [TH4656, ZH5145] (horrid thing), which is found twice in the Hebrew of this verse. The term *mipletseth* is meant to evoke a strong shudder of hatred and fear, but not necessarily sexual repulsion.

Kidron Valley. This valley is located directly east of Jerusalem and west of the Mount of Olives.

15:16 *constant war.* This is a repeated reference throughout these several chapters (see commentary on 15:1-8).

Baasha. See note on 15:27.

15:17 *fortified Ramah.* This was a Benjamite city (present-day village of er-Ram) just 5 miles (8 km) north of Jerusalem. By this action, Baasha effectively blockaded Asa in his own capital city (Cogan 2001:399) or, at least, controlled traffic on the main north–south route to and from Jerusalem (Pitard 1987:107).

15:18 *silver and gold that was left.* This was a desperate measure, but understandable from a desperate king (see the previous note). Presumably not all that much gold or silver was left (but cf. 15:15) after the notorious despoiling of the city of Jerusalem by Pharaoh Shishak in the days of Rehoboam (14:25-26).

Ben-hadad. This is Ben-hadad I, the first of at least two (and possibly three) Aramean monarchs who bore that name, which means "son of [the god] Hadad." Pitard (1987:107-110; also cf. Pitard in ABD 1.663-664) characterized this king as an early ninth-century king of Damascus, son of Tab-Ramman ("Ramman [the thundering one] is good"); cf. "Tabrimmon, son of Hezion," in the present verse.

15:19 *Let there be a treaty.* This follows the imperative verb of the LXX (*diathou* [TG1303, ZG1415]). There is no expressed verb in MT, but this is possibly its intended meaning as well (cf. GKC 453 [§141f], as noted by Pitard 1987:108; but contrast Cogan 2001:400; Japhet 1993:733).

Break your treaty. This would have far-reaching consequences—among other things, domination of Israel's northern territory and interruption of their main trade route to the coastal cities of Tyre and Sidon (Pitard 1987:109; Wiseman 1993:156). The symmetrical nature of these diplomatic and military maneuverings is self-evident (see note on 15:17).

15:20 *all the land of Naphtali.* This was the area west and southwest of Aram proper, and north and west of the Sea of Galilee (including Dan; cf. the note on 12:29).

15:21 *Tirzah.* Heb., *tirtsah* [TH8656A, ZH9574], meaning "pleasure, beauty." This was the early capital of the northern kingdom (14:17), probably to be identified with Tell el-Far'ah (north), 7 miles (11 km) northeast of Shechem along the highway running downhill to Beth-shan in the Jordan River valley (Cogan 2001:401).

15:22 *without exception.* Lit., "none was clean [innocent, exempt]"—that is, free from state obligations (cf. Deut 24:5, as noted by Cogan 2001:401).

15:23 *are recorded in* The Book of the History of the Kings of Judah. See "Literary Style" in the Introduction.

his feet became diseased. This is another brief, concluding notice, akin to 14:30 and 15:7b. Concerning the nature and the significance of this disease, see the commentary below.

15:24 *Jehoshaphat.* His formal accession formula will not be given until 22:41-42; for the earlier placement of this formula in the LXX, see the note on 16:28.

COMMENTARY

"A generation of hostilities between Judah and Israel reached new heights during the reign of Asa." This is how Cogan (2001:403) introduces his historical overview of the present passage of Scripture. Likewise, I have noted in the two preceding commentary sections how the refrain of constant warfare punctuates both these passages. By now, something more permanent had to be accomplished, and it was Baasha's provocative action of fortifying Ramah (just north of Jerusalem) that led Asa to respond. "In an open admission of weakness" (again, Cogan's comment), Asa sent a bribe to encourage Ben-hadad of Aram to break his nonaggression pact with Israel. And the stratagem worked—at least for Asa's generation. Soon enough, however, Aram again becomes an enemy (cf. ch 20; also 22:1-40).

"God moves in mysterious ways, his wonders to perform," an adaptation from the hymn by William Cowper, might well describe the present passage about Asa. We have been told a number of times in 1 Kings that both apparent successes and apparent disasters were the will of Yahweh (cf. the notes and commentary on 12:15, 24). Such is probably also the case here: Asa, in a desperate move, acted decisively (and deceitfully, it must be acknowledged) to protect the capital city of Jerusalem. And the results were positive: Both the Benjamite cites of Geba and Mizpah were eventually captured, thus guarding the northern approaches to Jerusalem itself (Cogan 2001:401). The capital city of David became secure; and it was apparently not threatened from without until the time of King Joash, some 50 years later (see

2 Kgs 12:17). Yahweh was truly protecting the city that bears his name (see "One Place of Worship" under "Major Themes" in the Introduction).

But in another mysterious move of God, King Asa is said to have had a disease of his feet (15:23). (For other royal illnesses, note Uzziah's "leprosy" [or contagious skin disease] in 2 Kgs 15:5, and Hezekiah's "deathly illness" in 2 Kgs 20:1-11 [termed a "boil" in Isa 38:21].) Unlike Hezekiah, who was miraculously healed, the implication in the present text seems to be that Asa's foot troubles (gout?) led to his death (Cogan 2001:402; DeVries 1985:191). Wiseman (1993:157) argues that this was a vascular disease with ensuing gangrene. Although in the Kings account the causal connection between disease and death is only implied by the editor, contrast 2 Chronicles 16:12-13.

In sum, Asa was a godly king who pleased his Lord. He significantly cleansed the land of idolatry, and he acted decisively to protect his capital city. Such protection was costly, but apparently necessary and apparently in God's will. Even his foot disease did not disqualify him from being reckoned positively as only 8 out of 19 southern kings (and *no* northern kings) would be. God does work in mysterious ways, his wonders to perform.

◆   ## 4. Nadab rules in Israel (15:25-31)

25Nadab son of Jeroboam began to rule over Israel in the second year of King Asa's reign in Judah. He reigned in Israel two years. 26But he did what was evil in the LORD's sight and followed the example of his father, continuing the sins that Jeroboam had led Israel to commit.

27Then Baasha son of Ahijah, from the tribe of Issachar, plotted against Nadab and assassinated him while he and the Israelite army were laying siege to the Philistine town of Gibbethon. 28Baasha killed Nadab in the third year of King Asa's reign in Judah, and he became the next king of Israel.

29He immediately slaughtered all the descendants of King Jeroboam, so that not one of the royal family was left, just as the LORD had promised concerning Jeroboam by the prophet Ahijah from Shiloh. 30This was done because Jeroboam had provoked the anger of the LORD, the God of Israel, by the sins he had committed and the sins he had led Israel to commit.

31The rest of the events in Nadab's reign and everything he did are recorded in *The Book of the History of the Kings of Israel.*

NOTES

15:25 *Nadab.* This was probably the second son of Jeroboam, first mentioned in 14:20, just after the sad narrative describing the untimely death of Jeroboam's son Abijah (probably his firstborn). Nadab's name probably means "generous" or "noble."

15:26 *the sins that Jeroboam had led Israel to commit.* This is a common formulaic condemnation found for most of the northern kings (see commentary on 12:25-33).

15:27 *Baasha son of Ahijah . . . Issachar.* He was already informally introduced in 15:16-22. Cogan (2001:405) notes that the identification of a usurper by his tribal affiliation is unique here. The tribal territory of Issachar was located just north of the western half of Manasseh, and south of the Sea of Galilee. Possibly the tribal affiliation was included so as to preclude any identification of Baasha's patronymic (father's name), "Ahijah," with the prophet of the same name mentioned repeatedly in the previous chapter (as well as prominently in 11:29-39). The meaning of Baasha's name is uncertain; it is possibly a contraction of "Baal hears" or "the sun is Baal" (see IDB 1.333). Here, "Baal" (which simply means "lord") need not refer explicitly to the Canaanite storm-god so infamously celebrated in the later years of Ahab and Jezebel.

Gibbethon. This was a Levitical city of the tribe of Dan, probably just west of Gezer (Cogan 2001:405). Sweeney (2007:196) suggests that the attack probably represented an attempt to extend Israel's power into the coastal plain to the west, perhaps by recovering land once belonging to the tribe of Dan. A similar reference (a doublet?) is found in 16:15.

15:29 *the prophet Ahijah.* This prophet "from Shiloh" (in the territory of Ephraim) is not to be confused with Baasha's father.

15:31 The Book of the History of the Kings of Israel. See "Literary Style" in the Introduction.

COMMENTARY

Usurpation (grabbing power by illegal, usually violent means) is never pleasant, and halfhearted measures will never lead to success in any endeavor to establish a new dynastic authority. The Bible does not flinch from conveying these ugly realities (cf. Judg 9:5; 2 Sam 4:1-12; and, infamously, 1 Kgs 2). The extermination of Jeroboam's family must have been a gruesome event indeed. Nadab's attack on the Philistines at Gibbethon was surely an understandable, even honorable undertaking, but it also obviously provided a convenient occasion for Baasha's coup d'etat. Nevertheless, two points must be made here: (1) Such violence is said to be part of the prophetic agenda—the same Ahijah from Shiloh who first announced Jeroboam's dynasty was also the first to announce its brief duration (see 11:29-39 and 14:7-16, respectively). (2) "Those who use the sword will die by the sword" (Matt 26:52). The fate of Baasha's regime would be the same as that of Jeroboam's (see 16:9-13). There is often poetic justice in life, and the biblical narratives recount many instances of such (see especially the comment found in 16:7b). As the modern mantra has it: "What goes around comes around." We forget such truths at our own peril (cf. the Teacher's admonitions in Eccl 1:9-11).

◆   5. Baasha rules in Israel (15:32–16:7)

³²There was constant war between King Asa of Judah and King Baasha of Israel. ³³Baasha son of Ahijah began to rule over all Israel in the third year of King Asa's reign in Judah. Baasha reigned in Tirzah twenty-four years. ³⁴But he did what was evil in the LORD's sight and followed the example of Jeroboam, continuing the sins that Jeroboam had led Israel to commit.

CHAPTER 16

This message from the LORD was delivered to King Baasha by the prophet Jehu son of Hanani: ²"I lifted you out of the dust to make you ruler of my people Israel, but you have followed the evil example of Jeroboam. You have provoked my anger by causing my people Israel to sin. ³So now I will destroy you and your family, just as I destroyed the descendants of Jeroboam son of Nebat. ⁴The members of Baasha's family who die in the city will be eaten by dogs, and those who die in the field will be eaten by vultures."

⁵The rest of the events in Baasha's reign and the extent of his power are recorded in *The Book of the History of the Kings of Israel.* ⁶When Baasha died, he was buried in Tirzah. Then his son Elah became the next king.

⁷The message from the LORD against

Baasha and his family came through the prophet Jehu son of Hanani. It was delivered because Baasha had done what was evil in the LORD's sight (just as the family of Jeroboam had done), and also because Baasha had destroyed the family of Jeroboam. The LORD's anger was provoked by Baasha's sins.

NOTES

15:32 *constant war.* See 15:16-22 and the commentary on 15:1-8 and 15:9-24. The formal, chronologically ordered nature of these regnal discussions leads to such repetitions as we see here. This stereotypical brevity is particularly ironic considering Baasha's 24-year reign was one of the longest of the 19 kings in the northern kingdom; only the reigns of Jehu (28 years) and Jeroboam II (41 years) were longer.

16:1 *the prophet Jehu son of Hanani.* He is otherwise unknown; the name Jehu probably means "Yah(weh) is he," or "Yah(weh) is the (true) one" (cf. the first note on 2 Kgs 9:2).

16:2 *you have followed the evil example of Jeroboam. You have provoked my anger by causing my people Israel to sin.* Sadly, in this respect Baasha qualified as following Jeroboam; the editor cites only the evil examples both kings gave. In 16:7b, Baasha is also condemned for wiping out Jeroboam's family. The formulaic nature of the Deuteronomistic editor is rarely better displayed than in this passage.

16:4 *dogs . . . vultures.* See note on 14:11.

16:5 **The Book of the History of the Kings of Israel.** See "Literary Style" in the Introduction.

16:6 *Elah.* See note on 16:8.

16:7 *the prophet Jehu son of Hanani.* This is yet another example of a duplication in the Kings text (see 16:1); such duplications probably signal some sort of literary structure or effect akin to an *inclusio* (cf. the first notes on 3:15 and 14:31; *inclusios* such as this signal the beginning and end of a narrative unit).

COMMENTARY

Usurpers are universally reviled by those who crave order, and such is undoubtedly the case here. Baasha is said to have reigned 24 years (see note on 15:32), but all we read in the present passage is that his reign was doomed from the start. In relation to Jeroboam, his reign simply represented more of the same. He radically removed Jeroboam and his family, but he retained their sinful practices. It seems in both respects he erred: Taking on the role of a usurper has its self-evident dangers, and the brief, negative summary of Baasha's lengthy reign stands as an enduring representative of that very fact. Unwittingly acting to accomplish God's clear will (15:29) hardly qualifies one for God's clear blessing. Sins of commission and sins of omission may both significantly mar the result.

◆   **6. Elah rules in Israel (16:8-14)**

⁸Elah son of Baasha began to rule over Israel in the twenty-sixth year of King Asa's reign in Judah. He reigned in the city of Tirzah for two years.

⁹Then Zimri, who commanded half of the royal chariots, made plans to kill him. One day in Tirzah, Elah was getting drunk at the home of Arza, the supervisor of the

palace. ¹⁰Zimri walked in and struck him down and killed him. This happened in the twenty-seventh year of King Asa's reign in Judah. Then Zimri became the next king.

¹¹Zimri immediately killed the entire royal family of Baasha, leaving him not even a single male child. He even destroyed distant relatives and friends. ¹²So Zimri destroyed the dynasty of Baasha as the LORD had promised through the prophet Jehu. ¹³This happened because of all the sins Baasha and his son Elah had committed, and because of the sins they led Israel to commit. They provoked the anger of the LORD, the God of Israel, with their worthless idols.

¹⁴The rest of the events in Elah's reign and everything he did are recorded in *The Book of the History of the Kings of Israel.*

NOTES

16:8 *Elah.* This was the doomed descendant of Baasha who, like Nadab before him (see 15:25-31), only reigned two years. The name Elah probably means "terebinth [tree]."

16:9 *Zimri.* See note on 16:15.

half of the royal chariots. Wiseman (1993:159), following Yadin, suggests that half the chariotry was probably based at Megiddo (cf. the second note on 10:26), the other half near Tirzah, ready for action against Judah to the south.

was getting drunk at the home of Arza. As Cogan (2001:412) memorably phrased it, "at a private party" (cf. 20:12, 16 for another such disaster). The Bible certainly does not endorse political or military leaders drinking to excess (see Prov 20:1; 31:4-7; also cf. Prov 23:29-35). Still, what a sad way for a usurper to gain an advantage.

the supervisor of the palace. He was the principal officer of the state, probably akin to the prime minister (Wiseman 1993:159); cf. the first note on 4:6.

16:11 *killed the entire royal family.* Sadly, this was the typical procedure to prevent possible reprisals (see commentary on 15:25-31).

a single male child. See the first note on 14:10.

16:14 The Book of the History of the Kings of Israel. See "Literary Style" in the Introduction.

COMMENTARY

If usurpers are universally reviled by those who crave order (see commentary on 15:32–16:7), privileged children are probably in a similar category. Accidents of birth should not lead to presumptions of privilege, as may have been the case here. The Deuteronomistic editor's insistence on strict chronological arrangement of these brief discussions of the northern and southern kings leads to anticipatory notices of "regime change" that can bewilder the casual reader (cf. the Asa material in 15:16-22, where, although not formally introduced, Baasha king of Israel is prominently featured). Such is the case with Zimri, the commander of half of the royal chariots, an exalted position for one of such humble background. The only thing we learn about Elah is that (at least once, but probably rather often) he got drunk at a private party (see third note on 16:9). Surely he did more in his two-year reign than attend private parties, but historical treatments are naturally quite selective in their emphases. This last point certainly gives pause to leaders of any age!

◆   ## 7. Zimri rules in Israel (16:15–20)

¹⁵Zimri began to rule over Israel in the twenty-seventh year of King Asa's reign in Judah, but his reign in Tirzah lasted only seven days. The army of Israel was then attacking the Philistine town of Gibbethon. ¹⁶When they heard that Zimri had committed treason and had assassinated the king, that very day they chose Omri, commander of the army, as the new king of Israel. ¹⁷So Omri led the entire army of Israel up from Gibbethon to attack Tirzah, Israel's capital. ¹⁸When Zimri saw that the city had been taken, he went into the citadel of the palace and burned it down over himself and died in the flames. ¹⁹For he, too, had done what was evil in the LORD's sight. He followed the example of Jeroboam in all the sins he had committed and led Israel to commit.

²⁰The rest of the events in Zimri's reign and his conspiracy are recorded in *The Book of the History of the Kings of Israel.*

NOTES

16:15 *Zimri.* With no patronymic given, Zimri (short for "strength of Yahweh") may have come from a lowly lineage (Cogan 2001:411). Wiseman (1993:159) suggests the name may be Aramean in origin. In any case, his significant military position (see 16:9) will soon be eclipsed by one with even higher standing.

seven days. The Old Greek (Codex Vaticanus) reads "seven years"; DeVries (1985:198) points out that the term *yamim* [TH8441, ZH3427] (days) can also mean "years" (e.g., 1 Sam 1:3), which may have led to the varying chronology found throughout the present section (so also Cogan 2001:103). The MT should be retained (cf. Barnes 1991:154-155 note e).

The army of Israel was then attacking the Philistine town of Gibbethon. This is eerily similar to the demise of Nadab (15:27). Some see the continuation of the siege of that city (at least intermittently), now for 24 years, as perhaps indicating the military weakness of Baasha's dynasty (Sweeney 2007:202; Wiseman 1993:160).

16:16 *Omri, commander of the army.* Thus, he was Zimri's superior. The name Omri may not be Israelite in origin (see note on 16:23).

16:17 *Tirzah, Israel's capital.* See note on 15:21.

16:18 *the citadel of the palace.* Heb., *'armon beth hammelek*, meaning "fortress/citadel of (?) the house of the king"; the term *'armon* [TH759, ZH810] probably refers to a specific structure in the palace complex (Cogan and Tadmor 1988:173).

died in the flames. This is possibly meant to be taken as a tragically heroic way to die (Cogan 2001:411; DeVries 1985:200), and not necessarily a cowardly way (cf. Samson's demise, essentially by his own hands; Judg 16:28-30). Although the Hebrew is imprecise as to who started the fire, most think it was of Zimri's own volition, not that of the besieging army of Omri.

16:19 *example of Jeroboam.* This is a repeated, stereotypical condemnation for most of the northern kings (see commentary on 12:25-33). Not too many of these sins could have taken place in only one week!

16:20 The Book of the History of the Kings of Israel. See "Literary Style" in the Introduction.

COMMENTARY

Once again, "Those who use the sword will die by the sword" (Matt 26:52; see commentary on 15:25-31). As Cogan (2001:412) puts it, Zimri's "breach of personal trust" lived on in popular memory (attacking Elah at a private party, thereby usurping the throne; cf. the notes and commentary on 16:8-14). Even Queen Jezebel cited Zimri's infamous act of treachery when confronting her own usurper, Jehu son of Nimshi, some 40 years later (2 Kgs 9:31; cf. Cogan and Tadmor [1988:307], who see this reference as insulting "in every sense"). If Zimri's reign truly only lasted seven days (see the second note on 16:15), at least he went out with a flourish—tragically heroic, the stuff of legends. Cogan (2001:413) cites the classical traditions about the last Assyrian king, Sin-shar-ishkun (probably corresponding to the infamous "Sardanapalus" of the classical texts), allegedly throwing himself into the fire of his burning palace so as not to fall into the hands of barbarians (a tradition probably derived from the fiery demise of Shamash-shum-ukin in Babylon some years earlier). In any case, it will soon be necessary for Zimri's successor, Omri, to relocate the capital from Tirzah to Samaria, after fighting his own way through to victory in a civil war. Violent usurpation is a sad political specter found repeatedly throughout the first half of the ninth century BC. But hope is on the way in the persons of Elijah and Elisha the prophets, who fearlessly confronted kings, Israelite and otherwise.

◆   ## 8. Omri rules in Israel (16:21-28)

²¹But now the people of Israel were split into two factions. Half the people tried to make Tibni son of Ginath their king, while the other half supported Omri. ²²But Omri's supporters defeated the supporters of Tibni. So Tibni was killed, and Omri became the next king.

²³Omri began to rule over Israel in the thirty-first year of King Asa's reign in Judah. He reigned twelve years in all, six of them in Tirzah. ²⁴Then Omri bought the hill now known as Samaria from its owner, Shemer, for 150 pounds of silver.* He built a city on it and called the city Samaria in honor of Shemer.

²⁵But Omri did what was evil in the LORD's sight, even more than any of the kings before him. ²⁶He followed the example of Jeroboam son of Nebat in all the sins he had committed and led Israel to commit. The people provoked the anger of the LORD, the God of Israel, with their worthless idols.

²⁷The rest of the events in Omri's reign, the extent of his power, and everything he did are recorded in *The Book of the History of the Kings of Israel.* ²⁸When Omri died, he was buried in Samaria. Then his son Ahab became the next king.

16:24 Hebrew *for 2 talents* [68 kilograms] *of silver.*

NOTES

16:21 *split into two factions.* Lit., "were divided into half"; some see here a division between the native Israelites versus the military (or mercenary elements therein), led by the "foreigner" Omri (Cogan 2001:415).

Tibni son of Ginath. He is otherwise unknown. In 16:22 the LXX includes the detail that when Tibni died, Joram his brother also died, a note that is likely to be original and perhaps signifies recognition that at the time, Tibni was considered king (cf. also the LXX addition of the phrase "after Tibni" following the accession notice "Omri became the next king" at the end of 16:22). Independent, early tradition such as this gives one pause when confronting the variant synchronism in 16:23.

16:23 Omri. With no patronymic given (cf. Zimri), Omri (*'omri* [TH6018, ZH6687]) probably came from a humble background; nonetheless, he is positively described as "commander of the army" in 16:16. The name Omri, while eventually becoming rather
well-known in the wider ancient Near Eastern world (see the commentary below), is of
uncertain etymology, with some taking it as Canaanite, and others as being of altogether
non-Israelite origin (thus Omri was perhaps a foreign mercenary; cf. Cogan 2001:416). If
derived from an Arabic root, the name may mean "(the) life which Yah(weh) has given"
(ABD 5.17).

thirty-first year. As already noted (see second note on 16:21; also DeVries 1985:198-202),
this is a seemingly aberrant synchronism in light of the information in 16:15. Many suggest
that this is the first year of Omri's sole reign, the previous civil war lasting four years, from
the fall of Zimri to the defeat of Tibni (e.g., Sweeney 2007:204). Thus, the regnal total of
"twelve years" for Omri found in this verse would include only eight or so of uncontested
rule (that this, however, hardly appears to be the plain meaning of the present text almost
goes without saying).

16:24 Samaria. Heb., *shomeron* [TH8111, ZH9076], modern Sebastiyeh. The precise etymology of the place-name "Shomron" is disputed; Cogan (2001:417) suggests that the name
was already an established name for the high hill (1400 ft [430 m] in elevation, well-
situated some 7 miles [11 km] northwest of Shechem on the road network connecting
the hill country to the coastal plain) when the site was purchased by Omri (cf. the other
"mountain names" akin to "Shomron": Tsion [Zion], Hermon, Lebanon, all ending in
"-on" [DeVries 1985:202 adds "Sirion" to this list as well]). This would make the reference
to "Shemer," the owner in the present verse, a secondary (yet still valid) etymology. In any
case, this lovely site would be the capital city of the northern kingdom until its fall more
than 150 years later; the familiar NT term "Samaritans" is also derived from this famous
place-name.

150 pounds of silver. Lit., "two talents of silver"; see the second note on 9:14 for the
probable weight of the Hebrew talent.

16:26 example of Jeroboam son of Nebat. This is the common refrain cited for nearly all
of the northern kings (see commentary on 12:25-33).

16:27 The Book of the History of the Kings of Israel. See "Literary Style" in the Introduction.

16:28 next king. At this point the LXX (identified from 1 Kgs 2:12–21:29 in Codex Vaticanus as the Old Greek; see the Introduction, "Canonicity and Textual History") inserts
the Judahite accession notice and regnal discussion for Jehoshaphat son of Asa (enumerated as 16:28a-h in Rahlfs [1935]; see note on 15:24 and endnote 17 in the Introduction). Some years ago, Shenkel, following the text-critical proposals of his (and my)
mentor, Frank Cross, suggested that the Old Greek reflects a significantly different, and
more accurate, chronology for the Omride kings (as well as some of their predecessors).
His proposal has not met with wide acceptance, but I think there is much merit to his
approach, at least for the Omrides. That the Old Greek reflects a different chronology is
quite evident to all (e.g., here, in the Old Greek, Jehoshaphat's accession is synchronized
with Omri's eleventh year [16:28a], whereas in the MT, it is synchronized with Ahab's
fourth year [22:41]); but most scholars have denied that the Old Greek chronology was
more accurate than that of the MT. I retained remnants of this Old Greek chronology in
my tentative chronology for the northern kings (see Barnes 1991:153-155, and especially
note "e" on pp. 154-155), but I will be the first to admit that certitude on this issue still
eludes us. Uncertainty notwithstanding, I still think that the LXX contains traces of earlier, and probably more accurate, traditions (chronological and otherwise) for both the

Omride kings and their immediate precursors (see, e.g., the notes on 16:15, 21, 23; also note Cogan's citation [2001:422] of Mazor's work on the primacy of the LXX both in Joshua and here in 1 Kings in reference to the curse on Jericho).

COMMENTARY

Omri's status in the ancient Near East was far more significant than these eight brief and largely formulaic verses in the Bible might indicate. For example, the Mesha Stele (commonly known as the Moabite Stone; see Cogan and Tadmor 1988:333-334 for a recent translation) forthrightly states that "Omri, king of Israel, oppressed Moab many years" (lines 4-5); and even the later Black Obelisk of Shalmaneser III (cf. Cogan and Tadmor 1988:335) refers to the tribute of Jehu, "son [descendant] of Omri" (cf. 2 Kgs 9:2, below). Cogan (2001:418-419) sees a "distinctly new turn in Israelite history" under Omri's reign with a probable alliance between Israel and Tyre (see also Barnes 2009:694); this led to profitable new markets for Israelite produce and Tyrian products (whether from the skilled artisans of Tyre and Sidon themselves, or imported wares from their trading partners throughout the entire eastern Mediterranean). The establishment of a new capital at Samaria, oriented to the western sea rather than the eastern wilderness (the situation at Tirzah, which may have been heavily damaged both by the suicidal actions of Zimri and the civil strife with Tibni), also proved propitious, as Sweeney (2007:204) points out:

> Omri's purchase of the hill of Samaria from Shemer, who is otherwise unknown, indicates an interest in establishing a capital for the Omride dynasty on much the same basis as Jerusalem—that is, Omri acquired Samaria as a personal possession, much as David acquired Jerusalem [a suggestion first made by Albrecht Alt]. Although Samaria was located in the territory of Manasseh, Omri would not be dependent on the northern tribes, giving him greater flexibility and power in ruling over the northern coalition.

Cogan (2001:419) notes further the nature of Omri's (and his son Ahab's) building project at Samaria: "The archaeological remains uncovered at Samaria attest to the impressive city constructed on the site; the design of the palace and its workmanship are evidence that Phoenician masons were employed in this project, just as they had been in Jerusalem in the days of Solomon. And considering that a good part of Omri's 'official' reign was spent in overcoming internal opposition, much of the work probably fell to Ahab."

Was Omri therefore a new David (cf. Leithart 2005:22-33), and Ahab a new Solomon? At least in one respect that would be the case: A foreign wife (Queen Jezebel from the Sidonian region [i.e., Tyre; cf. Wiseman 1993:162-163]) will again largely be the undoing of an Israelite or Judahite monarch. And note the corollaries to this observation: Both Solomon and Ahab would be denounced by Israelite prophets, yet with some concessions given in each case (cf. 11:34-39 and 21:27-29, respectively). Both Solomon's and Ahab's sons would be overthrown by usurpers who had been underlings, and who would, in turn, become significant kings in their own right (Jeroboam I and Jehu son of Nimshi [2 Kgs 9–10], respectively).

◆   ## 9. Ahab rules in Israel (16:29-34)

²⁹Ahab son of Omri began to rule over Israel in the thirty-eighth year of King Asa's reign in Judah. He reigned in Samaria twenty-two years. ³⁰But Ahab son of Omri did what was evil in the LORD's sight, even more than any of the kings before him. ³¹And as though it were not enough to follow the sinful example of Jeroboam, he married Jezebel, the daughter of King Ethbaal of the Sidonians, and he began to bow down in worship of Baal. ³²First Ahab built a temple and an altar for Baal in Samaria. ³³Then he set up an Asherah pole. He did more to provoke the anger of the LORD, the God of Israel, than any of the other kings of Israel before him.

³⁴It was during his reign that Hiel, a man from Bethel, rebuilt Jericho. When he laid its foundations, it cost him the life of his oldest son, Abiram. And when he completed it and set up its gates, it cost him the life of his youngest son, Segub.* This all happened according to the message from the LORD concerning Jericho spoken by Joshua son of Nun.

16:34 An ancient Hebrew scribal tradition reads *He killed his oldest son when he laid its foundations, and he killed his youngest son when he set up its gates.*

NOTES

16:29 *Ahab son of Omri.* He is the first Israelite king to be mentioned in a cuneiform inscription (the Kurkh Monolith). "Ahab the Israelite" is said to have contributed numerous chariots (2,000 if the text is accurate) and 10,000 foot soldiers to an anti-Assyrian coalition (see Cogan 2001:420, 506). The name Ahab (*'akh'ab* [TH256, ZH281]) may have been a non-Israelite name (cf. Omri his father; see the first note on 16:23); it may mean "My brother is Abba (the father-god)" (so Wiseman 1993:162), or else (if it is Israelite), "the brother of the father" (i.e., "resembling the father"; Gray 1970:367).

16:31 *Jezebel, the daughter of King Ethbaal of the Sidonians.* Jezebel, the soon-to-be-infamous queen, probably married early in Ahab's reign to cement political and economic ties between Israel and Phoenicia (cf. Wiseman 1993:163; see also the commentary on 16:21-28). The name Jezebel perhaps means "Zebul exists" where Zebul, "Prince," is an epithet for Baal (Cogan 2001:281, 420-421); but Appler (2008:313) prefers a reference to the Canaanite cultic chant, "where is the Prince?" (cf. Gray 1970:368). Ethbaal, the "Eithobalos" or "Ithobalos" of Josephus (see, at length, Barnes 1991:29-55), ruled 32 years in Tyre; his name probably means "Baal is alive" (Wiseman 1993:162-163; cf. Gray 1970:368), "Baal exists," or else, "Baal is with him" (HALOT 101-102). The term "Sidonians" probably at this time referred to the greater region of Tyre (i.e., the land of Phoenicia) as well as the port city of Sidon itself (Katzenstein 1997:130-136).

16:32 *a temple and an altar for Baal.* Blatant apostasy—here, the worship of other gods—is signified by this phrase. Cogan (2001:421) has pointed out that "Ahab's introduction of the cult of Baal in Samaria is hardly different from Solomon's installation of various high places in Jerusalem (cf. 11:7; both monarchs honored their wives by supporting the worship of their native gods." Nevertheless, Yahweh, the jealous God of Israel, would not allow this to continue for very long (see commentary on 12:25-33).

16:33 *an Asherah pole.* See note on 14:15. This particular Asherah symbol will apparently survive until after the reign of the reformer king, Jehu (cf. 2 Kgs 13:6).

He did more to provoke the anger of the LORD. This is the climax of an escalating refrain of harsh criticism (cf. 16:25, 30) unique to Omri and Ahab. With such severe censure, the mitigating refrain found later in 21:27-29 seems genuinely grace-filled ("Ahab . . . humbled himself before me. . . . I will not do what I promised during his lifetime. It will happen to his sons.").

16:34 *This all happened according to the message from the* LORD *concerning Jericho spoken by Joshua son of Nun.* Joshua placed a curse on anyone who would try to rebuild Jericho (Josh 6:26). The curse is fulfilled some 350 or more years later, at the cost of (A)hiel's oldest and youngest sons (concerning the name Hiel [MT] or Ahiel [cf. LXX], see Cogan 2001:421). Whether it's part of the curse of the *kherem* [TH2764, ZH3051] (see note on 9:21), or something particularly dangerous or distasteful about Jericho's particular location (later on, the prophet Elisha will have to heal its waters; see 2 Kgs 2:19-22), or a combination of both of these factors, the Kings editor reminds us that these sad events occurred during the already ill-starred reign of Ahab. In addition, this strong tie between the books of Joshua and Kings serves to strengthen the Deuteronomistic hypothesis that the editing of both books came from the same hand.

COMMENTARY

Once again, we find here mostly formulaic denunciations, but with even more "mustard" than in the past. Ahab is the worst king of all so far! Among other things, such statements prepare us for Elijah's harsh words of condemnation for both Ahab and Jezebel in the next chapters; and ironically, these words also prepare us to be shocked by the events of chapter 21, where Ahab's repentance brings about a startling delay of the inevitable disaster awaiting the dynasty and kingdom. (Cf. 21:27-29 with 2 Kgs 22:19-20, the only two places in 1-2 Kings containing the term "humble oneself," a Niphal of *kana'* [TH3665, ZH4044].) So, notwithstanding the present harsh, condemnatory passage, as well as the next several chapters of repeated, deserved prophetic denunciations, there is always hope, it would seem, for even the most wicked of leaders if they repent of their sins and change their ways. This seems to be the overall agenda of the editor(s) of 1-2 Kings. But for the present, it is only condemnation, severe condemnation, and, eventually, monstrously disastrous condemnation.

The concluding Jericho *inclusio* (cf. the first note on 3:15), found in the present passage (see note on 16:34; cf. Josh 6:26), serves effectively to prepare us for the prophetic chapters that lie ahead. For it is the *prophetic* role of Joshua son of Nun that is emphasized here—that is, a prophetic word coming from the "kinglike" Joshua, able military leader and mostly successful successor of Moses—who literally had the last word concerning the fate of Jericho. The firstfruits of the Israelite conquest, Jericho would be, as it were, the *last* city to be rebuilt in the land, and at a fearsome cost. As already discussed in the note on 16:34, the unfortunate actions of Hiel are probably meant to reflect negatively on the reign of Hiel's king, Ahab. While any king can repent and thus bring blessing to himself, his land, and perhaps to his future dynasty, no king can undo a truly prophetic word from God, whether it be from an unnamed "man of God" (cf. ch 13), or from the renowned leader Joshua. Perhaps the continuing conundrum of free will versus predestination has never been illustrated so clearly as in these parallel passages: God literally has the last word in history, but authentic repentance can remarkably change the future, at least to some extent (yet *not* rendering void any clear long-term prophecies from God). What a divine mystery this is! What a hope and what a warning to believers in any age!

♦   **C. Prophetic Stories from the Elijah Cycle (1 Kgs 17:1–19:21)**
     1. Elijah fed by ravens (17:1-7)

Now Elijah, who was from Tishbe in Gilead, told King Ahab, "As surely as the LORD, the God of Israel, lives—the God I serve—there will be no dew or rain during the next few years until I give the word!"

²Then the LORD said to Elijah, ³"Go to the east and hide by Kerith Brook, near where it enters the Jordan River. ⁴Drink from the brook and eat what the ravens bring you, for I have commanded them to bring you food."

⁵So Elijah did as the LORD told him and camped beside Kerith Brook, east of the Jordan. ⁶The ravens brought him bread and meat each morning and evening, and he drank from the brook. ⁷But after a while the brook dried up, for there was no rainfall anywhere in the land.

NOTES

17:1 *Elijah, who was from Tishbe in Gilead.* Traditionally translated "Elijah the Tishbite," thus understood as the name of the prophet followed by his gentilic (i.e., the name of his hometown or home region, often conveyed by the place-name followed by the suffix "-ite"). Cogan (2001:425) cites parallels with the names of other prophets such as Ahijah "the Shilonite" (11:29), as well as Elisha (19:16) and Jonah (2 Kgs 14:25). But in Elijah's case, there is no clear attestation of a town called "Tishbe" in the ancient sources (so Cogan 2001:425), and some have translated the following phrase in MT, *mittoshabe* [TH3427, ZH3782] *gil'ad*, as "from the settlers of Gilead," thereby indicating Elijah himself was perhaps a sojourner or immigrant in the land. In any case, the appellation "Elijah the Tishbite" is mentioned in the MT repeatedly throughout the Elijah and Elisha cycles (see 21:17, 28 [MT]; 2 Kgs 1:3, 8; 9:36). The name Elijah (*'eliyyahu* [TH452A, ZH489]) means "Yah(weh) is my God." This name will be particularly resonant in light of Elijah's bold assertion that "you, O [Yahweh], are God" in 18:36-37. Scholars have often speculated on this sudden introduction, even interruption, of the Ahab material by these Elijah narratives (see the commentary below for McKenzie's satisfying explanation for this otherwise unsettling phenomenon). In any case, the abrupt appearance of a true prophet of God will serve to eclipse any actions of any Israelite king (concerning the relative status of "king versus prophet," see the commentary on 1:5-27).

As surely as the LORD *. . . lives.* This is a classic oath formula. Cogan (2001:425) prefers translating this phrase as "by the life of Yahweh" (*yhwh* [TH3068, ZH3378]), with the deity understood as sanctioning the oath, thus asserting the truth of the words spoken, with punishment meted out for any falsehood given.

no dew or rain during the next few years. This is a classic short-term prediction (see notes on 13:2, 3). This threat was dire indeed, since rain (and dew) were crucial for Palestinian agricultural prosperity, in clear contrast to both the lands of Egypt and Mesopotamia, where great rivers were used to irrigate the land. In Palestine, the rains would generally fall during the wet winter season (early rains in late October, and the latter rains tapering off by March or April, but with much variation possible year by year); these rains were essential, especially for the cereal crops raised in this region of the Near East. The dew was crucial, too; it often falls heavily in Israel throughout the year, and it is also important for agricultural success, especially for the grapes, which ripen throughout the dry summer season (Baly 1974:44-46). Cogan (2001:426) cites Josephus's comment in *Antiquities* 8.13.3.324 that Elijah's threat corresponded to the yearlong drought mentioned by Menander of Ephesus, which took place during the reign of King Ethbaal of Tyre (i.e., Jezebel's father; see note on 16:31). For the particular theological threat that this drought would represent to the reputation of Baal the storm god, cf. the note on 17:12 and the commentary on 18:41-46. As Dillard (1999:18) points out, "There could be no clearer way to throw down the gauntlet to the worship of Baal."

17:3 *Kerith Brook.* This is of uncertain location, presumably "east" of the Jordan (so NLT), therefore probably in Elijah's home territory of Gilead (cf. Cogan 2001:426; contrast Wiseman [1993:165] who prefers a western location, noting that the Heb. *'al-pene* [TH5921/6440, ZH6584/7156] can simply mean "overlooking [the Jordan]"). In any case, an inaccessible location is clearly in view here.

17:4 *ravens.* Heb., *'orebim* [TH6158, ZH6854]; short-tailed, black birds (cf. Song 5:11) of prey. Several texts teach that God provides food even for the ravens and their young (Job 38:41; Ps 147:9; Luke 12:24) but here, instead of God feeding the ravens, the ravens were feeding God's servant. Some have suggested that one should slightly emend the pointing of the text to read *'arebim* [TH6163, ZH6861], "Arabs" or "merchants" or the like, but that would remove the essential element of the miraculous from the story (cf. Cogan 2001:426-427).

17:6 *bread and meat.* These are generous provisions; rarely would meat be eaten daily by the common people, still less, twice a day. The LXX reads "bread" (with no mention of meat) in the morning, and "meat" (with no mention of bread) in the evening, which is more typical of the Middle Eastern diet (Cogan 2001:427); this possibly represents a more original text (but note that it is parallel with Exod 16:8, as pointed out by Cogan). In any case, the emphasis here is on the abundant nature of God's provision for his servant.

17:7 *no rainfall.* As already noted (see third note on 17:1), this represents impending agricultural disaster for the already semiarid land of the Levant. Two years of drought would bring famine to the region and often the need to migrate away from the affected territory (Baly 1974:69-75). Elijah himself would soon be subject to this very same fate.

COMMENTARY

From the onset it should be noted that McKenzie (1991:81-100) argued effectively that 1 Kings 17:1–19:18 is a complex of stories about Elijah that have been "bound into a cycle"; he also concluded that they were inserted later into the preexisting Deuteronomistic work, in this case, the Deuteronomist's account of King Ahab (cf. 16:29-34). The stories themselves undoubtedly predate greatly their insertion into the Deuteronomistic work; but as they now stand, they interrupt the Deuteronomistic framework rather than being integrated into it. This is probably also true of much of chapters 20 and 22, 2 Kings 1, and the Elisha narratives that make up much of 2 Kings 2–8, plus 13:14-25). I would submit that many of the seemingly intrusive features of these remarkable stories in their present settings (which vary somewhat in the MT and LXX) should be seen in light of McKenzie's arguments.

In this present section (17:1-7) we see that God provided for his servant Elijah, the prophet, by means of ravens. It should be recalled that the ravens were considered unclean birds (Lev 11:15; Deut 14:14). Seow (1999:126-127) has nicely entitled the present section of 1 Kings as "Elijah is fed by ravens," and the beginning of the next section as "Elijah is fed by a Sidonian widow." What an effective comparison and contrast we find both here and in Jesus' later teachings: God will even provide for the common sparrows (Matt 10:29-31; cf. Matt 6:26), and, yes even the ravens and their young (Luke 12:24), as well as bring much beauty to the humble lilies of the field (Matt 6:28-30). How much more will he provide for his faithful human followers! We need to realize that God will provide a Kerith Brook in tough times, as well as meet our daily needs, both morning and evening. Our God is truly faithful.

◆   2. The widow of Zarephath (17:8-24)

8Then the LORD said to Elijah, 9"Go and live in the village of Zarephath, near the city of Sidon. I have instructed a widow there to feed you."

10So he went to Zarephath. As he arrived at the gates of the village, he saw a widow gathering sticks, and he asked her, "Would you please bring me a little water in a cup?" 11As she was going to get it, he called to her, "Bring me a bite of bread, too."

12But she said, "I swear by the LORD your God that I don't have a single piece of bread in the house. And I have only a handful of flour left in the jar and a little cooking oil in the bottom of the jug. I was just gathering a few sticks to cook this last meal, and then my son and I will die."

13But Elijah said to her, "Don't be afraid! Go ahead and do just what you've said, but make a little bread for me first. Then use what's left to prepare a meal for yourself and your son. 14For this is what the LORD, the God of Israel, says: There will always be flour and olive oil left in your containers until the time when the LORD sends rain and the crops grow again!"

15So she did as Elijah said, and she and Elijah and her family continued to eat for many days. 16There was always enough flour and olive oil left in the containers, just as the LORD had promised through Elijah.

17Some time later the woman's son became sick. He grew worse and worse, and finally he died. 18Then she said to Elijah, "O man of God, what have you done to me? Have you come here to point out my sins and kill my son?"

19But Elijah replied, "Give me your son." And he took the child's body from her arms, carried him up the stairs to the room where he was staying, and laid the body on his bed. 20Then Elijah cried out to the LORD, "O LORD my God, why have you brought tragedy to this widow who has opened her home to me, causing her son to die?"

21And he stretched himself out over the child three times and cried out to the LORD, "O LORD my God, please let this child's life return to him." 22The LORD heard Elijah's prayer, and the life of the child returned, and he revived! 23Then Elijah brought him down from the upper room and gave him to his mother. "Look!" he said. "Your son is alive!"

24Then the woman told Elijah, "Now I know for sure that you are a man of God, and that the LORD truly speaks through you."

NOTES

17:9 *the village of Zarephath, near the city of Sidon.* Zarephath lay on the Mediterranean seacoast 8 miles (13 km) south of Sidon. The irony of King Ahab's wife Jezebel, whose ancestry was "Sidonian" (see note on 16:31), coming to the land of Israel, over against Elijah the Israelite prophet being sent to the region of Sidon should not be missed (Wiseman 1993:165).

I have instructed a widow there to feed you. Whether it be wild ravens (17:1-7) or a foreign widow, God's methods of provision are often quite surprising. Sadly, in ancient (and still in contemporary) times, widows generally suffered disproportionate economic distress. Therefore, the Torah made special provisions for them (see Exod 22:22; Deut 10:18; 14:29;

24:17, 19, 21; 26:12-13). Cogan (2001:427) points out that widows often wore distinctive attire even long after the formal time for mourning had passed. They could easily be identified as such.

17:10-11 *a little water . . . a bite of bread.* These were modest requests (contrast the provisions of "bread and meat" twice a day in 17:6, MT) but still far beyond the widow's ability to supply. Those perhaps dismayed by Elijah's seeming selfishness here should be reminded that Yahweh had commanded Elijah to do this (17:9). Elijah, therefore, was to expect a miracle here (Cogan 2001:427, citing the medieval sage David Qimhi).

17:12 *I swear by the LORD your God.* This is a shorter version of the oath formula Elijah used in 17:1 (see note). If Jezebel (in chs 18–19) could force Israelites to worship the Phoenician god Baal Hadad ("Lord of the Storm"), the narrator here reminds us that Phoenicians could also acknowledge the power of Israel's God, Yahweh. After all, the worship of such a "storm god" as Baal Hadad had proven to be totally ineffective during this time of drought, even in Phoenicia!

a handful of flour . . . a little cooking oil. This was presumably enough only for one "cake"—hardly enough for two people, let alone three.

to cook this last meal. The NLT is a bit paraphrastic; the Hebrew simply reads "that I may go in and prepare it [the handful of flour] for myself and for my son." The widow's response in the final part of this verse is actually quite grim and to the point: "I will prepare it . . . and we will eat it and (then) we will die."

17:13 *Don't be afraid!* Elijah directly responded to her fatalism with this comforting command. Elijah, in turn, is so comforted in 2 Kgs 1:15, as is Elisha's anxious servant in 2 Kgs 6:16.

17:14 *flour and olive oil.* These are the identical commodities and containers mentioned back in 17:12 (cf. 17:16). Again, these represent modest but sufficient staples, until "the LORD sends rain and the crops grow again" (supposedly, the fundamental task of Baal in Phoenicia!).

17:17 *Some time later.* Elijah will apparently spend a considerable amount of time in this location, possibly a year or two (cf. 18:1).

17:18 *man of God.* See the note on 13:1 concerning this phrase as a synonym for "prophet" (cf. 17:24).

to point out my sins and kill my son? Interestingly, in the somewhat parallel story of Elisha and the Shunammite (see 2 Kgs 4:8-37), we find similar sentiments of anxiety and gloom (all the more ironic in the present story since Elijah and his God have already saved the son's life; 17:12-16). In a gentle and healing way, the present text touches on the issue of the woman's concern over her "sins" but then moves away—focusing in the rest of the story on the need for, and appropriateness of, the son's resurrection (cf. 17:20). Thus, we may conclude that the widow should not fixate on how her "sins" were necessarily the source of tragedy.

17:20 *why have you brought tragedy to this widow?* Lit., "Will you bring harm even to this widow . . . by killing her son?" The ancient Israelites attributed both blessing and tragedy directly to their God (see Deut 32:39; 1 Sam 2:6-7; and ironically in 2 Kgs 5:7). This raises the age-old question concerning the unfairness of life that we will explore at length in the commentary on 19:9b-18.

17:21 *stretched himself.* This is a unique form of the verb *madad* [TH4058, ZH4499], meaning "to measure, measure off." The exact procedure here is unclear, but it is probably akin to what Elisha does in 2 Kgs 4:34-35, bringing the Shunammite's son back to life by lying down on the child's body, "placing his mouth on the child's mouth, his eyes on the child's eyes, and his hands on the child's hands."

17:22 The LORD heard. The verb used in this phrase, *wayyishma'* [TH8085, ZH9048] *yhwh beqol* (Yahweh listened to the voice [of Elijah]) often means "to obey," when used of human subjects; hence Yahweh "hearkened unto" or, as it were, "obeyed" Elijah's plea for the child's resurrection.

17:23 upper room. The same term *'aliyyah* [TH5944, ZH6608] is used in 17:19 (NLT, "up the stairs to the room where he was staying"); here we find another parallel to the story about the Shunammite and Elisha in 2 Kgs 4, where Elisha stays in an *'aliyyah* (2 Kgs 4:10-11; cf. 2 Kgs 1:2; 23:12). Cogan (2001:429) translates the term *'aliyyah* in the present passage as "roof chamber"; Sweeney (2007:213) prefers "upper level," and he points out that many houses in ancient Israel and Phoenicia would have two levels; the lower one was used for the housing of livestock, as well as for storage and cooking, while the upper level would be used for the living and sleeping quarters. I have been told that one advantage of this living arrangement would be the warming of the upper level in winter by the cooking fires and the heat given off by the animals stabled below.

17:24 Now I know. As Cogan (2001:430) notes, "The gift of life aroused greater awe than the gift of food." Wiseman (1993:166) appropriately compares the testimony of another foreigner in Exod 18:11. I would, however, note the sobering contrast found in Matt 28:17 that some among the crowd of witnesses who saw the resurrected Christ still doubted the reality of his resurrection. Miracles are great sources of encouragement, but only to those who already have a predisposition to believe (cf. Luke 16:31).

COMMENTARY

As noted in the commentary on 17:1-7, Seow's apt characterization of the beginning of the present text (17:8-16) is "Elijah is fed by a Sidonian widow." But all too soon the tables are turned, and it will be Elijah and his God who will be the ones feeding the widow and her child. And as it so often does, personal tragedy strikes: The widow's son becomes sick and eventually dies (note the significant passage of time this represents). Elijah was still residing in his upper room or roof chamber (cf. 17:19, 23). The woman cried out to him in a guilty fashion (17:18), so he cried out in turn to his God, "Why have you brought tragedy to this widow who has opened her home to me?" Note that any mention of Baal, the patron deity of Phoenicia (and certainly of Jezebel, the Phoenician wife of King Ahab of Israel) is out of the question here: It is only Yahweh who "gives both death and life" (1 Sam 2:6)—even in the land of Baal.

One of the great mysteries of faith is that when tragedy strikes, God sometimes heals and sometimes seemingly does not. Texts such as the present one are not meant to give formulas or recipes on how to bring about healing (still less, resurrections!). But divine healings did and do occur; and from time to time there are, even today, resurrections. So it is here, and so it will be in the parallel Elisha story (2 Kgs 4). Here, a foreign widow, destitute, understandably reluctant to share her last meal with a prophet from Israel whom she has just met, is brought to genuine faith in Israel's God. She and her child were eventually fed for quite some time directly by that God; and so was Elijah, who brought blessings. Yahweh can and will bring the rain and the dew to bless the land in his own good timing, but now he brings food and (literally) renewed life to his chosen people (at least two of them) who happen to reside in a seaport village in the land of Phoenicia, far from Israel, and who have surely suffered already more than their share of life's heartaches. "Now I know for sure that you are a man of God, and that the LORD truly speaks through you," are the final words we hear from this unnamed widow (17:24).

What a testimony of faith, so appropriately recalled by Jesus (in Luke 4:25-26) to his hometown audience in the synagogue of Nazareth. Unfortunately, this hometown audience was provoked by the fact that Elijah was sent to a foreign widow in Zarephath, although there were surely many needy widows in Israel during his time. It was a reminder of how "hometown folk" may be bypassed by a sovereign God; and it was teaching that God would bring his kindness to Gentiles. Again in John 4 Jesus is pictured ministering to another "outsider," the Samaritan woman at Jacob's well. He brought life and hope to another ethnic group (the Samaritans) whom God's people at that time considered outside of the law and the covenant, and therefore to be despised and rejected. God's ways are not our ways, and God's ways of ministering are often unexpected. What a great God we serve!

◆ 3. The contest on Mount Carmel (18:1-40)

Later on, in the third year of the drought, the LORD said to Elijah, "Go and present yourself to King Ahab. Tell him that I will soon send rain!" [2]So Elijah went to appear before Ahab.

Meanwhile, the famine had become very severe in Samaria. [3]So Ahab summoned Obadiah, who was in charge of the palace. (Obadiah was a devoted follower of the LORD. [4]Once when Jezebel had tried to kill all the LORD's prophets, Obadiah had hidden 100 of them in two caves. He put fifty prophets in each cave and supplied them with food and water.) [5]Ahab said to Obadiah, "We must check every spring and valley in the land to see if we can find enough grass to save at least some of my horses and mules." [6]So they divided the land between them. Ahab went one way by himself, and Obadiah went another way by himself.

[7]As Obadiah was walking along, he suddenly saw Elijah coming toward him. Obadiah recognized him at once and bowed low to the ground before him. "Is it really you, my lord Elijah?" he asked.

[8]"Yes, it is," Elijah replied. "Now go and tell your master, 'Elijah is here!'"

[9]"Oh, sir," Obadiah protested, "what harm have I done to you that you are sending me to my death at the hands of Ahab? [10]For I swear by the LORD your God that the king has searched every nation and kingdom on earth from end to end to find you. And each time he was told, 'Elijah isn't here,' King Ahab forced the king of that nation to swear to the truth of his claim. [11]And now you say, 'Go and tell your master, "Elijah is here."' [12]But as soon as I leave you, the Spirit of the LORD will carry you away to who knows where. When Ahab comes and cannot find you, he will kill me. Yet I have been a true servant of the LORD all my life. [13]Has no one told you, my lord, about the time when Jezebel was trying to kill the LORD's prophets? I hid 100 of them in two caves and supplied them with food and water. [14]And now you say, 'Go and tell your master, "Elijah is here."' Sir, if I do that, Ahab will certainly kill me."

[15]But Elijah said, "I swear by the LORD Almighty, in whose presence I stand, that I will present myself to Ahab this very day."

[16]So Obadiah went to tell Ahab that Elijah had come, and Ahab went out to meet Elijah. [17]When Ahab saw him, he exclaimed, "So, is it really you, you troublemaker of Israel?"

[18]"I have made no trouble for Israel," Elijah replied. "You and your family are the troublemakers, for you have refused to obey the commands of the LORD and have

worshiped the images of Baal instead. ¹⁹Now summon all Israel to join me at Mount Carmel, along with the 450 prophets of Baal and the 400 prophets of Asherah who are supported by Jezebel.*"

²⁰So Ahab summoned all the people of Israel and the prophets to Mount Carmel. ²¹Then Elijah stood in front of them and said, "How much longer will you waver, hobbling between two opinions? If the LORD is God, follow him! But if Baal is God, then follow him!" But the people were completely silent.

²²Then Elijah said to them, "I am the only prophet of the LORD who is left, but Baal has 450 prophets. ²³Now bring two bulls. The prophets of Baal may choose whichever one they wish and cut it into pieces and lay it on the wood of their altar, but without setting fire to it. I will prepare the other bull and lay it on the wood on the altar, but not set fire to it. ²⁴Then call on the name of your god, and I will call on the name of the LORD. The god who answers by setting fire to the wood is the true God!" And all the people agreed.

²⁵Then Elijah said to the prophets of Baal, "You go first, for there are many of you. Choose one of the bulls, and prepare it and call on the name of your god. But do not set fire to the wood."

²⁶So they prepared one of the bulls and placed it on the altar. Then they called on the name of Baal from morning until noontime, shouting, "O Baal, answer us!" But there was no reply of any kind. Then they danced, hobbling around the altar they had made.

²⁷About noontime Elijah began mocking them. "You'll have to shout louder," he scoffed, "for surely he is a god! Perhaps he is daydreaming, or is relieving himself.* Or maybe he is away on a trip, or is asleep and needs to be wakened!"

²⁸So they shouted louder, and following their normal custom, they cut themselves with knives and swords until the blood gushed out. ²⁹They raved all afternoon until the time of the evening sacrifice, but still there was no sound, no reply, no response.

³⁰Then Elijah called to the people, "Come over here!" They all crowded around him as he repaired the altar of the LORD that had been torn down. ³¹He took twelve stones, one to represent each of the tribes of Israel,* ³²and he used the stones to rebuild the altar in the name of the LORD. Then he dug a trench around the altar large enough to hold about three gallons.* ³³He piled wood on the altar, cut the bull into pieces, and laid the pieces on the wood.*

Then he said, "Fill four large jars with water, and pour the water over the offering and the wood."

³⁴After they had done this, he said, "Do the same thing again!" And when they were finished, he said, "Now do it a third time!" So they did as he said, ³⁵and the water ran around the altar and even filled the trench.

³⁶At the usual time for offering the evening sacrifice, Elijah the prophet walked up to the altar and prayed, "O LORD, God of Abraham, Isaac, and Jacob,* prove today that you are God in Israel and that I am your servant. Prove that I have done all this at your command. ³⁷O LORD, answer me! Answer me so these people will know that you, O LORD, are God and that you have brought them back to yourself."

³⁸Immediately the fire of the LORD flashed down from heaven and burned up the young bull, the wood, the stones, and the dust. It even licked up all the water in the trench! ³⁹And when all the people saw it, they fell face down on the ground and cried out, "The LORD—he is God! Yes, the LORD is God!"

⁴⁰Then Elijah commanded, "Seize all the prophets of Baal. Don't let a single one escape!" So the people seized them all, and Elijah took them down to the Kishon Valley and killed them there.

18:19 Hebrew *who eat at Jezebel's table.* 18:27 Or *is busy somewhere else,* or *is engaged in business.*
18:31 Hebrew *each of the tribes of the sons of Jacob to whom the LORD had said, "Your name will be Israel."*
18:32 Hebrew *2 seahs* [12 liters] *of seed.* 18:33 Verse 18:34 in the Hebrew text begins here. 18:36 Hebrew *and Israel.* The names "Jacob" and "Israel" are often interchanged throughout the Old Testament, referring sometimes to the individual patriarch and sometimes to the nation.

NOTES

18:1 *Later on, in the third year of the drought.* There are interesting contrasts in the various chronological notices found throughout this chapter. This particular notice is nothing short of disastrous (see notes on 17:1 and 17:7); having to endure a drought lasting into the third year in Palestine would have been absolutely devastating.

Go and present yourself to King Ahab. Finally, it was time to meet the king and to see who would win this battle (cf. Elijah's comments to Ahab in 17:1).

18:3 *Obadiah, who was in charge of the palace.* Lit., "Obadiah who was over the house" ('al-habbayith [TH5921/1004, ZH6584/1074]); he was certainly a high royal official, possibly the prime minister or the like (see the first note on 4:6). This Obadiah (whose name probably means "worshiper of Yahweh") is not to be confused with the later minor prophet of the same name who prophesied mainly against Edom. Sweeney (2007:224) suggests that the prophetic figure may have been named after this ninth-century northern court official. In the Talmud (b. *Sanhedrin* 39b), the two individuals are indeed considered to be one and the same, and probably to be identified as a proselyte from Edom.

a devoted follower of the LORD. Lit., "one who greatly feared Yahweh." Even in pagan palaces, God will often have high officials who show respect to him, such as Mordecai in the book of Esther (palace gatekeeper, Esth 2:21), Nehemiah in the book that bears his name (cupbearer to the king, Neh 1:11), and Daniel, eventually under Darius the Mede (see Dan 6:3). Paul also knew believers who were strategically placed within Caesar's palace (cf. Phil 1:12-14).

18:4 *He put fifty prophets in each cave and supplied them with food and water.* This goes against the expressed wishes of Queen Jezebel earlier in the verse, but was presumably done with the tacit approval, or at least passive toleration, of King Ahab. The total number of 100 prophets of Yahweh certainly brings Elijah's later protestations of standing alone against all the Baal prophets (in 18:22) into question; perhaps the idea there is that he was the only Yahwistic prophet who was brave enough to stand publicly against the Baalists. That would be a very sad situation in Yahweh's own land. (On the implied comparison between Obadiah feeding these prophets and the widow of Zarephath feeding Elijah in 17:8-16, see Seow 1999:132 and the commentary below.)

18:5 *see if we can find enough grass.* This is at once both pathetic in effect, and oddly endearing. Ahab, caught between his assertive queen and his ancestral God, was doing what he could to assist the man who was perhaps his best friend, his trusted official, Obadiah. Still, Wiseman's contrast (1993:167) between Ahab's and David's response to famine is telling: Ahab foraged for fodder for his military forces, while David sought the Lord and tried to make amends for the sins of the house of Saul (see 2 Sam 21:1-14). It should be recalled, however, that Ahab himself did later repent, tearing his clothing in dismay, wearing sackcloth, fasting, and going about in deep mourning (1 Kgs 21:27-29).

18:6 *one way . . . another way by himself.* It is, ironically, the result of the king's prompting that Obadiah was able to meet Elijah alone.

18:7-8 *my lord . . . your master.* Heb., 'adoni [TH113, ZH123] and 'adoneka, "my lord," and "your lord(s)," respectively—the second word is probably an "intensive plural of rank" (BDB 11b).

18:9 *sending me to my death.* This is ironically parallel to the conundrum the Phoenician widow faced in 17:18. When a prophet of God shows up, the situation often escalates to life-or-death levels (see commentary below). Note that Obadiah says in his speech three times that Ahab will kill him (18:9, 12, 14).

18:12 *Spirit of the LORD.* Heb., *ruakh yhwh.* The term *ruakh* [TH7307, ZH8120] can mean "breath," "wind," or "spirit"; Elijah has come and gone as if the very wind had carried him about (for a NT paralleling of "wind" with "spirit," see John 3:5-8).

18:15 *I swear by the LORD Almighty, in whose presence I stand.* See the note on 17:1 concerning the oath formula "by the life of Yahweh." Prophets were characterized as "standing" in Yahweh's presence (cf. Jer 23:18-24, where twice [vv. 18, 22; cf. KJV] Yahweh asks rhetorically if the false prophets had ever "stood" in his presence).

18:16 *So Obadiah went to tell Ahab that Elijah had come.* The last reference we have to this anxious God-fearer is a positive one: Obadiah does what Elijah asked him to do in 18:8.

18:17 *you troublemaker of Israel.* This is perhaps a phrase better reserved for Queen Jezebel, or for that matter Ahab himself, as Elijah points out explicitly in the very next verse. The verb *'akar* [TH5916, ZH6579], used twice in these two verses, means "to entangle, put into disorder, bring into disaster or ruin" (HALOT 824).

18:19 *Mount Carmel.* This is the stunning mountain overlooking the Mediterranean Sea just south of the present city of Haifa, Israel. Cogan (2001:439) suggests that this was the border of Israel and Tyre in Elijah's day, since Solomon ceded the Cabul territory to the north to Hiram more than a half century earlier (9:10-14).

18:21 *How much longer will you waver, hobbling between two opinions?* This is not a conscious reference back to Obadiah, but not entirely incidental to him either. The Hebrew idiom here is akin to our English expression "sitting on the fence." Obadiah had finally come down publicly on Elijah's side in 18:16, but the people here would still remain publicly uncommitted until after the fire fell from heaven (18:39).

18:22 *the only prophet of the LORD who is left.* We already know that this is not literally the situation (see note on 18:4), although Elijah must surely have felt very much like it was an accurate summary of the case, both here and in 19:10, 14.

18:24 *The god who answers by setting fire.* Elijah shrewdly dictated the terms of the contest and seemingly gave the Baalists every advantage—Baal was often depicted as brandishing a club of thunder in one hand and a spear of lightning in the other (Toorn 2006:367; Dillard 1999:44-45).

18:26 *from morning until noontime.* That is, for half the day (in ancient times, the day in essence ended at sundown).

they danced, hobbling around the altar. Here the narrator uses a stronger (Piel) form of the verb "to limp, limp about" (*pasakh* [TH6452A, ZH7174]), whose simple form (Qal) is found in 18:21. Koehler and Baumgartner (HALOT 947) translate the Piel here as "to limp about in a cultic ceremony, perform a hobbling dance." Curiously, the Hebrew term for the Passover holiday (*pesakh* [TH6453, ZH7175]) apparently is derived from this same verbal root: Yahweh "limped or skipped over" the Hebrew homes where the blood of the Passover lamb or young goat was applied to the door lintels, so as not to kill the firstborn within (Exod 12:13, 23; cf. Cogan 2001:440).

18:27 *is relieving himself.* This is part of Elijah's mocking taunts to the Baal prophets; the rare term *sig* [TH7873, ZH8485; cf. TH5472, ZH6047] may here mean "to go to the side," either in the sense of wandering away or on business (cf. NLT mg), or indeed as the NLT text intimates, "defecating" (see HALOT 1319).

18:29 *They raved all afternoon.* Extreme, frantic behavior ensued—the prophets trying to arouse a deity's pity or attention in any way possible. Wiseman (1993:169) cites a Ugaritic text where people "bathed in their own blood like an ecstatic prophet." The verb translated "to rave" is the denominative verb *hitnabbe'* [TH5012, ZH5547] from the noun "prophet" (*nabi'* [TH5030, ZH5566]; cf. the first note on 13:11).

18:31 *twelve stones, one to represent each of the tribes of Israel.* The MT is more verbose: "twelve stones, according to the number of the tribes of the sons of Jacob, to whom Yahweh's word came: 'You will be named Israel.'" As the NLT mg indicates, this is a reference to the entirety of Israel and Judah as making up the people of God (see "Audience" in the Introduction).

18:32 *large enough to hold about three gallons.* The Hebrew here is difficult; it seems to read "as a house [= receptacle?] of 2 seahs of seed," which might refer to how much land one would sow with 2 seahs of seed (cf. HALOT 124), or else how much space 2 seahs of seed require. A "seah" would perhaps represent about 1½ gallons (6 or 7 L) of dry measure (cf. Cogan and Tadmor 1988:81, who prefer 7.3 L), but Powell (ABD 6.904-905) argues for nearly doubling that size, understanding the "seah" here as representing a postexilic measure. Considering that jars of water were poured into the trench, this last option seems the most probable.

18:33 *four large jars with water.* This was done presumably to increase the magnitude of the miracle (Cogan 2001:443, citing Qimhi). Finding so much water in the third year of a severe drought in order to douse the altar three times is admittedly problematic (leading some commentators to suggest the conflation of separate traditions here; cf. DeVries 1985:226-227); one possible harmonistic solution is using seawater, since Mount Carmel overlooks the Bay of Haifa and the Mediterranean Sea. Older suggestions by skeptical commentators that Elijah used naphtha or some other flammable liquid instead of water (and then waited for a lightning strike or the like!), are rendered implausible by the obvious curiosity of the crowd (cf. Elijah's invitation in 18:30 to "come over here"), as well as the close attention and evident hostility of the Baalists.

18:36 *offering the evening sacrifice.* Heb., *hamminkhah* [TH4503, ZH4966] (the meal offering), already mentioned in 18:29. This offering would be given in the early morning and again in the evening (see Exod 29:38-41; cf. Ezra 9:4-5, where this term is also used as a time indicator).

18:37 *these people will know that you, O LORD, are God and that you have brought them back to yourself.* As already pointed out (see the first note on 17:1), the actual meaning of Elijah's name is evoked in the first part of this citation. But the second half of the citation is less straightforward; the Hebrew seems to read, "and that you have turned their heart backward (= away?)" (cf. Cogan [2001:443], who cites Isa 63:17 as support for Yahweh being the cause of the sinful ways of humanity). A high view of the sovereignty of Yahweh (even in causing the people to forsake Yahweh) may well be in view here.

18:38 *Immediately.* Not explicitly stated as such in the Hebrew, but surely implied in the larger context of the verse. Up to now, there have been repeated, embarrassing delays in the alleged "response time" of the god Baal.

18:39 *The LORD—he is God!* Again, as noted in 18:37, this phrase echoes closely the etymological meaning of the name Elijah.

18:40 *Don't let a single one escape!* Presumably Elijah and his "converts" were more thorough than Jezebel was able to be (cf. 18:4).

Kishon Valley. This is the Wadi el-Muqatta, which flows northwest out of the Jezreel valley, reaching the Mediterranean on the north side of Mount Carmel; it was the site of Sisera's defeat back in the days of Deborah the judge (Judg 4:7, 13; 5:21). Cogan (2001:444) quotes the medieval Jewish philosopher Gersonides as suggesting the site was chosen "so that their blood would not pollute the land; and on this account, it was spilled into the wadi that would carry it far off."

killed. Heb., *shakhat* [TH7819, ZH8821], meaning "to slaughter"; it is used some 51 times as a technical term for the slaughter of a sacrifice on the altar. Hence, the demise of the Baal prophets may well have been understood in such terms. Concerning the justice of this, see the commentary below.

COMMENTARY

This is surely one of the most famous episodes in Elijah's life; it is the event when he called down fire from heaven to consume a sacrifice and converted a skeptical audience. The story continues on into the rest of the chapter, and, in essence, into the entirety of chapter 19, as well. The essence of Elijah's challenge to his audience is this: "Choose today whom you will serve—whether Yahweh or Baal" (cf. the aged Joshua's challenge to his own audience in Josh 24:15). By placing this story just after the story of a Phoenician widow "choosing" to serve Yahweh (or, at least, to be served by Yahweh and by Yahweh's emissary, Elijah), the editor has made his choice clear: There is only one living God anywhere in the Levant, let alone Israel, and his name is Yahweh (cf. 18:37 and 18:39 of the present passage, as well as the meaning of the name Elijah, as discussed in the first note on 17:1). Back then, such theological choices were often literally life-or-death decisions, as Elijah brought into effect in 18:40: "Seize all the prophets of Baal. Don't let a single one escape!" It is a sad bit of poetic justice that, when the rains finally fall (18:45-46), Jezebel will issue the very same command concerning Elijah himself: "By the gods, may they kill me, if, by this time tomorrow I have not done the same thing to you that you have done to them" (19:2, paraphrased). "Live by the sword, die by the sword"—such could very possibly be the fate Elijah had been led to bring about in the present passage, and such is the fate threatened for him, too. But that message belongs to chapter 19—let us not detract from Elijah's remarkable triumph, which is the major feature of the present chapter. This was the first time, but certainly not the last time (see 2 Kgs 1), that Elijah was able to call fire down from heaven to vindicate his God, as well as his own reputation as God's true prophet.

Today there is a movement in the church known as "power ministry"; its proponents believe in powerful acts of God performed through miracles. These miracles can sway people's opinions about the reality of God. Similarly, in the present passage, opinions about God swayed back and forth (18:21a), even if they were left unexpressed (18:21b; cf. Amos 5:13). But true faith doesn't always come from being dazzled. Real faith often grows, paradoxically, during times of persecution (cf. the two groups of 50 prophets that Obadiah had been sheltering; 18:4). Times of overwhelming triumph may (as here) prompt renewed persecution on the part of God's now embarrassed enemies, and may lead to increasingly uncomfortable visibility for God's human leadership (as in much of ch 19). Still, there is something particularly satisfying when God, to use the vernacular, "kicks some butt"—that is, when he demonstrates his eternal power in a very temporal way! Calling down fire from heaven, and "immediately" (18:38) seeing the results—now that is what I would call power ministry!

But there are other kinds of ministry. Obadiah seems to have exercised a kind of "covert ministry" as he, a highly placed royal official in Ahab's court, was also one who feared Yahweh (see note on 18:3; cf. also Hens-Piazza [2006:173-174], who points out, "Before the king, Obadiah lives up to his job description and his duty. Before the Lord, Obadiah lives up to his name"). Talk about being between a rock and a hard place! Seow (1999:137-138) has a wonderful word on the subject: "Here we find a story of a high government official furtively subverting a quasi-state-sponsored pogrom and paying homage to the most wanted dissident in the country." He goes on to point out:

> In Obadiah we have someone with whom most people in the community of faith might identify much more readily than with Ahab or even the people of Israel assembled on Mt. Carmel. Obadiah is a believer, a fearer of God. . . . Obadiah, however, has other allegiances and fears, as well: He has his boss to serve, his career to protect, his own life to preserve. He is one with whom we readily sympathize, and we wonder whether the narrator has been a tad too harsh in comparing him implicitly with the Sidonian widow, a woman outside the community of faith. The text warns us, however, of the dangers of the insidious or the seemingly excusable compromises, as well as the blatant ones. Herein lies the threat to faith for most of us. (Seow 1999:137-138)

So when we preach this great story, and what a great story it is, let us not forget about the highly placed palace administrator Obadiah. We may not be an Elijah, nor an Ahab, and God forbid we ever be a Jezebel, but how often are we an Obadiah—brave at times, but also timid as well, especially when confronted suddenly and unexpectedly by a radical man of faith? Will we respond with courage? Hopefully we will. In any event, it is sad to reflect on the fact that we never hear any further word about Obadiah after 18:16. Was he fired? Executed? Imprisoned? Or did he undertake further great things for God? Was the later, canonical prophet indeed named for him? Someday, when we are in a better place than this world, we may find out the rest of the story.

◆ 4. Elijah prays for rain (18:41-46)

⁴¹Then Elijah said to Ahab, "Go get something to eat and drink, for I hear a mighty rainstorm coming!"

⁴²So Ahab went to eat and drink. But Elijah climbed to the top of Mount Carmel and bowed low to the ground and prayed with his face between his knees.

⁴³Then he said to his servant, "Go and look out toward the sea."

The servant went and looked, then returned to Elijah and said, "I didn't see anything."

Seven times Elijah told him to go and look. ⁴⁴Finally the seventh time, his servant told him, "I saw a little cloud about the size of a man's hand rising from the sea."

Then Elijah shouted, "Hurry to Ahab and tell him, 'Climb into your chariot and go back home. If you don't hurry, the rain will stop you!' "

⁴⁵And soon the sky was black with clouds. A heavy wind brought a terrific rainstorm, and Ahab left quickly for Jezreel. ⁴⁶Then the LORD gave special strength to Elijah. He tucked his cloak into his belt* and ran ahead of Ahab's chariot all the way to the entrance of Jezreel.

18:46 Hebrew *He bound up his loins.*

NOTES

18:41 *get something to eat and drink.* It was now time for Ahab to rejoice (Sweeney 2007:229), or at least return to business as usual (Cogan 2001:444). Elijah himself, however, still had some work to do (cf. 18:42).

18:42 *bowed low . . . and prayed.* Cogan and Tadmor (1988:58), commenting on the use of the rare verb *gahar* [TH1457, ZH1566] in 2 Kgs 4:34-35 (where it is used twice to describe Elisha's physical posture when he is praying for the Shunammite's dead child), suggest the translation "to crouch." Both there and here Elijah is praying "with his face between his knees"; what is being depicted is deep meditative concentration.

18:43 *his servant.* Only in this passage and in 19:3 is there any mention of a servant for this generally solitary prophet.

Seven times. Persistence is sometimes the key!

18:44 *a little cloud . . . rising from the sea.* The rains often come from the west, off the Mediterranean Sea (see Beitzel 1985:52-53).

18:45 *black with clouds.* Once the storm arrived, it proved fierce indeed. Sweeney (2007:230) compares this storm to the earlier, providentially timed cloudburst during the days of Deborah, which also turned the Kishon into a muddy torrent, that time greatly impeding the chariots of Sisera (Judg 5:21). This is why it was so important that Ahab climb into his chariot and race home to Jezreel before the heavy rain arrived.

18:46 *special strength.* Elijah, however, did not need any chariot to make the journey to Jezreel—or to pass Ahab's chariot. The Hebrew literally says "the hand of Yahweh" was upon him (cf. 2 Kgs 3:15); the idiom connotes divine power invigorating the prophet, giving him strength to run the roughly 17 miles (27 km) to Ahab's estate at Jezreel.

Jezreel. This was probably the winter home of the king. Samaria, in the hills, would have been quite cold and, given enough precipitation, even snowy during that time of year. Jezreel, however, would have remained relatively warm even during the winter rainy season. It is now identified with the modern village of Zerin, some 9 miles (15 km) due east of Megiddo, overlooking the valley of Jezreel (whence its name; cf. Cogan 2001:477).

COMMENTARY

Fire from heaven was all well and good, but the persistent problem was the lack of rain. Yahweh was originally described as a desert God. Moses first encountered him in the land of Midian, a wilderness region (see Exod 3:1-6); and the famous image of Yahweh numbering the stars (Isa 40:26) is best understood as depicting the clear nighttime sky found in the desert. This "desert God" could certainly be expected to bring about fire and drought, but it was cloud and moisture that were needed desperately at this time in Israel (as well as in Baal's home turf of Phoenicia; cf. 17:8-24). Baal Hadad was the rain and fertility god of Phoenicia, and the fact that he could not bring life-giving moisture either to Israel or to Phoenicia was of little help to those who were waiting for any deity to do anything to bless the land. Earlier, the fire came down from heaven "immediately" (18:38), but this time the rain would not come until Elijah's servant was asked to go and look seven times, seemingly in vain. Of course, Yahweh could cause rain to fall immediately (cf. 1 Sam 12:16-18, where Samuel the prophet presumably prayed only once for "thunder and rain" to be heard and felt by the people during what was normally the dry harvest season). But our God works in his own ways, sometimes responding to prayer immediately, sometimes requiring persistent faith for his sovereign will to be effected. It is commonplace to point out that these great, faith-building stories are not meant to be recipes for how to bring about God's miracles of healing and prosperity, but such a point should still be stressed here: Sometimes God heals, sometimes he does not; sometimes God makes prosperous, sometimes he does not. Sometimes, a simple prayer of faith is all it takes; sometimes, seven steps of faith. But, sure enough, if it is God's will, a "terrific rainstorm" (18:45) will break the extended drought, and God's showers of blessing will fall on the just and the unjust alike (cf. Jesus' comments in Matt 5:45).

The Jezebels of the world will probably only renew their persecution (see 19:1-2), but the Elijahs of the church may still respond with supernatural strength (cf. 18:46), as Elijah ran roughly 17 miles before the king's chariot. Times are rarely boring for the person of faith—alternately facing times of triumph and times of trial, but rarely times of tedium! Elijah's time of testing will continue again (see 19:1-18), but for now let us celebrate his tremendous triumphs in the present chapter of his life—once and for all putting an end to any doubts about who is truly God in Israel, and finally bringing to an end that debilitating three-year drought which had ravaged the land. Our God is a powerful God, and his servants can certainly accomplish mighty exploits in his name.

◆   ## 5. Elijah flees to Sinai (19:1-9a)

When Ahab got home, he told Jezebel everything Elijah had done, including the way he had killed all the prophets of Baal. ²So Jezebel sent this message to Elijah: "May the gods strike me and even kill me if by this time tomorrow I have not killed you just as you killed them."

³Elijah was afraid and fled for his life. He went to Beersheba, a town in Judah, and he left his servant there. ⁴Then he went on alone into the wilderness, traveling all day. He sat down under a solitary broom tree and prayed that he might die. "I have had enough, LORD," he said. "Take my life, for I am no better than my ancestors who have already died."

⁵Then he lay down and slept under the broom tree. But as he was sleeping, an angel touched him and told him, "Get up and eat!" ⁶He looked around and there beside his head was some bread baked on hot stones and a jar of water! So he ate and drank and lay down again.

⁷Then the angel of the LORD came again and touched him and said, "Get up and eat some more, or the journey ahead will be too much for you."

⁸So he got up and ate and drank, and the food gave him enough strength to travel forty days and forty nights to Mount Sinai,* the mountain of God. ⁹There he came to a cave, where he spent the night.

19:8 Hebrew *to Horeb*, another name for Sinai.

NOTES

19:1 *the way he had killed all the prophets of Baal.* This is the most extreme of Elijah's actions in the previous chapter, and the one that would surely spur Jezebel to take action.

19:2 *So Jezebel sent this message.* This is a reciprocal threat, made even more evident by the LXX's opening phrase for the message, "as you are Elijah, so I am Jezebel," which does not appear in the MT but may well have been original (cf. Cogan 2001:450). Jezebel's threat is underscored by a typical oath formula, "may the gods strike me" (see note on 2:23; cf. 20:10; 2 Kgs 6:31).

19:3 Elijah was afraid. This reading follows LXX, Syriac, and Vulgate; the MT reads "Elijah saw" (a very slight change in vocalization of the Hebrew).

Beersheba. This is the famous patriarchal town (Gen 21:31), located 25 miles (40 km) southwest of Hebron. Beersheba was proverbially the southernmost city of the kingdom of Solomon (see note on 4:25).

left his servant there. See the first note on 18:43; Elijah's servant is mentioned only twice in the Elijah/Elisha cycles. Seemingly Elijah preferred to work alone.

19:4 a solitary broom tree. As Jones (1984:329-330) notes, the "broom tree" (*rothem* [TH7574, ZH8413]) is well-known in the Sinai, Petra (southern Jordan), and Dead Sea areas; it is a shrub that can grow to a height of over 3 meters (10 ft). Sweeney (2007:231) notes affinities between this text and Jonah 4, where the disaffected prophet there sits under a *qiqayon* [TH7021, ZH7813] plant and likewise expresses his desire to die (cf. Moses's strong words in Num 11:15).

no better than my ancestors. Elijah saw himself as not having any unique relationship with God, but just as any other mortal. But it is not for any man to decide when he should die. Wiseman (1993:172) says, "To ask God to *take my life* will always get a sure reply. But God will take his servant to himself in his own time and manner (2 Kg. 2:11)." Hens-Piazza (2006:187) points out that "Elijah wants to die but he does not want to be killed."

19:5 an angel touched him. The "angel" (*mal'ak* [TH4397, ZH4855]) is mentioned here and also in 19:7. The MT has the same term for "a messenger [from Jezebel]" in 19:2. God knows when to answer laments and when not to—sometimes, all we need is a good nap and some food.

19:6 bread. Heb., *'ugah* [TH5692, ZH6314], also found in 17:13, where the Zarephath widow is asked to make the same thing. There are a number of other parallels between the present text and God's supernatural provisions for Elijah in ch 17, whether it be by the ravens or by the Phoenician widow.

19:8 forty days and forty nights. Commentators have often noted the parallels between Elijah and Moses, and here is one of the most vivid ones (cf. Exod 24:18; 34:28). For more on this, see the commentary on 19:9b-18.

Mount Sinai. Lit., "Horeb" (so NLT mg). "Horeb" is a standard variant for designating Mount Sinai in the Pentateuch (see Exod 3:1; 33:6; Deut 1:2; 4:10; cf. Sweeney 2007:231).

COMMENTARY

Elijah's story rolls on from one scene to the next. We have had the public ecstasy, now we get the private agony. Seemingly, whenever individuals undertake great things for God, they can expect renewed opposition, often quite vicious in nature. So it is here in the narrative of Elijah. Elijah hardly expected Queen Jezebel to respond passively to his taunts in the previous chapter, still less to his commissioning the execution of her prophets! But her quick and decisive response surely unnerved the man of God. "The best defense is a good offense" is a maxim Jezebel seemingly understood well. She was evidently a devout, religious woman, and such effrontery to her god, Baal, simply could not be tolerated. Religion is a very dangerous thing—if it does not make a person very much better, it will make that person very much worse (cf. C. S. Lewis, writing to his friend and former student Dom Bede Griffiths, dated December 20, 1961 [Lewis 1966:301]).

Jezebel was determined to kill Elijah. This so depressed Elijah that he wanted to die. What a change of emotions—from the elation of victory in the previous chapter to the depression of defeat in the next. But this chapter (ch 19) can be very instructive to the many would-be Elijahs in the world who have just had (literal or metaphoric) mountaintop experiences, but then are, as it were, quickly and cruelly blindsided by the enemy. We all have been there, I suspect. Fortunately, God took care of Elijah's depression by speaking to Elijah and encouraging his downcast spirit (see next section).

◆ 6. The LORD speaks to Elijah (19:9b-18)

But the LORD said to him, "What are you doing here, Elijah?"

¹⁰Elijah replied, "I have zealously served the LORD God Almighty. But the people of Israel have broken their covenant with you, torn down your altars, and killed every one of your prophets. I am the only one left, and now they are trying to kill me, too."

¹¹"Go out and stand before me on the mountain," the LORD told him. And as Elijah stood there, the LORD passed by, and a mighty windstorm hit the mountain. It was such a terrible blast that the rocks were torn loose, but the LORD was not in the wind. After the wind there was an earthquake, but the LORD was not in the earthquake. ¹²And after the earthquake there was a fire, but the LORD was not in the fire. And after the fire there was the sound of a gentle whisper. ¹³When Elijah heard it, he wrapped his face in his cloak and went out and stood at the entrance of the cave.

And a voice said, "What are you doing here, Elijah?"

¹⁴He replied again, "I have zealously served the LORD God Almighty. But the people of Israel have broken their covenant with you, torn down your altars, and killed every one of your prophets. I am the only one left, and now they are trying to kill me, too."

¹⁵Then the LORD told him, "Go back the same way you came, and travel to the wilderness of Damascus. When you arrive there, anoint Hazael to be king of Aram. ¹⁶Then anoint Jehu grandson of Nimshi* to be king of Israel, and anoint Elisha son of Shaphat from the town of Abel-meholah to replace you as my prophet. ¹⁷Anyone who escapes from Hazael will be killed by Jehu, and those who escape Jehu will be killed by Elisha! ¹⁸Yet I will preserve 7,000 others in Israel who have never bowed down to Baal or kissed him!"

19:16 Hebrew *descendant of Nimshi;* compare 2 Kgs 9:2, 14.

NOTES

19:9, 13 *What are you doing here, Elijah?* Elijah was asked the same question twice, and he responded with the same answer each time (see next note).

19:10, 14 *I have zealously served the LORD God Almighty.* This is the grand *inclusio* (or narrative repetition; see the first note on 3:15) of the passage.

19:11-12 *a mighty windstorm . . . an earthquake . . . a fire.* These are paradoxical "non-theophanies." Presumably the comparison and the contrast are to Yahweh's theophany with Moses in Exod 32–34 (particularly Exod 33:22-23).

19:12 *the sound of a gentle whisper.* This is a difficult phrase to translate; the Hebrew reads, "the voice/sound of a crushed/thin/fine silence/whisper" (*qol demamah daqqah* [TH1827/1851, ^{ZH}1960/1987]). Cross (1973:194) translates this as "a thin whisper of sound." Certainly, a remarkable contrast with the more typical theophanic sound-and-light shows mentioned previously ("windstorm . . . earthquake . . . fire") is meant to be felt.

19:15 Go back the same way you came. In other words, it was time to get back to work (see the commentary below). The servant of God is not to worry about the Jezebels on life's journey.

19:15-16 anoint Hazael . . . anoint Jehu . . . anoint Elisha. Of the three assignments, Elijah did only one—he appointed Elisha (see 19:19-21, but with no actual anointing taking place). Elisha will be the one to designate Hazael as future king of Aram (see 2 Kgs 8:7-15, where once again no actual anointing is described), and Elisha's servant will be the one to anoint Jehu as future king of Israel (see 2 Kgs 9:1-10).

19:16 Elisha son of Shaphat from the town of Abel-meholah. This is a formal introduction providing both Elisha's patronymic and place of origin. The name Elisha probably means "God (El) saves, delivers" (Cogan 2001:454); the name Shaphat means "(Yahweh) has obtained justice." Abel-meholah is located in the Jordan River valley south of Beth-shan (cf. 4:12).

19:18 7,000 others. Finally, Elijah's repeated statement, "I am the only one left," is directly countered. What a rebuke for Elijah, even though it is treated only as an afterthought. God does not desire to make a grand display of our inaccurate understandings of reality, but he will not altogether allow them to stand uncorrected, either.

COMMENTARY

Was Elijah a second Moses? Commentators are not reluctant to make such a comparison, especially in their discussions of the present passage of 1 Kings. Both Elijah and Moses were considered, of course, prophets par excellence, and both were singled out, for example, by the prophet Malachi at the end of the Minor Prophets scroll as particularly relevant in the last days (see Mal 4:4-6). But the similarities between Moses and Elijah in the present chapter of Kings are particularly impressive (cf. Cogan 2001:456-457; also Dillard 1999:54-55):

1. Both Moses and Elijah escaped into the wilderness, fleeing from non-Israelite rulers who were actively seeking their death, after each had brought about the death of subordinate(s) of that ruler (see 18:40; 19:1-8; Exod 2:11-15).
2. Both Moses and Elijah at one point expressed their wish to die (see the first note on 19:4 for details).
3. For both of these "prophets," significant references are given to a period of "forty days and forty nights" (19:8; Exod 24:18; 34:28).
4. Moses took no food or water during his second stay on Mount Sinai (Exod 34:28); Elijah made his long trek to the mountain sustained only by the food he had eaten in the wilderness near Beersheba (19:8).
5. Elijah came to a cave on Mount Sinai (19:9), and was told to "stand before" Yahweh on the mountain as the deity "passed by" (19:11), just as Moses had stood "in the crevice of the rock" until Yahweh had "passed by" (Exod 33:22).
6. As Yahweh passed by, Elijah wrapped his face in his cloak (19:13); Moses was covered by Yahweh's hand, and thus protected while Yahweh passed by (Exod 33:22).

7. The fire and thunder of Yahweh at Sinai (Exod 19:18; cf. Exod 3:2) were reenacted for Elijah (19:11-12 of the present passage), although in Elijah's case, those signs did not serve adequately to represent the deity (they certainly did serve in that capacity, however, in the previous chapter of 1 Kings!). As Seow (1999:144) puts it, "The point is made quite deliberately that God is not locked into any one mode of appearing."

8. Less immediate, but nonetheless quite compelling, is the parallel between Moses and Elijah, both fierce servants of God who were not allowed to see the final fruit of their labors. Moses was eventually forbidden to enter the Promised Land, and Elijah did not personally experience the final triumph of Yahwism over Baalism in his lifetime; both had to trust that their successors (Joshua and Elisha, respectively) would meet with greater success.

And it is to this incomplete nature of Elijah's triumph that we now turn.

Some years ago, in his excellent commentary on Ruth, Edward F. Campbell Jr. (1975:167-168) commented on the nature of complaint in the Bible, and in particular how it is handled in the books of Ruth, Jonah, Job, Jeremiah, and here in 1 Kings (and also, in the portrayal of Jesus' passion in the synoptic Gospels). He concluded that in all these cases, the complainant is never given a satisfactory explanation of God's ways, but rather the matter is transferred into the future, and (this being particularly important for the present passage), "what resolution there is comes in terms of renewed vocations for the persons involved" (emphasis added). The only assurance given, in other words, is that God is still about his business, despite any appearance to the contrary, and his people should be about theirs! And that is exactly what we find here: Clearly no resolution of Elijah's complaints in 19:10 and 14 is ever offered, but instead, the disheartened prophet is given three new tasks to accomplish (see 19:15-16). "Go back home and get to work" is the essence of Yahweh's answer. Yes, Elijah needed some interim correction about how many others were also doing God's business—not just him alone, as he seemed to think, but 7,000 others! How true to life this is—when times get tough, we whine and complain and get no answers; but we should expect no answers, just the opportunity for more work to accomplish. After all, we are only unworthy servants, who have simply done our duty and must continue to do the same (see Luke 17:7-10). So we get no answers, only more work to do, but that is the answer: We are still worthy of being entrusted with such work. And we are not to worry about the seeming unfairness of all this, since Jesus later reminds us in Luke 18:29-30 that anyone who has given up house or family for the sake of the Kingdom of God will be repaid many times over in this life and have eternal life as well in the world to come.

So, was Elijah truly a second Moses? As we have seen, the answer must be "yes," on many accounts. But, as Brevard Childs (1980:135) has provocatively pointed out, we should not simplistically equate these two great leaders. First of all, although Elijah was expected to wait for the presence of Yahweh on Mount Sinai, as Moses had, Yahweh, this time, was *not* in the wind, earthquake, or fire, but rather in the "still small voice" (KJV). And secondly, that does not serve as the narrative climax of the Elijah story. Elijah was given three tasks to accomplish (see note on

19:15-16), the third of which was to acknowledge publicly his (already divinely chosen) prophetic successor, Elisha. Elijah has thus, as it were, been relieved of his mission, if not altogether dismissed (cf. Cogan [2001:457], who notes that a number of medieval Jewish commentators considered this chapter as indicating the effective end of Elijah's career). Finally, Childs comments on Yahweh's parting rebuke to Elijah about the 7,000 other loyal Yahwists who existed in Israel (thus introducing the concept of the "faithful remnant" in Israelite thought? [so Jones 1984:335, citing von Rad 1965:20-21]). Elijah, thus, need not stand entirely alone, nor would any such heroic figure have to do so from this time forward—there will always be a faithful remnant of God's chosen people ready to stand with an Elijah or, later, a Jeremiah or an Ezekiel. Elijah like a second Moses? Our conclusion must still be yes in many respects. After all, in the New Testament, these are the only two figures who have the honor to appear with Jesus on the Mount of Transfiguration (see Matt 17:1-9; Mark 9:2-10; Luke 9:28-36). And in the Christian Old Testament canon (Protestant, Catholic, and Orthodox), these are the only two figures worthy of citation in the final verses of the final book (Mal 4:4-6), "Remember to obey the Law of Moses, my servant. . . . Look, I am sending you the prophet Elijah before the great and dreadful day of the LORD arrives. His preaching will turn the hearts of fathers to their children, and the hearts of children to their fathers." Our own prayer should then be, let that day, the day of Moses and Elijah, soon come—Maranatha!

◆   ## 7. The call of Elisha (19:19-21)

¹⁹So Elijah went and found Elisha son of Shaphat plowing a field. There were twelve teams of oxen in the field, and Elisha was plowing with the twelfth team. Elijah went over to him and threw his cloak across his shoulders and then walked away. ²⁰Elisha left the oxen standing there, ran after Elijah, and said to him, "First let me go and kiss my father and mother good-bye, and then I will go with you!"

Elijah replied, "Go on back, but think about what I have done to you."

²¹So Elisha returned to his oxen and slaughtered them. He used the wood from the plow to build a fire to roast their flesh. He passed around the meat to the townspeople, and they all ate. Then he went with Elijah as his assistant.

NOTES

19:19 *Elisha son of Shaphat*. See note on 19:16.

***twelve teams of oxen*.** This probably indicates that Elisha was a wealthy man, who gave up a stable and secure life to serve Elijah (Sweeney 2007:233).

***threw his cloak*.** Elisha will get this cloak permanently when Elijah is taken to heaven (2 Kgs 2:7-14). Apparently, the throwing of this cloak is the sum total of Elijah's initial "call" to Elisha to follow him.

19:20 *kiss my father and mother good-bye*. Elisha will be known for his tenderness and sensitivity to the sons of the prophets (see the second note on 20:35) and their families in 2 Kgs 2–9. It should be noted that Jesus did not endorse any such delay as saying good-bye to parents (see Luke 9:61-62, which is a clear echo of the present passage), or even providing them proper burial (Luke 9:59-60).

think about what I have done to you. This is a strong challenge, possibly a rebuke to Elisha's request to say good-bye to his parents. At least, Elijah's response represents a sharp rhetorical reminder of how momentous Elisha's career change will be. Jesus likewise reminds us forcefully to "count the cost" carefully if we are thinking of becoming his disciples (see Luke 14:25-35).

19:21 Elisha returned to his oxen and slaughtered them. I like to kid in my lectures and sermons that when the people felt religious in the OT, the animals started flinching. They knew that they could well end up as sacrifices, whether on the altar, or here as the main course of Elisha's "farewell feast" (Wiseman 1993:175), with the wood from the plows serving as fuel (talk about burning bridges!). As I have already pointed out (see the second note on 1:9), the common people probably ate meat only about three times a year (during the pilgrim feasts), so this meal would have been a momentous celebration.

assistant. Heb., *wayesharethehu* [TH8334, ZH9250], "and he served/ministered to him"; Cogan (2001:455) translates "and [he] became his attendant." But Elisha would not be recognized formally as Elijah's preeminent successor until 2 Kgs 2 (see note on 2 Kgs 2:9 and the "double-portion" references found in 2 Kgs 2:9-14).

C O M M E N T A R Y

Here we reach the end of the lengthy Elijah narrative that started back in the beginning of chapter 17. Elijah literally had mountaintop experiences as well as those in the valleys, and then his successor Elisha was named. Elisha's final status is not confirmed until 2 Kings 2, but the narrative delay should not diminish for a moment the importance of the present passage. Elisha here responds, Jesus-disciple-like (at least, as described in Mark 1:16-20), to Elijah's brusque (apparently silent) invitation, marked only by the throwing of his cloak in 19:19. At least, Jesus spoke briefly when he commanded Peter, James, and John to "come, follow me" (Mark 1:17, 20). But as we have noticed, Elisha was permitted at least to kiss his parents good-bye (see note on 19:20), whereas Jesus discouraged a would-be follower from doing the same in Luke 9:61-62. Elisha's twelve yoke of oxen soon became a giant barbecue feast, an irrevocable public celebration of his sudden career change. The chapter then draws to a close with the brief notification of his new status as Elijah's assistant. God can, did, and does effect quick career changes, as any attentive visitor can recognize in Bible colleges and seminaries: People of all ages, attending class and chapel faithfully, respond to a clear (and often sudden) call from God. May our God be praised!

◆   D. Prophetic Stories about the Syro-Israelite Wars
        (1 Kgs 20:1–22:40)
        1. Ben-hadad attacks Samaria (20:1-12)

About that time King Ben-hadad of Aram mobilized his army, supported by the chariots and horses of thirty-two allied kings. They went to besiege Samaria, the capital of Israel, and launched attacks against it. ²Ben-hadad sent messengers into the city to relay this message to King Ahab of Israel: "This is what Ben-hadad says: ³'Your silver and gold are mine, and so are your wives and the best of your children!' "

⁴"All right, my lord the king," Israel's king replied. "All that I have is yours!"

⁵Soon Ben-hadad's messengers returned again and said, "This is what Ben-hadad says: 'I have already demanded that you give me your silver, gold, wives, and children. ⁶But about this time tomorrow I will send my officials to search your palace and the homes of your officials. They will take away everything you consider valuable!' "

⁷Then Ahab summoned all the elders of the land and said to them, "Look how this man is stirring up trouble! I already agreed with his demand that I give him my wives and children and silver and gold."

⁸"Don't give in to any more demands," all the elders and the people advised.

⁹So Ahab told the messengers from Ben-hadad, "Say this to my lord the king:

20:12 Or *in Succoth;* also in 20:16.

'I will give you everything you asked for the first time, but I cannot accept this last demand of yours.' " So the messengers returned to Ben-hadad with that response.

¹⁰Then Ben-hadad sent this message to Ahab: "May the gods strike me and even kill me if there remains enough dust from Samaria to provide even a handful for each of my soldiers."

¹¹The king of Israel sent back this answer: "A warrior putting on his sword for battle should not boast like a warrior who has already won."

¹²Ahab's reply reached Ben-hadad and the other kings as they were drinking in their tents.* "Prepare to attack!" Ben-hadad commanded his officers. So they prepared to attack the city.

NOTES

20:1 *About that time.* As already noted (cf. "Literary Style" in the Introduction), in the LXX the order of chs 20 and 21 is the reverse of that in the MT. McKenzie (1991:88-93) sees the Greek order as more likely the original, with the traditions in chs 20 and 22:1-38 independent of the Elijah and Elisha material, and, indeed, probably not originally referring to the reign of Ahab at all. On this last point he is reflecting a view rather widely held among scholars (cf., e.g., Pitard 1987:114-125; but contrast Cogan 2001:472-474 and Gooding 1964:269-280). The following notes will assume Ahab is the king in question, without pressing the issue too strongly in light of the many folkloristic flourishes to be found in both chs 20 and 22:1-38, a number of which will be singled out for special comment below.

King Ben-hadad of Aram. This king is probably Ben-hadad II (see the second note on 15:18 for a reference to Ben-hadad I; cf. the next note)—although if the events in this chapter occurred early in Ahab's reign, Ben-hadad I could have been the king (Cogan 2001:462). Once again, the historicity of these traditions in reference to King Ahab of Israel has been repeatedly brought into question.

thirty-two allied kings. This is certainly a large number; perhaps tribal chieftains or the like are in view here. Cogan (2001:462, 473-474) connects this "Ben-hadad II" (understood as a dynastic title) with the king known as Adad-idri (= Hadad-ezer) in the Assyrian inscriptions (cf. Wiseman 1993:175-176). Cogan sees the reference below in 20:24 to the replacement of these "kings" by "governors" (NLT, "field commanders") as perhaps reflecting Adad-idri's reorganization of his kingdom, where various Aramean tribal units were brought under a centralized administration (cf. 20:16).

20:3 *silver and gold . . . wives . . . best of your children.* These were typical demands for tribute and hostages (Sweeney 2007:241), with Ahab acting as a vassal (subordinate) in calling Ben-hadad "my lord the king" (thus, his suzerain or overlord). The adjective "best" might refer to both "wives" and "children" (cf. NRSV, NJPS), since masculine adjectives tend to predominate when both masculine and feminine nouns are modified (see Waltke and O'Connor 1990:258, #18); otherwise, presumably the strongest and healthiest children are here designated by the term "best."

20:6 *take away everything.* This represents nothing less than the virtual surrender of the city (Cogan 2001:463).

20:8 *Don't give in to any more demands.* King Ahab was not to give in to the extreme demands made by Ben-hadad.

20:10 *May the gods strike me and even kill me.* Concerning this oath formula, see note on 19:2.

if there remains enough dust from Samaria to provide even a handful for each of my soldiers. This is an unforgettable boast made effective by its "audacious hyperbole" (Cogan 2001:464); even cursory glances at photographs of the surviving archaeological evidence of Samaria's magnificent walls and architecture will indicate how audacious this boast really was (cf. ANEP, picture 718).

20:11 *A warrior putting on his sword for battle should not boast like a warrior who has already won.* The Living Bible famously paraphrased this with the saying, "Do not count your chickens before they hatch," which certainly conveys effectively the essence of the Hebrew. (For the use of proverbs in diplomatic negotiations, see Cogan and Tadmor 1988:156 for both biblical and Mesopotamian examples; cf. Wiseman 1993:176.)

20:12 *drinking in their tents.* This is a folkloristic theme for incompetence and overconfidence: The enemy was so comfortable that they literally let down their guard (see also 20:16; 16:9). Cogan (2001:464) prefers reading the place-name "Sukkoth" (which means "tents" or "booths," whence the NLT mg note on 20:12 ["Succoth"], also the name of the Jewish holiday [Deut 16:13]), both here and in 20:16. If it is to be identified with Tell Deir 'Alla, the town of Sukkoth was located in the central Jordan River valley about 20 miles (32 km) south of Beth-shan (cf. Cogan's notes [2001:268] on 7:46).

COMMENTARY

Ahab has been depicted as evil (and also indecisive) in the several previous chapters, and he will appear in a similar vein in chapter 21. So it is with some surprise that we find Ahab as seemingly sober-minded, in control, and even heroic to some degree in the present chapter. As noted above (see note on 20:1), this chapter follows chapter 21 in the Greek, thus linking the various battles with the Arameans together. Either way, Ahab is described as being under much pressure from the enemy to give away his silver, gold, wives, and children. But Ahab listened to the wishes of his elders and of his people not to give in. I think Hens-Piazza (2006:202-204) is right to remind us that "appearances can be deceptive," and that Ahab's apparent flexibility on the subject of paying tribute to Aram's king may bespeak more of his political and economic expediency (see below for more on this subject) than of his fidelity to his God. In any case, we will soon hear from an anonymous prophet (see 20:13) on this very subject.

◆   ## 2. Ahab's victory over Ben-hadad (20:13-22)

¹³Then a certain prophet came to see King Ahab of Israel and told him, "This is what the LORD says: Do you see all these enemy forces? Today I will hand them all over to you. Then you will know that I am the LORD."

¹⁴Ahab asked, "How will he do it?"

And the prophet replied, "This is what the LORD says: The troops of the provincial commanders will do it."

"Should we attack first?" Ahab asked.

"Yes," the prophet answered.

¹⁵So Ahab mustered the troops of the

232 provincial commanders. Then he called out the rest of the army of Israel, some 7,000 men. ¹⁶About noontime, as Ben-hadad and the thirty-two allied kings were still in their tents drinking themselves into a stupor, ¹⁷the troops of the provincial commanders marched out of the city as the first contingent.

As they approached, Ben-hadad's scouts reported to him, "Some troops are coming from Samaria."

¹⁸"Take them alive," Ben-hadad commanded, "whether they have come for peace or for war."

¹⁹But Ahab's provincial commanders and the entire army had now come out to fight. ²⁰Each Israelite soldier killed his Aramean opponent, and suddenly the entire Aramean army panicked and fled. The Israelites chased them, but King Ben-hadad and a few of his charioteers escaped on horses. ²¹However, the king of Israel destroyed the other horses and chariots and slaughtered the Arameans.

²²Afterward the prophet said to King Ahab, "Get ready for another attack. Begin making plans now, for the king of Aram will come back next spring.*"

20:22 Hebrew *at the turn of the year;* similarly in 20:26. The first day of the year in the ancient Hebrew lunar calendar occurred in March or April.

NOTES

20:13 *a certain prophet.* Throughout this chapter, all the prophets are anonymous (in contrast to chs 17–19, 21–22). Prophets were the ones who normally initiated the *kherem* [TH2764, ZH3051] or "holy war" (see the commentary on 1:5-27).

20:14 *troops of the provincial commanders.* Lit., "by the youths of the commanders of the provinces"; although the term "youths" (*ne'arim* [TH5288, ZH5853]) can be used for professional soldiers, probably a band of relatively untrained fighters is in view here (Cogan 2001:464-465).

20:16 *About noontime.* This was surely a time to be awake and alert!

thirty-two allied kings. For a discussion of who these 32 "kings" probably were, see the second note on 20:1.

drinking themselves into a stupor. For references to these infamous and ill-fated drinking bouts in 1 Kings, see note on 20:12.

20:20 *escaped on horses.* This is unusual because horses were normally employed only to pull chariots at this time in history (see the first note on 4:26).

20:22 *next spring.* This was the time "kings normally go out to war" (cf. 2 Sam 11:1), although winter battles were not unheard of (cf. Cogan 2001:466).

COMMENTARY

The arrival of a prophet often heralds God's will to bless a king, and although the king will often *not* recognize this as a blessing (cf. Ahab in 18:17 and 21:20; Ahaz in Isa 7:1–8:10), King Ahab was wise enough (or desperate enough) to listen here willingly to the prophet. (This will not, however, be the case later on in the chapter.) Once again, a king is supposed to defer to the prophet when initiating holy war (cf. the note on 20:13). Longman and Reid (1995:57-60) point out that when a king turned against Yahweh, it was the prophet who then performed holy war (using Samuel and Elijah as examples [18:18-40; 1 Sam 15:10-35]). Although not mentioned by Longman and Reid, this category probably also applies to the actions of both prophets in the present chapter (see 20:13, 22, and especially 20:35-43). Kings have been and will be chastised for usurping the roles of prophet and priest, but they are probably to be chastised even more for not performing the role they should exercise most diligently: acting as the head of the army and protector of the state. So far, Ahab's surprising victory does demonstrate that "he will know" that Yahweh is sovereign, but the overall campaign is far from over!

◆ 3. Ben-hadad's second attack (20:23-34)

²³After their defeat, Ben-hadad's officers said to him, "The Israelite gods are gods of the hills; that is why they won. But we can beat them easily on the plains. ²⁴Only this time replace the kings with field commanders! ²⁵Recruit another army like the one you lost. Give us the same number of horses, chariots, and men, and we will fight against them on the plains. There's no doubt that we will beat them." So King Ben-hadad did as they suggested.

²⁶The following spring he called up the Aramean army and marched out against Israel, this time at Aphek. ²⁷Israel then mustered its army, set up supply lines, and marched out for battle. But the Israelite army looked like two little flocks of goats in comparison to the vast Aramean forces that filled the countryside!

²⁸Then the man of God went to the king of Israel and said, "This is what the LORD says: The Arameans have said, 'The LORD is a god of the hills and not of the plains.' So I will defeat this vast army for you. Then you will know that I am the LORD."

²⁹The two armies camped opposite each other for seven days, and on the seventh day the battle began. The Israelites killed 100,000 Aramean foot soldiers in one day. ³⁰The rest fled into the town of Aphek, but the wall fell on them and killed another 27,000. Ben-hadad fled into the town and hid in a secret room.

³¹Ben-hadad's officers said to him, "Sir, we have heard that the kings of Israel are merciful. So let's humble ourselves by wearing burlap around our waists and putting ropes on our heads, and surrender to the king of Israel. Then perhaps he will let you live."

³²So they put on burlap and ropes, and they went to the king of Israel and begged, "Your servant Ben-hadad says, 'Please let me live!'"

The king of Israel responded, "Is he still alive? He is my brother!"

³³The men took this as a good sign and quickly picked up on his words. "Yes," they said, "your brother Ben-hadad!"

"Go and get him," the king of Israel told them. And when Ben-hadad arrived, Ahab invited him up into his chariot.

³⁴Ben-hadad told him, "I will give back the towns my father took from your father, and you may establish places of trade in Damascus, as my father did in Samaria."

Then Ahab said, "I will release you under these conditions." So they made a new treaty, and Ben-hadad was set free.

NOTES

20:23 *gods of the hills.* Chariots are useless in the hills, and most of the northern kingdom of Israel is hilly country, with the notable exception of the Plain of Jezreel. Israel knew, or should have known, that Yahweh is the God of all creation, whether the land is flat or hilly, but non-Israelites assumed that the various national gods lost their power beyond the borders of their realms (Sweeney 2007:243).

20:24 *replace the kings with field commanders!* Cogan (2001:466) prefers the term "governors" for the Aramaic (actually Akkadian; cf. Cogan and Tadmor 1988:232) loanword *pakhoth* [TH6346, ZH7068] (the term is so translated in the NLT in 10:15). On the probable historicity of this reference, see the second note on 20:1.

20:26 Aphek. Cogan (2001:466; cf. ABD 1.275-277) suggests that of the five or so locations in greater Israel that have borne this name, the most likely candidate here is the one in Transjordan near the Golan Heights (northeast of the Sea of Galilee). A later reference to Aphek (presumably the same location) may be found in 2 Kgs 13:17, which is probably an echo of the present passage (see Cogan and Tadmor 1988:148). Such echoes are common in folkloristic literature (cf. the numerous parallels between the Elijah and Elisha cycles, as illustrated in the "Elijah and Elisha Cycles: Comparisons and Contrasts" chart on p. 204).

20:27 two little flocks of goats. The Hebrew here is difficult; the NLT wisely follows the ancient versions. Cogan (2001:467) suggests translating the Hebrew as "two exposed [flocks of] goats."

20:29 camped opposite each other for seven days. Ben-hadad's forces were possibly seeking favorable omens from their god(s); cf. the extended procedure described in 22:1-28, below. But yet another folkloristic motif is to be found here (cf. Job 2:13; Ezek 3:15): Cogan (2001:467), citing Revell, says "the typological number 'seven' suggests that a literary device is being used 'to delay the progress of the narrative in order to increase its suspense.'" Commentators often compare the seven days here to the seven days the Israelites marched around Jericho (see Josh 6:1-21; cf. also the collapse of Aphek's wall in 20:30 of the present passage), but the Joshua passage plainly distinguishes the seventh day from the six that precede it, and that is not the case here. Still, the literary parallels are too close to be entirely coincidental (Leithart 2006:150).

20:29-30 100,000 . . . 27,000. These huge figures are typical of folklore; they presumably are indicative of large numbers of casualties, but the literal numbers themselves seem highly unlikely.

20:30 secret room. This is another folkloristic touch, akin to 22:25 and 2 Kgs 9:2, where the identical expression (*kheder bekhader* [TH2315, ZH2540], "a room [with]in a room") is found.

20:31 let's humble ourselves. The NLT adds this interpretive phrase, explaining what the sackcloth (NLT, "burlap") and the ropes on (or around) the head symbolize—mourning and submission (Wiseman 1993:178-179); cf. Ahab's own actions in 21:27.

20:32 He is my brother! This is diplomatic language indicating equal status. Ahab was a vassal of Ben-hadad, but Ahab's subsequent military successes had put them both on the same level (especially now that Ben-hadad entitles himself Ahab's "servant").

20:34 they made a new treaty. In this case, a parity treaty; neither would be suzerain nor vassal to the other. The economic benefits to Ahab and Israel are evident, but seemingly short-lived (22:1). As Hens-Piazza (2006:203) puts it, "Political and economic expediency motivate the release of the captured king, despite the mandate of holy war whereby this enemy is to be delivered up for destruction. . . . Despite the demands of holy war, Ahab uses his God-given military success to reclaim lost territories in the north, as well as to ensure economic advantages in Damascus."

COMMENTARY

"Then you [plural] will know that I am the LORD"—thus reads the end of 20:28 (also cf. 20:13, where the singular pronoun is indicated). Whether addressed to the later reader/hearer of the text or the original audience, the point is that believers often need to be reassured of their faith. Not rarely, God acts decisively to pique the curiosity of (or even frighten the wits out of) unbelievers; but most of the time it is the believer who needs to be reminded that the Lord truly is God. Ahab himself, however, seemed blind to all this—he focused only on the political and economic advantages to be found in the fortuitous turn of events Yahweh had brought about. Yahweh had clearly demonstrated that he is not only God of the hills, but of the plains, too— the Arameans had probably come to realize this as well. But the focus here is once again on Ahab himself and his apparent reasonableness in his responses to the newly humiliated and now humble-acting Arameans. As we know, however, the Bible rarely preaches reasonableness and accommodation in our walk of faith, and that certainly is the case here. Hens-Piazza (2006:203-204) has pointed this out quite well:

> *To the modern reader, this holy war ban [cf. the note on 20:34] that demands offering up to destruction everything and everyone in battle is morally difficult to accept, if not repugnant. . . . Nonetheless, woven into the layers of this text is a lesson that beckons us to self-examination. Here we are called to evaluate not so much our choices or our actions but rather the motives behind what we do. It is possible that our own choices, while appearing moral and of high standards, are actually motivated by that which is personally expedient or self-serving. On occasion, our deeds of mercy might really be acts of self-aggrandizement. Even the actions that serve as public expressions of both a kinship and fidelity to God might, actually, turn out to be betrayals of the very faith to which they purport to witness. Although the practices of warfare narrated in this story are quite removed from what we can accommodate under just war theory, the lessons that can be learned from the character Ahab are close at hand.*

I would submit that such comments are not only uncomfortably on target, but also help illustrate why the next and final section of the present chapter seems so harsh and unreasonable, for we serve an unreasonable God, who has high and unreasonable standards (but who nonetheless demonstrates unreasonable love and grace to an amazing number of people). Let us give our all to this wonderful and awe-ful God!

◆   ### 4. A prophet condemns Ahab (20:35-43)

35Meanwhile, the LORD instructed one of the group of prophets to say to another man, "Hit me!" But the man refused to hit the prophet. 36Then the prophet told him, "Because you have not obeyed the voice of the LORD, a lion will kill you as soon as you leave me." And when he had gone, a lion did attack and kill him.

37Then the prophet turned to another man and said, "Hit me!" So he struck the prophet and wounded him.

38The prophet placed a bandage over his eyes to disguise himself and then waited beside the road for the king. 39As the king passed by, the prophet called out to him, "Sir, I was in the thick of battle, and suddenly a man brought me a prisoner. He said, 'Guard this man; if for any reason he gets away, you will either die or pay a fine of seventy-five pounds* of silver!' 40But while I was busy doing something else, the prisoner disappeared!"

"Well, it's your own fault," the king replied. "You have brought the judgment on yourself."

41Then the prophet quickly pulled the bandage from his eyes, and the king of Israel recognized him as one of the prophets. 42The prophet said to him, "This is what the LORD says: Because you have spared the man I said must be destroyed,*

now you must die in his place, and your
people will die instead of his people." ⁴³So

the king of Israel went home to Samaria
angry and sullen.

20:39 Hebrew *1 talent* [34 kilograms].   20:42 The Hebrew term used here refers to the complete consecration of things or people to the LORD, either by destroying them or by giving them as an offering.

NOTES
20:35 *Meanwhile.* This term is an effective way to indicate the disjunction in the Hebrew text, "now, a particular member of the sons of the prophets." Leithart (2006:149-150) interestingly indicates that the appearance of the anonymous prophet here is contrary to the expected narrative sequence found twice in the present chapter (Arameans attack, prophet visits Ahab, Ahab wins battle, prophet advises Ahab, Ben-hadad's servants advise him, and Ben-hadad takes advice), inasmuch as the reader would have looked for the prophet to appear between 20:29 and 20:30 (as one similarly did back in 20:22 in the first narrative sequence). Thus, the prophet's delayed appearance here, and his eventual delivery of a harshly negative message directed to King Ahab, are narratively the whole point of the passage (cf. Seow 1999:146).

group of prophets. Lit., "sons of the prophets"; this is the first usage in Kings of what will be a commonplace reference in the Elisha cycle, which comprises 2 Kgs 2–9, 13. The phrase usually indicates a formal prophetic brotherhood (see 2 Kgs 2, 4, 6).

20:36 *a lion.* The folkloristic prediction-and-immediate-fulfillment motif is quite evident (cf. the lion killing the disobedient "man of God" from Judah back in 13:24). On folkloristic motifs see the note on 3:5. Concerning the existence of lions in biblical Israel, see the note on 13:24.

20:38 *disguise himself.* Ironically, Ahab himself will do the same thing in 22:30, but for a very different, selfish, and superstitious reason.

20:39 *seventy-five pounds of silver.* Lit., "one talent of silver"; for the weight of the Hebrew talent, see the second note on 9:14. This was an impossibly huge amount of money for any soldier to contemplate paying.

20:40 *You have brought the judgment on yourself.* This is similar to the result of Nathan's parable directed to King David regarding his adultery and commissioning of murder (2 Sam 12:5-6); to his credit, David acknowledged forthrightly the justice of the sentence.

20:42 *must be destroyed.* As already discussed, this is the main point of the passage: The demands of *kherem* [TH2764, ZH3051] or "holy war" (cf. NLT mg) must be met (see Hens-Piazza's comments as quoted in the commentary on 20:23-34; cf. note on 9:21).

20:43 *angry and sullen.* This same phrase will be found in 21:4 (MT), thus literarily linking Ahab's breach of the *kherem* law in the present chapter with his contemplated sin against the ancestral law of inheritance in the next. In both cases his actions or proposed actions seem reasonable, even generous on the surface, but they nevertheless stand in sharp violation of settled Hebrew custom—and in Israel, even the king must submit to the Torah.

COMMENTARY
We have here a poignant, unsettling conclusion to what should have been a time of triumph for King Ahab. But as I have argued in the previous commentary section, sweet reasonableness is often not the will of God, as is well illustrated in the present passage, with its violence and subterfuge leading to the peevish irritation of the king (20:43). Ahab had clearly not done God's will, and the narrator will not let him (or us) forget that fact for a moment. This is evident as we see an anonymous

prophet announce doom on another prophet for not hitting him as demanded (20:35-36; paralleling Ahab not smiting Ben-hadad as the demands of *kherem* [TH2764, ZH3051] would dictate), and the same prophet, wounded at his own request, act as an escapee from the battle who had lost his prisoner of war, thus "catching the conscience of the king" by his charade (20:38-42). These scenes parallel Ahab's focus on politics, economics, and new opportunities for personal and national gain rather than the stipulations of *kherem*, thus letting his prisoner of war Ben-hadad escape. Ahab could have repented of his hubris (as he does in the next chapter), but instead he became "angry and sullen," realizing perhaps that it would indeed be his life that would stand in for Ben-hadad's life, and his people's lives in place of the Arameans' lives. This is as Leithart (2006:150) further notes:

> Israel wins the victories over the Arameans purely through the Lord's strength, as Yahweh gives the enormous Aramean army into the hands of Ahab and brings the wall down on the remnants of the army. Yahweh even gives Ahab the battle strategy, as the commanding king of Israel's hosts. Ben-hadad is not Ahab's prisoner but Yahweh's. "Devoted to destruction" [i.e., the essence of kherem] essentially means "reserved for Yahweh," and Ahab should have known from everything about the battle that the decision whether Ben-hadad lived or died was not his to make. Ahab once again proves himself an Achan [the villain of Josh 7, who broke the kherem by keeping some of the plunder from the defeated city of Jericho], a "troubler in Israel" ([1 Kgs] 18:17).

Leithart goes on to suggest that the reference to the talent of silver in 20:39 (an incredibly huge sum of money for a commoner) hints at the possibility of atonement for the king. But Ahab refused any such possibility—at least in this chapter—so it would have to be his life for Ben-hadad's life ("a life for a life, an eye for an eye, a tooth for a tooth"; Exod 21:23-25). Thus, deservedly, the king was doomed to die, and seemingly his people and his kingdom also stood in that danger as well.

◆   ## 5. Naboth's vineyard (21:1-29)

Now there was a man named Naboth, from Jezreel, who owned a vineyard In Jezreel beside the palace of King Ahab of Samaria. ²One day Ahab said to Naboth, "Since your vineyard is so convenient to my palace, I would like to buy it to use as a vegetable garden. I will give you a better vineyard in exchange, or if you prefer, I will pay you for it."

³But Naboth replied, "The LORD forbid that I should give you the inheritance that was passed down by my ancestors."

⁴So Ahab went home angry and sullen because of Naboth's answer. The king went to bed with his face to the wall and refused to eat!

⁵"What's the matter?" his wife Jezebel asked him. "What's made you so upset that you're not eating?"

⁶"I asked Naboth to sell me his vineyard or trade it, but he refused!" Ahab told her.

⁷"Are you the king of Israel or not?" Jezebel demanded. "Get up and eat something, and don't worry about it. I'll get you Naboth's vineyard!"

⁸So she wrote letters in Ahab's name, sealed them with his seal, and sent them to the elders and other leaders of the town where Naboth lived. ⁹In her letters she commanded: "Call the citizens together for a time of fasting, and give Naboth a place of honor. ¹⁰And then seat two scoundrels across from him who will accuse him of cursing God and the king.

Then take him out and stone him to death."

¹¹So the elders and other town leaders followed the instructions Jezebel had written in the letters. ¹²They called for a fast and put Naboth at a prominent place before the people. ¹³Then the two scoundrels came and sat down across from him. And they accused Naboth before all the people, saying, "He cursed God and the king." So he was dragged outside the town and stoned to death. ¹⁴The town leaders then sent word to Jezebel, "Naboth has been stoned to death."

¹⁵When Jezebel heard the news, she said to Ahab, "You know the vineyard Naboth wouldn't sell you? Well, you can have it now! He's dead!" ¹⁶So Ahab immediately went down to the vineyard of Naboth to claim it.

¹⁷But the LORD said to Elijah,* ¹⁸"Go down to meet King Ahab of Israel, who rules in Samaria. He will be at Naboth's vineyard in Jezreel, claiming it for himself. ¹⁹Give him this message: 'This is what the LORD says: Wasn't it enough that you killed Naboth? Must you rob him, too? Because you have done this, dogs will lick your blood at the very place where they licked the blood of Naboth!' "

²⁰"So, my enemy, you have found me!" Ahab exclaimed to Elijah.

"Yes," Elijah answered, "I have come because you have sold yourself to what is evil in the LORD's sight. ²¹So now the LORD says,* 'I will bring disaster on you and consume you. I will destroy every one of your male descendants, slave and free alike, anywhere in Israel! ²²I am going to destroy your family as I did the family of Jeroboam son of Nebat and the family of Baasha son of Ahijah, for you have made me very angry and have led Israel into sin.'

²³"And regarding Jezebel, the LORD says, 'Dogs will eat Jezebel's body at the plot of land in Jezreel.*'

²⁴"The members of Ahab's family who die in the city will be eaten by dogs, and those who die in the field will be eaten by vultures."

²⁵(No one else so completely sold himself to what was evil in the LORD's sight as Ahab did under the influence of his wife Jezebel. ²⁶His worst outrage was worshiping idols* just as the Amorites had done—the people whom the LORD had driven out from the land ahead of the Israelites.)

²⁷But when Ahab heard this message, he tore his clothing, dressed in burlap, and fasted. He even slept in burlap and went about in deep mourning.

²⁸Then another message from the LORD came to Elijah: ²⁹"Do you see how Ahab has humbled himself before me? Because he has done this, I will not do what I promised during his lifetime. It will happen to his sons; I will destroy his dynasty."

21:17 Hebrew *Elijah the Tishbite;* also in 21:28.   21:21 As in Greek version; Hebrew lacks *So now the LORD says.*   21:23 As in several Hebrew manuscripts, Syriac, and Latin Vulgate (see also 2 Kgs 9:26, 36); most Hebrew manuscripts read *at the city wall.*   21:26 The Hebrew term (literally *round things*) probably alludes to dung.

NOTES

21:1 *Now there was a man named Naboth.* This begins a new narrative, presumably independent of the war narratives (ch 20 [MT], and 22:1-40) that surround it. Sweeney (2007:247) nicely characterizes this passage as a presentation of a number of major characters who interacted with King Ahab: first Naboth (21:1-4), then Jezebel (21:5-16), and then finally Elijah (21:17-29). Ironically, the name Naboth (borne by the vineyard owner) probably means "shoot" or "sprout" (cf. HALOT 660). Concerning the order of chs 20–21 in the Old Greek (LXX, Codex Vaticanus), see the note on 20:1.

Jezreel. See the second note on 18:46. The fact that Naboth was a native of this city is emphasized in the MT and is an integral part of the story (Cogan 2001:476).

21:2 *vegetable garden.* Wiseman (1993:181) makes a strong case for translating the Hebrew term *yaraq* [TH3419, ZH3763] as "green growth" rather than "vegetables" or the like;

royal gardens (which are probably what is in view here) naturally were located close to the royal palace, furnished with trees and shrubs for color and shade.

21:3 The LORD forbid that I should give you the inheritance. What follows is, in a nutshell, the ancestral law of inheritance that will be discussed at some length in the commentary below.

21:4 angry and sullen. This is identical to the phrase found in 20:43 (see note there). The seeming immaturity of the pouting king (turning his face away, refusing to eat) will find an ironic partial echo in the story of the good king Hezekiah (see 2 Kgs 20:2). (Note, however, that there is no specific Hebrew reference to the term "wall" in the present verse [although it is probably implied], in contrast to its clear inclusion in the Hezekiah passage.)

21:7 Are you the king of Israel or not? Jezebel, daughter of King Ethbaal of the Sidonians (see note on 16:31), may not have known (or cared) much about the Torah, but she certainly knew about the "divine right of kings" (at least in Phoenicia).

21:8 she wrote letters in Ahab's name, sealed them with his seal. Cogan (2001:485) cites David Noel Freedman's apt comment concerning this action as follows: "Ahab manipulated the manipulative Jezebel. He knew exactly what he was doing and what the outcome would be. Elijah's condemnation is correctly aimed at the king; the use of his name signet cannot be without his permission and knowledge." (Concerning the importance of the king's seal, or better the state seal, which showed the endorsement of the state rather than the king in his own person, see Andersen 1966:52.)

elders and other leaders. Commentators note the sociological delineation here of the two rankings (*zeqenim* [TH2205, ZH2418], "elders"; and *khorim* [TH2715, ZH2985], probably "nobles") of the Israelite aristocracy: the ancestral tribal leaders and the freemen or nobles who have been connected with the palace (Cogan 2001:479). The disturbingly remarkable cooperation of these groups of aristocrats sadly speaks loudly as to the corruptness of Israelite society at this time.

21:9 a time of fasting. How bitterly ironic such a summons must have been.

a place of honor. Lit., "at the head of the people." Such a conspicuous position would be natural for such a distinguished citizen and landowner of the city. (The identical Hebrew phrase is translated "at a prominent place" in 21:12.)

21:10 two scoundrels. We sadly have here a parody of the Deuteronomic insistence on the need for two witnesses in order to convict the accused (see Deut 17:6; 19:15). The term "scoundrels" refers literally to "sons of Belial," with the term Belial perhaps signifying "without worth" or, more intriguingly, "without [opportunity for] rising" (i.e., confined to the underworld, Sheol, with no chance for escape due to their wickedness [cf. Cogan 2001:479]).

cursing God and the king. These are capital offenses (see Exod 22:28; Lev 24:15-16). Cogan (2001:480) thinks only one offense is in view here: an abusive remark against the king, reinforced by a reference to the name of Yahweh. (Both here and in the parallel reference in 21:13, the Hebrew literally reads "bless" rather than "curse"; but this is a common Hebrew euphemism ensuring that no one reading or hearing the MT would encounter an impious expression; cf. Job 1:5, 11; 2:5, 9.)

21:11 followed the instructions. In typical folkloristic fashion, the next several verses repeat with very little variation the fulfilling of every detail of Jezebel's written orders (cf. the second note on 21:9).

21:13 dragged outside . . . stoned to death. Being executed "outside" the town would avoid contamination by contact with the dead (Lev 24:13-14, 23; Num 15:35-36). If the procedure detailed in Deut 17:2-7 was followed here, the accusers (here, the "two scoundrels" of 21:10) would have had to throw the first stones.

21:16 *immediately.* This word in the NLT is perhaps a bit too interpretive (there is no exact correspondence to it in the Hebrew), but the force of the Hebrew verbs, "arose to go down . . . to take possession of it," do imply quick action. The LXX softens this by adding the phrase "and he [Ahab] tore his garments and put on sackcloth."

21:17 *Elijah.* As the NLT mg indicates, the full title "Elijah the Tishbite" is used here in the MT (see the first note on 17:1 for details).

21:18 *Go down to . . . Samaria . . . Jezreel.* Repeating the two place-names reinforces the disparity—Ahab's capital is Samaria, not Jezreel. (One does indeed "go down" from Samaria to Jezreel inasmuch as the former location is significantly higher in elevation than the latter.)

21:19 *Must you rob him, too?* As Seow points out, the issue here is the breaking of the tenth commandment (Exod 20:17; Deut 5:21), the prohibition against coveting something that belongs to someone else:

> The danger lies in the intensity of the greed that prompts someone to commit acts of violence against others in order to achieve his or her goals. . . . Covetousness leads quickly to perjury and murder; disregard for the tenth commandment leads to violation of the ninth and the sixth. It is no accident either that the narrator of this passage views Ahab's sin as idolatry—that is, violation of the first and second commandments (21:26). Covetousness, in other words, is a form of idolatry: It is placing other priorities and desires before God; it is the elevation of material things to the status of gods. (Seow 1999:159)

dogs will lick. In regard to ancient people reckoning dogs only as opportunistic scavengers, see the note on 14:11. The present prophecy will be somewhat literally yet unexpectedly fulfilled, not in the city of Jezreel, but in Samaria (see 22:38; also cf. 2 Kgs 9:25-26 for Jehu's further fulfillment of the prophecy in regard to Joram, Ahab's son). As Wiseman (1993:183-184) notes, "the fulfillment of prophecy is sometimes by stages." Here, Ahab's dead body will eventually be exposed in Samaria with the dogs indeed licking up his blood; but, probably due to the reprieve promised by God in light of Ahab's later repentance (see 21:29), it is Ahab's son Joram who will be killed in Jezreel and his body left on Naboth's plot of land by the usurper Jehu and his officer Bidkar. Whether it's in the OT or in the NT, whether it's large or small, God reserves the right to fulfill his prophecies at the time he chooses, and in the ways he sovereignly chooses. The resultant interplay between divine sovereignty and human freedom often remains a wonder to behold.

21:20 *my enemy.* This is a literal translation of the term *'oyebi* [TH341, ZH367]. Ahab earlier had called Elijah a "troublemaker of Israel" (18:17). He will also characterize the prophet Micaiah in similar terms in 22:8.

21:21 *every one of your male descendants, slave and free alike.* See the first two notes on 14:10 concerning the two Hebrew idioms found here.

21:23 *at the plot of land in Jezreel.* As noted in the NLT mg, this follows a few witnesses in reading *kheleq* [TH2506, ZH2750] (which appears at 2 Kgs 9:36) for the MT's *khel* [TH2426, ZH2658]. Eissfeldt, cited by Cogan and Tadmor (1988:112-113), prefers the MT ("at the city wall" [*khel*]) both here and as an emendation for *kheleq* in 2 Kgs 9:36, since Jezebel was thrown from the palace window and probably died on the fortification wall of the city. The NLT follows the more likely original, with the MT representing a secondary (or even tertiary) harmonization (cf. Cogan 2001:482).

21:24 *dogs . . . vultures.* See note on 14:11.

21:26 *worshiping idols.* Concerning the actual meaning of the term *gillulim* [TH1544, ZH1658], see the second note on 15:12. More fundamentally, as was pointed out in the first note on

21:19, Ahab's sin of covetousness, and all that it leads to, is indeed nothing less than a form of idolatry.

Amorites. This is an ethnic designation of the Amurru or "westerners" (HALOT 67-68); the directional perspective is that from Mesopotamia, where the term carried a strongly negative connotation of a people who were basically uncivilized barbarians (cf. Mendenhall [ABD 1.199-200], who discounts the historical precision of this negative Mesopotamian categorization). In any case, wicked King Manasseh of Judah will also be condemned in terms quite similar to those found for Ahab here (2 Kgs 21:11).

21:27 But when Ahab heard this message. This is a remarkable change of action, filled with irony; Ahab fasted in sincere repentance here, instead of in self-pity as in 21:4, or symbolizing an occasion for so-called ethical outrage in 21:9 and 21:12. This fast was recognized by God as being genuine (cf. 21:29). Concerning the wearing of burlap or "sackcloth," see the note on 2 Kgs 6:30.

21:28 another message. Like good King Hezekiah after him (see 2 Kgs 20:1-11), Ahab's sincere actions led to a remarkable divine reprieve. It would seem that wicked King Ahab was a veritable Manasseh, but he instead was (at least for a bit) a veritable Hezekiah (or, indeed, like the repentant Manasseh of 2 Chr 33:10-20; cf. commentary below). The incredible nature of this passage of Scripture can hardly be overstated.

21:29 humbled himself. This is the Niphal of *kana'* [TH3665, ZH4044] (cf. commentary on 16:29-34). King Ahab is reckoned as nothing less than comparable to good King Josiah in this verse, and the mitigation of his punishment is appropriately akin to that of Josiah (see Huldah's prophecy as found in 2 Kgs 22:18-20). Apparently, there is nearly always hope for anyone, no matter how wicked their past actions (cf. Ezek 18). What an ironic encouragement texts like these can be for any would-be leader today!

COMMENTARY

Naboth's vineyard stood for something much more important than choice real estate; it was part of the family inheritance as ordained by God in the Torah (see comments below). Naboth was mindful of that fact, but King Ahab and Queen Jezebel showed utter disregard for it. This provides the setting for this unforgettable narrative.

Of the two royal personages, Jezebel is the more villainous. Ahab seems, once again, to be the picture of attempted accommodation in 21:1-6 (in contrast to a hardened villain who would not necessarily go home "angry and sullen," or to his bed "with his face to the wall," refusing to eat). Jezebel is the standard villainess "from central casting," as it were, but her way is the way of thwarted royalty in general: "Are you the king of Israel or not?" she asked Ahab rhetorically. And she certainly played the part of imperious queen to grand effect (21:7-16). Queen Jezebel was foreign by birth, married (presumably) not for love or even by choice but as a result of larger diplomatic purposes (see note on 16:31), and probably quite unaware of the peculiar and stringent way of Torah when it comes to ancestral inheritance rights (Wiseman 1993:181). Nonetheless, her actions were harsh and unfeeling, and she fully deserved her bloody death (see 2 Kgs 9:30-37). This was the poetic justice of God being meted out to one who deserved it (see, e.g., Pss 37 and 49). Lord Acton, years ago, reminded us most famously that "power tends to corrupt and absolute power corrupts absolutely." How true that is.

But let us not elevate pathetic King Ahab and garden-variety-despot Queen Jezebel to tragic heights they don't deserve. Whether it be power politics in church or state, innocent people are often hurt, and hurt grievously. The perpetrators of such hurt are often people, not unlike ourselves, who happen to have opportunities to wield power that we don't ourselves enjoy. That is the real tragedy of the present passage, and that is what makes its ending satisfying—where we see Ahab condemned most harshly (21:25-26), yet given a chance to repent. When he—surprise, surprise—takes that opportunity, he is given a reprieve by God akin to that of Manasseh in 2 Chronicles 33:10-20. Villainy may take the guise of weak-willed petulance, wily maneuverings, or strong-armed brazenness; villains must and will meet their just deserts, but repentance is available to all, no matter how far from God they may happen to be. Our God is always and ever a most faithful God, and it is he who remains sovereign in all situations.

Comment should also be made concerning the specific issue addressed in the present passage: the issue of social justice, and more specifically, that of ancestral land rights. In the present age, when the rich get richer, and, seemingly, the poor poorer, such preoccupations with preservation of ancestral wealth within tribes, clans, and families might seem hopelessly quaint; but there certainly was such pre-occupation in the Torah. The specific laws concerning the land and Yahweh's owner-ship of it are to be found in Leviticus 25:1-34 (cf. especially Lev 25:23); and some special cases are dealt with in Numbers 27:1-11; 36:1-12 (both in reference to the daughters of Zelophehad from the tribe of Manasseh), as well as in Deuteronomy 25:5-10 (cf. Ruth 4:1-12; Jer 32:1-15). But the book that deals most extensively with tribal land inheritances is Joshua—nearly half of that book consists of land divisions among the tribes, including boundary descriptions as well as lists of cities (see especially Josh 13–21). What is of great importance throughout that book is the repeated reminder that larger tribes merited larger tracts of land, smaller tribes, smaller tracts. The only criterion, it would seem, was the actual size of the tribal population: Famously, in Joshua 17:14-18 the Joseph tribes successfully petition for more land due to the size of their population (Joshua himself tells them in 17:17, "Since you are so large and strong, you will be given more than one portion"). Once again, the issue here is simply the number of people, not any increase or decrease in their per capita wealth; strenuous efforts were extended to ensure strict fairness in this regard. I would submit that such economic concerns should still be taken most seriously in our modern age, as I have recently tried to argue in another context:

This dividing of the land [in Joshua] sounds fair enough. But is all this too utopian, akin to the brief period in the Early Church when God's people had all things in common, as described in Acts 2:44-46? Certainly we cannot argue that the Bible insists that God's people must accept one particular political or economic system of government, be it feudalism, democracy, capitalism, socialism, or the like. Still less can we say that biblical Christians are expected to force fellow believers to share their material wealth with the less fortunate (or with us). But here, as in so many other instances, God's perfect plan seems to be in evidence: Those who care most about the kingdom of God and for God's glorious presence in their lives will care little for economic advantage. They will be most pleased when all of God's children are adequately blessed, and they will gladly give away some of their own economic excess so that others' needs may be met. (Barnes 2003:374-375)

This, I submit, is the real answer to the modern conundrum of the rich getting richer and the poor, poorer—a radical spiritual orientation and focus on what is really important in life. This economic conundrum did not concern King Ahab or his wife Jezebel very much, but it should have. And this conundrum *did* and *does* concern Ahab's God very much indeed; and so it is that we find in the Torah careful provisions concerning the Year of Jubilee (Lev 25:8-22, where every 50th year each Israelite is to return to their ancestral land). In particular, we read the following statement about the Jubilee (Lev 25:10): "Set this year apart as holy, a time to *proclaim freedom throughout the land for all who live there.*[1] It will be a jubilee year for you, when each of you may return to the land that belonged to your ancestors and return to your own clan" (with elaborate provisions being made in Lev 25:14-17 to adjust the buying and selling price of a piece of property in light of the number of years remaining until the next Jubilee). The law of redemption was also an important aspect of this Torah legislation, as found in the very next passage (Lev 25:23-34; cf. Deut 15:1-18; 25:5-10), reminding them and us that "the land must never be sold on a permanent basis, for the land belongs to me [Yahweh]." These are traditions Naboth the Jezreelite undoubtedly knew well, and that is why he uttered his famous oath to Ahab, "The LORD forbid that I should give you the inheritance that was passed down by my ancestors" (21:3). And the Lord will forbid—indeed, the Lord must forbid our trampling on the rights of his children in order to enlarge or beautify whatever may happen to be the modern equivalent of a king's winter palace. As Moses succinctly reminds us in Deuteronomy 15:4, "There should be no poor among you, for the LORD your God will greatly bless you in the land he is giving you."

One final note: Years later the usurper Jehu and his supporters made much rhetorical use of this infamous Naboth incident when they put an end to the Omride dynasty (see 2 Kgs 9:21-26). Cogan (2001:486) thinks it was Elijah and the prophetic circles associated with him who had kept the matter alive until Yahweh's judgments against Jezebel and Ahab's descendants would be finally and completely fulfilled, some 15 or so years after Naboth's death. And what a bloody fulfillment it would prove to be (2 Kgs 9:1-10:31). In any case, it certainly does prove once again to be the case that "what goes around comes around," and that human leadership (whether political or ecclesiastical) will eventually reap what it sows. Sadly, however, it is often the children who bear the brunt of their parents' transgressions, whether it be Ahaziah or Joram (the immediate sons of Ahab) or the later, sixth-century descendants of Manasseh of Judah in 2 Kings or, finally, the exilic and postexilic generations that were probably the intended audience of the Deuteronomistic editing of 1-2 Kings (for details, see "The 'Sins of Manasseh'" under "Major Themes" in the Introduction). This ironically proves in its own way the point of the present passage: "The LORD [will] forbid" that the ancestral customs of the Torah be ignored or trampled upon by present or future generations. Come to think of it, this message—that future generations may suffer because of our present-day literal or metaphorical trespasses—may be one of the most effective deterrents against our trespassing against their (and our—i.e., the church's) ancestral customs in the first place!

ENDNOTE

1. The italicized portion was inscribed in the KJV on the United States' "Liberty Bell," which was originally cast in 1753 and, now cracked, is currently located at the Independence National Historical Park, Philadelphia, Pennsylvania.

◆   6. Jehoshaphat and Ahab (22:1–9)

For three years there was no war between Aram and Israel. ²Then during the third year, King Jehoshaphat of Judah went to visit King Ahab of Israel. ³During the visit, the king of Israel said to his officials, "Do you realize that the town of Ramoth-gilead belongs to us? And yet we've done nothing to recapture it from the king of Aram!"

⁴Then he turned to Jehoshaphat and asked, "Will you join me in battle to recover Ramoth-gilead?"

Jehoshaphat replied to the king of Israel, "Why, of course! You and I are as one. My troops are your troops, and my horses are your horses." ⁵Then Jehoshaphat added, "But first let's find out what the LORD says."

⁶So the king of Israel summoned the prophets, about 400 of them, and asked them, "Should I go to war against Ramoth-gilead, or should I hold back?"

They all replied, "Yes, go right ahead! The Lord will give the king victory."

⁷But Jehoshaphat asked, "Is there not also a prophet of the LORD here? We should ask him the same question."

⁸The king of Israel replied to Jehoshaphat, "There is one more man who could consult the LORD for us, but I hate him. He never prophesies anything but trouble for me! His name is Micaiah son of Imlah."

Jehoshaphat replied, "That's not the way a king should talk! Let's hear what he has to say."

⁹So the king of Israel called one of his officials and said, "Quick! Bring Micaiah son of Imlah."

NOTES

22:1 *For three years.* This refers to the campaigns against Aram described back in ch 20 of the MT (ch 21, LXX). Note that with this verse, LXX (Codex Vaticanus) reverts back to the so-called "Kaige" recension (see "Canonicity and Textual History" in the Introduction for details concerning the various recensions found in the LXX of 1–2 Kings).

22:2 *King Jehoshaphat.* He is first mentioned in passing in Asa's burial notice (15:24). Jehoshaphat's formal accession formula will be found in 22:41-42 (MT). (For the placement of this formula in the Old Greek at 16:28a [Rahlfs's enumeration], and also in the Kaige recension [= MT] in 22:41-42 of the present chapter, see the note on 16:28.) Cogan (2001:489) sees a formal state visit in view here, during which plans for a joint offensive against Aram were being discussed. (For a formal introduction to King Jehoshaphat, including the meaning of his name, see the note on 22:41.)

22:3 *Ramoth-gilead.* The Levitical city and city of refuge (Josh 20:8; 21:38; cf. Deut 4:43) located in the border area between Israel and Aram (probably Tell Ramith, which is 4 miles [7 km] south of Ramthah near the modern border with Syria and the ancient King's Highway). The term Ramoth means "heights," which would fit well with Tell Ramith's prominent location as a height over the surrounding plain of Gilead (ABD 5.621, following Glueck 1943:10-13).

22:4 *You and I are as one.* Possibly parity in status is in view here (Cogan 2001:489), although Seow (1999:160-161) argues effectively that Jehoshaphat plays a subservient role throughout this narrative (cf. 22:30). In any case, the previous era of warfare between Israel and Judah has come to an end (apparently at Jehoshaphat's initiative; cf. 22:44).

22:5 *what the LORD says.* It is imperative to know what is the will of Yahweh (= "the LORD"; see endnote 4 of the Introduction). This is especially the case in the area of holy war (concerning the crucial role of the prophet in initiating holy war, see the commentary on 1:5-27). But it will often be ambiguous as to whether the various prophets we meet in this chapter are prophets of Yahweh or of Baal or of Asherah (or of some syncretistic combination of the three). And it will be somewhat unclear as to whether it is the will of Yahweh (for us) always to know the will of Yahweh! (For further comments on this conundrum, which we also face from time to time, see the commentary on 22:10-28.)

22:6 *about 400 of them.* An allusion to the 400 prophets of Asherah mentioned back in 18:19 may be what is in mind here, but we cannot be certain—the reference is too vague. In any case, this number once again represents a large and impressive contingent.

22:7 *Is there not also a prophet of the LORD here?* Again, there is some ambiguity in the original Hebrew; as Cogan (2001:490) notes, the LXX omits the word "another" (or "also") (*'od* [TH5750, ZH6388]), both here and in 22:8, probably to indicate more clearly that all the other prophets were *not* to be categorized as prophets of Yahweh (cf. the Vulgate; also Josephus *Antiquities* 8.15.4.402). But our narrator here is more subtle than this (see notes on 22:5; 22:8).

22:8 *I hate him.* We know by now whom King Ahab especially "hates": the prophet Elijah (cf. 18:17 and 21:20). So it is with some surprise that we hear here for the first time the name "Micaiah son of Imlah," who is further described as the prophet who never prophesies "anything but trouble" for Ahab. Possibly this surprise reference indicates the independent nature of the present text over against the extensive Elijah/Elisha traditions that surround it (cf. its appearance in 2 Chr 18:1-34, which lacks all the Elijah material up to and beyond this point); but in any case, it certainly demonstrates the masterful art of indirection displayed here by the author (or, at least, the editor) of these various prophetic texts. And, as noted below in the commentary, Ahab himself here also unwittingly fulfills the role of a true prophet.

Micaiah son of Imlah. This individual is only mentioned here and in the Chronicles parallel (2 Chr 18:1-27). The name Micaiah means "Who is like Yah(weh)?" and the name Imlah (especially as it is spelled in the Hebrew of 2 Chr 18:7-8) probably means "May he [Yahweh] fill" (the womb?).

C O M M E N T A R Y

Some time ago, DeVries (1978:25-51; cf. 1985:263-266) argued plausibly that the Micaiah material in 22:1-37 represents a composite of two originally independent narratives (cf. Jones 1984:360-362). Nonetheless, the view taken here will be that the present narrative(s) represents a coherent discussion of King Ahab's last days (see the first note on 20:1 for other views) as he campaigned in coalition with King Jehoshaphat of Judah against the Arameans to retake Ramoth-gilead. (Note that a particularly good, recent rehearsal of the many historical and narratological issues surrounding this text may be found in Sweeney 2007:254-258.)

In 22:1-28 we see prophet versus king versus another king; north versus south; true prophet versus false prophet. All these conflicts are to be found throughout the present passage, but perhaps the most immediate lesson to be found in these first nine verses of the chapter is that God-seeking leaders must stand their ground against less-God-seeking leadership. King Jehoshaphat is abruptly introduced as in coalition with Ahab in 22:2 without any prior formal accession formula (that is to be found in 22:41-50, in strict Deuteronomistic chronological order), and as a king who may not have had much choice in the matter (cf. the note on 22:4), but one who still was able to stand his ground, insisting that an unambiguous prophet of Yahweh be found, and, more importantly, heeded. This will, of course, cause some short-term discomfort to King Ahab, but it will prove to bring long-term benefits (maybe not for Ahab, who himself can "prophetically" predict the prophet's message; 22:8) at least to Jehoshaphat and to the future leadership of both kingdoms. We too must stand our ground in the presence of our less godly superiors, even at the risk of public discomfort, or else the results may prove disastrous indeed. Better some discomfort now than a great disaster later.

One ironic contrast illustrated briefly in this chapter is the difference between "prediction" and true prophecy. Ahab can make accurate predictions; in 22:8 he mutters that Micaiah never says anything good about him (cf. 22:7-18). But it is Micaiah who will prove to be a true prophet of God, for it is he who can see and hear the divine deliberations taking place concerning the fate of Ahab and of his kingdom (see 22:19-23). And, more to the present point, it is the positive word from a true prophet of God that is required for the initiation of holy war, and a king should not avoid this obligation (cf. Halpern's conclusions, as described in the commentary on 1:5-27). Interestingly, Cogan (2001:490) cites the present chapter as the earliest reference to the consultation of prophets (instead of priests) prior to battle (he contrasts Num 27:21 and 1 Sam 30:7-8). I suspect, however, that the need for the prophetic word is not all that new in Ahab's era (cf. 1 Sam 13:2-14, where Saul's transgression is probably against Samuel the prophet, rather than Samuel the priest), and I further suspect that both Ahab and Jehoshaphat knew this requirement quite well (whence the 400 prophets Ahab summoned). In any case, Jehoshaphat insisted upon a clearly authentic word from Yahweh through the prophet; and as Jeremiah sardonically reminded his wavering audience some 250 years later (see Jer 28:8-9), the "ancient prophets" often warned of war, disaster, and disease—and as for anyone who dares prophesy "peace," the burden of proof rests upon those words coming true. Thus, the default position, if you will, is pessimism; optimists must prove the divine inspiration of their words! And that, as we will see, was unlikely to take place in the days of Ahab.

◆   ## 7. Micaiah prophesies against Ahab (22:10-28)

[10]King Ahab of Israel and King Jehoshaphat of Judah, dressed in their royal robes, were sitting on thrones at the threshing floor near the gate of Samaria. All of Ahab's prophets were prophesying there in front of them. [11]One of them, Zedekiah son of Kenaanah, made some iron horns and proclaimed, "This is what the LORD says: With these horns you will gore the Arameans to death!"

[12]All the other prophets agreed. "Yes," they said, "go up to Ramoth-gilead and be victorious, for the LORD will give the king victory!"

[13]Meanwhile, the messenger who went to get Micaiah said to him, "Look, all the prophets are promising victory for the king. Be sure that you agree with them and promise success."

[14]But Micaiah replied, "As surely as the LORD lives, I will say only what the LORD tells me to say."

¹⁵When Micaiah arrived before the king, Ahab asked him, "Micaiah, should we go to war against Ramoth-gilead, or should we hold back?"

Micaiah replied sarcastically, "Yes, go up and be victorious, for the LORD will give the king victory!"

¹⁶But the king replied sharply, "How many times must I demand that you speak only the truth to me when you speak for the LORD?"

¹⁷Then Micaiah told him, "In a vision I saw all Israel scattered on the mountains, like sheep without a shepherd. And the LORD said, 'Their master has been killed.* Send them home in peace.' "

¹⁸"Didn't I tell you?" the king of Israel exclaimed to Jehoshaphat. "He never prophesies anything but trouble for me."

¹⁹Then Micaiah continued, "Listen to what the LORD says! I saw the LORD sitting on his throne with all the armies of heaven around him, on his right and on his left. ²⁰And the LORD said, 'Who can entice Ahab to go into battle against Ramoth-gilead so he can be killed?'

"There were many suggestions, ²¹and finally a spirit approached the LORD and said, 'I can do it!'

²²"'How will you do this?' the LORD asked.

"And the spirit replied, 'I will go out and inspire all of Ahab's prophets to speak lies.'

"'You will succeed,' said the LORD. 'Go ahead and do it.'

²³"So you see, the LORD has put a lying spirit in the mouths of all your prophets. For the LORD has pronounced your doom."

²⁴Then Zedekiah son of Kenaanah walked up to Micaiah and slapped him across the face. "Since when did the Spirit of the LORD leave me to speak to you?" he demanded.

²⁵And Micaiah replied, "You will find out soon enough when you are trying to hide in some secret room!"

²⁶"Arrest him!" the king of Israel ordered. "Take him back to Amon, the governor of the city, and to my son Joash. ²⁷Give them this order from the king: 'Put this man in prison, and feed him nothing but bread and water until I return safely from the battle!' "

²⁸But Micaiah replied, "If you return safely, it will mean that the LORD has not spoken through me!" Then he added to those standing around, "Everyone mark my words!"

22:17 Hebrew *These people have no master.*

NOTES

22:10 *dressed in their royal robes.* There will be intriguing interplay between this royal council and the divine council (see note on 22:19) that appears in Micaiah's vision (22:19-23; cf. Leithart 2006:161-162), with one of the ironies being the openness of the latter to "input from the floor" (i.e., suggestions from the lesser-status participants in the committee meeting). Maybe Yahweh's style of leadership is less autocratic than we might first surmise!

at the threshing floor near the gate of Samaria. The city gate is the place where both commercial and legal business were usually transacted, and the threshing floor (probably just outside the gate) may well have represented the only open space to be found near the city with its narrow streets and cramped quarters (cf. Cogan 2001:490).

22:11 *Zedekiah son of Kenaanah.* He is mentioned only here (cf. 22:24) and in the Chronicles parallel (2 Chr 18:10, 23); his name ironically means "Yah(weh) is righteousness." "Kenaanah" probably means "the Canaanite" or the like, possibly signifying a Phoenician background. Sweeney (2007:259-260) notes that, like Jeremiah versus Hananiah in Jer 27–28, the Israelites had to weigh the competing claims of both prophets before one was eventually proved true by future events.

made some iron horns. This was a typical prophetic sign action, meant to reinforce the verbal message (similar sign actions are found often in the books of Jeremiah and Ezekiel); for the specific image evoked here, see Deut 33:17.

22:13 Meanwhile. The MT has a simple disjunctive *waw* [TH2050.1, ZH2256] here (which means "and"), but the NLT nicely captures the Hebrew syntax here by using this term. (For a brief discussion of the disjunctive Waw, see "Literary Style" in the Introduction.)

22:15 sarcastically. This is not literally in the text but is surely implied by the context. The irony of Micaiah seeming to agree with the verbiage of the other prophets (cf. 22:15b with 22:12), but then hearing the king respond as he does in 22:16, leads us to surmise that Micaiah's tone of voice must have been indeed sarcastic.

22:16 speak only the truth. This is a worthy goal, to be sure, but one impeded by the messenger (cf. 22:13). The king's prediction (22:8) will also come true (see 22:18) if Micaiah declares "only the truth."

22:17 In a vision. This phrase is an appropriate, interpretive addition to the text. Elsewhere, we are told that in the early days prophets were termed "seers" (see 1 Sam 9:9; also the first note on 13:11). The visions they "saw" (*ra'ah* [TH7200, ZH8011]) represented the potential future, especially as planned and provided for by Yahweh and the divine council (see note on 22:19 for details). So it is here: Micaiah declares the probable—but *not inevitable* (cf. endnote 28 of the Introduction)—future for Kings Ahab and Jehoshaphat in regard to their planned campaign against Aram to retake Ramoth-gilead. Indeed, as bidden, Micaiah does declare the simple truth as best he can, and in terms that brook no confusion.

22:19 I saw the LORD. In terms reminiscent of the narrative of Isa 6, Micaiah beheld the deliberations of the divine council (the "heavenly host"; Cogan 2001:492; Seow 1999:164). A true prophet was given the opportunity to witness the proceedings of Yahweh's heavenly court with its attendants and their deliberations (Jer 23:18-22; also cf. Job 1:6; 2:1; Pss 103:20-21; 148:2 for other references to this divine entourage).

with all the armies of heaven. Heb., *wekol-tseba' hashamayim* [TH6635/8064, ZH7372/9028] (and all the hosts of the heavens), an expression commonly and appropriately translated in the NLT as found here. But military imagery (as implicit in "armies") is not clearly evident in the present verse (see previous note); rather, it is a committee meeting discussing future strategy.

22:22 inspire . . . to speak lies. Lit., "a lying spirit"; see 22:23 for a literal translation of the same Hebrew expression (*ruakh sheqer*).

22:24 Then Zedekiah . . . slapped him across the face. This is another sign action (cf. the second note on 22:11). The resultant ambiguity (which prophet is the true prophet of Yahweh?) is probably not fully resolved until the short-term prophecy of hiding in a secret or inner room is fulfilled (22:25). Presumably this prediction did come to pass; otherwise, we would not be reading about it in the inspired text (although, admittedly, this is an argument from silence). In any event, the more profound short-term prediction is to be found in 22:28.

22:25 trying to hide in some secret room. This is reminiscent of Ben-hadad's cowardly action (20:30; see note there), probably part of the same Ahab versus Aram battle tradition (but cf. 2 Kgs 9:2 for yet another use of the phrase). Sweeney (2007:260) intriguingly alludes to the "spirit" or "wind" of the previous verse in the present passage as giving rise to the crude rejoinder by Micaiah (it is not the "wind of Yahweh," but something quite different!).

22:26 Amon . . . Joash. Both names are otherwise unknown. "Amon" probably means "master workman" (BDB 54c), but it could refer to the famous Egyptian deity of that name. "Joash" ("Yahweh has given" [HALOT 393]) is probably literally a descendant from the royal family (Cogan 2001:492-493), despite scholarly proposals to reckon him as a low-ranking official or a deputy with police duties. (Concerning a clay bulla [seal impression] attesting the phrase "governor of the city," see second note on 2 Kgs 23:8.)

22:28 Everyone mark my words! Here is the culminating short-term prediction that sadly comes true in the very next section of the text—and that despite Ahab's superstitious attempt to disguise himself as a common soldier.

COMMENTARY

Ambiguity shrouds the details here—probably purposefully so—for even Yahweh gave approval to a lying spirit to deceive Ahab, who himself (superstitiously and/or brazenly) disguised himself to try to deceive Yahweh and his unwitting Aramean agents. But Yahweh revealed the lying spirit's commission to deceive Ahab when Ahab paradoxically insisted that the prophet Micaiah must be sure to tell the truth. What better deception than telling the simple truth if people are predisposed not to receive it? Indeed, the entire passage is a meditation on truth versus falsehood, and, yes, the conundrum of whether it is always God's will (for us) to know his will. In the book of Exodus, God famously hardened Pharaoh's heart, and here God seems to be doing the very same thing to King Ahab. Ahab would simply not seek the truth because he was seemingly satisfied by his prophetic extravaganza (22:6). It took the more suspicious King Jehoshaphat to compel Ahab to seek out the Yahwistic prophet Micaiah (22:8). All this was in God's will, for God reveals his plans to his servants the prophets (Amos 3:7), and then allows (or, indeed, causes) a "lying spirit" to disguise those very same plans! Seow has an excellent word concerning this:

> In this story we see just how recalcitrant human beings can be. Here is Ahab, a man who has personally witnessed the manifestation of God's power, who has heard the word of the Lord through several prophets, and, despite his sins, has experienced the grace of God when he expresses penitence. Still, he does not seem to understand what it is that God demands. He has little understanding of the nature of God He has a personal agenda that he is determined to carry out. So he musters all his resources. He gets his subordinates and allies to do his bidding and does not hesitate to manipulate the religious establishment to support his questionable goals. He ignores what he knows to be the truth and suppresses any voice of dissent. He even tries to thwart God's will by deceit in order to achieve his goal. Ahab is a model of what we can become when we are not attentive to the will of God [emphasis added]. (Seow 1999:166)

But, as Seow himself goes on to point out, the will of God is often not easy to discern! As is the case here, we may be confronted with competing truth claims, which can only be verified or falsified unequivocally after the event. Certainly, majority opinion may well prove misleading, and feel-good messages can be positively pernicious. And as Seow points out there always will be those "who are all too ready to pander to the powerful. . . . Perhaps we should listen especially carefully when the word makes us uncomfortable" (Seow 1999:166).

And there is yet more to this. Our God can be very tricky, too! As Seow puts it,

> God may not fit our preconceived image of unimpeachable goodness. The passage
> jolts us into the realization that such a notion of deity, ironically, is too limiting for
> God. Such a god would be an idol, a god of our own creation. . . . The God of the
> Bible is a sovereign deity who oversees all that goes on in the world, darkness as well
> as light, woe as well as weal (Isa 45:7). . . . The sovereign God will use whatever
> means necessary to bring about divine will—whether in judgment or in salvation.
> (Seow 1999:166-167)

This, I submit, is the basic message of the "hardening of the heart" passages in
Exodus (as even the Philistines ironically recognize in 1 Sam 6:5-6). This is also, I
submit, the difficult teaching found in Job 42:2-6. God is absolutely sovereign, but
at times, inscrutable. And this is the message of the present passage. King Ahab may
attempt to bypass his God, but God may choose to bypass him, too. For it is not
only Ahab who knows about "lying spirits." In short, it may well be God's will (for
us) not to know God's will. In any case, to God be the glory!

◆   8. The death of Ahab (22:29-40)

29So King Ahab of Israel and King Jehoshaphat of Judah led their armies against
Ramoth-gilead. 30The king of Israel said to
Jehoshaphat, "As we go into battle, I will
disguise myself so no one will recognize
me, but you wear your royal robes." So the
king of Israel disguised himself, and they
went into battle.

31Meanwhile, the king of Aram had issued these orders to his thirty-two chariot commanders: "Attack only the king of
Israel. Don't bother with anyone else!"
32So when the Aramean chariot commanders saw Jehoshaphat in his royal
robes, they went after him. "There is the
king of Israel!" they shouted. But when
Jehoshaphat called out, 33the chariot
commanders realized he was not the king
of Israel, and they stopped chasing him.

34An Aramean soldier, however, randomly shot an arrow at the Israelite troops
and hit the king of Israel between the
joints of his armor. "Turn the horses* and
get me out of here!" Ahab groaned to the
driver of his chariot. "I'm badly wounded!"

35The battle raged all that day, and the
king remained propped up in his chariot
facing the Arameans. The blood from his
wound ran down to the floor of his chariot,
and as evening arrived he died. 36Just as the
sun was setting, the cry ran through his
troops: "We're done for! Run for your lives!"

37So the king died, and his body was
taken to Samaria and buried there. 38Then
his chariot was washed beside the pool of
Samaria, and dogs came and licked his
blood at the place where the prostitutes
bathed,* just as the LORD had promised.

39The rest of the events in Ahab's reign
and everything he did, including the story
of the ivory palace and the towns he built,
are recorded in *The Book of the History of
the Kings of Israel.* 40So Ahab died, and his
son Ahaziah became the next king.

22:34 Hebrew *Turn your hand.*   22:38 Or *his blood, and the prostitutes bathed [in it]; or his blood, and they
washed his armor.*

NOTES

22:30 *I will disguise myself.* Seow (1999:165) suggests that Jehoshaphat was to wear the
garb of the *Israelite* king (so LXX; but this might be an internal Greek corruption exchang-
ing *mou* [TG1473, ZG1609] for *sou* [TG4771, ZG5148], i.e., "my" for "your"). Montgomery

(1951:345) prefers here an intentional alteration in the Greek to heighten Ahab's treachery. The MT, however, clearly reads "your (own) robes" (also cf. 22:10 where both kings are dressed in their own royal robes). In any case, the motif of disguising oneself has already been presented in 20:38, and it will also be found in the Chronicler's description of the demise of King Josiah (see 2 Chr 35:22), a story that has been strongly influenced by the present narrative (see Japhet 1993:1042-1043 for details). Disguise represents deception, and it betrays insecurity and probably also a guilty conscience (see the first note on 14:2).

22:31 thirty-two. This is possibly a reference back to the leaders mentioned in 20:1, 16 (see the third note to 20:1); this number is lacking in the Chronicles parallel (2 Chr 18:30) and may well be a gloss.

Attack only the king of Israel. It is unclear if the enemy even knows that the Judahite king is in the battle. In any case, they were obviously seeking King Ahab of Israel, who had initiated the hostilities.

22:34 randomly shot an arrow. As the reader knows, there is really nothing random at all about this event. The Hebrew rendered "randomly" is literally "in his innocence" (*letummo* [TH8537, ZH9448]); the same expression is found in 2 Sam 15:11 where 200 Jerusalemites followed the rebel Absalom "but they knew nothing of his intentions."

between the joints of his armor. As Cogan (2001:494) has noted, a vivid example of this may be seen on one of the exterior carved panels located on the chariot of Thutmose IV, where the armor of an enemy chariot driver is depicted as being pierced by an arrow through one of the joints (see ANEP, illustration 314 [at detail no. 11]).

22:35 propped up. Heb., *hayah mo'omad* [TH5975, ZH6641] (he was caused to stand); this posture surely was meant to encourage the Israelites that the king had not fled the battle scene. Yet again, the theme of deception is exemplified.

22:36 the cry ran through his troops. This fulfills the prophecy found back in 22:17. In particular, what is sad here is the fact that this did not have to happen; indeed, the prophecy was given so that it would *not* have to take place (cf. the note on 22:17).

22:38 dogs . . . licked his blood. See the second note on 21:19.

at the place where the prostitutes bathed. The original text here is problematic (cf. the various suggestions given in the NLT mg). The MT is straightforward enough, if a bit unexpected; it is reflected in the above translation, as well as in the first alternative given in the NLT mg. But the LXX refers to dogs and pigs (both here and in the anticipatory prophecy back in 21:19 [20:19, LXX]); the word "pigs" is *khazirim* [TH2386, ZH2614] in Hebrew, somewhat similar to the Hebrew for "the prostitutes" (*hazzonoth* [TH2181B, ZH2390]), possibly leading to the varying textual traditions (although the LXX does include the "prostitute" reference as well). Cogan (2001:495) notes that both dogs and pigs (the scavengers found in cities) were often invoked in formulaic curses of the ancient Near East. The Targum and Syriac Peshitta seem to understand the term *zonoth* (prostitutes) yet differently, along the lines of *zeyanoth* ("weapons, armor"; cf. Jastrow 388, 393). Further complicating the situation is their understanding that the term "dogs" (*kelabim* [TH3611, ZH3978]) could refer to male prostitutes, as in Deut 23:18 [19]. I suspect that such an understanding of *kelabim* (in parallel with *hazzonoth*) may underlie the MT as well (cf. the use of both terms in close proximity in the Deuteronomy text). In any case, if the MT (in the sense of the NLT text) be retained, the idea might simply be that the place where Ahab's blood was washed off the chariot was a well-known place where prostitutes usually did their bathing (cf. NIV text; also Wiseman 1993:189). And if the first alternative translation in the NLT mg be selected (which is also a plausible rendition of the MT), the idea was that the prostitutes at this time bathed in the king's blood (or bloody water) due to the alleged fructifying effects of royal blood (cf. Gray 1970:455; Jones 1984:371-372). In conclusion, certitude still eludes us at this point in our understanding of this difficult and intriguing text.

22:39 *ivory palace.* Amos 6:4 notes the use of ivory carvings to decorate furniture (cf. 10:22; Amos 3:15; for some magnificent examples of such ivory carvings and panels, see ANEP, pictures 125-132). Cogan (2001:495) suggests that the reference here may be to a building that was particularly ostentatious, though Wiseman (1993:190) notes that "there are no known instances of ivory panelling of whole rooms or exteriors."

The Book of the History of the Kings of Israel. See "Literary Style" in the Introduction.

COMMENTARY

The theme of deception continues. Ahab heeded Micaiah's message, at least to the superstitious extent of disguising himself as a common soldier (an ironic contrast to his heroic cast in ch 20). Despite the disguise, Ahab's day in battle would end on a tragic but heroic note—his mortally wounded body (presumably no longer disguised), propped up in the chariot until sundown. This was, on the one hand, yet another ruse to encourage his troops and discourage the enemy, but on the other, a testimony to his dying conviction that he must not quit the field of battle early. Here Ahab's words from 20:11 come true with a vengeance: "A warrior putting on his sword for battle should not boast like a warrior who has already won." Ahab had fair warning that his God did not favor his endeavors (although, admittedly, the contest of prophet versus prophet probably made this warning more ambiguous than we might otherwise surmise; cf. the commentary on 22:10-28). Ahab's ally King Jehoshaphat, although remaining dressed in royal robes as bidden (see note on 22:30), was the only king who providentially survived, apparently unscathed. Ahab's dynasty (or more accurately, the dynasty of his father, Omri) would hang on for 11 more years; but it, like Ahab himself, was already as good as dead.

In summary, Ahab was a complicated person. He did have moments of heroism (mainly in ch 20, but even there, the evidence is mixed), and he certainly had many moments of treachery (much of chs 18, 21, and also here in ch 22). His marriage to Jezebel was probably not by choice, but rather arranged by his parents (see note on 16:31), and certainly he represented the result of diplomatic pressures that we rarely face today. He did repent at one point (21:27-29), but such repentance seems not to have lasted very long. In short, Ahab was a crafty, conniving, sometimes cowardly leader during an era when such personality traits were probably necessary to survive long on the throne. But the final verdict on King Ahab must be as negative as the initial verdict found back in 16:30-33: "He did more to provoke the anger of the LORD, the God of Israel, than any of the other kings of Israel before him." What a sad legacy to leave to posterity. We must be suitably chastened so that we are in no danger of following him in his fate. Truly, "a (spiritual) warrior girding for battle should not boast like one who has already won" (an adaptation of Ahab's apt words as found in 20:11; cf. Paul's similarly sober words in Phil 3:12-14: "Forgetting the past . . . I press on to reach the end of the race and receive the heavenly prize"). Let us redouble our dedication to run the good race and fight the good fight to the very end.

◆   E. Synchronistic History of the Divided Monarchy, Resumed
       (1 Kgs 22:41-53 [22:41-54])
       1. Jehoshaphat rules in Judah (22:41-50 [22:41-51])

⁴¹Jehoshaphat son of Asa began to rule over Judah in the fourth year of King Ahab's reign in Israel. ⁴²Jehoshaphat was thirty-five years old when he became king, and he reigned in Jerusalem twenty-five years. His mother was Azubah, the daughter of Shilhi.

⁴³Jehoshaphat was a good king, following the example of his father, Asa. He did what was pleasing in the LORD's sight. *During his reign, however, he failed to remove all the pagan shrines, and the people still offered sacrifices and burned incense there. ⁴⁴Jehoshaphat also made peace with the king of Israel.

⁴⁵The rest of the events in Jehoshaphat's reign, the extent of his power, and the wars he waged are recorded in *The Book of the History of the Kings of Judah.*

⁴⁶He banished from the land the rest of the male and female shrine prostitutes, who still continued their practices from the days of his father, Asa.

⁴⁷(There was no king in Edom at that time, only a deputy.)

⁴⁸Jehoshaphat also built a fleet of trading ships* to sail to Ophir for gold. But the ships never set sail, for they met with disaster in their home port of Ezion-geber. ⁴⁹At one time Ahaziah son of Ahab had proposed to Jehoshaphat, "Let my men sail with your men in the ships." But Jehoshaphat refused the request.

⁵⁰When Jehoshaphat died, he was buried with his ancestors in the City of David. Then his son Jehoram became the next king.

22:43 Verses 22:43b-53 are numbered 22:44-54 in Hebrew text.   22:48 Hebrew *fleet of ships of Tarshish.*

NOTES

22:41-50 The Old Greek has a doublet of much of this Jehoshaphat material in 16:28a-h (see note on 16:28 for details); this represents a varying, and possibly more original, chronological schema than that found here in the MT.

22:41 *Jehoshaphat son of Asa.* Although mentioned several times already in the Ahab material (cf. 22:2), the Deuteronomistic accession formula (in the MT) has been postponed until this verse, following the death and burial formula for Ahab. This is normal practice (see "Literary Style" in the Introduction). The name Jehoshaphat means "Yah(weh) judges" or "Yah(weh) has judged" (the sense of the verb *shapat* [TH8199, ZH9149] is to vindicate, or bring positive justice to a negative situation). Jehoshaphat has already been pictured somewhat as a pawn of Ahab of Israel (see commentary on 22:1-9), but he is generally described in quite positive terms here in Kings and especially in the more extensive material to be found about him in 1-2 Chronicles (2 Chr 17-20).

22:43 *a good king.* For a listing of these "good" kings, see endnote 2 of the Introduction (much of the present evaluative material is formulaic in nature, as is discussed at some length in endnote 33 of the Introduction).

22:44 [45] *made peace.* This is already alluded to in the note on 22:4.

22:45 [46] **The Book of the History of the Kings of Judah.** See "Literary Style" in the Introduction.

22:46 [47] *male and female shrine prostitutes.* See note on 14:24.

22:47 [48] *There was no king in Edom.* This laconic comment probably anticipates Jehoshaphat's subsequent campaign in the area as presented in 2 Kgs 3 (especially note the comment about the "king of Edom" in 2 Kgs 3:9; cf. the first note on that verse concerning the apparent contradiction between that statement and the one found here). The present comment also prepares the hearer/reader for the reference to Ezion-geber, an Edomite port, in the next verse (22:48).

22:48 [49] *a fleet of trading ships*. Lit., "ships of Tarshish"; see the first note on 10:22 for details. For the Solomonic parallels, both positive and negative, that are meant to be noticed here, see the commentary below.

***Ophir*.** See note on 9:28.

COMMENTARY

The Deuteronomistic verdict on King Jehoshaphat is quite positive (as is that of the Chronicler; see note on 22:41). Nevertheless, Seow (1999:168) has made a good case for finding here both a comparison and some subtle criticism of Jehoshaphat in terms of great King Solomon in the following areas: (1) the issue of local sanctuaries as a negative for both kings (see 22:43b; cf. 3:2-3); (2) the enactment of peace with Israel and dominion over Edom as two positive developments for both kings (see 22:44, 47; cf. 4:24; 5:12), thus gaining dominion over the Edomite port of Ezion-geber (22:48; cf. 9:26-27); and (3) the attempt to send a fleet of ships to the port of Ophir for gold (see 22:48; cf. 9:26-28, as well as Solomon's marked success in this endeavor [10:11-12]). In this last comparison, however, Jehoshaphat was clearly no equal to Solomon, for Solomon succeeded most remarkably with the nautical help proffered by the Phoenician king Hiram (9:27); whereas Jehoshaphat, rejecting the help offered by Ahaziah, king of Israel, failed most miserably (22:49)—Ahaziah perhaps representing a latter-day Hiram, as it were (see Barnes 2009:694, where I point out the significant Phoenician influence on the northern kingdom of Israel at this time; cf. the commentary on 16:21-28). I suspect that both these Solomonic parallels and contrasts were meant to be recognized by the reader/hearer of the text.

Jehoshaphat tried, like a veritable King Solomon, to dominate his time and his region; he succeeded somewhat, but he eventually proved to be nothing like Solomon in nautical stature (cf. Japhet 1993:803). Still, as Seow concludes, he was still a Solomon in that he too was a Davidic ruler, and that is no small consideration in the overall scheme of history (see the commentary on 22:51-53 for further reflections on this issue). Meanwhile, Jehoshaphat was nevertheless reckoned in Deuteronomistic terms as a "good" king—no small thing in the eyes of the Lord and not the case for most of the descendants of David (only 8 of the 19 candidates after Solomon were so reckoned; cf. endnote 2 of the Introduction).

◆   **2. Ahaziah rules in Israel (22:51-53 [22:52-54])**

51Ahaziah son of Ahab began to rule over Israel in the seventeenth year of King Jehoshaphat's reign in Judah. He reigned in Samaria two years. 52But he did what was evil in the LORD's sight, following the example of his father and mother and the example of Jeroboam son of Nebat, who had led Israel to sin. 53He served Baal and worshiped him, provoking the anger of the LORD, the God of Israel, just as his father had done.

NOTES

22:51 [52] *Ahaziah.* This was the first of two sons of Ahab who succeeded their father to the throne (cf. 2 Kgs 1:17). Ahaziah's name probably means "Yah(weh) has grasped, taken hold of." It is interesting that Ahab's children seem to bear Yahwistic names (cf. Joram, and also Joash [22:26], if indeed Joash was literally the king's son).

COMMENTARY

We will hear more about Ahaziah in the very next chapter (i.e., 2 Kgs 1, as the book is now divided); this is a good reminder that the division of Kings into two volumes is secondary and not editorially significant (cf. "Canonicity and Textual History" in the Introduction).

The Deuteronomistic denunciation here for Ahaziah is general and formulaic (cf. endnote 1 of the Introduction), nothing more. Perhaps a modicum of sympathy may be extended by the modern hearer/reader of this ancient text for this seemingly colorless descendant and successor of the vigorous King Ahab of Israel, whose dramatic story has just been told at some length. Still, all the northern kings were deemed "evil" to some extent (see endnotes 1 and 33 of the Introduction), and Ahaziah proved to be no exception. What a sad way to end 1 Kings: "Like father, like son" (cf. 22:53)—end of subject. But that, in its own way, is the epitaph of the entirety of 1–2 Kings: The fathers sin, and the children do the same, and eventually, exile (northern, and later southern) has to happen.

Seow (1999:198) contrasts the legacy of Jehoshaphat in 22:50 ("buried with his ancestors in the City of David") with that of Ahaziah in 22:53 ("provok[ed] the anger of the LORD . . . just as his father [Ahab] had done"). One king's legacy is relatively positive, the other utterly negative. But the real difference between the two is that one of them was heir to the throne of David, the other was not; and this was due only to the sovereign will of God. (Our legacies, likewise, depend much on God's utter sovereignty and the resulting parental legacy we inherit.) This will be the burden, not so much of the brief discussions found in the final 13 verses of the present chapter (22:41-53), but of the entirety of the next. "Is there no God in Israel?" (2 Kgs 1:3, 16) is the question repeated therein. Thus, in conclusion, we need to realize that we cannot control either our parental legacies or our birthright, but we can control our theological responses to whatever setting they may place us in (cf. 2 Kgs 3:2 about Ahab's other son, Joram). And we are indeed responsible for those responses. This very biblical message is something we can and must take away from the present short passages about Jehoshaphat of Judah and Ahaziah of Israel.

◆   F. Another Prophetic Story from the Elijah Cycle:
        Elijah Confronts King Ahaziah (2 Kgs 1:1-18)

After King Ahab's death, the land of Moab rebelled against Israel.

²One day Israel's new king, Ahaziah, fell through the latticework of an upper room at his palace in Samaria and was seriously injured. So he sent messengers to the temple of Baal-zebub, the god of Ekron, to ask whether he would recover.

³But the angel of the LORD told Elijah, who was from Tishbe, "Go and confront the messengers of the king of Samaria and ask them, 'Is there no God in Israel? Why are you going to Baal-zebub, the god of Ekron, to ask whether the king will recover? ⁴Now, therefore, this is what the LORD says: You will never leave the bed you are lying on; you will surely die.' " So Elijah went to deliver the message.

⁵When the messengers returned to the king, he asked them, "Why have you returned so soon?"

⁶They replied, "A man came up to us and told us to go back to the king and give him this message. 'This is what the LORD says: Is there no God in Israel? Why are you sending men to Baal-zebub, the god of Ekron, to ask whether you will recover? Therefore, because you have done this, you will never leave the bed you are lying on; you will surely die.' "

⁷"What sort of man was he?" the king demanded. "What did he look like?"

⁸They replied, "He was a hairy man,* and he wore a leather belt around his waist."

"Elijah from Tishbe!" the king exclaimed.

⁹Then he sent an army captain with fifty soldiers to arrest him. They found him sitting on top of a hill. The captain said to him, "Man of God, the king has commanded you to come down with us."

¹⁰But Elijah replied to the captain, "If I am a man of God, let fire come down from heaven and destroy you and your fifty men!" Then fire fell from heaven and killed them all.

¹¹So the king sent another captain with fifty men. The captain said to him, "Man of God, the king demands that you come down at once."

¹²Elijah replied, "If I am a man of God, let fire come down from heaven and destroy you and your fifty men!" And again the fire of God fell from heaven and killed them all.

¹³Once more the king sent a third captain with fifty men. But this time the captain went up the hill and fell to his knees before Elijah. He pleaded with him, "O man of God, please spare my life and the lives of these, your fifty servants. ¹⁴See how the fire from heaven came down and destroyed the first two groups. But now please spare my life!"

¹⁵Then the angel of the LORD said to Elijah, "Go down with him, and don't be afraid of him." So Elijah got up and went with him to the king.

¹⁶And Elijah said to the king, "This is what the LORD says: Why did you send messengers to Baal-zebub, the god of Ekron, to ask whether you will recover? Is there no God in Israel to answer your question? Therefore, because you have done this, you will never leave the bed you are lying on; you will surely die."

¹⁷So Ahaziah died, just as the LORD had promised through Elijah. Since Ahaziah did not have a son to succeed him, his brother Joram* became the next king. This took place in the second year of the reign of Jehoram son of Jehoshaphat, king of Judah.

¹⁸The rest of the events in Ahaziah's reign and everything he did are recorded in *The Book of the History of the Kings of Israel.*

1:8 Or *He was wearing clothing made of hair.*   1:17 Hebrew *Jehoram,* a variant spelling of Joram.

NOTES

1:1 *After King Ahab's death.* The reference is to the preceding chapter (1 Kgs 22), where Ahab dies tragically, and to some degree heroically, on the battlefield (see 1 Kgs 22:34-38).

Moab. The Mesha Stela from ancient Moab states, "Omri, king of Israel, oppressed Moab many years" (cf. the commentary on 1 Kgs 16:21-28). Presumably this would include the 22 years of his son Ahab as well. We will read much more about Moab and its king Mesha in ch 3.

rebelled against Israel. In clear contrast to Jehoshaphat's presumed control over Edom (1 Kgs 22:47), Ahaziah is not able to retain control over Moab. Leithart (2006:166) succinctly points out the contrast: "While Jehoshaphat controls Gentiles, Ahaziah loses control over Gentiles . . . the kingdom is as sick as the king, and the dynasty is dying."

1:2 Ahaziah. See 1 Kgs 22:51 for an introduction to this successor to Ahab. The "latticework of an upper room at his palace" probably refers to wood slats found in clerestory windows or roof skylights protecting the interior room from the rays of the sun, yet giving access to free-flowing air; the "upper room" would probably represent the second-floor throne room (or possibly bedroom) of a *bit hilani* or colonnaded palace structure (see Sweeney 2007:269, and his reference to Halpern 1988:45-54; cf. especially Halpern's diagram on p. 53; also cf. Cogan and Tadmor 1988:24).

Baal-zebub, the god of Ekron. The Hebrew "name" for this god means "lord of the flies," but this was not his original name or title! Presumably, the deity in question is a local manifestation of Baal Hadad (cf. the commentary on 1 Kgs 18:41-46 for details), otherwise known in Phoenicia as Baal Zebul ("Baal the prince"). The Hebrew here thus employs the similar-sounding pejorative word *zebub* ("flies") for the original epithet *zebul* ("prince"). This mocking substitution is also attested in the New Testament references to Satan as "Beelzeboul" and "Beelzebub" (cf. the NLT mg for Matt 10:25; 12:24; Mark 3:22; Luke 11:15). A comparable phenomenon in the OT is the sarcastic pattern of substituting the term *bosheth* [TH1322, ZH1425] (shame) for Israelite names containing references to Baal. See, e.g., "Ishbosheth" for Esh-baal in 2 Sam 4:1 (cf. NLT mg); "Mephibosheth" for Merib-baal in 2 Sam 4:4 (cf. NLT mg); and "Jerub-besheth" for Jerub-baal (another name for Gideon) in 2 Sam 11:21 (cf. NLT mg).

Ekron. This is one of the five Philistine cities, located on the border between Judah and Philistia (cf. Josh 13:3), thus some distance southwest of Samaria. Perhaps the unexpectedness of this location (Baal Zebul was worshiped particularly in the land of Phoenicia, northwest of Israel) was an attempt to confuse Elijah and his God (cf. the similar pattern, in a number of respects, found in 1 Kgs 14:1-18, which also involved the life-threatening illness of a royal personage and an analogous attempt to disguise the nature of the formal inquiry being made to the deity as to the likelihood of his recovery). Wiseman (1993:192) proffers the intriguing suggestion that this god may also have been renowned for his healing qualities.

to ask. The verb *darash* [TH1875, ZH2011] is used here, in 1:3, 6, and twice in 1:16, as well as in the similar context of 1 Kgs 14:5. This verb is a technical term signifying making an oracular inquiry of the deity (see Cogan and Tadmor 1988:24-25); that such a formal inquiry is made of a *foreign* god in the present passage helps explain the extreme anger of Yahweh, as well as of his prophet Elijah, which is conveyed to the emissaries of the king.

1:3 Elijah. See the first note on 1 Kgs 17:1 for the meaning of his name, as well as the reference here to "Tishbe." The present chapter is usually considered to be the last chapter of the so-called "Elijah cycle" (see the "Elijah and Elisha Cycles: Comparisons and Contrasts" chart on p. 204). Elijah's translation into heaven in the next chapter, then, is considered part of the "Elisha cycle," which includes 2:1–8:15 and the concluding story in 13:14-21. (For a later, curious reference to a letter sent from Elijah to King Jehoram of Judah, see 2 Chr 21:12-15. About this, see Boda 2010:337-338.)

Is there no God in Israel? This famous query is also found in 1:6, 16 (see the third and fourth notes to 1:2, above, for reasons for Elijah's righteous anger as displayed here). The close parallelism of Elijah's repetitive answers to the various groups of emissaries sent by the king (cf. 1:3-4, 6, 16) is characteristic of folkloristic storytelling (see the various notes on 1 Kgs 20; cf. Hobbs 1985:4-5).

1:8 *He was a hairy man.* Lit., "a man, baal [i.e., owner] of hair" (*'ish ba'al se'ar* [TH8181, ZH8552]), which some take as indicating a garment or clothing of hair (i.e., a hairy garment or mantle; cf. the NLT mg, also John the Baptist as described in Matt 3:4; Mark 1:6). Cogan and Tadmor (1988:26), however, argue convincingly for the traditional translation found here (also see Hobbs 1985:10); Leithart (2006:168) nicely contrasts Elijah as a "Baal of Hair" in place of the "Baal-zebub" mentioned earlier in the chapter. I myself would further contrast the apparently quite "hairy" Elijah with the relatively "hairless" Elisha mocked by the insolent boys ("Go away, baldy!") in 2:23-25. In any case, the king immediately recognized which famous person his emissaries had encountered, based only on a simple description of his physical appearance.

1:9 *an army captain with fifty soldiers.* A repetitive motif of "fifties" will pervade both this chapter (1:10-14) and the next (cf. 2:7, 16-17; cf. also 1 Kgs 18:4, 13, where Obadiah hid the Yahwistic prophets in two caves, fifty in each). Fifty men typically comprise a military unit, headed, as here, by an "officer" or "captain" (*sar* [TH8269, ZH8569]; cf. Cogan and Tadmor 1988:26).

1:11 *demands.* This is an effective, if periphrastic, translation, conveying the harsher language found here in the second command (*meherah redah* [TH4120/3381, ZH4559/3718], "hurry, come down!") in contrast to the first command in 1:9.

1:13 *Once more.* As is commonly the case in folkloristic literature, the third time proves to be the charm (see further the commentary below). Another folkloristic motif is also illustrated by the approach taken by the third "captain of fifty": "Honey attracts more flies than vinegar." The second captain (1:11-12) had tried arrogance and assertiveness to get his way, with disastrous results, but the third captain showed more wisdom than that—he appealed to Elijah's concern over loss of innocent life, and his "honey" of a request proved far more effective than the "vinegar" that the first and especially the second commander had to offer.

1:15 *the angel of the LORD.* This presumably is the same angel who first apprised Elijah of the king's secret mission (1:3); now he ironically confirms that it is indeed God's will to follow the first two captains' messages to "go down" to meet the king. Considering the fate of the king's emissary's two predecessors, I assume Elijah did have some reason to fear him; but even if not, the angel's reassurance to the prophet, "don't be afraid of him," was surely a welcome addition.

1:17 *Joram.* Here is the first example of what will be a repeated phenomenon: the interspersing of the names "Joram" and "Jehoram" (basically, two different pronunciations of the same name), referring to both the king of Israel and the concurrent king of Judah (see the NLT mg note to 8:21a for variations in the naming of the Judahite monarch). The name Joram/Jehoram means "Yah(weh) is high, exalted."

second year of . . . Jehoram. As Shenkel (1968:74) notes, this synchronism is at variance with the one found in 3:1; it probably represents an alternate chronological system elsewhere preserved mostly in the Old Greek translation of Kings (see the note on 1 Kgs 16:28 and "Canonicity and Textual History" in the Introduction). Codex Vaticanus here omits this reference, instead inserting 1:18a-d, which is largely a doublet of 3:1-3. To state the obvious, the chronological data represented by the varying synchronisms in the MT and LXX here and elsewhere rule out any dogmatism as to which dates are primary and which are secondary. I do suspect, however, that here the MT attestation of Joram's accession as taking place in the "second year of . . . Jehoram [of Judah]," although betraying the Hebrew syntax of a later, secondary insertion into the text (see Hobbs 1985:3-4; cf. Cogan and Tadmor 1988:27), may well attest an earlier (and more accurate?) comparative chronology also attested in the otherwise aberrant synchronism found in 1 Kgs 16:23 (MT and LXX), which the Masoretes also retained in the text. (See also my comments on the varying locations of Jehoshaphat's accession formula in the MT and the LXX, as discussed in the note on 1 Kgs 16:28.)

1:18 *are recorded in* **The Book of the History of the Kings of Israel.** See "Literary Style" in the Introduction.

COMMENTARY

The major transgression presented in this chapter is King Ahaziah's "making formal inquiry of" Baal, the god of Ekron, instead of Yahweh, the God of Israel (see fourth note on 1:2). It has become commonplace in commentaries on Kings to highlight Yahweh's strong jealousy of any worship of any other god (see, e.g., the commentary on 1 Kgs 12:25-33). This basic observation must once more be emphasized here. Yahweh simply will not tolerate (for the good of his people) any formal religious "inquiries" of any other deities (who, after all, do not even exist; cf. Isa 43:10-13; 44:6-8; 45:14). Whether it be the notorious Baal Hadad of Phoenicia, the patron god of Jezebel the queen mother (cf. the note on 1 Kgs 16:31), or the otherwise unknown "Baal of Ekron" mentioned in the present passage (and mockingly entitled "Baal-zebub" by the Hebrew writers; cf. the second note on 1:2), or any other alleged deity or ideological system of ancient or modern times (e.g., astrology, secularism, materialism), Yahweh will not be mocked. His people and their leadership, if they try to sneak off to seek direction from such "deities," had better be ready to face disaster as severe as any described in the present chapter. It cannot be otherwise. Of course, our God is a God of love, incredible patience, and amazing grace; but even in the New Testament, lies and subterfuge on the part of God's people (such as Ananias and Sapphira in Acts 5:1-11) may lead to sudden death and severe fear falling upon "the entire church and everyone else who heard what had happened" (Acts 5:11). That is surely the primary message of the present chapter of 2 Kings.

But there is more. As Gina Hens-Piazza (2006:230-232) has effectively argued, King Ahaziah participated in a kind of dangerous deception even beyond his attempt to fool Elijah and Elijah's God:

[The] refusal to acknowledge God's ultimate reign in all matters encourages delusions that one can manipulate reality. It supports our inclinations to serve our self-interests and to use others to do so.

Ahaziah participated in this kind of deception. First, he believed he could be privy to what is beyond human capacity to know. He refused to acknowledge his human limitations regarding the ultimate questions surrounding life and death. . . . Confronted by his officers with evidence of an alternative power in the form of the word of the Lord through Elijah, the king must make a choice. Either he must give up his self-deceiving belief system, acknowledge his vulnerability, and embrace the Lord, or he must become even more fixed and adamant in his false sense of being in charge. . . .

When human power competes with divine power it often yields tragic outcomes. The first two companies of men that Ahaziah sends up the mountain are destroyed. Innocent lives are put in harm's way. But to keep the delusion alive, the abuse of power becomes imperative. . . . Thus a third company of men is sent.

Such power that functions without controls, believing it can manipulate reality— even ultimate reality—eventually self-destructs. Ahaziah's death confirmed the prophet's word and thus became a witness to the ultimate truth and power of God's word. But it also teaches something else. It illustrates the relationship between lack of faith in the omnipotent Lord and the human potential for abuse of power. When we lose sight of the all-powerful God who controls matters of life and death, we are drawn to other false groundings for our hope. In turn, putting trust in other false controls over our destiny can breed a misuse of power. Keeping such delusions alive not only leads to using or sacrificing others for our self-interests, but can eventually cost us our own lives as well. Ahaziah's story serves as a witness.

This story is a simple, repetitive tale, with characteristic folkloristic flourishes. (Let the reader be reminded that "folklore" can contain as much literal truth as any other storytelling technique—the truthfulness of the tale is *not* the issue here, but rather the technique that the divinely inspired author used to convey such truth.) The simple sequencing of threefold repetition (with subtle variations) can be most effective in storytelling, as D. N. Freedman has pointed out regarding the analogous folkloristic retelling of the story of Queen Esther: "The third time is the charm in literary accounts. It is like the acrobat or magician who deliberately fails twice in trying to perform his most difficult feat, before succeeding on the third try. This enhances the suspense and the expectation of the audience, as well as winning for the performance the applause he deserves but is not likely to get if the audience thinks that there is no danger or limited need of skill to succeed" (cited in Moore 1971:58, in reference to Esth 4–5). So it is here in chapter 1 (as well as in the very next chapter, where we again find a threefold repetition in 2:2, 4, and 6). But in Elijah's threefold threat of fire from heaven, who is the "winner" (besides the third captain and his fifty men!)? Certainly not King Ahaziah, as we have just seen—he does ironically get his wish that Elijah come "down" and be "captured" (of course, it took the reassuring words of the "angel of the LORD" to help effect that accomplishment [see the note on 1:15]), but all the king gets for his efforts is the repeated refrain of judgment and death found in 1:16 (cf. 1:3-4, 6). No, I guess the "winner," if there is one, is Elijah, who succeeds in going "down" to the king (presumably to Samaria), but eventually "up" with a flourish, as he is translated into heaven in the very next chapter. Thus, Elijah's ministry ends on a high note. The God of Elijah will literally and literarily have the last word here: "you [King Ahaziah] will surely die." So the king does die, and his brother takes over the throne (1:17). The fact that Elijah, in turn, does not die (here, or ever!) will of course be the major focus of the next chapter.

Finally, the Christian reader will recall that the New Testament makes curious use of the present story, as follows: In Luke 9:51-56, James and John ask Jesus if they should call down "fire from heaven" upon some Samaritans who did not welcome them (some of the later Greek mss add the phrase "as Elijah did" in 9:54, making the parallel with the present passage even more explicit). Jesus totally disagrees, rebuking them and, in some manuscripts, explicitly reminding them that he had come to save people's lives, not to destroy them! It is tempting to wish violence and destruction upon our enemies when our efforts at bringing in the Kingdom meet unreasoning opposition, but we know that Jesus promoted a "higher way" than this, instructing us to bless those who curse us, and pray for those who persecute us (Matt 5:44; Luke 6:28).

In light of such teachings, I wonder if the "fire from heaven" motif in the present chapter is brought under subtle critique even by the narrator of the passage, for it takes the words of a gently persistent angel and a honey-tongued captain to tame the fiery, rash actions of the enraged prophet. Neither the hot temper of Elijah, nor that of his greater predecessor, the prophet Moses, won them all that much favor from their God.

◆   ## G. Stories from the Elisha Cycle (2 Kgs 2:1–8:15)
1. Elijah taken into heaven (2:1-18)

When the LORD was about to take Elijah up to heaven in a whirlwind, Elijah and Elisha were traveling from Gilgal. ²And Elijah said to Elisha, "Stay here, for the LORD has told me to go to Bethel."

But Elisha replied, "As surely as the LORD lives and you yourself live, I will never leave you!" So they went down together to Bethel.

³The group of prophets from Bethel came to Elisha and asked him, "Did you know that the LORD is going to take your master away from you today?"

"Of course I know," Elisha answered. "But be quiet about it."

⁴Then Elijah said to Elisha, "Stay here, for the LORD has told me to go to Jericho."

But Elisha replied again, "As surely as the LORD lives and you yourself live, I will never leave you." So they went on together to Jericho.

⁵Then the group of prophets from Jericho came to Elisha and asked him, "Did you know that the LORD is going to take your master away from you today?"

"Of course I know," Elisha answered. "But be quiet about it."

⁶Then Elijah said to Elisha, "Stay here, for the LORD has told me to go to the Jordan River."

But again Elisha replied, "As surely as the LORD lives and you yourself live, I will never leave you." So they went on together.

⁷Fifty men from the group of prophets also went and watched from a distance as Elijah and Elisha stopped beside the Jordan River. ⁸Then Elijah folded his cloak together and struck the water with it. The river divided, and the two of them went across on dry ground!

⁹When they came to the other side, Elijah said to Elisha, "Tell me what I can do for you before I am taken away."

And Elisha replied, "Please let me inherit a double share of your spirit and become your successor."

¹⁰"You have asked a difficult thing," Elijah replied. "If you see me when I am taken from you, then you will get your request. But if not, then you won't."

¹¹As they were walking along and talking, suddenly a chariot of fire appeared, drawn by horses of fire. It drove

between the two men, separating them, and Elijah was carried by a whirlwind into heaven. ¹²Elisha saw it and cried out, "My father! My father! I see the chariots and charioteers of Israel!" And as they disappeared from sight, Elisha tore his clothes in distress.

¹³Elisha picked up Elijah's cloak, which had fallen when he was taken up. Then Elisha returned to the bank of the Jordan River. ¹⁴He struck the water with Elijah's cloak and cried out, "Where is the LORD, the God of Elijah?" Then the river divided, and Elisha went across.

¹⁵When the group of prophets from Jericho saw from a distance what happened, they exclaimed, "Elijah's spirit rests upon Elisha!" And they went to meet him and bowed to the ground before him. ¹⁶"Sir," they said, "just say the word and fifty of our strongest men will search the wilderness for your master. Perhaps the Spirit of the LORD has left him on some mountain or in some valley."

"No," Elisha said, "don't send them." ¹⁷But they kept urging him until they shamed him into agreeing, and he finally said, "All right, send them." So fifty men searched for three days but did not find Elijah. ¹⁸Elisha was still at Jericho when they returned. "Didn't I tell you not to go?" he asked.

NOTES

2:1 *up to heaven in a whirlwind.* As noted in 2:11, it is the "whirlwind" (*se'arah* [TH5591A, ZH6194]), and not the accompanying "chariot of fire," which actually impels the prophet Elijah into heaven.

Gilgal. As Cogan and Tadmor (1988:31) indicate, this is probably not the famous Gilgal located near the city of Jericho (Josh 4:19), but a site to the west, in the hill country of Ephraim (modern Jiljilia), near the road between Bethel and Shechem (ABD 2.1023). Note that after Elisha refuses to leave his master (2:2), they are said to go "down" to Bethel—an unlikely verb to use if they had been in the Gilgal near Jericho since they then would have been going uphill to Bethel.

2:2 *Stay here.* This is the first of three times (cf. 2:4, 6) Elijah tells Elisha this. Concerning the use of such a threefold reference in folkloristic storytelling, see the previous commentary section.

As surely as the LORD lives and you yourself live. This is repeated three times (cf. 2:4, 6). Concerning the meaning of this oath formula, see the second note on 1 Kgs 17:1.

Bethel. See the note on 1 Kgs 12:29 concerning the location and prominence of this significant site.

2:3 *The group of prophets.* See the second note on 1 Kgs 20:35. The phrase here (lit., "sons of the prophets") denotes a formal prophetic brotherhood (10 of the 11 occurrences of this phrase refer to prophetic groups connected with Elisha). Hobbs (1985:25-27) argues effectively that they were probably "lay supporters" of Elisha rather than an organized guild of prophetic disciples under Elisha's formal leadership (see next note).

your master. Heb., *'adoneka* [TH113, ZH123]. The term used for "lord" or "master" is the typical term used by the "sons of the prophets" and others to refer to the prophets Elijah (2:3, 5) and Elisha (2:16, 19; 4:16, 28; 5:20, 22; 6:5, 15; 8:12; cf. Hobbs 1985:25-26). Only twice is the term "father" used of Elisha, both times by a king of Israel (6:21; 13:14; cf. Elisha's similar usage for Elijah in 2:12); and as Hobbs notes, this should give pause to those who would argue that Elisha (or Elijah before him) was reckoned as the formal leader or "father" of the "sons of the prophets."

2:4 Jericho. The well-known city is located in the rift (or Jordan River) valley five miles (8 km) west of the Jordan River; it has the distinction of being the lowest city on earth (825 ft [250 m] below sea level). In 1 Kgs 16:34 (cf. the note there), we were reminded that Joshua's ancient curse on this city was fulfilled at fearsome cost (the death of two children), and now no longer operative (see also 2:19-22).

2:6 the Jordan River. This is presumably the lowest point in elevation for the entire trip, giving point to the contrast of Elijah's going up to heaven in 2:11, and to the repeated taunting of Elisha to do the same ("Go on up, you baldhead!") by the group of insolent boys in 2:23, NIV.

2:8 folded his cloak together. The Hebrew root galam [TH1563, ZH1676] (to roll or fold up) is found only here and as a noun in Ezek 27:24 (gelom [TH1545, ZH1659], "wrappings, garments"). Therefore, it is hard to specify the precise action depicted here, although the subsequent action of "striking" the water (cf. Elisha's similar action in 2:14) is quite clearly specified by the verb nakah [TH5221, ZH5782] (to strike).

2:9 a double share of your spirit. This is the prophetic "spirit" Yahweh has placed on his prophet, which is transferable to others (cf. 2:15; also Num 11:16-17, 24-30). The "double share" (pi-shenayim [TH6310/8147, ZH7023/9109], lit., "a double mouth") means "a double portion" (BDB 805 [5b]), which is the portion of the inheritance allotted for the firstborn son (see Deut 21:17). Although the "Elijah and Elisha Cycles: Comparisons and Contrasts" chart (p. 204) indicates a literary motif of duality concerning Elisha vis-à-vis Elijah (e.g., two resurrections of the dead over against one for Elijah; multiple food miracles over against a single one for Elijah), Elisha is to be reckoned as the eldest "son" of his "father" Elijah—not as a prophet of twice the significance or the like. However, that status in and of itself is still of great significance.

2:10 a difficult thing. The Hiphil of qashah [TH7185, ZH7996] here signifies "to make difficult, (ask) a difficult thing" (BDB 904); it is used elsewhere of making something severe or burdensome, or even of stiffening the neck. The present context represents a test of whether, as a typical ninth-century prophet, Elisha can "see" or "behold" heavenly realities (cf. the notes on 1 Kgs 22:19, concerning his contemporary, Micaiah son of Imlah, especially in regard to his seeing the "armies of heaven").

2:11 a chariot of fire . . . horses of fire. This is a literal translation of the Hebrew, but it should be noted (cf. Wiseman 1993:195-196) that it was the "whirlwind" (a repetition of the word found in 2:1) that actually bore Elijah into heaven. Nonetheless, this fiery appearance evokes the familiar imagery of the essence of Yahweh as "fire within cloud" (see Exod 3:2; 13:21; 19:18; 40:38; cf. Deut 4:24 [and its citation in Heb 12:29]; 18:16; also Yahweh as "Rider of the Clouds," an epithet often connected with the Canaanite storm god Baal; cf. Dillard 1999:83-85). Possibly plural chariots are in view (so Seow 1999:179), although the term used here (rekeb [TH7393, ZH8207]) is grammatically singular. In Hab 3:3-16, Yahweh's heavenly "chariots" (plural) are also connected with storm winds. In any case, Elisha clearly passed the test Elijah posed (cf. 2:10).

2:12 the chariots and charioteers of Israel! As in 2:11, the grammatically singular term rekeb [TH7393, ZH8207] (chariot) is used (see the previous note). Cogan and Tadmor (1988:32) suggest that these words probably represent an exclamatory phrase made popular during the mid-ninth-century Aramean wars (see 13:14; cf. 6:8-17). Certainly, the idea here is that the presence of the prophet was more militarily efficacious than any number of royal chariots or charioteers. (Concerning the suggested translation of parashim [TH6571A, ZH7305] as "charioteers," rather than "cavalry" or the like, see notes on 1 Kgs 4:26.)

2:15 *Elijah's spirit rests upon Elisha!* The unmistakable presence of the prophetic spirit sent by Yahweh is what is meant here (see note on 2:9).

2:16 *fifty of our strongest men.* See the note on 1:9.

Perhaps the Spirit of the LORD has left him on some mountain or in some valley. Elijah had been known to appear and disappear quite unpredictably (1 Kgs 18:12), and in any case, it would be important to avoid the disgrace of allowing a corpse to lie unburied (Wiseman 1993:196-197).

2:17 *they shamed him.* Lit., "until shame, or embarrassment" (*'ad bosh* [TH954, ZH1017]); the phrase probably came simply to signify "for a long while" (cf. Cogan and Tadmor 1988:33, citing G. F. Moore). This is also probably the sense of the difficult text found in 8:11.

COMMENTARY

As John H. Walton (2001:424-425) has reminded us (particularly in reference to the book of Genesis), "Biblical narratives generally resist moralization," and when we try to resist that observation, we usually end up imposing our own preconceptions on the text, which is not a good thing to do! Such is the case here in chapter 2. To interpret Elisha's dogged persistence as preaching a positive example of faithfulness (although I certainly do think perseverance is a positive attribute of the prophetic disciple) is probably to read into the text a spiritual presupposition that can certainly be sustained in general by citing such texts as Luke 18:1-8 (the parable of the persistent widow and the unjust judge) and Philippians 3:12-21 (Paul pressing on to receive the prize, and urging us to do the same), but which the present text does not assert. The familiar distinction in seminaries between *exegesis* (deriving a timeless teaching *out of* the text) versus *eisegesis* (reading meaning *into* the text) is another way to say the same thing. So let us not be guilty of eisegesis when handling this timeless text.

Elisha is persistent, just as his master was back in 1 Kings 18:42-44, when praying for the three-year drought to be broken. And persistence can surely be a good thing. When the various groups of prophets repeatedly reminded him of the imminent departure of his "master," Elijah, Elisha did not demur. When Elijah repeatedly showed apparent disinterest (and not for the first time; cf. the commentary on 1 Kgs 19:19-21), Elisha persisted, offering oaths in Yahweh's name that he not only knew the eternal significance of the present day in his master's life, but also the enduring seriousness of his prior call by that same master when the cloak was thrown across his shoulders. Elisha would not be put off, whether by circumstance (traveling the nearly 30 miles [50 km] between Ephraimite Gilgal and Elijah's eventual destination at the Jordan River), or by negative peer pressure from the groups of prophets (see 2:3, 5), or even by repeated refusals from the master himself (see 2:2a, 4a, 6a). Elisha was serious about being Elijah's "firstborn" successor (see the note on 2:9), as the old master himself acknowledged (2:9-10; see the notes on 2:10, 2:11). And that is undoubtedly a good thing. Transitions in spiritual leadership are often tenuous in nature, and Elisha's present persistence, in clear contrast to the abrupt "career change" he was not actively pursuing back in 1 Kgs 19:19-21, bodes well for the future of the often precarious prophetic enterprise in Israel. The end result—that Elisha was indeed able to "see" Elijah quite clearly as he was taken into heaven by the heavenly host—is surely meant to confirm this.

But what are we to do with the present narrative? Of course we are to celebrate successful, heroic changes of leadership over God's people, and certainly we are to appreciate the persistent stubbornness of Elisha in appropriating that role. The Kingdom of Heaven is "forcefully advancing," and it belongs particularly to those who take it by force, as Jesus repeatedly reminds us (see Matt 11:12; Luke 16:16 NIV). But are we all to manifest this trait of Elisha's? Sometimes we must doggedly persevere, but sometimes we are meant to graciously give in (as Elisha himself soon did to the repeated, misguided demands of that "group of prophets" who sought to discover the remains of Elijah). Perhaps Elisha grudgingly recognized the similar spirit of perseverance they showed, although in their case it led evidently to a foolish (and certainly to a fruitless) three-day endeavor. Wise and foolish persistence in the same text? Indeed, it is so!

Therefore, let us celebrate stubborn Elisha as well as his equally stubborn prophetic peers. The peerless narrator here reminds us gently (and yes, persistently) that persistence can be a good or a bad thing, depending entirely on the leading of the Spirit of God. Once again, the timeless biblical narrative transcends simple moralizing or "principlizing" (the latter term is often the stated goal of evangelical hermeneutics, or biblical interpretation) to remind us that the Bible is hardly a book of straightforward formulas on how to follow God and determine his will, but rather a wonderful set of historical illustrations and, yes, paradoxical examples, of the agony and the ecstasy of such godly discipleship. If it be God's will, may we also experience a "double portion" of God's Spirit as we are sovereignly called to positions of leadership.

Commentators commonly cite comparisons of Elijah and Elisha with Moses and Joshua (three of whom had occasion to dry up the Jordan River, while Moses in turn dried up the Red Sea). Extensive comparisons between Moses and Elijah may be found in the commentary on 1 Kings 19:9b-18. Suffice it to say here that Elisha does appear to serve somewhat as a "Joshua" to Elijah's "Moses," especially in the transfer of the spirit of leadership (see Num 27:18-23; Deut 34:9), as well as in the drying up of waters (Josh 4:21-24). But Joshua was no Moses, whereas Elisha stands literally as Elijah's equal (if not superior, at least in the number of his miracles); and Jesus' identification of John the Baptist as an Elijah ("And if you are willing to accept what I say, he is Elijah" [Matt 11:14; cf. Mark 9:11-13; Luke 1:17]) begs the question of whether Jesus himself should be seen as an Elisha. But we will have more to say about that in the next number of chapters (also see Leithart 2006:171).

With reference to the broader structure of 1–2 Kings, this narrative is generally regarded as the beginning of the Elisha cycle (2:1–8:15). This group of narratives is often compared and contrasted with those of the preceding Elijah cycle (1 Kgs 17:1—2 Kgs 1:18). The material is summed up in the following chart for easy reference:

ELIJAH AND ELISHA CYCLES: COMPARISONS AND CONTRASTS

Elijah—drought, fire; usually worked alone; often associated with mountains	Elisha—famine, water; worked with Gehazi his servant, also with disciples; often associated with rivers
1 Kings	2 Kings (also cf. 1 Kgs 19:19-21)
17:1-7 Announcement of **drought**; hiding **alone** at Kerith Brook	2:1-18 Tenaciously following Elijah into Transjordan (crossing the **water**)
17:8-24 Widow of Zarephath: flour and oil replenished; her son resurrected	2:19-22 Healing of Jericho's **water**
18:1-19 Elijah meets Obadiah (a Yahwistic prophet), also King Ahab	2:23-25 Cursing of the lads at Bethel
18:20-46 Contest on **Mount Carmel**; **fire** from heaven	3:1-27 Elisha's prophecy concerning **water** in Moab
19:1-18 Hiding **alone** at Horeb, "the **mountain** of God"	4:1-7 Multiplying the oil of the widow (originally wife of a **disciple**)
19:19-21 Call of Elisha—throwing his cloak on him	4:8-37 Shunammite's son resurrected
21:1-29 Naboth's vineyard: a curse on Ahab and Jezebel	4:38-41 Poisonous stew of the **disciples** purified
2 Kings	4:42-44 Bread multiplied
1:1-18 Calling down **fire** from heaven on Israelite soldiers (Elijah on top of the **hill**)	5:1-27 Naaman from Aram healed of leprosy (**Jordan River**); Gehazi, Elisha's **servant**, afflicted instead
2:1-18 Ascension into heaven; chariots and horses of **fire** (seemingly wishes to be **alone**)	6:1-7 Floating ax head in the **Jordan** (used by the **disciples**)
	6:8-23 Arameans' plot to seize Elisha foiled (Elisha's **servant** reassured)
	6:24–7:20 Miraculous lifting of the siege of Samaria
	8:1-6 The Shunammite's land restored (Gehazi his **servant** reappears)
	8:7-15 Hazael becomes king of Aram
	9:1–10:36 Jehu becomes king of Israel; Jezebel killed
	13:14-21 Death of Elisha—a second resurrection at his grave site

◆   ## 2. Elisha's first miracles (2:19-25)

¹⁹One day the leaders of the town of Jericho visited Elisha. "We have a problem, my lord," they told him. "This town is located in pleasant surroundings, as you can see. But the water is bad, and the land is unproductive."

²⁰Elisha said, "Bring me a new bowl with salt in it." So they brought it to him. ²¹Then he went out to the spring that supplied the town with water and threw the salt into it. And he said, "This is what the LORD says: I have purified this water. It will no longer cause death or infertility.*" ²²And the water has remained pure ever since, just as Elisha said.

²³Elisha left Jericho and went up to Bethel. As he was walking along the road, a group of boys from the town began mocking and making fun of him. "Go away, baldy!" they chanted. "Go away, baldy!" ²⁴Elisha turned around and looked at them, and he cursed them in the name of the LORD. Then two bears came out of the woods and mauled forty-two of them. ²⁵From there Elisha went to Mount Carmel and finally returned to Samaria.

2:21 Or *or make the land unproductive*; Hebrew reads *or barrenness.*

NOTES

2:19 Jericho. See the note on 2:4 concerning the previous fulfillment of Joshua's curse on this city.

the water is bad, and the land is unproductive. Whether this represents residual aspects of Joshua's curse on the city is unclear, but the "healing" of Jericho's water source will be the first (or second, if the crossing of the Jordan is included) example of numerous instances where Elisha's ministry is connected with bodies of water (see the chart "Elijah and Elisha Cycles: Comparisons and Contrasts" on p. 204). "Unproductive" (*meshakkaleth* [TH7921, ZH8897]) literally means "causing barrenness or abortion" (BDB 1013), leading some to see an actual curse on humans and animals described here (see 2:21). Wiseman (1993:197) cites two possible naturalistic explanations for the miracle: a geologic shift removing the effects of radioactivity in the region, or else the removal of some sort of parasitic infection from the water itself.

2:20 a new bowl with salt. The term for "bowl" is the rare word *tselokhith* [TH6746, ZH7504] (used only here in the MT); Cogan and Tadmor (1988:36) insist that it should be translated as "jar, flask," not "dish" or the like. The "salt" (readily available from the nearby Dead Sea) probably was symbolic of preservation, and the "newness" of the bowl symbolic of purity (Wiseman 1993:197; cf. the helpful discussion of Dale Brueggemann [2008:332] concerning the permanent nature of the "salt covenant" as found in Num 18:19 and 2 Chr 13:5, cf. NLT mg).

2:21 death or infertility. As pointed out in the second note on 2:19, the term *meshakkaleth* [TH7921, ZH8897] signifies the bringing about of barrenness or abortion (hence, e.g., the NLT mg note for the present verse). Whether the trouble comes from the land (2:19) or the water (as here), both humans and animals are presumably affected—possibly also plants, as can be inferred from the use of the verbal form of the same root in Mal 3:11: "Your grapes will not fall from the vine before they are ripe" (*lo'-teshakkel* [TH7921, ZH8897]).

2:22 ever since. Lit., "until this day." As Childs (1963:279-292) has pointed out, the phrase here is an example of a secondary etiological formula added to the account to give a personal testimony by the narrator or editor (in this case confirming the effectiveness of the word of Yahweh as mediated through the prophet Elisha). For other examples of such confirmatory testimonies, see 8:22; 10:27 (cf. LXX); 14:7; 16:6; 17:23, 34, 41; also 1 Kgs 8:8; 9:13, 21; 12:19.

2:23 a group of boys. Heb., *ne'arim qetannim,* lit., "small youths"; the same expression is found in the singular in 5:14. The noun *na'ar* [TH5288, ZH5853] can refer to a boy, or a young man, such as the 17-year-old Joseph (Gen 37:2) or the warrior Absalom (2 Sam 18:5, 12). It is also used commonly to designate a household servant or attendant. But here with the adjective "small" or "young" (*qatan* [TH6996, ZH7783]), the phrase probably emphasizes their immaturity. Cogan and Tadmor (1988:39) characterize them as "jeering urchins," and they note that such a scene can often discomfort the unwary urban traveler in the Middle East even today.

began mocking and making fun of him. The phrase *wayyithqallesu-bo* [TH7046, ZH7840] also
conveys the idea of mockery and derision in Ezek 22:5; Hab 1:10.

Go away, baldy! Lit., "go on up, baldy" (*'aleh qereakh* [TH7142, ZH7944]). The root *'alah*
[TH5927, ZH6590] regularly conveys the idea of "going up" or "ascending," and that is the
idea here (the same root is already used twice in the verse, indicating Elisha's "going up" to
Bethel and "walking along" the road [uphill?]). A number of commentators, however, prefer the basic idea of "going away" or "departing" for the present text (cf. NRSV; also Cogan
and Tadmor 1988:38), so the NLT translation here is quite defensible. Still, those who read
here a sardonic challenge for the bald Elisha to "go on up" as the very hairy Elijah (cf. 1:8)
recently did, have a point. (This might help explain the ferocious fate that a significant
number of the boys soon face.) Some see here a reference to a characteristic close haircut
said to be typical of some prophets (cf. the four references cited in Cogan and Tadmor
1988:38; but they themselves prefer the possibility that Elisha's "extreme natural baldness"
caught the boys' attention). In any case, a clear contrast with the well-known hairiness of
Elisha's master Elijah is probably in view here.

2:24 cursed them in the name of the LORD. A somewhat symmetrical reference to the
effective "word" of Yahweh is to be found in the preceding passage (see 2:21). That time
it was God's message through Elisha to the people, but here it is Elisha's word (in God's
name), again directed to the people. (In Deuteronomy, we are reminded several times that
the people, Levites, prophets, and priests are to speak only in the "name" of Yahweh; cf.
Deut 6:13; 10:8; 18:18-20; 21:5.)

two bears. Heb., *dubbim* [TH1677, ZH1800], here clearly feminine in gender (KJV, "she bears"),
as indicated by the feminine form of the accompanying verb. Bears roamed the hill country
of Palestine even up to the early twentieth century (ABD 6.1143), and mother bears robbed
of their cubs are known to be especially fierce (cf. Hos 13:8).

forty-two. This is possibly a typical number representing a quite sizable group (cf. the number of Jehu's victims cited in 10:14). But whether a precise tally or not, surely the unforgettable image here is of the sudden, gruesome deaths of a shockingly large number of youths.

2:25 Mount Carmel . . . Samaria. These are the sites of Elijah's great miracle against the
prophets of Baal, and the capital city of the queen mother, Jezebel, supporter of those Baal
prophets, respectively.

COMMENTARY

With the return of Elisha to Jericho (see 2:18), we read about a recurring problem
there: the dangerous water supply. But Elisha, whose ministry will be repeatedly
connected with waters and rivers, effects a miraculous healing of Jericho's water
source by means of a "new bowl" and some Dead Sea salt, and, more fundamentally,
by means of an effective, timely word from Yahweh. This "healing" is confirmed by
the story's narrator (or editor) as remaining in effect "to this day" (see the note on
2:22). Yet, when Elisha returns to Bethel (2:23) we read about what could become
another recurring problem: the insolence of a mob of shameless street urchins (see
the notes on 2:23). A miracle of destruction, however, soon takes place, and once
again a sharply negative situation is effectively eliminated by a timely word in the
name of Yahweh. A miracle of healing and restoration, followed by a miracle of
judgment and destruction—such are the introductory miracles connected with the
newly installed prophet Elisha.

We like miracles of restoration and chafe at miracles of judgment, but we need to hear about both of them, and probably best in tandem, as they occur here. Immediately, one thinks of a similar phenomenon in the book of Acts: The judgment of sudden death for the deceivers Ananias and Sapphira (Acts 5:1-11) is sandwiched between the account of the incredible growth of the early church (Acts 2–4) and that of the instant healings done by the apostles (Acts 5:12-16). "Great fear" came upon the entire church as a result of those sudden deaths (Acts 5:11), and great reserve and reverence came upon the crowds (Acts 5:13) as a result of those healings. Gladsome delight, surely, as a result of all those healings, but stern respect, too. Such literary juxtapositions represent shrewd knowledge of human nature—without the fear of God and of God's human leadership, miracles of healing and restoration may soon become trite in perspective and shallow in result. It seems to take some sharp signs of judgment to restore balance and perspective to the people of God.

Many commentators and critics have taken extreme umbrage over the destructive "miracle" of the she-bears, and it is not my task to explain away the offensive nature of that story. But we know in our heart of hearts that "it is the fear of the LORD which is the beginning of [true] knowledge and those who spurn wisdom and discipline are [nothing more than] fools" (my expanded paraphrase of Prov 1:7, the motto of that great book of godly wisdom). God will honor his servant-leaders, and sometimes it might tragically take some she-bears to reinforce the point. Thankfully, from this point on we will read mostly positive messages about the ministry of the prophet Elisha and how he effected, time and again, only healing and blessing on young and old, male and female, Jew and Gentile alike. Only a greedy Gehazi (see 5:20-27) or some hostile Arameans (see 6:8-20) need fear harsh, judgmental miracles; and even those seemingly last only for a season (cf. 8:5 and 6:20-23, respectively).

◆   3. War between Israel and Moab (3:1-27)

Ahab's son Joram* began to rule over Israel in the eighteenth year of King Jehoshaphat's reign in Judah. He reigned in Samaria twelve years. ²He did what was evil in the LORD's sight, but not to the same extent as his father and mother. He at least tore down the sacred pillar of Baal that his father had set up. ³Nevertheless, he continued in the sins that Jeroboam son of Nebat had committed and led the people of Israel to commit.

⁴King Mesha of Moab was a sheep breeder. He used to pay the king of Israel an annual tribute of 100,000 lambs and the wool of 100,000 rams. ⁵But after Ahab's death, the king of Moab rebelled against the king of Israel. ⁶So King Joram promptly mustered the army of Israel and marched from Samaria. ⁷On the way, he sent this message to King Jehoshaphat of Judah: "The king of Moab has rebelled against me. Will you join me in battle against him?"

And Jehoshaphat replied, "Why, of course! You and I are as one. My troops are your troops, and my horses are your horses." ⁸Then Jehoshaphat asked, "What route will we take?"

"We will attack from the wilderness of Edom," Joram replied.

⁹The king of Edom and his troops joined them, and all three armies traveled along a roundabout route through the wilderness for seven days. But there was no water for the men or their animals.

¹⁰"What should we do?" the king of Israel cried out. "The LORD has brought the three of us here to let the king of Moab defeat us."

¹¹But King Jehoshaphat of Judah asked,

"Is there no prophet of the LORD with us? If there is, we can ask the LORD what to do through him."

One of King Joram's officers replied, "Elisha son of Shaphat is here. He used to be Elijah's personal assistant.*"

¹²Jehoshaphat said, "Yes, the LORD speaks through him." So the king of Israel, King Jehoshaphat of Judah, and the king of Edom went to consult with Elisha.

¹³"Why are you coming to me?"* Elisha asked the king of Israel. "Go to the pagan prophets of your father and mother!"

But King Joram of Israel said, "No! For it was the LORD who called us three kings here—only to be defeated by the king of Moab!"

¹⁴Elisha replied, "As surely as the LORD Almighty lives, whom I serve, I wouldn't even bother with you except for my respect for King Jehoshaphat of Judah. ¹⁵Now bring me someone who can play the harp."

While the harp was being played, the power* of the LORD came upon Elisha, ¹⁶and he said, "This is what the LORD says: This dry valley will be filled with pools of water! ¹⁷You will see neither wind nor rain, says the LORD, but this valley will be filled with water. You will have plenty for yourselves and your cattle and other animals. ¹⁸But this is only a simple thing for the LORD, for he will make you victorious over the army of Moab! ¹⁹You will conquer the best of their towns, even the fortified ones. You will cut down all their good trees, stop up all their springs, and ruin all their good land with stones."

²⁰The next day at about the time when the morning sacrifice was offered, water suddenly appeared! It was flowing from the direction of Edom, and soon there was water everywhere.

²¹Meanwhile, when the people of Moab heard about the three armies marching against them, they mobilized every man who was old enough to strap on a sword, and they stationed themselves along their border. ²²But when they got up the next morning, the sun was shining across the water, making it appear red to the Moabites—like blood. ²³"It's blood!" the Moabites exclaimed. "The three armies must have attacked and killed each other! Let's go, men of Moab, and collect the plunder!"

²⁴But when the Moabites arrived at the Israelite camp, the army of Israel rushed out and attacked them until they turned and ran. The army of Israel chased them into the land of Moab, destroying everything as they went.* ²⁵They destroyed the towns, covered their good land with stones, stopped up all the springs, and cut down all the good trees. Finally, only Kir-hareseth and its stone walls were left, but men with slings surrounded and attacked it.

²⁶When the king of Moab saw that he was losing the battle, he led 700 of his swordsmen in a desperate attempt to break through the enemy lines near the king of Edom, but they failed. ²⁷Then the king of Moab took his oldest son, who would have been the next king, and sacrificed him as a burnt offering on the wall. So there was great anger against Israel,* and the Israelites withdrew and returned to their own land.

3:1 Hebrew *Jehoram*, a variant spelling of Joram; also in 3:6.   3:11 Hebrew *He used to pour water on the hands of Elijah.*   3:13 Hebrew *What is there in common between you and me?*   3:15 Hebrew *the hand.*   3:24 The meaning of the Hebrew is uncertain.   3:27 Or *So Israel's anger was great.* The meaning of the Hebrew is uncertain.

NOTES

3:1 Joram. See the first note on 1:17 concerning the spelling of this name.

eighteenth year. This more expected synchronism is discussed in the second note to 1:17, where a different, seemingly aberrant synchronism for Joram's accession (the second year of Jehoshaphat's son Jehoram of Judah) is to be found. It is essential that Jehoshaphat, the only king of the three for whom the prophet Elisha has any respect (see 3:14), be reckoned as still alive throughout the present chapter.

3:2 *not to the same extent.* See endnote 1 of the Introduction regarding this mitigation of the formulaic condemnation here.

sacred pillar of Baal that his father had set up. This is not included in the condemnatory material about Ahab found in 1 Kgs 16:31-33, but perhaps it was an event too typical of a syncretistic king like Ahab to merit specific comment there (so Cogan and Tadmor [1988:42-43], who go on to cite Albright's suggestion of identifying this Baal with Baal Melqart of Tyre [cf. the note on 1 Kgs 16:31]).

3:4 *King Mesha of Moab.* Mesha is the famous king mentioned repeatedly in the so-called "Moabite Stone," which he had erected in honor of his victories over "the son of Omri" of Israel (see the commentary on 1 Kgs 16:21-28).

an annual tribute of 100,000 lambs and the wool of 100,000 rams. Such immense quantities are characteristic of folkloristic literature (see the first note on 1 Kgs 20:1 and the comments throughout 1 Kgs 20:1–22:40).

3:5 *rebelled.* This is an annalistic note basically repeating 1:1 (see the notes there).

3:7 *You and I are as one.* Jehoshaphat gave a nearly identical response to King Ahab (1 Kgs 22:4), leading some to see that story and the present one as two different versions of the same event (see the commentary below). In any case, Jehoshaphat is clearly depicted as the weaker partner in both texts (Seow 1999:181).

3:8 *the wilderness of Edom.* Lit., "the road of the wilderness of Edom" (*derek midbar 'edom* [TH4057/123, ZH4497/121]), which Cogan and Tadmor (1988:44; following Glueck) take as a road leading east of the Jordan rift valley (south of the Dead Sea), following the Zered Brook to Edom. This region is also commonly known as the "Arabah," which probably means "dry" or "dusty." Undoubtedly the motive for such an odd, roundabout route to confront Moab was the element of surprise, since the closer northern border was more heavily fortified.

3:9 *king of Edom.* This is in evident contradiction with 1 Kgs 22:47, probably indicating a different source for the tradition (so Cogan and Tadmor [1988:44], who cite a similar contrast in the bilingual Tel Fekharye inscription, where a local ruler is termed "king" in the Aramaic text, but "governor" in the Akkadian text).

roundabout route through the wilderness for seven days. This confirms the likelihood that the southern route around the Dead Sea described in the note on 3:8 was followed.

3:11 *we can ask the LORD what to do.* As in the similar text in 1 Kgs 22:5 (see note there for general context), the technical term *darash* [TH1875, ZH2011] is used here, signifying that a formal oracular inquiry should be made (cf. the fourth note on 1:2 for similar inquiries of the deity). For other examples of prophets or diviners accompanying troops into battle, see Cogan and Tadmor 1988:45.

Elijah's personal assistant. As the NLT mg indicates, the Hebrew here reads "he (is the one who) used to pour water on the hands of Elijah." Although this precise expression is unparalleled in the OT, the meaning of the idiom is transparent (cf. 1 Kgs 19:21, and the second note found there). As illustrated in the chart, "Elijah and Elisha Cycles: Comparisons and Contrasts" (p. 204), it is Elisha who is especially associated with rivers and bodies of water, so we find here in the present verse an apt echo of his typical area of ministry, especially pertinent during this time of severe water shortage that the armies were facing in the southern desert ("the Arabah"; see the note on 3:8).

3:13 *Why are you coming to me?* As the NLT mg indicates, the Hebrew reads, "What (is there in common) to me and to you." The same expression is used by the widow of Zarephath back in 1 Kgs 17:18, again in a context of consternation and impending hostility (cf. Judg 11:12; 2 Sam 16:10; 19:22 [23]).

3:14 *As surely as the LORD . . . lives.* See the second note on 1 Kgs 17:1 concerning the meaning of this classic oath formula.

except for my respect for King Jehoshaphat of Judah. Some have seen the emphasis here on the inclusion of Jehoshaphat as part of the anti-Moabite coalition assembled *after* the death of King Ahab of Israel (1 Kgs 22:40) as a significant reason for the varying chronologies that exist for this period of Israelite history (see the second note on 3:1). In any case, Elisha's appreciation for King Jehoshaphat's demanding an oracle of victory from a Yahwistic prophet (see 3:11; cf. 1 Kgs 22:5) is what undoubtedly prompted his comment here.

3:15 *someone who can play the harp.* This is one of the classic texts linking the phenomenon of prophecy to the playing of music (see 1 Sam 10:5; cf. 1 Chr 25:1-3, where twice we are told that prophecies were delivered to the accompaniment of the harp or lyre). Not incidental to all this is the tradition that young David son of Jesse was celebrated not only for his military prowess but also for his harp-playing and his ability to soothe the "tormenting spirit" that afflicted King Saul (1 Sam 16:23; 18:10-11).

the power of the LORD. Lit., "the hand of Yahweh" (see the first note on 1 Kgs 18:46).

3:18 *a simple thing.* There is a sense of gradation to the upcoming miracles that Yahweh will provide for the anti-Moabite coalition; these lead, however, to the final ironic twist in the story (3:27).

3:19 *cut down . . . stop up . . . ruin.* These actions are in clear violation of the Torah (see, e.g., Deut 20:19-20, which specifically forbids the cutting down of trees in enemy territory); the hearer/reader is therefore expected to grow uneasy at the prospect of the fulfillment of what is "prophesied" here (cf. Leithart 2006:180-181).

3:20 *about the time when the morning sacrifice was offered.* A similar reckoning of time is to be found in the Elijah account in 1 Kgs 18:29, 36, where the "evening sacrifice" is twice mentioned. In the present case, the "morning sacrifice" refers to the cereal offering (*minkhah* [TH4503, ZH4966]) that accompanied the '*olah* [TH5930, ZH6592] or "whole burnt offering," both in the morning and in the evening (Sweeney 2007:283; cf. Exod 29:38-41; Num 28:1-8).

there was water everywhere. Flash flooding during the rainy (winter) season can occur when this normally dry region experiences sudden cloudbursts, and most of the water runs quickly off the generally impermeable rocks and soil down the wadis and ravines toward the Dead Sea. The expression about seeing "neither wind nor rain" (3:17) implies that the anti-Moabite coalition was in low-lying land, distant from the sudden rainfall (Sweeney 2007:283).

3:22 *like blood.* The anti-Moabite coalition was presumably camping near the Wadi Zered south of the Dead Sea (see the note on 3:8), where the terrain is known for its red, sandstone features (indeed, the place-name "Edom" comes from the Semitic root for the color red).

3:24 *destroying everything as they went.* The NLT text ably conveys what is indeed a difficult Hebrew original (cf. NLT mg). The basic question in the MT is whether the root *bo'* [TH935, ZH995] (to come, to go) or the root *nakah* [TH5221, ZH5782] (to hit, smite) should be read: The Kethiv (what is "written") argues for the former (albeit oddly spelled with no Aleph), whereas the Qere (what is "read") attests the latter (thus reading a Kaph for the Beth). Context favors the second option, but the LXX and the other versions favor the first (as do Cogan and Tadmor 1988:46). Happily, there is little difference in the overall flow of the narrative in either case.

3:25 *covered . . . stopped up . . . cut down.* See 3:19, where these same aggressive actions are listed in reverse order, with only minor variations in vocabulary (cf. the note on 3:19, regarding these actions in relation to the Torah). The Hebrew imperfect forms of the verbs used in the present verse vividly denote the actions as ongoing in nature, and thus convey "a graphic picture of the progress of the battle" (Cogan and Tadmor 1988:46, citing Driver).

Kir-hareseth. This was a major city of southern Moab, identified with modern Kerak (ABD 4.84); the city sits next to the King's Highway, and it is located on a major promontory overlooking the Dead Sea, whose slopes rendered the site particularly difficult to capture. (Note that although Codex Leningradensis spells this name "Kir-hareseth," a number of Hebrew Bibles spell it "Kir-haresheth," with a Shin instead of a Sin.)

men with slings. Heb., *haqqalla'im* [TH7051, ZH7847] (the slingers); this actual term is found only here in the MT, but the concept of "slinging stones" is familiar from such texts as 1 Sam 17:40, 48-50 (David vs. Goliath) and Judg 20:16 (700 left-handed Benjamites who could sling rocks and hit a target "within a hairsbreadth without missing").

3:27 *sacrificed him as a burnt offering on the wall.* This is the horrific ending to what has been a remarkable set of victories for the anti-Moabite coalition. Sadly, the reality of such child-sacrifices has been repeatedly attested, both within and without Israel, especially during times of emergency (Sweeney 2007:284; cf. Cogan and Tadmor 1988:47 for numerous extrabiblical parallels, especially from Phoenicia and its colonies in north Africa). The possibility that King Ahaz sacrificed his son under similar circumstances is discussed in the second note on 16:3.

great anger against Israel. Heb., "and there was great anger (*qetsep-gadol* [TH7110/1419, ZH7912/1524]) upon/against ('*al* [TH5921, ZH6584]) Israel." The question is whether the anger was directed at Israel or not; Leithart (see the commentary) argues forcefully that it was, while Sweeney (2007:284) suggests that this would render Yahweh's previous oracle of victory void: "Israel became angry at the sight of Mesha's sacrifice of his son, and consequently withdrew from Kir Haresheth [*sic*]" (see also Wiseman [1993:201-202], tentatively). But as Sweeney himself acknowledges, the normal meaning of the preposition '*al* with *qetsep* is in reference to anger directed *against* wrongdoers. And this, in my opinion, seems to be the situation here as well.

COMMENTARY

In his discussion of the present chapter Leithart (2006:179) provocatively points out: "If the story ended at 3:26, it would be comfortably, reassuringly familiar. But it goes on for another verse, and that verse deconstructs the story and disturbs our complacency, as the writer of Kings does habitually. . . . The surprise ending transforms the story from an exodus into a satire of exodus, from a story of Israel's holy war to a parody of holy war, a story of Gentile victory over Israel." It is from this angle that I want to discuss whether the present chapter of 2 Kings serves as a doublet (i.e., another version) of 1 Kings 22:1-40, as is often alleged, and what is meant to be the message of the present chapter. Is Leithart correct to suggest that we actually find here a story about a "doubly crafty God who traps Israel at the very moment he appears to be trapping Moab"? I have a feeling that he is. And, furthermore, that may well be the major message we are meant to take away from what otherwise seems to be just another example of Israelite military triumph over her enemies, effortlessly enabled by Yahweh, the powerful God of the prophet Elisha.

The notes to the individual verses cite a number of parallels between this chapter and 1 Kings 22:1-40, not the least of which is the starring role of King Jehoshaphat of Judah in both stories. (Indeed, as already noted, some see the overall chronology of 1–2 Kings as having been secondarily adjusted to accommodate Jehoshaphat's presence in this narrative—cf. the second note on 1:17 and the references cited there.) In both stories, there is another compelling parallel we also must not ignore: clear evidence of prophetic disfavor toward the Omride kings (Ahab and Joram, respectively) on the part of Elijah and Elisha. In fact, in the 1 Kings 22 story, the divine intention to send King Ahab to an untimely death is the major motivation for the entire passage (see especially 1 Kgs 22:19-23), and that may be the case for Joram here as well. (One should read the Greek addition in 1:18d [a text which otherwise parallels 3:1-3]: "And the Lord was very angry with the house of Ahab," a passage which finds no correspondence in the Hebrew in either chapter, but which, nevertheless, provides further textual support for Leithart's "doubly crafty God" theory.) Yes, it appears that Israel's God "has it in" for the Omride dynasty, clearly so in 1 Kings 22, but evidently also in 2 Kings 3.

Once again, however, we need to ask if these two stories are doublets. (That is, are they essentially two versions of the same story?) Commentators have long noted the remarkable similarities between the two traditions (some of which are noted above; cf. Cogan and Tadmor 1988:49 for others). Indeed, attempts to read "Aram" ('rm [TH758, ZH806]) for "Edom" ('dm [TH123, ZH121]) in 3:26, based on the Old Latin (cf. Wiseman 1993:201, who, however, wisely discounts such a reading) are probably predicated on such parallels. But such "parallelitis" can work both ways, with originally quite disparate stories attracting, as it were, parallel details in their sequence of events, as the stories are told and retold over the years. I give two brief examples: (1) Both evil King Ahab of Israel and good King Josiah of Judah are said to have "disguised themselves" (Hitpael of khapas [TH2664, ZH2924]) as they went into battle, after both kings were strongly advised not to go (1 Kgs 22:30; 2 Chr 35:22); and (2) both the Israelites of Joshua 8 and the Israelites of Judges 20, after unexpected previous defeats by their enemies (the people of Ai and the Benjamites at Gibeah, respectively) and with clear instructions from Yahweh to set ambushes and draw out their opponents from the city walls, gain decisive victories as their demoralized opponents see smoke rising from their suddenly captured cities (see Josh 8:20; Judg 20:38-41). No one would suggest that these examples are "doublets" of each other, and I suspect that the burden of proof for claiming the present chapter as a doublet with 1 Kings 22 remains heavier than some older scholars might have reckoned. Indeed, the current trend in scholarship is to see two separate events being described by these two "Jehoshaphat/Omride/Elijah-Elisha/Aram-Edom" accounts (see Cogan and Tadmor 1988:49-50; Wiseman 1993:199-200; Sweeney 2007:279-281). Although the precise coordination of the present chapter with the historical evidence attested on the Moabite Stone (see the first note on 3:4) remains somewhat problematic (cf. Sweeney 2007:280-282; also Cogan and Tadmor 1988:50-51 and the references cited there), the general import remains clear: Israel under an Omride king, allied with her presumably junior partners, Judah and Edom, successfully attacked Moab unexpectedly from the south with devastating results on both land and people. Then, in a desperate move, Mesha the Moabite king offered his own son as a human sacrifice to stave off total defeat. As a result, "great anger" descended upon the Israelite coalition, and they broke off their attack and returned home (cf. the notes on 3:27 for details). But, once again, what is the nature of this "great anger"? It is to that topic that we now must turn.

It is probably not coincidental to all of this that the Moabite Stone attributes Mesha's own previous military misfortunes to the "anger" (Moabite verbal root '-n-p, akin to the identical Hebrew root found in 1 Kgs 8:46; Ps 2:12; etc.; see 'anap [TH599, ZH647]) of Chemosh (the patron deity of Moab)—that was the reason why "Omri king of Israel" had "oppressed Moab for many days" (lines 4-5 of the Moabite Stone). Although the precise Semitic roots are different in this passage (qatsap [TH7107, ZH7911] is used in 3:27), the theology is identical. "Great anger" of the patron deity manifested itself in notorious public humiliation on the part of the monarch of the land. While some argue that the present text of 2 Kings is indicating that Chemosh indeed had such power (cf. Cogan and Tadmor 1988:51-52), surely the more likely conclusion the narrator wishes us to accept is that Yahweh may well have been the deity who was "angry" with his people, therefore allowing their "Gentile" opponents to gain the victory (whence Leithart's comments which were quoted at the beginning of this commentary). To be sure, we have hints as to the reasons for such disfavor scattered throughout the text—Elisha's Elijah-like contempt for the house of Omri; the trampling of "holy war" or kherem [TH2764, ZH3051] laws (see notes on 1 Kgs 9:21; 16:34; 20:13, 42, 43); indeed, the odd syncretistic nature of the coalition itself and their clear disinterest in any oracle at all from a Yahwistic prophet. But the surprise ending so nicely delineated by Leithart is precisely the point of the passage. Yahweh did "have it in" for the Omrides; and furthermore, Yahweh would not passively abide the breaking of his Torah by his people, not even by an otherwise godly Davidic king. "The ends do not justify the means," not then, not today. We do serve a tricky God, but tricky only in the sense of his remaining ever faithful to his nature and to his word. Let the would-be leader beware!

◆ 1. Elisha helps a poor widow (4.1-7)

One day the widow of a member of the group of prophets came to Elisha and cried out, "My husband who served you is dead, and you know how he feared the LORD. But now a creditor has come, threatening to take my two sons as slaves."

²"What can I do to help you?" Elisha asked. "Tell me, what do you have in the house?"

"Nothing at all, except a flask of olive oil," she replied.

³And Elisha said, "Borrow as many empty jars as you can from your friends and neighbors. ⁴Then go into your house with your sons and shut the door behind you. Pour olive oil from your flask into the jars, setting each one aside when it is filled."

⁵So she did as she was told. Her sons kept bringing jars to her, and she filled one after another. ⁶Soon every container was full to the brim!

"Bring me another jar," she said to one of her sons.

"There aren't any more!" he told her. And then the olive oil stopped flowing.

⁷When she told the man of God what had happened, he said to her, "Now sell the olive oil and pay your debts, and you and your sons can live on what is left over."

NOTES

4:1 *widow.* This is the first of a number of parallels between this chapter and 1 Kgs 17, as the commentary below will point out in more detail. The widow was an economically distressed member of society (see the second note on 1 Kgs 17:9 for details).

the group of prophets. Lit., "the sons of the prophets" (see the first note on 2:3).

slaves. Israelite wives and children could be sold for nonpayment of debts (Neh 5:5; cf. Exod 21:7; Deut 15:12; Isa 50:1; Amos 2:6); they were, however, to be freed in the Year of Jubilee (Lev 25:39-43).

4:2 *What can I do to help you?* A similar question is to be found in 4:13; both the rich and the poor have needs, but often only the poor are desperate enough to seek out the prophet.

a flask of olive oil. Heb., *'asuk* [TH610, ZH655] *shemen*; the first term is a hapax legomenon, presumably signifying a small vessel (cf. Cogan and Tadmor 1988:56). The parallel with the "handful of flour" and the "little cooking oil" of 1 Kgs 17:12 will immediately be evident.

4:3 *empty jars.* Heb., *kelim reqim* [TH7386, ZH8199]; the first word is a familiar term for vessels both large and small.

4:4 *shut the door behind you.* God's miracles often occur in private (cf. Wiseman 1993:202-203).

4:6 *every container.* Heb., *kelim* [TH3627, ZH3998]. Some of these storage vessels could hold well over 10 gal. (40 L) of oil!

4:7 *pay your debts.* Or with the LXX, "satisfy your creditor" (the Hebrew here is difficult; cf. Cogan and Tadmor 1988:56).

COMMENTARY

We begin here with the first of a number of "miracle stories" about Elisha's relationship with the "sons of the prophets" (see the chart, "Elijah and Elisha Cycles: Comparisons and Contrasts," p. 204), and more to the immediate point, the first of two narratives concerning women, specifically mothers whose children were facing dire threats (Sweeney 2007:287). The preceding notes mention some parallels between these passages and Elijah's ministry to the widow of Zarephath in 1 Kings 17:8-24; additional parallels between these texts would include the supernatural provision of everyday commodities in severe times of need, as well as the special attention given to the least significant members of society, whether Israelite or foreign. Yet, as Cogan and Tadmor (1988:59-60) point out, "The reader is not necessarily faced here with literary borrowing, for the folkloristic motifs which are at the heart of these stories [referring to the entirety of the present chapter of 2 Kings] could have developed independently within both the Elijah and Elisha cycles. One cannot deny that within the circles of the sons of the prophets among whom these stories circulated, motifs crossed back and forth to the enrichment of each individual story." So let us enjoy the uniqueness of these Elisha traditions for what they present—a prophet who was quick to bring life-changing blessings to those who needed them.

God's miracles are often copious in their results but remarkably reticent in their actual outworkings—indeed, often to a bewildering degree for those of us who wish to impress them upon unbelievers and compel skeptics to accept the unquestionable reality of such a powerful and loving deity. So it is here: We see God provide extravagant quantities of olive oil, perhaps limited only by the woman's lack of faith in her procurement of the total number of empty vessels (but note that any so-called "lack of faith" on her part is *not* the main point of the present narrative, in contrast to other stories found in the Elisha cycle; see 5:11-14; 6:15-17; 13:14-19). In any case, God's provision here proves more than adequate—for redeeming both her sons from debt-slavery as well as for providing for her and their future economic needs—and that is all the story states. The actual miracle, however, takes place quietly and privately, probably necessarily so in order to forestall needless grandstanding (as well as needless embarrassment on the part of the widow and her family), although the eventual results of the miracle become quite public soon enough. How typical of God: lavish generosity coupled with intimate sensitivity as to immediate surroundings. We may want it differently, but God truly and always knows best what to do and how to do it. After all, he wants people's authentic faith, their openness to his surprising ways, not merely their grudging acknowledgment of his sovereign power. Those who do have faith can testify to the one who can and will meet such needs, with provision to spare. This will also be evident in the very next passage for a wealthy woman who seemingly already had everything she needed. And it is to this unforgettable story that we now turn.

◆   ## 5. Elisha and the woman from Shunem (4:8-37)

⁸One day Elisha went to the town of Shunem. A wealthy woman lived there, and she urged him to come to her home for a meal. After that, whenever he passed that way, he would stop there for something to eat.

⁹She said to her husband, "I am sure this man who stops in from time to time is a holy man of God. ¹⁰Let's build a small room for him on the roof and furnish it with a bed, a table, a chair, and a lamp. Then he will have a place to stay whenever he comes by."

¹¹One day Elisha returned to Shunem, and he went up to this upper room to rest. ¹²He said to his servant Gehazi, "Tell the woman from Shunem I want to speak to her." When she appeared, ¹³Elisha said to Gehazi, "Tell her, 'We appreciate the kind concern you have shown us. What can we do for you? Can we put in a good word for you to the king or to the commander of the army?' "

"No," she replied, "my family takes good care of me."

¹⁴Later Elisha asked Gehazi, "What can we do for her?"

Gehazi replied, "She doesn't have a son, and her husband is an old man."

¹⁵"Call her back again," Elisha told him. When the woman returned, Elisha said to her as she stood in the doorway, ¹⁶"Next year at this time you will be holding a son in your arms!"

"No, my lord!" she cried. "O man of God, don't deceive me and get my hopes up like that."

¹⁷But sure enough, the woman soon became pregnant. And at that time the following year she had a son, just as Elisha had said.

¹⁸One day when her child was older, he went out to help his father, who was working with the harvesters. ¹⁹Suddenly he cried out, "My head hurts! My head hurts!"

His father said to one of the servants, "Carry him home to his mother."

²⁰So the servant took him home, and his mother held him on her lap. But

around noontime he died. ²¹She carried him up and laid him on the bed of the man of God, then shut the door and left him there. ²²She sent a message to her husband: "Send one of the servants and a donkey so that I can hurry to the man of God and come right back."

²³"Why go today?" he asked. "It is neither a new moon festival nor a Sabbath."

But she said, "It will be all right."

²⁴So she saddled the donkey and said to the servant, "Hurry! Don't slow down unless I tell you to."

²⁵As she approached the man of God at Mount Carmel, Elisha saw her in the distance. He said to Gehazi, "Look, the woman from Shunem is coming. ²⁶Run out to meet her and ask her, 'Is everything all right with you, your husband, and your child?' "

"Yes," the woman told Gehazi, "everything is fine."

²⁷But when she came to the man of God at the mountain, she fell to the ground before him and caught hold of his feet. Gehazi began to push her away, but the man of God said, "Leave her alone. She is deeply troubled, but the LORD has not told me what it is."

²⁸Then she said, "Did I ask you for a son, my lord? And didn't I say, 'Don't deceive me and get my hopes up'?"

²⁹Then Elisha said to Gehazi, "Get ready to travel*; take my staff and go! Don't talk to anyone along the way. Go quickly and lay the staff on the child's face."

³⁰But the boy's mother said, "As surely as the LORD lives and you yourself live, I won't go home unless you go with me." So Elisha returned with her.

³¹Gehazi hurried on ahead and laid the staff on the child's face, but nothing happened. There was no sign of life. He returned to meet Elisha and told him, "The child is still dead."

³²When Elisha arrived, the child was indeed dead, lying there on the prophet's bed. ³³He went in alone and shut the door behind him and prayed to the LORD. ³⁴Then he lay down on the child's body, placing his mouth on the child's mouth, his eyes on the child's eyes, and his hands on the child's hands. And as he stretched out on him, the child's body began to grow warm again! ³⁵Elisha got up, walked back and forth across the room once, and then stretched himself out again on the child. This time the boy sneezed seven times and opened his eyes!

³⁶Then Elisha summoned Gehazi. "Call the child's mother!" he said. And when she came in, Elisha said, "Here, take your son!" ³⁷She fell at his feet and bowed before him, overwhelmed with gratitude. Then she took her son in her arms and carried him downstairs.

4:29 Hebrew *Bind up your loins.*

NOTES

4:8 Shunem. This was a town near Mount Moreh in the hill country of Issachar (see the note on 1 Kgs 1:3).

wealthy woman. Lit., a "great woman"; cf. Lev 19:15, which contrasts "great" (*gadol* [TH1419, ZH1524]; so ESV, NASB, NIV) with "poor" (*dal* [TH1800, ZH1924]). Surely the clear contrast of this enterprising woman with the destitute woman of 4:1-7 (who in her own way was perhaps equally enterprising) is meant to be noticed.

4:11 upper room. Heb., *'aliyyah* [TH5944, ZH6608]; see the note on 1 Kgs 17:23 for details. In the previous verse of the present passage, the room is described more fully in the MT as an *'aliyyat qir* [TH7023, ZH7815] ("an upper room, walled up" [?], possibly walled off for privacy [perhaps a pertinent detail in light of 4:21], or else set off "by the wall," thus describing its separate access from the outside [cf. Cogan and Tadmor 1988:56-57]).

4:12 Gehazi. This is the first mention of Elisha's famous (and in ch 5, infamous) servant. Gehazi's name may mean "valley of vision" or possibly "avaricious" (5:20-27), in which case it may have been a nickname (Gray 1970:495). Cf. 4:43, however, where the name of Elisha's servant is not supplied.

4:13 What can we do for you? The question is essentially repeated in the next verse, and a similar query is to be found in 4:2 as well (see the first note found there). Innocent questions such as these can ultimately lead to life-changing actions!

4:14 She doesn't have a son, and her husband is an old man. Hence, as Gehazi intimates, there is always the possibility that the Shunammite may become a childless widow, which is a worse plight than that of the anonymous woman of 4:1, who at least had two children to carry on the family name, even if they were debt-slaves for a time. Wealth has many benefits, but it cannot eliminate childlessness, nor can it fully control the future.

4:16 Next year at this time. Nearly the same expression is used for predicting the birth of Isaac to an aged Sarah (Gen 18:10, 14). The precise meaning of the expression (*ka'eth khayyah* [TH2416A, ZH2645]) remains uncertain (it seems to mean "as the time of life/reviving" [i.e., the springtime?]), but Gen 17:21 parallels the prediction of Isaac's birth with clearer wording indicating "next year," and this gives significant support for the NLT translation here (cf. Cogan and Tadmor 1988:57 for pertinent Mesopotamian parallels).

4:19 My head hurts! The Hebrew simply reads "My head! My head!" with no verb. But the father's actions (note that this is the last time in the story that the father takes the initiative) imply strongly that something is obviously wrong with the child (sunstroke [?]; cf. Ps 121:6).

4:21 shut the door. For privacy (cf. 4:33; also the comments found in the note on 4:11).

4:23 neither a new moon festival nor a Sabbath. These were typical holidays (the "new moon" being the first of each month) when normal work was suspended; for other places where these holidays are mentioned together, see Num 28:9-15; Isa 1:13; Hos 2:11. Presumably such travel was not yet forbidden on the Sabbath, as it was by NT times (cf. Wiseman [1993:204], who, following Keil, further notes that the pious at that time may have gone to the prophet's house during such holidays for worship and teaching).

4:26 Is everything all right . . . ? The rich term *shalom* [TH7965, ZH8934] is used four times in this verse. It is often translated "peace" or the like, but it includes the concept of "one's current state of being or welfare," as it commonly does in modern Hebrew (see the second note on 1 Kgs 2:13 for further discussion of the root *sh-l-m*). This same term will be used as a haunting refrain throughout ch 9.

4:27 she fell to the ground before him and caught hold of his feet. The MT simply reads here "she took hold of his feet" (*wattakhazeq* [TH2388, ZH2616] *beraglayw* [TH7272, ZH8079]), but the NLT's longer rendition effectively captures the nuance of the abrupt Hebrew text. In any case, we are reminded once again that the Shunammite will not be deterred from her mission—any more than Elisha himself would be deterred from his mission to follow Elijah in ch 2.

4:29 Get ready to travel. The NLT mg note effectively indicates the more literal Hebrew idiom, colorfully rendered in the KJV as "gird up thy loins"—the idea being that the long tunic the Israelites customarily wore would hinder fast movement unless its bottom edges were temporarily tucked up into the belt.

4:30 As surely as the LORD lives and you yourself live. For the oath formula used here, see the note on 1 Kgs 2:24 and the second note on 17:1 (cf. the second note on 2:2, where, as here, the life of a person of spiritual authority is also invoked). Cogan and Tadmor (1988:58) note that by such an oath the Shunammite compelled Elisha to return with her home to her dead son, who had been the gift of the prophet. She would not take "no" for an answer!

4:34-35 *stretched out on him . . . stretched himself out again.* The rare root *gahar* [TH1457, ZH1566] is used only here (twice) and in 1 Kgs 18:42 for the prophet Elijah (see note there).

4:37 *overwhelmed with gratitude.* This is an interpretive addition by the NLT; the Hebrew simply reads "she fell at his feet and bowed to the ground." But such actions surely imply such an overwhelming feeling.

COMMENTARY

As already intimated in the notes, this lengthy and unforgettable miracle story finds a number of parallels (and some differences) with the Elijah traditions. First and most obviously, we find the account of the resurrection of a child, effected by the prophet "stretching himself" over the dead body of the boy (4:34; cf. 1 Kgs 17:21, where a different Hebrew verb is used). We have two wary women, concerned that the presence of a prophet may bring tragedy to their lives (4:16, 28; cf. 1 Kgs 17:18). And finally, we have the persistence of those prophets, wrestling with God, as it were, to reverse the awful, always tragic event of a child's death. Elisha prayed to the Lord his God (4:33) before commencing his literally life-changing actions (4:34-35); in the similar Elijah account, that prophet challenged his God as to why such a horrible event had to happen to such an innocent and generous widow (1 Kgs 17:20). Other more incidental parallels include the dual references to the "upper room" in both accounts (see the note on 4:11), as well as the conclusion in both stories of the prophet presenting the resurrected sons to their mothers (4:36-37; cf. 1 Kgs 17:23-24). In short, these parallels are too numerous to be coincidental in nature, but they surely represent not the result of a simple literary doublet (concerning this literary category, see the commentary on 3:1-27), but rather another example of the intentional literary device emphasizing both the parallels and the differences between the lives of these two great men of God (see the "Elijah and Elisha Cycles: Comparisons and Contrasts" chart for details, p. 204). In short: Elisha has inherited a "double share" of Elijah's spirit (see the note on 2:9). The reminder that Elisha, in effect, further effects a second "resurrection" even after his own death and burial (see 13:20-21) only further proves the point! Elisha, just like Elijah, his spiritual father, can bring the dead back to life. No one else, not even a king, could ever contemplate possessing such power as this (see 5:7; cf. 6:26-31; 8:4-6).

"Allow God to mess with your life!" This is the advice my pastor once gave me, and this may well sum up quite effectively the theology we find in this unforgettable story of the Shunammite woman and her family (and, it should be recalled, the story does not end here, but continues in 8:1-6). The Shunammite lived a comfortable life before she met Elisha, but her entirely commendable initiative in urging that prophet to spend time with her and her family led to what seemed at the time to be unnecessary, guarded elation (see 4:11-17), then almost inevitable, yet heart-rending despair (see 4:18-28), and then finally, tenacious, compelling emergency actions (again, 4:21-28; also 4:30), leading to the miracle of her son's resurrection (4:31-37). Thus, for the second time in the present chapter of 2 Kings, the compelling words and actions of a desperate woman elicit a timely miracle from the prophet Elisha. The hearers/readers of this ancient story could only marvel at what the God of such a prophet can and will accomplish in their lives, if only they remain tenacious in their faith.

This passage of Scripture has long intrigued me with its realistic and compelling characters, its overwhelming pathos, and its well-earned happy ending. How like life for the relatively well-to-do believer this story is! Many of us who have the good fortune of being able to make economic ends meet (at least for the most part!) are therefore able and willing to seek more of God in our lives, and we thus welcome occasions to get to know better the men and women of God who encounter us on our faith journeys. We are leery of getting too unbalanced in our spiritual walks of faith, but we correctly sense that spiritual "business as usual" is not enough and that it is probably not God's perfect will for our lives anyway. So it is that we seek out opportunities for God's authority figures to challenge our ways and change our lives; but we also may flinch when we realize that such challenges and changes are exactly that. These new realities can often lead to some quite uncomfortable circumstances and the unexpected need for drastic actions! So we, like the Shunammite in 4:16, steel ourselves against unreasonable hope; and we also, like the Shunammite in 4:28, remain quick to remonstrate when such hope, short of a miracle, is seemingly dashed for good. What a quandary we are in! Boring, banal predictability or a scary, exciting roller-coaster ride. These seem to be our only choices (cf. Luke 12:49-53). But we do not really have a choice anyway. Those who seek to "turn the world upside down" (cf. Acts 17:6, KJV) must have a strong dose of unpredictability in their lives! And even kings will take notice when such unpredictability leads to future occasions for witness, as we will soon see when the present story resumes in 8:1-6. You never know who might be affected when you allow God "to mess with your life."

◆   ## 6. Miracles during a famine (4:38-44)

38 Elisha now returned to Gilgal, and there was a famine in the land. One day as the group of prophets was seated before him, he said to his servant, "Put a large pot on the fire, and make some stew for the rest of the group."

39 One of the young men went out into the field to gather herbs and came back with a pocketful of wild gourds. He shredded them and put them into the pot without realizing they were poisonous. 40 Some of the stew was served to the men. But after they had eaten a bite or two they cried out, "Man of God, there's poison in this stew!" So they would not eat it.

41 Elisha said, "Bring me some flour." Then he threw it into the pot and said, "Now it's all right; go ahead and eat." And then it did not harm them.

42 One day a man from Baal-shalishah brought the man of God a sack of fresh grain and twenty loaves of barley bread made from the first grain of his harvest. Elisha said, "Give it to the people so they can eat."

43 "What?" his servant exclaimed. "Feed a hundred people with only this?"

But Elisha repeated, "Give it to the people so they can eat, for this is what the LORD says: Everyone will eat, and there will even be some left over!" 44 And when they gave it to the people, there was plenty for all and some left over, just as the LORD had promised.

NOTES

4:38 Gilgal. Presumably the site in western Ephraim is in view here (see the second note on 2:1).

the group of prophets. Lit., "sons of the prophets"; see the first note on 2:3.

his servant. Presumably this was Gehazi (also in 4:43). For possible meanings of his name, see the note on 4:12.

large pot. Heb., *hassir* [TH5518, ZH6105] *haggedolah*, a familiar term for a vessel for cooking meat. The overall image is probably that of a common meal in honor of the visiting prophet, wherein he might impart his "blessing" on the assembled community (Gray 1970:500).

4:39 wild gourds. Heb., *paqqu'oth sadeh* [TH6498, ZH7226], "cucumbers/gourds of (the) field"; commentators often connect this reference with the so-called "apples of Sodom" (*Citrullus colcynthus*), small melons that are yellow and fruitlike, which have strong purgative properties that can indeed lead to death (Cogan and Tadmor 1988:58).

4:40 there's poison in this stew! Lit., "there is death in the pot." Leithart (2006:186) properly notes the repetition of the theme of death which pervades the chapter.

4:41 some flour. Heb., *qemakh* [TH7058, ZH7854], the common term for flour or meal. Elisha's throwing the flour into the pot is akin to his earlier response to the impure water of Jericho (2:20-21); this is another occasion of purifying a liquid commodity that was producing death.

4:42 Baal-shalishah. This was a town possibly located in the region of Mt. Ephraim (Cogan and Tadmor 1988:59), but Herion (ABD 1.553) argues for the more traditional western location, overlooking the Plain of Sharon. In any case, the Talmud (*b. Sanhedrin* 12a) comments on the region's remarkable reputation for agricultural productivity.

a sack of fresh grain. The phrase here (*karmel betsiqlono* [TH3759A/6861, ZH4152/7638]) is difficult; it seems to read "new grain/corn in his bag/sack," or the like, but the second word is a hapax legomenon (i.e., it occurs only once). In light of an Ugaritic parallel, Cogan and Tadmor (1988:59, following Cassuto) suggest translating the phrase as "some fresh ears of grain." Wiseman (1993:206) prefers "roasted ears of corn," and he notes that it was a delicacy (cf. Sweeney 2007:292). R. K. Harrison (1980:56), in his commentary on Lev 2:14-16, points out that roasted ears of young corn were a common food item among the poor. Thus it was probably a simple delicacy enjoyed by rich and poor alike, similar to our modern popcorn.

twenty loaves of barley bread made from the first grain of his harvest. The barley harvest takes place around Passover time (March or April). Barley bread is less desirable than bread made from wheat flour, but the wheat harvest is significantly later (typically around Pentecost, May or June) and presumably had not yet taken place. Any fresh bread would have been greatly welcomed at this time!

to the people. Heb., *la'am* [TH5971A, ZH6639], a phrase repeated in the next verse. More than just Elisha's disciples will receive bread.

4:43 Feed a hundred people. This is possibly a round numbering of the "sons of the prophets" (Hobbs 1985:54), but probably it is better understood as a reminder of the larger crowd that will also be fed by the miracle-working prophet.

some left over. Thus, something more than bare sufficiency is in view, just as it was when the greater Elisha, Jesus, also fed a "huge crowd" (Matt 14:13-21; 15:32-39).

COMMENTARY

Another crisis, this time a famine (presumably both incidents described in this section of the chapter are related, at least thematically, by that rubric), leads to two remarkable miracles enacted by the prophet both for the benefit of the "group of prophets," and for the "people" (see 4:38, 42, respectively). Whether the "healing" of tainted food, or the multiplying of particularly welcome grain products (see the notes on 4:42 for details), the prophet proves most able and willing to bless those who, largely due to circumstances beyond their control, have great need for that very thing. Jesus reminds us in the Sermon on the Mount to pray for "our daily bread" (Matt 6:11, NIV); God is quite aware of our basic need for food and clothing (Matt 6:31-33), so we should not worry ourselves over such things. The timely and seemingly effortless miracles wrought by Elisha here must have reinforced such teachings most memorably for disciple and bystander alike, and they are meant to do the same thing for the believer of any age.

An interesting feature of both stories (akin to the initial provision of a few loaves and fishes in Jesus' feeding of the multitudes) is the "contributions" of two well-meaning individuals (that of the naive disciple in 4:39 and that of the visitor from Baal-shalishah in 4:42). The former "contribution" nearly ruined the entire pot of stew, while the latter probably could only serve to whet the appetite of such a large group of people. God and God's servants can always use such contributions, and surely he and they welcome at any time such offerings when given with good intent. After all, even the proverbial widow's mite (Luke 21:1-4) could be properly reckoned the most generous contribution of all by our Lord, and the two swords proffered during times of great trial might well prove sufficient (Luke 22:36-38). Therefore, let us never hesitate to offer whatever we can to help enable the miraculous work of God and of God's human leadership. God can always take our humble offerings and multiply them, altering them if necessary, for lasting effect for his Kingdom.

◆   ## 7. The healing of Naaman (5:1-19)

The king of Aram had great admiration for Naaman, the commander of his army, because through him the LORD had given Aram great victories. But though Naaman was a mighty warrior, he suffered from leprosy.*

²At this time Aramean raiders had invaded the land of Israel, and among their captives was a young girl who had been given to Naaman's wife as a maid. ³One day the girl said to her mistress, "I wish my master would go to see the prophet in Samaria. He would heal him of his leprosy."

⁴So Naaman told the king what the young girl from Israel had said. ⁵"Go and visit the prophet," the king of Aram told him. "I will send a letter of introduction for you to take to the king of Israel." So Naaman started out, carrying as gifts 750 pounds of silver, 150 pounds of gold,* and ten sets of clothing. ⁶The letter to the king of Israel said: "With this letter I present my servant Naaman. I want you to heal him of his leprosy."

⁷When the king of Israel read the letter, he tore his clothes in dismay and said, "This man sends me a leper to heal! Am I God, that I can give life and take it away? I can see that he's just trying to pick a fight with me."

⁸But when Elisha, the man of God, heard that the king of Israel had torn his clothes in dismay, he sent this message to him: "Why are you so upset? Send Naaman to me, and he will learn that there is a true prophet here in Israel."

⁹So Naaman went with his horses and chariots and waited at the door of Elisha's house. ¹⁰But Elisha sent a messenger out to him with this message: "Go and wash yourself seven times in the Jordan River.

Then your skin will be restored, and you will be healed of your leprosy."

¹¹But Naaman became angry and stalked away. "I thought he would certainly come out to meet me!" he said. "I expected him to wave his hand over the leprosy and call on the name of the LORD his God and heal me! ¹²Aren't the rivers of Damascus, the Abana and the Pharpar, better than any of the rivers of Israel? Why shouldn't I wash in them and be healed?" So Naaman turned and went away in a rage.

¹³But his officers tried to reason with him and said, "Sir,* if the prophet had told you to do something very difficult, wouldn't you have done it? So you should certainly obey him when he says simply, 'Go and wash and be cured!' " ¹⁴So Naaman went down to the Jordan River and dipped himself seven times, as the man of God had instructed him. And his skin became as healthy as the skin of a young child, and he was healed!

¹⁵Then Naaman and his entire party went back to find the man of God. They stood before him, and Naaman said, "Now I know that there is no God in all the world except in Israel. So please accept a gift from your servant."

¹⁶But Elisha replied, "As surely as the LORD lives, whom I serve, I will not accept any gifts." And though Naaman urged him to take the gift, Elisha refused.

¹⁷Then Naaman said, "All right, but please allow me to load two of my mules with earth from this place, and I will take it back home with me. From now on I will never again offer burnt offerings or sacrifices to any other god except the LORD. ¹⁸However, may the LORD pardon me in this one thing: When my master the king goes into the temple of the god Rimmon to worship there and leans on my arm, may the LORD pardon me when I bow, too."

¹⁹"Go in peace," Elisha said. So Naaman started home again.

5:1 Or *from a contagious skin disease.* The Hebrew word used here and throughout this passage can describe various skin diseases.   5:5 Hebrew *10 talents* [340 kilograms] *of silver, 6,000 [shekels]* [68 kilograms] *of gold.* 5:13 Hebrew *My father.*

NOTES

5:1 Naaman. This is a well-attested name in Aram (the southern region of present-day Syria). Wiseman (1993:206) notes parallels in the Alalakh and Ras Shamra (Ugaritic) texts. The name Naaman probably means "gracious" or the like (cf. the Hebrew name Naomi). Ironically, the MT here piles on the high terms of praise for this foreign military leader: "captain of the guard"; "a great man in the view of his master" (*'ish gadol* [TH1419, ZH1524] *lipne 'adonayw*); "highly respected" (*nesu' panim* [TH5375/6440, ZH5951/7156]); "a man of valor" (*gibbor khayil* [TH1368A/2428, ZH1475/2657]; concerning this last phrase cf. the first note on 1 Kgs 11:28). The effect is remarkably positive. But the single last word in the verse breaks the spell: *metsora'* [TH6879, ZH7665], "[he was] a leper."

the LORD had given Aram great victories. Continuing the almost other-worldly tenor of this tradition, Yahweh, the national God of Israel, was the one who had given great victories to her powerful enemy Aram (see Amos 9:7 for a similar international perspective).

leprosy. Biblical "leprosy" (*tsara'ath* [TH6883, ZH7669]) probably signified infectious skin conditions such as psoriasis and vitiligo (see NLT mg note; also Cogan and Tadmor 1988:63; ABD 4.277-279); it included molds and fungi on clothing and even on buildings (the classic Torah discussion concerning such "leprosy" is Lev 13–14). In contrast, "true leprosy" (Hansen's disease), with its hideous swellings and mutilations, was probably not known in the Bible. This would explain both Naaman's continued access to the Aramean court, as well as Gehazi's analogous access to the Israelite court later on (cf. 8:3-6), even though he too had previously been stricken with the same "leprosy" Naaman had (see 5:27, where this condition is further described as lasting "forever").

5:2 *as a maid.* This phrase is not found in the Hebrew, but it surely depicts the status of the young Israelite girl. Contrasts between various ethnic, economic, and social statuses pervade the chapter.

5:3 *the girl said.* This was a simple action with great consequences.

in Samaria. Elisha had "returned" to this capital city back in 2:25, and presumably it was there that he joined the Israelite king and his army when they marched out in their campaign against Moab (cf. 3:6).

5:5 *the king of Aram.* Presumably Ben-hadad II (also known as Adad-idri; see the second note on 1 Kgs 20:1; cf. 2 Kgs 6:24).

letter of introduction. Such letters about medical matters are attested throughout the ancient Near East (Wiseman 1993:207; see also Hobbs 1985:62 and Sweeney 2007:299 for details concerning such correspondence). Similarly, the practice of giving gifts to ensure an audience finds parallels elsewhere; but the total weights of the silver and gold cited here are remarkably large (10 talents of silver; 6,000 shekels of gold; see the second note on 1 Kgs 9:14 for modern-day equivalents). For other examples of large quantities of silver and gold as gifts to royalty, see the commentary on 1 Kgs 10:14-29.

5:7 *Am I God . . . ?* Only God (*'elohim* [TH430, ZH466]) can "give life and take it away" (see Deut 32:39; 1 Sam 2:6). Such expansive descriptions as these confirm the OT perspective on Yahweh's power to influence the future: Yahweh is all-powerful to bring about good or evil; that was never really under debate. The issue that remained was whether he would do so, and under what circumstances. In any case, Yahweh was never beholden to the words or actions of a king (cf. 1 Sam 12:12-25), although he in a sense had chosen to be beholden to those of a prophet (cf. Amos 3:7).

he's just trying to pick a fight with me. Lit., "he is seeking an occasion (to quarrel) with me" (*mith'anneh* [TH579, ZH628] *hu' li*). The narcissism of the king here, while deplorable, is understandable in light of the demise of King Ahab in 1 Kgs 22 at the hands of the self-same Arameans (indeed, Josephus *Antiquities* 8.15.5.414 and the Targum on 2 Chr 18 both identify Naaman as the Aramean archer whose randomly shot arrow killed King Ahab).

5:8 *Why are you so upset?* This phrase is not a literal translation of the Hebrew (which repeats, "Why have you torn your clothes?"), but it does convey effectively the gist of Elisha's message to the king.

5:9-10 *waited at the door . . . sent a messenger.* Regarding the remarkably prosaic way that Elisha here communicates with Naaman, see the commentary.

5:10 *seven times in the Jordan River.* A remarkably simple procedure in a relatively accessible location. Sweeney (2007:296-297) notes that both here and in the next narrative (6:1-7), the Jordan Valley is singled out as "the holy center of creation," and that such traditions may well have stemmed from the sanctuary at Gilgal.

5:12 *the Abana and the Pharpar.* These are more impressive rivers in their own right, to be sure, but not as efficacious as the Jordan in the present instance. The "Abana," or, more properly, "Amana" (as it is attested in some textual traditions), is probably the present-day Barada, which waters the plain of Damascus; the "Pharpar" may be the river el-Auwaj, which is south of the city (see Cogan and Tadmor 1988:64-65 for details). God, however, often chooses the unimpressive to bring about his miracles.

5:13 *Sir.* As the NLT mg note indicates, the Hebrew reads "my father" (*'abi* [TH1, ZH3]); this term, however, is an odd expression for servants (the NLT's "officers" are lit. "servants" in the Hebrew) to use to address their master (Cogan and Tadmor 1988:65). If the term is retained as is (it is omitted in the earliest manuscripts of the LXX), the NLT translation indicates the genuine concern the servants (officers) evidently have for their master, a concern paralleled earlier in 5:3 by the anonymous Israelite servant girl.

5:16 *As surely as the LORD lives, whom I serve.* Lit., "as Yahweh lives, before whom I stand." As Naaman and his party "stood" (*'amad* [TH5975, ZH6641]) before Elisha in the preceding verse, Elisha "stands" before Yahweh (also see 5:9, where the NLT's translation "waited" refers to the same root). Hobbs (1985:66) correctly emphasizes the nuance of worship in the present phrase. (For a less exalted, indeed ironic, repetition of the familiar expression "as the LORD lives," see 5:20, where Gehazi vows to profit from the prophet's healing power!)

5:17 *to load two of my mules with earth from this place.* This is apparently the earliest known example of what later became a widespread custom (cf. Montgomery 1951:377). A motif of duality is seen here and is found repeatedly in the next section; see the first note on 5:22.

5:18 *the god Rimmon.* This is an epithet (originally Ramman, "the thundering one") connected with Hadad, the storm god of the Levant (cf. the second note on 1 Kgs 15:18). The Masoretic pointing sarcastically renders this epithet as identical with the Hebrew term for "pomegranate" (cf. Gray 1970:507-508).

5:19 *Go in peace.* This is a brief and conventional response (in sharp contrast to the rambling remarks of Naaman (Cogan and Tadmor 1988:65). But Wiseman (1982:323-324) sees a covenantal relationship actually being confirmed here. However, in the Gehazi sequel this same term will soon be used in an ironic sense (see the note on 5:21 for details). For further details concerning the meaning inherent in the rich term *shalom*, see the note on 4:26.

COMMENTARY

Jesus makes an unforgettable reference to this first part of the Naaman story in his hometown sermon in Luke 4:27. This part celebrates the health-giving victory of Yahweh over a distinguished foreigner and his entourage, a victory in which the Israelite king plays no part, but in which the prophet plays an essential, if understated, role. The story at first appears to be a small but self-contained whole and need not necessarily presuppose its successor (i.e., the Gehazi debacle in 5:20-27). But later on we do find that the proffered "reward," spurned by the prophet in the present section, will lead to one later being given under false pretenses to the prophet's servant (see Cohn 1983:171-184 for a strong defense of the unity of the entire chapter). In short, in the present passage, Naaman is given a gift no money can buy, by a prophet who seeks no material reward. The prophet's role is surprisingly modest: He declines to meet personally with Naaman at all, sending out a messenger instead (5:10). The suggested "procedure" for the healing (wash seven times in the Jordan) is also remarkably understated, leading Naaman to dismiss the entire process in an angry huff, until his servants restore him to a more reasonable frame of mind (see 5:11-14). And later, the restored Aramean, gushing with gratitude and insisting on blessing the Israelite prophet in turn with a gift (5:15-16), merely receives a curt (but not unkind) dismissal of his attempts at generosity. Even after Naaman's memorable peroration on his new desire to serve only Yahweh while on "foreign" soil (as well as on transplanted Israelite soil! [5:17-18]), he only receives the brief response: "Go in peace." This part of the story, therefore, is all about Naaman the Aramean, not so much about the Israelite prophet Elisha, still less about the king of Israel (unnamed, but presumably Joram son of Ahab [cf. 1:17]).

It is no wonder Jesus used this story in his Nazareth discourse about God sending prophets to Gentiles (Luke 4:16-27), seemingly as his final "scriptural reference" in his sermon. (In the next several verses, the hometown folk are ready to put him to death!) In contrast, however, with Jesus' sermon in Luke 4, the main conflict in the present Kings text is *not* between two normally rival ethnic groups, Jews and Gentiles (see the second note on 5:1), but rather between king and prophet (and perhaps also between servant and master; I will have more to say about that in the next section). The conflict of kings versus prophets has occupied our thoughts already a number of times in 1–2 Kings (see the commentary on 1 Kgs 1:5-27 for the classic delineation of their respective roles), but here this perennial conflict seems to play a somewhat secondary note to a remarkably optimistic and universalistic depiction of Yahweh as sovereign God over all people and all situations.

Another particularly notable feature of this story is the contrasting levelheadedness and reasonableness of the underclass over against the impatience and impudence of those in authority. Whether it be the suddenly suspicious Israelite king (5:7) or the seemingly spurned Naaman himself (5:11-12), strong emotional outbursts characterize the responses of the higher class, while more rational rejoinders come from the prophet (5:8) and unnamed military underlings (5:13), respectively. (And it should be recalled that it was a captured Israelite "maid" [5:2-3] who first set Naaman on the path to healing.) Servants wiser than their masters—this is the theme in many literary works, and certainly this has become a significant theme here as well. (Also note that once Naaman is healed of his "leprosy," his skin is described as becoming as healthy as that of a "young child" [5:14].) It will not be until the final act of the story (presented, probably correctly, in the NLT as a separate section, below, but still to be connected rather closely with what precedes it) that we find an unexpected reversal where the master (Elisha) proves more prescient than the servant (Gehazi), a reversal all the more vivid due to the numerous examples already mentioned of underlings demonstrating more insight than their superiors.

Finally, specific comment should be given to the healed Naaman's "servant" speeches found in 5:15-19, especially the speech which includes his remarks that from now on he will worship only Yahweh, the God of Israel, and that to enable this to take place, he will take two mule-loads of Israelite soil back to Aram! Cohn (1983:178-179) has isolated the following palistrophe (i.e., ABCBA literary structure, with particular emphasis on the middle section [here delineated by "X"]) found in the literal translation of 5:18:

A. For this thing
  B. may Yahweh pardon your servant
    C. when my lord comes to the house of Rimmon to worship there
      X. *and he leans on my hand,*
    C'. and I worship in the house of Rimmon (in my worshiping in the house of Rimmon),
  B'. may Yahweh pardon your servant
A'. for this thing

Thus, Naaman the trusted "servant" of the Aramean king (see 5:1), the one whose very hand can be "leaned on" (the same idiom appears in 7:2, 17, in reference to an important official of the Israelite king), will himself henceforth be a secret worshiper of the foreign God Yahweh! As Cohn further points out, by the end of the present section of the story Naaman has been both cleansed and thoroughly "converted," with his original journey to Elisha now balanced by his impending departure from the prophet. But the larger story is not yet over. (For Cohn's further contrast of the God-fearing foreign servant Naaman with the ignoble Israelite servant Gehazi, see the commentary on 5:20-27.) Once again, who is servant and who is really master? Elisha knows, Naaman now knows, but Gehazi has yet to learn that there is no other God in all the world except for Yahweh (5:15), and it is Elisha the prophet who is uniquely his special servant. As will be clearly demonstrated in the next section of the story, the high and impartial morality of Yahweh transcends even his astounding miraculous power.

◆   8. The greed of Gehazi (5:20–27)

²⁰But Gehazi, the servant of Elisha, the man of God, said to himself, "My master should not have let this Aramean get away without accepting any of his gifts. As surely as the LORD lives, I will chase after him and get something from him." ²¹So Gehazi set off after Naaman.

When Naaman saw Gehazi running after him, he climbed down from his chariot and went to meet him. "Is everything all right?" Naaman asked.

²²"Yes," Gehazi said, "but my master has sent me to tell you that two young prophets from the hill country of Ephraim have just arrived. He would like 75 pounds* of silver and two sets of clothing to give to them."

²³"By all means, take twice as much* silver," Naaman insisted. He gave him two sets of clothing, tied up the money in two bags, and sent two of his servants to carry the gifts for Gehazi. ²⁴But when they arrived at the citadel,* Gehazi took the gifts from the servants and sent the men back. Then he went and hid the gifts inside the house.

²⁵When he went in to his master, Elisha asked him, "Where have you been, Gehazi?"

"I haven't been anywhere," he replied.

²⁶But Elisha asked him, "Don't you realize that I was there in spirit when Naaman stepped down from his chariot to meet you? Is this the time to receive money and clothing, olive groves and vineyards, sheep and cattle, and male and female servants? ²⁷Because you have done this, you and your descendants will suffer from Naaman's leprosy forever." When Gehazi left the room, he was covered with leprosy; his skin was white as snow.

5:22 Hebrew *1 talent* [34 kilograms].   5:23 Hebrew *take 2 talents* [68 kilograms].   5:24 Hebrew *the Ophel.*

NOTES

5:20 *Gehazi.* Possibly his very name means "greedy" or "avaricious" (see note on 4:12).

5:21 *Is everything all right?* Lit., "is there peace?" (*hashalom* [TH7965, ZH8934]). Although not evident in the NLT, the term *shalom* is also found in Gehazi's response to Naaman at the beginning of 5:22: "there is peace" (or, "everything is all right"). Both of these uses of the rich term *shalom* stand in sharp irony to its prior use in Elisha's brief parting comment to Naaman in 5:19. Here is yet another connection between the two sections of the Naaman story, showing that the present Gehazi material was unlikely to have been added at a later time.

5:22 two young prophets. A motif of duality pervades 5:22-23: two prophets, two sets of clothing, "twice as much silver," two bags, two servants—all this echoing, thematically, the two mule-loads of earth mentioned in 5:17.

75 pounds of silver. Lit., "a talent of silver" (see the second note on 5:5 and, for modern-day equivalences, the second note on 1 Kgs 9:14).

5:24 the citadel. Heb., ha'opel [TH6077, ZH6755], probably a topographical term denoting the elevated part of a city (so Cogan and Tadmor [1988:66], who further note the definition of "Ophel" that Yigal Shiloh, the excavator of Jerusalem's Ophel, the City of David, proposed: It is "an urban architectural term denoting the outstanding site of the citadel or acropolis"). In the present passage, the "Ophel" would presumably refer to a prominent part of the city of Samaria.

5:26 I was there in spirit. Lit., "did my heart (leb [TH3820, ZH4213]) not go [with you]?"; the NLT renders this by means of the contemporary expression of being somewhere "in spirit" if one is not there in the physical sense. Thus, Elisha was there with Gehazi both in his concern for, and knowledge of, the servant's duplicitous attitudes and actions. Wiseman (1993:208-209) lists these as avarice (5:22), deception (5:23-25), derogation of superiors ("this Aramean," 5:20), swearing deceitfully (5:20, contrasted with 5:16), and attempting to cover up the results of his actions (5:24-25).

5:27 his skin was white as snow. For the characteristics of such "leprosy," see the third note on 5:1. The concluding reference here to "leprosy" forms a clear *inclusio* (on the term *inclusio*, see the first note on 1 Kgs 3:15) with the first verse of the chapter—further indication that the entire chapter is to be considered a literary unity.

COMMENTARY

As Cohn has reminded us (see previous commentary section for details), this section of the chapter has close ties with what precedes, with the result that the servant of Elisha (Gehazi) suffers greatly in comparison with the servant of the king of Aram (Naaman). This is a bold, internationalist touch on the part of the "theologian" (Cohn's characterization) who put together this unforgettable narrative in its present form. Gehazi, in the end, is the one who "inherits" Naaman's leprosy, and the reader can only reflect on the fitness of his final fate. As Cohn puts it (1983:184): "The theologian wanted the moral to transcend the miraculous," and thus he balanced Elisha's acceptance of Naaman with his rejection of Gehazi. That is how the story sadly has to end: Greedy, duplicitous Gehazi, who could not let "this Aramean" (5:20) get away with a "free" healing, must receive his just desserts—the same affliction for himself and his descendants "forever" (see 5:27). What a long-term price to pay for such a crass, impulsive attempt to make a quick profit!

Seow (1999:198) reminds us: "There are people in every era who are so terribly afflicted with diseases and other ailments, who are desperate to find any word of hope from spiritual leaders. And there are always opportunists like Gehazi who are ready to make a quick profit in the name of the Lord. This text sternly warns against such opportunism." But as Seow himself points out, it may well be the unnamed Israelite slave back in the beginning of the chapter who is in a very real sense the proper foil to unfaithful Gehazi, and therefore the true role model of proper faith in her God, Yahweh. Although a hopeless captive in a foreign land, her "eyes of faith" perceived, and thus provided, hope for her foreign master, and through him, for his entourage as well. Thus, as greedy Gehazi fails, the unnamed servant girl succeeds in advancing the Kingdom of God beyond the borders of Israel. We today smile at Naaman's overly literal transporting of Israelite soil to his Aramean homeland to worship his new God, but we surely recognize that none of that could have happened without the brave, simple testimony of a captive Israelite servant girl, whose name our storyteller probably never even knew. One never knows what simple word of testimony might well change forever the course of salvation history.

◆ ## 9. The floating ax head (6:1-7)

One day the group of prophets came to Elisha and told him, "As you can see, this place where we meet with you is too small. ²Let's go down to the Jordan River, where there are plenty of logs. There we can build a new place for us to meet."

"All right," he told them, "go ahead."

³"Please come with us," someone suggested.

"I will," he said. ⁴So he went with them. When they arrived at the Jordan, they began cutting down trees. ⁵But as one of them was cutting a tree, his ax head fell into the river. "Oh, sir!" he cried. "It was a borrowed ax!"

⁶"Where did it fall?" the man of God asked. When he showed him the place, Elisha cut a stick and threw it into the water at that spot. Then the ax head floated to the surface. ⁷"Grab it," Elisha said. And the man reached out and grabbed it.

NOTES

6:1 *group of prophets.* Lit., "the sons of the prophets" (see first note on 2:3).

too small. Lit., "too narrow/tight for us" (*tsar* [TH6862, ZH7639] *mimmennu*). "Too cramped for us" is a felicitous translation suggested by Cogan and Tadmor (1988:69).

6:2 *Jordan River.* Sweeney (2007:295-301) has argued effectively that the present section of ch 6 should be connected syntactically with the preceding narrative (5:1-27). As he points out, "both episodes are concerned with Elisha's divinely granted powers, and both portray those powers in relation to the Jordan River" (see note on 5:10). To be sure, the narratives undoubtedly arose from different settings, but they are closely linked together in their present form—giving even more force to the strong contrast in Elisha's behavior highlighted in the next note.

6:3 *I will.* In clear contrast with Elisha's marked nonappearance to Naaman in the preceding chapter (see commentary on 5:1-19), his willingness to participate here is especially emphasized in the Hebrew (*'ani 'elek* [TH1980, ZH2143], "I myself will go").

6:5 *ax head.* Lit., "the [tool of] iron" (*habbarzel* [TH1270, ZH1366]). In this era, iron tools would still be rather rare and quite valuable (cf. 1 Sam 13:19-22, which describes the situation about 200 years prior to this time).

It was a borrowed ax! Lit., "it was asked for" (*hu' sha'ul* [TH7592, ZH8626]). Not only was the ax head valuable in and of itself, but the borrower was responsible to make recompense to the owner for its loss (cf. Exod 22:14-15). As Sweeney (2007:301) points out, the narrative presents two related problems here: the problem of the borrower's powerlessness in recovering the lost ax head from the water and also his moral obligation to give recompense to the original owner for its loss.

6:6 *the ax head floated to the surface.* Some commentators suggest that in the original story Elisha took a stick to poke around and thus find and retrieve the lost ax head (Gray 1970:511-512); or, more fancifully, he cut a stick to resemble the original ax handle, so that the head would float miraculously to join its handle (Cogan and Tadmor 1988:70, citing the medieval sage David Qimchi). As is the case with the other miraculous actions of Elisha (see commentary on 2:19-25), one's presuppositions will significantly govern one's inter-pretation of the text, but a plain reading of the narrative as we have it would indicate that a most timely and remarkable miracle took place.

COMMENTARY

Elisha was most willing once again to guide and to instruct his various "groups of prophets" scattered throughout the land of Israel (cf. Cogan and Tadmor 1988:69); here the "Jordan River" group had seemingly been brought together for that very purpose. But they had a problem: They had run out of room and needed to build a larger facility. This, to be sure, is a "problem" that both churches and schools would generally be pleased to face! Such opportunities, however, can lend themselves to annoying ancillary difficulties, and such a situation arose here—or, literally, sank here, as the borrowed ax head flew off the handle and then sank into the water, seemingly lost for good.

How like life this is: We endeavor to do something for God only to find that pesky problems arise, bedeviling us, as it were—frustrating circumstances that can instantly destroy any spiritual momentum we may have been experiencing. But we know that God is sovereign in all situations, even over the smallest detail. And often God's choice servant may be the very person who knows what to do and who is providentially present with us to bring about the very blessing we need. Miracu-lously, God's servant will be led by God's Spirit to rectify the situation and to restore the momentum. Nothing catches God by surprise, of course, and not much catches God's servant by surprise either (but see 4:27). We should cry out, state the problem plainly, and then watch with amazement as God, and God's representative, prove equal to the situation, no matter how desperate it might suddenly seem. To God be the glory!

◆   10. Elisha traps the Arameans (6:8-23)

⁸When the king of Aram was at war with Israel, he would confer with his officers and say, "We will mobilize our forces at such and such a place."

⁹But immediately Elisha, the man of God, would warn the king of Israel, "Do not go near that place, for the Arameans are planning to mobilize their troops there." ¹⁰So the king of Israel would send word to the place indicated by the man of God. Time and again Elisha warned the king, so that he would be on the alert there.

¹¹The king of Aram became very upset over this. He called his officers together and demanded, "Which of you is the trai-tor? Who has been informing the king of Israel of my plans?"

¹²"It's not us, my lord the king," one of the officers replied. "Elisha, the prophet in Israel, tells the king of Israel even the words you speak in the privacy of your bedroom!"

¹³"Go and find out where he is," the king commanded, "so I can send troops to seize him."

And the report came back: "Elisha is at Dothan." ¹⁴So one night the king of Aram sent a great army with many chariots and horses to surround the city.

¹⁵When the servant of the man of God got up early the next morning and went outside, there were troops, horses, and chariots everywhere. "Oh, sir, what will we do now?" the young man cried to Elisha.

¹⁶"Don't be afraid!" Elisha told him. "For there are more on our side than on theirs!" ¹⁷Then Elisha prayed, "O LORD, open his eyes and let him see!" The LORD opened the young man's eyes, and when he looked up, he saw that the hillside around Elisha was filled with horses and chariots of fire.

¹⁸As the Aramean army advanced toward him, Elisha prayed, "O LORD, please make them blind." So the LORD struck them with blindness as Elisha had asked.

¹⁹Then Elisha went out and told them, "You have come the wrong way! This isn't the right city! Follow me, and I will take you to the man you are looking for." And he led them to the city of Samaria.

²⁰As soon as they had entered Samaria, Elisha prayed, "O LORD, now open their eyes and let them see." So the LORD opened their eyes, and they discovered that they were in the middle of Samaria.

²¹When the king of Israel saw them, he shouted to Elisha, "My father, should I kill them? Should I kill them?"

²²"Of course not!" Elisha replied. "Do we kill prisoners of war? Give them food and drink and send them home again to their master."

²³So the king made a great feast for them and then sent them home to their master. After that, the Aramean raiders stayed away from the land of Israel.

NOTES

6:8 *the king of Aram.* See the second note on 6:24 for the probable identity of this king.

at such and such a place. Heb., *'el-meqom peloni 'almoni* [TH6423/492, ZH7141/532]; cf. 1 Sam 21:2 [3]; or in reference to an unnamed person, Ruth 4:1.

6:9 *immediately.* There is no precise equivalent for this term in the original, although the overall point of these verses is that Elisha was able to warn the Israelite king well in advance about any such intended Aramean military actions.

Elisha, the man of God. Both here and in the next verse, the MT merely reads "the man of God," while the LXX merely reads "Elisha." It is not until 6:12 that we find "Elisha, the prophet" in the MT. (Concerning the phrase "man of God" as an early synonym for "prophet," see the note on 1 Kgs 13:1.)

6:10 *warned the king.* The antipathy between prophet and king found in ch 5 (and elsewhere) is certainly not reflected here (but cf. 6:31!).

6:11 *Which of you is the traitor?* This phrase is not in the MT (but the LXX reads "who has betrayed me?" [cf. Vulgate and Targum]); in any case, the added phrase does convey effectively the full force of the king's fury.

6:12 *in the privacy of your bedroom!* Even such "pillow talk" was not hidden from "Elisha, the prophet in Israel"—much less discussions taking place in supposedly secret councils of war. (Concerning the "prophet" being particularly privy to the deliberations of the heavenly council, see notes on 1 Kgs 22:17, 19.)

6:13 *Go and find out where he is.* Lit., "go and see," which is particularly ironic inasmuch as complete blindness will soon be their fate (Hens-Piazza 2006:269).

Dothan. This is a town (modern Tell Dotha) located 9 mi. (14 km) north of Samaria, whose imposing mound is strategically situated on the main road leading from there into the Jezreel Valley (ABD 2.226-227). Dothan serves also as an important site mentioned in the Joseph story at Gen 37:17, the only other place where the city is mentioned in the Hebrew Bible.

6:15 *the servant.* Unnamed (as in 4:38, 43), but probably meant to be understood as Gehazi (see the third note on 4:38 for details). Literary variations like this (unnamed servants, prophets, and kings [of Israel and of Aram]) attest to the variegated provenances of these Elisha stories.

Oh, sir, what will we do now? As Seow (1999:201) points out, in the Hebrew the first part of this question ("alas, my lord"; *'ahah 'adoni* [TH113, ZH123]) is identical to the first part of the plaintive appeal the "son of the prophet" directed to Elisha in 6:5.

6:16 *Don't be afraid!* This is the exact same response Elijah gave to the widow of Zarephath in 1 Kgs 17:13 (see note there).

there are more on our side. See the commentary for a discussion about this remarkable statement of faith (which in the present instance will soon also be a statement of sight).

6:17 *horses and chariots of fire.* See 2:11 for the similar phenomenon of Elijah being borne up to heaven in the whirlwind (see the note there for details). There the question was whether Elisha would be able to "see" the fiery host and Elijah's heavenly departure. Now he can not only see them, but he prays that his servant can do so too.

6:18 *with blindness.* As will be noted further in the commentary below, the present story juxtaposes supernatural sight and supernatural blindness. The term used here for "blindness" (*sanwerim* [TH5575, ZH6177]) is a rare term, and probably represents an Akkadian loanword which has come to denote "a numinous flash of light which temporarily disables" (Cogan and Tadmor 1988:74; cf. the similar phenomenon found in Gen 19:11).

6:19 *Samaria.* See the first note on 1 Kgs 16:24 for details concerning this capital city.

6:21 *My father.* Heb., *'abi* [TH1, ZH3], a very positive term of address (see note on 5:13, where, however, the text is more dubious). In 2:12, Elisha called the recently departed Elijah his "father," and King Jehoash of Israel will use the same term for Elisha in 13:14.

6:22 *Do we kill prisoners of war?* In sharp contrast to the normal practices of holy war, we find remarkable clemency being advised here (contrast the perspective found in 1 Kgs 20:23-34, as well as 1 Kgs 20:35-43, where King Ahab is roundly condemned for similar acts of clemency). Yet, despite these sharp differences, the overall lesson remains remarkably the same—it is the prophet, not the king, who is to initiate holy war, and as it is here, it is the prophet, not the king, who is given the final say in whether or not the strictures of holy war are to be observed. Here, the Israelite victory is of entirely supernatural origin, so the bewildered captives evidently deserve special status. Furthermore, as Cogan and Tadmor (1988:75) point out, we may also find a parallel here with the neo-Assyrian practice of sparing enemy captives so that they might sing the praises of their captors and their gods.

COMMENTARY

Physical sight and spiritual blindness can often occur together, but rarely are these phenomena juxtaposed so dramatically as in the present text of 2 Kings. Elisha can see, spiritually—and sometimes literally—heavenly realities, and for a brief instance, so can his servant (6:16-17). Elisha can also pray for supernatural blindness to fall upon his foes (6:18), so that the enemies of God's people Israel can be led helplessly into the very center of the Israelite capital. Finally, Elisha can ask that Yahweh open the enemies' eyes (6:20), so that they could see immediately what predicament they were in and be moved to reach an amicable military solution with a minimum of bloodshed. In sharp contrast to the next several sections of 2 Kings, the present passage ends with a peaceful resolution between Arameans and Israelites, including a "great feast" celebrating the onset of that very status. Equally surprisingly, hints are given concerning continued peaceful relations between Israelite prophet and king (see 6:9-10, 21), with the latter following the advice of the former, and even calling him "my father" (see note on 6:21). When God's leadership stands united, absolutely amazing things can happen.

It will be evident by now that the Elisha cycle—no less than the Elijah cycle—represents a careful editing of various stories and traditions with somewhat different emphases and points of view. In the present case we find (rather atypically) Israelite king and prophet working in delightful harmony with each other, and thus vanquishing their common enemy in an effortless and almost humorous way—with the result that, as it were, whatever the Aramean king says even in the privacy of his own bedroom might well become public knowledge throughout the land of Israel (6:12). But even more importantly, we also find here one of the clearest confirmations anywhere in the Old Testament of what is normally an unseen spiritual reality for them and for us: "There are more [spiritual forces] on our side than on theirs" (6:16). With the more familiar New Testament parallels (Matt 26:53; cf. 1 John 4:4; and, perhaps, Heb 12:1-2) also in mind, we should be profoundly encouraged by the present passage. Time and again, the enemy's secret plans can be publicly exposed and thereby thwarted, if it is God's will to do so (6:10). Whether it be an expensive lost ax head or a powerful enemy army, God's people need not fear the onset of apparent calamity because God's leaders are equal to the situation. And the results will be a blessing (not only to God's needy people, but also paradoxically to the "enemy," as 6:22-23 makes clear). Surely the original owner of the ax (cf. 6:5-7) received a blessing when his valuable tool was safely returned, and in a similar way so did the Aramean army, when they were repatriated peacefully as prisoners of war. The present story illustrates God's triumphant sovereignty, with king and prophet working in true harmony, and that is the intended lesson. We will, however, soon notice that life does not always turn out this way, for the divinely inspired editor of 2 Kings will juxtapose with this passage the heart-wrenching tradition of the siege of Samaria by these same Arameans in the very next portion of the Elisha cycle. Nonetheless, there, just as here, "there are more on our side than on theirs" (cf. 7:5-7).

◆   ## 11. Ben-hadad besieges Samaria (6:24–7:2)

[24]Some time later, however, King Ben-hadad of Aram mustered his entire army and besieged Samaria. [25]As a result, there was a great famine in the city. The siege lasted so long that a donkey's head sold for eighty pieces of silver, and a cup of dove's dung sold for five pieces* of silver.

[26]One day as the king of Israel was walking along the wall of the city, a woman called to him, "Please help me, my lord the king!"

[27]He answered, "If the LORD doesn't help you, what can I do? I have neither food from the threshing floor nor wine from the press to give you." [28]But then the king asked, "What is the matter?"

She replied, "This woman said to me: 'Come on, let's eat your son today, then we will eat my son tomorrow.' [29]So we cooked my son and ate him. Then the next day I said to her, 'Kill your son so we can eat him,' but she has hidden her son."

[30]When the king heard this, he tore his clothes in despair. And as the king walked along the wall, the people could see that he was wearing burlap under his robe next to his skin. [31]"May God strike me and

even kill me if I don't separate Elisha's head from his shoulders this very day," the king vowed.

³²Elisha was sitting in his house with the elders of Israel when the king sent a messenger to summon him. But before the messenger arrived, Elisha said to the elders, "A murderer has sent a man to cut off my head. When he arrives, shut the door and keep him out. We will soon hear his master's steps following him."

³³While Elisha was still saying this, the messenger arrived. And the king* said, "All this misery is from the LORD! Why should I wait for the LORD any longer?"

CHAPTER 7

Elisha replied, "Listen to this message from the LORD! This is what the LORD says: By this time tomorrow in the markets of Samaria, five quarts of choice flour will cost only one piece of silver,* and ten quarts of barley grain will cost only one piece of silver.*"

²The officer assisting the king said to the man of God, "That couldn't happen even if the LORD opened the windows of heaven!"

But Elisha replied, "You will see it happen with your own eyes, but you won't be able to eat any of it!"

6:25 Hebrew *sold for 80 [shekels]* [2 pounds, or 0.9 kilograms] *of silver, and ¼ of a cab* [0.3 liters] *of dove's dung sold for 5 [shekels]* [2 ounces, or 57 grams]. *Dove's dung* may be a variety of wild vegetable. 6:33 Hebrew *he.*   7:1a Hebrew *1 seah* [6 liters] *of choice flour will cost 1 shekel* [0.4 ounces, or 11 grams]; also in 7:16, 18.   7:1b Hebrew *2 seahs* [12 liters] *of barley grain will cost 1 shekel* [0.4 ounces, or 11 grams]; also in 7:16, 18.

NOTES

6:24 *Some time later, however.* This translation, although a bit heavy for the Hebrew, does correctly indicate the marked shift in setting and perspective we now encounter (see the commentary below; also Seow 1999:202-203).

King Ben-hadad of Aram. In contrast to the unnamed Aramean king mentioned in 5:1 and 6:8, we find a specific (and familiar) name (or dynastic title?) in this new section (cf. 8:7, 9). The complicated issues surrounding this name or title have been rehearsed in the notes on 1 Kgs 15:18 and 20:1, where the traditional enumeration of Ben-hadad I and Ben-hadad II (= Adad-idri) has been cautiously followed. But here, the king in question may well be neither of those two monarchs (Cogan and Tadmor 1988:78-79; Kelle 2006), but a third Ben-hadad (son of Hazael; cf. 13:3). Those who argue for such an identification would then see the historical events underlying the present literary tradition as representing a time of clear Aramean supremacy over Israel, which is more typical of the end of the ninth century BC (which is precisely the time presupposed in the final Elisha story found in 13:14-21).

6:25 *donkey's head . . . dove's dung.* From feast (6:23) to famine: These are examples of normally disgusting items being sold for exorbitant prices due to the length and severity of the Aramean siege of the city. But the specific identities of these items are quite uncertain; Cogan and Tadmor (1988:79) argue convincingly that "dove's dung" was the popular term for inedible husks (carob pods?), and possibly "donkey's heads" was another such term. In any case, the references to cannibalism in the next several verses certainly underscore the extremity of the famine, as well as the absolute powerlessness of the king to alleviate it.

cup. Heb., *roba' haqqab* [TH6894, ZH7685] ("¼ of the *qab*"). This is the only place where the term *qab* occurs in the MT, so its exact size is uncertain. Rabbinic sources suggest that it was ¹⁄₁₈ of an ephah (which is equivalent to about 36 L, or ½ bushel); hence a *qab* would indeed be about 2 L, and ¼ of that, about a cup (cf. ABD 6.904-905; also Kletter 2009:834-835). (For present-day equivalences to the Israelite shekel, see the second note on 1 Kgs 9:14.)

6:26 *a woman called to him.* See the note on 8:3 concerning the possible legal ramifications of the verb used here.

6:27 *food from the threshing floor . . . wine from the press.* This is probably another pair of proverbial references: There is neither food nor drink available. Wine, usually drunk diluted, was the basic beverage for the people, partly due to the fact that water by itself often came from unsanitary sources (cf. 2 Macc 15:39).

6:28 *eat your son . . . eat my son.* Sadly, fulfillment of the covenantal curses of Deut 28:53-57 is probably in view. The genius of the author here is in evident display with the repeated references to specific details of the awful siege, meant surely to startle the reader (also see the next note).

6:30 *wearing burlap under his robe next to his skin.* The unnamed king here is certainly no hero for the author, yet there is a strange tenderness to the author's depiction of him: bitterly despondent (6:27), yet willing to listen to a woman's plea for help (6:28); publicly despairing (6:30a), and also privately mournful as well (6:30b). The burlap or "sackcloth" (*saq* [TH8242, ZH8566]) was a "coarsely woven piece of material, generally made of goat's hair and therefore usually black in the Near East. . . . In the ancient Near East, just as in ancient Israel, the *saq* was worn in situations of personal mourning, as well as in those involving communal mourning. It functioned as a visible representation of distress and humiliation" (Wolff 1977:29-30). In 1 Kgs 21:27, we are told that the repentant King Ahab went around dressed in sackcloth, even sleeping in it. If the present king was indeed Joram son of Ahab, it would be a positive example of "like father, like son."

6:31 *May God strike me and even kill me.* Concerning this oath formula, see the note on 1 Kgs 2:23. Coupled with the king's gloomy pronouncement in 6:27 ("If the LORD doesn't help you, what can I do?"), the reader is reminded by the king's oath that (1) seemingly, only the prophet can intercede positively with the deity to alleviate the horrific results of the siege, but also (2) the king can still take the initiative to punish the prophet for apparently not doing so. Thus, the present verse presents the king not merely as vengeful or hot-headed, but as deeply despairing.

6:32 *with the elders of Israel.* This is a passing comment, but highly illustrative of the important status of Elisha, a status which the king's profane oath in the preceding verse also attests.

murderer. As if to contradict what has just been asserted in the note on 6:31, Elisha's characterization of the king is succinct: He is nothing more than an assassin or murderer (*ben-hameratseakh* [TH7523, ZH8357], "son of the murderer/assassin"—the term "son" representing that the person in question partakes of the qualities of the category being cited, not that the king's father literally was an assassin or murderer).

We will soon hear. Elisha's comments here represent the well-known phenomenon of "short-term" prediction so characteristic of the classical prophets (see the note on 1 Kgs 13:3). The prophets usually know in advance what plans are being made by their antagonists, even before (but often just briefly before) they are publicized by conventional means.

6:33 *messenger . . . the king.* The word "king" does not appear in the MT, and in Hebrew there is little difference between the word for "messenger" (*mal'ak* [TH4397, ZH4855]) and the word for "king" (*melek* [TH4428, ZH4889]). Many commentators (see Cogan and Tadmor 1988:80-81) prefer reading "king" rather than "messenger" here (cf. 7:2, 18). Like the NLT, the NIV and NRSV include "messenger," but then introduce the king as the speaker in the second half of the verse (cf. the paraphrase of these events in Josephus *Antiquities* 9.4.4.69-70). In any case, the concluding statement ("All this misery is from the LORD! Why should I wait for the LORD any longer?") surely came from the mouth of the king.

7:1 *five quarts of choice flour . . . ten quarts of barley grain.* This phrase is repeated in 7:18 in a different order (in the MT), helping delineate what appeared to medieval scribes to be the natural chapter division we find here today (cf. the various *inclusios* [literary repetitions] noted in Leithart 2006:206). Lit., the phrase reads, "a seah of choice flour . . . 2 seahs of barley"—a "seah" ($^1/_3$ of an ephah) representing about 12 L, or $^2/_3$ peck (so ABD 6.904-905; Kletter 2009:834-835). Cogan and Tadmor (1988:81) prefer a smaller measure of 7.3 L. In any case, the prices listed here—1 shekel each (see the second note on 1 Kgs 9:14 for present-day equivalences for the shekel)—are still significantly higher than normal (probably at least fivefold, cf. Cogan and Tadmor; also Kletter 2009:838), but they are of course much lower than they would have been had the siege not been lifted.

7:2 The officer assisting the king. Heb., *shalish* [TH7991B, ZH8957], a word clearly related to the Hebrew word for the number three (*shalosh* [TH7969, ZH8993]), but otherwise uncertain in meaning here. Mastin (1979:125-154) suggests it denotes an officer of the "third rank."

windows of heaven! This phrase too is repeated below (in 7:19); it is familiar imagery found in Gen 7:11 where the "floodgates of heaven" are opened wide (cf. NLT "rain . . . from the sky") to help bring about the great flood (and in Gen 8:2 they are then closed, so the flood can dissipate). Also, in Mal 3:10 the "windows of heaven" are opened to provide copious rainfall to bless the crops of all those who bring "all the tithes into the storehouse."

COMMENTARY

This is the first of the three sections in the NLT that together form the single extended narrative (6:24–7:20) concerning Ben-hadad's awful siege of the capital city of Samaria, as well as Elisha's adversarial role vis-à-vis the king of Israel. Literary links found in this narrative include several repeated notes concerning the relative prices of food during and after the siege (6:25; 7:1, 16, 18), as well as two repeated comments concerning Yahweh's opening "the windows of heaven," and the king's officer seeing it happen but not being able to enjoy its benefits (7:2, 19). Like the entirety of chapter 5, this extended story features some unlikely heroes and villains, as well as a complicated, unexpected (but ultimately quite satisfying) plot progression. Even lepers can be heroes and royal officials, villains—that is one of the messages we are expected to take away from this most intriguing story.

In sharp contrast to the previous section where Israelite king and prophet generally worked in smooth harmony, the present story points to a sadly more typical circumstance, pitting Israelite king against Israelite prophet, each vying for supremacy, with the results leading to unnecessary hardship for the people of God (as in much of the Elijah cycle, especially 1 Kgs 21). The king is despairing throughout, whereas the prophet seems oddly serene, perhaps even a bit haughty in his demeanor (6:32). In any case, the latter knows, and the former will soon find out, that the very next day will bring amazing relief both to the inhabitants of Samaria and to the king and his court (cf. 8:3-6). Sadly, however, one member of the royal court will not be so fortunate, for it is prophesied that he will not be able to eat any of the suddenly available food (7:2); and the end of the story further specifies that the poor man was indeed trampled to death as the suddenly excited populace rushed out the city gate to plunder the abandoned enemy camp (7:17, 20).

Although this story fits into the relatively common category of prophet versus king, the author refused to present either as a stock, stereotypical figure. The king was, to be sure, powerless, desperate, and, because of that, blaspheming the reputation of Yahweh his God. But he was also attentive to the pleas of a despairing woman (6:26-31; see the note on 6:30), and his profane oath to separate the head of the prophet from his body is viewed in the context of genuine grief for the fate of the city and its inhabitants, who have been reduced to survival by cannibalism. Thus, this son of Ahab and Jezebel (assuming Joram is the king in question) was not one simply to emulate the coldly cruel actions of his mother (cf. especially her active part in the execution of Naboth in 1 Kgs 21). Rather, this king was genuinely heartbroken over the fate of his people. But he was a villain nonetheless, for he did seek the severed head of the prophet rather than the prophetic word from the prophet's mouth, the only word which could save the city. As for the prophet, he was found sitting serenely in his house in the city—with the elders of the city in attendance! What did he focus on? His own fate, to be sure, for he calmly predicted the imminent appearance of that "murderer" the king (cf. 6:32). Did he care about the city? We do not know. (Of course, we assume he did, and his calm reply [7:1] to the king's histrionics [in 6:33] shows he already had received a prophetic word that things would soon be remarkably back to near normal.) But the understandably excitable king, contrasted with the oddly serene prophet, does not entirely fit into our stereotypical categories of good and evil—and that is truly the mark of a gifted storyteller. (For concluding theological comments concerning the overall import of this story, which extends all the way to the end of chapter 7, see the commentary on 7:12-20.)

◆   12. Lepers visit the enemy camp (7:3-11)

3 Now there were four men with leprosy* sitting at the entrance of the city gates. "Why should we sit here waiting to die?" they asked each other. 4 "We will starve if we stay here, but with the famine in the city, we will starve if we go back there. So we might as well go out and surrender to the Aramean army. If they let us live, so much the better. But if they kill us, we would have died anyway."

5 So at twilight they set out for the camp of the Arameans. But when they came to the edge of the camp, no one was there! 6 For the Lord had caused the Aramean army to hear the clatter of speeding chariots and the galloping of horses and the sounds of a great army approaching. "The king of Israel has hired the Hittites and Egyptians* to attack us!" they cried to one another. 7 So they panicked and ran into the night, abandoning their tents, horses, donkeys, and everything else, as they fled for their lives.

8 When the lepers arrived at the edge of the camp, they went into one tent after another, eating and drinking wine; and they carried off silver and gold and clothing and hid it. 9 Finally, they said to each other, "This is not right. This is a day of good news, and we aren't sharing it with anyone! If we wait until morning, some calamity will certainly fall upon us. Come on, let's go back and tell the people at the palace."

10 So they went back to the city and told the gatekeepers what had happened. "We went out to the Aramean camp," they said, "and no one was there! The horses and donkeys were tethered and the tents were all in order, but there wasn't a single person around!" 11 Then the gatekeepers shouted the news to the people in the palace.

7:3 Or *with a contagious skin disease.* The Hebrew word used here and throughout this passage can describe various skin diseases.   7:6 Possibly *and the people of Muzur,* a district near Cilicia.

NOTES

7:3 *four men with leprosy.* Unlikely heroes, to be sure! (Concerning the exact nature of biblical "leprosy," see the third note on 5:1.) A number of parallels between this story and the Naaman story (ch 5), besides the phenomenon of heroes with leprosy, will be discussed in the commentary.

the entrance of the city gates. The city gate (or "gates"; although the Hebrew is singular here, there were probably at least two gates in the gate complex) is the standard location where both commercial and legal business were transacted. Presumably, the lepers were quarantined outside of the city (cf. Lev 13:1-8, 45-46; Num 12:14-16). Such a status would normally represent a severe burden on the men, but here it ironically leads to a very favorable outcome, both for them and for the "protected" people in the city. As Leithart (2006:209) puts it: "The world is turned upside down, as lepers save a city they cannot even enter."

7:4 *If they let us live . . . if they kill us.* Cogan and Tadmor (1988:82) cite a similar example where Aramean elders approached the victorious Assyrian king Ashurnasirpal II on bended knee, stating, "If it pleases you, kill! If it pleases you, spare! If it pleases you, do what you will!" Of course, death and life are really in the hand of Yahweh (cf. the first note on 5:7).

7:6 *chariots . . . horses.* The parallels with God's heavenly army described in 6:17 will be explored in the commentary on 7:12-20.

Hittites and Egyptians. This is the traditional (and probably correct) translation, although a number of commentators want to emend the reference to "Egyptians" (*mitsrayim* [TH4714, ZH5213]) to "the people of Mutsur" or the like (cf. NLT mg, "Muzur"; also cf. the note on 1 Kgs 10:28). But the north-Syrian or Anatolian kingdom of Mutsur had already been annexed to Assyria by the late tenth century BC (so Cogan and Tadmor 1988:82-83; cf. Kitchen 1996:326-327).

7:9 *a day of good news . . . some calamity will certainly fall upon us.* Both "good news" and "calamity" represent translations of strong terms in the Hebrew. The root *b-s-r* generally indicates the giving of "good news" (traditionally, "glad tidings"), and the Hebrew participle of this verb is used famously in Isa 52:7 twice to refer to the messenger who brings "good news." The Hebrew word for "calamity" (*'awon* [TH5771, ZH6411]) is often translated "iniquity," "punishment for iniquity," or the like; it is related to the root *'awah* [TH5753, ZH6700], which signifies sin or iniquity as well as awareness of the culpability of one's action (Eichrodt 1967:381, 415-417; cf. von Rad 1962:266). So, the lepers recognized both the remarkably good news they had to proclaim to their fellow inhabitants of Samaria and also the just punishment that they would experience if they delayed in issuing such a proclamation.

7:10 *gatekeepers.* See the second note on 7:3 concerning the importance of the city gate. Obviously, this "choke point" in the city wall will figure prominently in the trampling death of the king's unfortunate official in 7:17.

COMMENTARY

As has already been noted, the present story in the Kings text contains some remarkable echoes—some ironic, some quite comical—with several of the Elisha stories which precede it. Probably the most vivid echo is the reference to lepers as heroes. Naaman the Aramean leper makes a most unusual hero in the story that comprises chapter 5 (cf. the commentary on 5:1-19). Certainly our four Israelite lepers here, with their humorous deliberations, supply a much-needed diversion from the horribly grim setting of the extended siege. They also represent some of the most unlikely heroes to be found anywhere in the Bible. But there are other echoes as well, such as the seeming reappearance of the heavenly army in 7:6 (cf. 6:16-17), which in both instances leads to miraculous vanquishing of the Aramean foe; as Nelson (1987:187) points out (in reference to 6:8-23), "the awesome power of government, be it totalitarian or democratic, is something of a joke when compared to the horses and chariots of Yahweh, operative through the word of God's true spokesperson." How true that is in reference to our present section: lepers, suddenly wealthy, feasting and drinking wine (7:8), Aramean animals tethered and their tents all in order, but not a single enemy soldier to be found (7:10). God's armies can easily vanquish any human foe—and the results may well be as comical as they are tragic.

Other echoes of preceding stories include the embarrassing impotence of royal power, whether Aramean or Israelite (6:8-12, 27-31); servants convincing their masters as to the proper way to respond (6:12; 7:13; cf. the similar examples found in 5:2-3, 13); and "seeing and eating" in connection with the fates of the vanquished Aramean army (6:20, 23) and the Israelite officer (7:2). Finally, and most obviously, the unifying feature of these stories is the prophet Elisha—in both cases, kings blame Elisha for the problems they face, and in both cases, the kings send soldiers to capture or kill the prophet. And in both cases, Elisha, as it were, provides food (a banquet for the captured Arameans in 6:23, and plunder from the abandoned Aramean camp for the lepers and the other inhabitants of Samaria in ch 7). Our editor was truly inspired when he or she was led by the Spirit to juxtapose these quite different Elisha stories to form a unified whole (cf. Nelson 1987:187-188 and Leithart 2006:205-207 for these and other noteworthy parallels).

The present story is not yet over, but we have heard enough of it at this point to shed some new light on Jesus' teaching in the Nazareth synagogue concerning lepers in Israel in the days of the prophet Elisha (Luke 4:27; cf. the commentary on 5:1-19). Jesus reminded his hometown audience that "there were many lepers in Israel . . . but the only one healed was Naaman, a Syrian." Of course, Jesus was correct in what he asserted about Naaman. But in the present story, we do find out about four Israelite lepers, who although not healed, were mightily blessed and became a mighty blessing to others. What an encouragement for us today that God can use anyone of any social class or standing to effect his work. And, once again, what a reminder of how "unorthodox" God's methods may at times prove to be! (Concluding theological comments concerning the overall import of the present story may be found in the commentary on 7:12-20.)

◆   ## 13. Israel plunders the camp (7:12–20)

[12]The king got out of bed in the middle of the night and told his officers, "I know what has happened. The Arameans know we are starving, so they have left their camp and have hidden in the fields. They are expecting us to leave the city, and then they will take us alive and capture the city." [13]One of his officers replied, "We had

better send out scouts to check into this. Let them take five of the remaining horses. If something happens to them, it will be no worse than if they stay here and die with the rest of us."

¹⁴So two chariots with horses were prepared, and the king sent scouts to see what had happened to the Aramean army. ¹⁵They went all the way to the Jordan River, following a trail of clothing and equipment that the Arameans had thrown away in their mad rush to escape. The scouts returned and told the king about it. ¹⁶Then the people of Samaria rushed out and plundered the Aramean camp. So it was true that five quarts of choice flour were sold that day for one piece of silver, and ten quarts of barley grain were sold for one piece of silver, just as the LORD had promised. ¹⁷The king

appointed his officer to control the traffic at the gate, but he was knocked down and trampled to death as the people rushed out.

So everything happened exactly as the man of God had predicted when the king came to his house. ¹⁸The man of God had said to the king, "By this time tomorrow in the markets of Samaria, five quarts of choice flour will cost one piece of silver, and ten quarts of barley grain will cost one piece of silver."

¹⁹The king's officer had replied, "That couldn't happen even if the LORD opened the windows of heaven!" And the man of God had said, "You will see it happen with your own eyes, but you won't be able to eat any of it!" ²⁰And so it was, for the people trampled him to death at the gate!

NOTES

7:12 *in the middle of the night.* The Hebrew merely reads "night" (*laylah* [TH3915A, ZH4326]), but this is the sense of the time reference. For an extended discussion of the various time references in the story, see the commentary below.

I know what has happened. The king was entirely mistaken here in his "predictions," in clear contrast to the earlier predictions of the prophet (see 6:32; 7:1-2). This is particularly ironic since the Arameans themselves were equally mistaken in their "prediction" as to the reason for the arrival of the "Israelite" army back in 7:6. I suspect that quite often we today make similar mistakes in our assumptions and "predictions" about the activities of God.

leave the city. The ruse suspected here is in and of itself quite plausible; for example, both Joshua (Josh 8:1-29) and Abimelech (Judg 9:22-57) used it to great effect earlier in Israelite history.

7:13 The NLT is paraphrastic throughout this verse, but conveys effectively the overall force of the original (at least as reflected in the LXX, Syriac, and Vulgate; contrast the MT, which has a lengthy dittography [double reading] here—for details, see Cogan and Tadmor 1988:83; Jones 1984:437-438).

7:15 *They went all the way to the Jordan River.* Thus, they retreated to the east; but no matter what interim route they took, they would have to pass through much hostile territory (cf. Hobbs 1985:91-92).

7:16, 18 *choice flour . . . barley grain.* See the note on 7:1.

7:17 *his officer.* See the first note on 7:2.

So everything happened exactly. This is a summary comment (cf. "And so it was" in 7:20) drawing attention in a chiastic fashion to Elisha's prescient statements in 6:32–7:2 (see the note on 7:1 and the commentary below for details).

COMMENTARY

We come now to the end of this lengthy and intriguing story, with the promised demise of the king's official, and with the "farm market report" of the next day's crop prices (cf. Nelson [1987:190] for this felicitous phrase) proving to be right on target. Brief spans of time are noted throughout this story. Besides the next-day fulfillment of the "farm report" itself (7:1), we find Elisha's earlier prediction of a "murderer" at the door (6:32-33) fulfilled as he "was still saying this." Other time references include the lepers entering the now-abandoned enemy camp at "twilight" of the same day (7:5), the king's sleep also interrupted "in the middle of the night" (7:12; see the first note on that verse), and the final reminder of Elisha's prediction, "by this time tomorrow" (7:18), together indicating that all these events took place in about 24 hours! When God brings about a miracle, it can happen quickly. Finally, the king himself planned to "separate Elisha's head from his shoulders *this very day*" (6:31, emphasis added), but the only Israelite to meet death in the next 24 hours or so (as far as we know) was the unfortunate "officer assisting the king," who voiced his disbelief of Elisha's seemingly ridiculous "farm market report" in 7:1-2. The king had asked, "Why should I wait for the LORD any longer?" (6:33). Little did he know that he had less than one calendar day to wait to behold God's absolutely amazing grace. Back in my seminary days, I remember the comment we used to make about God's timing: "never late, but seldom early." How true that was then in my younger years, how true that is today, and, more to the present point, how true that proved to be in the days of Elisha the prophet. God's timing is always perfect, but it often seems otherwise in a given moment.

Some Concluding Theological Comments on 6:24–7:20. Sweeney (2007:307) has recently pointed out the effective contrast between Elisha's (unnamed) faithful servant in 6:15-17 and the king's (unnamed) faithless, disbelieving servant in chapter 7. Although the two stories came from originally independent traditions (an observation that Sweeney himself embraces), their current juxtaposition by the inspired editor strongly encourages the audience to seek to emulate the example of Elisha's servant, rather than that of the king's faithless officer. (I would also note that the next section of the Elisha cycle [8:1-6] will contribute to this end as well.) Thus, we today, especially in reference to the existence and efficaciousness of Yahweh's "heavenly armies," are also encouraged to rely upon the faithful word that God's prophet imparted to his servant ("there are more on our side than on theirs" [6:16]), rather than the blasphemous words that the king gave to his officer ("All this misery is from the LORD!" [6:33]). In both stories we are informed that the armies of the true God are ever present—even if rarely seen—and that they can easily encamp in immense numbers all around the city of Dothan when needed (6:13-17), as well as effortlessly chase the Aramean enemy well away from the besieged capital city of Samaria (7:6-7). "Contrary to the expectations of the Israelite king, YHWH took action to protect the Israelite nation," Sweeney (2007:313) reminds us. Even when the king does hear the news of Yahweh's deliverance, he still does not believe it (7:12); such disbelief puts the king on the same level with his own skeptical officer, and I suspect that for the original narrator of the story, it was the king himself who should have been trampled at the city gate instead of his unfortunate underling.

In any case, neither the palace entourage nor the despairing citizens of the capital city should have given up on the saving power of the God of Israel, who is often called "Yahweh, the God of the Heavenly Armies." Literally, "Yahweh of Hosts" (*yhwh tseba'oth* [TH3068/6635, ZH3378/7372]), this phrase was a traditional epithet used for the Israelite God, Yahweh, as demonstrated some years ago by Cross (1973:68-71, 90-111, 121-144; cf. the classical formulation found at the beginning of the "Song of the Sea" back in the days of Moses [Exod 15:3; cf. NLT mg note there]). Although rare in the books of 1–2 Kings, the epithet "Yahweh of Hosts" occurs some 285 times in the Hebrew Bible (TDOT 12.216-217), and, as is made quite clear in David's diatribe against Goliath in 1 Samuel 17:45, the epithet is clearly military in nature. (As David himself insists, "everyone assembled here will know that the LORD rescues his people. . . . This is the LORD's battle, and he will give you to us!" [1 Sam 17:47]). Thus, it is once again Yahweh who is the true Divine Warrior of the land of Israel. (For further details concerning the characterization of Yahweh as "Divine Warrior," cf. ABD 6.876-880; Coogan 2009.)

A word of caution must be given here, however. The great Old Testament theologian Eichrodt, for example, has reminded us that the use of the epithet "Yahweh of Hosts" in the prophets (some 247 times, or more than 85 percent of the total occurrences in the OT) tends to be significantly less nationalistic than the above comments might suggest:

> If the prophets could appeal to Yahweh [of Hosts] as the Judge exalted both over
> his own nation and over all the nations to support their threats against Israel, then
> both for themselves and for their hearers this name must have connoted more than
> simply the national deity. . . . This [supranational] assumption throws a brilliant
> light on the prophetic usage of the [phrase Yahweh of Hosts]; but it also shows that
> there is a universalistic tendency in the older Israelite conception of Yahweh, and
> proves that the primitive concept of the high God El had not been forgotten. (Eichrodt
> 1961:192-194)

Thus, whether early or late, the phrase "Yahweh of Hosts" represents something far more than a simple reference to a national deity who automatically fights for his people against their military adversaries.

It is, I suspect, along these lines that we should also interpret the twice-repeated statement in 2 Kings that it is the Israelite prophet (once Elijah [2:12], once Elisha [13:14]) who is to be identified with "the chariots and charioteers of Israel." (Not coincidentally, both contexts for the use of this phrase are at or near the end of the ministry of the prophet so addressed.) Yahweh can and does fight on behalf of his people Israel. But Yahweh has also sent his servants the prophets (Amos 3:7) as special representatives for his people and, in a sense, for all peoples (Amos 9:7; cf. 1 Kgs 19:15-16, especially the anointing of Hazael, which is fulfilled in 2 Kgs 8:7-15). Yahweh is an *international* God (as was El in northwest Semitic theology), and so must be the focus of his human leaders. Yes, Yahweh and his "heavenly armies" did once fight against the enemies of God's people back in the days of Deborah the prophet (Judg 5:20-21), but those same "heavenly armies" (or at least, their earthly counterparts) may well be sent *against* God's people Israel and Judah if necessary (cf. 24:2-4; Isa 10:5-19; Joel 2:1-11). Yahweh is indeed "a man of war" (the literal translation of Exod 15:3), who can vanquish the mighty gods of Egypt (Exod 12:12), but he and his armies (seen or unseen) will advance against not only the enemies of his people, but also, if necessary, the arrogant leadership of his own people (Zeph 3:1-13). It is a foolish king indeed who does not reckon with this fact. As the king of Israel had said to the starving mother (6:27), "If the LORD doesn't help you, what can I do?" If only that king had possessed enough faith to wait properly upon the Lord (who is aptly termed "Yahweh, the God of the Heavenly Armies"), the history of the northern kingdom of Israel would have turned out far less disastrously.

◆   ## 14. The woman from Shunem returns home (8:1-6)

Elisha had told the woman whose son he had brought back to life, "Take your family and move to some other place, for the LORD has called for a famine on Israel that will last for seven years." ²So the woman did as the man of God instructed. She took her family and settled in the land of the Philistines for seven years.

³After the famine ended she returned from the land of the Philistines, and she went to see the king about getting back her house and land. ⁴As she came in, the king was talking with Gehazi, the servant of the man of God. The king had just said, "Tell me some stories about the great things Elisha has done." ⁵And Gehazi was telling the king about the time Elisha had brought a boy back to life. At that very moment, the mother of the boy walked in to make her appeal to the king about her house and land.

"Look, my lord the king!" Gehazi exclaimed. "Here is the woman now, and this is her son—the very one Elisha brought back to life!"

⁶"Is this true?" the king asked her. And she told him the story. So he directed one of his officials to see that everything she had lost was restored to her, including the value of any crops that had been harvested during her absence.

NOTES

8:1 *Elisha had told the woman.* This brief sequel builds on the moving story about the Shunammite woman and her family found in 4:8-37. As Wiseman (1993:213) points out, the present event (the audience before the unnamed king, with Elisha's servant Gehazi in attendance) may have taken place before Gehazi was stricken with leprosy back in 5:27 (or else, like Naaman, Gehazi's "leprosy" may have been relatively mild; cf. the third note on 5:1).

Take your family. Commentators see Elisha's direct command to the woman as indicating that she may now have become a widow (cf. Hobbs 1985:100; after all, her husband had been described as "old" in 4:14), but even in ch 4, the woman usually took the initiative in family decisions (see the commentary on 4:8-37). In any case, the family was to "move to some other place" (lit., "sojourn wherever you would sojourn"; *weguri ba'asher taguri* [ᵀᴴ1481, ᶻᴴ1591]), an *idem per idem* expression indicating a purposeful lack of definitiveness (Cogan and Tadmor 1988:86, citing S. R. Driver).

seven years. Long famines are recorded both in biblical texts (Gen 41:30-31; Ruth 1:1-6) and extrabiblical texts; the present famine (which was "called" by the Lord) need not be related to the "famine" described in the city of Samaria in the preceding story. Perhaps it was, however, the same famine mentioned in 4:38. Possibly we are also to notice that this famine was twice the length of the infamous famine or drought in Elijah's time (Luke 4:25; cf. 1 Kgs 17:1; 18:1-2). This is another literary signal of Elisha as a "twofold" prophet in comparison with Elijah.

8:2 *the land of the Philistines.* In clear contrast to Elijah's words in 1:6, 16 (cf. the third note on 1:2 for the location of Ekron in Philistia), here the land of Philistia serves as a positive, or at least innocuous, location for the Shunammite woman. As in the book of Ruth, a family from the tribes of Israel, eventually headed by a woman, sought shelter in a nearby foreign land whose people were often Israel's bitter enemies. In Naomi's case it was Moab, and in the present case, Philistia. Inasmuch as Elisha told the Shunammite merely to move "to some other place" (see the second note on 8:1), Philistia represented a logical choice: relatively close to her home town and likely to be quite fertile since it would generally receive adequate rainfall (Hobbs 1985:100).

8:3 *she went to see the king.* Lit., "to cry out (*lits'oq* [TH6817, ZH7590]) to the king." Here (and very possibly also in 6:26), the verb *tsa'aq* indicates that a formal, legal appeal is being made to the king as chief arbiter (see Jones 1984:440; cf. Cogan and Tadmor 1988:79-80, especially for Assyrian and Babylonian parallels). The "king," as in a number of other Elisha stories, is unnamed. The Deuteronomistic editing would suggest that Joram is the king in question (see the notes on 1:17; cf. the commentary on 6:24–7:2, where the [unnamed] king there is also described in not entirely negative terms). Wiseman (1993:213), however, suggests that the king in question here may have been Jehu, since Joram presumably already knew Elisha quite well.

8:4 *Gehazi.* This was Elisha's famous, and eventually, infamous, servant (see the first note on 8:1; for the possible meanings of Gehazi's name, see the note on 4:12).

8:5 *At that very moment.* The NLT is a bit paraphrastic here, but it does convey the force of the chronological juxtaposition of Gehazi telling about the Shunammite's son's amazing resurrection just as the Shunammite herself shows up to reclaim her house and land (cf. the careful time indicators found in the previous story, as discussed in the commentary on 7:12-20).

8:6 *one of his officials.* Heb., *saris* [TH5631, ZH6247], lit., "a eunuch," but here, as often in the MT, the term more generally signifies a high official of the royal court (cf. Cogan and Tadmor 1988:112 for an extended discussion of this loanword from Akkadian).

including the value of any crops that had been harvested during her absence. Possibly the land had become crown property during her absence (Gray 1970:527; see de Vaux 1965:124-126; but cf. Cogan and Tadmor 1988:87-88 for other possibilities). In any case, the political authorities were expected to take care of the poor, especially widows and orphans (cf. Deut 15:4-11; Ps 72:1-4, 12-14 [ironically directed to King Solomon, according to the psalm's title]; Isa 1:17; Jer 7:6-7; and the numerous references to Yahweh as the one who provides particularly for widows and orphans [e.g., Deut 10:17-18; Prov 15:25]). Even if the woman were still wealthy (cf. 4:8), she had every right to make a legal claim for the restoration of her lands, as well as the income they yielded during her extended absence. Some commentators suggest that the seven-year hiatus mentioned in 8:1-2 may allude to some sort of fulfillment of the Torah legislation that debts be cancelled at the end of seven years (Deut 15:1-4; cf. Exod 21:2; 23:10-11). This interesting chronological correspondence, although germane, is not specified in the text—we have no sense that the Shunammite was seeking legal redress for debts or the like, just the return of her land.

COMMENTARY

This sequel to the Shunammite story found in 4:8-37 may seem oddly placed in the Elisha cycle, but that may say more about our own literary tastes than those of the ancient compilers of the prophetic traditions. For example, Leithart (2006:207) has helpfully isolated the following palistrophe, which incorporates this story with its immediate predecessor, thus shedding significant light on how we should understand its editorial underpinnings:

A. King's impotence: woman's appeal; king wants to kill Elisha (6:24-31)
    B. Elisha's prophecy (6:32–7:2)
        C. Four lepers discover the camp: They plunder it (7:3-8: If we die, we die)
        D. Lepers bring good news (7:9-10)
        C'. Five horses discover the camp: Samarians plunder it (7:11-16a: If they die, they die)
    B'. Elisha's prophecy fulfilled (7:16b-20)
A'. King's potence: Shunammite's appeal; king honors legacy of Elisha (8:1-6)[1]

Here we find that the king of Israel is the primary character both at the beginning and at the end of this editorial sequence (a sequence which has incorporated two separate stories, including the sequel to the Shunammite tradition found in ch 4). And it is the king, of all people, who has changed the most! Perhaps due to the remarkable miracle that the lepers (of all people!) discovered, the king now seemingly wants to hear about the exploits of Elisha (from, of all people, Gehazi—himself now a leper?). Cogan and Tadmor (1988:88) note that the detail about Gehazi regaling his royal audience with Elisha stories shows us how the great exploits of Elisha were told and retold, not only by the "sons of the prophets," but also at the royal court of Samaria and at Damascus, too (cf. 8:7). This time, the king (presumably the same king as in 6:24–7:20) was willing to do his part to vindicate both Elisha and his patron, the Shunammite. With the Shunammite's resurrected son standing right next to her (8:5), what else could the king do? I would submit that, contrary to expectations (but in line with some hints from the Samaria-siege story), this king, who had already exhibited a number of appealing qualities (cf. the commentary on 6:24–7:2), was never entirely beyond redemption. In any case, both king and prophet end up, in a sense, redeemed (not necessarily indicating that the king here is vindicated *over against* the prophet, as, e.g., Hobbs [1985:96-98] argues; cf. my rejoinder to that suggestion found in Barnes 1997a:407-411). In any event, this corresponds quite nicely with the *literal* redemption of the Shunammite's property. Thus, we find a proper end to the Israelite portion of the Elisha cycle (except for its sequel in 13:14-21): prophet and king properly exercising their redemptive roles to bring salvation and blessing to both rich and poor alike in the land of Israel.

ENDNOTE
1. I have slightly modified the wording of Leithart's palistrophe.

◆   **15. Hazael murders Ben-hadad (8:7-15)**

[7]Elisha went to Damascus, the capital of Aram, where King Ben-hadad lay sick. When someone told the king that the man of God had come, [8]the king said to Hazael, "Take a gift to the man of God. Then tell him to ask the LORD, 'Will I recover from this illness?'"

[9]So Hazael loaded down forty camels

with the finest products of Damascus as a gift for Elisha. He went to him and said, "Your servant Ben-hadad, the king of Aram, has sent me to ask, 'Will I recover from this illness?' "

¹⁰And Elisha replied, "Go and tell him, 'You will surely recover.' But actually the LORD has shown me that he will surely die!" ¹¹Elisha stared at Hazael* with a fixed gaze until Hazael became uneasy.* Then the man of God started weeping.

¹²"What's the matter, my lord?" Hazael asked him.

Elisha replied, "I know the terrible things you will do to the people of Israel. You will burn their fortified cities, kill their young men with the sword, dash their little children to the ground, and rip open their pregnant women!"

¹³Hazael responded, "How could a nobody like me* ever accomplish such great things?"

Elisha answered, "The LORD has shown me that you are going to be the king of Aram."

¹⁴When Hazael left Elisha and went back, the king asked him, "What did Elisha tell you?"

And Hazael replied, "He told me that you will surely recover."

¹⁵But the next day Hazael took a blanket, soaked it in water, and held it over the king's face until he died. Then Hazael became the next king of Aram.

8:11a Hebrew *He stared at him.*   8:11b The meaning of the Hebrew is uncertain.   8:13 Hebrew *a dog.*

NOTES

8:7 *Damascus.* This ancient city (cf. Gen 14:15; 15:2) was (and still is) the capital city of Aram (present-day Syria). Possibly this journey by Elisha was to fulfill Elijah's original mountaintop commission to "anoint Hazael to be king of Aram" (1 Kgs 19:15). Although the present text does not indicate that this was the actual reason for Elisha's trip, the end result is largely—but not literally—the same (i.e., no actual anointing is said to have taken place; cf. the note on 1 Kgs 19:15-16). (For other parallels between 1 Kgs 18–19 and 2 Kgs 6–9, see Leithart 2006:213.)

King Ben-hadad. See the second note on 6:24 for a rehearsal of the issues surrounding this repeated Aramean dynastic name (or title). Following the enumeration of the various "Ben-hadads" listed there, the king here should probably be identified as Ben-hadad II (= Adad-idri). Some scholars, however, would see the present section of 2 Kings as indicating the existence of yet another Ben-hadad, one who reigned briefly after Adad-idri before being assassinated by Hazael (Kelle 2006:427).

8.8 *Hazael.* Heb., *khaza'el* [TH2371, ZH2599] (El [God] sees). This is the infamous Aramean usurper or, at least, commoner (see the note on 8:13), well-attested in the Assyrian inscriptions (cf. the note on 1 Kgs 12:29). Hazael reigned some 40 years (a lengthy reign by contemporary standards). He applied increasing military pressure to Israel, Philistia, and Judah throughout his reign; he eventually annexed Gilead outright and almost certainly reduced Israel west of the Jordan River to nothing more than a vassal state (cf. ABD 3.83). He also resisted repeated attacks from Shamanezer III of Assyria, who was able to besiege Damascus at one point, forcing Hazael to pay heavy tribute. Amos 1:3-4, probably written a century after Hazael's reign, typifies both the mighty power and the notorious cruelty of King Hazael (cf. the horrific litany of atrocities in 2 Kgs 8:12).

Take a gift. This was an "audience gift" similar to that of Naaman (see the second note on 5:5; cf. 1 Kgs 14:3). As with Naaman's gift, this gift of 40 camel-loads of Damascus's finest products (see 8:9) is immense in scope, a typical feature of folkloristic literature (cf. the commentary on 1:1-18).

Will I recover from this illness? Ironically, this is identical to the question found in 1:2, but there the Israelite king Ahaziah asks it of Baal-zebub, "the god of Ekron." In the present passage, the question is directed to Yahweh, the God of Israel (still, presumably a "foreign" God for the Arameans—unless Naaman's evangelistic zeal so evident back in 5:17-18 had borne fruit!).

8:9 *Your servant Ben-hadad.* Lit., "your son Ben-hadad," possibly a wordplay on the term *ben* [TH1121, ZH1201] (son), but more likely simply a term of filial devotion (cf. the use of "father" in 5:13, NLT mg note; 6:21). "The portrayal of the king is entirely positive, and so the reader is set up to expect a positive word from the man of God" (Seow 1999:212).

8:10 *will surely recover . . . will surely die!* This brief sequence represents a whole host of exegetical and theological difficulties (for an extended discussion, see Barnes 1997a:411-415; most of these issues will also be dealt with in summary form in the commentary).

8:11 *Hazael.* The subject of the verb "to stare" (lit., "to set, make stand his face") is unspecified; commentators and translators therefore differ on how to read the first half of the verse (Who stared at whom? And who became uneasy?). In any case, it is clear that the "man of God" was the one who started weeping, realizing in the Spirit what a scourge to Israel Hazael would prove to be (cf. the first note on 8:8 for details).

until . . . became uneasy. This is the same expression (*'ad bosh* [TH954, ZH1017], lit., "until embarrassment") found in 2:17 (cf. the note there); possibly both there and here the expression simply signifies a long period of time. The fact that this odd expression, however, appears only at the beginning and the end of the Elisha cycle may also hint at an editorial *inclusio* (a narrative device signaling by some sort of repetition the beginning and the end of a prose or poetic unit). Thus, *embarrassment* occurs at the beginning of Elisha's career—by means of the well-meaning but obtuse "group of prophets"; and again, *embarrassment* occurs at the end of his career—as he ends up endorsing (virtually anointing?) an Aramean king who will eventually cause Israel so much heartache.

8:12 *terrible things.* See the first note on 8:8 for a brief summary of Hazael's military career; see Cogan and Tadmor (1988:91) for biblical and extrabiblical parallels for the horrific actions listed here.

8:13 *a nobody like me.* Lit., "a dog" (*hakkeleb* [TH3611, ZH3978]); cf. Hazael's Assyrian epithet, "son of a nobody," which means his lineage is not recorded and he is probably reckoned as a commoner (Wiseman 1993:214). Regarding the low estimation of dogs in the ancient Near East, see the note on 1 Kgs 14:11; for similar usages in the Lachish letters of the phrase "your servant (is but) a dog" as self-disparagement, see Cogan and Tadmor 1988:91.

8:15 *a blanket.* Heb., *hammakber* [TH4346, ZH4802], a word found only here in the MT, and usually understood as "something woven, meshwork, netting" (possibly mosquito netting, or the like [Gray 1970:532; cf. Jones 1984:445]). When "soaked in water," it could thus act as a kind of natural air conditioner (cf. modern desert coolers or "evaporative coolers") when hung over the bed or in the window. For a discussion of what Hazael actually did to the king, including its ethical implications, see the commentary.

COMMENTARY

Despite the interest in Hazael here, this is yet another story largely focusing on the prophet Elisha, and is most likely a part of the original Elisha cycle (perhaps strategically placed in its present position by the editor; cf. the second note on 8:11). It is, of course, also a significant story about two kings of Aram (indeed, two dynasties), the second of which eventually leads to major trouble for Israel (for details, see the notes on 8:7 and 8:8). Still, it is the Elisha tradition that I want to focus on here, and there is much to reflect on concerning his actions in this murky episode. I will organize these reflections as follows: (1) What did Elisha actually say to Hazael in 8:10? And what were his motives? (2) What did Hazael actually do to Ben-hadad in 8:15? And what were *his* motives? Textual uncertainties cloud the first question especially, but I suspect they should not prove insurmountable. Lexical uncertainties cloud the second question somewhat, but again, significant clarity is not beyond reach. So let us begin:

(1) In 8:10, according to the NLT, Elisha tells Hazael to inform his master Ben-hadad that he will indeed *recover* from his illness (which was, after all, the original subject of the inquiry and the reason for the gift in 8:9), but then Elisha immediately seems to contradict himself and tell Hazael that Ben-hadad will surely *die* (the Hebrew infinitives for "recover" and "die" emphasize the absolute certainty of those respective fates). Some commentators suggest that what Elisha actually meant by this apparent contradiction was that Ben-hadad will recover from his present illness, but will soon die anyway from other causes (which, after all, does prove to be the case). Others suggest that *Hazael* is the one who will "recover" (in the sense of "thrive" or the like), while *Ben-hadad* will die (it is certainly possible to read the Hebrew that way; cf. Labuschagne 1965:327-328). To complicate things further, the Qere (reading tradition) of the MT suggests reading *lo* [TH3807.1/2050.2, ZH4200/2257] ("to him"; thus the NLT, NIV, etc.), but the Kethiv (written version) reads *lo'* [TH3808, ZH4202] ("not," i.e., "he will surely *not* live" [cf. NIV footnote]). (In the Hebrew the difference between these readings is only one letter: a Waw in place of an Aleph.) The Kethiv smooths out Elisha's otherwise apparently contradictory message, rendering his response regarding Ben-hadad's future as entirely negative (and, once again, historically accurate). But then, how are we to understand Hazael's report to Ben-hadad in 8:14? Was he misrepresenting Elisha's answer? We have no clear reason to think so (the Hebrew is virtually identical to that in 8:10a). Another alternative, explored by Gray (1970:529-531), is that perhaps the oracle was meant to be Delphic (i.e., intentionally ambiguous), thus testing Hazael's actual commitment to the ailing king; the Hebrew particle *lo* or *lo'* could then be read as *lu* [TH3863, ZH4273], "would that [the king live]"). In any case, the oracle is indeed presented positively to the king in 8:14, "you will surely recover," and we again have no reason to think Hazael is misrepresenting what he heard Elisha say. So we are back to the original question: Did Elisha lie, or did he deliberately deceive Hazael? Or, as effectively posed by Seow (1999:212), is it the case that Elisha is actually and deliberately setting up Hazael for his role in usurping the throne?

I think that perhaps Seow is posing the question too baldly but that he is definitely on the right track. Attempts to soften this difficult text (i.e., to exonerate the prophet from censure or blame) appear to be special pleading and therefore suspect (cf. Cogan and Tadmor 1988:90). Elisha knows the bitter truth—all agree to that—and the question is not therefore knowledge, but rather causality. As I argued some years ago (Barnes 1997a:413):

The main point is that Elisha knew full well what Hazael was about to do, both against his own master the king, as well as against Israel in the future (cf. vv. 11-13). Thus the present statement is probably in line with Jesus' advice to Judas Iscariot in John 13:27, "What you are about to do, do quickly." Jesus was hardly telling Judas to hurry up and make the decision to betray him. Rather he was demonstrating that he knew all along what was in Judas' mind, and that Judas was determined to accomplish his dastardly deed. He might as well get on with it. This is probably the gist of Elisha's curious response to Hazael [here in v. 10]. Elisha could see the future, and there was no stopping Hazael, so he might as well get on with it. Go ahead, lie to the king, and then kill him—you are going to do it anyway.

In any case, whether my thoughts bear the test of time or not, we can agree on three general conclusions: First, the present text somehow represents a significant fulfillment of Elijah's commission (1 Kgs 19:15) to anoint Hazael king of Aram (cf. the first note on 8:7)—with all the complicated ethical ramifications that commission would entail. Second, it will be obvious, despite those horrendous ramifications, that Yahweh retains his sovereignty over *all* the earth—the land of Aram as well as the lands of Israel and Judah—and he retains ultimate control over *all* human leadership, whether it be the dynasty of Omri (which will soon come to a bloody end), the dynasty of Ben-hadad, or the dynasty of Hazael (or, for that matter, the dynasty of David). Finally, Yahweh's servants the prophets (the "men of God") are given special foreknowledge of his will—with the heart-rending implications to which such foreknowledge can lead.

(2) In 8:15 it is clear that the very next day Hazael becomes the new king of Aram, but that is about all that is clear in the verse! We do know that some sort of "blanket" (or "netting") is involved (see the above note on the verse for details), as well as the action of "dipping/soaking in water" (*tabal* [TH2881, ZH3188] usually means "to dip" something into something; cf. BDB 371), and finally, some sort of "spreading" the blanket or netting (*paras* [TH6566, ZH7298]) upon or over the king's face (which may simply refer to a general direction of the "spreading"). The note on 8:15 makes reference to Gray's intriguing suggestion that wetting the "netting" here represents something entirely benign, with the water thus cooling the bedstead or room, and Hazael's actions (or conceivably the actions of an unnamed person—the Hebrew verbs here permit such an interpretation) then to be construed as completely innocent (even though the rewetted "netting" will also serve to disguise for a time the fact that the king had expired). But that is not the prevailing view of most modern commentators, who see Hazael's actions as far from benign. While some medieval commentators suggest that Hazael may simply have been applying cool compresses to assuage the king's fever (cf. Cogan and Tadmor 1988:91), most moderns would follow Josephus (*Antiquities* 9.3.6.92-93) in simply asserting that Hazael killed the king by means of suffocation (so NLT; cf. NIV, KJV). Although Wiseman (1993:215) is correct to state that "the manner of Ben-Hadad's death is disputed," the tenor of the text hardly makes Hazael appear innocent, and I suspect we are to regard him as nothing less than an Old Testament Judas Iscariot: It was he who betrayed his master, bringing about in a very short time his most untimely death. No wonder Elisha wept (8:11b).

H. Synchronistic History of the Divided Monarchy, Resumed (2 Kgs 8:16-29)

1. Jehoram rules in Judah (8:16-24)

¹⁶Jehoram son of King Jehoshaphat of Judah began to rule over Judah in the fifth year of the reign of Joram son of Ahab, king of Israel. ¹⁷Jehoram was thirty-two years old when he became king, and he reigned in Jerusalem eight years. ¹⁸But Jehoram followed the example of the kings of Israel and was as wicked as King Ahab, for he had married one of Ahab's daughters. So Jehoram did what was evil in the LORD's sight. ¹⁹But the LORD did not want to destroy Judah, for he had promised his servant David that his descendants would continue to rule, shining like a lamp forever.

²⁰During Jehoram's reign, the Edomites revolted against Judah and crowned their own king. ²¹So Jehoram* went with all his chariots to attack the town of Zair.* The Edomites surrounded him and his chariot commanders, but he went out at night and attacked them* under cover of darkness. But Jehoram's army deserted him and fled to their homes. ²²So Edom has been independent from Judah to this day. The town of Libnah also revolted about that same time.

²³The rest of the events in Jehoram's reign and everything he did are recorded in *The Book of the History of the Kings of Judah.* ²⁴When Jehoram died, he was buried with his ancestors in the City of David. Then his son Ahaziah became the next king.

8:21a Hebrew *Joram,* a variant spelling of Jehoram; also in 8:23, 24.   8:21b Greek version reads *Seir.*
8:21c Or *he went out and escaped.* The meaning of the Hebrew is uncertain.

NOTES

8:16 *Jehoram.* See the first note on 1:17 for the probable meaning of this name. The spellings "Joram" and "Jehoram" are found in connection with both the northern and the southern kings, whose reigns substantially overlapped chronologically.

son of King Jehoshaphat of Judah. Already this king has been mentioned twice in 1–2 Kings (see 1:17; 1 Kgs 22:50), but in typical Deuteronomistic style, Jehoram's accession formula is postponed until all the Joram (the concurrent king in Israel) material has been presented (concerning this practice, see "Literary Style" in the Introduction; see also the commentary on 1 Kgs 15:1-8). Curiously, the MT repeats the phrase "and Jehoshaphat [being/having been] king of Judah"; some (e.g., Cogan and Tadmor 1988:95) interpret this phrase as a dittograph (double reading), while others (e.g., Thiele 1951:36; 1974:174; but cf. Barnes 1991:20-21) understand it as overtly confirming the coregency between Jehoram and his father Jehoshaphat (see the next note).

in the fifth year of the reign of Joram son of Ahab, king of Israel. Comparing this datum with that found in 3:1 (cf. the second note on that verse), Thiele and others (e.g., the medieval sage David Qimchi) have posited a coregency (probably about four years in length) between Jehoshaphat and his son Jehoram (cf. Cogan and Tadmor 1988:95).

8:18 *as wicked as King Ahab.* This is the infamous king of Israel, son of Omri. First Kings 16:33 claims that he did more to provoke Yahweh's anger than any of the other kings before him (cf. 1 Kgs 21:25-26). For a general overview of these evaluative formulas for the kings of Israel and Judah, see endnotes 1 and 2 of the Introduction.

married one of Ahab's daughters. This was done for diplomatic reasons. Still, as with Ahab himself (1 Kgs 16:31; cf. the note there), and with Solomon on a notoriously large scale (1 Kgs 11:1-6; cf. the note on 1 Kgs 11:2), marrying foreign royalty can lead only to disastrous results. (For more information concerning Athaliah, the particular woman Jehoram married, see the second note on 8:26.)

8:19 *shining like a lamp forever.* See "The 'Lamp' of David" under "Major Themes" in the Introduction for this very important catchphrase found several times in 1–2 Kings. In the present instance, we are encouraged that despite the negative events which attend Jehoram's reign, Yahweh will be faithful to his covenant with David.

8:20 *the Edomites . . . crowned their own king.* In 1 Kgs 22:47 we were told there was no king in Edom during the days of Jehoshaphat, Jehoram's father, so this is a clear indication that Judah's political and military power had waned in the interval. (Curiously, 3:9 does make passing reference to a king of Edom in the days of Jehoshaphat; cf. the first note on that verse for a possible explanation.)

8:21 *Jehoram.* See the first note on 8:16 concerning the spelling variants.

Zair. This is a name otherwise unattested; possibly equivalent to "Zoar" (= "Smallville") of Gen 19:22, etc., at the southern edge of the Dead Sea; or else "Zior" of Josh 15:54, near Hebron in Judah, but that seems too close to Jerusalem (cf. Lawlor 2009).

he went out at night and attacked them. As the NLT mg indicates, the Hebrew here is difficult; indeed, we are not even sure if Edom was attacked or did the attacking! In any case, the Judahite army "fled" home, evidently in ignominious defeat (Wiseman 1993:216).

8:22 *to this day.* See Childs (1963:284, 289) for this phrase being understood as a "political etiology" added to an archival note: "and Edom revolted from the rule of Judah (as is the situation today)." (See the note on 2:22 for the other instances of this familiar phrase throughout 1–2 Kings.)

Libnah. This was a Levitical city near the Philistine border, not far from Lachish (cf. 19:8 and its parallel in Isa 37:8); it is probably to be identified with Tell Bornat, or else Tell es-Safi (ABD 4.322-323). This laconic notice thus indicates that rebellion took place to the west as well as the southeast in the days of Jehoram of Judah. (Libnah, however, reverted back to Judahite control by the time of King Hezekiah.)

8:23 *are recorded in* The Book of the History of the Kings of Judah. See "Literary Style" in the Introduction.

COMMENTARY

We are back in the "leapfrog" treatment of the Israelite and the Judahite kings so typical of the Deuteronomistic editor (see second note on 8:16). But the placement of the Elisha material, especially the Hazael pericope (with its dire implications for the northern kingdom), casts a tragic light on the present passage, especially in its seemingly incidental details. Not so incidentally, Judah was at this time experiencing a significant loss of its political supremacy over the southern Levant (including independent access to the trade route to the Red Sea), and again, not so incidentally, that may have been due more to the pernicious northern Israelite, even Tyrian traditions present even in the south (cf. 8:18), rather than the time-honored traditions more typical of the Davidic dynasty. Up to now, only two southern kings have been censured by the editor (Rehoboam [1 Kgs 14:22, LXX] and Abijam [1 Kgs 15:1-3]), but both Jehoram and his son Ahaziah (8:27) will sadly fall into this category. As Cogan and Tadmor (1988:97) point out, the two brief annalistic excerpts in 8:20-22a and 22b, although unclear in some details (see the third note on 8:21), are very clear about the decline of Judah in the mid-ninth century BC. Edom's revolt may have been inspired by Moab's example in chapter 3, but the loss of the city of Libnah in territorial Judah may hint at internal Judahite monarchical instability. It may well be, therefore, that Judah's joining Israel in foreign wars during this time (3:7; 8:28-29; 1 Kgs 22:1-4) "was as much due to imposition by the stronger partner as it was to shared economic and political interests" (so conclude Cogan and Tadmor; cf. Seow's similar perspective, cited in the notes on 1 Kgs 22:4, 30). (Concerning the dangers of intermarriage with unbelievers, a major factor in the condemnation of both Jehoram and Ahaziah, see the commentary on the next section.)

◆   ## 2. Ahaziah rules in Judah (8:25-29)

25Ahaziah son of Jehoram began to rule over Judah in the twelfth year of the reign of Joram son of Ahab, king of Israel.

26Ahaziah was twenty-two years old when he became king, and he reigned in Jerusalem one year. His mother was Athaliah, a granddaughter of King Omri of Israel. 27Ahaziah followed the evil example of King Ahab's family. He did what was evil in the LORD's sight, just as Ahab's

family had done, for he was related by marriage to the family of Ahab.

28Ahaziah joined Joram son of Ahab in his war against King Hazael of Aram at Ramoth-gilead. When the Arameans wounded King Joram in the battle, 29he returned to Jezreel to recover from the wounds he had received at Ramoth.* Because Joram was wounded, King Ahaziah of Judah went to Jezreel to visit him.

8:29 Hebrew *Ramah*, a variant spelling of Ramoth.

NOTES

8:25 *Ahaziah.* See the note on 1 Kgs 22:51 for the likely meaning of this name. As is the case with Joram/Jehoram, there are two "Ahaziahs" (an Israelite, and here a Judahite monarch) reigning around the same time; for both of these duplicated names, the correspondences can hardly be coincidental, since intermarriage has taken place (cf. Sweeney 2007:320).

in the twelfth year of the reign of Joram son of Ahab. In 9:29, this verse is essentially repeated, but with the ordinal "eleventh" rather than "twelfth," an alteration which some scholars interpret as indicating that two different chronological systems were in use (i.e., so-called "antedating," where the king's first [partial] regnal year is reckoned as the first year of his reign; and "postdating," where the first *complete* year of reign is reckoned as year one, with the partial "accession" year not counted in his regnal total at all [cf. Barnes 1991:6 n. 14]). Thus, Thiele (1983:58) uses this "double synchronism" to buttress his claim that the scribes of Judah switched from postdating to antedating just around this time, probably under the influence of Athaliah. (For an alternate interpretation, where the ordinal "twelfth" of the MT found here is emended to "eleventh," see Cogan and Tadmor 1988:98.)

8:26 *he reigned . . . one year.* An anomalous total, representing probably only several months on the throne (assuming antedating practice; cf. Thiele 1983:101, Wiseman 1993:217; but contrast Tadmor, as cited in Barnes 1991:155 note h).

Athaliah, a granddaughter of King Omri of Israel. Lit., "Athaliah, daughter (*bath*) of Omri, king of Israel." Most commentators, noting that *bath* [TH1323, ZH1426] can signify "granddaughter" as well as "daughter," suggest that Athaliah was actually the daughter of Omri's son Ahab and his notorious wife, Jezebel (so NLT). Cogan and Tadmor (1988:98-99) suggest "this Israelite princess proved herself to be cut from the same autocratic mold as her mother, Queen Jezebel, as shown in her seizing the throne in Jerusalem after the murder of her son by Jehu's riders (11:1-3)." That Athaliah emulated Jezebel, no one would deny. But not all agree that she was literally Ahab's daughter (cf. the unnamed woman in 8:18, who is probably Athaliah); see the notable suggestion of Katzenstein (1955:194-197; cf. Gray 1970:534) that Athaliah was indeed the *daughter* of Omri, and that she grew up as a young orphan at the court of Ahab, under the tutelage of Queen Jezebel (after all, the chronology is very tight if the traditional view is maintained). As far as the name Athaliah (*'athalyahu* [TH6271A, ZH6976]) is concerned, it is clearly Yahwistic, but its exact meaning still eludes us (BDB 800 suggests tentatively, "Yah is exalted" [so also Hobbs 1985:138]; but see ABD 1.511 for other possibilities). In any case, I suspect that Jezebel did not choose the name!

8:27 *evil example.* Cf. the first note on 8:18.

8:28 *Hazael.* Concerning this important Aramean king, see the first note on 8:8.

Ramoth-gilead. Lit., "Heights of Gilead." This was the infamous spot where King Ahab received his mortal wound (1 Kgs 22:34); see especially the note on 1 Kgs 22:3.

8:29 *Ramoth.* Heb., *ramah* [TH7413, ZH8229] (heights); probably, as the NLT mg indicates, this is an alternative form for Ramoth (i.e., Ramoth-gilead; cf. NIV, also Wiseman 1993:218).

COMMENTARY

"Like father, like son" is the theme of this brief section. And this is true in a number of respects: Ahaziah of Judah emulated his father Jehoram, just as Jehoram emulated the evil kings of Israel, Omri and his son Ahab (cf. 8:18, 27). And Ahab in turn emulated (to some degree) the pagan ways of Queen Jezebel. Athaliah, in turn, will emulate the ways of her queen mother, Jezebel (perhaps her literal mother as well; see the second note on 8:26). Like parent, like child—how true that is (cf. Prov 22:6, which may be a negative as well as a positive proverb [lit., "train up your child in the way he *would* go . . ."]; cf. Stuart 1984:51-52). Thus, I have jokingly commented to my students that I hope they picked their parents most carefully!

Influence of parents notwithstanding, the major issue in both this and the preceding section must be the dangers of intermarriage with foreigners, that is, non-believers (at that time, non-Israelites would normally worship their own national god, not Yahweh, the national God of Israel or Judah). Of course, most such intermarriages took place for diplomatic reasons, and in a real sense, the royal family of the northern kingdom of Israel did not fit completely into the category of "foreigners"; but still, the danger of foreign influence had long been recognized in Judah (highlighted especially in the book of Deuteronomy; cf. the note on 1 Kgs 11:2 for references), and for the Deuteronomistic Historian, the results of borrowing practices from non-believers can only be disastrous. To be sure, things get tricky when mothers-in-law get involved and arranged marriages take place, but the warning remains—marry the unbeliever, get the unbelief (thrown in for free, as it were). This is especially true when the marriage partner is vigorous in personality or from a home with parents of vigorous personalities. Ahaziah in his single year of reign (perhaps encompassing only several months or so; see the first note on 8:26), would hardly have done much actual harm, but the Deuteronomistic evaluation must nonetheless be given (see endnotes 1 and 2 of the Introduction for details; see also the case of Zimri of Israel who was apparently on the throne for only one week and yet was still roundly condemned by the Deuteronomist [1 Kgs 16:15-20]). As is generally the case, the history here is written with a clear contemporary agenda. And in this case it is that thou shalt not marry unbelievers (cf. 2 Cor 6:14, also the commentary on 1 Kgs 11:1-13 for Solomon's particularly notorious failings in this area).

◆   I. Prophetic Stories about the Coup of Jehu (2 Kgs 9:1–10:36)
        1. Jehu anointed king of Israel (9:1-13)

Meanwhile, Elisha the prophet had summoned a member of the group of prophets. "Get ready to travel,"* he told him, "and take this flask of olive oil with you. Go to Ramoth-gilead, ²and find Jehu son of Jehoshaphat, son of Nimshi. Call him into a private room away from his friends, ³and pour the oil over his head. Say to him, 'This is what the LORD says: I anoint you to be the king over Israel.' Then open the door and run for your life!"

⁴So the young prophet did as he was told and went to Ramoth-gilead. ⁵When he arrived there, he found Jehu sitting around with the other army officers. "I have a message for you, Commander," he said.

"For which one of us?" Jehu asked.

"For you, Commander," he replied.

⁶So Jehu left the others and went into the house. Then the young prophet poured the oil over Jehu's head and said, "This is what the LORD, the God of Israel, says: I anoint you king over the LORD's people Israel. ⁷You are to destroy the family of Ahab, your master. In this way, I will

avenge the murder of my prophets and all the LORD's servants who were killed by Jezebel. ⁸The entire family of Ahab must be wiped out. I will destroy every one of his male descendants, slave and free alike, anywhere in Israel. ⁹I will destroy the family of Ahab as I destroyed the families of Jeroboam son of Nebat and of Baasha son of Ahijah. ¹⁰Dogs will eat Ahab's wife Jezebel at the plot of land in Jezreel, and no one will bury her." Then the young prophet opened the door and ran.

¹¹Jehu went back to his fellow officers, and one of them asked him, "What did that madman want? Is everything all right?"

"You know how a man like that babbles on," Jehu replied.

¹²"You're hiding something," they said. "Tell us."

So Jehu told them, "He said to me, 'This is what the LORD says: I have anointed you to be king over Israel.'"

¹³Then they quickly spread out their cloaks on the bare steps and blew the ram's horn, shouting, "Jehu is king!"

9:1 Hebrew *Bind up your loins.*

NOTES

9:1 *Meanwhile.* We are now back to the prophetic traditions, probably part of the Elisha cycle, or even part of the Elijah materials, since the Hazael pericope may have served to close the Elisha cycle proper (see the second note on 8:11), and since the anointing of Jehu is the *only* part of the Elijah recommissioning in 1 Kgs 19:15-17 that is fulfilled literally. In any case, we once again (and for the last time) hear about the "group of prophets" that is so often connected with Elisha.

the group of prophets. Lit., "sons of the prophets"; cf. notes on 2:3.

Get ready to travel. See the note on 4:29 concerning the colorful Hebrew idiom underlying this phrase.

this flask of olive oil. Heb., *pak* [TH6378, ZH7095] *hashemen hazzeh*; the only other use of the word *pak* in the MT is in 1 Sam 10:1, where it also designates a flask of oil used for anointing a king (in that case, Samuel anointing Saul). "Anointing" (*mashakh* [TH4886, ZH5417]; cf. 9:3, 6, 12) involves the pouring of seemingly copious amounts of oil upon the head (cf. Ps 133); probably it was originally a hygienic rite (to kill head lice; cf. Stuart 1987:360), but it came to denote the ceremonious transferal of sanctity from God to the "anointed one" or "messiah" (*mashiakh* [TH4899, ZH5431]; cf. McCarter 1980:178).

Ramoth-gilead. Obviously the warfare against Aram described in 1 Kgs 22:1-38, as well as that mentioned in 2 Kgs 8:28, still raged on. It does appear that for the moment, Israel has the upper hand. (For the location and significance of the site, see the note on 1 Kgs 22:3.)

9:2 Jehu son of Jehoshaphat, son of Nimshi. Typically appearing as "Jehu son of Nimshi," the use of this threefold name is unusual (Cogan and Tadmor 1988:106). Perhaps the grandfather was better known in the community, or else the third generation was included so as to preclude confusion with King Jehoshaphat of Judah. The name Jehu probably means "Yah(weh) is the (true) one" (Wiseman 1993:219), but the meaning of Nimshi is less certain (Gray [1970:540], citing Noth, suggests the nickname "weasel"; Penner [2009] suggests "drawn out"). (See the note on 1 Kgs 22:41 for the meaning of the name Jehoshaphat. For the irony of the repeated Assyrian identification of Jehu with the House of Omri, see the commentary below.)

private room. Heb., *kheder bekhader* [TH2315, ZH2540] ("a room [with]in a room"); see the notes on 1 Kgs 20:30 and 22:25. Leithart (2006:220) points out how the private nature of this action is reminiscent of other aspects of the ministry of Elisha—healing behind closed doors (4:32-35), remaining inside when Naaman comes for healing (5:9-10), knowing what the king of Aram says in his bedroom (6:12; and I would add the reference in 6:32 to Elisha being at home when the king's messenger arrives). But there was a private aspect to Elijah's ministry as well—e.g., when he healed the son of the widow of Zarephath in the upper room in 1 Kgs 17:19-23 (and to a lesser degree, his remaining aloof and alone at the Kerith Brook [1 Kgs 17:2-7], and when he fled to the wilderness near Beersheba and eventually to Mount Sinai [1 Kgs 19:4-15]). However, Babylonian coronation ceremonies also partly took place in an inner room (Wiseman 1993:219).

9:3 I anoint you . . . king over Israel. See the fourth note on 9:1 concerning the nature and significance of this action. Possibly the original concept of such anointing was for the prophetic representative to identify an appropriate "king-designate," which would have been later ratified by the tribal leadership after clear military success (see the commentary on 1 Kgs 1:5-27 for details). In any case, the nearly immediate, spontaneous approval of Jehu's fellow officers certainly confirms the popularity of this originally private procedure. As the Israelite army brought Omri to power (cf. 1 Kgs 16:15-16), the army will also bring about the downfall of his dynasty (Wiseman 1993:218).

run for your life! The precariousness of this totally unanticipated action will be evident, as will its drastic implications concerning Jehu's future career as usurper of the Omride dynasty (cf. Queen Jezebel's words in 9:31). It is thus entirely up to Jehu as to how to proceed publicly at this point (9:11-12).

9:5 Commander. Heb., *hassar* [TH8269, ZH8569]; the plural has been used for the other army officers previously in the verse, with the indication that Jehu is, as it were, first among equals.

9:8 every one of his male descendants, slave and free alike. See the first two notes on 1 Kgs 14:10 regarding the two Hebrew idioms found here. The expression is also found in the Elijah diatribe against Ahab in 1 Kgs 21:21; in fact, most of the rest of 9:7-10 in the present passage finds parallels in 1 Kgs 21:20-24, giving further support for its origin in the Elijah (rather than the Elisha) cycle.

9:11 What did that madman want? Lit., "Why did this madman (*meshugga'* [TH7696, ZH8713]) come to you?" For the larger significance of this comment, see the commentary. At this point, the tenor of the give-and-take between Jehu and his fellow officers is akin to locker-room banter ridiculing prophets in general.

Is everything all right? Lit., "is it peace?" (*hashalom* [TH7965, ZH8934]), a *Leitwort* (recurring word or word root; cf. Olyan 1984:653, citing Martin Buber; also cf. Hendel 2008:93) that will be repeated some nine times throughout the chapter (see commentary on 9:14-29).

9:12 You're hiding something. Lit., "a lie!" (*sheqer* [TH8267, ZH9214]). The NLT is paraphrastic here (contrast NIV, "that's not true!"), although it does convey effectively the overall ebb and flow of the conversation.

9:13 spread out their cloaks. This is akin to what the crowd did when greeting Jesus on his Triumphal Entry into Jerusalem on the day that has become known as Palm Sunday (Matt 21:8; Mark 11:8; Luke 19:36). A similar gesture of profound respect was also given to Cato of Utica (Cato the Younger) by his fellow soldiers when he was about to leave military service (Plutarch *Cato Minor* 12.1). I have come to wonder if the Palm Sunday gesture was more military in nature than I would have originally surmised.

blew the ram's horn. See the second note on 1 Kgs 1:34.

COMMENTARY

Some years ago Saul Olyan (1984:652-668) wrote an important article on the entirety of chapter 9; we will have occasion to analyze in some detail his work concerning the *shalom* refrain (or better, *Leitwort*; cf. the second note on 9:11) in the next section of commentary. Yet there is another important observation Olyan made concerning the double use of the Hebrew root *sh-g-'* ("to be mad or crazy" [TH7696, ZH8713]) in this chapter that must be discussed at this point: He highlighted the intriguing parallel between the "crazy" actions of the prophetic emissary in 9:11 ("that madman") and Jehu's later driving his chariot "like a madman" to Jezreel in 9:20. As Olyan pointed out (following Robert Wilson [1980:204-205]), the ecstatic prophets would often have been seen as crazy or mad by the more conservative circles such as the army and the governmental bureaucracy (which explains the bemused reactions of Jehu's fellow officers in 9:11), but Jehu will soon act as "crazy" as any of those prophets. As Olyan puts it, "it seems fairly apparent that the writer of this passage is using the root (*sh-g-'*) in a subtle and artful manner," and "The words (from the root *sh-g-'*) become symbolic of the service of Yahweh. Both the prophets and Jehu are instruments of Yahweh's restoration of *shalom*." Whether it be Elisha bringing about the rise of Hazael of Aram (cf. 8:7-15), or, as here, the rise of Jehu, there will be no question that the work of Elijah and Elisha will inevitably bring about the demise of the Omride dynasty, both from without and from within.

But that is not necessarily how the Assyrians recorded it. King Jehu "son of Omri" is famously (or perhaps infamously) depicted in the second register of the Black Obelisk from Nimrud (see ANEP, pictures 351, 355) as bowing down in abject humility to the Assyrian king Shalmaneser III, and Jehu's tribute is listed as follows: silver, gold, a golden bowl, a golden vase (?), golden goblets, golden buckets, etc. (cf. Cogan and Tadmor 1988:335). Now, Jehu was hardly the "son of Omri," but that is nevertheless how various Assyrian inscriptions repeatedly refer to him, even well into the second half of the eighth century (cf. Cogan and Tadmor [1988:106], who note that the Assyrian scribes were aware that Jehu had seized the throne but chose to acknowledge Omri as the first significant dynast in Israel; also cf. Stith 2008:213-214, who sees Jehu as a vassal of Hazael in light of the Tel Dan inscription [see the note on 1 Kgs 12:29 for details]). (For McCarter's suggestion, generally discredited, that it is Jehoram "son of Omri," and not Jehu, who is depicted on the Black Obelisk, see Cogan and Tadmor 1988:106; Barnes 1991:35 n. 14.) Thus we end up with the acute irony that Jehu, the infamous usurper of the Omride dynasty, was remembered in Assyria as a petty vassal king linked with the dynasty he usurped. The irony will become even more acute when one realizes that Jehu's dynasty lasted over 100 years (Omri's lasted at most some 42 years), and Jehu's great-grandson Jeroboam II was remembered as one of the most powerful kings in Israelite history (see 14:23-29).

Such are the vicissitudes of history and of historiography—one cannot control how one will be remembered. And as we shall see in the commentary on 10:1-17 and 10:18-31, even the biblical record concerning Jehu is mixed: clear appreciation of his zeal for Yahweh, yet clear hesitation in reference to his bloodthirsty way of exhibiting such zeal (cf. Hos 1:4-5). But one thing is most clear: The dynasty of Omri has come to an end, and that end is clearly the will of Yahweh, as repeatedly stated through his prophets Elijah and Elisha. The blood of Naboth most definitely will be avenged (cf. 9:26)!

◆   ## 2. Jehu kills Joram and Ahaziah (9:14-29)

14So Jehu son of Jehoshaphat, son of Nimshi, led a conspiracy against King Joram. (Now Joram had been with the army at Ramoth-gilead, defending Israel against the forces of King Hazael of Aram. 15But King Joram* was wounded in the fighting and returned to Jezreel to recover from his wounds.) So Jehu told the men with him, "If you want me to be king, don't let anyone leave town and go to Jezreel to report what we have done."

16Then Jehu got into a chariot and rode to Jezreel to find King Joram, who was lying there wounded. King Ahaziah of Judah was there, too, for he had gone to visit him. 17The watchman on the tower of Jezreel saw Jehu and his company approaching, so he shouted to Joram, "I see a company of troops coming!"

"Send out a rider to ask if they are coming in peace," King Joram ordered.

18So a horseman went out to meet Jehu and said, "The king wants to know if you are coming in peace."

Jehu replied, "What do you know about peace? Fall in behind me!"

The watchman called out to the king, "The messenger has met them, but he's not returning."

19So the king sent out a second horseman. He rode up to them and said, "The king wants to know if you come in peace."

Again Jehu answered, "What do you know about peace? Fall in behind me!"

20The watchman exclaimed, "The messenger has met them, but he isn't returning either! It must be Jehu son of Nimshi, for he's driving like a madman."

21"Quick! Get my chariot ready!" King Joram commanded.

Then King Joram of Israel and King Ahaziah of Judah rode out in their chariots to meet Jehu. They met him at the plot of land that had belonged to Naboth of Jezreel. 22King Joram demanded, "Do you come in peace, Jehu?"

Jehu replied, "How can there be peace

as long as the idolatry and witchcraft of your mother, Jezebel, are all around us?" ²³Then King Joram turned the horses around* and fled, shouting to King Ahaziah, "Treason, Ahaziah!" ²⁴But Jehu drew his bow and shot Joram between the shoulders. The arrow pierced his heart, and he sank down dead in his chariot.

²⁵Jehu said to Bidkar, his officer, "Throw him into the plot of land that belonged to Naboth of Jezreel. Do you remember when you and I were riding along behind his father, Ahab? The LORD pronounced this message against him: ²⁶'I solemnly swear that I will repay him here on this plot of land, says the LORD, for the murder of Naboth and his sons that I saw yesterday.' So throw him out on Naboth's property, just as the LORD said."

²⁷When King Ahaziah of Judah saw what was happening, he fled along the road to Beth-haggan. Jehu rode after him, shouting, "Shoot him, too!" So they shot Ahaziah* in his chariot at the Ascent of Gur, near Ibleam. He was able to go on as far as Megiddo, but he died there. ²⁸His servants took him by chariot to Jerusalem, where they buried him with his ancestors in the City of David. ²⁹Ahaziah had become king over Judah in the eleventh year of the reign of Joram son of Ahab.

9:15 Hebrew *Jehoram*, a variant spelling of Joram; also in 9:17, 21, 22, 23, 24.   9:23 Hebrew *turned his hands*.
9:27 As in Greek and Syriac versions; Hebrew lacks *So they shot Ahaziah*.

NOTES

9:14 *led a conspiracy.* Lit., "conspired with each other," a Hitpael (reciprocal form) of the verb *qashar* [TH7194, ZH8003] (to tie a knot). See 12:20 [21] for the Qal form of this verb and for the noun *qesher* [TH7195, ZH8004] (conspiracy, treason); cf. Athaliah's words in 11:14.

9:15 *King Joram was wounded.* This was already mentioned in 8:29 as the reason for the ill-fated presence in Jezreel of King Ahaziah of Judah (see also 9:16). (Concerning the variant spellings of Jehoram/Joram for the Israelite king, see the first note on 1:17.)

Jezreel. See the second note on 1 Kgs 18:46 concerning this city.

9:20 *he's driving like a madman.* See the commentary on 9:1-13 for the literary parallel. More specifically, Jehu's typical style of chariot driving must have been notorious (contrast Josephus and the Targum which have him driving calmly; cf. Cogan and Tadmor 1988:110).

9:21 *Naboth of Jezreel.* See the notes on 1 Kgs 21:1 concerning this unfortunate landowner, whose plot of ground was coveted by King Ahab. (See also 9:26 concerning the tragic death of his children.)

9:22 *your mother, Jezebel.* This is the infamous Tyrian wife of Ahab; see the note on 1 Kgs 16:31 for Jezebel's royal background. See also the note on 1 Kgs 21:8 for Freedman's comment regarding her imperious proclivities and how they were probably manipulated by Ahab to procure Naboth's vineyard.

9:23 *turned the horses around.* Or "signaled his team of chariots to change directions," by pulling up on one of the reins (so Cogan and Tadmor 1988:110); the same expression (lit., "turn the hand[s]") is found in 1 Kgs 22:34 in a similar context of a quick reversal of fortune in chariot warfare.

Treason. Heb., *mirmah* [TH4820, ZH5327], "deceit, treachery" (BDB 941); cf. NIV. Olyan (1984:666-667) suggests that this term functions as "the diametrical opposite" of *shalom* [TH7965, ZH8934] (see the commentary for details). This is the only time *mirmah* appears in 1-2 Kings.

9:24 *The arrow pierced his heart.* This is a relatively literal translation of *wayyetse'* [TH3318, ZH3655] *hakhetsi millibo*, "and the arrow went out from his heart" (cf. NRSV, NIV). Although the Hebrew terms for "heart" (*leb* [TH3820, ZH4213] and *lebab* [TH3824, ZH4222]) often do not refer to the actual organ but rather to one's inner self, or even one's life in general (cf. HALOT 514-515), the physical organ is what is meant here (cf. Ahab's similar demise in 1 Kgs 22:34-35).

9:25 Bidkar, his officer. This individual is otherwise unknown, but he is nevertheless important in the present context as a second witness to attest the particulars of Naboth's death (Sweeney 2007:334). Concerning the meaning of the name Bidkar (that is, if it is a proper name at all—the initial Beth may refer to *ben* [TH1121, ZH1201] or "son"), see Gray 1970:547; also Montgomery 1951:406. Concerning the term used here for "officer" (*shalish* [TH7991B, ZH8957]), see the first note on 7:2.

plot of land that belonged to Naboth of Jezreel. See the second note on 1 Kgs 21:19 for details concerning the fulfillment of Elijah's original prophecy.

9:26 for the murder of Naboth and his sons that I saw yesterday. This is the only reference to the death of Naboth's children to be found in 1–2 Kings, and it reflects a tradition evidently independent from that underlying 1 Kgs 21. Certainly, the sudden death of Joram the son of Ahab which has just been narrated, a prince who was presumably innocent of the juridical murder of Naboth (see the commentary), gains a bit more legitimacy in light of this firsthand reference. Concerning the probable meaning of the word *'emesh* [TH570, ZH621] (= "yesterday"?), see Cogan and Tadmor 1988:111.

9:27 King Ahaziah of Judah. See the first note on 8:25; it is also noteworthy that, in sharp contrast to the assassination of Joram of Israel, there is no rationale given for the killing of this king (Gray [1970:548] suggests that he was struck down since he was closely related in marriage to Joram and thus a possible avenger of his death). An ironic benefit for chronographers of the double assassination of both the northern and southern kings at the same time (842/841 BC) is the firm chronological peg this affords us (cf. Barnes 1991:156 note j)!

Beth-haggan. This is modern Jenin (ABD 1.687); thus Ahaziah was fleeing south on the main road to Samaria (and, presumably, Judah).

Ascent of Gur, near Ibleam. After being ambushed just south of Beth-haggan (Ibleam was about a mile [2 km] south of Jenin; cf. ABD 2.1099), Ahaziah's chariot made a sharp turn to the northwest, going all the way to Megiddo where he died (Jehu in turn eventually ends up in Samaria [cf. 10:12]).

9:29 eleventh year. See the second note on 8:25.

COMMENTARY

"Is it peace?" This is a literal translation of the refrain (*hashalom* [TH7965, ZH8934], a single word in Hebrew) which occurs a total of four times in this part of the chapter (9:17, 18, 19, 22), and twice more elsewhere (9:11, 31). There are three analogous usages of the root *sh-l-m* in 9:18, 19, and 22 as well. As noted in the previous commentary section, Saul Olyan has explored this phenomenon in some detail (1984:652-668); a number of his conclusions merit summarizing here. First of all, the very fact of Jehu traveling away from the military front at Ramoth-gilead may well have prompted the initial question *hashalom?* ("Is there peace?") in 9:17-18. Jehu, although secretly anointed to become king, publicly represented the military arm of the Omride regime at this point (note that in 9:18a, it is none other than the king himself who is asking *hashalom?*). But in a deeper sense, as we know, the king's messenger himself represents the fatally corrupt dynasty, so how can there be any possibility of *shalom*? Jehu therefore answers the messenger's question with his own question: "What do you know about *shalom*?" And he then commands in true military style: "Fall in [lit., 'turn around'] behind me!" If the original question was in reference to the front, Jehu's response clearly changes the point of reference: The messenger must decide immediately which side he will join before "war" breaks out—not at Ramoth-gilead but here at home in Jezreel.

Joram, the king of Israel, himself has no idea (or at least no clear idea; cf. 9:22-23) about what is soon to take place, so he duly orders a second messenger to be dispatched, with similar results (9:19-20). Finally, the king himself (accompanied by King Ahaziah of Judah) rides out to meet Jehu, to ask him directly the familiar question *hashalom?* (9:21-22a). This is when Jehu utters his fatal retort: "How can there be *shalom* as long as the idolatry and witchcraft of your mother, Jezebel, are all around us?" (9:22b). Whether or not Joram thought a direct confrontation by the two kings with Jehu, the "crazy driver" (cf. the note on 9:20), might still stem the tide and preserve the "peace" (cf. Wiseman 1982:321), the results of his move proved fatal. Still, as Olyan himself notes (1984:665-666):

> In the face of extreme danger, Joram turns to hope in a hopeless situation. The writer has brought us to the point of confrontation between the representative of Yahweh's justice and the representative, through no fault of his own, of Ahab's undoing of shalom. A comment on pathos is in order here. However necessary and compelling the execution of Yahweh's justice was perceived to be by the writer, he nonetheless portrays Joram as a figure of great pathos, eliciting sympathy from the reader. Joram himself is not responsible for the murder of Naboth. He is weak and defenseless in the presence of Jehu, and up to now unable to perceive the situation accurately, or at least to act intelligently on such a perception. We feel acutely the tension between Joram's weakness and Jehu's strength.

Once face-to-face with Jehu, Joram recognizes clearly the desperate situation: not *shalom* but its polar opposite, *mirmah* ("treachery" [see the second note on 9:23]). Both Joram and Ahaziah will soon die at the hands of Jehu—Joram at the very plot of land that had originally belonged to Naboth. And as Olyan (1984:667-668) concludes, it is not until after Joram's death that the narrator discloses the real reason for that assassination: It was none other than the explicit will of Yahweh that Joram die at that very spot (9:25-26)—in order to avenge the death of Naboth (and, I would add, of Naboth's sons, a detail we find only here in the text [see the note on 9:26]). Thus, it is at this point that we find the final example of pathos in the story: Before his own death, Joram is confronted with the sins of Jezebel, his mother; but it is due to the sins of Ahab, his father, that his death is irrevocably decreed. This is ironic in the extreme.

In contrast to Joram, Jezebel is portrayed by the writer as all too aware of Jehu's true intentions—and hardly as ignorant or as deluded as her now-dead son. Her own *hashalom* query in 9:31 betrays no false hope, just clear awareness of her hopeless situation, and she prepares to die as full of defiance as ever. Here, irony works on an entirely different level: As Olyan (1984:668) points out, "Jezebel asks sarcastically if all is in order, implying *mirmah*. She may understand that Jehu has come with violent intentions, but she also has no idea that he is really the restorer of *shalom*: with her death, order will be one step closer." As Olyan himself concludes his analysis of this carefully constructed story: "We have seen how *Leitwörter* and conceptual motifs add depth to the story. Behind a simple question like *hashalom* lies a multiplicity of meanings." (Concerning *Leitwort*, see the second note on 9:11.)

In have already noted the recent suggestion of Stith (2008:213) that Jehu may have been acting as a vassal of Hazael the king of Aram. Wouldn't it be the ultimate irony that somehow it was the will of God to bring about Aramean hegemony over the northern kingdom of Israel—and thus to avenge the innocent deaths of Naboth and his children? (Concerning the Transjordanian territories lost to Hazael during Jehu's reign, cf. 10:32-33.) Thus, God commissioned through his prophets Elijah and Elisha not one but two usurpers to bring the dynasty of Omri to an irrevocable end. It is indeed a fearsome thing to fall into the hands of the living God (cf. Heb 10:31).

◆   ## 3. The death of Jezebel (9:30-37)

30When Jezebel, the queen mother, heard that Jehu had come to Jezreel, she painted her eyelids and fixed her hair and sat at a window. 31When Jehu entered the gate of the palace, she shouted at him, "Have you come in peace, you murderer? You're just like Zimri, who murdered his master!"*

32Jehu looked up and saw her at the window and shouted, "Who is on my side?" And two or three eunuchs looked out at him. 33"Throw her down!" Jehu yelled. So they threw her out the window, and her blood spattered against the wall and on the horses. And Jehu trampled her body under his horses' hooves.

34Then Jehu went into the palace and ate and drank. Afterward he said, "Someone go and bury this cursed woman, for she is the daughter of a king." 35But when they went out to bury her, they found only her skull, her feet, and her hands.

36When they returned and told Jehu, he stated, "This fulfills the message from the LORD, which he spoke through his servant Elijah from Tishbe: 'At the plot of land in Jezreel, dogs will eat Jezebel's body. 37Her remains will be scattered like dung on the plot of land in Jezreel, so that no one will be able to recognize her.' "

9:31 See 1 Kgs 16:9-10, where Zimri killed his master, King Elah.

NOTES
9:30 *Jezebel, the queen mother.* See the note on 9:22.

painted her eyelids and fixed her hair and sat at a window. A classic example of ancient Near Eastern iconography (study of visual images or symbols) is the "woman in the window" (often understood as an alluringly coiffed prostitute) depicted on carved ivory plaques found throughout the region (see, e.g., ANEP, picture 131). Cogan and Tadmor (1988:111-112) discount the significance of the parallels here (e.g., Jezebel is certainly not trying to seduce Jehu) and instead cite Freedman's apt comment, "The idea is that (as) a queen, (she) meets her destiny in full regalia and made up for the occasion" (contrast Sisera's mother as depicted in Judg 5:28-30). (Typically, *kohl*, or powdered antimony, was used to paint the lids, lashes, and brows of the eyes black [cf. the famous bust of Queen Nefertiti of Egypt].)

9:31 *Have you come in peace, you murderer?* See the previous commentary concerning the repetition of the phrase *hashalom* [TH7965, ZH8934]. The NLT's paraphrastic addition, "you murderer," does not reflect the Hebrew text, although that is surely the intent of Jezebel's apt "Zimri" insult.

Zimri. This is the infamous Israelite king who apparently reigned only a week after assassinating his predecessor, Elah (see commentary on 1 Kgs 16:15-20).

9:32 *eunuchs.* Heb., *sarisim* [TH5631, ZH6247]. The term is here best translated literally, as in the NLT, since these servants evidently wait upon the queen; elsewhere the term takes on the more general nuance of "court officials" or the like (cf. the first note on 8:6).

9:34 *ate and drank.* He was apparently carrying on as if nothing amiss had taken place.

bury this cursed woman, for she is the daughter of a king. This is a belated acknowledgment of the royal background of Jezebel (concerning Israelite burial practices, see the commentary on 1 Kgs 13:1-34).

9:36 *dogs.* Thus Elijah's prophecy concerning Jezebel is finally fulfilled (1 Kgs 21:23; see the note there for details; cf. 9:10). Deborah Appler (2008) has recently suggested that since dogs served as healers and guides to the afterlife in Canaanite myth, the present account acts also as an Israelite parody of that tradition.

9:37 *scattered like dung.* In contrast to the preceding verse, this verse finds no parallel in 1–2 Kings, thus attesting to the independent nature of the present account.

COMMENTARY

The previous commentary section characterized Jezebel as clear-eyed and eerily composed as she confronted her soon-to-be assassin Jehu. Not much more need be said here other than to recognize grudgingly that Queen Jezebel—so often portrayed by commentators as the classic villainess of the books of Kings—plays her part with studied class up to the very end (cf. Freedman's comment, as cited in the second note on 9:30). The final depiction of Jezebel is more tragic than triumphant, I submit, although one is never to dismiss entirely the evident poetic justice of her meeting a fate similar to that which she had earlier arranged for Naboth and his family (see the commentary on 1 Kgs 21:1-29 for further thoughts on this subject). Jehu nevertheless remains the "low-class" cad, an impostor who seizes the throne like Zimri, whom he did indeed emulate (Jezebel pegged him accurately). Still, the prophetic word is to be fulfilled, and Jezebel's end is as pathetic as any zealous prophet of Yahweh could wish: the pampered child of a Tyrian king becoming nothing more than food for scavenging Israelite dogs. *Sic semper tyrannis* ("Thus always to tyrants").

Even so, it is easy to dismiss Jezebel's death too cavalierly, as Jehu did when he went in to eat and drink. As Hens-Piazza (2006:296) reminds us, "It is not necessary to be innocent to be a victim," and:

> *The case of Jezebel is an instance of the ease with which outsiders may be vilified. How we read and remember her not only occasions the opportunity to rehearse her misdeeds but to be mindful of the violence done to her. It also invites us to reconsider those identified as the "Jezebels" of our own world: those who suffer the violence of sustained or disproportionate blame; those who incur damaged reputations because of their gender, ethnic identity, or their status as "other"; and those who are excoriated for their wrongdoings and are deemed undeserving of forgiveness.*

It probably is not entirely coincidental, therefore, that the Latin phrase already cited, *sic semper tyrannis*, was not only attributed to Marcus Junius Brutus when he helped assassinate Julius Caesar, but also to John Wilkes Booth when he assassinated

Abraham Lincoln (it also appears prominently on the State Seal of the Commonwealth of Virginia). Sometimes, it seems that a "tyrant" becomes one largely in the eyes of the beholder!

◆ ## 4. Jehu kills Ahab's family (10:1-17)

Ahab had seventy sons living in the city of Samaria. So Jehu wrote letters and sent them to Samaria, to the elders and officials of the city,* and to the guardians of King Ahab's sons. He said, 2"The king's sons are with you, and you have at your disposal chariots, horses, a fortified city, and weapons. As soon as you receive this letter, 3select the best qualified of your master's sons to be your king, and prepare to fight for Ahab's dynasty."

4But they were paralyzed with fear and said, "We've seen that two kings couldn't stand against this man! What can we do?"

5So the palace and city administrators, together with the elders and the guardians of the king's sons, sent this message to Jehu: "We are your servants and will do anything you tell us. We will not make anyone king; do whatever you think is best."

6Jehu responded with a second letter: "If you are on my side and are going to obey me, bring the heads of your master's sons to me at Jezreel by this time tomorrow." Now the seventy sons of the king were being cared for by the leaders of Samaria, where they had been raised since childhood. 7When the letter arrived, the leaders killed all seventy of the king's sons. They placed their heads in baskets and presented them to Jehu at Jezreel.

8A messenger went to Jehu and said, "They have brought the heads of the king's sons."

So Jehu ordered, "Pile them in two heaps at the entrance of the city gate, and leave them there until morning."

9In the morning he went out and spoke to the crowd that had gathered around them. "You are not to blame," he told

them. "I am the one who conspired against my master and killed him. But who killed all these? 10You can be sure that the message of the LORD that was spoken concerning Ahab's family will not fail. The LORD declared through his servant Elijah that this would happen."

11Then Jehu killed all who were left of Ahab's relatives living in Jezreel and all his important officials, his personal friends, and his priests. So Ahab was left without a single survivor.

12Then Jehu set out for Samaria. Along the way, while he was at Beth-eked of the Shepherds, 13he met some relatives of King Ahaziah of Judah. "Who are you?" he asked them.

And they replied, "We are relatives of King Ahaziah. We are going to visit the sons of King Ahab and the sons of the queen mother."

14"Take them alive!" Jehu shouted to his men. And they captured all forty-two of them and killed them at the well of Beth-eked. None of them escaped.

15When Jehu left there, he met Jehonadab son of Recab, who was coming to meet him. After they had greeted each other, Jehu said to him, "Are you as loyal to me as I am to you?"

"Yes, I am," Jehonadab replied.

"If you are," Jehu said, "then give me your hand." So Jehonadab put out his hand, and Jehu helped him into the chariot. 16Then Jehu said, "Now come with me, and see how devoted I am to the LORD." So Jehonadab rode along with him.

17When Jehu arrived in Samaria, he killed everyone who was left there from Ahab's family, just as the LORD had promised through Elijah.

10:1 As in some Greek manuscripts and Latin Vulgate (see also 10:6); Hebrew reads *of Jezreel.*

NOTES

10:1 *seventy sons.* This is certainly a large number, and very possibly a round one, but not one without parallel (see Judg 9:5; and cf. Gen 46:27 [MT] and Exod 1:5 [MT]; also cf. Num 11:16). The eighth-century Panammua Inscription from Sam'al (southern Turkey) similarly cites the "seventy kinsmen" of the king who had been killed by a usurper (Wiseman 1993:224-225). As Wiseman concludes concerning the present passage, "The large numbers would certainly cover all those likely to seek reprisals or have any legitimate claim to the throne."

letters. Jehu's letter is cited in a fashion that reflects a common structure of ancient Israelite and Aramean letters; a greeting and list of addressees is followed by an opening expression (in Heb., *we'attah* [TH6258, ZH6964], "and now"). This occurs with the lit. clause "and now, with the arrival of this letter," found at the beginning of 10:2 in the MT and reflected in the NLT by the words at the end of 10:2. (For references to recent scholarly analyses of such standard features of Hebrew letter-writing, see the second note on 5:5.) In light of the precise transmission of letter-writing style we find here, it is ironic that "writing is often associated with deception in Samuel and Kings" (Leithart [2006:222], who cites David's deceptive letter to Joab in 2 Sam 11, as well as Jezebel's literary efforts against Naboth in 1 Kgs 21).

elders and officials of the city. This was presumably all who were based in Samaria, and not just visiting there (contrast the MT, which reads "to the rulers of Jezreel, the elders" [cf. NLT mg]). Reading "city" with the ancient versions (as NLT does; contrast NRSV, NIV) makes for a smoother text, and lines up better with 10:5-6. The MT could be retained, however, if the rulers/elders of Jezreel had traveled to Samaria, perhaps seeking advice from the royal officials in the capital city (so Qimchi, as cited in Cogan and Tadmor 1988:113; cf. Hobbs 1985:26).

10:3 *fight for Ahab's dynasty.* The name Ahab is not found in the original, which simply reads "put him on the throne of his father" (who was Ahab). Strictly speaking, Ahab's father Omri was the founder of the dynasty, but time and again it is the name Ahab that the narrator uses to designate that line of kings (cf. 1 Kgs 21:29). (For the overall effectiveness of Jehu's aggressive directives here, see the commentary.)

10:6 *a second letter.* This is an example of the deceptive nature of the letter-writing found in Kings (see the second note on 10:1)—did Jehu want their actual "heads" severed from their bodies? (Cf. Leithart 2006:222, " 'I didn't mean *literal* heads,' we can hear him protesting on the evening news.")

by this time tomorrow. Not coincidentally, this is the same threat Jezebel made against Elijah in 1 Kgs 19:2.

10:8 *Pile them in two heaps at the entrance of the city gate.* This would frighten the surviving citizens of the city into submission, a tactic also used by contemporary Neo-Assyrian kings (Cogan and Tadmor 1988:113). For an Assyrian image of severed heads as part of a scene where scribes of King Sennacherib are compiling lists of war booty and of the slain, see ANEP, picture 236.

10:9 *You are not to blame.* Lit., "you are innocent" (*tsaddiq* [TH6662, ZH7404]). Sweeney (2007:337) characterizes this as a standard judicial formula used to state innocence as decided in a court of law. (For the alternate view that this phrase could signify that the people are "righteous judges," see the commentary.)

10:10 *Elijah.* As is the case throughout the Jehu story (cf. 9:36 and 10:17), this is the prophet who is repeatedly cited as responsible for the demise of Ahab and his family (cf. the first note on 9:1 and the note on 9:8 concerning the likelihood that the Jehu narrative may reflect materials taken from the Elijah [rather than the Elisha] cycle). That Ahab was left "without a single survivor" (10:11) testifies to the literal fulfillment of Elijah's original prophecy that Yahweh would destroy every one of Ahab's male descendants, whether slave or free, anywhere in Israel (cf. 9:8; 1 Kgs 21:21).

10:12 Beth-eked of the Shepherds. Heb., *beth-'eqed haro'im* [TH1044A/7473, ZH1118/8286]. The specific identification of this location between Jezreel and Samaria remains uncertain. It is traditionally identified with Bayt Qad, 3 mi. [5 km] east of Jenin, or else Kafr Ra'i ("village of the shepherd"), 5 mi. [8 km] southwest of Jenin (ABD 1.685).

10:13 to visit. Lit., "to seek the peace/welfare of" (*lishlom* [TH7965, ZH8934]). This is yet another reference to *shalom*, the *Leitwort* so prominent in the previous chapter (see the commentary on 9:14-29). Once again, what Jehu brings is quite the opposite of "shalom," for either the northern or (as here) the southern kingdom. Most commentators think these "relatives" of Ahaziah were entirely innocently motivated and were simply in the wrong place at the wrong time; but Hobbs (1985:128) has argued plausibly that these Judahites were actually quite aware of recent events, and were thus on the march to avenge Ahaziah's death. This would largely explain Jehu's bloodthirsty response when he encountered them.

10:14 forty-two. This is a large, and presumably exact, total (but cf. the third note on 2:24).

10:15 Jehonadab son of Recab. Here and in Jer 35 Jehonadab is famously reckoned as the leader of an Israelite ascetic movement harkening back to an earlier, more simplified nomadic lifestyle. They did not plant vineyards, cultivate the land, build houses, or drink wine (this last prohibition was of particular import to the Jeremiah text). Therefore, it is assumed that they would have been natural allies of a zealous leader attempting to root out the "newfangled" Baalism in the land of Israel. Frick (1971:279-287), however, has suggested that the Recabites were actually a guild of metalworkers—an occupation which would necessarily be nomadic in nature—and that their prohibition against drinking wine was largely to protect trade secrets! Since the term "Recab" is virtually identical with that used for chariotry (*rekeb* [TH7393, ZH8207]), some commentators have further suggested that these metalworkers were especially involved with the manufacture and repair of chariots (Hobbs 1985:128-129).

put out his hand. This is "a gesture of promise and compact" (Greenberg 1983:315, in reference to Ezek 17:18; cf. 1 Chr 29:24; 2 Chr 30:8; Ezra 10:19). A striking parallel to this "handshake" may be found in a relief carved on the throne base of the contemporary Assyrian king Shalmaneser III, where he is depicted as extending his hand in friendship to one Marduk-zakir-shumi, a king he had helped reinstate to the Babylonian throne (see Oates 1963:21-22, also Plate VIIc; concerning Jehu's abject bowing to this same king, see the commentary on 9:1-13).

10:16 how devoted I am to the LORD. Lit., "my zeal for Yahweh" (*beqin'athi layhwh* [TH7068/3068, ZH7863/3378]); the phrase evokes the prophet Elijah's own repeated protestation that he has "zealously served the LORD" (1 Kgs 19:10, 14).

10:17 Elijah. See the note on 10:10.

COMMENTARY

Alas, the killing continues in what Cogan and Tadmor (1988:117) have described as the "longest sustained narrative in 2 Kings" (the entirety of the Jehu tradition in chs 9–10). The penetrating intensity of the present narration equals that of the main protagonist, Jehu himself. This passage presents the relentless, wholesale extermination of anyone, relative or friend, who could possibly bring back Ahab's dynasty (or properly, Omri's dynasty; cf. the note on 10:3) or even stand up in its defense (thus the eventual killing of all the relatives and friends of King Ahaziah of Judah in 10:12-14). As is often said, the best defense is a good offense, and Jehu is clearly very much on the offensive here. But even by Old Testament standards, the violence seems extreme. As is typical of many of the narratives of Samuel—Kings, we read "just the facts," with the editorializing mostly left to others (of course, that does not include the repetitive Deuteronomistic evaluation-summary concerning the sins of Jeroboam I, as found in 10:29, 31). The idea that there may be subtle indications even in the present narrative of editorial distaste for Jehu's extremes will be explored in the commentary on 10:32-36. But for the present, the perverse brilliance of Jehu's fanatic excesses is mainly meant to be noticed and, in a strange sense, appreciated.

In an earlier study on the present chapter (Barnes 1997a:439), I categorized the first Jehu letter (10:1-4) as "a master-stroke of indirection"—by ostensibly urging the town and court officials to prepare energetically to fight for their master's house (and, not least, to pick without delay a new king to lead them), the letter powerfully undermined any possibility that such would happen! Jehu thus effectively called their bluff. How could they withstand the crazy usurper who had already killed two kings? (Concerning Jehu's "craziness," see the commentary on 9:1-13.) But it is the second letter, with its apparently carefully written ambiguity—delivering the "heads" of the 70 sons to Jehu in Jezreel "by this time tomorrow"—that really takes the cake. Sadly, there exist ancient Near Eastern parallels to the literal decapitation and display of the heads of enemy warriors to forestall further rebellion (see note on 10:8). But decapitating all of Ahab's children? And by their own guardians? ("Whoever is in power will find willing executioners who try to save their own lives" [Würthwein 1984:2.336, as cited in Fritz 2003:287].) Surely the words of Elijah about destroying every male, slave or free, in Ahab's dynasty have come true with a savage vengeance (see the note on 10:10).

But what about Jehu's words to the citizens of Jezreel in 10:9 ("You are not to blame")? Are they truly innocent of all charges? Who, then, was guilty in regard to the cruel killing of all of Ahab's children? Again, Jehu was masterful in his carefully contrived speech. Since neither Jehu nor the Jezreelites were to blame, perhaps the the other leaders in Samaria were to be held guilty (cf. 10:2, 5, 6b-7)? No matter— Jehu reminded them that it was ultimately the will of God, as Elijah the prophet had declared years earlier (10:10). An alternative view is that Jehu's statement in 10:9 should be understood to mean "you are fair judges"; he thus appeals to the people as able to decide whether his actions should be approved and whether divinely inspired circumstances indeed led to the massacre of the rest of Ahab's family (cf. Gray 1970:555; Jones 1984:466-467). In any case, the narrator's conclusion is clear enough: "So Ahab was left without a single survivor" (10:11; cf. 10:17).

The final section introducing Jehonadab the Recabite represents a brief respite from all the killing, but it too will eventually lead to further bloodshed (cf. 10:23). Meanwhile, Jehu has run into a willing ally (cf. the second note on 10:15), one who will serve an ambiguous role in the butchery to follow. Later tradition remembers

Jehonadab kindly (see Jer 35) and reckons the Recabites as a kind of Amish brother-hood, both quaint and appealing in their anachronistic simplicity. But it would be wrong to import such warm feelings into the present text, which merely recalls the (opportunistic?) friendship and bond between the two Israelite leaders, presumably united in their deep hatred of the Baal cult. If indeed the Recabites were a guild of metalworkers (cf. the first note on 10:15), we may have a "marriage of convenience" between two nonagricultural groups: the military and the metalworkers (indeed, probably the fashioners and repairers of chariots for the military). The power of this "military-industrial complex," however, is to be resisted by the reader (at least in modern times; cf. the farewell speech of U.S. President Dwight Eisenhower given in 1961). At the very least, it had better be examined most closely! This is true even though the narrator's editorial neutrality has sometimes led to misunderstanding by later commentators, who in their own laudable efforts to resist Baalism may have welcomed uncritically any and all apparent allies. In short, the enemy of our enemy may not be our friend, a fact modern Christians must be reminded of time and again, especially in the realm of partisan politics. And as the next section of the Jehu story will illustrate vividly (see the "cunning plan" of Jehu described in 10:18-19), even his "zeal for Yahweh" (see note on 10:16) does not necessarily permit the abrogation of the common—and properly prophetic—evangelical Christian teach-ing that "the ends do not justify the means." Laudable goals do not justify mass deception and mass murder any more than they do present-day uses of torture and "ethnic cleansing." The enemy of our enemy is not necessarily our friend.

◆   ## 5. Jehu kills the priests of Baal (10:18-31)

18 Then Jehu called a meeting of all the people of the city and said to them, "Ahab's worship of Baal was nothing compared to the way I will worship him! 19 Therefore, summon all the prophets and worshipers of Baal, and call together all his priests. See to it that every one of them comes, for I am going to offer a great sacrifice to Baal. Anyone who fails to come will be put to death." But Jehu's cunning plan was to destroy all the worshipers of Baal.

20 Then Jehu ordered, "Prepare a solemn assembly to worship Baal!" So they did. 21 He sent messengers throughout all Isra-el summoning those who worshiped Baal. They all came—not a single one remained behind—and they filled the temple of Baal from one end to the other. 22 And Jehu in-structed the keeper of the wardrobe, "Be sure that every worshiper of Baal wears one of these robes." So robes were given to them.

23 Then Jehu went into the temple of Baal with Jehonadab son of Recab. Jehu said to the worshipers of Baal, "Make sure no one who worships the LORD is here—only those who worship Baal." 24 So they were all inside the temple to offer sacrifices and burnt offerings. Now Jehu had stationed eighty of his men outside the building and had warned them, "If you let anyone es-cape, you will pay for it with your own life."

25 As soon as Jehu had finished sacrific-ing the burnt offering, he commanded his guards and officers, "Go in and kill all of them. Don't let a single one escape!" So they killed them all with their swords, and the guards and officers dragged their bodies outside.* Then Jehu's men went into the innermost fortress* of the temple of Baal. 26 They dragged out the sacred pil-lar* used in the worship of Baal and burned it. 27 They smashed the sacred pil-lar and wrecked the temple of Baal, con-

verting it into a public toilet, as it remains to this day.

²⁸ In this way, Jehu destroyed every trace of Baal worship from Israel. ²⁹ He did not, however, destroy the gold calves at Bethel and Dan, with which Jeroboam son of Nebat had caused Israel to sin.

³⁰ Nonetheless the LORD said to Jehu, "You have done well in following my instructions to destroy the family of Ahab. Therefore, your descendants will be kings of Israel down to the fourth generation." ³¹ But Jehu did not obey the Law of the LORD, the God of Israel, with all his heart. He refused to turn from the sins that Jeroboam had led Israel to commit.

10:25a Or *and they left their bodies lying there;* or *and they threw them out into the outermost court.*
10:25b Hebrew *city.*   10:26 As in Greek and Syriac versions and Latin Vulgate; Hebrew reads *sacred pillars.*

NOTES

10:18 *Ahab's worship of Baal was nothing compared to the way I will worship him!* Lit., "Ahab served/worshiped (*'abad* [TH5647, ZH6268]) Baal a little; Jehu will serve/worship him a lot."

10:19 *prophets . . . worshipers . . . priests.* There are textual irregularities here concerning these terms (the term "worshipers" is lacking altogether in two Hebrew mss, and it is placed after the term "priests" in the Lucianic version of the LXX); many surmise that the reference here in the MT to "worshipers" (or, perhaps better, "cult-personnel" or "ministrants"; see Cogan and Tadmor 1988:115; cf. NIV, "ministers") may have come from its appearance in 10:21, 23. (For the implications of *'obedim* [TH5647, ZH6268] meaning "cult-personnel" and not "worshipers," see the commentary.)

Jehu's cunning plan. Lit., "but Jehu acted with *insidiousness.*" The root *'-q-b* [TH6117, ZH6810] found here is also famously attested in the name Jacob, which leads to Esau's plaintive wordplay in Gen 27:36: "No wonder his name is Jacob, for now he has cheated me twice."

10:22 *keeper of the wardrobe.* Heb., *la'asher 'al-hammeltakhah* [TH4458, ZH4921]; the last term is a hapax legomenon (a word used only once) in the MT. The exact translation is therefore uncertain, but, largely due to context, most commentators concur with the rendering found in the NLT.

robes. Concern for proper clothing for approaching the deity is also attested in Gen 35:2; Exod 19:10 (and possibly Zeph 1:8; cf. KJV).

10:23 *Jehonadab.* See the first note on 10:15.

10:25 *Don't let a single one escape!* This is nearly identical to Elijah's words in 1 Kgs 18:40 (but with a different Hebrew verb).

dragged their bodies outside. This is a traditional rendering of the MT, but, as noted in the translation proffered by Cogan and Tadmor (1988:105, 116), "they left [them] lying [there]," this Hiphil of the verb *shalak* [TH7993, ZH8959] probably means "to expose, leave unburied" (cf. Cogan 1968:133-135). This explains the first alternative translation suggested in the NLT mg. The second alternative represents a possible emendation (substituted reading) for the admittedly difficult Hebrew text, akin to that found in Gray 1970:558 note d.

innermost fortress of the temple of Baal. Lit., "as far as the city (*'ir* [TH5892, ZH6551]) of the house of Baal." Inasmuch as it is now uncertain where the precise location of this notorious (cf. 10:27) Baal temple was, possibly the normal meaning of "city" should here be retained (i.e., denoting a municipal area next to the Baal temple); alternatively, the term *'ir* might here denote "fortress" (Hobbs 1985:130).

10:26 *sacred pillar.* The MT contains the plural *matseboth* [TH4676, ZH5167] (cf. NLT mg), but then has a singular reference in the next verbal form, "and they burned *it*"; hence, most (like NLT) emend the Hebrew to a singular form as found in the next verse.

10:27 *public toilet.* The MT's Kethiv reads *makhara'oth* [TH4280, ZH4738], "places of dung," hence probably "latrines, cesspools" or the like; the Qere reads *motsa'oth* [TH4163, ZH4606], "places of withdrawal," probably a euphemism for toilets or latrines (see the note on 3:24 concerning the terms Kethiv and Qere). Possibly, however, the consonantal of the Kethiv merely indicated a public dump (Cogan and Tadmor 1988:116).

to this day. This is a good translation of *'ad hayyom* ("until today"; cf. the note on 2:22), which is found in the MT. The more expected, fuller phrase *'ad hayyom hazzeh* [TH2088, ZH2296] (until this day) is attested in the LXX, Targum, and Vulgate.

10:28 *destroyed every trace of Baal worship from Israel.* Lit., "wiped out, exterminated [Hiphil of the verb *shamad* [TH8045, ZH9012]] Baal from Israel."

10:29 *Jeroboam.* Concerning the nature of these infamous "sins of Jeroboam," see the commentary on 1 Kgs 12:25-33.

10:30 *done well.* See the commentary for a discussion of this disquieting note of high praise from Yahweh.

fourth generation. Jehu's dynasty was the longest of any in the northern kingdom; it encompassed some 100 years.

10:31 *did not obey the Law of the LORD.* This is a variation on the negative Deuteronomistic evaluative refrain for the northern kings (see endnote 1 of the Introduction for details).

COMMENTARY

"Zeal for the LORD" indeed! If we have encountered extended "genealogical cleansing" in the previous sections, now we encounter rigorous "religious cleansing." And surely both are as repugnant to modern minds as the "ethnic cleansings" of the late twentieth century. But that is our modern Christian perspective. What about the attitudes and expectations of the original hearers/readers of the present passage? Answering such queries is a major part of the task of exegesis. Yet in the present instance, answering such questions is hard to do, inasmuch as our narrator once again basically presents "just the facts," and lets our own perspectives and prejudices take precedence over any overt theologizing (apart from the general commendation from Yahweh [10:30] that Jehu had "done well" to destroy Ahab's family). Cunning, clever, effective, all-encompassing—these are proper characterizations of Jehu's actions as he successfully exterminates every single prophet, priest, and minister of Baal he can find. (That this is the nearly exact counterpart of Jezebel's original actions against the prophets of Yahweh [cf. 1 Kgs 18:4, 13] is surely meant to be noticed.) But as was the case with Jehonadab's earlier compact with Jehu back in 10:15-16, we cannot be sure what the narrator thought about the horrific actions he or she recorded here with such storytelling fervor. A smile surely crossed the narrator's face when the "public toilet" (see note on 10:27) reference was delivered and, as Sweeney (2007:339) has pointed out, this reference does provide "a focal point" for the prior references to the killing off of all the males from the house of Ahab—literally, "all who urinate against the wall" (9:8; 1 Kgs 21:21; cf. the first note on 1 Kgs 14:10 for details concerning this idiom).

So what are we to make of the present narrative? Jezebel had indeed been ruthless in her attempts to exterminate the Yahwistic prophets back in 1 Kings 18. That surely horrified the narrator as much as it does us. So, is turnabout fair play? I think, even for the ancient narrator, it was not quite that simple. First of all, the question arises over whether the "ministers" (i.e., cult-personnel) of Baal were wiped out (see the first note on 10:19), or if, indeed, all the *worshipers* of Baal were also wiped out (so NLT, NRSV, etc.). If the latter, as Hobbs (1985:132) notes, "the cost to the country in manpower must have been great." (In any case, Jehu apparently had declared his allegiance as a vassal-king to Shalmaneser III; cf. the commentary on 9:1-13 for details.) Even if only the former was the case, it implies hundreds, possibly thousands of deaths—certainly comparable with Elijah's own slaughter of the 450 prophets of Baal in 1 Kings 18:40 (cf. the parallel command not to let any escape [10:25]). Could this possibly be God's will? Certainly not, if the traditional understanding of Hos 1:4-5 is followed: "I [Yahweh] am about to punish King Jehu's dynasty to avenge the murders he committed at Jezreel [cf. 2 Kgs 9:16-37; 10:6-11].... I will break [Israel's] military power in the Jezreel Valley."[1]

Recently, I had the privilege of talking with Greg Boyd, an eminent evangelical Christian author and pastor living in Minnesota. He proposed an idea for a new book he wanted to write, *Crucifixion of the Warrior God*, which would address the "incarnational nature" of God working through Old Testament society and culture. He would suggest that as in the New Testament incarnation of Jesus (God becoming truly human, with all the ramifications that situation entails—limited power and knowledge, frailty and fatigue, etc.), so also in the Old Testament, God worked in and through the very human culture of Israel, with, for example, its bloodthirsty conceptions of holy war (this would help explain the fierce delight found in the horrific war directives found in Deuteronomy and their fulfillment in Joshua). Yahweh, the true God, does not agree completely with such fierceness, but he has chosen to work incarnationally with that culture to bring about deliverance from idolatry. Perhaps such a concept is helpful here as well. For, with proper caveats (see the next commentary section), it appears that the present narrator generally approves of Jehu's bloodthirsty ways here, certainly citing with approval Yahweh's own attitude concerning those ways (or at least the end result of those ways; cf. the first note on 10:30). Thus, we are told that Jehu did (largely for his own political purposes, I suspect) bring about an abrupt end to Baalism in Israel, and that (1) this was clearly and unequivocally the will of God, and (2) it served to fulfill quite literally the words of Elijah, his prophet. That is the message of the present text. And that is the reason why Jehu was promised descendants on the throne down to the fourth generation.

ENDNOTE

1. Some time ago, my mentor, the late Thomas E. McComiskey [1992:18-22], argued that these verses in Hosea should rather be understood as merely equating historically the bloodshed at Jezreel in Jehu's time with the later prediction of bloodshed in the same location bringing Jehu's own dynasty to an end (cf. the second note on 2 Kgs 15:10 for details). Although my respect for Professor McComiskey is considerable, I suspect that the traditional understanding of Hos 1:4-5 is still to be preferred.

◆   6. The death of Jehu (10:32–36)

³²At about that time the LORD began to
cut down the size of Israel's territory. King
Hazael conquered several sections of the
country ³³east of the Jordan River, including all of Gilead, Gad, Reuben, and Manasseh. He conquered the area from the
town of Aroer by the Arnon Gorge to as
far north as Gilead and Bashan.

³⁴The rest of the events in Jehu's reign—
everything he did and all his achievements—are recorded in *The Book of the
History of the Kings of Israel.*
    ³⁵When Jehu died, he was buried in Sa-
maria. Then his son Jehoahaz became the
next king. ³⁶In all, Jehu reigned over Israel from Samaria for twenty-eight years.

NOTES

10:32 *to cut down.* This is a good, rather literal translation of the infinitive *leqatsoth* [TH7096,
ZH7894] (cf. Cogan and Tadmor 1988:117; also NRSV's "began to trim off parts of Israel").

Hazael. See the first note on 8:8 for details concerning this important Aramean king,
including his eventual oppression (and outright annexation) of much of the land of Israel.

several sections of the country. See Cogan and Tadmor (1988:117) for details. Suffice it
to say here that evidently the entirety of the Transjordanian regions of Israel were lost to
Hazael. ("Aroer" in the south was located directly east of the Dead Sea, while "Bashan"
corresponds to the present-day Golan Heights, northeast of the Sea of Galilee, stretching
toward Damascus.) The overall irony of this extensive loss of territory will be evident: By
abandoning the battle for Ramoth-gilead in 9:14-15, Jehu ultimately ceded all that territory to the enemy. (For the suggestion that Jehu actually became a vassal of Hazael, see the
commentary on 9:1-13.)

10:34 *are recorded in* **The Book of the History of the Kings of Israel.** See "Literary Style"
in the Introduction.

10:35 *Jehoahaz.* See 13:1-9.

10:36 *Jehu reigned . . . for twenty-eight years.* There has been no regnal total given for
Jehu up to this point, presumably due to the insertion of the Elijah-Elisha material in
chs 9–10 (cf. Gray 1970:563). Although the present location of this regnal total is odd,
it is not without parallel (cf. 1 Kgs 2:11; 11:42; 14:20).

COMMENTARY

In the place where we would expect some discussion of Jehu's 28-year reign, we
find instead the abrupt notice that it was Yahweh's will to "cut down" the size of
Israel's territory (10:32-33). King Hazael of Aram is the human agent, and we are
probably meant to recall that he too was "anointed" by Elisha seemingly to take
from Israel (see 8:11-12). As Hens-Piazza (2006:302) points out, "While we have a
rather extended account of . . . Jehu's violent coup to overthrow the house of Ahab
in establishing himself as Israel's ruler (2 Kgs 9–10), we have no account of his
actual tenure as king."

    So what are we to make of the melancholy list of all the territories conquered by
Hazael that we find here? I have already suggested (in the commentary on 10:1-17)
that these verses may represent "editorial distaste" for Jehu's extreme actions. Perhaps we find here a subtle dig at Jehu's results, too—a mocking of the inevitable
aftermath of so much murder, which was nothing less than abject military defense-
lessness against Israel's perennial enemies to the east. But perhaps I am being too

subtle here; maybe this notice is simply a resumption of the Deuteronomistic History which left off at 1 Kings 16:34 when it was interrupted by the insertion of the extensive Elijah-Elisha narratives (cf. Gray 1970:563). In any case, the sharp diminution of Jehu's territory listed here is said to represent ultimately the very will of Yahweh (10:32). Still, we are also reminded that Jehu did enjoy a relatively long reign and that he was afforded a proper burial in his capital city, with his son Jehoahaz securely on the throne (eventualities quite different from those experienced by his predecessor). Earlier we were also reminded that his dynasty would endure (and, as we will later see, even at times flourish) for four generations—a generous span of history by the brutal standards of the ancient Near East. Such is our final impression of this strangely bold, clearly gifted, but bizarrely zealous king, who did not bring *shalom* [TH7965, ZH8934] (peace) but rather *mirmah* [TH4820, ZH5327] (treachery) to the land of Israel (cf. 9:23; see the commentary on 9:14-29).

◆   **J. Synchronistic History of the Late Divided Monarchy (2 Kgs 11:1-13:13)**

1. Queen Athaliah rules in Judah (11:1-3)

When Athaliah, the mother of King Ahaziah of Judah, learned that her son was dead, she began to destroy the rest of the royal family. ²But Ahaziah's sister Jehosheba, the daughter of King Jehoram,* took Ahaziah's infant son, Joash, and stole him away from among the rest of the king's children, who were about to be killed. She put Joash and his nurse in a bedroom, and they hid him from Athaliah, so the child was not murdered. ³Joash remained hidden in the Temple of the LORD for six years while Athaliah ruled over the land.

11:2 Hebrew *Joram*, a variant spelling of Jehoram.

NOTES

11:1 *Athaliah.* See the second note on 8:26. Athaliah was the Judahite queen mother (*gebirah* [TH1377, ZH1485]) and the daughter or granddaughter of King Omri of Israel. Since her son Ahaziah was dead, her previously secure position as *gebirah* was now in danger (Sweeney 2007:344; but cf. Ben-Barak 1991:28).

11:2 *Ahaziah's sister Jehosheba, the daughter of King Jehoram.* Presumably, then, Jehosheba was a daughter of Athaliah (see Cogan and Tadmor [1988:126], who also point out that "the narrative carefully notes that the queen's own daughter was her undoing"). The parallel text in 2 Chr 22:11 further specifies that Jehosheba was the wife of the high priest Jehoiada (11:4). The name Jehosheba ("Jehoshabeath" in Chronicles, basically an alternative spelling) probably means "Yahweh is abundance," or else "Yahweh is an oath" or the like (cf. the name Bathsheba, as discussed in the note on 1 Kgs 1:13). Concerning the use here of "Joram" for Jehoram of Judah (cf. NLT mg), see the first note on 8:16 (and cf. the first note on 1:17).

Joash. See the note on 12:1.

11:3 *remained hidden in the Temple of the LORD.* Possibly in the high priest's apartment within the Temple precinct, but not within the Temple itself (cf. Cogan and Tadmor 1988:126). In any case, Athaliah, as a foreigner, presumably was not allowed to enter the Temple complex (Sweeney 2007:345).

COMMENTARY

In what may be an excerpt from an originally longer story (see the second note on 11:4), we now read with horror about a veritable "Judean Jehu"—someone in the dynasty-killing business, but this time a female, and this time related to the very dynasty of Ahab which Jehu himself had detested and had sought to exterminate (so she is also in a very real sense a "Judean Jezebel" as well). Sadly, we also hear about yet more killing of innocent children. But what must perhaps concern us even more, as it would have the original Deuteronomistic audience, is the existential threat all this posed to the Davidic dynasty itself, which Yahweh promised would be eternal (2 Sam 7; see "Date and Occasion of Writing" in the Introduction). Could it be that Jehu would in essence (i.e., through Athaliah's vengeful actions) cause the end of *that* dynasty as well as the one he had ended in the north? But there is hope—and from a strange quarter it comes, the priesthood. I indicated earlier in passing (see the commentary on 1 Kgs 1:5-27) that the priesthood naturally had misgivings about the formation of the monarchy. As Halpern says (1981:78), "In the new arrangement [the monarchy] it was the priesthood that stood to lose most." It is thus ironic that it will be nothing other than the institution of the priesthood that will preserve the monarchy's stable existence during this perilous time. The present-day reader will hardly need to be reminded that this is not the only occasion where God has used a rival institution to further his will.

◆   2. Revolt against Athaliah (11:4-12)

⁴In the seventh year of Athaliah's reign, Jehoiada the priest summoned the commanders, the Carite mercenaries, and the palace guards to come to the Temple of the LORD. He made a solemn pact with them and made them swear an oath of loyalty there in the LORD's Temple; then he showed them the king's son.

⁵Jehoiada told them, "This is what you must do. A third of you who are on duty on the Sabbath are to guard the royal palace itself. ⁶Another third of you are to stand guard at the Sur Gate. And the final third must stand guard behind the palace guard. These three groups will all guard the palace. ⁷The other two units who are off duty on the Sabbath must stand guard for the king at the LORD's Temple. ⁸Form a bodyguard around the king and keep your weapons in hand. Kill anyone who tries to break through. Stay with the king wherever he goes."

⁹So the commanders did everything as Jehoiada the priest ordered. The commanders took charge of the men reporting for duty that Sabbath, as well as those who were going off duty. They brought them all to Jehoiada the priest, ¹⁰and he supplied them with the spears and small shields that had once belonged to King David and were stored in the Temple of the LORD. ¹¹The palace guards stationed themselves around the king, with their weapons ready. They formed a line from the south side of the Temple around to the north side and all around the altar.

¹²Then Jehoiada brought out Joash, the king's son, placed the crown on his head, and presented him with a copy of God's laws.* They anointed him and proclaimed him king, and everyone clapped their hands and shouted, "Long live the king!"

11:12 Or *a copy of the covenant.*

NOTES

11:4 *In the seventh year.* This chronological synchronism, like its counterpart in 11:3, reminds us that the brief discussion of Athaliah's "reign" was neither introduced nor concluded with typical regnal formulas, thus signaling by silence its illegitimacy (Sweeney 2007:342). Yet, its seven years must be included in any chronological reckoning of the Davidic dynasty (cf. Cogan and Tadmor 1988:133; also Barnes 1991:140 [citing Bin-Nun 1968:423], 153).

Jehoiada the priest. The Hebrew reads only "Jehoiada"; some LXX mss add the phrase "the priest" (cf. 2 Chr 22:11). His abrupt introduction gives support to the view that the present story is an excerpt from a longer account which had previously mentioned the priest (Cogan and Tadmor 1988:126). (Concerning this interesting collusion between royalty and priesthood, see the previous commentary section.) The name Jehoiada probably means "Yahweh knows" or "Yahweh has regarded."

Carite mercenaries. This was apparently a group of foreign mercenaries loyal to the Davidic house (ABD 1.872), but it is a term (*kari* [TH3746, ZH4133]) of uncertain origin (= the Kethiv of 2 Sam 20:23 [Qere = "Kerethites"]). Sweeney (2007:345), noting its similarity to the noun *kar* [TH3733, ZH4119] (ram), suggests it signifies a military rank akin to the modern-day noncommissioned officer. In any case, these soldiers (who reappear in 11:19) are not to be confused with the "Kerethites and Pelethites" of 1 Kgs 1:38, 44 and elsewhere (cf. NLT mg; also cf. the note on 1 Kgs 1:38). Cogan and Tadmor (1988:126) liken them to the "Swiss Guard" of the Davidides, loyal to that family ever since the early days of David himself.

palace guards. Heb., *ratsim* [TH7323, ZH8132], traditionally, the "outrunners"; Hobbs (1985:139), however, notes that such military terms can change with time, and he would define this group as "the elite royal bodyguard" (cf. 1 Kgs 14:27).

11:5-6 *A third . . . Another third . . . And the final third.* Some of the details concerning this complicated and carefully coordinated set of military maneuvers remain unclear (11:6 is particularly hard to follow in the Hebrew), but its overall import is reasonably clear: All Temple and palace guards, both those normally off duty and those currently on duty, will be strategically deployed to facilitate the crowning of the heretofore-hidden seven-year-old king-designate. In particular (and some of the details of this reconstruction are hazy in places), on or around the Sabbath, when both the soldiers about to go off duty and those just reporting for duty can be mustered at the Temple precincts without undue suspicion, Jehoiada deployed the guards as follows: Of those still on duty, one third of them were divided and sent to the royal palace, another third to the "Sur Gate" (see the next note), and the final third to the gate where the palace guard (*haratsim* [TH7323, ZH8132]; see previous note) would normally enter (this gate is also mentioned in 11:19). The other two-thirds of the total guard (11:7), who had been off duty (cf. the three shifts of Adoniram's labor force in 1 Kgs 5:14), would take up positions throughout the Temple proper to guard the arrival and coronation of the new king. This reconstruction basically follows Cogan and Tadmor (1988:127; cf. Montgomery 1951:419-420). In this way, forces loyal to Queen Athaliah would find it most difficult to interrupt the coronation of Joash.

11:6 *Sur Gate.* Otherwise unknown; the parallel in 2 Chr 23:5 reads "Foundation (*yasod* [TH3247A, ZH3572]) Gate," also otherwise unknown.

11:8 *Kill anyone who tries to break through.* Parallels with the Jehu narrative in the previous chapter are evident (cf. 10:24-25), although here the command is given in a defensive, not offensive, context. (The offensive maneuverings against the "temple of Baal" in Jerusalem will take place in 11:18.)

11:10 *spears and small shields that had once belonged to King David.* Thus, they were apparently over 150 years old! Whether these were the actual spears and shields literally from the time of David (cf. 2 Sam 8:7-8) or some replacement weaponry (cf. 1 Kgs 14:27-28), they probably served as much to signify the continuity of the Davidic dynasty as actual weapons of war.

small shields. This is the NLT translation of the plural form of the word *shelet* [TH7982, ZH8949], a relatively rare term with varying translations in the ancient and contemporary versions. Cogan and Tadmor (1988:128) argue plausibly for the translation "quivers" (cf. Hobbs 1985:141; HALOT 1522-1523).

11:12 *crown.* Heb., *nezer* [TH5145, ZH5694], mentioned as worn by Saul (2 Sam 1:10), also as emblematic of the Davidic kings (cf. Pss 89:39 [40]; 132:18, NIV).

a copy of God's laws. Heb., *ha'eduth* [TH5715, ZH6343], often translated as "the covenant" or "the testimony," and probably signifying some sort of covenant documents (Seow 1999:230). The term *'eduth* is connected with David's kingship in Ps 132:12, and it probably presumes some sort of fulfillment of the "law of the king" in Deut 17:18-20, where a "copy of this Torah" is to be kept with the king at all times. Wiseman (1993:232-233) notes that the British custom of presenting the monarch with a copy of the Bible during the coronation service probably echoes this procedure. In any case, such an action clearly affirms that the power of the monarch is not absolute; rather, the ruler stands under the Torah and the kingship of Yahweh. (For the suggestion that *'eduth* here signifies a second symbol of royal office [the "jewels"], in parallel with the preceding reference to the crown or diadem, see Cogan and Tadmor 1988:128; Yeivin 1974:17-20.)

anointed. See the fourth note on 9:1; the note on 9:3.

Long live the king! See the note on 1 Kgs 1:25.

COMMENTARY

"Beware the changing of the guard!" This dictum, occasionally referenced in business and politics, warns that changes at the top of an organization mean that all the lower-level "troops" must beware of the changes and new dangers they will face. This is a good parallel to the present chapter of 2 Kings. The original changing of the Temple guard at or around the Sabbath seems to have made an excellent time to change the "palace guard" as well—meaning the installation of the new king, unbeknownst to the current queen who thought she (like Jehu) had already exterminated any and all such threats to her reign. How wrong she was, and how fatal that mistake proved to be—but that is the subject of the next part of the story, as we soon shall see.

The changing of the guard, at least in modern times, is a very carefully choreographed procedure (as seen, for example, at Buckingham Palace in London), and this, too, provides a good comparison to the carefully planned positioning of the various contingents of the Temple guard (and others) by the high priest Jehoiada. Seemingly leaving nothing to chance, he first swore the commanders and the soldiers to secrecy, then revealed Joash's existence, then gave orders for careful deployment throughout the Temple and palace complex, and then started the coronation ceremony. His efforts, however, will hardly end there—he will command both the time and the location of Athaliah's death (see the next section), as well as effecting the double covenant (cf. the note on 11:17), the destruction of the Baal temple, and the choreographing of the final scene where King Joash will take his throne and the people rejoice. (Jehoiada will continue to play a prominent part in the Temple repairs in the next chapter as well.) In sum, it is fair to say that Jehoiada easily takes first place in any comparison to the other high priests mentioned in 1–2 Kings (cf. the Introduction for their listing). It is indeed a good thing when Temple and palace act in harmony to further their common goal of bringing God's blessing to the people, especially in times of crisis when continuity of leadership is far from guaranteed. The changing of the guard, elaborate as it was, had as its primary purpose that very goal.

◆   ## 3. The death of Athaliah (11:13-16)

¹³When Athaliah heard the noise made by the palace guards and the people, she hurried to the LORD's Temple to see what was happening. ¹⁴When she arrived, she saw the newly crowned king standing in his place of authority by the pillar, as was the custom at times of coronation. The commanders and trumpeters were surrounding him, and people from all over the land were rejoicing and blowing trumpets. When Athaliah saw all this, she tore her clothes in despair and shouted, "Treason! Treason!"

¹⁵Then Jehoiada the priest ordered the commanders who were in charge of the troops, "Take her to the soldiers in front of the Temple,* and kill anyone who tries to rescue her." For the priest had said, "She must not be killed in the Temple of the LORD." ¹⁶So they seized her and led her out to the gate where horses enter the palace grounds, and she was killed there.

11:15 Or *Bring her out from between the ranks;* or *Take her out of the Temple precincts.* The meaning of the Hebrew is uncertain.

NOTES

11:14 *place of authority by the pillar.* Cf. 23:3, where King Josiah also stands "beside the pillar" and renews the covenant "in the LORD's presence." Possibly one of the Temple pillars is in view (cf. 1 Kgs 7:21-22, and especially their names "Jakin" and "Boaz," as discussed in the note on 1 Kgs 7:21; cf. Gray 1970:575-577).

people from all over the land. This is the NLT rendering for the recurring Hebrew phrase "people of the land" (*'am ha'aretz* [TH5971A/776, ZH6639/824]), which many scholars see as a distinct group (e.g., landed aristocracy?) in preexilic Judah. The only problem is that scholars differ on what the group represents, and whether every reference to this group signifies the same thing. So the NLT translation here can be defended, especially by those who see the "people of the land" as largely outside the confines of Jerusalem and its political entities (see the lengthy discussion in Jones 1984:483-484; cf. Cogan and Tadmor 1988:129-130).

Treason! Treason! This is a different term (*qesher* [TH7195, ZH8004]) than that used by Joram in 9:23 (cf. second note there). The present reference connotes "conspiracy" or the like. For another *qesher,* this time against Joash, see 12:20 [21].

11:15 *Take her to the soldiers in front of the Temple.* As the NLT mg indicates, the Hebrew is hard to follow (especially the reference to "between the ranks"), and commentators suggest that at least one gloss (i.e., a later, explanatory addition) may be present here. Japhet (1993:834) is probably right to emphasize that the overall idea here is to isolate Athaliah from any potential support: "The uprising is presented as a classic *coup d'état;* with the exception of Athaliah's execution, there is no bloodshed."

COMMENTARY

As Seow (1999:230) succinctly puts it, "Athaliah is caught off guard." Apparently completely surprised and entirely unaware of all the elaborate preparations Jehoiada had made for "the changing of the guard" (see the previous commentary), Athaliah first learned of her future fate from the noise of celebration accompanying Joash's coronation ceremony—shouting, rejoicing, the blowing of trumpets. But, like Jezebel, she quickly surmised the situation and correctly labeled it "treason" (at least in the sense of "conspiracy"—cf. the third note on 11:14). She seemingly had no time to escape, however, as she was seized by the guard and led helplessly beyond the horse gate out of the Temple-palace complex, where she soon met her death. As far as we know, besides the death of Mattan the priest of Baal, who was killed in front of the altars (11:18; cf. the pagan priests of Josiah's day in 23:20), these are the only executions that took place that day—a change of power effected with much less violence than those under Jehu and Athaliah herself. Any such executions warrant a moment of sadness, but as Sweeney (2007:343) intimates, not until Athaliah's death is Elijah's prophecy about the killing of every male (and female?) from the house of Ahab finally fulfilled. And yet, as Sweeney further notes, Athaliah, from the house of Ahab, is also an ancestor of the entire house of David beginning with the reign of Ahaziah (8:25-29), a fact that has strong repercussions felt in the days of Josiah, over two centuries later (e.g., Josiah's Ahab-like repentance will forestall destruction and exile until after his death [cf. 22:18-20; 1 Kgs 21:28-29]). The fact that females are involved (Jezebel, Athaliah, and later, Huldah the prophetess) only heightens the comparisons between the episodes. As William Faulkner reminded us, "The past is never dead. It's not even past."

◆   4. Jehoiada's religious reforms (11:17-21 [11:17–12:1])

¹⁷Then Jehoiada made a covenant between the LORD and the king and the people that they would be the LORD's people. He also made a covenant between the king and the people. ¹⁸And all the people of the land went over to the temple of Baal and tore it down. They demolished the altars and smashed the idols to pieces, and they killed Mattan the priest of Baal in front of the altars.

Jehoiada the priest stationed guards at the Temple of the LORD. ¹⁹Then the commanders, the Carite mercenaries, the palace guards, and all the people of the land escorted the king from the Temple of the LORD. They went through the gate of the guards and into the palace, and the king took his seat on the royal throne. ²⁰So all the people of the land rejoiced, and the city was peaceful because Athaliah had been killed at the king's palace.

²¹*Joash* was seven years old when he became king.

11:21a Verse 11:21 is numbered 12:1 in Hebrew text.   11:21b Hebrew *Jehoash*, a variant spelling of Joash.

NOTES

11:17 *a covenant . . . a covenant.* Thus, two different covenants are probably in view: the first, between Yahweh, the king, and the people, representing a renewal of the Davidic (2 Sam 7) and Mosaic covenants between Yahweh and the people (cf. Exod 19:3-8; 24:3-8); and the second (implied in the Hebrew, but not literally stated as such), a political covenant between the king and the people, similar to that made by David with the elders of Israel at Hebron (2 Sam 5:3; cf. 1 Kgs 12:1-20). In this delineation of the covenants I am largely following Gray 1970:579-580 (cf. Cogan and Tadmor 1988:132-133). The likelihood of a double covenant here provides, at best, weak evidence for broader hypotheses concerning, for example, a seven-year cycle of covenant renewal by the Davidic monarchs. As Cogan and Tadmor put it: "No rigid pattern as to how covenants were concluded is discernible in Kings" (1988:132-133).

11:18 *temple of Baal.* A separate "house" or temple apparently existed near, or even within, the walls of Jerusalem, either within the palace complex, perhaps as a shrine for Athaliah, or else outside the walls but nearby. Yadin (1978:127-135) locates it at Ramat Rahel, a prominent hilltop location halfway between Jerusalem and Bethlehem, thus some 2 mi. (3 km) south of the Davidic city, akin to the relative location of the Baal temple near Samaria (cf. the third note on 10:25). In any case, in a frenzy that anticipates Josiah's actions, the altars are demolished, the idols smashed, and the priest Mattan put to death (the name Mattan simply means "gift"; whether "gift [of Baal]" or the like cannot be determined [Wiseman 1993:234-235]). Thus, again in parallel with Israel under Jehu, Baal worship was decisively curtailed in Judah.

11:20 *all the people of the land rejoiced.* Echoes of the time of Solomon's coronation (1 Kgs 1:40, 45) are surely intended here (concerning the "people of the land," see the second note on 11:14).

COMMENTARY

"So all the people of the land rejoiced" (11:20). Such is the final impression we get from this most intriguing chapter of Scripture. As the soldiers cheered Jehu's impending coronation back in 9:13, the "people of the land" rejoiced when his Judahite counterpart Joash, all of seven years old, assumed the throne as well. Whether the "people of the land" represent only part of the Judahite populace is perhaps secondary at this point (see the second note on 11:14), for they, assuredly in coalition with the priests and presumably the military as well, acted to reinstate the Davidic dynasty (they evidently do so again in 14:21; 21:23-24; 23:30). Only two deaths are reported in connection with these events, those of Athaliah and Mattan, the priest of Baal (see the preceding commentary). This was a relatively bloodless coup, not unlike that of Solomon (over Adonijah), which began the book of 1 Kings. No wonder the people rejoiced. Sadly, however, the end of Joash's reign will be like that of his grandmother Athaliah—assassination at the hands of his own officials, who once again plan a conspiracy (*qesher* [TH7195, ZH8004]) against the reigning monarch (cf. 12:20 [21]). At least in regard to his promising start followed by an ignominious end, Joash, alas, resembles both Solomon, the original Temple builder, and Josiah (chs 22–23), another famous Temple cleanser and restorer.

◆   5. Joash repairs the Temple (12:1-16 [12:2-17])

[1]*Joash* began to rule over Judah in the seventh year of King Jehu's reign in Israel. He reigned in Jerusalem forty years. His mother was Zibiah from Beersheba. [2]All his life Joash did what was pleasing in the LORD's sight because Jehoiada the priest instructed him. [3]Yet even so, he did not destroy the pagan shrines, and the people still offered sacrifices and burned incense there.

⁴One day King Joash said to the priests, "Collect all the money brought as a sacred offering to the LORD's Temple, whether it is a regular assessment, a payment of vows, or a voluntary gift. ⁵Let the priests take some of that money to pay for whatever repairs are needed at the Temple."

⁶But by the twenty-third year of Joash's reign, the priests still had not repaired the Temple. ⁷So King Joash called for Jehoiada and the other priests and asked them, "Why haven't you repaired the Temple? Don't use any more money for your own needs. From now on, it must all be spent on Temple repairs." ⁸So the priests agreed not to accept any more money from the people, and they also agreed to let others take responsibility for repairing the Temple.

⁹Then Jehoiada the priest bored a hole in the lid of a large chest and set it on the right-hand side of the altar at the entrance of the Temple of the LORD. The priests guarding the entrance put all of the people's contributions into the chest. ¹⁰Whenever the chest became full, the court secretary and the high priest counted the money that had been brought to the LORD's Temple and put it into bags. ¹¹Then they gave the money to the construction supervisors, who used it to pay the people working on the LORD's Temple—the carpenters, the builders, ¹²the masons, and the stonecutters. They also used the money to buy the timber and the finished stone needed for repairing the LORD's Temple, and they paid any other expenses related to the Temple's restoration.

¹³The money brought to the Temple was not used for making silver bowls, lamp snuffers, basins, trumpets, or other articles of gold or silver for the Temple of the LORD. ¹⁴It was paid to the workmen, who used it for the Temple repairs. ¹⁵No accounting of this money was required from the construction supervisors, because they were honest and trustworthy men. ¹⁶However, the money that was contributed for guilt offerings and sin offerings was not brought into the LORD's Temple. It was given to the priests for their own use.

12:1a Verses 12:1-21 are numbered 12:2-22 in Hebrew text.   12:1b Hebrew *Jehoash*, a variant spelling of Joash; also in 12:2, 4, 6, 7, 18.

NOTES

12:1 [2] Joash. He is not to be confused with "Jehoash" son of Jehoahaz (see 13:10-13); both kings have identical spellings for their names: *yo'ash* [TH3101, ZH3409] or *yeho'ash* [TH3060, ZH3371]; cf. the second NLT mg note on this verse. The Davidic king was introduced in 11:2; he was the only survivor of Athaliah's purge. The name Joash/Jehoash probably means "Yahweh has given" (HALOT 393).

12:2 [3] did what was pleasing. This is a welcome respite from the frequent negative evaluations given to these monarchs (see the Introduction, endnotes 2 and 33). Here, uniquely, credit is given to the high priest Jehoiada for such a positive development (Cogan and Tadmor [1988:137] note that such a reference to the high priest may have been added under the influence of 2 Chr 24:2, 15-22, where Joash's fidelity to Yahweh deteriorates markedly after Jehoiada's death).

12:3 [4] did not destroy the pagan shrines. See endnote 33 of the Introduction for this formulaic Deuteronomistic condemnation, which will be repeated in 14:4; 15:4, 35; in each case it occurs just after an otherwise "pleasing" evaluation of a Davidic ruler.

12:4 [5] a regular assessment, a payment of vows, or a voluntary gift. The Hebrew here is difficult, probably representing "shorthand" for various priestly levies (so Cogan and Tadmor 1988:137). In any case, it should be observed how intense the focus is throughout this chapter on Temple matters (this account possibly stemming from some sort of separate Temple history; cf. Jones 1984:488).

12:5 [6] *repairs.* Heb., *bedeq* [TH919, ZH981], "breach or fissure," a term found a number of times only in this chapter and in 22:5, giving further evidence of the literary ties between the Joash tradition here and the later Josiah Temple-repair tradition (see the commentary).

12:6 [7] *twenty-third year.* A remarkably precise chronological datum, unusual in Kings (but cf. Josiah's 18th year in 22:3; 23:23; also cf. the first note on 1 Kgs 14:25). How this remarkable delay fits in with Joash's desperate attempt to buy off King Hazael with, among other things, the Temple treasury (see 12:18) remains unclear, although some sort of historical connection surely must have existed.

12:7 [8] *From now on.* This was an obvious change in plans, initiated by the king. (Concerning the fact that the king was particularly responsible for the national Temple, see the commentary.)

12:9 [10] *a large chest.* Such "cash boxes" located near temple gates were typical features in Mesopotamia in the first millennium BC. Cogan and Tadmor (1988:138) further note that the Judahite contributor would actually give his offering to the Levitical guard at the gate, who would then deposit the offering in the box on the right side of the altar some distance away in the center of the court.

12:10 [11] *court secretary and the high priest.* Thus both royal and priestly representatives were present, presumably to ensure an honest tally.

put it into bags. The probable meaning of *wayyatsuru* [TH6696, ZH7443], "and they bound, tied up (something into bags?)"; cf. 5:23, where the same verb is used. The silver would then have to be weighed to determine its value, coinage not yet being widely employed (see the next note; also see Wiseman 1993:237; Hurowitz 1986:289-294).

12:11 [12] *money.* Lit., "the silver that was weighed" (*hakkesep hamethukkan* [TH8505, ZH9419], "be weighed"); see previous note.

12:13 [14] *silver bowls, lamp snuffers, basins, trumpets, or other articles of gold or silver.* These Temple vessels and implements were also listed back in 1 Kgs 7:50 (when they were first fashioned in the days of King Solomon); several of these categories of objects will again be listed in 25:14-15 (cf. Jer 52:18-19), when Nebuchadnezzar seizes them as plunder after he has conquered the city of Jerusalem in 586 BC.

12:15 [16] *No accounting . . . was required.* This is paralleled later in the days of King Josiah (22:7), where another form of the same verb (*khashab* [TH2803, ZH3108]) is used (see the commentary for other parallels). As Wiseman (1993:238) reminds us, "Our use of money is always a test of faithfulness."

COMMENTARY

In terms that bring to mind the great reformer king, Josiah (the "hero" of the Deuteronomistic editor—see "Earlier Editions of Kings?" under "Date and Occasion of Writing" in the Introduction), who also took the throne at a young age after his father's assassination, we read that King Joash orchestrated necessary Temple renovations effectively. As Sweeney (2007:351) notes, "Temple renovation is frequently a sign of national restoration as well." And as Wiseman (1993:236) points out, "The maintenance of the main national temple was the responsibility of the king, for the temple served also as a chapel royal. All ancient Near Eastern monarchs record their care for such shrines." So, especially after times of political turmoil and religious apostasy, such "Temple care" would be most expected of a Judahite monarch, especially one who "did what was pleasing" in Yahweh's sight (12:2).

But two issues mar this positive record somewhat. The second is addressed in the next section of commentary, and the first appears here: the role of the high priest Jehoiada. Up to now, his role has been aggressively positive, at least from the point of view of the Deuteronomistic Historian (cf. the entirety of the preceding chapter). But that seems less the case here (probably at least partly due to his advanced age; cf. 2 Chr 24:15). For whatever reason, perhaps laxity on his part (as well as that of Joash himself), actual repairs were not begun until the king's 23rd year of reign (see 12:6)! By this time, the 30-year-old king acted most appropriately in remonstrating, "Why haven't you repaired the Temple?" (12:7). He upbraided the priests, including Jehoiada specifically, and he changed the system of contributions in accord with accepted ancient Near Eastern practice (see Hurowitz 1986:289-294; cf. the notes on 12:9-11). Using fiscally sound practices akin to the modern system of double signatures on church checks (cf. 12:10), the king ensured that the priests would no longer spend the money foolishly. As I wrote some years ago (Barnes 1997a:467), "Whether it be the high priest planning carefully the accession of the youthful King Joash in the previous chapter, or the king urging on the high priest to complete the temple repairs [here], each had his own calling and profession, yet each acted properly to bring about positive change in the other's sphere of influence." We, likewise, should remain open to such mutual occasions for blessings for (and from) others, so that God's true Kingdom can continue to grow and to flourish.

◆   ## 6. The end of Joash's reign (12:17-21 [12:18-22])

[17]About this time King Hazael of Aram went to war against Gath and captured it. Then he turned to attack Jerusalem. [18]King Joash collected all the sacred objects that Jehoshaphat, Jehoram, and Ahaziah, the previous kings of Judah, had dedicated, along with what he himself had dedicated. He sent them all to Hazael, along with all the gold in the treasuries of the LORD's Temple and the royal palace. So Hazael called off his attack on Jerusalem.

[19]The rest of the events in Joash's reign and everything he did are recorded in *The Book of the History of the Kings of Judah.* [20]Joash's officers plotted against him and assassinated him at Beth-millo on the road to Silla. [21]The assassins were Jozacar* son of Shimeath and Jehozabad son of Shomer—both trusted advisers. Joash was buried with his ancestors in the City of David. Then his son Amaziah became the next king.

12:21 As in Greek and Syriac versions; Hebrew reads *Jozabad.*

NOTES

12:17 [18] *King Hazael of Aram.* See the first note on 8:8 concerning this notorious king.

Gath. One of the cities of the original Philistine pentapolis, probably located at Tell es-Safi, where the massive destruction level and a siege trench surrounding the city on three sides accord with the campaign of Hazael cited in the present verse (see Ehrlich 2007; cf. ABD 2.908-909). Tell es-Safi, a prominent mound which can be seen for some distance, is located on the south bank of the Wadi Elah (Wadi 'Ajjur), about 5 mi. (8 km) northwest of Beit Guvrin and 10 mi. (16 km) southeast of Tel Miqne (Ekron). Any takeover of such a strategic site, less than 25 mi. (40 km) from Jerusalem (and on a significant secondary route up to that city), would indeed be cause for panic.

12:18 [19] *sacred objects . . . gold.* It is difficult to date this extensive and desperate payment to the Aramean king (cf. the note on 12:6), but it presumably was made late in Joash's reign, after (ironically) more efficient collection of Temple funds had been effected. In this way, he unwittingly acted like his great-great-grandfather Asa did when confronted by an earlier Aramean king, Ben-hadad I (cf. 1 Kgs 15:18; also see the commentary for further discussion).

12:19 [20] *are recorded in* **The Book of the History of the Kings of Judah.** See "Literary Style" in the Introduction.

12:20 [21] *plotted . . . assassinated.* The Hebrew for "plotted" (lit., "conspired a conspiracy") comes from the root *qashar* [TH7194, ZH8003], seen earlier in Athaliah's cry (11:14). "And assassinated" (*wayyakku* [TH5221, ZH5782]) is literally "and they struck down." Apart from Athaliah herself, this is the first example of a Davidic ruler being killed by conspirators (although Amaziah, Joash's son, will eventually suffer a similar fate [see 14:19], as will Amon son of Manasseh a century later [21:23]). The motive for this assassination is unclear in the present Kings account; in 2 Chr 24:25 it is stated that it took place because Joash had previously put Zechariah son of Jehoiada to death.

Beth-millo. Presumably, "house of the Millo;" this location remains obscure, although, if the assassination took place in Jerusalem (which is quite probable), the "Millo" here may be a reference to the famous "filling" or supporting terraces located on the northeast side of the City of David (cf. the second note on 1 Kgs 9:15 for details). Another Beth-millo, however, was located in Shechem during the period of the judges (Judg 9:6, 20).

Silla. This reference also remains very obscure. Possibilities include some sort of "ramp" or street in Jerusalem, or even a commercial district in that city; or else this possibly is a reference to going toward "Sela," an Edomite city to the southeast of the Dead Sea (Jones 1984:495-496; ABD 6.23).

12:21 [22] *Jozacar . . . Jehozabad.* The MT (Codex Leningradensis) reads *yozabad* and *yehozabad* [TH3075, ZH3379] (cf. NLT mg), basically two versions of the same name (cf. 2 Chr 24:26, which also reflects the same Hebrew root [*zabad*] for both names). This is indeed possible, given that the men have different patronymics (fathers' names); cf. NIV. But since many Hebrew mss read *yozakar* for the first name, a simple confusion of Beth for Kaph and Daleth for Resh may have taken place, confusions that could easily occur in the transmission of Hebrew names throughout much of this era (the LXX, Targum, Vulgate, and the Peshitta also reflect Jozacar).

both trusted advisers. The NLT is probably too interpretive here; the MT simply reads "his servants" (*'abadayw* [TH5650, ZH6269]), which, to be sure, can often refer to high officials in the palace.

Amaziah. See 14:1-21.

COMMENTARY

This second negative note marring the reign of Joash is, alas, significant indeed. Here, Joash is more resonant with Asa than with Josiah. Asa bribed an Aramean king to relieve pressure from the northern kingdom (Israel) on Judah and Jerusalem (see the note on 12:18), while Josiah ironically sought occasion to needlessly oppose an Egyptian expedition through the Levant to help relieve Assyria (see 23:29). Joash purchased Aramean peace by stripping both palace and Temple of treasure. Ironically, he also emulated "good" King Hezekiah, who did much the same thing to pay off the Assyrian king Sennacherib when the latter was also threatening the city of Jerusalem (18:13-16). What are we to think of these emergency allocations of

Temple funds? As Cogan and Tadmor (1988:141) laconically put it, "The occasional seizure of temple treasures to pay off foreign attackers was not to a king's credit."

We who live in the United States often forget what it must have been like to live in a small, militarily weak country, often facing severe pressure from powerful enemies. But neither the preexilic Judahite royal annalists nor their exilic and postexilic audiences could ever entertain that luxury. In my discussion of the Asa "payoff" to Ben-hadad I (see the commentary on 1 Kgs 15:9-24), I refrained from harsh censure of his desperate action to preserve his capital city. I even intimated that this was, somehow, part of the mysterious activity of the true God, moving in mysterious ways, his wonders to perform. Is Asa to be censured for his action to save his city? The evidence remains, like it so often does in real life, mixed. And that is what I suspect is the case with Joash as well. Choon-Leong Seow (1999:233) is on target in his helpful summary of these Asa/Joash parallels:

> All the efforts of Joash to do right seem to be negated, however, when Hazael of Aram threatens Jerusalem. To buy Hazael off, Joash takes from the temple treasury the votive gifts deposited there by his predecessors, Jehoshaphat, Joram, and Ahaziah. History seems to repeat itself, for the reformist king Asa had long ago taken from the same treasury in order to buy off the Arameans (1 Kgs 15:18). The temple treasury, which was depleted by Asa and slowly replenished by his successors, is again being raided by a reformist king in the face of an Aramean threat. Even reformist kings like Asa and Joash do not perform adequately in the interest of the Lord's house.

I suspect, however, Seow's last sentence could be subjected to some critique. It is true that both the reformer kings Asa and Joash (as is also the case with the "best" kings of all, Hezekiah and Josiah) paid a high price for some of their international policies, especially when they bought off, or attempted to thwart militarily, their powerful enemies. And that is certainly far from "adequate" performance as we might measure it today. But Asa did secure some 50 or so years of peace. Hezekiah did survive Sennacherib's siege of the city. (Josiah's final military adventure had a less positive outcome, an issue which will have to be addressed in turn.) Here, King Joash does succeed in avoiding near-certain military disaster at the hands of Hazael (in vivid contrast to his northern counterpart, Jehoahaz, as the very next passage [13:3-7] will soon make clear). The reasons for Joash's assassination, to be sure, remain murky in the present passage (cf. the first note on 12:20); possibly they are meant to be seen as a reaction to his emptying the treasury to pay off Hazael. But, in any case, both he as well as his predecessor, Asa, enjoyed relatively long reigns on the throne of David (41 and 40 years, respectively). That will not be quite the case for either Hezekiah or Josiah (29 and 31 years, respectively). Life is rarely as formulaic as our moralistic preaching would make it, and that may well be one of the teaching points of the present chapter of 2 Kings.

◆   ## 7. Jehoahaz rules in Israel (13:1-9)

Jehoahaz son of Jehu began to rule over Israel in the twenty-third year of King Joash's reign in Judah. He reigned in Samaria seventeen years. [2]But he did what was evil in the LORD's sight. He followed the example of Jeroboam son of Nebat, continuing the sins that Jeroboam had led Israel to commit. ³So the LORD was very angry with Israel, and he allowed King Hazael of Aram and his son Ben-hadad to defeat them repeatedly.

⁴Then Jehoahaz prayed for the LORD's help, and the LORD heard his prayer, for he could see how severely the king of Aram was oppressing Israel. ⁵So the LORD provided someone to rescue the Israelites from the tyranny of the Arameans. Then Israel lived in safety again as they had in former days.

⁶But they continued to sin, following the evil example of Jeroboam. They also allowed the Asherah pole in Samaria to remain standing. ⁷Finally, Jehoahaz's army was reduced to 50 charioteers, 10 chariots, and 10,000 foot soldiers. The king of Aram had killed the others, trampling them like dust under his feet.

⁸The rest of the events in Jehoahaz's reign—everything he did and the extent of his power—are recorded in *The Book of the History of the Kings of Israel.* ⁹When Jehoahaz died, he was buried in Samaria. Then his son Jehoash* became the next king.

13:9 Hebrew *Joash,* a variant spelling of Jehoash; also in 13:10, 12, 13, 14, 25.

NOTES

13:1 Jehoahaz son of Jehu. This is the second of what will be a total of five northern kings from the Jehu dynasty (if Zechariah's six months on the throne before his assassination [15:8] is included in the list). The name Jehoahaz probably means "Yahweh has grasped, taken hold of" (cf. the name "Ahaziah," as well as the shortened form, "Ahaz"). The identical name of the late-seventh-century Judahite king, Jehoahaz son of Josiah (cf. 23:30), has recently been attested on a stamp seal (Cogan and Tadmor 1988:142, 303).

twenty-third year. As already noted (see notes on 8:25 and 8:26; cf. the "Excursus on Chronology" in the Introduction), some of these synchronisms seem to be secondary calculations. Unless there is some sort of coregency implied by these numbers, antedating practice (counting the first partial year of reign as "year one") is clearly now in effect (Cogan and Tadmor 1988:142-143; Thiele 1983:56-60).

13:2 Jeroboam. Concerning the nature of the infamous "sins of Jeroboam," see the commentary on 1 Kgs 12:25-33.

13:3 Hazael . . . Ben-hadad. Concerning these Aramean kings, as well as the possibility that the "Ben-hadad" of 6:24 refers to the same person, see the second note on that verse.

13:5 someone to rescue. This is a rather diffuse translation for a seemingly specific reference to a "savior" or "rescuer" (*moshia'* [TH3467B, ZH4635]), akin to those mentioned in the book of Judges (Judg 3:9, 15). See the commentary for details.

13:6 But they continued to sin. This is a resumption of the formulaic reference to the sins of Jeroboam (13:2) and their aftermath (13:3). Cogan and Tadmor (1988:143-144, 213) term this a *Wiederaufnahme* (resumptive repetition), where an interrupted narrative or exposition is taken up and continued by repeating a key word or phrase (thus implying that in the present instance the Deuteronomistic writer has incorporated the earlier, sympathetic northern tradition found in 13:4-5 into the present narrative; thus, those verses do not represent a later interpolation).

Asherah pole. See the note on 1 Kgs 14:15 for a discussion about the nature and significance of this popular cultic symbol. This particular Asherah pole seems to date to the days of Ahab (cf. 1 Kgs 16:33); thus it survived Jehu's actions against the Baal cult (for other references to the incomplete nature of Jehu's reforms, see 2 Kgs 10:29, 31).

13:7 reduced. The chariot corps are indeed reduced drastically from the numbers attested in Ahab's time (cf. the note on 1 Kgs 16:29), though the number of foot soldiers listed still represents a sizable army (but hardly a potent one; as Cogan and Tadmor [1988:143] point out, it was the number of mobile units deployed that would largely determine who gained the victory between Aram and Israel).

dust. Heb., *'apar* [TH6083, ZH6760], here connected with the verb *dush* [TH1758, ZH1889], "to trample" or even "to thresh" (cf. NIV, NRSV; also the imagery found in Isa 41:15; Amos 1:3).

13:8 *are recorded in* The Book of the History of the Kings of Israel. See "Literary Style" in the Introduction.

COMMENTARY

In what is yet another example of the "leapfrog" treatment of the kings of Israel and Judah (for details concerning this Deuteronomistic editorial patterning, see both "Literary Style" in the Introduction and the commentary on 1 Kgs 15:1-8), we now turn back to the north, with a brief and largely formulaic examination of the first of two kings from the Jehu dynasty, Jehoahaz. Actually there are very few specifics included in these first nine verses (with 13:7 being the notable exception), but there is nonetheless a fair amount of theology to be found in this brief section. Besides the formulaic condemnation of the king for following the ways of Jeroboam (13:2), there is a surprising interlude found in 13:4-5 concerning Jehoahaz's intercession to Yahweh (akin in a sense to that of the later hero, King Hezekiah, in 19:1-7), as well as Yahweh's clear and positive response in providing a "savior" (see the note on 13:5) to bring about "safety" for Israel as they had experienced in days of yore. I use that quaint expression since the original Hebrew in 13:5 makes an equally quaint reference to the northerners living "in their tents as in times past." Although the expression is both quaint and vague in its intended timeframe, it is hardly insignificant, recalling as it does parallels in the book of Judges where, as the result of earnest supplication, Yahweh responded by providing a "savior" or "deliverer" to effect such blessing, often for an entire generation (cf. "forty years" in Judg 3:11; 5:31; 8:28; and "eighty years" [!] in Judg 3:30). In sum, the fact that the Deuteronomistic editors preserve such optimistic historical references (see the first note on 13:6), a phenomenon we will run into again (see 13:23), shows that they are not as monolithic in their theology as some scholars allege. Certainly their "pet peeve" is evident in the repeated denunciation of the "sins of Jeroboam," but that hardly exhausts their theological repertoire, even in reference to the northern kings. (Still, the negative, anti-Jeroboam refrain is currently placed in a dominant position vis-à-vis the "savior" theology in the present editing of the book, a status not to be dismissed lightly.)

Nevertheless, it is the "savior" reference that I want to focus on at this juncture. In the first of at least three examples (see also 13:23; 14:26-27), Yahweh's compassion for the northern kingdom of Israel has become evident, even emphasized. In terms more reminiscent of the cycle of apostasy, oppression, supplication, and deliverance found in Judges (cf., e.g., Judg 2:11-19), Yahweh raised up these "heroes" to give some relief to his often wayward, but still very needy, people (see Judg 2:18; cf. Seow [1999:234], who notes that in the period of the Jehu kings, "Israel seemed to have been treated in a manner more typical of Judah: The ruling dynasty endured, and Israel experienced the persistence of God's grace despite the sins of the kings").

But who specifically is this "savior" (13:5; NLT, "someone to rescue")? Commentators vary in their answers (see Cogan and Tadmor 1988:143 for an extensive listing of the various possibilities, both Israelite and non-Israelite); but an immediately attractive option, exegetically, must be the prophet Elisha (cf. 13:14-21). Always in the Judges parallels, the "savior"—whether *moshia'*[TH3467B, ZH4635], as here (cf. Judg 3:9, 15); or else "judge" (*shopet* [TH8199A, ZH9149]), as in Judg 2:16, 18; or even "prophet" (*nabi'* [TH5030, ZH5566]; see Judg 6:8; cf. Judg 4:4)—is an Israelite, and is often a spiritual leader as well as a military one (admittedly, the prophet in Judg 6:8 is an imperfect parallel, inasmuch as Gideon, not he, brings deliverance and military leadership). (For those who see the "Ben-hadad" of 6:24 as referring to this time, the antipathy between prophet and king described in 6:24–7:20 would detract from the Elisha option, to be sure, but all such parallels must, at best, remain hypothetical.) But a strong historical case may be made that the savior here is the Assyrian king Adad-nirari III (see, especially, Wiseman 1993:240-241), whose vigorous attacks finally brought Aram to bay. Or possibly, Jehoahaz's son Jehoash may be the "savior" (*moshia'*) in question. Cogan and Tadmor point to the use of other forms of the cognate verb *hoshia'* [TH3467, ZH3828] (to deliver) in connection with that king and his son Jeroboam II (13:17; 14:27), but I would submit that the prophet Elisha remains a better candidate.

Admittedly, all this speculation represents the classic "argument from silence," inasmuch as the biblical text remains quiet concerning any specific identity of the present "savior" (contrast Hobbs 1985:167-168 [citing Carroll 1969:400-415], who makes a strong case for parallels here with Deut 26:5-9, where Moses himself would serve as the prophetic archetype for a string of prophets, Elisha being the present example [cf. Leithart 2006:232]). In any case Jehoahaz, the Israelite king, was correct to call upon Yahweh, the Israelite deity, who in turn had compassion on his people and sent the "savior" to deliver them from their enemies and allow them to live in "safety" as heretofore. God is faithful, as is especially evident when his human king acts in humility and obedience. And that is the clear message of the present nine verses of 2 Kings.

◆ 8. Jehoash rules in Israel (13:10-13)

¹⁰Jehoash son of Jehoahaz began to rule over Israel in the thirty-seventh year of King Joash's reign in Judah. He reigned in Samaria sixteen years. ¹¹But he did what was evil in the LORD's sight. He refused to turn from the sins that Jeroboam son of Nebat had led Israel to commit.

¹²The rest of the events in Jehoash's reign and everything he did, including the extent of his power and his war with King Amaziah of Judah, are recorded in *The Book of the History of the Kings of Israel.* ¹³When Jehoash died, he was buried in Samaria with the kings of Israel. Then his son Jeroboam II became the next king.

NOTES

13:10 *Jehoash son of Jehoahaz.* Now, the third of the five northern kings from the Jehu dynasty is dealt with. Jehoash (not to be confused with his similarly named southern counterpart [cf. the note on 12:1]) is sometimes called "Joash" (cf. the NLT mg note on 13:9). The name of this king is attested on an Assyrian stela found at Tell al-Rimah in northern Mesopotamia, dated to the reign of Adad-nirari III (Wiseman 1993:240; cf. Page 1968:139-153, especially pp. 144-145, 148-149). Significantly, Jehoash is called "the Samarian" (*Yu-'a-su Sa-mer-ri-na-a*), with any reference to the "dynasty of Omri" no longer to be found (see the commentary on 9:1-13 regarding Assyrian references to Jehu).

13:11 *Jeroboam.* See note on 13:2.

13:12-13 These verses in their entirety are repeated in 14:15-16, giving further evidence of the complicated nature of the Deuteronomistic editing of this material (cf. the first note on 13:6). Cogan and Tadmor (1988:145) see these verses as secondary, taken from their counterparts in the next chapter when the entire northern tradition about Jehoash's victory over Amaziah was removed to its present location in the latter's regnal material.

13:12 *war with King Amaziah.* See 14:8-14 for the details of this northern victory.

***are recorded in* The Book of the History of the Kings of Israel.** See "Literary Style" in the Introduction.

13:13 *Jeroboam II.* See 14:23-29.

C O M M E N T A R Y

The formulaic and stereotypic nature of this passage, evident enough to the casual reader or hearer of this book, is further emphasized by the repetition of the contents of 13:12-13 in 14:15-16. In the present regnal summary, however, there is no hint of Jehoash's remarkable victory over Amaziah at Beth-shemesh and his subsequent sack of Jerusalem, just a brief note that he "fought" with him. Thus, I would see the primacy of the Judahite material once again illustrated in 1–2 Kings, a hypothesis I have entertained for some time in light of the importance of the regnal totals from the Judahite king-list in the overall scheme of the book (see "Excursus on Chronology" in the Introduction).

Pertinent historical information which might also have fit in the present passage of 2 Kings has been placed in the material concerning Amaziah (cf. the note on 13:12-13). Analogously, the subsequent reference to Jehoash's repeated victories over the Arameans (13:24-25) is placed rather awkwardly, some verses after his own death notice has been given (13:13). Still, the overall "leapfrog" ordering of all these regnal notices reinforces the essential completeness of the formal listing of all the kings, northern and southern, included in the Deuteronomistic work, as well as editorial attempts to be relentlessly chronological in placement. (For a remarkable succession of such bare-bones notices, with no less than seven northern and southern kings chronologically interleaved, see ch 15.)

◆   **K. A Prophetic Story from the Elisha Cycle: Elisha's Final Prophecy (2 Kgs 13:14-25)**

¹⁴When Elisha was in his last illness, King Jehoash of Israel visited him and wept over him. "My father! My father! I see the chariots and charioteers of Israel!" he cried.

¹⁵Elisha told him, "Get a bow and some arrows." And the king did as he was told. ¹⁶Elisha told him, "Put your hand on the bow," and Elisha laid his own hands on the king's hands.

¹⁷Then he commanded, "Open that eastern window," and he opened it. Then he said, "Shoot!" So he shot an arrow. Elisha proclaimed, "This is the LORD's arrow, an arrow of victory over Aram, for

you will completely conquer the Arameans at Aphek."

¹⁸Then he said, "Now pick up the other arrows and strike them against the ground." So the king picked them up and struck the ground three times. ¹⁹But the man of God was angry with him. "You should have struck the ground five or six times!" he exclaimed. "Then you would have beaten Aram until it was entirely destroyed. Now you will be victorious only three times."

²⁰Then Elisha died and was buried.

Groups of Moabite raiders used to invade the land each spring. ²¹Once when some Israelites were burying a man, they spied a band of these raiders. So they hastily threw the corpse into the tomb of Elisha and fled. But as soon as the body touched Elisha's bones, the dead man revived and jumped to his feet!

²²King Hazael of Aram had oppressed Israel during the entire reign of King Jehoahaz. ²³But the LORD was gracious and merciful to the people of Israel, and they were not totally destroyed. He pitied them because of his covenant with Abraham, Isaac, and Jacob. And to this day he still has not completely destroyed them or banished them from his presence.

²⁴King Hazael of Aram died, and his son Ben-hadad became the next king. ²⁵Then Jehoash son of Jehoahaz recaptured from Ben-hadad son of Hazael the towns that had been taken from Jehoash's father, Jehoahaz. Jehoash defeated Ben-hadad on three occasions, and he recovered the Israelite towns.

NOTES

13:14 *last illness.* Lit., "the illness from which he would die."

My father! See note on 6:21.

chariots and charioteers of Israel! See the note on 2:12. If the speaker here is indeed the king (cf. Wiseman 1993:241), he stands in the place of the prophet Elisha vis-à-vis Elijah in 2:12 (cf. Seow 1999:237).

13:15 *Get a bow and some arrows.* The necessary prerequisite for the following two sign actions dictated by the prophet Elisha, the first of which is to shoot an arrow out the eastern window (13:17), the second, to strike the ground repeatedly with the remaining arrows (13:18).

13:16 *Elisha laid his own hands on the king's hands.* This is a physical act of solidarity with the compliant king (see the commentary).

13:17 *an arrow of victory.* The word for "victory" (*teshu'ah* [TH8668, ZH9591]) comes from the same root as "savior" (*moshia'* [TH3467B, ZH4635], 13:5; cf. the note there). The action of shooting the arrow (as well as the later striking of the ground with the remaining arrows in 13:18) represents a "miniature" of the future events they prefigure (Hobbs 1985:169, citing H. Wheeler Robinson 1946:35-36: "a miniature of that larger activity of God which it [the symbolic act of the prophet] initiates"), rather than "sympathetic magic" aimed to effect change through paranormal means.

Aphek. The precise location of this city in Transjordan remains uncertain (see note on 1 Kgs 20:26).

13:19 *victorious only three times.* Although the reason for Elisha's unexpected, harsh criticism of the king for striking the earth only three times with the arrows remains obscure, the overall message of grave concern for the northern kingdom in the face of Aram remains oddly touching (see the commentary). Elijah's parting words to King Ahaziah (1:16-17), though harshly critical like Elisha's words here, betray no such concern for the nation and its future.

13:20 *Groups of Moabite raiders.* There is possibly an indication of Elisha being buried near Jericho or Gilgal or somewhere in the lower Jordan River valley (Gray 1970:598), which would, among other things, fit typologically with Elijah's previous place of translation into heaven at or near the Jordan River not far from Jericho (2:1-18; cf. especially 2:11-13, 18). The actual location of Elisha's burial spot, however, remains unknown.

13:21 *the dead man revived.* Resurrections have already been effected by the prophets Elijah (1 Kgs 17:17-24) and Elisha (2 Kgs 4:8-37). Perhaps in another literary acknowledgment of the "double portion" of Elijah's spirit resting on Elisha (see note on 2:9), we find yet another one taking place here. But in contrast to Elijah, who never actually dies or is buried, Elisha, after a ministry of some 60 years, does grow ill and die, and he is presumably given a conventional burial (for details concerning Israelite burial practices, see the commentary on 1 Kgs 13:1-34). Elisha, however, is able to bring forth life even after his own sad demise.

13:22, 24 *Hazael . . . Ben-hadad.* See note on 13:3. Regarding the lengthy (and probably not original) Lucianic addition found in some Greek mss at 13:22, see Cogan and Tadmor 1988:149.

13:23 *covenant.* Here is one of the most remarkable theological references to be found in 1–2 Kings. In contrast to the repeated references to the Davidic covenant for the southern kings (see "The 'Lamp' of David" in "Major Themes" in the Introduction for details), we find here a unique reference to some sort of "northern" covenant, made in the names of Abraham, Isaac, and Jacob (see 1 Kgs 18:36 for the only other reference to these patriarchs in 1–2 Kings; for the patriarchal covenant itself, see Gen 15:17-21; 17:1-14). Yahweh thereby ensured that his people Israel would never be destroyed (the reference "to this day," however, probably dates the tradition found in this verse as preexilic, and possibly pre-Hezekian [see the next note]). For further discussion of this notable covenant and God's love and grace as relates to the northern kingdom, see the commentary.

And to this day. Lit., "until now" ('*ad-'attah* [TH6258, ZH6964]). Although not literally one of the "until this day" formulas examined by Childs (1963:279-292; for details, see the note on 2:22), this reference still confirms the firsthand (hence relatively early) dating of this unique verse (cf. the previous note), as well as the confirmatory testimony of its original author.

13:25 *Israelite towns.* These are probably towns west of the Jordan that had been lost in the days of Jehoahaz, since the entire northern Transjordanian area had been taken over by Aram in the days of Jehu (cf. 10:32-33). Jehoash's son Jeroboam II will eventually reverse these humiliating defeats (see 14:25, 28).

COMMENTARY

In this odd confluence of short vignettes, we find a curious concern for the welfare of the northern kingdom that is not characteristically found in 1–2 Kings (but see the commentary on 13:1-9). To be sure, we encounter here once again a familiar example of prophetic exasperation with the king, which can be compared to Elijah's frustration with King Ahaziah of Israel in 1:1-18—a story that is all the more parallel to the present one inasmuch as it depicts the last recorded event in Elijah's life and prophetic ministry, with a particular focus on patterns of "three." But the three battles (13:25) against Ben-hadad (at least one taking place at Aphek) in the present text find a closer parallel with the battles against an earlier Ben-hadad (one at Aphek) in the days of King Ahab (1 Kgs 20:1-34; curiously, in that text there is also a sequel condemning the king for not treating Ben-hadad more severely [1 Kgs 20:35-43; cf. 13:19]). But of more immediate interest is the intriguing commingling of prophet and king in King Jehoash's words (13:14): "My father! My father! I see the chariots and charioteers of Israel!" As Seow has intimated (1999:237), this parallel seems to place King Jehoash in the same relationship with the soon-to-depart Elisha as Elisha himself had with the soon-to-depart Elijah in chapter 2. As Leithart (2006:235-236) argues from a more general overview of this chapter:

> Even in his death, Elisha continues to minister life, but after 2 Kgs. 13 Elisha is gone, and his memory vanishes instantly. . . . Nor is there any mention of the 'sons of the prophets' after one of them anoints Jehu (9:1). . . . [Both Elijah and Elisha effected many miracles, which Leithart lists in turn.] And what was the long-term result of this burst of miraculous activity? Almost nil. After a long and wild ride with the prophets, the narrator turns back to the dry-as-dust chronicle, chanting out the irreversible march toward the now-inevitable disaster of exile.

I would quibble with some of the specifics of Leithart's simplistic summary statements here, but I think he is nevertheless on to something important: The prophets are dead and gone, but the history continues with king after king marching toward inevitable exile. This is where Seow's earlier observation gains poignancy. In almost a tactile way (see note on 13:16), it is now the king who takes the place of the prophet—it is none other than Jehoash who will replace Elisha, hardly perfectly, but still significantly. How do we know this? I submit that it is not just the parallel in 13:14 (or, for that matter, in 13:4-5) that "seals the deal." As Leithart puts it, "Elisha gave life from the grave, but—and this is crucial—his bones *remained* there" (2006:236, emphasis in the original). And Leithart's conclusion is inevitable (to the Christian reader) and poignant: "Clinging to the prophet is the way of life, but what happens to that life when the prophet dies and stays dead? Israel will not be saved by any ordinary prophet or by any extraordinary one. Israel needs a prophet who would give life on the other side of the grave by triumphing, once for all, over the grave."

How true that observation is—and how profound. Yet we can have more hope than Leithart seems to have in regard to the interim time period between Elisha and the greater Elisha, Jesus (for this typology, see the commentary on 2:1-18 and with regard to Elijah, 1 Kgs 19:19-21). I say this because of the clear, unequivocal, surprising—yet strangely satisfying—comments in 13:23 that do the job. Yahweh has *not* forgotten his people Israel, nor his covenant with the ancient patriarchs Abraham, Isaac, and Jacob (from whom *all* the tribes of Israel have descended). And if the book of Revelation is to be taken literally, he *will* not forget any of his tribes or any of his people (cf. Rev 7:1-8). Elisha the prophet is gone, but the king remains. He is hardly the same in status as the prophet, but perhaps that observation actually matters less than we might think—after all, Jehoash's father Jehoahaz knew how to intercede with God as well as any prophet (13:4-5). And Jehoash's son Jeroboam II knew how to "win through" as well as any previous prophet-led king (14:25-28). No, the king can stand in, at least to some degree, for the prophet—at least, in some of the verses found in the present chapter. Of course, the Deuteronomists have condemned all the northern kings, and mostly because they "refused to turn from the sins [of Jeroboam I]" (13:11; cf. the commentary on 1 Kgs 12:25-33); but that should not obscure the apparently earlier, and certainly more optimistic, literary stratum that commends these three Jehuite kings.

What are we to make of Elisha's stern words to the king for his striking the ground only three times? Whether due to lack of effort or enthusiasm, or lack of prophetic foresight, surely these words represent the kind of sharp rebuke a master would have for his disciple (seen also with *the* Master and his disciples—e.g., Matt 16:7-11, 21-23; 17:17; Mark 10:13-16). Could the king be a disciple of the prophet? Could the king be seen as one of the "sons of the prophets"? Why not? Moses, the greatest of the prophets (see Deut 34:10-12), was also the political leader of the nation of Israel for some 40 years. When kings arose in the land (see Deut 17:14-20, the so-called "law of the king"), they were commanded to know well Moses's words. Might not kings (even Jehuite ones) also follow later prophets (who were "like Moses"; cf. Deut 18:15-18), acting to intercede and to proclaim his words, among the monarchy? And if this seems too strange to traditional biblical interpreters—what else are we to do with 13:4-5? In any case, we truly know that God's people have *not* been forgotten by their loving and gracious deity—that is the unequivocal message we can take away from the present chapter. And that is no small consolation to any contemporary reader of this ancient portion of the Word of God.

◆   ## L. Synchronistic History of the Late Divided Monarchy, Concluded (2 Kgs 14:1–17:41)

1. Amaziah rules in Judah (14:1-22)

Amaziah son of Joash began to rule over Judah in the second year of the reign of King Jehoash* of Israel. ²Amaziah was twenty-five years old when he became king, and he reigned in Jerusalem twenty-nine years. His mother was Jehoaddin from Jerusalem. ³Amaziah did what was pleasing in the LORD's sight, but not like his ancestor David. Instead, he followed the example of his father, Joash. ⁴Amaziah did not destroy the pagan shrines, and the people still offered sacrifices and burned incense there.

⁵When Amaziah was well established as king, he executed the officials who had assassinated his father. ⁶However, he did not kill the children of the assassins, for he obeyed the command of the LORD as written by Moses in the Book of the Law: "Parents must not be put to death for the sins of their children, nor children for the sins of their parents. Those deserving to die must be put to death for their own crimes."*

⁷Amaziah also killed 10,000 Edomites in the Valley of Salt. He also conquered Sela and changed its name to Joktheel, as it is called to this day.

⁸One day Amaziah sent messengers with this challenge to Israel's king Jehoash, the son of Jehoahaz and grandson of Jehu: "Come and meet me in battle!"*

⁹But King Jehoash of Israel replied to King Amaziah of Judah with this story: "Out in the Lebanon mountains, a thistle sent a message to a mighty cedar tree: 'Give your daughter in marriage to my son.' But just then a wild animal of Lebanon came by and stepped on the thistle, crushing it!

¹⁰"You have indeed defeated Edom, and you are proud of it. But be content with your victory and stay at home! Why stir up trouble that will only bring disaster on you and the people of Judah?"

¹¹But Amaziah refused to listen, so King Jehoash of Israel mobilized his army against King Amaziah of Judah. The two

armies drew up their battle lines at Beth-shemesh in Judah. [12]Judah was routed by the army of Israel, and its army scattered and fled for home. [13]King Jehoash of Israel captured Judah's king, Amaziah son of Joash and grandson of Ahaziah, at Beth-shemesh. Then he marched to Jerusalem, where he demolished 600 feet* of Jerusalem's wall, from the Ephraim Gate to the Corner Gate. [14]He carried off all the gold and silver and all the articles from the Temple of the LORD. He also seized the treasures from the royal palace, along with hostages, and then returned to Samaria.

[15]The rest of the events in Jehoash's reign and everything he did, including the extent of his power and his war with King Amaziah of Judah, are recorded in *The Book of the History of the Kings of Israel.*

[16]When Jehoash died, he was buried in Samaria with the kings of Israel. And his son Jeroboam II became the next king.

[17]King Amaziah of Judah lived for fifteen years after the death of King Jehoash of Israel. [18]The rest of the events in Amaziah's reign are recorded in *The Book of the History of the Kings of Judah.*

[19]There was a conspiracy against Amaziah's life in Jerusalem, and he fled to Lachish. But his enemies sent assassins after him, and they killed him there. [20]They brought his body back to Jerusalem on a horse, and he was buried with his ancestors in the City of David.

[21]All the people of Judah had crowned Amaziah's sixteen-year-old son, Uzziah,* as king in place of his father, Amaziah. [22]After his father's death, Uzziah rebuilt the town of Elath and restored it to Judah.

14:1 Hebrew *Joash*, a variant spelling of Jehoash; also in 14:13, 23, 27.   14:6 Deut 24:16.   14:8 Hebrew *Come, let us look one another in the face.*   14:13 Hebrew *400 cubits* [180 meters].   14:21 Hebrew *Azariah,* a variant spelling of Uzziah.

NOTES

14:1 Amaziah. Already cited in 12:21 as succeeding his father Joash to the throne after the latter's assassination, he is the 10th king of the Davidic dynasty. Amaziah's name means "Yahweh has been strong, mighty" (cf. the short form of the name, "Amoz," borne by the father of the prophet Isaiah [Isa 1:1]).

14:2 twenty-five years old . . . reigned in Jerusalem twenty-nine years. The length of reign here seems excessive if it doesn't include any coregencies (Barnes 1991:156 notes l and m; also Cogan and Tadmor 1988:154); possibly a 15-year coregency with his son Uzziah (or Azariah) should be included here as part of the regnal total (cf. 14:17). In any case, the curious "25/29" correspondence with Hezekiah (who also comes to the throne at the age of 25 and reigns 29 years [see 18:2]) led me some time ago to posit some sort of grand *inclusio* between these two kings in a hypothetical Judahite king-list used by the final Deuteronomist (see Barnes 1991:147-148; cf. "Literary Style" in the Introduction for a basic introduction to this Judahite king-list).

14:3 did what was pleasing. This is the second in a string of five positive notices for the Judahite kings (see endnote 33 of the Introduction for details); in every case, however, the positive notice is tempered with a reminder that the pagan shrines still had not been removed.

14:5 executed the officials who had assassinated his father. See 12:20-21. Unfortunately, Amaziah himself eventually suffered the same fate as his father.

14:6 obeyed. Here is a positive indication that Amaziah was implicitly fulfilling the requirement specified in the "law of the king" (Deut 17:14-20; cf. the previous commentary): The monarch was to make a copy of the Torah for himself and read from it all the days of his life. The actual "law" he obeys here is found in Deut 24:16 (cf. Ezek 18), and it limits blood revenge (contrast the excesses of Queen Athaliah, as described in 11:1-2, a bloodbath whose repercussions must have made a vivid impression on Joash, Amaziah's father). Commentators differ on whether Amaziah here follows customary procedure in his relative leniency toward the families of the assassins (Jones 1984:508) or represents a departure from traditional practice (Cogan and Tadmor 1988:155), but all are united in seeing the Deuteronomistic editor as implicitly commending the king for his mercy. It should not be ignored that during this time, dynastic stability is more evident among the Jehuites than it is among the Davidides. Adopting, as it were, policies more congruent with the peaceful dynastic succession of the northern kingdom (1) makes Amaziah's later stubbornness toward King Jehoash of Israel even more incomprehensible (see 14:8-14), and (2) opens the way for—maybe even encourages—those who eventually bring about his assassination (see 14:19-20; as Hens-Piazza [2006:327] points out, "Ironically though, the very ones he spared may be those who are later responsible for his death").

14:7 10,000 Edomites in the Valley of Salt. This is an archival reference, presumably, and one of a number of references to the land of Edom vis-à-vis Judah (and occasionally Israel) to be found throughout 1–2 Kings (3:9; 8:20-22; cf. 14:22; 16:6; 1 Kgs 9:26; 22:47 [48]). The "10,000" slain, a very large number, accords exactly with the number of foot soldiers previously left to King Jehoahaz of Israel by the Arameans (13:7; cf. Wiseman 1993:244); possibly that is one reason Amaziah thought he could take on Jehoahaz's son Jehoash. In any event, as Seow (1999:241) notes, "Judah's relation with Edom has been something of a gauge of the status of the Davidic king in the eyes of God." (The "Valley of Salt" is probably somewhere in the Arabah south or southeast of the Dead Sea [cf. 2 Sam 8:13, reading "Edom" for "Aram," as in 1 Chr 18:12; also cf. the title of Ps 60].)

Sela. This is a term meaning "rock," "crag," or "cliff" in Hebrew (cf. 2 Chr 25:12, where it is used twice as a common noun), but probably it is a proper noun here (often identified as Petra [cf. LXX] but more likely al-Sela', 20 mi. [32 km] south of the Dead Sea and 2.5 mi. [4 km] northwest of Buseira [biblical Bozrah]; cf. Jones 2009; Hart 1986:91-95).

Joktheel. Renaming a captured location implied control over it (cf. Israelite "Dan" for the originally Canaanite city of "Laish" in Judg 18:29). For the significance of the eyewitness testimony implied in the phrase "to this day," see the note on 2:22. The meaning of the name Joktheel is uncertain.

14:8 Come and meet me in battle! Lit., "Come, let us look at each other (in the) face" (cf. NLT mg), an expression used only here and in 14:11 (there in a clear context of military confrontation). It is less certain whether the intent here is hostile or not, which may be the very point the narrator wishes to make. Was Amaziah open to Jehoash's suggestion that he refrain from further military action, or was his mind already made up? Cogan and Tadmor (1988:156) cite semantically equivalent Akkadian examples signifying both peaceful meetings or, less often, hostile confrontations.

14:9 thistle . . . mighty cedar tree. Thus begins a brief parable or "fable" (cf. Solomon 1985:114-125 for an excellent discussion of this literary genre), which Jehoash (the "mighty cedar tree" of Lebanon) uses to try to "disarm" Amaziah (the "thistle" of Lebanon). As is the case with parables, the details should not be pressed (e.g., whether an actual marriage proposal had ever been proffered or who was represented by the "wild animal of Lebanon"; cf. Japhet 1993:868). Plant and animal fables are attested elsewhere in the Bible (e.g., Jotham's fable in Judg 9:8-15), as well as throughout the ancient Near East (e.g., in the Amarna letters [see the commentary on 1 Kgs 10:14-29 for details], as when King Labayu of Shechem writes the Pharaoh: "When an ant is struck, does it not fight back and bite the hand of the man that struck it?" [Moran 1992:305-306; cf. Sweeney 2007:365]). Cogan and Tadmor (1988:156) cite other examples from Mesopotamia, and Wiseman (1993:245), from Ugarit.

14:10 *be content*. Jehoash, who was presumably allied with Adad-nirari III of Assyria at this time (see the note on 13:10), shows "judicious patience" in his advice to Amaziah to remain satisfied with his victory over Edom. The northern provenance of the present tradition is once again quite evident (see the first note on 13:6), with Jehoash appearing in a positive light vis-à-vis Amaziah.

14:11 *Beth-shemesh in Judah*. This is an important site (Tell al-Rumeileh) 15 mi. (24 km) west of Jerusalem in the Shephelah (lowlands). As a border town with Philistia in the Sorek Valley, it plays a prominent role in the story of the capture and return of the Ark (cf. 1 Sam 6:9-15). In the present text, inclusion of the phrase "in Judah" again indicates the likely northern origin of this material (although it may merely be used to distinguish the well-known Judahite site from other, northern "Beth-shemeshes" mentioned in Josh 19:22 [in Issachar] and in Josh 19:38 [in Naphtali]).

14:13 *600 feet of Jerusalem's wall*. Lit., 400 cubits; concerning the length of the "cubit," see the note on 1 Kgs 6:2. Jerusalem's northern wall, its most crucial, was thus extensively breached and the city immediately rendered defenseless (steep ravines helped protect Jerusalem on the western and eastern sides, as well as to some degree on the narrow southern side).

***Ephraim Gate . . . Corner Gate*.** The former was probably the main gate in the center of the northern wall, and the latter the gate in the northwest corner tower (Cogan and Tadmor 1988:157).

14:14 *gold . . . silver . . . articles . . . treasures*. This embarrassed Amaziah as thoroughly as Hazael the Aramean had embarrassed Joash his father (see 12:17-18). This sad similarity between father and son will soon extend to the manner of their deaths (see the commentary for a discussion on whether these violent deaths represent further fulfillment of Elijah's curse against the house of Ahab).

***hostages*.** This is an unusual Hebrew idiom, lit., "sons of pledges" (*bene hatta'aruboth* [TH8594, ZH9510]). Cogan and Tadmor (1988:157) note that in contemporary Assyrian records, family members related to the defeated king were often carried off and kept under guard in order to ensure good behavior of the king left on the throne; such hostages could also be held for ransom at a later time.

14:15-16 The information presented in these verses appears with only slight differences in 13:12-13 (see the note there, which includes the observation that the present location of these verses was probably original). Recently, Provan (1995:236-237) has argued persuasively that the inclusion of these verses concerning Jehoash of Israel here may well indicate that it was he (and not Amaziah) who was in essence the real ruler of Judah at this time (also see Leithart 2006:240).

14:17 *lived for fifteen years*. This was presumably part of Amaziah's 29-year reign (see the note on 14:2 for details).

14:18 *are recorded in* The Book of the History of the Kings of Judah. See "Literary Style" in the Introduction.

14:19 *a conspiracy*. Heb., *qesher* [TH7195, ZH8004]; the verbal form is also used. This same phrase was used concerning the sadly analogous fate of Amaziah's father, Joash (cf. the first note on 12:20). Whether the Jehoash debacle is the cause of this conspiracy is not clearly stated, but it is definitely implied (this is similar to the evident cause of his father's untimely death, again at the hands of assassins; see 12:20-21).

***Lachish*.** This was an important and heavily fortified site in the Shephelah (Tell al-Duweir), 30 mi. (50 km) southwest of Jerusalem (Ussishkin 2008). Sweeney (2007:366) suggests that it served as a sort of "second capital" to Jerusalem, projecting Judahite power onto the Philistine plain and the coastlands; it thus served as an appropriate spot for Amaziah to rally support against the conspirators.

14:21 Uzziah. Or "Azariah"; see the first note on 15:1 for details.

14:22 Uzziah rebuilt the town of Elath and restored it to Judah. This is yet another reference to Edom vis-à-vis Judah. Elath is an Edomite seaport near Ezion-geber (1 Kgs 9:26); see the first note on 14:7 concerning such continuing focus on Edomite locations (cf. 16:6). Possibly, this took place after the death of King Jehoash of Israel, the de facto power over Judah at the time (so Na'aman 1993:228-230; also see the note on 14:15-16).

C O M M E N T A R Y

The material regarding Amaziah represents a paradox: A king who was said to be good (14:3) is generally presented in quite a bad light. This is in part due to the inclusion of tradition that is probably northern in origin (see 14:10), but rather than explaining this as the result of unintended editorial inconsistency, I would submit that we end up with an evaluation remarkably accurate as well as subtle in overall effect. King Amaziah did try to do well (cf. 14:3), both in internal (14:5-6) and external affairs (14:7). But he eventually overreached in the latter category, prompting King Jehoash of Israel to caution him with the famous fable about the thistle and the cedar tree of Lebanon (14:9-10, with the threefold reference to "Lebanon" in the north acting as an obvious literary contrast to Amaziah's exploits in the south just enumerated). Along with other signs of northern origin, this narrative ends with a sober recitation of an abject, humiliating defeat for Amaziah (14:11-14) at the hands of the north, an ignominious debacle almost on par with Nebuchadnezzar's victory over Jerusalem and its Temple, described in the last chapter of Kings. As in the days of Joash his father (12:17-18) and Hezekiah his great-grandson (see 18:14-16), so also during Amaziah's reign: Foreigners brought about nothing less than the embarrassing emptying of the Temple treasury, as well as much other mischief.

Leithart (2006:238) makes much of the symmetry between Joash of Judah as a second Solomon and his son Amaziah as a second Rehoboam (son of Solomon); this certainly does seem fitting in reference to the ransacking of the Temple by powerful foreigners, which takes place in each of their reigns (14:11-14; cf. 1 Kgs 14:25-26). Though artificial, such symmetries nonetheless do gain some currency in light of the curious chronological symmetries I have found between Amaziah and Hezekiah (see the first note on 14:2 for details). But what to do with Amaziah himself? I guess, as with life in general, we must remain open to the intriguing inconsistencies here. Amaziah was a "good" king, yet not like David but rather like his father, Joash (14:3). Amaziah commendably followed the strictures of Mosaic Torah as found in the book of Deuteronomy (14:6). Amaziah attained some stability in his reign through bold actions (14:5), and he also attained some remarkable victories over the Edomites, Judah's persistent nemesis (14:7). But he eventually overreached—and that may have been the reason for his demise (14:11-14, 19). Thus, he was a complicated king for a complicated time, serving under a complicated God (cf. Leithart 2006:239), who was sovereign not only of his kingdom of Judah, but also of Jehoash's kingdom of Israel (13:23-25). Then, as today, things get very complicated when the people of God go to war against other people of God.

But the most intriguing, continuing parallel between Amaziah and his Judahite predecessors when compared with Jehoash and his Israelite predecessors has not been discussed up to this point. I owe this insight to Sweeney (2007:343, 349, 363), who traces with considerable detail the eventual fulfillment of Elijah's prophecy against the whole house of Ahab (1 Kgs 21:20-26), which in its entirety would encompass all the related kings both northern and southern. As was seen in chapters 9–10, Jehu exterminated every possible candidate for kingship over the northern house of Israel (cf., particularly, 10:10-11, 17) and, for that matter, nearly every candidate for the southern house of Judah as well (cf. 10:14). And in chapter 11, Athaliah (daughter or granddaughter of Omri [see the note on 11:1], and thus also subject to Elijah's curse) met her own untimely death, but not until after she had attempted to exterminate the rest of the southern royal family. Joash (Athaliah's grandson) was hidden from her and in due course was crowned king. But he too was eventually assassinated (12:20-21), as was his son Amaziah (14:19-20). The various events and vicissitudes facing these southern monarchs preclude simple moralizing, but it does seem that Elijah's curse continued in its effect at least "to the third and fourth generation" of those who hated him (concerning that famous phrase, originally found in the Ten Commandments, see "The 'Sins of Manasseh'" under "Major Themes" in the Introduction). Sweeney provocatively also sees the end of 2 Kings, where Jehoiachin (Mephibosheth-like) is released from prison to eat at the table of the Babylonian king (thus bringing the Davidic dynasty effectively to an end [25:27-30; cf. 2 Sam 9:1-13; 19:24-30]), as representing the final fulfillment of Elijah's stern pronouncement against any and all possible descendants of the house of Ahab! (Talk about a powerful prophecy!) The Davidic hope for Christian believers is by no means snuffed out with the effective end of the Davidic dynasty, but it is no longer to be personified by political kings on a Judean throne.

Finally, and on a more practical note, we find in the present passage perhaps the most vivid negative example in Scripture of the importance of Jesus' sobering reminder (in Luke 14:31-32) that we are to "count the cost" before we even consider entering into battle against an obviously superior foe. Amaziah evidently did not, and that ended up costing him dearly—from the loss of the Temple and palace treasuries to the effectual loss of his capital city, Jerusalem, as a defensive bulwark, and even the eventual loss of his own life. We disciples of the ultimate Son of David should count the cost carefully as well, for Jesus bids us to contemplate nothing less than the giving of everything we own as the continuing price of following him (Luke 14:33). For those who are willing, the price is worth it, for what else in this world truly matters (cf. John 6:68-69)?

◆   ## 2. Jeroboam II rules in Israel (14:23-29)

23 Jeroboam II, the son of Jehoash, began to rule over Israel in the fifteenth year of King Amaziah's reign in Judah. He reigned in Samaria forty-one years. 24 He did what was evil in the LORD's sight. He refused to turn from the sins that Jeroboam son of Nebat had led Israel to commit. 25 Jeroboam II recovered the territories of Israel between Lebo-hamath and the Dead Sea,* just as the LORD, the God of Israel, had promised through Jonah son of Amittai, the prophet from Gath-hepher.

²⁶For the LORD saw the bitter suffering of everyone in Israel, and that there was no one in Israel, slave or free, to help them. ²⁷And because the LORD had not said he would blot out the name of Israel completely, he used Jeroboam II, the son of Jehoash, to save them.

²⁸The rest of the events in the reign of Jeroboam II and everything he did— including the extent of his power, his wars, and how he recovered for Israel both Damascus and Hamath, which had belonged to Judah*—are recorded in *The Book of the History of the Kings of Israel.* ²⁹When Jeroboam II died, he was buried in Samaria* with the kings of Israel. Then his son Zechariah became the next king.

14:25 Hebrew *the sea of the Arabah.* 14:28 Or *to Yaudi.* The meaning of the Hebrew is uncertain. 14:29 As in some Greek manuscripts; Hebrew lacks *he was buried in Samaria.*

NOTES

14:23 *Jeroboam II.* He was the fourth and most important king of the dynasty of Jehu (for the probable meaning of the name Jeroboam, see the first note on 1 Kgs 11:26). A stamp seal "of exquisite design" found at Megiddo attests his name; it reads "belonging to Shema', servant of Jeroboam," and a striking image of a roaring lion dominates the seal design (see Cogan and Tadmor 1988:160, also Plate 12[a]; cf. ANEP, picture 276).

forty-one years. This is an impressive regnal total—in fact, the longest of any of the 19 kings of the northern kingdom. The fact that we have so little annalistic information given here concerning this significant northern king will be discussed further in the commentary.

14:24 *sins that Jeroboam son of Nebat had led Israel to commit.* Once again, we see the Deuteronomistic formulaic judgment concerning the "sins" of Jeroboam I appended to 15 of the 19 northern kings (cf. endnotes 1 and 27 of the Introduction for details). For a discussion concerning the actual nature of these infamous "sins of Jeroboam," see the commentary on 1 Kgs 12:25-33.

14:25 *recovered the territories of Israel between Lebo-hamath and the Dead Sea.* In essence, this represents the territorial limits of the vast kingdom of Solomon (Cogan and Tadmor 1988:160-161; cf. Amos 6:14).

Lebo-hamath. See the first note on 1 Kgs 8:65 for the location of this site; also see Na'aman (1993:230-231), who argues that the powerful kingdom of Hamath never was actually conquered or subjugated by Jeroboam, whose northern boundary probably extended only to the region of Damascus (see the first note on 14:28 for details). Nevertheless, this still represented an impressive display of Israelite power, for the kingdom of Aram (southern Syria), whose capital was indeed Damascus, had been a powerful nemesis of Israel for well over a century (Haran 1967:266-284).

Dead Sea. Lit., "the Sea of the Arabah" (cf. NLT mg); the "Arabah" is the Judahite desert region including the rift valley of the Jordan River extending south to Elath (cf. Josh 3:16, NET).

Jonah son of Amittai. This is the only reference in the OT to this nationalistic prophet apart from the book that bears his name.

14:26 *For the LORD saw.* Once again (see the note on 13:23), this is a remarkably positive reference to Yahweh's love and concern for the northern kingdom of Israel.

slave or free. Concerning this Hebrew idiom, see the second note on 1 Kgs 14:10; but note that this is the only occasion where the phrase is used in a tragic sense—there was, alas, no one, "slave or free," able to help Israel (Sweeney 2007:368-369).

14:27 *blot out the name.* This is an idiom found only here in 1–2 Kings (cf. Deut 9:14; 29:20 for the only other uses in the OT). The image is that of washing a papyrus scroll clean prior to its reuse (Cogan and Tadmor 1988:161).

to save them. See the notes on 13:5 and 13:17, as well as the commentary on 13:1-9, for further discussion of terms related to *yasha'* [TH3467, ZH3828].

14:28 *Damascus.* The capital of Aram (southern Syria; cf. the first note on 8:7), which Na'aman (1993:230-231) thinks represented the actual northern boundary of Jeroboam's domain: "It is inconceivable that Jeroboam was able either to conquer it [the Kingdom of Hamath to the north of Damascus] or to make it a tributary kingdom." Rather, Jeroboam's realm came to include most or all of Aram, and his northern boundary abutted the southern border of Hamath (which itself consisted of both Hamath proper in central Syria on the Orontes River [modern Hamah], and Hadrach to the north, near Aleppo).

Hamath, which had belonged to Judah. There was apparently another "Hamath" to the south although, as the NLT mg indicates, the precise meaning of this text remains obscure (the alternative reading, "Yaudi" [taken as an Akkadian reference for Sam'al in Asia Minor], instead of biblical "Judah," now appears to be untenable [cf. Cogan and Tadmor 1988:162]). For a plausible emendation of the present text, see Na'aman (1993:230-234); he suggests translating, "and how he restored Damascus, and the war(s) of Judah against Israel" (thus reading *wmlkhmwt* [TH4421, ZH4878] *yhwdh*, "and the war(s) of Judah," for the MT's *w't khmth* [TH2574, ZH2828] *lyhwdh*, "and Hamath (belonging) to Judah"). Na'aman goes on to show how recently uncovered archaeological evidence from Kuntillet 'Ajrud in northeast Sinai (southwest of Judah) includes "Samaria ware" originating from the northern kingdom of Israel, thus indicating that in the first half of the eighth century BC, the valuable caravan trade from Israel apparently had to bypass Judah, following a western path through the Sinai (a less direct route). Among other things, this evidence corroborates the notice in 14:22 that, after the death of King Jehoash of Israel (cf. the note on that verse), Uzziah of Judah was able to regain control of the town of Elath at the north end of the gulf (and thus deny Israel access to that location).

are recorded in **The Book of the History of the Kings of Israel.** See "Literary Style" in the Introduction.

COMMENTARY

With the accession of Jeroboam II to the throne in the first decade or so of the eighth century BC, we move finally into the era of the so-called "writing prophets" (note the citation of Amos 6:14 in the first note on 14:25 [cf. Amos 1:1; 7:10-17]). Indeed, the only Old Testament reference to "Jonah son of Amittai," apart from those found in the book that bears his name, is to be found in 14:25. Finally, the important northern prophet Hosea should also be dated to about this time (see Hos 1:1). We know from both Amos and Hosea that the nation of Israel became militarily and economically powerful during the reign of Jeroboam II, but we also know that it sadly experienced a widening disparity between the rich and the poor (see the economic data found in the Samaria Ostraca [ABD 5.921-926]). Once again, the present seven verses of 2 Kings only hint at Jeroboam's power and prestige, as well as his apparently rocky relations with Uzziah of Judah (cf. Na'aman's conclusions as cited in the notes on 14:28). As Cogan and Tadmor (1988:162) put it, "Jeroboam II's forty-one year reign, the longest of all kings of Israel, is presented tersely and in no way proportionally to his notable accomplishments in political and military affairs."

Probably not coincidentally, Jeroboam's reign largely corresponded with an extended era of Assyrian weakness, although our available sources lack specifics.

For example, the occurrence of the notoriously evil omen of a total solar eclipse on June 15, 763 BC, may well have been understood as presaging the arrival of uprisings, plagues, and other troubles in the land (as well as, ironically, greatly helping modern scholars to establish the absolute chronology of this period; cf. Cogan and Tadmor 1988:163). And some modern commentators have indeed linked this eclipse with the remarkable revival brought about by Jonah and his reluctant preaching in Nineveh (Jonah 3; cf. Archer 1974:311; also Stuart 1987:491-492). Regardless of one's views on the extent of the impact of the eclipse, with both Aram and Assyria largely out of the picture, and with Egypt beset by continuing internal divisions, only the relatively weak nations of Phoenicia and Philistia (as well as the apparently now-independent kingdom of Judah [see the second note on 14:28]) could serve to dampen Jeroboam's military ambitions. Most scholars, therefore, characterize his reign as vigorous and powerful. But, as we have already seen, Yahweh did speak through two important prophets—Amos and Hosea—concerning its actual tenuousness. And so we will not be surprised to read in the very next chapter (cf. 15:8-12) that Jeroboam's son Zechariah lasted only some six months on the throne. Then, finally, the mighty dynasty of Jehu came to its ignominious and inevitable end.

Several comments are made in this passage about Yahweh's love and concern for the northern kingdom of Israel, this time during Jeroboam's reign (see the first note on 14:26 and the commentary on 13:14-25 for previous parallels). This flies in the face of the Deuteronomistic editor's overall agenda of emphasizing the importance of the Davidic dynasty in the south while generally denigrating the northern kings (which, if Na'aman's conclusions [cited in the first two notes on 14:28] about the relative power of Uzziah vis-à-vis Jeroboam are on target, would have been easy to do here). Hence, the present text seemingly harkens back not to Deuteronomistic theology but to an earlier tradition of Yahweh's blessing on the Jehu kings (see the second note on 14:27 for parallels). In any case, it is clear that Yahweh is not yet ready to consign *either* the northern or the southern kingdom to utter annihilation. And that results in "salvation" mediated here through none other than King Jeroboam II.

This is, however, the last time we read such positive sentiments concerning the north or any of its kings. Although six northern kings are yet to be discussed, their history basically goes downhill from here. As Amos straightforwardly prophesied in reference to the future of King Jeroboam's nation: "The people of Israel will certainly become captives in exile, far from their homeland" (Amos 7:17b; cf. Amos 7:10-11). As will also be the case with Judah's King Manasseh, son of Hezekiah, a lengthy period of time on the throne may well come to represent something quite different than the clear blessing of God. Present successes can still lead to future disasters. Therefore, let us not lose sight of such sobering realities: In any era, a long and seemingly successful career, whether in politics, academia, or even ministry, may not necessarily indicate the unequivocal seal of God's approval on an individual or that individual's accomplishments. Maybe it is, after all, quite appropriate that we find here little discussion about the accomplishments of King Jeroboam II of Israel, but a fair amount about the love and faithfulness of his (and our) God.

3. Uzziah rules in Judah (15:1-7)

Uzziah* son of Amaziah began to rule over Judah in the twenty-seventh year of the reign of King Jeroboam II of Israel. ²He was sixteen years old when he became king, and he reigned in Jerusalem fifty-two years. His mother was Jecoliah from Jerusalem.

³He did what was pleasing in the LORD's sight, just as his father, Amaziah, had done. ⁴But he did not destroy the pagan shrines, and the people still offered sacrifices and burned incense there. ⁵The LORD struck the king with leprosy,* which lasted until the day he died. He lived in isolation in a separate house. The king's son Jotham was put in charge of the royal palace, and he governed the people of the land.

⁶The rest of the events in Uzziah's reign and everything he did are recorded in *The Book of the History of the Kings of Judah.* ⁷When Uzziah died, he was buried with his ancestors in the City of David. And his son Jotham became the next king.

15:1 Hebrew *Azariah*, a variant spelling of Uzziah; also in 15:6, 7, 8, 17, 23, 27.   15:5 Or *with a contagious skin disease*. The Hebrew word used here and throughout this passage can describe various skin diseases.

NOTES

15:1 *Uzziah.* Or "Azariah," as in the MT (cf. the NLT mg). Commentators suggest that "Uzziah" was his throne name (cf. Isa 1:1; 6:1; 7:1; Hos 1:1; Amos 1:1; Zech 14:5) and "Azariah" was his personal name, which he probably used after his "leprosy" forced him off the throne (McKenzie 2009:722; cf. Cogan and Tadmor [1988:165-166], who note that the Hebrew roots '*azaz* [TH5810, ZH6451] and '*azar* [TH5826, ZH6468] are semantically very close, both conveying the idea of "victory, valor, strength"). The conventional translation of "Azariah" is "Yahweh is my help"; of "Uzziah," "Yahweh is my strength."

twenty-seventh year of . . . Jeroboam II. This is an odd synchronism; 14 or 15 years would have been expected in light of the earlier chronological data where Amaziah, reigning 29 years (14:2), has his 15th year synchronized with the accession of Jeroboam II (14:23). Since Amaziah presumably reigned 14 more years (or maybe less in actuality; cf. the note on 15:2), his son Uzziah would have come to the throne *at the latest* in Jeroboam's 14th or 15th year (even earlier if a coregency is posited). I know of no way to explain the high number found here, except to suggest that it partakes of the same 12-year dislocation found later in connection with Ahaz and Hezekiah in relation to Hoshea of Israel (Barnes 1991:19; cf. the second note on 17:1).

15:2 *fifty-two years.* This is another impressive regnal total, and frankly, one difficult to reconcile within the chronological constraints of the middle of the eighth century BC (cf. McKenzie 2009:723). It should, nonetheless, be noticed that the various synchronisms found in 15:8, 13, 17, 23, and 27 for the Israelite kings presuppose this regnal total.

15:3 *did what was pleasing.* This is the third (cf. 12:2; 14:3) in a string of five positive notices for the Judahite kings (see endnote 33 of the Introduction for details); but here again the positive notice is tempered with the formulaic reminder that the pagan shrines still had not been removed.

15:5 *leprosy.* See the third note on 5:1 concerning the characteristics of biblical "leprosy."

lived in isolation in a separate house. Lit., "he lived in the house of freedom/separation" (*wayyesheb bebeth hakhopshith* [TH2669, ZH2931]). Although the exact meaning of the last two Hebrew words still eludes us, most would suggest that some sort of sanatorium (or place of quarantine) is in view, although the alternative view that Uzziah was "freed" of his duties as king is also possible (Gray 1970:618-620; cf. Cogan and Tadmor 1988:166-167). In any case, an inscribed plaque written in Aramaic and dated to the first century BC was discovered in Jerusalem some time ago (cf. Sukenik 1931:217-220, and Plates I and II); the inscription reads, "Here were brought the bones of Uzziah, King of Judah. Do not open!"

Albright (1931:10), commenting on this unique find, concluded, "Since our inscription cannot be dated less than six hundred years after the death of Uzziah, it is quite likely that the bones in question did not belong to the king at all, but were found during the clearance of a tomb which was traditionally assigned to him. In this case it is a most interesting illustration of the growing reverence paid to the graves and relics of great men of the past" (also see Cogan and Tadmor [1988: Plate 5] for a photograph of the plaque).

was put in charge of the royal palace. Lit., "was over the house"; Sweeney (2007:370, citing the work of Nili Sacher Fox) specifies this as taking on the role of the chief administrator of the kingdom. Many would see this annalistic note as also attesting a coregency—indeed, as representing the only clearly attested coregency to be found anywhere in 1–2 Kings (so Albright; cf. Barnes 1991:8-9).

the people of the land. See the second note on 11:14 for details concerning this recurring reference (cf. 21:24; 23:30, 35). Sweeney (2007:370) notes that these "people" were also probably the ones responsible for placing Uzziah on the throne after the assassination of his father Amaziah (cf. 14:21).

15:6 *are recorded in* **The Book of the History of the Kings of Judah.** See "Literary Style" in the Introduction.

15:7 *Jotham.* See 15:32-38 for details.

COMMENTARY

The entirety of the present chapter consists of seven examples of the chronological "leapfrog" treatment of the northern and southern kings typical of 1–2 Kings, with the kings' order of presentation based solely on their chronological succession as determined by the Deuteronomistic editor, probably working from two different king-lists, one for each kingdom (for further discussion concerning these hypothetical king-lists, as well as the concomitant Deuteronomistic regnal accession notices, evaluations, and concluding summaries, see "Literary Style" in the Introduction).

To be remembered largely for leprosy and for living in separate accommodations from the palace is a curious way to be commemorated. We never know how (or even if—see Eccl 2:16) we will be remembered! Uzziah had been celebrated for his rebuilding of the town of Elath back in 14:22, and thus his reassertion of Judahite dominance over the region of Edom is strongly implied (see the note to that verse; cf. the second note on 14:28, which discusses Na'aman's conclusion that during the time of King Uzziah, Judah also exhibited clear independence from Israel. That, after decades of Judahite submission to Israel, was indeed something to commemorate.) The text could celebrate Uzziah's remarkably long reign (even if the 52 years literally attributed to him seem excessive), but no, it rehearses instead the onset of his leprosy and the resulting quarantine of his living arrangements. Once again, we never know how we will be remembered!

An important event mentioned several times in other biblical texts goes unnoticed here—a powerful earthquake (see Amos 1:1 [cf. Amos 8:8 and 9:1?]; cf. Zech 14:5). Later on, Josephus (*Antiquities* 9.10.4.225) and others connected the onset of this earthquake with the exact moment when Yahweh struck the king with leprosy (cf. Cogan and Tadmor 1988:166). In Chronicles, much additional material is given regarding Uzziah, both positive and negative (see 2 Chr 26:3-23). There, Uzziah's leprosy is attributed directly to divine punishment for his attempt to encroach upon the role of the priests by offering incense on the altar. But once again in 2 Kings we have the problem of silence; we cannot conclude much at all from what the text chooses not to say!

One more chronological datum found elsewhere, however, deserves mention here: the famous reference in Isaiah 6:1 to "the year King Uzziah died," when Isaiah son of Amoz "saw the Lord." This, of course, introduces Isaiah's incredible vision of Yahweh and the seraphim in the Temple (Isa 6:1-8), ending with the famous query, "Whom should I send as a messenger to this people? Who will go for us?" Isaiah instantly volunteered: "Here I am. Send me." When King Uzziah finally met his demise (usually dated to c. 740 BC), the presumed period of national uncertainty was immediately met by the calling of one of the most famous prophets of Old Testament times.

Again, we read nothing about Isaiah's call in our present passage—just the briefest details about some positive actions by the king, and then an inexplicable strike from Yahweh with its life-changing results. This is followed by his death and then (for once) the completion of a smooth transition of the throne to his son Jotham (with no reference to any conspiracies, in contrast to what befell his predecessors Ahaziah, Joash, and Amaziah). So, to sum up: Like Naaman, the important Aramean army official (cf. 5:1), Uzziah was a great man. But also like Naaman, Uzziah (or Azariah; see note on 15:1) was a leper. And that, evidently, is how we are meant to remember him. As Cogan and Tadmor (1988:167) succinctly point out: "Azariah is the only 'leper king' attested in antiquity."

◆   ## 4. Zechariah rules in Israel (15:8-12)

⁸Zechariah son of Jeroboam II began to rule over Israel in the thirty-eighth year of King Uzziah's reign in Judah. He reigned in Samaria six months. ⁹Zechariah did what was evil in the LORD's sight, as his ancestors had done. He refused to turn from the sins that Jeroboam son of Nebat had led Israel to commit. ¹⁰Then Shallum son of Jabesh conspired against Zechariah, assassinated him in public,* and became the next king.

¹¹The rest of the events in Zechariah's reign are recorded in *The Book of the History of the Kings of Israel*. ¹²So the LORD's message to Jehu came true: "Your descendants will be kings of Israel down to the fourth generation."

15:10 Or *at Ibleam*.

NOTES

15:8 *Zechariah*. This is the fifth and final king from the dynasty of Jehu. Zechariah's name means "Yahweh has remembered." Interestingly, there are over 30 different Zechariahs named in the Bible.

15:9 *Jeroboam son of Nebat*. See note on 14:24.

15:10 *Shallum son of Jabesh*. The town of Jabesh (Gilead) may well be in view here (cf. Cogan and Tadmor 1988:170); if so, we find a reference to Shallum's clan affiliation rather than to the specific name of his father. Shallum's name probably means "he for whom compensation has been made" (cf. ABD 5.1154, which further points out [following Jones 1984:521] that Shallum's usurpation here may well have represented the result of Transjordanian opposition to the house of Jehu).

assassinated him in public. This is a defensible translation of the difficult Hebrew—or actually partly Aramaic—text which reads *qabol-'am* [TH6904/5971A, ZH7692/6639] ("before [the] people"; the word *qebol* is Aramaic). Many commentators, however, want to emend the text to read beyible'am [TH2991, ZH3300] ("at Ibleam") or the like (cf. NLT mg; this would involve the shift of only one letter [Qoph to Beth and Yodh] in the consonantal text). Lucianic mss of the LXX read "in Ibleam," and as Cogan and Tadmor (1988:170-171) point out, one would expect the site of the attack to be specified (cf. 9:27 where it was "near Ibleam" that Jehu assassinated Ahaziah of Judah [see the third note on that verse for the probable location of the town]). If this reading is accepted, we would find, among other things, an ironic *inclusio* (literary repetition) linking together the beginning and the end of Jehu's dynasty (Jones 1984:521-522). In any case, Sweeney (2007:371) is probably correct to see Shallum's motivation as the desire to bring an end to that dynasty and its historic alignment with Assyria as opposed to Aram.

15:11 *are recorded in* **The Book of the History of the Kings of Israel.** See "Literary Style" in the Introduction.

15:12 *down to the fourth generation.* See 10:30; also the commentary on 10:18-31.

COMMENTARY

Ironically, as we come to the end of a string of assassinations in Judah (cf. the previous commentary section), we begin to read about a number of them in Israel ("In my anger I [Yahweh] gave you kings, and in my fury I took them away" [Hos 13:11]). Indeed, as has already been seen (see the commentary on the reign of Jeroboam II [14:23-29]), this also represents the beginning of the end for the northern kingdom, with Jeroboam II the last powerful king to reign over it. Although there will be six kings after him, none will be anywhere near as important as he was.

Here we also reach the end of the Jehu dynasty, with its remarkable stability. Zechariah's brief six months on the throne represent indeed a "fourth" generation of kings beyond Jehu himself, and since the Hebrews tended to reckon years inclusively (e.g., the "50th" Year of Jubilee probably occurred on the seventh sabbatical year, which we would count as year 49), Zechariah as the "fifth" king in that dynasty (counting Jehu himself), would be an extra, "bonus" monarch. Be that as it may, nothing good could be said about his half-year on the throne (cf. Zimri back in 1 Kgs 16:19 [see the note there], who apparently sat on the throne for only one week). Sometimes, it seems, one can be a "placeholder" in history and still be tainted by the sins of predecessors. At least, this is how 2 Kings "remembers" Zechariah son of Jeroboam II.

◆   **5. Shallum rules in Israel (15:13-15)**

[13]Shallum son of Jabesh began to rule over Israel in the thirty-ninth year of King Uzziah's reign in Judah. Shallum reigned in Samaria only one month. [14]Then Menahem son of Gadi went to Samaria from Tirzah and assassinated him, and he became the next king.

[15]The rest of the events in Shallum's reign, including his conspiracy, are recorded in *The Book of the History of the Kings of Israel.*

NOTES

15:13 *Shallum son of Jabesh.* See note on 15:10.

Menahem son of Gadi. Once again (cf. 15:10), probably a clan name is used for the patronymic (cf. Cogan and Tadmor [1988:171, 178-179], who suggest the possibility that Menahem was a "Gadite," hence like Shallum also from Transjordan).

Mariottini (2009a:40), however, following the tradition cited by Josephus (*Antiquities* 9.11.1.228-229), holds that Menahem was an army general who had served under Zechariah; he prefers identifying Menahem (with "Gadi" indeed being his actual father's name) as coming from the tribe of Manasseh and stationed at Tirzah at the time of Shallum's assassination of Zechariah (cf. the following note). In any case, he obviously acted precipitately and decisively to avenge Zechariah's death. Ironically, the name Menahem means "comforter" or the like.

15:14 *Tirzah*. See the note on 1 Kgs 15:21 for the probable site of this city, which was the early capital of the northern kingdom, located about 10 mi. (15 km) directly east of Samaria. See also the previous note.

15:15 *are recorded in* The Book of the History of the Kings of Israel. See "Literary Style" in the Introduction.

COMMENTARY

As in 1 Kings 15–16, we move into a bewildering list of various Israelite usurpers and assassins of usurpers. The dizzying array of five kings in little more than a quarter of a century (at most), as well as the distinct difficulty of squeezing in the regnal totals recorded for these kings, has led some chronographers to suggest that there was more than one king on the throne in various regions of Israel during this time, a possibility which gains plausibility inasmuch as such was definitely the case at this time in Egypt (see Kitchen [1996:467-468], who lists pharaohs from Dynasties 22, 23, and 24 as ruling concurrently in the middle of the eighth century BC and later; cf., e.g., Higginbotham 2007:215). Indeed, it is apparently not until the year 712 that the resurgent 25th (Nubian) Dynasty under Shabako exercised control over all Egypt (cf. Barnes 1991:97-100, and the references cited there). Parallel "dynasties" in Egypt at this time—quite certain; parallel "dynastic houses" in Israel at this time—quite possible (cf. Cogan and Tadmor 1988:173-174, and the references cited there).

◆   ### 6. Menahem rules in Israel (15:16-22)

¹⁶At that time Menahem destroyed the town of Tappuah* and all the surrounding countryside as far as Tirzah, because its citizens refused to surrender the town. He killed the entire population and ripped open the pregnant women.

¹⁷Menahem son of Gadi began to rule over Israel in the thirty-ninth year of King Uzziah's reign in Judah. He reigned in Samaria ten years. ¹⁸But Menahem did what was evil in the LORD's sight. During his entire reign, he refused to turn from the sins that Jeroboam son of Nebat had led Israel to commit.

¹⁹Then King Tiglath-pileser* of Assyria invaded the land. But Menahem paid him thirty-seven tons* of silver to gain his support in tightening his grip on royal power. ²⁰Menahem extorted the money from the rich of Israel, demanding that each of them pay fifty pieces* of silver to the king of Assyria. So the king of Assyria turned from attacking Israel and did not stay in the land.

²¹The rest of the events in Menahem's reign and everything he did are recorded in *The Book of the History of the Kings of Israel.* ²²When Menahem died, his son Pekahiah became the next king.

15:16 As in some Greek manuscripts; Hebrew reads *Tiphsah*.   15:19a Hebrew *Pul*, another name for Tiglath-pileser.   15:19b Hebrew *1,000 talents* [34 metric tons].   15:20 Hebrew *50 shekels* [20 ounces, or 570 grams].

NOTES

15:16 Tappuah. This follows the Lucianic mss of the LXX; the MT reads "Tiphsah" (*tipsakh* [TH8607, ZH9527]), but a reference to this city on the Euphrates River seems most unlikely here. Cogan and Tadmor (1988:171) suggest that a confusion between the letters Samekh and Waw in the early Aramaic period led to the confusion. Tappuah, located on the border between Ephraim and Manasseh (ABD 6.319-320), would only have been 12 mi. (20 km) or so south of Tirzah (see the note on 15:14 for the location of that city). But then that means Menahem committed cruel atrocities against, in essence, his own people.

ripped open the pregnant women. Cf. the horrendous actions of the Aramean king Hazael as described back in 8:12, which caused the prophet Elisha to weep bitterly over the prospect. For an Assyrian parallel attesting this kind of atrocity, see Cogan (1983:755-757).

15:17 Menahem son of Gadi. See the second note on 15:14.

ten years. Possibly a round number; it is hard to fit this length of reign in literally (cf. Barnes 1991:157 note o, where I opted for eight years). In any case, Menahem is cited in the annals of Tiglath-pileser III as paying tribute to him in 738 BC (15:19; cf. Cogan and Tadmor 1988:172; also Wiseman 1993:254).

15:18 Jeroboam son of Nebat. See the note on 14:24.

15:19 King Tiglath-pileser of Assyria. More formally Tiglath-pileser III (but cited here simply as "Pul"), the vigorous new king who ascended the Assyrian throne in 745 BC. For the use of the nickname "Pul" for Tiglath-Pileser ("Pulu," meaning "limestone [block]," and probably representing a folk-etymological reference to "Pileser"), see Roberts 2009:594; Cogan and Tadmor 1988:172. We will be hearing more about this king throughout the reigns of the next several kings of Israel and Judah (for the equation of the death of Tiglath-pileser in 727 BC with the possibly concurrent death of Ahaz of Judah in that same year, see Tadmor's conclusions detailed in Barnes 1991:115-116).

thirty-seven tons of silver. Lit., "1,000 talents" (for the probable weight of the talent in modern terms, see the second note on 1 Kgs 9:14).

15:20 fifty pieces of silver. Lit., "50 shekels" (again, see the second note on 1 Kgs 9:14 for the modern-day equivalents). Wiseman (1993:255), noting that this was the current price of a slave in Assyria, suggests that this levy was not unduly oppressive for the "leading class," who otherwise would have been compelled to furnish men of war.

15:21 are recorded in The Book of the History of the Kings of Israel. See "Literary Style" in the Introduction.

COMMENTARY

Usurper of a usurper, and an assassin of an assassin, Menahem truly embodies both the cruelty and the cowardice which would typify the role of such an individual—brutally terrorizing the weak (15:16) and cravenly groveling before the strong (15:19-20). In contrast to the kings from the family of Jehu, there is no positive comment whatsoever appended to the brief discussion here of the rather substantial reign of Menahem (that is, substantial in length of time in contrast to the reigns of his immediate predecessor and successor). Menahem became a vassal king of Assyria. Even the Israelite "rich" had little reason to appreciate Menahem (see 15:20), for he brought no clear "comfort" their way. There is, however, one dubious distinction to be attached to his reign: He was able successfully to establish Pekahiah his son as his successor—but apparently the latter lasted only two years.

As the prophet Hosea put it, "They kill their kings one after another, and no one cries to me [Yahweh] for help" (Hos 7:7b). This was surely a miserable time to be living in the land of Israel.

◆   ## 7. Pekahiah rules in Israel (15:23-26)

23Pekahiah son of Menahem began to rule over Israel in the fiftieth year of King Uzziah's reign in Judah. He reigned in Samaria two years. 24But Pekahiah did what was evil in the LORD's sight. He refused to turn from the sins that Jeroboam son of Nebat had led Israel to commit.

25Then Pekah son of Remaliah, the commander of Pekahiah's army, conspired against him. With fifty men from Gilead, Pekah assassinated the king, along with Argob and Arieh, in the citadel of the palace at Samaria. And Pekah reigned in his place.

26The rest of the events in Pekahiah's reign and everything he did are recorded in *The Book of the History of the Kings of Israel.*

NOTES

15:23 *Pekahiah.* The only king of Israel among the last five who doesn't come to the throne through assassination; he probably was appointed early to be Menahem's successor in light of the new pressure from Assyria (Wiseman 1993:255). The name Pekahiah probably means "Yahweh has opened [the eyes/the womb]" (HALOT 960).

15:24 *Jeroboam son of Nebat.* See the note on 14:24.

15:25 *Pekah son of Remaliah.* "Pekah" is basically a short form for a name such as "Pekahiah"—i.e., the name of the very king he usurped (see the note on 15:23 for the probable meaning of that name). In the Hebrew text of Isaiah (Isa 7:4, 5, 9; 8:6) Pekah is merely designated as the "son of Remaliah" (with no mention of the name Pekah at all); this probably indicates that the prophet considered his reign illegitimate (cf. Mariottini [2009b:426], who also suggests that when Pekah took the throne, he may have purposely taken on the name of his predecessor as well). In any case, events indicate (cf. 15:29) that Pekah was rebelling against Menahem's (and presumably Pekahiah's) costly policy of cooperation with Assyria.

conspired This is yet another clear example of the military rebelling against a seated king (see the commentary).

along with Argob and Arieh. This is a difficult text. Cogan and Tadmor (1988:179) suggest that the various details we find throughout this chapter concerning the Israelite kings may have been taken from a scroll listing details derived from contemporary Israelite chronicles, and that, as we are now near the end of the scroll, we find textual confusion [e.g., in 15:16 and 25], perhaps stemming from physical damage to the scroll. In any case, the MT here reads *'eth-'argob we'eth-ha'aryeh* [TH709A/745, ZH759/794], which the NLT reads as proper names (cf. NRSV and NIV), but which are otherwise unknown. Other possibilities include place names displaced from the listing found in 15:29 (cf. Jones 1984:527), or gateway figures of an eagle (*'rgb*) and a lion (*'ryh* [TH738A, ZH793]) found in "the citadel of the palace" (see next note) in Samaria (Geller 1976).

in the citadel of the palace. For this translation, see the first note on 1 Kgs 16:18.

15:26 *are recorded in* The Book of the History of the Kings of Israel. See "Literary Style" in the Introduction.

COMMENTARY

Yet again we read of an assassination and usurpation of the throne of Israel, and yet again it is brought about by the military (for the probable political reasons for this action, see the next commentary section). Perhaps at this point it would be useful to tally the number of assassinations of the kings of Israel and Judah we have encountered so far, and to connect this melancholy total to attested and implied activities of the military. The results: ten assassinations (six northern [with one more to come—see 15:30], and four southern [counting Queen Athaliah]). Six of these are clearly military in origin (9:24, 27; 12:20; 15:25; 1 Kgs 15:27; 16:9-10; plus 1 Kgs 16:18, where Zimri kills himself while under military attack [thus, strictly speaking, it is not counted as an assassination here]); and two more have implied military connections (see the notes on 15:10, 17). Only the assassinations of Queen Athaliah (11:16, where the palace guard take an active role) and King Amaziah (14:19, where the professions of his "enemies," as well as their motives, remain unspecified) are not evidently military in origin.

Some quick conclusions from all this: If you are a king of Israel or of Judah, stay on good terms with the military! We have already noted the military background of both Saul and David, with Solomon as the vivid counterexample to this (see the note on 1 Kgs 3:7 for details). But we perhaps need to be reminded once again that, despite the principle of dynastic stability the monarchy brought to both those countries, the military had to be placated, or an untimely death might be the result. This becomes even more evident in the second half of the eighth century BC, with the renewed politico-military pressure that a revitalized Assyria brought onto the scene. With Israel (and, soon, also Judah) relentlessly reduced essentially to vassal status vis-à-vis Assyria, restive military officials would have to act more circumspectly as they too came under acute pressure from foreign powers. Nevertheless the abrupt assassination of Amon son of Manasseh a century later by his own palace officials after sitting on the throne for only two years (see 21:23; these officials need not have represented military interests) does serve to remind us that a long life and a natural death were by no means guaranteed, even to Davidic kings, and even given the circumstances (also, note that King Josiah himself died at a relatively young age at the hands of Pharaoh Neco [23:29], and three of the final four Judahite kings ended up in exile [23:34; 24:15; 25:7]). The life of a king back then was indeed often "nasty, brutish, and short" (cf. Thomas Hobbes's depiction of the life of humanity in its natural state: "solitary, poor, nasty, brutish, and short" [*Leviathan*, ch 13, paragraph 9]). Yes, Jesus' sober reminder remains as apt as ever: "Those who use the sword will die by the sword" (Matt 26:52).

◆   8. Pekah rules in Israel (15:27-31)

27 Pekah son of Remaliah began to rule over Israel in the fifty-second year of King Uzziah's reign in Judah. He reigned in Samaria twenty years. 28 But Pekah did what was evil in the LORD's sight. He refused to turn from the sins that Jeroboam son of Nebat had led Israel to commit.

29 During Pekah's reign, King Tiglath-pileser of Assyria attacked Israel again, and he captured the towns of Ijon, Abel-beth-

maacah, Janoah, Kedesh, and Hazor. He also conquered the regions of Gilead, Galilee, and all of Naphtali, and he took the people to Assyria as captives. ³⁰Then Hoshea son of Elah conspired against Pekah and assassi-nated him. He began to rule over Israel in the twentieth year of Jotham son of Uzziah.

³¹The rest of the events in Pekah's reign and everything he did are recorded in *The Book of the History of the Kings of Israel.*

NOTES

15:27 *Pekah son of Remaliah.* See note on 15:25.

twenty years. It is simply impossible to fit this lengthy period into the less than seven years separating the reigns of Pekahiah and Hoshea, Pekah's successor to the throne (see Barnes 1991:157-158 note q, and the references cited there). Perhaps this high regnal total includes some years chronologically overlapping with Menahem and Pekahiah (i.e., Pekah ruling as a rival king in Gilead, a situation that is not without parallel at the time [cf. the commentary on 15:13-15]); or perhaps Pekah considered the reigns of Menahem and Pekahiah as illegitimate (since they both were, in essence, vassals of Assyria), and therefore appropriated their years of reign as his own. More likely, some sort of textual error has occurred (which, however, brings up additional problems inasmuch as the synchronisms in 15:30 and 16:1 depend on the present regnal total). At one time I suggested reducing Pekah's sole reign over Israel in Samaria to around five years (Barnes 1991:154), simply because that was the largest number I could fit into the available chronological space! Although not totally satisfactory, a textual error is probably the best explanation.

15:28 *Jeroboam son of Nebat.* This is the last of some 15 times where we have found this Deuteronomistic refrain used against a northern king (see the note on 14:24 for details).

15:29 *Tiglath-pileser.* See the first note on 15:19 for details concerning this vigorous king of Assyria.

captured the towns . . . conquered the regions. For a comprehensive study of these names and locations, see Cogan and Tadmor (1988:174-175); it will be obvious that the geographical extent of this "Galilean" campaign is simply overwhelming, with only the territory immediately surrounding Samaria left in Israelite hands (Wiseman 1993:256; Younger 2007b:900).

took the people to Assyria as captives. This is the first time we read in Kings about this devastating practice of the Assyrian Empire; deporting leaders and other selected individuals into permanent exile indicated a further step toward complete vassal status of the offending nation, representing as it did both physical removal of the actual offenders as well as clear intimidation of any would-be insurgents. Entire populations were sometimes removed—in this case a figure of 13,520 is cited in Tiglath-pileser's annals as the sum total of captives taken during his Galilean campaign (Cogan and Tadmor 1988:175-178).

15:30 *Hoshea.* See 17:1-4 for details.

15:31 *are recorded in* The Book of the History of the Kings of Israel. See "Literary Style" in the Introduction.

COMMENTARY

The infamous "son of Remaliah," mentioned five times in Isaiah 7–8 as a coalition partner with King Rezin of Aram, has already made a brief appearance in 2 Kings as Pekahiah's assassin in 15:25, but he is now featured in his own "regnal" account. (I put the term in quotation marks since Isaiah probably did not consider him a legitimate king; see the first note on 15:27.) In any case, the de facto ruler of this entire region will soon be the Assyrian king Tiglath-pileser III, as his own annals describe it: "Pekah their king [I/they killed], and I installed Hoshea as king over them" (see Cogan and Tadmor 1988:175).

But why did this Pekah rebel against Assyria in the first place? Whether it was the initiative of King Rezin of Aram, or of Pekah himself, surely it was, among other things, the result of extreme discomfort over Israel's abject subjection to Assyria, manifested by such things as the very expensive tribute that Menahem and the Israelite upper class had been forced to pay some years prior (cf. 15:19-20). But King Rezin of Aram was probably the actual ringleader (see Pitard [ABD 5.708-709], who further notes that he, too, was probably a usurper). Tyre and Philistia (but *not* Judah) also joined this Israelite-Aramean coalition against Assyria, with the disastrous results already discussed (see the notes on 15:29). In any case, as a result of the otherwise obscure "Syro-Ephraimite War" (c. 734 BC), in which Rezin and Pekah had invaded Judah to compel them to join the anti-Assyrian coalition, we encounter the unforgettable reference of the prophet Isaiah to a certain "sign of Immanuel" (meaning "God with us"; cf. Isa 7:1-17). This sign, among other things, functioned as a sure indication to King Ahaz that this northern coalition would *not* succeed either in usurping the house of David or in overrunning their land. All that as a result of an obscure Israelite usurper who seemingly borrowed his very throne name from the predecessor he deposed. Virtually no one today knows much about "Pekah"; but nearly everyone has heard much about "Immanuel." The fates of names and their would-be bearers are indeed funny things, unpredictable in the extreme, but nevertheless totally under the sovereignty of the true God, Yahweh.

◆   ## 9. Jotham rules in Judah (15:32-38)

³²Jotham son of Uzziah began to rule over Judah in the second year of King Pekah's reign in Israel. ³³He was twenty-five years old when he became king, and he reigned in Jerusalem sixteen years. His mother was Jerusha, the daughter of Zadok.

³⁴Jotham did what was pleasing in the LORD's sight. He did everything his father, Uzziah, had done. ³⁵But he did not destroy the pagan shrines, and the people still offered sacrifices and burned incense there. He rebuilt the upper gate of the Temple of the LORD.

³⁶The rest of the events in Jotham's reign and everything he did are recorded in *The Book of the History of the Kings of Judah.* ³⁷In those days the LORD began to send King Rezin of Aram and King Pekah of Israel to attack Judah. ³⁸When Jotham died, he was buried with his ancestors in the City of David. And his son Ahaz became the next king.

NOTES

15:32 *Jotham.* Already introduced as Uzziah's regent in 15:5, Jotham's name probably means "Yahweh is complete/perfect." A seal that was thought to attest the name of this king was found at Tell el-Kheleifeh near Elath some time ago (it reads *lytm*, "to YTM"), but it is Edomite in origin and probably should be translated "Belonging to Yatom [i.e., 'the orphan']" (so Cogan and Tadmor 1988:181; but cf. ABD 3.1021). According to the genealogical records cited in 1 Chr 5:17, King Jotham is to be connected chronologically with the time of Jeroboam II, another datum pointing to a probable early reign for Jotham (cf. the next note).

15:33 *sixteen years.* This is, once again, a surprisingly large number, unless a coregency is included (cf. the third note on 15:5). As is increasingly the custom among scholars, I will suggest an early date for the accession of King Hezekiah (see note on 18:1), thus pushing back significantly Ahaz's accession date and thereby shrinking the chronological window for Jotham. I did tentatively retain his regnal total of 16 years (see Barnes 1991:153-154; 157, notes n and p), but I had to shorten Ahaz's reign to 10 years or so. Chronological certitude still eludes us, even though it does appear that we can now date the year of King Ahaz's death to c. 727 BC (cf. the first note on 15:19 for details). Curiously, Cogan and Tadmor (1988:182) place the entirety of Jotham's reign within the lifetime of his father Uzziah.

15:34 *did what was pleasing.* See note on 15:3.

15:35 *the upper gate.* This is a literal translation; the gate was probably on the north side (the side hardest to defend; cf. the first note on 14:13), but we cannot be certain. Commentators compare the references found in Jer 20:2 (the "Benjamin Gate" probably facing the north; cf. Thompson 1980:454) and Ezek 9:2 (cf. Ezek 8:3). In any case, here is yet another brief example of the Deuteronomistic editor's interest in Temple matters (cf. the notes on 12:4, 5, and 13, as well as the commentary on that section).

15:36 *are recorded in* The Book of the History of the Kings of Judah. See "Literary Style" in the Introduction.

15:37 *the LORD began to send.* This seems to be the first reference in Kings to what has been labeled the "Syro-Ephraimite War" (for details, see the previous commentary). Thus, Jotham must still have been on the throne in or around 735 BC. The curious bias of the Deuteronomistic editor displayed here also deserves comment—stating directly that it was the will of Yahweh that such Israelite and Aramean pressure be placed upon the land of Judah and the throne of David. Such testimony should be included especially when Isaiah 7–8 comes under discussion; commentators generally disregard any possibility that the attacks from Rezin and Pekah could be in accordance with the will of God.

COMMENTARY

In clear contrast to his son Ahaz (see the entirety of the next chapter), we read little here about King Jotham. Indeed, as already noted (see notes on 15:5, 33), we are not even sure for how long, or even if, Jotham actually reigned as "sole king" on the throne. Although the position of Jotham as son of Uzziah and father of Ahaz is quite secure in the Bible (Isa 1:1; Hos 1:1; cf. Mic 1:1), any independent activities of Jotham (apart from his work on the Temple gateway noted in 15:35) must be found in the later account of Chronicles (see 2 Chr 27:1-9, especially the curious double date formula found in vv. 1 and 8 [cf. Barnes 1991:142-144]).

So, King Jotham is a sort of "placeholder," a "Zechariah of the south," as it were (cf. the commentary on 15:8-12), a nondescript loop in the chain of Davidic kings linking the lengthy and mostly positive reign of his father Uzziah to the relatively short and mostly disastrous reign of his son Ahaz. But not all of the present description of Jotham's reign is so colorless. As already noted, 15:37 gives us the unsettling indication that something new is on the horizon. God is again at work, and as Isaiah put it (in reference to events not far from that time), God's work may well be characterized as "a strange thing" and "an unusual deed" (see Isa 28:21-22). So it is here. For it was certainly God's prerogative, and evidently it was God's plan, to send the two infamous kings (both usurpers?), Rezin of Aram and Pekah of Israel, against his own people in Judah—and for reasons which seem clear only to him. We will have to wait for the Ahaz passage, and its parallels in Chronicles and Isaiah, to find out more. King Jotham remains, for the moment, the calm before the storm (cf. Isa 8:5-10). Placeholders do have their rightful place in the Kingdom of God.

◆ 10. Ahaz rules in Judah (16:1-20)

Ahaz son of Jotham began to rule over Judah in the seventeenth year of King Pekah's reign in Israel. ²Ahaz was twenty years old when he became king, and he reigned in Jerusalem sixteen years. He did not do what was pleasing in the sight of the LORD his God, as his ancestor David had done. ³Instead, he followed the example of the kings of Israel, even sacrificing his own son in the fire.* In this way, he followed the detestable practices of the pagan nations the LORD had driven from the land ahead of the Israelites. ⁴He offered sacrifices and burned incense at the pagan shrines and on the hills and under every green tree.

⁵Then King Rezin of Aram and King Pekah of Israel came up to attack Jerusalem. They besieged Ahaz but could not conquer him. ⁶At that time the king of Edom* recovered the town of Elath for Edom.* He drove out the people of Judah and sent Edomites* to live there, as they do to this day.

⁷King Ahaz sent messengers to King Tiglath-pileser of Assyria with this message: "I am your servant and your vassal.* Come up and rescue me from the attacking armies of Aram and Israel." ⁸Then Ahaz took the silver and gold from the Temple of the LORD and the palace treasury and sent it as a payment to the Assyrian king. ⁹So the king of Assyria attacked the Aramean capital of Damascus and led its population away as captives, resettling them in Kir. He also killed King Rezin.

¹⁰King Ahaz then went to Damascus to meet with King Tiglath-pileser of Assyria. While he was there, he took special note of the altar. Then he sent a model of the altar to Uriah the priest, along with its design in full detail. ¹¹Uriah followed the king's instructions and built an altar just like it, and it was ready before the king returned from Damascus. ¹²When the king returned, he inspected the altar and made offerings on it. ¹³He presented a burnt offering and a grain offering, he poured out a liquid offering, and he sprinkled the blood of peace offerings on the altar.

¹⁴Then King Ahaz removed the old bronze altar from its place in front of the LORD's Temple, between the entrance and the new altar, and placed it on the north side of the new altar. ¹⁵He told Uriah the priest, "Use the new altar* for the morning sacrifices of burnt offering, the evening grain offering, the king's burnt offering and grain offering, and the burnt offerings of all the people, as well as their grain offerings and liquid offerings. Sprinkle the blood from all the burnt offerings and sacrifices on the new altar. The bronze altar will be for my personal use only." ¹⁶Uriah the priest did just as King Ahaz commanded him.

¹⁷Then the king removed the side panels and basins from the portable water carts. He also removed the great bronze basin called the Sea from the backs of the bronze oxen and placed it on the stone pavement. ¹⁸In deference to the king of Assyria, he also removed the canopy that had been constructed inside the palace for use on the Sabbath day,* as well as the king's outer entrance to the Temple of the LORD.

¹⁹The rest of the events in Ahaz's reign and everything he did are recorded in *The Book of the History of the Kings of Judah.* ²⁰When Ahaz died, he was buried with his ancestors in the City of David. Then his son Hezekiah became the next king.

16:3 Or *even making his son pass through the fire.* 16:6a As in Latin Vulgate; Hebrew reads *Rezin king of Aram.* 16:6b As in Latin Vulgate; Hebrew reads *Aram.* 16:6c As in Greek version, Latin Vulgate, and an alternate reading of the Masoretic Text; the other alternate reads *Arameans.* 16:7 Hebrew *your son.* 16:15 Hebrew *the great altar.* 16:18 The meaning of the Hebrew is uncertain.

NOTES

16:1 *Ahaz.* He was the 14th king from the line of David. Ahaz's name is a shortened form of "Jehoahaz" or the like (see 23:30; cf. the first note on 13:1, concerning the Israelite King Jehoahaz, for details). The name of the present king is attested in Assyrian inscriptions as *Iauhazi* (cf. Cogan and Tadmor 1988:183), thus confirming that "Ahaz" is the shortened form.

16:2 *did not do what was pleasing.* After a string of four relatively positive evaluations for the Davidides (cf. the note on 15:3), we find a starkly negative note here, yet one which is couched in identical terms with the previous four evaluations, all of which employed the expression *'asah hayyashar* [TH3477, ZH3838] (did what was proper/pleasing).

16:3 *Instead, he followed the example of the kings of Israel.* As Sweeney (2007:381-382) points out, Ahaz is presented here as an apostate king, failing the Deuteronomistic tests for a good and faithful king in no less than three areas: following the sins of the kings of Israel rather than the positive example of his own Judahite ancestor David; engaging in child sacrifice (see the next note) like the pre-Israelite inhabitants of the land; and offering sacrifices at the illicit high places over against the Deuteronomistic requirement of worship in one central sanctuary (Deut 12:2-7; cf. "One Place of Worship" under "Major Themes" in the Introduction for details).

even sacrificing his own son in the fire. The Hebrew text here (*he'ebir* [TH5674, ZH6296] *ba'esh*; cf. 17:17; 21:6; 23:10; Deut 18:10 for the same expression) literally means "making [someone, here 'his son'] pass through the fire" (cf. NLT mg notes here and on those verses). Most commentators see the practice of child sacrifice as indeed indicated by this expression (cf. the first note on 3:27 for details on that grisly practice). Although a few maintain that this was not carried out literally (cf. Cogan and Tadmor [1988:266-267], who cite Deller and others as suggesting the children were dedicated to the Temple to circumvent this harsh penalty), most would see here (sadly) a reference to literal child sacrifice (as, e.g., was clearly the case in connection with Mesha in 3:27 and as presupposed in the extreme imagery of twisted devotion cited for rhetorical effect in Mic 6:7 [cf. Green 1975:173-179, who also analyzes parallel passages in Jeremiah and Ezekiel equating "passing through the fire" with verbs indicating actual child sacrifice]). The Chronicler (2 Chr 28:3) interpreted the present passage in this way, stating that Ahaz "burnt his sons in the fire" (*wayyab'er* [TH1197, ZH1277] *eth-banayw ba'esh*), although some of the versions of the Chronicles text read the same Hebrew root as found here in Kings (the only difference is the transposition of Beth and 'Ayin).

16:4 *on the hills and under every green tree.* This expression is found three times in the book of Jeremiah (Jer 2:20; 3:6; 17:2), perhaps attesting Baruch as author/editor both of that book as well as the Deuteronomistic literature (cf. 17:10; Deut 12:2; 1 Kgs 14:23).

16:5 *Rezin . . . Pekah.* This "Syro-Ephraimite" coalition has already been discussed in the commentary on 15:27-31. Note also that this attack was said in 15:37 to have commenced already in the reign of Jotham (cf. Oded 1972:153-165) and to have been in accordance with the will of Yahweh.

16:6 *king of Edom.* As already noted briefly in the commentary on 3:1-27, the only difference between the place names "Aram" and "Edom" in the Hebrew consonantal text is one letter (Daleth and Resh, which are easily confused in the Aramaic square script, as attested in the ancient versions; cf. the NLT mg). The present verse seems therefore to have been originally another archival entry concerning the fate of the Edomites (cf. 8:20-22; 14:7, 22). But since this time it directly follows the reference to Rezin king of Aram in the previous verse, textual confusion led to what we now find in the MT (cf. Cogan and Tadmor

1988:186-187; also the Kethiv/Qere variants in the MT [Edomites/Arameans] near the end of the verse [for the terms Kethiv and Qere, see note on 3:24]). It is extremely unlikely that Rezin could have extended his direct influence all the way south to the town of Elath on the Gulf of Aqabah (see the note on 14:22 for its location), although Sweeney (2007:383) does argue that Rezin's northern exertions may have contributed indirectly to Edomite attacks (cf. 2 Chr 28:17). In any case, Pratico's reinterpretations of Glueck's excavations at Tell el-Kheleifeh (in the vicinity of biblical Elath) confirm Edomite presence in this area at this time (see Glueck and Pratico 1993:867-870; cf. Pratico 1985:1-32). This will be the last reference to Edom and/or its territory in 2 Kings (but see the note on 24:2).

to this day. This is yet another secondary etiological formula giving confirmatory testimony by the narrator (see the note on 2:22; cf. the third note on 14:7). Cogan and Tadmor (1988:193-194) point out that this phrase was used three times in 2 Kings in reference to "territorial contexts," and more specifically in Judahite-Edomite connections (8:22; 14:7; 16:6). They suggest that such concerns probably became paramount during the time of Josiah, with his renewed Judahite territorial expansions, especially in regard to the seaport of Elath and the Gulf of Aqaba.

16:7 King Tiglath-pileser of Assyria. See the first note on 15:19 for details concerning this vigorous king of Assyria.

I am your servant and your vassal. Lit., "your servant and your son" (*'abdeka ubineka* [TH1121, ZH1201]); cf. NLT mg. Cogan and Tadmor (1988:187) discount the likelihood that Ahaz would have actually used the latter term, which would have conveyed "familial dependency" (contrast Jones 1984:536; Sweeney 2007:383). In any case, Wiseman (1993:261) is surely correct to castigate Ahaz for trusting in Assyria rather than in Yahweh, against the direct advice of the prophet Isaiah (Isa 7:10-16; cf. the discussion found in the commentary on 15:27-31).

16:8 took the silver and gold . . . and sent it as a payment to the Assyrian king. This is becoming a melancholy refrain in regard to a number of the Judahite kings forfeiting wealth to foreigners (cf. Joash back in 12:18 [19], as well as Amaziah, unwillingly, in 14:14). Intriguingly, Ahaz's son, the "good" king Hezekiah, does much the same thing (but with a strikingly different outcome) in 18:15-16 (cf. 20:17).

16:9 Kir. This site was presumably in Mesopotamia (see Isa 22:6; cf. Amos 9:7 for its depiction of "Kir" as the origin of the Arameans [cf. Amos 1:5]), but its specific geographical location remains uncertain (cf. ABD 4.83).

16:10 took special note of the altar. Much of the material found in 16:10-18 may have come from Temple records (Wiseman 1993:262; cf. the note on 15:35). Opinions vary, however, as to the intended meaning of the phrase "took special note" of the altar in Damascus. Does it represent an aesthetic preference for a Syro-Phoenician- or Aramean-type altar, or does it indicate a specific example of Judah's new status as a vassal state, subservient to Assyria? The latter is less likely inasmuch as Cogan, in his major study on the subject (1974:42-64), has shown that the Assyrians did not impose their own religious practices on conquered peoples. Of course, that would not preclude Ahaz from showing such abject obeisance on his own initiative.

Uriah the priest. Presumably one of the two "honest men" mentioned in Isa 8:2, Uriah is one of only a handful of priests mentioned by name in 1–2 Kings (see the Introduction for details). Presumably he was the high priest during Ahaz's reign, but his name is not found in the list of Zadokite priests in 1 Chr 6:1-15, so he may have been a member of a rival priestly family (cf. Cogan and Tadmor 1988:189; but contrast Cross [1973:211-212], who notes the numerous textual difficulties attending this list).

its design in full detail. The evocative term *tabnith* [TH8403, ZH9322] (pattern) is used here, a term memorably used also for Moses's Tabernacle as well as its furnishings (Exod 25:9, 40). "In place of the heavenly [*tabnith*], Ahaz follows a Gentile model" (Leithart 2006:247).

16:14 *removed the old bronze altar.* There is no word in the MT specifically corresponding with the NLT's term "old," but the import of the present reference to the "bronze altar" is that it was indeed removed to a different (and presumably less conspicuous) location north of the newly constructed "great altar" (concerning this, see next note).

16:15 *new altar.* As the NLT mg indicates, the MT reads, "the great altar" (*hammizbeakh haggadol* [TH1419, ZH1524]), possibly an oblique reference to the criticism found back in 1 Kgs that the bronze altar had proved to be of insufficient size even in Solomon's day (see the commentary on 1 Kgs 8:54-66).

personal use only. The meaning of the term here (*lebaqqer* [TH1239, ZH1329]) is uncertain (cf. Cogan and Tadmor [1988:189], who tentatively argue for a translation analogous to that found here).

16:17 *portable water carts.* See 1 Kgs 7:27-39a for details. Presumably the bronze "side panels" and the "basins" were removed as part of the tribute paid to Assyria, although the text does not say so directly.

great bronze basin. See 1 Kgs 7:23-26, 39b for details. Again, tribute to Assyria may be the underlying cause for the removal of the 12 bronze oxen (as Wiseman [1993:263] points out, "all this to get hold of metal which was primarily dedicated to the worship of God alone").

16:18 *canopy . . . king's outer entrance.* These are two further architectural features Ahaz apparently "removed" (or altered) from the Temple area, but the precise nature of the first item remains most obscure. The MT's Qere reads *musak hashabbath* [TH4329A, ZH4590], "covering [?] for the Sabbath," whereas the LXX reads "base of the throne" or the like, probably reflecting a slightly different Hebrew original (cf. NIV footnote; see Cogan and Tadmor 1988:190 for details). Both the NRSV and NIV (text), however, concur with the NLT. As for the second item, "the king's outer entrance," here the general meaning of the Hebrew is clear enough, even if remaining obscure concerning specific architectural details (for example, would the "removal" of this entrance line up with Ahaz's previous relocation of the bronze altar to the "north" [see 16:14] and/or Jotham's previous rebuilding of the Temple gate also in that vicinity [see 15:34]?). In any case, it appears probable that both these actions were undertaken "in deference to the king of Assyria" (and, perhaps more immediately, in deference to an Assyrian representative possibly posted at Ahaz's court [cf. the commentary on 15:16-22]). See the commentary below concerning the muted nature of this Assyrian reference in the original Hebrew.

16:19 *are recorded in* The Book of the History of the Kings of Judah. See "Literary Style" in the Introduction.

16:20 *Hezekiah.* See chs 18–20 for details.

COMMENTARY

As will be evident in the commentaries (especially in reference to Isa 7–8), King Ahaz's reputation has suffered much in later tradition. To be sure, he is roundly condemned by the Deuteronomistic formulas in 2 Kings as well (see the notes on 16:2-3), but the chapter as a whole presents the gloomy details of Ahaz's reign in a relatively nonjudgmental way (cf. Seow 1999:251). Apparently drawing largely from a Temple tradition (cf. the first note on 16:10), the present account does spend time on Ahaz's Solomon-like (or Jeroboam I-like) dedication of the new altar with the full panoply of offerings (see 16:15), but without any overt theological commentary. (The fact that Wiseman [1993:262] connects Ahaz with Solomon but Leithart [2006:246] connects him with Jeroboam I illustrates well the narrative subtlety we find here.) Let us be clear: To the Deuteronomistic editor, Ahaz was an evil king. But he was no Manasseh, whose discussion (21:1-18), though similar in length, is filled with harsh and extended theological condemnation. After all, it was due to the sins of Manasseh, and not those of Ahaz or any other king before or after him, that the Judahite exile became inevitable (for details, see "The 'Sins of Manasseh'" under "Major Themes" in the Introduction).

How then are we to evaluate King Ahaz? Not entirely negatively, in my opinion. First, he was a survivor (cf. 16:5b). During one of the most difficult crises in Judahite history, he was able to withstand the full onslaught of the Syro-Ephraimite coalition (cf. the note on 16:5, and the references cited there; also cf. Isa 7–8). Second, he probably was a realist. He sought help successfully from Assyria (again, an action which was roundly condemned by the prophet Isaiah), but he was able to stay on the throne—something few of his northern counterparts were able to enjoy (cf. the five northern kings discussed in ch 15, plus Hoshea in 17:1-6). Of course, he did have to pay a high price (literally) for this (see 16:8, 17-18); but, as far as that issue is concerned, so did his "godly" successor Hezekiah (see 18:14-16, a section of 2 Kings conspicuous by its omission in the otherwise closely parallel Hezekiah material found in Isa 36–39). Maybe this is why the writer's treatment of Ahaz here is curiously muted: The hero Hezekiah's actions toward Assyria were at first quite analogous to those of the less-than-heroic Ahaz!

Third, Ahaz was apparently a bit of a Temple architect and renovator: A new altar to replace the clearly deficient bronze altar from the era of Solomon? No problem! Ahaz took the initiative to make sure this happened (16:10-13), along with alterations of the portable water carts and of the Sea (16:17), as well as the removal of the "Sabbath canopy" and of the king's outer entrance to the Temple (16:18). Whether all these actions were undertaken due to Assyrian pressure, the text does not say (see the first note on 16:10; 16:18 admittedly does intimate that the actions described in that verse were "in deference" to the Assyrian king, but the Hebrew is less emphatic than the NLT translation might suggest [cf. Cogan and Tadmor 1988:190]). Hezekiah will also famously be an innovator in regard to the old Moses cult (18:4, where he destroys the bronze serpent Moses had made). And Hezekiah too will come under criticism from the prophet Isaiah. Indeed, the last specific word we read concerning good King Hezekiah is his thought that "at least there will be peace and security during my lifetime" (20:19b), hardly the final words of a timeless hero. Ahaz and his son Hezekiah were both survivors. One was a hero, the other a clear villain (at least in Isaiah and in 2 Chr 28). But here, Ahaz is, yes, a survivor—and one who will ensure (even through less-than-heroic actions) that the Davidic hope will also continue to survive. As Seow (1999:251) concludes in reference to the entirety of chapters 15–16 of 2 Kings:

The narrator conveys a subtle, even subliminal, message: God's sovereign will is being worked out in separate tracks. On the one hand, the [northern] kingdom is moving inexorably toward destruction because its leader will not turn the nation away from the sinful course on which it has been set. On the other hand, another nation [Judah] is being preserved because of God's promise, despite the inadequacies of its rulers.

It will be our task in the next several chapters of 2 Kings to observe the final out-workings of both of these tracks: final, inexorable destruction for Samaria and its kings (ch 17), but nothing less than miraculous, divine deliverance for Jerusalem and for the Davidic hope (chs 18–19).

◆ ## 11. Hoshea rules in Israel (17:1-4)

Hoshea son of Elah began to rule over Israel in the twelfth year of King Ahaz's reign in Judah. He reigned in Samaria nine years. ²He did what was evil in the LORD's sight, but not to the same extent as the kings of Israel who ruled before him.

³King Shalmaneser of Assyria attacked King Hoshea, so Hoshea was forced to pay heavy tribute to Assyria. ⁴But Hoshea stopped paying the annual tribute and conspired against the king of Assyria by asking King So of Egypt* to help him shake free of Assyria's power. When the king of Assyria discovered this treachery, he seized Hoshea and put him in prison.

17:4 Or *by asking the king of Egypt at Sais.*

NOTES

17:1 *Hoshea.* He was the 19th and final king of the northern kingdom. Hoshea's name means "salvation" (cf. the original name for Moses's successor, Joshua son of Nun, as attest-ed in Num 13:8, 16 [cf. Deut 32:44]; the name Joshua means "Yahweh is salvation," and it comes from the same root as Hoshea, *y-sh-'* [TH3467, ZH3828]). An assassin and usurper (see 15:30), Hoshea was said to have been placed on the throne by the Assyrian king Tiglath-pileser III (see the commentary on 15:27-31).

twelfth year. This synchronism, as well as those found in 18:1, 9, 10, seems to be about 12 years too late when compared with 15:32 and 16:1 (Barnes 1991:16-20; cf. the direct synchronism of Jotham's 20th year as Hoshea's year of accession in 15:30). If Ahaz did indeed die in 727 BC (see the first note on 15:19 for Tadmor's suggestion that Ahaz died in the same year as Tiglath-pileser III), this synchronism, ironically, may be historically on target, while the numerous synchronisms in chs 15–16 tied to Uzziah's long reign (as well as that of Pekah) are more problematic. We will have more to say about this in connection with the major problem of the dating of Hezekiah's accession year (see the second note on 18:1).

17:2 *did what was evil.* Nearly all the northern kings are described in such terms (see endnote 1 of the Introduction for details), but here the Deuteronomistic notice is uniquely tempered by the additional phrase, "but not to the same extent" (as those who reigned before him). I.e., for once, the paradigmatic "sins of Jeroboam" are not cited as criticism of his theological predilections (see the note on 14:24 for references to this otherwise com-mon refrain appended to the evaluations of the northern kings; cf. Seow 1999:252-253). No specific reason is given for the relatively restrained evaluation of Hoshea; perhaps the Deuteronomistic writer is softening his usual criticism of the northern kingdom since the end of that kingdom is close at hand. However, there might be a kernel of specificity to be found here in that the originally pro-Assyrian puppet king may have—for whatever reason—actually downgraded activities that were typical of nearly all of his predecessors (although he was not necessarily required to do so by his Assyrian overlords). (For the nature of the infamous "sins of Jeroboam," see the commentary on 1 Kgs 12:25-33; and concerning the fact that the Assyrians did not, as a rule, impose their own religious practices on their subject peoples, see the first note on 16:10; Cogan 1974:42-64.)

17:3 *King Shalmaneser of Assyria.* Known as Shalmaneser V, this son and successor of Tiglath-pileser III (see note on 15:19) only reigned for five years (727–722/721 BC; cf. Cogan and Tadmor 1988:198-200). Although both the Assyrian and Egyptian sources are meager for this time, it appears that Shalmaneser spent most of his brief reign on military campaigns, most famously besieging the city of Samaria for at least two calendar years (but cf. the note on 17:5 concerning the eventual fall of that city, also attributed to Shalmaneser's successor, Sargon II).

17:4 *asking King So of Egypt.* I have argued at some length that the alternative found in the NLT mg note ("asking the king of Egypt at Sais") is more likely (see Barnes 1991:131-135); it is unnecessary to rehearse the arguments at length here (cf. Cogan and Tadmor [1988:196, also p. 199 n. 5] for a concise summary [also cf. ABD 6.75-76]; contrast Kitchen [1996:372-375], who prefers "So" as a shortened form or nickname for Osorkon IV). The problem of identifying the specific pharaoh in view here is compounded by the fact that there were no less than three "pharaohs" on the throne in various locations in Egypt at this time (cf. the commentary on 15:13-15)!

COMMENTARY

In this portion of the Deuteronomistic History, muted ironies continue to present themselves. If Ahaz serves unwittingly as a foil for his much more successful son, Hezekiah (see previous commentary section), here Hoshea (Hezekiah's northern counterpart), in a different sense, does much the same. For it becomes clear that both Hoshea and Hezekiah rebelled against Assyria and sought help from Egypt (see 17:4 for Hoshea; and 18:7; 19:9 for Hezekiah). To be sure, Hezekiah's help came mainly from Yahweh, and whatever aid Egypt proffered was marginal. Still, the parallels do exist, as well as their dramatically different outcomes. As was the case with Ahaz, Hoshea was an "evil" king, although, as was also the case with Ahaz, actual instances of Hoshea's "evil" were downplayed. Thus, the final "placeholder" in Israelite history (see the commentary on 15:8-12 and 15:32-38) serves more as a melancholy reminder of the inevitable fate of that land than as a noteworthy example of good or evil.

◆   **12. Samaria falls to Assyria (17:5-23)**

⁵Then the king of Assyria invaded the entire land, and for three years he besieged the city of Samaria. ⁶Finally, in the ninth year of King Hoshea's reign, Samaria fell, and the people of Israel were exiled to Assyria. They were settled in colonies in Halah, along the banks of the Habor River in Gozan, and in the cities of the Medes.

⁷This disaster came upon the people of Israel because they worshiped other gods. They sinned against the LORD their God, who had brought them safely out of Egypt and had rescued them from the power of Pharaoh, the king of Egypt. ⁸They had followed the practices of the pagan nations the LORD had driven from the land ahead

of them, as well as the practices the kings of Israel had introduced. 9The people of Israel had also secretly done many things that were not pleasing to the LORD their God. They built pagan shrines for themselves in all their towns, from the smallest outpost to the largest walled city. 10They set up sacred pillars and Asherah poles at the top of every hill and under every green tree. 11They offered sacrifices on all the hilltops, just like the nations the LORD had driven from the land ahead of them. So the people of Israel had done many evil things, arousing the LORD's anger. 12Yes, they worshiped idols,* despite the LORD's specific and repeated warnings.

13Again and again the LORD had sent his prophets and seers to warn both Israel and Judah: "Turn from all your evil ways. Obey my commands and decrees—the entire law that I commanded your ancestors to obey, and that I gave you through my servants the prophets."

14But the Israelites would not listen. They were as stubborn as their ancestors who had refused to believe in the LORD their God. 15They rejected his decrees and the covenant he had made with their ancestors, and they despised all his warnings. They worshiped worthless idols, so they became worthless themselves. They followed the example of the nations around them, disobeying the LORD's command not to imitate them.

16They rejected all the commands of the LORD their God and made two calves from metal. They set up an Asherah pole and worshiped Baal and all the forces of heaven. 17They even sacrificed their own sons and daughters in the fire.* They consulted fortune-tellers and practiced sorcery and sold themselves to evil, arousing the LORD's anger.

18Because the LORD was very angry with Israel, he swept them away from his presence. Only the tribe of Judah remained in the land. 19But even the people of Judah refused to obey the commands of the LORD their God, for they followed the evil practices that Israel had introduced. 20The LORD rejected all the descendants of Israel. He punished them by handing them over to their attackers until he had banished Israel from his presence.

21For when the LORD* tore Israel away from the kingdom of David, they chose Jeroboam son of Nebat as their king. But Jeroboam drew Israel away from following the LORD and made them commit a great sin. 22And the people of Israel persisted in all the evil ways of Jeroboam. They did not turn from these sins 23until the LORD finally swept them away from his presence, just as all his prophets had warned. So Israel was exiled from their land to Assyria, where they remain to this day.

17:12 The Hebrew term (literally *round things*) probably alludes to dung.   17:17 Or *They even made their sons and daughters pass through the fire.*   17:21 Hebrew *he*; compare 1 Kgs 11:31-32.

NOTES

17:5 the king of Assyria. The events as described here (17:5-6) and in the parallel text in 18:9-11 have obscured somewhat the roles that the Assyrian kings Shalmaneser V and his successor, Sargon II, played in the fall of Samaria (for a very helpful delineation of these roles, see Cogan and Tadmor 1988:198-201; cf. Younger 2009a, and the references cited there). It seems that Shalmaneser did besiege the city for at least two calendar years, and indeed was successful in capturing it just before his death in the winter of 722/721 BC, as attested in the Babylonian Chronicle. (It will be recalled that King Hoshea already had been captured and deported before the siege began [cf. 17:4].) However, Sargon II (a royal prince but not the direct heir) took the Assyrian throne in 721 under circumstances which remain unclear. (Younger notes that although Shalmaneser had evidently died of natural causes, Assyrian texts indicate that internal struggles attended Sargon's accession to the throne, apparently preventing him from conducting any foreign campaigns until his second year.) Nevertheless, it is probably Sargon who in 720 deported the Israelites to the sites listed in 17:6. (Younger [2009a] notes that Sargon asserted in eight different inscriptions that he had conquered Samaria in that year.) Indeed, Sargon boasted of taking captive 27,000 inhabitants from Samaria and resettling most of them within Assyria (as cited in Cogan and Tadmor 1988:200, cf. 336-337). It is unlikely, therefore, that the activities of Shalmaneser and Sargon should be conflated into one event, as some have tried to do. It appears, rather, that the Assyrian evidence attests that in essence both kings should be given credit for capturing the city.

17:6 Halah . . . Gozan . . . cities of the Medes. These were locations both northwest and northeast of Nineveh, hence deep within Assyrian territory (note the identical list in 18:11 and the slightly different version of it in 1 Chr 5:26). Despite later romantic attempts to identify the "10 lost tribes of Israel," it seems that most or all of these forcibly transplanted Israelites were indeed lost permanently to history.

17:7 This disaster came. Many commentators would suggest that the lengthy Deuteronomistic sermon which stretches to the end of the chapter begins here (cf. the textual division as found in NIV).

17:9 secretly done many things. This is the traditional translation (cf. NIV, NRSV; so also BDB, which draws on *khapah* [TH2645, ZH2902]) of this hapax legomenon (a Piel of *khapa'* [TH2644, ZH2901]); but Cogan and Tadmor (1988:205) have strongly questioned it (cf. HALOT 339, "ascribe, impute"), preferring to render the phrase "ascribed untruths (to Yahweh)"—citing targumic and rabbinic support for their alternative translation (they, however, reject an alleged Akkadian parallel which is commonly cited—e.g., in Gray 1970:646). In their very next note, however, they suggest "cultic embellishment" could also (instead?) be the meaning of the rare term used here. At this point, it is evident that linguistic certainty still eludes us as to the meaning of this phrase (cf. Hobbs 1985:232).

17:10 sacred pillars and Asherah poles. Concerning the "sacred pillars," see the note on 1 Kgs 14:23; and concerning the "Asherah poles," see the note on 1 Kgs 14:15. We are told that both Kings Hezekiah and Josiah later removed such "pillars" and "poles" from the land of Judah (see 18:4; 23:14; cf. 23:6, where an Asherah pole was removed from the Jerusalem Temple itself!).

at the top of every hill and under every green tree. Again, a typical expression found in Deuteronomy and in Jeremiah (cf. the note on 16:4).

17:12 idols. Heb., *gillulim* [TH1544, ZH1658], "round(ed) things" (?); see the second note on 1 Kgs 15:12 for plausible translations for this term, which is used six times in 1-2 Kings (and nearly 40 times in the book of Ezekiel).

17:13 Again and again. This is strongly implied in the context, although there is no exact counterpart to these words in the Hebrew. It should be noted, however, that the root idea of the verb "to warn" (Hiphil of *'ud* [TH5749, ZH6386]) used here is "to repeat, do again."

17:16 two calves from metal. See 1 Kgs 12:26-33 (and cf. Exod 32:1-35).

17:17 even sacrificed their own sons and daughters in the fire. Concerning this somewhat paraphrastic, but very defensible translation of the Hebrew, see the second note on 16:3 for a detailed discussion; see also the note on 17:31.

17:18 Judah. Concerning the references to Judah found several times in this Deuteronomistic sermon focusing on Israel, see the commentary.

17:21 the LORD. Not clearly specified, but strongly implied as the subject of the verb "to tear away" (cf. NLT mg; also Cogan and Tadmor 1988:206).

Jeroboam son of Nebat. Perhaps the most vivid of the numerous references characteristic of the Deuteronomistic writer concerning the paradigmatic sin of Jeroboam (cf. the note on 14:24).

17:23 *to this day.* See the notes on 2:22; 1 Kgs 12:19.

COMMENTARY

We find in this section the tail end of the Hoshea discussion (17:5-6), coupled with the first half of the most complete Deuteronomistic sermon in 1–2 Kings concerning the reasons for the fall of Israel to Assyria (the next half of the "sermon" [17:24-41] will largely focus on the fate of the transplanted foreigners Assyria brought in to replace the exiled Israelites). As the note on 17:5 spells out in some detail, it was probably Sargon II, rather than his predecessor Shalmaneser V, who actually brought about those sizable transfers of populations, but for our author the specifics were of less concern than the basic theological motivations of Yahweh, the true God of Israel, who was the real cause for such population transfers. Actually, the reasons for such action were simple enough: Yahweh's people consistently "worshiped other gods" (17:7), and they insisted on practicing idolatry, bowing down to "worthless idols, so they became worthless themselves" (17:15). This continued violation of the first two of the Ten Commandments (cf. Exod 20:3-6; Deut 5:7-10) could only prove fatal—after all, no one is worth more than the deities they embrace; and in a sense almost merciful in intent, the true God must eventually put an end to such empty foolishness, both for the sake of the people involved and for the sake of anyone else watching from the sidelines (cf. the Philistines, of all people, learning a positive lesson from the hardening of Pharaoh's heart in the time of Moses [1 Sam 6:5-6]).

As was also the case with the Ten Commandments (Exod 20:2; Deut 5:6), the present sermon begins with the reminder that it was Yahweh who had brought the Israelites (and, of course, the Judahites as well) out of the land of Egypt and from under the oppressive power of Pharaoh (cf. 17:36b). The Israelites were Yahweh's own special people (cf. Exod 19:4-6), and they were supposed to be a blessing to the surrounding nations, especially in reference to the latter's truly debased forms of worship (cf. 17:8, 11, 15b); but as this homily makes very clear through its melancholy repetition of details (cf. 17:9-11, 16-17), Israel eventually became as debased as anyone around them. Once again, what choice did Yahweh have? He sent prophet after prophet—both to Israel and to Judah (see 17:13)—but they would not listen to the prophets, who were to emulate Moses (cf. Deut 18:15-19), any more than their ancestors had heeded Moses himself (cf. 17:14). That is why they are reckoned as worthless as the worthless idols they foolishly insisted on venerating.

As already noted, the nation of Judah is addressed here as well as Israel. Viviano (1987:552-553, 556) has made a strong case that the sins listed throughout this section are more characteristic of Judah than of Israel, and she concludes: "In the guise of accounting for the fall of the North, 2 Kings 17 actually highlights Judah's failings." In any case, specific references to Judah are found in 17:13, 19-20; and contrary to some scholars' desire to excise them as intrusive, they are (at least now) integral to the text. Whether or not this concern was part of the earliest version of the Deuteronomistic homily, it certainly is a major feature of its present form, and the etiological reminder in the concluding verse, "to this day," clinches the case, for it is meant to remind the original (as well as contemporary) hearers or readers that something more than dry history is being rehearsed here (cf. Sweeney 2007:391). Judah's fate will sadly be no better than that of Israel, but a full discussion of that topic must await the concluding chapter of 2 Kings. Meanwhile, Yahweh is no respecter of persons (Acts 10:34).

Concerning the likely dating of the present homily, as well as its overall shape, see the next commentary section.

◆   13. Foreigners settle in Israel (17:24-41)

[24]The king of Assyria transported groups of people from Babylon, Cuthah, Avva, Hamath, and Sepharvaim and resettled them in the towns of Samaria, replacing the people of Israel. They took possession of Samaria and lived in its towns. [25]But since these foreign settlers did not worship the LORD when they first arrived, the LORD sent lions among them, which killed some of them.

[26]So a message was sent to the king of Assyria: "The people you have sent to live in the towns of Samaria do not know the religious customs of the God of the land. He has sent lions among them to destroy them because they have not worshiped him correctly."

[27]The king of Assyria then commanded, "Send one of the exiled priests back to Samaria. Let him live there and teach the new residents the religious customs of the God of the land." [28]So one of the priests who had been exiled from Samaria returned to Bethel and taught the new residents how to worship the LORD.

[29]But these various groups of foreigners also continued to worship their own gods. In town after town where they lived, they placed their idols at the pagan shrines that the people of Samaria had built. [30]Those from Babylon worshiped idols of their god Succoth-benoth. Those from Cuthah worshiped their god Nergal. And those from Hamath worshiped Ashima. [31]The Avvites worshiped their gods Nibhaz and Tartak. And the people from Sepharvaim even burned their own children as sacrifices to their gods Adrammelech and Anammelech.

[32]These new residents worshiped the LORD, but they also appointed from among themselves all sorts of people as priests to offer sacrifices at their places of worship. [33]And though they worshiped the LORD, they continued to follow their own gods according to the religious customs of the nations from which they came. [34]And this is still going on today. They continue to follow their former practices instead of truly worshiping the LORD and obeying the decrees, regulations, instructions, and commands he gave the descendants of Jacob, whose name he changed to Israel.

[35]For the LORD had made a covenant with the descendants of Jacob and commanded them: "Do not worship any other gods or bow before them or serve them or offer sacrifices to them. [36]But worship only the LORD, who brought you out of Egypt with great strength and a powerful arm. Bow down to him alone, and offer sacrifices only to him. [37]Be careful at all times to obey the decrees, regulations, instructions, and commands that he wrote for you. You must not worship other gods. [38]Do not forget the covenant I made with you, and do not worship other gods. [39]You must worship only the LORD your God. He is the one who will rescue you from all your enemies."

[40]But the people would not listen and continued to follow their former practices. [41]So while these new residents worshiped the LORD, they also worshiped their idols. And to this day their descendants do the same.

NOTES

17:24 *The king of Assyria*. Presumably Sargon II is in view (see the note on 17:5 for details).

***Babylon, Cuthah, Avva, Hamath, and Sepharvaim*.** These were presumably locations both southeast and southwest of Assyria proper (Cogan and Tadmor 1988:209-210). It should be noted that this sequence of locations is generally followed in the more detailed discussion of the deities listed in 17:30-31.

17:25 *lions*. Probably the infamous incident found in 1 Kgs 13:23-30 in which a wayward Judahite prophet is killed by a lion is meant to be recalled here. See 1 Kgs 20:36 for another, brief reference to a disastrous prophetic encounter with a lion sent by Yahweh.

17:26-27 *the religious customs of the God of the land*. Three times in 17:26-27 the Hebrew reads *'eth-mishpat* [TH4941, ZH5477] *'elohe ha'arets* (the law/custom of the God of the land). As Viviano (1987:554) points out, these three phrases are bracketed in by two references to "fearing Yahweh" (17:25a, 28b), a "ring construction" (A-B-B-B-A) that serves to emphasize the need to fear Yahweh rather than fearing the other gods, which will be listed in 17:30-31.

17:27 *Send one of the exiled priests . . . Let him live there and teach the new residents*. This is an action which finds a close analogue in one of Sargon's own inscriptions where he stated that he had Assyrian officials sent to Dur-Šarrukin (Khorsabad) to give "correct instruction" (cf. the previous note for the Hebrew analogue to this phrase) to various deportees from throughout the vast Assyrian Empire, so that they might thus know how to "serve god and king." See Shalom Paul (1969:73-74), who terms this procedure "religious homogenization of the disparate elements of the populace," and who points out the apparent literary influence of Sargon's policy on the almost verbatim parallel found here in the biblical text.

17:29 *their own gods*. The next two verses cite various locations with their deities; a number of the names found there, however, remain problematic (see Cogan and Tadmor 1988:210-211 for details; cf. Sweeney 2007:396 and the references cited there).

17:31 *burned their own children as sacrifices*. Here the unambiguous verb *sarap* [TH8313, ZH8596] is to be found in the Hebrew (contrast the second note to 16:3 for the more euphemistic "passing through the fire" in apparent reference to Israelite child sacrifice).

17:32 *appointed from among themselves all sorts of people as priests*. This follows the negative example of Jeroboam I (see 1 Kgs 12:31-32).

17:34 *the descendants of Jacob, whose name he changed to Israel*. See Gen 32:28; 35:10; cf. 1 Kgs 18:31(NRSV and NIV) concerning this reference.

17:36, 39 *worship only the LORD*. Concerning the probable preexilic provenance of this repeated command, and its reference to exiled Israelites rather than to displaced foreigners, see the commentary.

17:41 *to this day*. This is the third time this etiological formula has been found in this chapter (see 17:23, 34); cf. Cogan's literary analysis as discussed in the commentary.

COMMENTARY

The preceding portion of this Deuteronomistic sermon mostly focused on the Israelites being forced to leave their land, but it now turns to the nature of the people who were compelled by the Assyrians to take the Israelites' place, closing with statements, however, that once again focus on Israelite idolatry—apparently even in exile (cf. Deut 4:27-29, especially 4:28). In 17:24-33 the newly arrived people (who will in 17:29 be called "Samaritans" for the first and only time in the OT [cf. ESV, KJV; cf. also Cogan and Tadmor 1988:211]) must be given the most basic information about how to live with the "God of the land" (see the note on 17:26-27); otherwise, they will be consumed by lions sent by Yahweh! So, ironically, a priest from Samaria was sent home to "save" the foreigners from such a fate. A list of their ancestral deities then is given (17:30-31), with the sobering reminder that in one case the people had been practicing child sacrifice as part of the worship of their gods. And then we find a subtle reminder about Israelite syncretistic tendencies from the past, with an oblique reference back to Jeroboam I and his tendency to appoint priests from "all sorts of people" (see the note on 17:32). There is no comment given (or probably needed) concerning Israelite and Judahite child sacrifice (cf. the second note on 16:3), or the excesses of Solomon in his reverence toward foreign gods (cf. 1 Kgs 11:1-13, 33-39)—just the reminder that such was still going on "to this day."

The chapter then wraps up with several verses giving reference to the Israelite covenant (17:34b-40), written in rich Deuteronomistic language, but fitting somewhat oddly in their present context, if they are meant to be connected with the foreigners now living in the land. But as already noted, Cogan has suggested a different approach in reference to these verses: He has argued plausibly that 17:34-40 was meant to apply, not to the newly arrived "Samaritans," but to the Israelites they displaced (see Cogan 1978; cf. Cogan and Tadmor 1988:213-214). In fact, there are clear literary signs that signal this transfer of subject: Both the repetition of the key phrase "until this day" (see the note on 17:41), as well as the repeated reference to "follow[ing] their former practices" (17:34b, 40) represent the literary device of "resumptive repetition" (German *Wiederaufnahme*), thus signaling that 17:34-40 refers not to the foreigners (the subject of 17:24-33), but to the now-exiled Israelites (the subject of 17:7-23). As Cogan (1978:41) aptly argues, how could foreigners be described as "sons of Jacob" bound by the covenant obligations of Yahweh's Torah (cf. 17:34-35, 37)—or, I would add, be further described as those whom Yahweh had brought out of Egypt "with great strength and a powerful arm" (17:36)? Cogan's conclusion is also apt (1978:41): The historiographic viewpoint expressed in this section simply states that "even after punishment, i.e., exile, Israel persisted in its 'former ways' (17:34-40) and sought no return."

What is the likely date for such a powerful sermon? Cogan suggests that the Josianic period would fit quite nicely. As he puts it, "Late preexilic Judah, the reign of Josiah, in particular, provides an appropriate setting for attention to be focused on the Israelite kingdom and its inhabitants, former and present." And, "The Israelite exiles, by their continued idolatry, forfeit any rights to their former inheritance. Our historian denies them legitimacy; their exile is proof of rejection" (1978:43). It should be recalled, however, that Viviano has argued for a focus on Judahite culpability throughout the chapter (see the previous commentary section), such that the overall sermon found in the present chapter is directed more immediately at the sins of the south, as much as rehearsing the apostasy of the remnants of the north. But, I would submit, these perspectives need not be mutually exclusive. After all, that is the way most sermons, past and present, work: Traumatic events of the past as well as controversial actions in the present are evoked to promote a change of agenda for the near-term future. Judah should repent so as to avoid exile (or possibly return from it; see Deut 4:29-31; 1 Kgs 8:46-53, and elsewhere), unlike Israel, which has continued in idolatry and therefore remains in exile. We are to learn carefully from the past, as well as survey closely the present, in order not to repeat past or present mistakes in the future, mistakes that would otherwise lead to future divine judgments equivalent to what has already taken place elsewhere among God's wayward people. Let us be sure that we too have ears to heed its message.

◆ III. History of the Kings of Judah up to the Exile (2 Kgs 18:1–25:30)
     A. Hezekiah: Good, Successful King of Judah (2 Kgs 18:1–20:21)
        1. Hezekiah rules in Judah (18:1-12)

Hezekiah son of Ahaz began to rule over Judah in the third year of King Hoshea's reign in Israel. ²He was twenty-five years old when he became king, and he reigned in Jerusalem twenty-nine years. His mother was Abijah,* the daughter of Zechariah. ³He did what was pleasing in the LORD's sight, just as his ancestor David had done. ⁴He removed the pagan shrines, smashed the sacred pillars, and cut down the Asherah poles. He broke up the bronze serpent that Moses had made, because the people of Israel had been offering sacrifices to it. The bronze serpent was called Nehushtan.*

⁵Hezekiah trusted in the LORD, the God of Israel. There was no one like him among all the kings of Judah, either before or after his time. ⁶He remained faithful to the LORD in everything, and he carefully obeyed all the commands the LORD had given Moses. ⁷So the LORD was with him, and Hezekiah was successful in every-

thing he did. He revolted against the king of Assyria and refused to pay him tribute. ⁸He also conquered the Philistines as far distant as Gaza and its territory, from their smallest outpost to their largest walled city.

⁹During the fourth year of Hezekiah's reign, which was the seventh year of King Hoshea's reign in Israel, King Shalmaneser of Assyria attacked the city of Samaria and began a siege against it. ¹⁰Three years later, during the sixth year of King Hezekiah's reign and the ninth year of King Hoshea's reign in Israel, Samaria fell. ¹¹At that time the king of Assyria exiled the Israelites to Assyria and placed them in colonies in Halah, along the banks of the Habor River in Gozan, and in the cities of the Medes. ¹²For they refused to listen to the LORD their God and obey him. Instead, they violated his covenant – all the laws that Moses the LORD's servant had commanded them to obey.

18:2 As in parallel text at 2 Chr 29:1; Hebrew reads *Abi,* a variant spelling of Abijah.   18:4 *Nehushtan* sounds like the Hebrew terms that mean "snake," "bronze," and "unclean thing."

N O T E S

18:1 *Hezekiah.* The 15th king from the line of David. Hezekiah's name probably means "Yahweh was strong, prevailed." Cogan and Tadmor (1988:216) note that the Akkadian transcription Ḫa-za-qi-ya-ú supports this interpretation; they also note the spelling found on a Hebrew seal inscription "[belonging] to Yehozarah son of Hilkiah servant of Hezekiah [ḥzqyhw]"; cf. Hestrin and Dayagi (1974:27-29) for details.

third year. As pointed out in the second note on 17:1, this synchronism (along with the ones in 18:9-10) remains at variance with the synchronisms found in 15:32; 16:1; and elsewhere. What is important here is the clear testimony by the Deuteronomistic editor that Hezekiah did indeed ascend the throne of Judah well *before* the fall of Samaria in 722 BC.

As I noted some time ago (see Barnes 1991:3), it seems most unlikely that the editor would have misremembered a fact so basic as who was on the throne of Judah when the northern kingdom fell to the Assyrians—it would be like confusing Abraham Lincoln with his predecessor, James Buchanan, in reference to who was the US president when the Confederacy seceded from the Union. See the commentary for further discussion concerning this fundamental issue of chronology.

18:2 *twenty-five years old . . . reigned in Jerusalem twenty-nine years.* Curiously, both of these numbers correspond exactly to those found previously for Amaziah, which would lend support to the view that some of the numbers are secondary in origin (see the note on 14:2 for details; also the first note on 18:13).

18:3 *did what was pleasing.* Apart from the sharply negative evaluation of Hezekiah's father, Ahaz, which is couched in similar phraseology (see note on 16:2), we have had a string of positive evaluations couched in this stereotypical Deuteronomistic language (see the note on 15:3 for details), but heretofore always with the added caveat that the "pagan shrines" had not been removed. In the present instance, the "pleasing" evaluation needs no such qualification—the shrines *were* finally removed (18:4a), just as Deut 12:2-7 mandates (see "One Place of Worship" under "Major Themes" in the Introduction for details).

18:4 *sacred pillars . . . Asherah poles.* See the first note on 17:10 for references to descriptions of these pagan images.

bronze serpent. This is the only reference in 1–2 Kings to the *nekhash hannekhosheth* [TH5175/5178, ZH5729/5733], which, as the present verse goes on to indicate, was also known as the "Nehushtan" (cf. the NLT mg). The reference to Moses originally making this object is to be found in Num 21:8-9. Like Moses's destruction of Aaron's golden calf (as described in Deut 9:21; Exod 32:20 uses a different verb), Hezekiah "broke up" (Piel of *kathath* [TH3807, ZH4198]; the Qal stem is used in Deut 9:21) this metal object, which, ironically, by Hezekiah's time had become an object of idol worship. Cogan and Tadmor (1988:217) term the serpent a "venerated cult object." Thus, Hezekiah acted as decisively in the face of popular tradition as Moses had done in the calf incident, thus bringing about ruthlessly the reform agenda strongly urged in the homily found in the preceding chapter of 2 Kings.

18:5 *no one like him.* For the uniqueness of King Hezekiah as "the best king of all," see "Earlier Editions of Kings?" under "Date and Occasion of Writing" in the Introduction (cf. the nuanced comments found in Sweeney 2007:403).

18:7 *successful.* The revolts against Assyria probably took place rather late in Hezekiah's reign (see Kuan 2007:819; Wiseman 1993:271), while those against Philistia, which are cited in the next verse, would have represented analogous attacks against an Assyrian client state after the death of Sargon II in 705 BC (Cogan and Tadmor 1988:217). To the Deuteronomistic writer, these acts of rebellion are positive moves, to be sharply contrasted with the accommodationist policies of Hezekiah's father, Ahaz (cf. the notes on 16:7, 8, as well as the commentary on 16:1-20). In the north, however, King Hoshea had also recently rebelled against Assyria, but the results of his attempts at independence were singularly *unsuccessful*—in fact, they resulted in nothing less than the complete demise of his kingdom (see the note on 17:5 for details).

18:8 *Philistines.* This area had been under Assyrian authority since the days of Tiglath-pileser (cf. Cogan and Tadmor [1988:217], who suggest Hezekiah's actions took place in 705–702 BC). The literary reference to the "Philistines" here (the last time in Kings where they are mentioned) evokes positive parallels with King David (see 18:3; see also Seow 1999:260; Sweeney 2007:409-410 concerning the strategic importance of this action in blocking Egyptian advances from the south).

Gaza. See the note on 1 Kgs 4:24, where "Gaza" is the southernmost city of the Philistines—in essence, the farthest one can go in conquering that area.

18:9-11 Most of the material found in these verses has already been presented in 17:5-6 (see the notes there).

18:12 *they refused to listen . . . they violated his covenant.* In essence, this verse represents a brief summary of the indictment of the Israelites that encompasses most of ch 17.

COMMENTARY

We now come to the final section of 1-2 Kings, a section which can perhaps simply be entitled, "Judah Alone." For Israel, the northern kingdom, has now irrevocably disappeared from the scene. After the stirring sermon of chapter 17 describing the reasons for its fate, we know that Israel was doomed by its continued preoccupation with idolatry and religious syncretism. We also suspect that Judah will eventually be subjected to the same fate, unless something dramatically different takes place. And sure enough, with the onset of the reign of good King Hezekiah (chs 18-20), the dramatic turnaround we are seeking seems indeed on the horizon (see "Earlier Editions of Kings?" under "Date and Occasion of Writing" in the Introduction for details). This will, however, prove to be only a delay in the demise of the southern kingdom, as Hezekiah himself will come to recognize (see 20:19). In fact, even good King Josiah (22:1-23:30), the great-grandson of Hezekiah and probably the "hero" of the Deuteronomistic History, will not succeed in halting permanently the seemingly inevitable course of this tragic history (see 22:15-20). Inevitably doomed, yet always containing a glimmer of hope—that is Judah's nature in the final section of 1-2 Kings. And this section is indeed the conclusion of the whole Deuteronomistic History, the work that stretches from Joshua through Kings, spanning some seven centuries to the demise of Judah in 586 BC, and on to the faint preservation of the Davidic hope which still lingers in 561, the last incident described in the book (25:27-30; cf. "Date and Occasion of Writing" in the Introduction). Israel gone, Judah doomed, but the Davidic hope still alive—this is the theme of the final section of 1-2 Kings.

One of the biggest conundrums in Old Testament chronology is the dating of the accession of King Hezekiah. The Deuteronomistic Historian is quite clear about Hezekiah's positive impact on the nation of Judah and is equally clear in insisting that Hezekiah's accession to the throne of David took place a few years *before* the fall of Samaria in 722 BC (see the second note on 18:1 for details). But however plainly this dating is stated and restated in the biblical text, it hardly represents the consensus of biblical historians of the last century or so—whether liberal or conservative (see Barnes 1991:74 and the references cited there). To simplify a complicated issue, these historians remain (understandably) fixated on another important chronological datum also firmly established in the biblical record, namely the synchronism found in 18:13, which states that it was in Hezekiah's 14th year that Sennacherib invaded Judah (an event firmly dated to 701 BC; see Cogan and Tadmor 1988:228; Barnes 1991:3, 83-84). What are we to do with these conflicting chronological notices? That is the crux of the problem of the dating of Hezekiah's accession. First of all, we should acknowledge the existence of these incompatible synchronisms and explicate the problems they represent (problems, by the way, that the ancient chronographers would probably not have noticed, since they would not have been privy to the Assyrian annals and the absolute dating of a solar eclipse, which can now coordinate their relative dates to an absolute calendar). Second, we can attempt to find solutions to the resultant chronological incompatibility, whether by the now mostly discredited attempt to posit two different invasions of Judah by Sennacherib (see Barnes 1991:79-86 for an overview; cf. Cogan and Tadmor 1988:246-251) or by the more attractive suggestion of emending the 14th-year synchronism to the 24th year to minimize its incongruity (an easy "fix" in the Hebrew [*'arba' 'esreh* to *'arba' 'esrim*]; cf. Rowley 1962:410-413 [discussed in Barnes 1991:80-84]; also Oswalt 1986:631), or by other suggestions similar to the previous (cf. Barnes 1991:83 for those possibilities). Third, we should recognize the irresolvable incompatibility—at least as far as we can now determine—of the two sets of synchronisms and choose the more likely option (if either). I myself prefer the accession synchronisms placing Hezekiah firmly on the throne around 727 BC, and so I must somehow discount the 701 synchronism to Hezekiah's 14th year (I have suggested the possible artificiality of this synchronism in the note on 18:2 [cf. the first note on 18:13], but I will be the first one to admit that this smacks of special pleading). Finally, we must remain open to the results of new discoveries—whether archaeological, textual (i.e., ancient texts, Assyrian, Egyptian, or otherwise), or literary (e.g., new ways to understand clearly nonchronological arrangements of biblical narratives; cf. the discussion of Hezekiah's illness and recovery as described in ch 20).

Whenever it was that Hezekiah became king, his reign (or at least the earlier part of his reign) is described as a good one. One recent indication from archaeological evidence is the remarkable standardization at this time of the shekel weight used in balance-beam scales (to about 11.33 g; see the second note on 1 Kgs 9:14 for details). As Dever (2001:226-227) points out, religious "revival" can thus be objectively documented by such mundane economic realia as the comparison of shekel weights found in various Judahite archaeological sites (cf. the plaintive lament of the prophet Micah, "How can I tolerate your merchants who use dishonest scales and weights?" [Mic 6:11, written probably just before the time of Hezekiah]). Another dramatic result from archaeology is the evidence of the apparent doubling (or even tripling, or more) of the size of the city of Jerusalem around this time (Broshi 1974:21-26), with most of the western hill becoming part of the city (or at least its unwalled suburb; cf. the reference to the "New Quarter" or the "Second Quarter" in the days of Josiah, 22:14). Many of the refugees from the north probably settled in the Jerusalem area around this time (those who were able to escape Assyrian deportation; cf. 17:6); Broshi thinks refugees from Judahite provinces ceded by Sennacherib to the Philistines in 701 BC may also have led to the city's remarkable surge in size. The new wall to the west, although itself representing a doubling of the size of the city, probably only surrounded part of it, with unwalled suburbs to the west and probably also to the north also coming into existence. Indeed, it was an exciting time to be living in Jerusalem.

So, in conclusion, Hezekiah proved to be a good king, but one who would for a little while grow quite desperate in the face of continued Assyrian aggression, as we will see in the next section. But let the reader not worry—the embarrassing moments for this able king will eventually pass, and with unforgettable (but not entirely positive) results for the future, especially during the time of Jeremiah and the late history of the Judahite monarchy, as the "inviolability" of the Temple becomes a cardinal article of faith in Judah (cf. Jer 7, his so-called "Temple Sermon," where he inveighs repeatedly against false faith in the continued existence of "the Temple of Yahweh"). Sometimes evident success, especially if later misunderstood, can lead to theological excess and eventual disaster. But in the case of Judah, that is a story which can be postponed for another hundred years or so. As Hezekiah himself says, "Good. . . . There will be peace in my time."

◆   ## 2. Assyria invades Judah (18:13-18)

¹³In the fourteenth year of King Hezekiah's reign,* King Sennacherib of Assyria came to attack the fortified towns of Judah and conquered them. ¹⁴King Hezekiah sent this message to the king of Assyria at Lachish: "I have done wrong. I will pay whatever tribute money you demand if you will only withdraw." The king of Assyria then demanded a settlement of more than eleven tons of silver and one ton of gold.* ¹⁵To gather this amount, King Hezekiah used all the silver stored in the Temple of the LORD and in the palace treasury. ¹⁶Hezekiah even stripped the gold from the doors of the LORD's Temple and from the doorposts he had overlaid with gold, and he gave it all to the Assyrian king.

¹⁷Nevertheless, the king of Assyria sent his commander in chief, his field commander, and his chief of staff* from Lachish with a huge army to confront King Hezekiah in Jerusalem. The Assyrians took up a position beside the aqueduct that feeds water into the upper pool, near the road leading to the field where cloth is washed.* ¹⁸They summoned King Hezekiah, but the king sent these officials to meet with them: Eliakim son of Hilkiah, the palace administrator; Shebna the court secretary; and Joah son of Asaph, the royal historian.

18:13 The fourteenth year of Hezekiah's reign was 701 B.C.   18:14 Hebrew *300 talents* [10 metric tons] *of silver and 30 talents* [1 metric ton] *of gold.*   18:17a Or *the rabshakeh;* also in 18:19, 26, 27, 28, 37.   18:17b Or *bleached.*

NOTES
18:13 *fourteenth year.* The NLT mg is correct to connect Sennacherib's invasion of Judah to 701 BC, but as the previous commentary discusses at some length, this may well *not* have corresponded historically with Hezekiah's 14th year of reign (which might itself have been a secondary calculation; cf. the notes on 14:2 and 20:6 for the remarkable "25/29/15" set of chronological parallels with Amaziah).

King Sennacherib of Assyria. Successor of Sargon II (see the note on 17:5), he was probably Sargon's son (see Younger 2009b:167). Sargon's ignominious death on the battlefield in 705 BC probably was an embarrassment to Sennacherib (cf. Younger 2009a:111); in any case, it helped lead to significant revolts throughout the vast Assyrian kingdom. After crushing rebellion in the south in 704–702, Sennacherib campaigned in the west (his so-called "third campaign"), fighting against Phoenicia and then Judah. He eventually captured Lachish (see the first note on 18:14), as well as some 46 Judahite cities in all, finally placing Jerusalem itself under siege, thus shutting up Hezekiah "like a bird in a cage" (as described in the Rassam Prism Inscription; cf. Cogan and Tadmor 1988:337-339). Of course, Sennacherib was unsuccessful in his attempt to capture Jerusalem, but he did extract heavy tribute from Hezekiah (cf. the notes on 18:14, 16).

18:14 *Lachish.* See the second note on 14:19 concerning this important city in the Shephelah (for a recent discussion of the extensive archaeological remains of Level III, which are almost certainly to be connected with Sennacherib's destruction of the city in 701 BC, see Ussishkin 2008:559-561). Assyrian reliefs from Sennacherib's palace at Nineveh illustrate strikingly his capture of this city, as well as the subsequent deportation of its inhabitants (ANEP, pictures 371-374).

more than eleven tons of silver and one ton of gold. As the NLT mg indicates, this is more literally 300 talents of silver—an immense amount—and 30 talents of gold—also immense. It is of no little interest that Sennacherib's own annals cite "30 talents of gold and 800 talents of silver" (plus many other objects) as being received from Hezekiah as tribute (see Cogan and Tadmor [1988:229, 338-339], who suggest that the higher amount of silver in the Assyrian annals totals may include the precious metals stripped from the Temple doors and doorposts). (For the probable weight of the talent in modern terms [about 75 lb., or 35 kg], see the second note on 1 Kgs 9:14; cf. the recent article by John Holladay [2009:211]).

18:16 *gold.* This word is used twice in this verse in the NLT (cf. NIV, NRSV), but there is no explicit counterpart in the MT (which simply reads that Hezekiah had stripped the doors and the doorposts, which he had previously plated), whence the suggestion mentioned in the previous note that (unspecified) precious metals (presumably silver) stripped from the Temple doors and doorposts may have been included in the higher Assyrian totals for tribute received from Hezekiah. (Both the doors and doorposts of the Temple had, however, indeed been plated with gold back in the days of Solomon; see 1 Kgs 6:31-35.)

gave it all. In a way, King Hezekiah was no better than his predecessors, including his "evil" father, King Ahaz (see the note on 16:8). What a humiliating image we have here of Hezekiah scraping the bottom of the barrel, so to speak, to pay off the Assyrians! (The omission of 18:14-16 in the Isaiah parallel will be discussed in the commentary.)

18:17 *Nevertheless.* The Hebrew simply reads, "and the king of Assyria sent . . ." (*wayyish-lakh* [TH7971, ZH8938] *melek 'ashur*), but the NLT translation effectively conveys the idea that we are probably beginning a new section of narrative here ("Account B"; see the commentary for details).

commander in chief . . . field commander . . . chief of staff. Heb., *tartan* [TH8661, ZH9580] . . . *rab-saris* [TH7227B/5631, ZH8042/6247] . . . *rab-shaqeh* [TH7262, ZH8072], three titles now familiar to us from their Akkadian parallels (see Cogan and Tadmor 1988:229-230 for details). The third refers to the main spokesperson here, the "chief of staff" (or more precisely, the "chief butler," often transliterated "Rabshakeh"), who was a high court official whose duties did not normally include military affairs, but since Sennacherib himself was participating in this particular campaign, he naturally accompanied him into the field. The *rab-shaqeh* may have himself been an Israelite of noble birth previously exiled to Assyria; in any case, his fluency in the Judahite dialect (cf. 18:26) probably qualified him to be the chief spokesperson for the Assyrians over against his immediate military superiors (cf. the references found in the NLT mg note on this verse concerning how often he is referred to, in contrast to the other Assyrian officials).

upper pool. This location is also mentioned in nearly identical terms in Isa 7:3 in connection with King Ahaz's inspection of the Jerusalem defenses in the days of Tiglath-pileser. The "aqueduct" (*te'alah* [TH8585, ZH9498]) is not to be confused with Hezekiah's famous tunnel, which is only mentioned in passing in 20:20 as bringing water "into the city" from the Gihon Spring (the main water source for Jerusalem) down to the pool of Siloam (presumably the "lower" pool). The location of the "upper" pool, however, remains uncertain.

Wiseman (1993:276) plausibly suggests it was near the Gihon Spring itself, while Cogan and Tadmor (1988:230) cite Mazar's identification with the location of the "camp of the Assyrians" outside the city walls to the northwest (cf. Ussishkin 1979:137-142; Hobbs 1985:260-262).

to the field where cloth is washed. Heb., *sedeh kobes* [TH3526, ZH3891], "field of washing" or "field of bleaching" (cf. NLT mg). Koehler and Baumgartner (HALOT 459) translate here, "to full, clean cloths by treading, kneading, and beating them," whence the traditional rendering of "fuller's field"; but they also note the suggestion that this field was where fulled cloths were spread out "in order to dry and bleach."

18:18 *Eliakim . . . Shebna . . . Joah.* Thus, three Judahite high court officials counterbalance the three members of the Assyrian delegation mentioned in the previous verse. Eliakim was the "royal steward" or "palace administrator" (*'al habbayith* [TH1004, ZH1074], lit., "over the palace/house"; cf. the first note on 1 Kgs 4:6). Shebna was the "scribe" or "court secretary" (*soper* [TH5608A, ZH6221])—in Isa 22:15 he had been termed both the "steward" (*soken* [TH5532B, ZH6125]; cf. Oswalt 1986:418 for this suggested translation) and the "palace administrator" (*'al habbayith*), but Isaiah prophesied that he would soon be demoted and replaced by Eliakim [Isa 22:20], a prediction which has seemingly taken place, at least partially, here in 2 Kings). Finally, Joah was listed as the "state recorder" or "royal historian" (*mazkir* [TH2142C, ZH4654]), but he is otherwise unknown.

COMMENTARY

We have just read a remarkably "terse, factual account" (18:13-16; so Cogan and Tadmor 1988:240-241) concerning Hezekiah's actions during the invasion of Sennacherib in 701 BC. Commentators have come to label this "Account A," describing it as an annalistic or archival record utterly devoid of theological reflection (cf. the commentary on 16:1-20 for similar, nonjudgmental records cited concerning King Ahaz). But starting with 18:17, another account begins, usually labeled "Account B": a lengthy and discursive narrative, heavily theological throughout, and according to some, describing an entirely different campaign (cf. the references cited in the previous commentary section for details). Although once championed by no less a figure than W. F. Albright, few today would be open to such a radical historical reconstruction. But that then leaves us in a quandary: Can "Account B" (traditionally delineated as 18:17–19:37, with the possibility that all or part of the last two verses properly belong to "Account A") actually be an account of the same campaign so tersely presented in Account A and represent such an embarrassing set of events for King Hezekiah?

Complicating matters even further, scholars such as Childs (1967:73-103; cf. Barnes 1991:77-79) generally subdivide Account B into two subsections: B[1] (18:17–19:9a, 36-37) and B[2] (19:9b-35). Both subsections are largely parallel, with B[1] containing the speeches of the Rabshakeh (NLT, "chief of staff"; see the second note on 18:17 for details concerning this title), the first response of King Hezekiah and the prophet Isaiah, and the latter's confident prediction that Sennacherib would hear a rumor and return to his own land where he would fall by the sword; and B[2] containing another speech (and/or letter) from unnamed Assyrian messengers, another response from Hezekiah and from Isaiah, and a prediction that Yahweh himself would defend his city, Jerusalem. Thus, Account B[1] concludes with

Sennacherib's abrupt departure home to Nineveh after receiving word that Tirhakah (later a very famous pharaoh [cf. the note on 19:9] but here possibly an Egyptian royal commander of the army) was on the march against him, and then Sennacherib's assassination by his own sons; while Account B² ends with Yahweh's miraculous slaying of some 185,000 Assyrian soldiers. Childs characterizes B¹ as a unified narrative largely based upon ancient historical tradition (cf. Barnes 1991:108-109), but B² as more legendary, more heavily theological (e.g., the role of Hezekiah as pious king), and containing a lengthy prophetic interpolation (19:21b-31), which is more akin to oracles found in the book of Isaiah. Thus, a complicated analysis of what seems to be a relatively straightforward (if repetitive) narrative account.

Childs's analysis has won many followers (I think there is a lot to be said for it, myself); but its subtlety is mostly beyond the scope of the present commentary, which mainly looks at the text in its final form. And not all have followed his source-critical approach anyway. Sweeney (2007:411-412), for one, largely discounts the validity of such an analysis: "The report of successive delegations does not mark independent narratives, but points instead to the development of dramatic tension in the midst of a confrontation between the two groups, portrayed at the surface level by the numerically balanced groups of three Assyrian and three Israelite officers." Childs, however, in his recent Isaiah commentary (2001:271-272), gives an effective response: "I do not agree . . . that because of the possibility of rendering the text as a coherent literary composition, the synchronic reading undercuts the case for seeing an earlier, diachronic diversity. Without adequate recognition of a history of development the danger can be acute of flattening the tensions and subtle nuances that are clearly present." Suffice it to say that, as we have found already throughout the books of 1–2 Kings, annalistic material has been combined with more heavily theological discourses, and that definitely appears to be the case here. It will be our task to tease out these historical and theological messages as a whole, leaving behind diachronic analyses (i.e., those reflecting different editorial eras and times), which are in any case largely hypothetical in nature. But simply to suggest that we have a unified, straightforward narrative here about Hezekiah, Isaiah, the Rabshakeh, and the arrogant Assyrian King Sennacherib is to miss much of the richness of the traditions which comprise most of chapters 18 and 19 of the book of 2 Kings.

Commentators have, as we have just seen, taken seriously the lengthy parallels between these chapters of 2 Kings and Isaiah 36–37 (actually the parallels extend through 2 Kgs 20 and Isa 39), and they have naturally debated which was the more likely original source, Kings or Isaiah? Most these days think Kings was used by Isaiah (e.g., Cogan and Tadmor 1988:257), with the "Poem of Praise of Hezekiah" (Isa 38:9-20) added to the account "at a late stage in its development" (Williamson 1996:47-52). But proponents of Isaiah's primacy have not been found entirely lacking (cf. the nuanced discussion in Blenkinsopp 2000:458-461).

In such cases, each parallel text must be weighed on its own, and overarching hypotheses resisted in the case of individual variations. One such variation should be cited to make the point: the notable absence of 18:14-16 in the otherwise closely parallel account about King Hezekiah found in Isaiah 36. As we have seen, these three verses in Kings present a very negative image of Hezekiah scurrying around trying to raise the immense tribute Sennacherib demanded as his price for withdrawing from the land and leaving Hezekiah on the throne. Naturally, commentators are quick to assume that the Isaiah editor purposely omitted these verses so as not to present Hezekiah in such a negative light—a suggestion which certainly appears plausible enough at first sight. But Childs (1967:69-70) proposed a simpler text-critical solution: We find here a case of haplography in which where a scribe's eye skipped from the verb "and he sent" (*wayyishlakh* [TH7971, ZH8938]) at the beginning of 18:14 to the identical verb at the beginning of 18:17, resulting in his omission of 18:14-16 in the parallel Isaiah text. I cite this example merely to show how mechanical textual corruption may be the underlying cause of what might otherwise seem to be tendentious editing of the otherwise parallel texts. In sum: We may never know for sure why something is left out—it is our job rather to focus upon what is *not* left out, and why!

◆   ## 3. Sennacherib threatens Jerusalem (18:19-37)

¹⁹Then the Assyrian king's chief of staff told them to give this message to Hezekiah:

"This is what the great king of Assyria says: What are you trusting in that makes you so confident? ²⁰Do you think that mere words can substitute for military skill and strength? Who are you counting on, that you have rebelled against me? ²¹On Egypt? If you lean on Egypt, it will be like a reed that splinters beneath your weight and pierces your hand. Pharaoh, the king of Egypt, is completely unreliable!

²²"But perhaps you will say to me, 'We are trusting in the LORD our God!' But isn't he the one who was insulted by Hezekiah? Didn't Hezekiah tear down his shrines and altars and make everyone in Judah and Jerusalem worship only at the altar here in Jerusalem?

²³"I'll tell you what! Strike a bargain with my master, the king of Assyria. I will give you 2,000 horses if you can find that many men to ride on them! ²⁴With your tiny army, how can you think of challenging even the weakest contingent of my master's troops, even with the help of Egypt's chariots and charioteers? ²⁵What's more, do you think we have invaded your land without the LORD's direction? The LORD himself told us, 'Attack this land and destroy it!' "

²⁶Then Eliakim son of Hilkiah, Shebna, and Joah said to the Assyrian chief of staff, "Please speak to us in Aramaic, for

we understand it well. Don't speak in Hebrew,* for the people on the wall will hear."

²⁷But Sennacherib's chief of staff replied, "Do you think my master sent this message only to you and your master? He wants all the people to hear it, for when we put this city under siege, they will suffer along with you. They will be so hungry and thirsty that they will eat their own dung and drink their own urine."

²⁸Then the chief of staff stood and shouted in Hebrew to the people on the wall, "Listen to this message from the great king of Assyria! ²⁹This is what the king says: Don't let Hezekiah deceive you. He will never be able to rescue you from my power. ³⁰Don't let him fool you into trusting in the LORD by saying, 'The LORD will surely rescue us. This city will never fall into the hands of the Assyrian king!'

³¹"Don't listen to Hezekiah! These are the terms the king of Assyria is offering: Make peace with me—open the gates and come out. Then each of you can continue eating from your own grapevine and fig tree and drinking from your own well. ³²Then I will arrange to take you to another land like this one—a land of grain and new wine, bread and vineyards, olive groves and honey. Choose life instead of death!

"Don't listen to Hezekiah when he tries to mislead you by saying, 'The LORD will rescue us!' ³³Have the gods of any other nations ever saved their people from the king of Assyria? ³⁴What happened to the gods of Hamath and Arpad? And what about the gods of Sepharvaim, Hena, and Ivvah? Did any god rescue Samaria from my power? ³⁵What god of any nation has ever been able to save its people from my power? So what makes you think that the LORD can rescue Jerusalem from me?"

18:26 Hebrew *in the dialect of Judah;* also in 18:28.

³⁶But the people were silent and did not utter a word because Hezekiah had commanded them, "Do not answer him."

³⁷Then Eliakim son of Hilkiah, the palace administrator; Shebna the court secretary; and Joah son of Asaph, the royal historian, went back to Hezekiah. They tore their clothes in despair, and they went in to see the king and told him what the Assyrian chief of staff had said.

NOTES

18:19 *chief of staff.* Heb., *rab-shaqeh* [TH7262, ZH8072]; cf. the second note on 18:17 for details.

great king. The Hebrew equivalent of the Assyrian term *šarru rabû,* the "foremost title of every Assyrian king from the days of Shamshi-Adad [c. 1750 BC] on" (Cogan and Tadmor 1988:231). Cogan and Tadmor also note that in contrast, the "chief of staff" or Rabshakeh in his speech always refers to Hezekiah by his personal name, never using a royal title.

18:21 *On Egypt?* Whether or not we accept Childs's B¹ and B² analysis (see the previous commentary section for details), we certainly are meant to note the parallelism between trusting in Egypt and trusting in Yahweh, parallelism insufficiently noted in the commentaries (but see Barnes 1991:109-111, 119-124; cf. the commentary on 19:1-19). The characterization of Egypt as a "reed that splinters beneath your weight and pierces your hand" resonates with Yahweh's similar comments about Egypt in Ezek 29:6-7. The reed imagery evokes the canes which grew profusely in Egypt's marshy waters. Isaiah had also repeatedly denounced seeking help from Egypt (see Isa 30:1-5; 31:1-3; cf. Isa 20:6 [from the days of Sargon II]), in addition to delivering Yahweh's condemnations of Egypt and Cush (NLT, "Ethiopia") found in Isa 18:1-7; 19:1-17.

18:22 *trusting in the LORD our God!* The logic here is most ironic, inasmuch as it includes an oblique reference (surely historical in origin—cf. Childs 1967:82) to Hezekiah following the Deuteronomic tradition (cf. Deut 12:8-14) in its insistence that in the future (from Moses's point of view) Yahweh will place "his name" on only one site in Israel, and it is to that spot that all are to travel to worship him (see "One Place of Worship" under "Major Themes" in the Introduction). Aharoni, in his excavations at Beersheba in 1973, discovered the remains of a large four-horned stone altar calculated to be some 63 in. (157 cm) in height (= 3 royal cubits?), but with its stones reused as part of a repaired wall of a storehouse complex around the end of the eighth century BC (see Aharoni 1974:2-6). Here is conclusive proof that the demolition of the altar and the reuse of its stones took place during the reign of King Hezekiah, probably as part of his religious reform so sarcastically noted here by the Rabshakeh—no more altars to Yahweh (or any other god) permitted anywhere except Jerusalem.

18:23 *2,000 horses.* These horses were probably meant to pull chariots rather than to be ridden as cavalry (see the note on 1 Kgs 4:26). Still, this "offer" was meant to be thoroughly demoralizing in any case (the sarcastic echo of the "law of the king" in Deut 17:14-20— the king is not to multiply horses, and especially not to go back to Egypt to get them!—is surely also meant to be noticed [cf. the commentary on 1 Kgs 10:14-29 for details]).

18:26 *speak to us in Aramaic.* That is, the international diplomatic language of the western half of the Assyrian Empire (Machinist 1983:733). Obviously, the Judahite leaders wanted the people *not* to understand what the Assyrian "chief of staff" was saying! (Cf. the second note on 18:17 concerning the probable fluency of the Rabshakeh in the local Judahite dialect.)

18:27 *eat their own dung and drink their own urine.* This is a literal translation. The Kethiv of the MT reads *kharehem* [TH2716, ZH2989], "their excrement," and *shenehem* [TH7890, ZH8875], "their urine." The Qere, however, reads *tso'atham* [TH6675, ZH7363], "their filth," and *meme-raglehem* [TH4325/7272, ZH4784/8079], "water of their legs/feet"—more euphemistic expressions for the harsh words found in the Kethiv. (Concerning Kethiv and Qere, see the note on 3:24.) The ugly realities of a protracted siege are effectively portrayed here!

18:31 *eating . . . drinking.* See the second note on 1 Kgs 4:25 for this stereotypical description of "ideal" life in the land of Israel (or Judah).

18:32 *another land like this one.* Concerning the Assyrian policy of deporting large portions of subject peoples, see the third note on 15:29. Here the Rabshakeh puts the best face possible on this terrifying prospect facing the Judahites, although as Cogan and Tadmor (1988:233) point out, "[This] was not mere rhetoric. It was in Assyria's interest to care for the deportees both during the journey to the lands of resettlement, as well as in their new homes, an interest motivated by a desire to make maximum use of the manpower and resources these exiles represented. . . . Deportees from the West were resettled within Assyria proper, and in Sennacherib's days many were brought to Nineveh to populate the newly rebuilt capital."

18:33 *Have the gods of any other nations ever saved their people from the king of Assyria?* This is an effective rhetorical question, even if the places mentioned in the next verse had been defeated by previous Assyrian kings (Cogan and Tadmor 1988:34) and not by Sennacherib himself, who had only come to the throne four years previously. (A similar listing of references to defeated peoples is also found in 19:11-13, where the previous Assyrian kings are clearly cited as gaining the victories.)

18:34 *Did any god rescue Samaria . . . ?* Of course, the God who would have been expected to rescue Samaria was none other than Yahweh himself; for reasons that he did not rescue them, see 17:7-12, 18a. Samaria had fallen to the Assyrians in 722 BC, with credit given to both Shalmaneser V and his successor Sargon II (see note on 17:5). Whether the Assyrians were aware of the fact that Yahweh was the national God of both Israel and Judah is uncertain, but presumably the Rabshakeh (if he was indeed from northern Israel) would have been quite clear on the subject—hence, the devastating reference to Samaria's recent demise being left to the end.

18:37 *Eliakim . . . Shebna . . . Joah.* See the note on 18:18 for details.

COMMENTARY

Hezekiah and his people are in the middle of a crisis that will extend to the end of the next chapter (cf. the textual and form-critical analysis discussed in the previous commentary section for details). The crisis is acute, and it is overwhelming. The Rabshakeh (NLT, "chief of staff"; see the second note on 18:17) has given his speeches (in the native dialect of Judah; see note on 18:26), and their conclusions seem to be unanswerable for Hezekiah: (1) You can't trust in Egypt, your erstwhile ally, to be of any assistance; (2) you can't trust in Yahweh, your national God, to help you out; and (3) it is in fact Yahweh himself who has ordered us to attack you! As is evident, the underlying issue here is that of "trust" (*batakh* [TH982, ZH1053]; cf. Seow 1999:265). Whom should one trust?

With regard to these questions of trust, Egypt will prove to be of some assistance and *not* be "a reed that splinters" (18:21; cf. the note there and the note on 19:9), in spite of past indicators to the contrary (cf. 17:4). The major concern, however, was trust in Yahweh: Maybe Yahweh himself is acting against his people Judah (he certainly acted quite recently against his people Israel [see the note on 18:34], an observation the Deuteronomistic editor has just made at some length in the previous chapter of 2 Kings). This too will prove false, to the relief of Hezekiah.

Two subpoints in the Rabshakeh's diatribes should also be cited here: (a) Yahweh might well be angry over the recent removal of the Yahwistic high places by Hezekiah (cf. the note on 18:22); and in any case, (b) it is most difficult to argue against the impressive track record of previous Assyrian successes. Which other nation or kingdom has been able to withstand its military might (cf. 18:32b-35)? Both are reasonable and persuasive, but both err. Subpoint (a) asserts that because Hezekiah has uniquely (and surely for some, paradoxically) shut down many of Yahweh's own sanctuaries, Yahweh has sent the Assyrians to punish Judah. Ironically enough, the prophet Isaiah stated something similar to this in Isaiah 10:5-19 (Assyria, "the rod of my anger" [Isa 10:5a] was sent by Yahweh against Jerusalem [Isa 10:12], but for different reasons than those given by the Rabshakeh [Isa 10:1-2]). Subpoint (b) asserts that Assyria's power cannot be resisted by any god and history will repeat itself. But Assyria misunderstood the reason for its successes, foolishly claiming, "By my own powerful arm I have done this" (Isa 10:13a), and would soon suffer much due to that misunderstanding ("[Yahweh] will send a plague among Assyria's proud troops. . . . [as a fire] burning up the enemy in a single night" [Isa 10:16-17]). At this point in the story, the end is not yet, but the end is certain. It is, however, incumbent upon Hezekiah to act in faith, and in faith he will act. As we soon shall see, he will change nothing less than the course of world history by his prayers!

◆   ### 4. Hezekiah seeks the Lord's help (19:1-19)

When King Hezekiah heard their report, he tore his clothes and put on burlap and went into the Temple of the LORD. ²And he sent Eliakim the palace administrator, Shebna the court secretary, and the leading priests, all dressed in burlap, to the prophet Isaiah son of Amoz. ³They told him, "This is what King Hezekiah says: Today is a day of trouble, insults, and disgrace. It is like when a child is ready to be born, but the mother has no strength to deliver the baby. ⁴But perhaps the LORD your God has heard the Assyrian chief of staff,* sent by the king to defy the living God, and will punish him for his words. Oh, pray for those of us who are left!"

⁵After King Hezekiah's officials delivered the king's message to Isaiah, ⁶the prophet replied, "Say to your master, 'This is what the LORD says: Do not be disturbed by this blasphemous speech against me from the Assyrian king's messengers. ⁷Listen! I myself will move against him,* and the king will receive a message that he is needed at home. So he will return to his land, where I will have him killed with a sword.'"

⁸Meanwhile, the Assyrian chief of staff left Jerusalem and went to consult the king of Assyria, who had left Lachish and was attacking Libnah.

⁹Soon afterward King Sennacherib received word that King Tirhakah of Ethiopia* was leading an army to fight against him. Before leaving to meet the attack, he sent messengers back to Hezekiah in Jerusalem with this message:

¹⁰"This message is for King Hezekiah of Judah. Don't let your God, in whom you trust, deceive you with promises that Jerusalem will not be captured by the king of Assyria. ¹¹You know perfectly well what the kings of Assyria have done wherever they have gone. They have completely destroyed everyone who stood in their way! Why should you be any different? ¹²Have the gods of other nations rescued them—such nations as Gozan, Haran, Rezeph, and the people of Eden who were in Tel-assar? My predecessors destroyed them all! ¹³What happened to the king of Hamath and the king of Arpad? What happened to the kings of Sepharvaim, Hena, and Ivvah?"

¹⁴After Hezekiah received the letter from the messengers and read it, he went up to the LORD's Temple and spread it out before the LORD. ¹⁵And Hezekiah prayed this prayer before the LORD: "O LORD, God of Israel, you are enthroned between the mighty cherubim! You alone are God of all the kingdoms of the earth. You alone created the heavens and the earth. ¹⁶Bend down, O LORD, and listen! Open your eyes, O LORD, and see! Listen to Sennacherib's words of defiance against the living God.

¹⁷"It is true, LORD, that the kings of Assyria have destroyed all these nations. ¹⁸And they have thrown the gods of these nations into the fire and burned them. But of course the Assyrians could destroy them! They were not gods at all—only idols of wood and stone shaped by human hands. ¹⁹Now, O LORD our God, rescue us from his power; then all the kingdoms of the earth will know that you alone, O LORD, are God."

19:4 Or the rabshakeh; also in 19:8.   19:7 Hebrew I will put a spirit in him.   19:9 Hebrew of Cush.

NOTES

19:1 burlap. Traditionally, "sackcloth" (cf. note on 6:30).

19:2 Isaiah son of Amoz. Ironically not mentioned by name in 1–2 Kings up to this point, this very famous Judahite prophet has already played a large role in King Ahaz's life and reign, and he will do that and more here and in the next chapter in connection with Ahaz's son Hezekiah (cf. the commentary on 15:1-7 and on 19:20-37).

19:3 ready to be born. Lit., "children have come to the breaking forth, or breach [of the womb]" ('ad-mashber [TH4866, ZH5402]); cf. Hos 13:13 for the same idiom.

19:4 chief of staff. Or, "the Rabshakeh" (see the second note on 18:17 for details).

19:7 I myself will move against him. As indicated in the NLT mg, the Hebrew reads "I will put a spirit in him" (hineni nothen [TH5414, ZH5989] bo ruakh); other usages of the term ruakh [TH7307, ZH8120] occur in 2:9; 1 Kgs 18:12 (cf. the notes on those verses).

19:8 Lachish . . . Libnah. For the city of Lachish, see the note on 18:14, as well as the second note on 14:19. For Libnah, see the second note on 8:22.

19:9 King Tirhakah of Ethiopia. The third (as reckoned in Manetho) and best-known of the pharaohs of the 25th (Nubian or "Kushite") Dynasty of Egypt. Spelled "Thrk" in Egyptian ("Taharqa" in Nubian), "Tarkos" in Greek, and "Tarqu" in Assyrian, he reigned 690–664 BC, so the invasion of Sennacherib in 701 BC took place some 11 years prior to Tirhakah's accession to the throne as "of Kush" (which is what the Hebrew reads here). This chronological incongruity has been a major impetus for positing a second Palestinian invasion by Sennacherib late in his reign (cf. the commentary on 18:13-18). The Nubian kingdom of Napata (located on the Nile River south of Egypt in what roughly corresponds with the northern part of present-day Sudan; cf. Barnes 1991:73) had placed considerable pressure during and before 712 BC on the balkanized regions in the delta area (which had no fewer than three different "pharaohs" on the throne at the same time; cf. the commentary on 15:13-15). But in that year, one Shabako, "King of Kush" (see Spalinger 1973:97;

also the convenient summary in Barnes 1991:97-99), had taken over, and this is, effectively, the first year of the reign of the 25th Dynasty over all of Upper and Lower Egypt. Tirhakah (son of Piye [or Piankhy, c. 735–712 BC], who was the effectual founder of the dynasty) was probably the brother of Shebitku, his immediate predecessor on the throne (accession c. 701 or earlier [cf. Kitchen 1996:155-156, 557]; recently, Kahn [2001:1-18] has argued for 706 BC). In any case, he easily transcends in fame all the family who preceded him, both in his building projects ("for the first time in five centuries Egypt experienced a building boom of major proportions" [ABD 6.572]), as well as in his military prowess (Redford 1992:355-358; cf. Spalinger 1978). In summary, the ancient Greek traditions of Tirhakah as a conquering warrior, though roundly discounted by many moderns, are not without foundation (see Barnes 1991:106-108; cf. Redford 1992:355-356, and the references cited there; also cf. Morkot 2000:262-264).

The historicity, however, of Tirhakah actually leading an Egyptian force against Sennacherib in 701 BC remains problematic for many (of course, he was hardly "King of Kush" at the time, but the title may be taken as proleptic). Kitchen (1996:154-161, 553-558) has argued vigorously for its accuracy, and he has been followed by several others (cf. Barnes 1991:103). But this must be discussed in the light of the battle on the plain of Eltekeh, a prominent military confrontation between Egypt and Assyria that took place during Sennacherib's third campaign (Eltekeh was a Levitical city in the original territory allotted to the tribe of Dan [Josh 21:23]; it was located near Timnah, although its precise location remains uncertain [cf. ABD 2.483-484]). According to Sennacherib's annals, the Assyrians were victorious (cf. Cogan and Tadmor 1988:338 for the text), but some scholars doubt their accuracy (Redford 1992:353 suggests that it was "an unexpected and serious reverse" for Assyria); and if the present verse in 2 Kings has any connection with this—which I strongly suspect is the case— we would have independent corroboration for this conclusion. However the cryptic notice is meant to be understood, it could not be a good omen for Assyria.

In summary: Tirhakah was a powerful pharaoh, but not in 701 BC. He could have been a military leader of some prominence then, but this remains, at best, problematic. However, the positive reality of an effective Egyptian force sent against Sennacherib is indicated by this brief notice. And Egypt is therefore no longer to be characterized simply as a "reed that splinters beneath your weight and pierces your hand," as the Rabshakeh asserts in 18:21. Both Egypt and Yahweh have proven to be dependable allies for the beleaguered little land of Judah.

19:12 *Have the gods of other nations rescued them . . . ?* See the notes on 18:33; 18:34 (and the related commentary) concerning this effective line of reasoning on the part of the Assyrians (also see Hezekiah's own words concerning these embarrassing assertions in his prayer to Yahweh in 19:17-18).

19:14 *spread it out before the LORD.* Cogan and Tadmor (1988:236) suggest that, because of the national emergency, Hezekiah was allowed to enter the Holy of Holies where the wings of the cherubim stretched over the Ark of the Covenant, a privilege normally restricted to the priests.

19:15 *enthroned between the mighty cherubim!* See the first note on 1 Kgs 6:23. Sweeney (2007:417-418) points out that this form of address was also frequently associated with the procession of the Ark (1 Sam 4:4; 2 Sam 6:2; Ps 80:1 [2]; cf. Ps 99:1).

19:16 *listen!* Hezekiah's impassioned pleas for Yahweh "the living God" to "see" and to "listen" to Sennacherib's defiant words against him recall Solomon's prayer of dedication (1 Kgs 8:23-53) for Yahweh to see and to hear from heaven (cf. 1 Kgs 8:52) and respond favorably to the petitions of his people addressed toward the Temple.

19:19 *then all the kingdoms of the earth will know that you alone, O LORD, are God.*
This is a powerful concluding petition, truly international in scope (cf. the figure of Solomon back in 1 Kgs 4:20-34; and also, to some degree, Moses himself with his reference to the Egyptians in Exod 32:11-13; Num 14:13-16).

COMMENTARY

As noted in "Earlier Editions of Kings" in the Introduction, King Hezekiah is one of the two Deuteronomistic kings considered "incomparable"; that is, to be placed in a category uniquely above and beyond all the others (the other king in this category is King Josiah). A commonplace conundrum among Kings commentators is to ask, then, which of these two kings was the better (contrast 18:5 with 23:25, and then try to decide!). And a commonplace response is to say the answer is "yes"; or if any distinction is to be made, that King Hezekiah was incomparable in the area of trusting in Yahweh (cf. 18:5; also the commentary on 19:20-37), whereas Josiah was clearly incomparable in the area of cult-reform (virtually the entirety of 23:1-25 illustrates that with a vengeance). But I suspect more should be said about our current hero, King Hezekiah, and his "incomparability": In light of the text we have just read, Hezekiah is clearly incomparable in the area of prayer.

In my conservative Protestant circles, I recall senior pastors and church officials some years ago saying something to the effect of: "Now make that a $5,000 prayer." Obviously $5,000 was reckoned as needed at the time, so a "$5,000 prayer" was also what was perceived to be needed—that is, a prayer to move the people (and to move God?) to meet that monetary goal. Well, Hezekiah needed a city to be saved miraculously from a ferocious Assyrian army, so he had to offer a "Jerusalem-sized prayer" to accomplish the task. And that is exactly what he did. (Later on, he will have to offer a prayer for personal healing from an apparently mortal wound [see 20:1-11, and especially 20:2-3], and he will do so once again.) That king could pray!

So I suspect that, just as Josiah was *incomparable* in reforming the worship system to match the Deuteronomic ideal, Hezekiah was nothing less than *incomparable* in the intercessory prayers he could, and did, offer up to Yahweh. And just as the prophet Isaiah would later change his direction of walking (20:4-5) in reference to another such prayer from the king, in the present passage it would appear that Isaiah had to change his mind completely about the future of the city of Jerusalem—and not least, about the place that Egypt would play in such a future (cf. the note on 18:21)—again, due largely to the powerful prayer of King Hezekiah. Whether or not that was precisely the case, Isaiah will offer up a stirring, powerful prophecy about the fatal hubris of Assyria and the newly acquired inviolability of Jerusalem in the very next section of this chapter. As James (Jas 5:16) says, "The earnest prayer of a righteous person has great power and produces wonderful results."

Now whether Egypt was somehow involved in this victory, or whether the victory was won by Yahweh alone, is a question to which the answer is still uncertain (cf. the extended discussion on Tirhakah in the note on 19:9). But certainly, the current structuring of Account B would suggest that one consider the idea that Egypt was indeed involved (see the commentary on 18:13-18 regarding Account B). Perhaps in deference to the previous "anti-Egyptian" policy of the prophet Isaiah (see note on 18:21), the narrator is soft-pedaling the subject; but I do see the present Tirhakah reference in 19:9 serving as a clear rejoinder to the Rabshakeh's mocking remarks back in 18:19b-25 that it was futile to trust either in Egypt or in Yahweh. Of course, Yahweh was the reason Jerusalem was spared and the prayers of Hezekiah answered, but Egypt *did* indeed play a role, however minor. The narrator draws our attention to that fact, at least in passing. We should not miss this signal, as so many commentators these days seem to do. Pharaoh Tirhakah, whatever his role may have been in 701 BC, grew to be a very significant force in the Levant over the next number of years. Yahweh was faithful; Egypt apparently also (at least to some degree), and Isaiah, on this occasion, was led to change his mind about Egypt—they were no longer simply to be characterized as a "reed which splinters and pierces your hand" (cf. Ezek 29:6-7). And somehow, I don't think this great prophet minded one bit that he may have been proven inconsistent about the power of that nation, for his powerful words about Jerusalem and about Hezekiah did indeed carry the day (see 19:21-34 and the miraculous fulfillment in 19:35-37). (On the idea that the prophet may have been proven "wrong" about Hezekiah's personal future, see the commentary on 20:1-11; and for a reminder that a prophet need not be "woodenly" correct in his or her predictions to be a true prophet of God, see endnote 28 of the Introduction.)

In summary, a true prophet must predict the future accurately (Deut 18:15-22; cf. the note on 1 Kgs 13:3, where I have labeled this important criterion "the test of short-term prediction"), but with the proviso that either individual and/or corporate "free will" can alter the result (Jer 18:1-12). Isaiah was of course a true prophet, yet at least in 2 Kings 20:1-11 (and I suspect in the present text as well) his initial prophecy proved to be "inaccurate" (in the sense that Hezekiah's free will significantly altered the future result). This would not be a problem for the ancients, and we today make it a problem only if we interpret biblical prophecy as some sort of inflexible and inalterable fortune-telling.

◆   5. Isaiah predicts Judah's deliverance (19:20–37)

20Then Isaiah son of Amoz sent this message to Hezekiah: "This is what the LORD, the God of Israel, says: I have heard your prayer about King Sennacherib of Assyria. 21And the LORD has spoken this word against him:

"The virgin daughter of Zion
despises you and laughs at you.
The daughter of Jerusalem
shakes her head in derision as
you flee.

22 "Whom have you been defying and
ridiculing?
Against whom did you raise your
voice?
At whom did you look with such
haughty eyes?

It was the Holy One of Israel!
23 By your messengers you have defied
the Lord.
You have said, 'With my many
chariots
I have conquered the highest mountains—
yes, the remotest peaks of Lebanon.
I have cut down its tallest cedars
and its finest cypress trees.
I have reached its farthest corners
and explored its deepest forests.
24 I have dug wells in many foreign lands
and refreshed myself with their
water.
With the sole of my foot
I stopped up all the rivers of Egypt!'
25 "But have you not heard?
I decided this long ago.

Long ago I planned it,
  and now I am making it happen.
I planned for you to crush fortified
    cities
  into heaps of rubble.
²⁶ That is why their people have so little
    power
  and are so frightened and confused.
They are as weak as grass,
  as easily trampled as tender green
    shoots.
They are like grass sprouting on a
    housetop,
  scorched before it can grow lush
    and tall.
²⁷ "But I know you well—
  where you stay
and when you come and go.
  I know the way you have raged
    against me.
²⁸ And because of your raging against me
    and your arrogance, which I have
    heard for myself,
  I will put my hook in your nose
    and my bit in your mouth.
I will make you return
  by the same road on which you
    came."

²⁹Then Isaiah said to Hezekiah, "Here is
the proof that what I say is true:

"This year you will eat only what
    grows up by itself,
  and next year you will eat what
    springs up from that.
But in the third year you will plant
    crops and harvest them;
  you will tend vineyards and eat
    their fruit.
³⁰ And you who are left in Judah,
  who have escaped the ravages of
    the siege,

will put roots down in your own soil
  and will grow up and flourish.
³¹ For a remnant of my people will
    spread out from Jerusalem,
  a group of survivors from
    Mount Zion.
The passionate commitment of the
    LORD of Heaven's Armies*
  will make this happen!

³²"And this is what the LORD says about
the king of Assyria:

"His armies will not enter Jerusalem.
  They will not even shoot an arrow
    at it.
They will not march outside its gates
    with their shields
  nor build banks of earth against
    its walls.
³³ The king will return to his own
    country
  by the same road on which he came.
He will not enter this city,
  says the LORD.
³⁴ For my own honor and for the sake of
    my servant David,
  I will defend this city and protect it."

³⁵That night the angel of the LORD went
out to the Assyrian camp and killed
185,000 Assyrian soldiers. When the surviving Assyrians* woke up the next morning, they found corpses everywhere.
³⁶Then King Sennacherib of Assyria broke
camp and returned to his own land. He
went home to his capital of Nineveh and
stayed there.
³⁷One day while he was worshiping in
the temple of his god Nisroch, his sons*
Adrammelech and Sharezer killed him
with their swords. They then escaped to
the land of Ararat, and another son, Esarhaddon, became the next king of Assyria.

19:31 As in Greek and Syriac versions, Latin Vulgate, and an alternate reading of the Masoretic Text (see also Isa 37:32); the other alternate reads *the Lord.*   19:35 Hebrew *When they.*   19:37 As in Greek version and an alternate reading of the Masoretic Text (see also Isa 37:38); the other alternate reading lacks *his sons.*

NOTES
19:21 *The daughter of Jerusalem shakes her head in derision.* Cities are uniformly considered to be "daughters" of the state, so probably "daughter Jerusalem" would have been a
better translation (as well as "daughter Zion" in 19:21a); cf. the translation found in Cogan

and Tadmor 1988:226. The entire poem is a taunt-song or mocking song, written in a dirge-like *qinah* meter, and thus sarcastically imitating an elegy written in honor of the dead.

19:22 the Holy One of Israel! This is a characteristic reference to Yahweh found 29 times in the book of Isaiah, and only 7 times elsewhere in the OT (counting this occurrence; cf. Oswalt 1986:19).

19:23 I have cut down . . . cedars . . . cypress trees. This is typical language of Assyrian propaganda indicating both the appropriation of such prized wood from Lebanon and elsewhere for local building projects, as well as "the heroism of the king and the long range of his might" (Machinist 1983:723).

19:24 dug wells . . . stopped up all the rivers of Egypt! As Cogan and Tadmor (1988:237) note, Esarhaddon (cf. 19:37), the first Assyrian king to reach Egypt, boasted of providing his troops with water drawn from wells dug in the desert. The word for "Egypt" here (*matsor* [TH4693, ZH5191]) is unusual (but cf. Isa 19:6); some commentators have therefore proposed alternative translations (Calderone [1961:423-432] suggests "mountain streams" and Tawil [1982:195-206] prefers "Mt. Musri" [near Nineveh]). But the traditional translation is still probably the best (the "rivers" of Egypt would then refer to the branches of the Nile found in the delta).

19:28 my hook . . . my bit. These are ironic reversals of what normally were *Assyrian* actions taken against their defeated enemies when they were led into exile or put on public display in Nineveh (cf. Cogan and Tadmor 1988:238; also ANEP, picture 447).

19:29 the proof. Lit., "this is the sign" (*ha'oth* [TH226, ZH253]). For another famous reference to a "sign" as guaranteeing a miraculous future deliverance of Judah and the line of David, see Isa 7:14-16, where the virgin's conceiving and bearing a son, and calling his name "Immanuel," is a sign (*'oth* [TH226, ZH253]) guaranteeing the impending defeat of an enemy coalition that was terrifying King Ahaz (Hezekiah's father). (Concerning the use of such "short-term" predictions by the prophets, see the note on 1 Kgs 13:3.)

19:31 a remnant of my people. Again, this is quite typical of the Isaianic remnant theology; see, e.g., Isa 6:13; 10:20-23; and the naming of Isaiah's first son, "a remnant will return" (*she'ar* [TH7610, ZH8639] *yashub*; cf. Isa 7:3 and mg note). Wiseman (1993:283) notes that since many Israelites had fled to Judah at this time, Judah became in a sense the "remnant" of Israel (see the commentary on 18:1-12 concerning the doubling of the size of the city of Jerusalem at about this time).

LORD of Heaven's Armies. This is the common NLT rendering of the Hebrew epithet *yhwh tseba'oth* [TH3068/6635, ZH3378/7372] (traditionally, "the LORD of hosts"). As the NLT mg indicates, this is the reading found in the Isaiah parallel (Isa 37:16) and in some of the MT mss (and versions); Codex Leningradensis, however, simply reads the consonants for Yahweh here, plus the vowels for *tseba'oth* [TH6635, ZH7372].

19:32-33 will not enter. This phrase is used twice in the Hebrew, forming an *inclusio* (a repetition at the beginning and end of a literary unit) that brackets Isaiah's bold oracle, setting it off from the rest of the narrative. The prophet clearly asserts here that Jerusalem will survive, quite handily, any Assyrian attempt to besiege it (cf. Wiseman [1993:283], who, in contrast to some commentators, sees no contradiction here with the reference to an encircling group of "watch-posts" found in Sennacherib's annals [also cf. Cogan and Tadmor 1988:238]).

19:34 my servant David. Both here and in 20:6, Yahweh's "honor" is coupled with focus on the Davidic dynasty (see "The 'Lamp' of David" under "Major Themes" in the Introduction).

19:35 the Assyrian camp. On the probable location of this camp northwest of the city, see the third note on 18:17.

killed 185,000 Assyrian soldiers. We find here an impossibly large number, if taken literally (cf. the characteristics of such "folkloristic" figures, as discussed briefly in the note on 1 Kgs 20:29-30; see also the second note on 1 Kgs 3:5). For attempts to reinterpret this figure, see Wiseman 1993:284 ("a hundred and eighty-five officers"); also Cogan and Tadmor 1988:239. There is an intriguing tradition related in Herodotus's *History* (2.141) of a multitude of field mice swarming over an Assyrian camp in the days of Sennacherib, which was said to be located at Pelusium on the Egyptian frontier, with the mice devouring quivers, bows, and the handles of shields, thus rendering the Assyrian army unarmed and forced to flee with many casualties. Some see in this an independent (if garbled) confirmation of the biblical account (e.g., mice are notorious bearers of plague; cf. 1 Sam 6:3-5), while others see Herodotus's tradition as actually stemming from the present account (with a third possibility being that two different incidents are in view; cf. Wiseman). Whatever happened that night, some remarkable miracle must have taken place, changing forever the course of Judahite history. Na'aman (1979:86) concluded in his study of the Hezekiah *lmlk* seal impressions, "Then suddenly, some factor or factors, whose exact nature is obscure but which certainly did not emanate from internal Judean causes, forced the Assyrian army to retreat. Jerusalem, the Judean hill country and other regions not yet conquered were thus saved. This miraculous deliverance was attributed by the biblical narrator to the God of Israel and, in the course of years, developed into a tradition regarding Jerusalem's divine inviolability." For the suggestion that some sort of plague, augmented by the lack of any dependable water source for the Assyrian army as well as the brutal heat of late summer, brought about this deliverance, see Barnes 1991:123-124 and the references cited there.

19:37 *his god Nisroch.* This is an obscure reference, if taken literally (no such god is known); therefore, some take the term as a derogatory Hebrew pun on an Assyrian word such as *matsrukhu* ("divine standard" or "weapon") or the like (see Scurlock [2009], who concludes that the Hebrew spelling signifies in a single word the narrator's "judgment on Sennacherib as a boastful and ultimately humbled 'weapon' in the hand of God").

his sons Adrammelech and Sharezer. A single assassin, one "Arda-milissu," who was bypassed in the line of succession, is attested in the Mesopotamian sources. See Cogan and Tadmor (1988:239-240), who note, however, that there is no reason to discount the second name as a possible accomplice.

Esarhaddon. This was a younger son of Sennacherib (cf. the previous note) who was named by his father as successor to the throne; he reigned from 680 to 669 BC (see Younger 2007a). Although mentioned by name only three times in the Bible (here and in the parallel text in Isa 37:38; also in Ezra 4:2 in reference to the transplanted "Samaritans" brought in to resettle the northern territory of Israel [see 17:24-33]), Esarhaddon's influence on Judah, and especially on King Manasseh, must have been considerable.

COMMENTARY

We continue to find here, as well as in the parallel text of Isaiah 37:21-38, close parallels (and stunning reversals) with Isaiah's original stance toward Egypt (cf. the Isaianic references cited in the note on 18:21), as well as the original braggadocio of the Rabshakeh, cited at length in chapter 18. Nothing less than a miracle is described here, and it would seem nothing less than a miracle was able to rescue King Hezekiah from otherwise certain disaster for the city and death (or at least humiliating exile) for the king himself. (The fact that exactly such disaster and humiliating exile prove to be the fate for Zedekiah, the final king of Judah, will not be lost on the hearer or reader of the present text.) Yes, it does appear that Egypt (in the person of Tirhakah, eventual "King of Kush") did mitigate the Assyrian onrush (see the previous commentary for details), but the major focus of chapters 18 and 19 is the action of Yahweh in striking down, in the nick of time, an immense number of Assyrian soldiers (see the second note on 19:35). The prophet Isaiah, in clear response to Hezekiah's most timely prayer for the city and the nation (19:15-19), gives the audacious retort found in 19:21-28 ("[daughter] Jerusalem shakes her head in derision as you flee. . . ."), as well as the daring prediction found in 19:29-31 ("This year . . . next year. . . . But in the third year you will plant crops and harvest them . . . tend vineyards and eat their fruit"), and finally, the direct pronouncement of 19:32-34: "[He] will not enter. . . . The king will return to his own country. . . . I [Yahweh] will defend this city." And defend the city he does! Hezekiah proposes and Yahweh disposes, while Isaiah "counterposes." No wonder the popular theology of the "inviolability" of the city of Jerusalem later grew so powerful—and so pernicious (cf. the end of the commentary on 18:1-12).

In light of the stunning action of the "angel of Yahweh" in 19:35, the vivid *non-action* of the Assyrian god (or gods) in 19:37 should not be missed. It will be recalled that much of the Rabshakeh's sarcasm in chapter 18 was directed at the nonaction of the various deities cited for the peoples defeated by Assyria (this is also the case for the "message" given in 19:10-13 as well). Yahweh will equally be as ineffective as all those other national deities—or so the Assyrian propagandists boldly stated. In fact, it might be the case that Yahweh had actually sent the Assyrians in the first place (see 18:25). It was, in any case, clearly the will of Yahweh (either by commission or by omission) to humble Hezekiah and to humiliate his city. Eventually, however, there turns out to be, not one, but two "messages" that develop from this crisis (see 19:9, 20)—one from Sennacherib and another one from Yahweh (through his prophet Isaiah). And, as one would expect, it is the second message that will truly prove to be the prophetic one. To the alert hearer and reader of the book of Isaiah, this will bring to mind another Judahite king who was also faced with two messages, one from his intimidating military enemy, the other directed through Isaiah the prophet from Yahweh his God—namely, King Ahaz (see Isa 7:1-16). Alas, Ahaz did not heed the right message and, of all things, seemingly sought help from a third source—Assyria (see Isa 7:17–8:10). But perhaps the better comparison is between Hezekiah and his earlier northern counterpart, King Hoshea of Israel. For both had rebelled against Assyria, and both had sought help from *Egypt* (see the commentary on 17:1-4). But only one succeeded (or at least survived) as a result of his risky endeavor. And that would be King Hezekiah—the best king of all in the area of prayer, who will indeed "top" his record of success in the first half of the next chapter. But as was the case with kings Ahaz and Hoshea in chapters 16 and 17, the last word for King Hezekiah will *not* be success. Not the Assyrians but the Babylonians will have the last word. That, however, will come to pass well after Hezekiah's lifetime, and the little nation of Judah will outlast the powerful nation of Assyria—and that, to no small degree, will be due to the bold actions and the powerful prayers of heroic King Hezekiah.

◆   6. Hezekiah's sickness and recovery (20:1-11)

About that time Hezekiah became death-ly ill, and the prophet Isaiah son of Amoz went to visit him. He gave the king this message: "This is what the LORD says: Set your affairs in order, for you are going to die. You will not recover from this illness." ²When Hezekiah heard this, he turned his face to the wall and prayed to the LORD, ³"Remember, O LORD, how I have al-ways been faithful to you and have served you single-mindedly, always doing what pleases you." Then he broke down and wept bitterly.

⁴But before Isaiah had left the middle courtyard,* this message came to him from the LORD: ⁵"Go back to Hezekiah, the leader of my people. Tell him, 'This is what the LORD, the God of your ancestor David, says: I have heard your prayer and seen your tears. I will heal you, and three days from now you will get out of bed and go to the Temple of the LORD. ⁶I will add fif-teen years to your life, and I will rescue you and this city from the king of Assyria. I will defend this city for my own honor and for the sake of my servant David.' "

⁷Then Isaiah said, "Make an ointment from figs." So Hezekiah's servants spread the ointment over the boil, and Hezekiah recovered!

⁸Meanwhile, Hezekiah had said to Isaiah, "What sign will the LORD give to prove that he will heal me and that I will go to the Temple of the LORD three days from now?"

⁹Isaiah replied, "This is the sign from the LORD to prove that he will do as he promised. Would you like the shadow on the sundial to go forward ten steps or backward ten steps?*"

¹⁰"The shadow always moves forward," Hezekiah replied, "so that would be easy. Make it go ten steps backward instead." ¹¹So Isaiah the prophet asked the LORD to do this, and he caused the shadow to move ten steps backward on the sundial* of Ahaz!

20:4 As in Greek version and an alternate reading in the Masoretic Text; the other alternate reads *the middle of the city.*   20:9 Or *The shadow on the sundial has gone forward ten steps; do you want it to go backward ten steps?*   20:11 Hebrew *the steps.*

NOTES

20:1 *About that time.* This is a vague time marker, yet appropriate in the context since both events described in the present chapter evidently took place *before* the events described in the previous two chapters (see endnote 24 of the Introduction for further discussion concerning this important observation).

you are going to die. Concerning the "finality" of such a disturbing prediction, as well as the use of the same Hebrew verb both here ("set your affairs in order") and in the text concern-ing the aged King David in 1 Kgs 2:1, see the commentary. In ironic contrast to King David in 1 Kings 2, Hezekiah's "last words" will not be found immediately after this notice, but after a later notice given by Isaiah concerning the doomed future of the nation of Judah.

20:2 *he turned his face to the wall.* As observed in the note on 1 Kgs 21:4, King Ahab of Israel did much the same thing when he disliked a message he had just heard. But in fol-lowing this with a prayer, Hezekiah acted quite differently than Ahab did. Instead of refus-ing to eat, as Ahab did, Hezekiah refused to acquiesce to the status quo—so he prayed. And by now we know that this is a person who knows how to pray most powerfully (even though, to the proverbial "untrained ear," I must admit that his actual prayer followed by bitter weeping has the quality of petulant complaint).

20:4 *middle courtyard.* This is a grammatically difficult phrase in the MT. The Qere is fol-lowed here in the NLT (see NLT mg; cf. NRSV, NIV), while the Kethiv reads "the city" rather than "courtyard" (basically, there is only a difference of two similar-looking consonants plus the vowel-letter Yodh). For other references to various courtyards in the Temple, see 21:5; 23:12; 1 Kgs 7:12. In both readings, the main idea is that Isaiah had not even been able to return home before he received a new message from Yahweh.

20:5 Go back. Lit., "return" (*shub* [TH7725, ZH8740]), a word which often is used metaphorically to mean "change" or "repent" (cf. "The 'Sins of Manasseh'" in the Introduction for further discussion). Here Isaiah, both literally and metaphorically, "returns" to King Hezekiah with a new and very different message from Yahweh. (Concerning the "changeableness" of Isaiah's prophecy here over against the commonly argued view that a true prophet of Yahweh must declare the [seemingly unalterable] future with 100 percent accuracy the first time, see the commentary on 19:1-19, as well as the references cited there.)

20:6 I will add fifteen years to your life. The number of additional years promised here for Hezekiah corresponds precisely to the length of time cited for King Amaziah at the end of his life (14:17; cf. notes on 14:2; 15:1). Accepting the early date for Hezekiah's accession, as I have already argued (see the commentary on 18:1-12 for details), results in understanding Sennacherib's invasion in 701 BC as taking place during these additional years as well (cf. Isaiah's additional comment later on in the present verse that "[Yahweh] will rescue you and this city from the king of Assyria," thus implying that the city had not yet been rescued from the army of Sennacherib).

my servant David. See note on 19:34.

20:7 ointment from figs. Lit., "lump of pressed figs" or "poultice of figs"; figs were widely believed in antiquity to have medicinal qualities (cf. Pliny *Natural History* 23.122). (Concerning the odd placement of this verse in the overall narrative sequence about Hezekiah's healing, cf. Cogan and Tadmor [1988:256-257], who argue that this "fig cake" tradition, analogous to that of the miracles of Elijah and Elisha, was probably originally independent of the rest of the present narrative [also see the next note].)

boil. Neither here nor in the Isaiah parallel (cf. Isa 38:21, which represents a sort of footnote to Hezekiah's psalm of praise found in Isa 38:10-20) are we prepared for this abrupt reference to a "boil" or "skin eruption" (*shekhin* [TH7822, ZH8825]). Since it was apparently acute and life-threatening, a case of severe blistering known as *pemphigus* may have actually been what was afflicting the king (cf. Cogan and Tadmor 1988:255). (It may be only an odd coincidence, but it is intriguing how King Uzziah [15:5] was also afflicted with a skin disease ["leprosy"; cf. the first note on that verse for details] after visiting the Temple, at least according to the Chronicler [see 2 Chr 26:16-21].)

20:8 What sign . . . ? Heb., *mah 'oth* [TH4100/226, ZH4537/253]; cf. the note on 19:29 concerning the *'oth* (sign) as a preliminary guarantee, so to speak, of the certitude that the major prophetic promise will come to pass (here, the granting of 15 more years of life to Hezekiah). As already hinted in that note, Hezekiah's demand for a "sign" here is meant to be sharply contrasted with his father Ahaz's overly "pious" refusal to seek one (Isa 7:10-12), a fact that explains Isaiah's exasperated response to that king in Isa 7:13-14 (cf. Hens-Piazza 2006:371-372).

20:11 sundial. Lit., "stairs" (*ma'aloth* [TH4609A, ZH5092]) of Ahaz; most commentators, however, see here some sort of sundial or systematic marker of the movement made by a shadow from the sun (cf. NLT mg notes on 20:9, 11; also cf. Cogan and Tadmor [1988:256], who note an Egyptian parallel where flights of stairs were used for telling time). Although not specifically mentioned elsewhere (except in the brief parallel text found in Isa 38:8), this innovation of Ahaz (in honor of the sun god? [cf. 23:11-12]) may have been part of his extensive architectural renovations detailed in 16:10-18. As far as the sun's shadow moving forward or backward, Hezekiah obviously sought the more impressive sign, reversing the progress of time itself, as it were (he was hardly in the mood to speed up time!). Concerning this, Oswalt (1986:678) cites Smith to great effect: "[Smith] paints a graphic picture of the dying king watching from his sickroom as the shadow inexorably descended the steps. How easily he could have associated his own ebbing strength with that lengthening shadow and contemplated the coming sunset with dread. Thus, when the prophet offered to move the shadow forward ten steps, one can imagine the king reacting with alarm. Much better to move it backward, up the steps, as a sign of the divine reprieve." (As far as the exact nature of this miracle, some commentators insist on the actual reversal of the earth's rotation [cf. Ramm 1954:161-163]; Oswalt suggests some sort of local refraction of the sunlight as actually marking the miracle.)

COMMENTARY

Now we encounter a second stupendous miracle from Yahweh mediated through the prophet Isaiah and presented as the result of a prayer made by King Hezekiah. What are we to conclude from this? In my several decades of being a Christian believer, I have found that much of the Christian life of prayer revolves around the twin poles of "prayer as protest against the status quo" and "not my will, but thine be done." Even Jesus, it will be recalled, included both perspectives in his prayer in the garden of Gethsemane: "My Father! If it is possible, let this cup of suffering be taken away from me. Yet I want your will to be done, not mine" (Matt 26:39; cf. Mark 14:36; Luke 22:42). Ironically, in the two stories we find here in chapter 20, we encounter examples of each of the twin poles of prayer just given. For "prayer as protest" against (or at least, as clear rejection of) the status quo, we find Hezekiah sharply contesting the stated will of God as just presented by the prophet Isaiah ("You will not recover from this illness" [20:1]). And in the next section, we will find this same king meekly acquiescing to what is again the stated will of God as declared by Isaiah ("The time is coming when everything in your palace . . . will be carried off to Babylon" [20:17]). Hezekiah strongly refused to accept the first prediction (in contrast, e.g., to King David's perspective back in 1 Kgs 2:1-2a, where the same Hebrew expression, "to give one's last injunctions, make one's will" is to be found [see Gray 1970:697; the Hebrew verb used in both cases is generally understood as deriving from the root *tsawah* [TH6680, ZH7422], "to command, commission"; but cf. Gray's own alternative analysis from an Arabic cognate; also cf. HALOT 1011]). And, as we soon shall see, Hezekiah quite unexpectedly accepts without any protest whatsoever Isaiah's second prediction ("At least there will be peace and security during my lifetime" [20:19b]). But, once again, the biblical narrative resists simple moralization (see the commentary on 2:1-18). Whatever the narrator (or "editor," inasmuch as both of these stories are also told with many parallels—and a number of variations—in Isa 38–39) wishes for us to conclude concerning Hezekiah's prayerful actions and non-actions, there is certainly a reminder here that humans do have free will, and such free will (especially in the hands of people in leadership positions) can markedly change the course of history. Even direct pronouncements from God can—and at times should—be challenged (cf. Moses [e.g., Exod 32:7-14; Num 14:10b-25] and Job [e.g., Job 6:2-13; 10:1-22; 13:13-28; 16:7-17]). But the key is to know *when* to do so—for the popular pagan proverb does contain much truth when it reminds us, "Those whom the gods hate, they answer their prayers."

Hezekiah did pray, and he was *no* pagan. And by now we know that man could *pray*! But was he right to do so here? Did he get what he really wanted?

Some commentators have calculated, especially in light of his age at accession being only 12 years (so 21:1), that the birth of Manasseh, Hezekiah's son and successor, stands as an unfortunate by-product of Hezekiah receiving these 15 additional years of life. Chronologically speaking, that does appear to be the case (but then did Hezekiah have no suitable heir at all until Manasseh's birth?). It must, however, be pointed out that the Deuteronomistic editor drew no such conclusion. We must, therefore, offer such an observation only most tenuously and prefer rather to emphasize the conclusions that are plainly asserted in the text itself. And one of those is the fact that Hezekiah did receive 15 more years of life largely because he dared to pray for them. Rather clear as well is the corollary observation that he evidently deserved such favor—and it is clearly presented as a *favorable* action by God—largely because of his previous track record of faithfulness to God (cf. 20:3). Hezekiah deserved more years of life, it would seem, and he received them, due ultimately to God's sovereign grace. But Hezekiah still had to ask for those years! At times, therefore, it appears that God's will can include the bold rejection by God's faithful people of what has been presented as God's (evident) will. What a conundrum this can represent! But also, what a note of fierce and stubborn hope it can engender. "May God's will be done!" must remain our defiant (rather than defeatist) cry. (The events addressed in the next commentary section also bear on this most intriguing topic.)

◆ ## 7. Envoys from Babylon (20:12-21)

[12]Soon after this, Merodach-baladan* son of Baladan, king of Babylon, sent Hezekiah his best wishes and a gift, for he had heard that Hezekiah had been very sick. [13]Hezekiah received the Babylonian envoys and showed them everything in his treasure-houses—the silver, the gold, the spices, and the aromatic oils. He also took them to see his armory and showed them everything in his royal treasuries! There was nothing in his palace or kingdom that Hezekiah did not show them.

[14]Then Isaiah the prophet went to King Hezekiah and asked him, "What did those men want? Where were they from?"

Hezekiah replied, "They came from the distant land of Babylon."

[15]"What did they see in your palace?" Isaiah asked.

"They saw everything," Hezekiah replied. "I showed them everything I own—all my royal treasuries."

[16]Then Isaiah said to Hezekiah, "Listen to this message from the LORD: [17]The time is coming when everything in your palace—all the treasures stored up by your ancestors until now—will be carried off to Babylon. Nothing will be left, says the LORD. [18]Some of your very own sons will be taken away into exile. They will become eunuchs who will serve in the palace of Babylon's king."

[19]Then Hezekiah said to Isaiah, "This message you have given me from the LORD is good." For the king was thinking, "At least there will be peace and security during my lifetime."

[20]The rest of the events in Hezekiah's reign, including the extent of his power and how he built a pool and dug a tunnel* to bring water into the city, are recorded in *The Book of the History of the Kings of Judah.* [21]Hezekiah died, and his son Manasseh became the next king.

20:12 As in some Hebrew manuscripts and Greek and Syriac versions (see also Isa 39:1); Masoretic Text reads *Berodach-baladan.*   20:20 Hebrew *watercourse.*

NOTES

20:12 *Soon after this*. See the first note on 20:1 concerning this time indicator (lit., "at that time"), especially in light of the nonchronological arrangement of the Hezekiah stories.

***Merodach-baladan*.** As the NLT mg indicates, the MT here reads "Berodach-baladan," but the Isaiah parallel (Isa 39:1) attests the NLT spelling, as do some Hebrew mss as well as the Greek and Syriac versions. Merodach-baladan was a prominent chieftain of the Yakin tribe of southern Babylonia who assumed kingship over the entirety of Babylonia soon after the death of Shalmaneser V in 722 BC; he was not ousted from that position until 710 by Sargon II (concerning these Assyrian kings, see the notes on 17:3, 5). During his reign Babylon prospered to a great degree, despite Assyrian claims to the contrary (ABD 4.704-705). When deposed, Merodach-baladan was able to flee to his ancestral homeland in the southern marshes of Babylonia and Elam; and by the time of Sennacherib (cf. the second note on 18:13), Merodach-baladan was again active in Babylonian affairs, ascending the throne of that city around 703 BC after removing the usurper Marduk-zakir-shumi; in fact, Sennacherib's self-styled "first campaign" was directed against him. At this time, Merodach-baladan's allies included Elamites and Arabs, as well as Chaldeans and Arameans (and possibly Hezekiah of Judah as well; see the next note). Nevertheless, Sennacherib succeeded in ousting him from the city, and after a second campaign in 700, Sennacherib was able to place his own son, Asshur-nadin-shumi, on the Babylonian throne. Merodach-baladan again fled south, and eventually died in Elam around 694 BC.

***his best wishes and a gift*.** Lit., "letters and a gift," which probably included personal greetings from the king as well as monetary benefactions to encourage Hezekiah's support of his military endeavors (cf. Barnes 1991:117-118 n. 128, and the references cited there). Sweeney (2007:413) suggests this represented a two-pronged attack against Sennacherib, with Hezekiah in the west and Merodach-baladan in the east putting simultaneous pressure on the Assyrian monarch. Whatever dating one may follow, it must be admitted that this hypothesis does make excellent strategic sense, with the Assyrian evidence pointing to roughly the year 701 BC for the sending of the Babylonian delegation to Jerusalem to "feel out" the willingness of Hezekiah to risk such a gambit. (Alternatively, such a visit could have taken place earlier, around 713 [which would have indeed been Hezekiah's "14th year" if the earlier chronology is accepted], which was another time of Palestinian revolt against Assyria [cf. Barnes 1997a:573, following Cogan and Tadmor 1988:261].)

20:13 *Hezekiah received the Babylonian envoys*. Cogan and Tadmor (1900.259, cf. note b on p. 258) have argued strongly that the Isaianic variant verb (in Isa 39:2) should be read here in Kings as well (i.e., reading *samakh* [TH8055, ZH8523], "be happy, pleased," for the MT's *shama'* [TH8085, ZH9048], "listen to"). I however think the NLT's translation "received" (with its variation "was delighted with" in the Isaiah text) is quite defensible.

***showed them everything*.** The obvious fact that Hezekiah had much to show the Babylonian delegation should be duly noted (contrast his later status as impoverished due to his trying to buy off Sennacherib, as described in 18:14-16!). Here again we see further evidence for the nonchronological arrangement of these Hezekiah texts (cf. the first note on 20:1). The extensive listing of his (and his nation's) wealth that is found here will make Isaiah's startling prophecy in 20:17 ("All [of this] will be carried off to Babylon") all the more chilling.

20:14 *distant land of Babylon*. Emphasis is placed on the land of Babylon as a "distant land"—hence unlikely under normal circumstances to have any reason or opportunity to seize Judah's wealth. But they did that very thing in the early sixth century, as the last two chapters of 2 Kings describe in detail.

20:17 *The time is coming.* Isaiah announces the certitude of the Babylonian exile *prophetically*, and he may be doing so *legally* as well (cf. Barnes 1991:113 n. 123, following Peter R. Ackroyd [1974:339-341]). Ackroyd notes that the very act of formally viewing all this property may have signified some sort of legal transfer of ownership (such was usually the case for the sale of something unable physically to be handed over to the new owner, such as a house or land). As Ackroyd (1974:341) puts it, "By letting these ambassadors see everything, Hezekiah has handed over the possession of everything in Judah to the enemy and has anticipated the exile. Though the disaster itself belongs to the future . . . the essential legal take-over has already ensured that exile will take place." Oblique support for this proposal may also be found in Cogan and Tadmor (1988:259, 262-263), who argue that the language in 20:17-19 is actually quite characteristic of Jeremiah, not of Isaiah—hence, probably to be dated to around the sixth-century exile itself.

20:19 *This message you have given me from the LORD is good.* As Seow (1999:272) has pointed out, this public comment stands sharply at odds with Hezekiah's private response, "At least there will be peace and security during my lifetime." This short-sighted response also contrasts sharply with the later view held by many Judahites that the Temple and the city remained under Yahweh's miraculous protection, and were thus inviolable.

20:20 *built a pool and dug a tunnel.* As pointed out in the third note on 18:17, this is the only reference to Hezekiah's remarkable tunnel, which brought water from the Gihon Spring down to the Pool of Siloam located inside the walls of Jerusalem (see Wiseman 1993:289 for details, including the text of the famous inscription originally located in the tunnel near the Siloam entrance and giving details of its construction; cf. ANEP, pictures 275, 744).

are recorded in **The Book of the History of the Kings of Judah.** See "Literary Style" in the Introduction.

COMMENTARY

Alas, here "the third time is *not* the charm" (see previous commentary section). This time there is another crisis—personal *and* national—and this time there is another startling message for Hezekiah given by the prophet Isaiah. But this time there is inexplicably *no* prayer offered by the king to change the status quo! So this time, there will be no miracle—no national deliverance either of the city of Jerusalem or the nation of Judah. And, it will be recalled, the final chapter of 2 Kings describes the destruction of both of these geographical entities in unforgettable detail. Perhaps the only positive development one can find from these sections of Kings is the emphatic dismissal, once and for all, of any naive theology of the eternal inviolability of the Temple of Yahweh or the city of Jerusalem, a belief which seemingly held sway for the next century or so, giving the prophet Jeremiah such fits (see the end of the commentary on 18:1-12 for details). If Baruch, Jeremiah's scribe, was involved prominently with the Deuteronomistic school (as I, following Friedman, have suggested; cf. "Author" in the Introduction), this would help explain the emphasis we find here in the text (cf. the note on 20:17). Hezekiah's seemingly short-sighted neglect of the future only grows deeper in incomprehensibility in light of the horrors of the eventual exile to Babylonia. But that must have been the author's point: Present-day acquiescence will lead to future disaster. The prophetic word is sure: Disaster will come, and it will come from Babylon (cf. 20:17).

But that cannot be our final word concerning King Hezekiah. The present text

does conclude with some positive references to Hezekiah's accomplishments, especially his famous tunnel bringing water into the city of Jerusalem (see 20:20). It's as
if the Deuteronomistic editor wanted to leave a relatively positive memory of this
most noteworthy king in the mind of the audience. As is the case with King Josiah
as well, a dubious ending should not obscure all the good work this Davidide had
accomplished. And so, it is only appropriate that a concluding summary of "good
king" Hezekiah will draw our own discussion to a close.

First of all, there are more verses in 1–2 Kings devoted to King Hezekiah (three
chapters of 2 Kings; 95 verses in all) than even to "good king" Josiah (most of two
chapters, 50 verses in all). Only "relatively good king" Solomon merits more space
(the first 11 chapters of 1 Kings, with a total of 434 verses—but with a significant
number of those describing the Temple and its furnishings). To be sure, "not-so-
good king" Ahab occupies much literary territory as well (1 Kgs 16:29–22:40; a total
of 209 verses), but most of those verses stem from the Elijah cycle. And the Deuteronomistic editor exempts none of these kings from criticism, whether Solomon,
whose sins are listed in 1 Kings 11, or Hezekiah (here), or Josiah (2 Kgs 23:29-30).
Hezekiah was a reformer par excellence, a risk-taker who nearly lost his kingdom
(and certainly did lose most of its wealth) contending against the mighty empire
of Assyria. He was one who also had to contend (in essence) with the prophet Isaiah several times. And in a sense, he had to contend even with Yahweh (at least in
the matter of his sudden death sentence in 20:1-3). Whether there actually was a
Hezekian recension of the Deuteronomistic History or not (see "Earlier Editions of
Kings?" under "Date and Occasion of Writing" in the Introduction for details), this
much is clear: Hezekiah proved to be a powerful role model for the later reformer
king Josiah, and thus supported the major agenda of the book itself. And thus it
truly was the case with King Hezekiah that "there was no one like him among all
the kings of Judah, either before or after his time" (18:5). No wonder the book of
Isaiah devotes four chapters to this king (plus numerous allusions to him elsewhere
in the book), and the book of 2 Chronicles four lengthy chapters as well (with three
of them [2 Chr 29–31] nearly totally independent of the Kings material). Hezekiah
was a great king—flawed to be sure, but nevertheless a truly great king. And that
man could pray!

◆ **B. Manasseh and Amon: Evil Kings of Judah (2 Kgs 21:1-26)**
   1. Manasseh rules in Judah (21:1-18)

Manasseh was twelve years old when he
became king, and he reigned in Jerusalem
fifty-five years. His mother was Hephzi-
bah. ²He did what was evil in the LORD's
sight, following the detestable practices of
the pagan nations that the LORD had driv-
en from the land ahead of the Israelites.
³He rebuilt the pagan shrines his father,
Hezekiah, had destroyed. He constructed
altars for Baal and set up an Asherah pole,
just as King Ahab of Israel had done. He
also bowed before all the powers of the
heavens and worshiped them.

⁴He built pagan altars in the Temple of
the LORD, the place where the LORD had
said, "My name will remain in Jerusalem
forever." ⁵He built these altars for all the
powers of the heavens in both courtyards
of the LORD's Temple. ⁶Manasseh also
sacrificed his own son in the fire.* He

practiced sorcery and divination, and he consulted with mediums and psychics. He did much that was evil in the LORD's sight, arousing his anger.

⁷Manasseh even made a carved image of Asherah and set it up in the Temple, the very place where the LORD had told David and his son Solomon: "My name will be honored forever in this Temple and in Jerusalem—the city I have chosen from among all the tribes of Israel. ⁸If the Israelites will be careful to obey my commands—all the laws my servant Moses gave them—I will not send them into exile from this land that I gave their ancestors." ⁹But the people refused to listen, and Manasseh led them to do even more evil than the pagan nations that the LORD had destroyed when the people of Israel entered the land.

¹⁰Then the LORD said through his servants the prophets: ¹¹"King Manasseh of Judah has done many detestable things. He is even more wicked than the Amorites, who lived in this land before Israel. He has caused the people of Judah to sin with his idols.* ¹²So this is what the LORD, the God of Israel, says: I will bring such

disaster on Jerusalem and Judah that the ears of those who hear about it will tingle with horror. ¹³I will judge Jerusalem by the same standard I used for Samaria and the same measure* I used for the family of Ahab. I will wipe away the people of Jerusalem as one wipes a dish and turns it upside down. ¹⁴Then I will reject even the remnant of my own people who are left, and I will hand them over as plunder for their enemies. ¹⁵For they have done great evil in my sight and have angered me ever since their ancestors came out of Egypt."

¹⁶Manasseh also murdered many innocent people until Jerusalem was filled from one end to the other with innocent blood. This was in addition to the sin that he caused the people of Judah to commit, leading them to do evil in the LORD's sight.

¹⁷The rest of the events in Manasseh's reign and everything he did, including the sins he committed, are recorded in *The Book of the History of the Kings of Judah.* ¹⁸When Manasseh died, he was buried in the palace garden, the garden of Uzza. Then his son Amon became the next king.

21:6 Or *also made his son pass through the fire.*   21:11 The Hebrew term (literally *round things*) probably alludes to dung; also in 21:21.   21:13 Hebrew *the same plumb line I used for Samaria and the same plumb bob.*

NOTES

21:1 Manasseh. He was the 16th king from the line of David. Manasseh's name probably means "[Yahweh is] the one who causes to forget [the loss of an earlier child?]" or the like (see Wiseman 1993:290; cf. the commentary on 20:1-11 concerning the chronological circumstances surrounding Manasseh's birth and the apparent absence of any older brother as a suitable heir to the throne). As Cogan and Tadmor (1988:265) point out, King Manasseh is well attested in the contemporary records of the Assyrians; they knew him as *Menasí/ Minsí šar māt Iaudi* (Manasseh, king of Judah).

fifty-five years. He had the longest reign of any king from either Israel or Judah, and we can date Manasseh's reign closely to 697-642 BC by means of the Assyrian records. Some scholars see a 10-year coregency with his father Hezekiah as part of this total, but inasmuch as I have argued for an early date for Hezekiah's accession to the throne (see the commentary on 18:1-12 for details), every one of these 55 years for Manasseh would then represent his sole reign, with no overlap at all with his father. Also, as already pointed out, a number of Manasseh's early years would correspond with those of the powerful Assyrian king Esarhaddon (680–669 BC; cf. the third note on 19:37), perhaps a dubious status for Manasseh, to be sure, but also one which would contribute to a long and prosperous reign as long as one remained loyal to Assyria. This would also be the case under Esarhaddon's son and successor, Ashurbanipal, whose long reign (668–627 BC) represented the zenith of neo-Assyrian power—his empire would stretch "from Egypt to Elam" (so Kim [2006]); and his famous library in Nineveh with its thousands of surviving texts would provide us with the single greatest treasure trove of information we have concerning the history and culture of the ancient Near East.

21:2 did what was evil. A typical Deuteronomistic condemnation (see endnotes 1 and 2 of the Introduction), but here we also meet with a clear conundrum: How can it be that any king who was so evil reigned this long? In Deuteronomic theology, a long life generally connotes blessing from God (see Deut 4:40; 5:33; 6:2; 11:9; 17:20; 30:20; 32:47). See the commentary for further thoughts on this important topic.

21:2b-4 pagan nations . . . pagan shrines . . . pagan altars. In none of these cases is there a precise Hebrew counterpart for the term "pagan." But it is clearly implied in the first instance; it stands as an understandable translation in the second instance (the Hebrew reads *habbamoth* [TH1116, ZH1195], usually translated as "the high places"); and in the final instance, where the Hebrew merely indicates "altars" with no further specification, the NLT's interpretation is again possible, but not certain. Concerning the nature of the so-called "high places," which may well have been shrines dedicated to Yahweh, see the note on 1 Kgs 3:3 and the references cited there.

21:3 an Asherah pole. See the note at 1 Kgs 14:15 for details concerning this popular "pagan" deity. In 21:7, we are told that such a pole was even set up in the Jerusalem Temple!

all the powers of the heavens. These certainly did represent "pagan" deities (cf. 23:5), although not necessarily Mesopotamian in origin as commentators used to suggest (cf. Cogan and Tadmor 1988:266). Once again, it should be emphasized that Assyria did *not* insist on its subject peoples worshiping its deities, as long as they acknowledged the sovereignty of the Assyrian gods in reference to enforcement of the suzerainty treaty (see Wiseman 1993:290; also see the first note on 16:10 concerning Cogan's seminal work [1974] in this area).

21:4 My name. Concerning the "name theology" found here and in 21:7, see the note on 1 Kgs 5:5; see also "One Place of Worship" under "Major Themes" in the Introduction.

21:5 in both courtyards. Only the "inner court" was specified in 1 Kgs 6:36, but there is brief mention of a "great [outer?] courtyard" as well in 1 Kgs 7:12 (cf. the first note on that verse).

21:6 sacrificed his own son in the fire. For details concerning this heinous practice, see the second note on 16:3 (where King Ahaz, Manasseh's grandfather, did the very same thing).

sorcery . . . divination . . . mediums . . . psychics. These were all occult practices clearly forbidden in the Torah, especially Deut 18:9-14. (Concerning the last two terms, see the note on 23:24.)

21:9 the people refused to listen. Although this entire section represents sharp condemnation of the king as "leading" the people into evil, quite similar to what Jeroboam I had done for Israel (cf. the note on 1 Kgs 15:26; also Leithart 2006:264), there are also a few reminders in this section that the people were far from guiltless (cf. 21:13-15; as well as the commentary on 17:5-23 for the condemnations found there directed against Judah's sins as well as those of Israel).

pagan nations. Once again (cf. the note on 21:2b-4), the term "pagan" does not render a specific word in the Hebrew, although the idea is quite clearly implied. And, in this instance, the parallels with the "pagan-like" King Ahab of Israel (cf. 21:3, 13) are probably also meant to be recalled (see the reference to the "Amorites" in 21:11; also see the second note on 1 Kgs 21:26).

21:10 *his servants the prophets.* The reference here is quite vague, perhaps intentionally so. Historically, Manasseh's reign (and indeed much of the seventh century) was a time of judicious silence for the Yahwistic prophets, broken only (as far as we know) by the ministry of Zephaniah sometime during the reign of King Josiah (cf. Zeph 1:1; also cf. Jer 15:4, which represents the only place in the OT outside of Kings and Chronicles where Manasseh is mentioned by name).

21:11 *idols.* Lit., "round(ed) things" (*gillulim* [TH1544, ZH1658], mentioned both here and in 21:21—so "like father, like son"); for possible interpretations of these *gillulim*, see the note on 17:12; cf. the second note on 1 Kgs 15:12.

21:12 *the ears . . . will tingle with horror.* The image is that of a resounding ringing or echoing in the ears caused by the terrible news of the impending disaster (Cogan and Tadmor 1988:268-269; cf. 1 Sam 3:11; Jer 19:3).

21:13 *same standard . . . same measure.* Lit., by the same "measuring line" or "plumb line" (*qaw* [TH6957, ZH7742]) that was used for Samaria, and by the same "plummet, plumb bob" (*mishqoleth* [TH4949, ZH5487]) that was used for the family (house) of Ahab. Both architectural terms are also found in Isa 28:17, where the larger context again refers to the future of both Samaria and Jerusalem. Some, however, translate the second term as "mason's level" or the like (i.e., a horizontal, not vertical, leveling instrument; see BDB 1054; HALOT 652-653).

as one wipes a dish and turns it upside down. The image here is not of thoroughly washing and drying a dish, but of wiping it clean to get each and every morsel of food, leaving absolutely nothing behind (see Cogan and Tadmor 1988:269).

21:15 *ever since.* Lit., "from the day (their ancestors came out of Egypt) until this day"; this relentlessly pessimistic assessment of the people (also see 21:9) corresponds with Yahweh's gloomy assessment of the earlier generations cited at length in Ezek 20:1-44.

21:16 *filled . . . with innocent blood.* The phrase "to shed innocent blood" signified in the late monarchical period the oppression of the poor and the underprivileged (Cogan and Tadmor 1988:269; see Jer 7:6; 22:3, 17; cf. Ezek 22:6-12, 25-29). More literally, however, some commentators, in line with Josephus (*Antiquities* 10.3.1.38) and the Talmud (*b. Sanhedrin* 103b), suggest that Manasseh actually sought to put to death many of the righteous, including Isaiah and other Yahwistic prophets, in an attempt to eliminate all opposition to his policies. In the pseudepigraphical *Ascension of Isaiah*, the prophet Isaiah was said to be sawn in half by Manasseh using a wooden saw (cf. Heb 11:37 and *b. Yevamot* 49b).

21:17 *are recorded in* **The Book of the History of the Kings of Judah.** See "Literary Style" in the Introduction.

21:18 *buried in the palace garden.* Cogan and Tadmor [1988:269-270] point out that after King Hezekiah, there seem to be no more burials within the City of David, perhaps due to lack of space (strictly speaking, however, we are not told where Hezekiah himself was buried; cf. 20:21). In their massive study of the death and burial notices (as well as the references to the queen mothers), Halpern and Vanderhooft (1991:194-197) have emphasized a different approach; they have argued for a change of author as the more likely explanation of the phenomenon of no more references to burials in the City of David (although, on other grounds, they do acknowledge that there may have been a shift in burial practices around the time of King Hezekiah, as well—most likely due to Hezekiah's successes in discouraging ancestor cults among the elite). (Concerning the evidence for a change in author at the time of Hezekiah, see "Earlier Editions of Kings?" under "Date and Occasion of Writing" in the Introduction.) In sum, the location of the "palace garden" mentioned here, as well as details concerning the "garden of Uzza" (mentioned both here and in 21:26), still remains uncertain, as does its editorial significance.

COMMENTARY

As already noted, this section about King Manasseh is relatively sparse on details (especially for a 55-year reign!), but very heavy on editorial denunciation. In fact, if there is one particular villain of the Deuteronomistic literature, it *must* be Manasseh (see "The 'Sins of Manasseh'" under "Major Themes" in the Introduction). And as the notes on the individual verses indicate, King Manasseh is compared to the other most notorious kings of either kingdom: Jeroboam I (21:9); Ahab (21:9b, 13); and Ahaz (21:6). In fact, there doesn't appear to be a sinful practice that Manasseh neglected; no wonder the Deuteronomistic Historian singles him out for such overwhelming opprobrium.

Still, 55 years on the throne! How can that be explained? As in the commentary for Ahaz (16:1-20), a more balanced look may be necessary (such a look is already to be found in 2 Chr 33:1-20, which describes Manasseh's sins in great detail, but also notes his humbling by the Assyrians [under Ashurbanipal?], his repentance and restoration, and his successful building projects in Jerusalem). But I want to review here the provocative work of Ahlström (1982:75-81, as also cited in Wiseman 1993:292-293): It may well be the case that Manasseh was able to recover at least some of the considerable Judahite territory lost by Hezekiah (cf. the second note on 18:13); and his restoration of the high places, as well as some of his other cultic innovations, represented the status quo during the "good old days" of Ahaz. As 2 Chronicles 33:17 reminds us, the people worshiped at the high places, "though only to [Yahweh] their God." Ahlström also makes reference to Broshi's conclusions about the city of Jerusalem more than doubling its size during this time (cf. the commentary on 18:1-12 for details); such expansion would require major building projects, especially new walls and fortifications (the very activities described in 2 Chr 33:14). As Ahlström concludes:

> [According to later editorial perspectives] Hezekiah's reform was the ideal against which the religious customs of the pre-exilic era were to be evaluated. In Manasseh's eyes, however, the policies of Hezekiah had led the country to the brink of disaster. Therefore, Manasseh's cultic reform may have been nothing more than a return to the religious situation that existed before Hezekiah's innovations. . . . If the above interpretation is correct, Manasseh cannot be called an "apostate," as many scholars prefer to label him. He was rather a traditionalist in religious matters, and as such he came into conflict with those groups still advocating the religious ideas and the radical, utopian innovations of his "unorthodox" father. Therefore, Manasseh had to neutralize those elements; they may be seen as enemies of the state. (Ahlström 1982:81)

So was Manasseh a "survivor," akin to his grandfather Ahaz? (See the conclusions concerning that king to be found in the commentary on 16:1-20.) Manasseh, like Ahaz, was given a difficult role to play (and so was Hezekiah, to be sure!). Ahaz survived, and kept the little kingdom of Judah intact. And so did Manasseh—for some 55 years.

As noted throughout this commentary, the agenda of the Deuteronomistic Historian was to explain the Exile. Manasseh violated the core values of Deuteronomic theology—so he became the villain of 1–2 Kings. Hezekiah was the bold hero, and so was his great-grandson, Josiah, the peerless cult reformer. But Manasseh too had his reasons to "un-reform" the cult; and it is to the credit of the Chronicler that Manasseh is given some credit for surviving the Assyrians. But that is not the Deuteronomist's agenda, for the very term "Deuteronomist" signifies allegiance to the Mosaic theology of the book of Deuteronomy. And that theology is crystal clear: only one God, and only one place of worship for that God. In light of that overarching criterion, Hezekiah was a hero and Josiah was also a hero, but Manasseh was the villain. That is why we read so little about what King Manasseh had accomplished but so much about what he shouldn't have done. All history is propaganda (i.e., it urges a present perspective and course of action by means of selective rehearsal of the past), and in this section of 2 Kings, that is basically all it seems to be. Manasseh was undoubtedly a realist and probably a very able king, but Moses (as presented in Deuteronomy) was nothing less than the greatest of the prophets. And the editor of Kings stands firmly behind Moses's agenda, not Manasseh's.

◆   ## 2. Amon rules in Judah (21:19-26)

[19] Amon was twenty-two years old when he became king, and he reigned in Jerusalem two years. His mother was Meshullemeth, the daughter of Haruz from Jotbah. [20] He did what was evil in the LORD's sight, just as his father, Manasseh, had done. [21] He followed the example of his father, worshiping the same idols his father had worshiped. [22] He abandoned the LORD, the God of his ancestors, and he refused to follow the LORD's ways.

[23] Then Amon's own officials conspired against him and assassinated him in his palace. [24] But the people of the land killed all those who had conspired against King Amon, and they made his son Josiah the next king.

[25] The rest of the events in Amon's reign and what he did are recorded in *The Book of the History of the Kings of Judah.* [26] He was buried in his tomb in the garden of Uzza. Then his son Josiah became the next king.

NOTES

21:19 Amon. He was the 17th king from the line of David. Amon's name, ironically, probably means "faithful" (so McMurray [2006]); but other possibilities include "master-workman" (so BDB 54) or even a reference to the Egyptian god Amon (but since most commentators suspect King Amon was, if anything, pro-Assyrian [like his father], rather than pro-Egyptian, this last option is unlikely). Amon's reign of "two years" need only include a small portion of one year (his accession year), plus a small portion of the next year (if antedating is practiced [see "Excursus on Chronology" in the Introduction; but as noted there, many chronographers argue for the Babylonian practice of postdating as being practiced in Judah at this time]).

21:20 did what was evil. A stereotypical Deuteronomistic evaluation (cf. endnote 2 of the Introduction); after all, how much "evil" could occur in a short "two-year" reign? Probably the idea is that such "evil" kings allowed pagan ritual practices to continue.

21:22 abandoned. The same verb (*'azab* [TH5800, ZH6440]) was also used in Elijah's bitter refrain found in 1 Kgs 19:10, 14, as well as in Huldah's prophecy to Josiah in 22:17 (cf. 17:16); in all those cases it was Yahweh's rebellious people who "abandoned" him and his ways (see the first note on 21:9).

21:23 conspired. This will be the last "palace coup" (so Cogan and Tadmor [1988:275]; cf. ABD 1.198-199) in 1–2 Kings (although four of the next five Davidic kings, including Zedekiah, the final Davidide reigning in Jerusalem, will either meet premature death or be exiled by foreign powers). So, whether it was the result of international interests or domestic politics, this drastic resort to regicide represents a rare but devastating event in Judah. On the international front, Assyria was clearly waning in power by this time, whereas Egypt was resurgent. On the domestic front, the Jerusalem priesthood's power and influence had been suppressed during Manasseh's long reign, and more importantly, those bypassed in the line of succession to the throne—Amon is unlikely to have been Manasseh's eldest son—would likely engage in palace intrigue.

21:24 *the people of the land.* See the second note on 11:14 for details concerning these recurring references to a distinct group of powerful individuals (landed aristocrats?), who remained loyal to the Davidic ancestral line, stepping forward whenever that dynasty was threatened (cf. 23:30, 35 [?]; also cf. the earlier references listed in the fourth note on 15:5). Such a stabilizing influence by a group largely independent of Jerusalem and its palace intrigues probably contributed greatly to the remarkable length of the Davidic dynasty, which, after all, represented something far more important than just another obscure line of petty kings who happened to reign in the ancient Near East.

21:25 *are recorded in* **The Book of the History of the Kings of Judah.** See "Literary Style" in the Introduction, and cf. 21:17.

21:26 *garden of Uzza.* See the note on 21:18.

COMMENTARY

Is King Amon another "cipher," merely a generational placeholder between two prominent kings, Manasseh, the notoriously evil villain, and Josiah, one of the best kings of all? Or does Amon, brief though his reign was (see the note on 21:19), deserve to be condemned in terms equivalent to those used for the apostate Manasseh? Can one truly be so "evil" and still remain, as it were, only a footnote of history? Obviously, with the paucity of information we now have, these questions must remain without definite answer. But we do know this much: Amon followed his father, literally and theologically, and that fact apparently led directly to his own all-too-quick assassination. The "people of the land" (21:24), to be sure, did step in and ensure that the Davidic dynasty would not come to an untimely end, and they also made certain that those who had threatened it for whatever reason (rival claimants to the throne from Manasseh's own family?) were quickly and properly dealt with. (For further comments on the "people of the land" and the lasting implications of their actions, see the next commentary section.) Thus, to sum up, we find here an evil son slavishly following his notoriously evil father. End of story. But not really—for Amon's quick demise will open the doors for a very young King Josiah to take the throne and eventually change irrevocably the course of theological history.

◆   C. Josiah: Good Reformer King of Judah (2 Kgs 22:1–23:30)
       1. Josiah rules in Judah (22:1-7)

Josiah was eight years old when he became king, and he reigned in Jerusalem thirty-one years. His mother was Jedidah, the daughter of Adaiah from Bozkath. ²He did what was pleasing in the LORD's sight and followed the example of his ancestor David. He did not turn away from doing what was right.

³In the eighteenth year of his reign, King Josiah sent Shaphan son of Azaliah and grandson of Meshullam, the court secretary, to the Temple of the LORD. He told him, ⁴"Go to Hilkiah the high priest and have him count the money the gatekeepers have collected from the people at the LORD's Temple. ⁵Entrust this money to the men assigned to supervise the restoration of the LORD's Temple. Then they can use it to pay workers to repair the Temple. ⁶They will need to hire carpenters, builders, and masons. Also have them buy the timber and the finished stone needed to repair the Temple. ⁷But don't require the construction supervisors to keep account of the money they receive, for they are honest and trustworthy men."

NOTES

22:1 Josiah. He was the 18th king from the dynasty of David and definitely one of the most important. Already, in the late tenth century, the name Josiah has been invoked as the one who will avenge the notorious sins of Jeroboam I of Israel (see the note on 1 Kgs 13:2 for details). The meaning of Josiah's name remains uncertain; Althann (ABD 3.1015) suggests it comes from the root '-w-sh, meaning "to give"; while other possibilities include the Hiphil (causative form) from the root y-sh-h, meaning "to bring forth, produce"; or else from the root '-sh-h, meaning "to heal" (which is also the likely etymology of the name Asa).

22:2 did what was pleasing. After the sharply negative evaluations of Manasseh and Amon, which we have seen in the previous chapter (cf. 21:2, 20), we return to the string of positive evaluations typical of Hezekiah (cf. 18:3) and four of his five predecessors, all of which were couched in this phraseology (and Ahaz's negative evaluation is also presented in analogous terms; see the note on 16:2). For details concerning Ahaz's predecessors who "did what was pleasing," see the notes on 15:3, 34.

his ancestor David. See 18:3; contrast 16:2 (and to some degree, 14:3).

He did not turn away from doing what was right. Lit., "he did not turn aside either to the right or to the left," which is a key criterion from the book of Deuteronomy; curiously, however, this description has not been applied to any other king of Judah (cf. Sweeney [2007:441], who cites Moses's repeated exhortation to the people as well as the king to observe the Torah, so as not to stray "to the right or to the left" [Deut 5:32; 17:11; 28:14; also Deut 17:20, in the "law of the king"]). The literary connection between Josiah and the Deuteronomistic tradition could not be illustrated more clearly.

22:3 In the eighteenth year. This year can be closely dated to 622 BC. Ironically, and perhaps only coincidentally—although there is a distinct sense of intentional literary compression in the Kings account concerning the numerous events that were packed into this single year (cf. Williamson 1982a:398)—Josiah's reforms are dated as taking place exactly 100 years after the infamous fall of Samaria to the Assyrians (for details concerning the dating of the fall of that city, see the note on 17:5). In any case, Josiah's "eighteenth year" will figure most prominently in the extended narrative stretching from this verse all the way to 23:24 (cf., particularly, 23:23). Also, as I have argued elsewhere, the parallel references in the Chronicles account to this same year of Josiah's reign (see 2 Chr 34:8; 35:19) are particularly significant in their own right, singling out Josiah as the 15th Davidic king of the divided monarchy (see Barnes 1991:142-144). I have also pointed out (ibid.) that the 5th Davidic king, Jehoram, has a double regnal formula in the Chronicles account (2 Chr 21:5, 20), as does the 10th king, Jotham (2 Chr 27:1, 8). These odd repetitions, unique in Chronicles except for the present Josiah notices, are surely not coincidental, but their significance remains obscure. As for the Chronicler's references to Josiah's "eighth" and "twelfth" years (2 Chr 34:3), the independent historicity of those references remains problematic. They most certainly stem from the Chronicler's own reckoning (so Williamson 1982a:397-399; cf. Wiseman 1993:294; also Barnes 1997b:108-111, 128-129).

22:4 Hilkiah the high priest. One of the relatively few high priests mentioned by name in 1-2 Kings (see the first section of the Introduction), and possibly the same "Hilkiah" who was the father of the prophet Jeremiah (see Jer 1:1). Cogan and Tadmor (1988:281-282) note, however, that there is no clear evidence that these priests from Anathoth ever served in the Temple in Jerusalem (cf. Thompson [1980:140], who also dismisses this identification as "most unlikely").

22:5-6 to repair the Temple. This is the agenda also discussed in 12:1-16, in the days of King Joash (who also came to the throne as a child); and there is distinctive Hebrew vocabulary found only there and here—most notably, *bedeq* [TH919, ZH981], "breach or fissure" (12:5); but also *muba'* [TH935, ZH995], "(money) being brought in, donated," a Hophal participle of *bo'*; and a Niphal of *khashab* [TH2803, ZH3108], "(not) require to keep account (of the donated money)"; (see note on 12:15). These parallels give further support for a Temple tradition underlying significant sections of 1-2 Kings (see the note on 12:4 for details; cf. Sweeney 2007:444). For some pertinent observations concerning the importance of Temple maintenance and repair, see the commentary on 12:1-16; and for further intriguing parallels between Kings Joash and Josiah, including the striking symmetry of the aftermath of both reigns, see Leithart 2006:266.

COMMENTARY

Nearly the entire reign of Josiah can be carefully arranged in a palistrophe (or A-B-C-B-A literary structure), as presented in detail in the commentary on 23:1-20. This may well have served as the climax of the Josianic edition (see "Earlier Editions of Kings?" under "Date and Occasion of Writing" in the Introduction for details)— hence, the careful arrangement of these texts, as well as the programmatic nature of their detailed exposition (with 23:26-30 presumably added at a later date). In short, this is *the* culminating example of the program of restoration and cult centralization as ideally envisioned in the book of Deuteronomy.

With this brief introduction to the reign of King Josiah, we begin a nearly two-chapter discussion of his efforts at cult-reform (see "One Place of Worship" under "Major Themes" in the Introduction regarding the Deuteronomic basis of his reform). Since his reform spans this whole lengthy narrative, summarizing remarks are to be found in the commentary on 23:21-30. At this juncture, we read only about Josiah's first actions to repair and cleanse the Temple, not realizing that the resultant discovery of the "Book of the Law" will even take place, let alone irrevocably change the course of theological history. A veritable second "King Joash" (as already noted, Joash was another son of an assassinated father who came to the throne at a very young age [see 11:21–12:1] and was greatly focused on repairing the Temple), Josiah acted with great dispatch, even before he heard about the terrible indictment found in the "Book of the Law" concerning cultic laxity. And it is to his credit that once he heard those words, he continued to act with undiminished forcefulness to cleanse the cult, despite the personal word Huldah the prophet had given him concerning his own exemption from the coming wrath. (See the next commentary section for further thoughts concerning this remarkable focus.)

Before Josiah's efforts at renovating and cleansing the Temple were initiated, the "people of the land" (cf. the note on 21:24) probably remained largely in control of palace politics (cf. Cogan and Tadmor [1988:276], who suggest that this control amounted to "a decade of rule" during Josiah's minority and beyond). Presumably conservative in orientation, and demonstrably loyal to the house of David, they may or may not have had any effect on Josiah's determination to reverse the "pagan" perspective of the brief reign of his father Amon and the very lengthy reign of his grandfather Manasseh. In any case, for 10 long years, Josiah in essence bided his time as he reached maturity (for the Chronicler's alternative chronology for Josiah's first reforms, see the note on 22:3); but when his 18th year finally came, Josiah was apparently all action. This contrast in behavior leads to some interesting historical and psychological reflections on "radical" versus "conservative" leadership. Both Josiah and the "people of the land" were undoubtedly sincere, dedicated Yahwists. And both parties did much good in connection with the history of monarchical Judah. But that is where the similarities end. The "people of the land" acted intermittently, as needed during a monarchical crisis, and therefore usually in the sense of remaining reactive rather than proactive in their accomplishments. Josiah, however, was as proactive as they come. Neither party stands at fault here; both parties effectively advanced Yahweh's will for his people over against significant opposition. But supporters of the earlier status quo represent something quite different than those who find that same status quo quite limiting. Jesus' comments about the Kingdom advancing violently certainly come to mind, as well as putting new wine into fresh wineskins (Matt 11:12; Mark 2:22). This is not to put down the valuable work the "people of the land" accomplished when the situation called for it. But the Deuteronomistic author celebrates here the radical, even extreme, actions of King Josiah. And so, in the next two chapters, let us do the same!

◆   2. Hilkiah discovers God's law (22:8-20)

⁸Hilkiah the high priest said to Shaphan the court secretary, "I have found the Book of the Law in the LORD's Temple!" Then Hilkiah gave the scroll to Shaphan, and he read it.

⁹Shaphan went to the king and reported, "Your officials have turned over the money collected at the Temple of the LORD to the workers and supervisors at the Temple." ¹⁰Shaphan also told the king, "Hilkiah the priest has given me a scroll." So Shaphan read it to the king.

¹¹When the king heard what was written in the Book of the Law, he tore his clothes in despair. ¹²Then he gave these orders to Hilkiah the priest, Ahikam son of Shaphan, Acbor son of Micaiah, Shaphan the court secretary, and Asaiah the king's personal adviser: ¹³"Go to the Temple and speak to the LORD for me and

for the people and for all Judah. Inquire about the words written in this scroll that has been found. For the LORD's great anger is burning against us because our ancestors have not obeyed the words in this scroll. We have not been doing everything it says we must do."

¹⁴So Hilkiah the priest, Ahikam, Acbor, Shaphan, and Asaiah went to the New Quarter* of Jerusalem to consult with the prophet Huldah. She was the wife of Shallum son of Tikvah, son of Harhas, the keeper of the Temple wardrobe.

¹⁵She said to them, "The LORD, the God of Israel, has spoken! Go back and tell the man who sent you, ¹⁶'This is what the LORD says: I am going to bring disaster on this city* and its people. All the words written in the scroll that the king of Judah has read will come true. ¹⁷For my people

have abandoned me and offered sacrifices to pagan gods, and I am very angry with them for everything they have done. My anger will burn against this place, and it will not be quenched.'

¹⁸"But go to the king of Judah who sent you to seek the LORD and tell him: 'This is what the LORD, the God of Israel, says concerning the message you have just heard: ¹⁹You were sorry and humbled yourself before the LORD when you heard what I said against this city and its people—that this land would be cursed and become desolate. You tore your clothing in despair and wept before me in repentance. And I have indeed heard you, says the LORD. ²⁰So I will not send the promised disaster until after you have died and been buried in peace. You will not see the disaster I am going to bring on this city.' "

So they took her message back to the king.

22:14 Or *the Second Quarter,* a newer section of Jerusalem. Hebrew reads *the Mishneh.* 22:16 Hebrew *this place;* also in 22:19, 20.

NOTES

22:8 *the Book of the Law.* Heb., *seper hattorah* [TH8451, ZH9368], meaning "the Book (Scroll) of the Torah." It is later also termed "the Book of the Covenant," *seper habberith* [TH1285, ZH1382] (see 23:2, 21; cf. Exod 24:7). This reference is the classic citation for source-critical scholars to identify all or part of the book of Deuteronomy with what was found in the Temple (and thus also with the so-called "D" [= "Deuteronomic"] source of the Penta-teuch). Concerning the term "Torah" as better understood as "Teachings" rather than "the Law," see the commentary on 1 Kgs 2:1-12. Concerning the phenomenon of discovering old documents during the repairing of temples, as attested elsewhere in the ancient Near East, see Cogan and Tadmor 1988:294.

22:9 *turned over the money.* Lit., "poured out [or melted] the silver" (cf. Cogan and Tad-mor [1988:282, also 138-139], who note that the melting down of metal into ingots of standard size was a common procedure in the ancient Near East, inasmuch as coinage was not yet widely used). See the references cited in the second note on 12:10 concerning such practices.

22:11 *When the king heard.* This truly seems to signify that the words of this section of the Torah were unfamiliar to the king. In any case, he did the right thing; he sought, without hesitation, any further word that Yahweh would have for him and for the people.

22:13 *Go to the Temple and speak to the LORD.* As 22:13b will indicate, this kind of "speaking" may also be termed "inquiring" (*darash* [TH1875, ZH2011]), a technical term in this context, meaning to make inquiry of the deity through a designated prophet (cf. the fourth note on 1:2). Again, it should be noted that even the Davidic king had to seek Yahweh's word by means of the prophet (cf. the commentary on 1 Kgs 1:5-27).

22:14 *New Quarter.* See the commentary on 18:1-12 for details concerning this "Second Quarter" to the west of the City of David, the original city of Jerusalem (also see the refer-ence in Zeph 1:10).

Huldah. Prophets could be either male or female, as Deborah "the prophet" unforgettably illustrates in the book of Judges (see Judg 4:4). Although the prophet Zephaniah (and possibly the youthful Jeremiah) was presumably also available for consultation, rabbinic tradition suggests Josiah consulted Huldah because he thought a woman would be more merciful! (See Sweeney 2007:445; cf. Cogan and Tadmor 1988:283-284 for further details, including the existence of women prophets at this time in the court of Assyrian kings.) Huldah's first oracular statement (22:15-17), however, was as severe as anything in Scrip-ture, although her second oracle (22:18-20) contained significantly more hope, at least for the near-term future (concerning the parallels here with Isaiah's similar prophecies to haughty King Hezekiah in 20:16-18, see the commentary).

wife of Shallum. This Shallum may have been an uncle of the prophet Jeremiah (Jer 32:7); cf. Wiseman 1993:298.

22:16 *I am going to bring disaster on this city and its people.* As noted in the NLT mg, the Hebrew term *maqom* [TH4725, ZH5226] literally means "place"; so Huldah's prophecy would affect not only the city of Jerusalem but also every other part of Josiah's realm (which might still be labeled only a "city-state," but probably by this time, after Manasseh's efforts to enlarge the territory [cf. the commentary on 21:1-18], could indeed be labeled a country or "kingdom." Certainly that is what is in view in the Chronicler's version of Josiah's reign; cf. 2 Chr 34:6-7; also cf. Sweeney 2007:445). Still, Koehler and Baumgartner (HALOT 627) do cite this particular verse in their suggestion that *maqom* could be used as an epithet for Jerusalem (also see Wiseman 1993:299). In any case, the referent of the phrase "on this place" will depend partly on whether the interpreter sees this part of Huldah's prophecy as original to Josiah's time or as a later adaptation from exilic times (see Cogan and Tadmor 1988:295-296 for details).

22:18 *But go to the king of Judah who sent you.* This is a little more respectful than the brusque "go back and tell the man who sent you" found in 22:15. However, as Sweeney points out, "The initial anonymity [in v. 15] aids in building up the mystique of an oracular consultation."

22:20 *after you have died and been buried in peace.* This is a good, idiomatic translation of the Hebrew, which more literally reads, "therefore, I will gather you to your ancestors, and you will be gathered to your grave in peace." It is imperative to note that the parallelism here signifies a peaceful death *and* burial. Josiah's death in actuality turns out to be hardly peaceful at all (see the second note on 23:29 and the commentary on 23:21-30). Concerning the custom of "gathering [one's bones] to the grave" as representing proper burial, see the commentary on 1 Kgs 13:1-34.

C O M M E N T A R Y

We have a recent memory of another godly king who faced a clear prophetic word of future destruction of his kingdom, but exemption for the king himself. That would be King Hezekiah of Judah (cf. 20:16-19). He was indeed a good king and one who could react decisively in a crisis, whether personal (20:1-11) or national (18:13–19:35). He was highly praised by the Deuteronomistic editor (see 18:5-6); in fact, he was lauded for, among other things, his significant efforts at cult-reform (cf. 18:3-4). But when faced with a prophecy of doom for his kingdom, he deferred, consoling himself that "at least there will be peace and security during my lifetime" (see the note on 20:19). Whether literally shortsighted or not, this comment hardly reflects heroism. And it certainly does not reflect the kind of reaction our hero Josiah had. It is to a brief meditation on that reaction that I now turn.

Josiah had no more reason to suspect a sharply negative result from a prophetic word stemming from his well-intentioned efforts to cleanse the Temple of Yahweh than Hezekiah, three-quarters of a century earlier, would have had from his efforts to show off the wealth and power of his kingdom to some Babylonian visitors. And Josiah was equally blindsided by the prophetic words read to him by Shaphan the court secretary from the "Book of the Law"; he had no reason to suspect their ferocity. People say that our true nature is revealed during a totally unexpected crisis. Well, if that is the case, it appears that Josiah acted more nobly than Hezekiah did (at least in this case, for at other times Hezekiah's bravery and nobility are truly without peer). In any case, Josiah certainly did the right thing; he sought out a prophet (see the second note on 22:14) and listened carefully to her word from Yahweh (which showed that she was quite aware that Yahweh knew all about Josiah's previous acts of contrition and repentance [cf. 22:19; these are details the narrator had only mentioned in the briefest fashion back in 22:11]). As a result, he would act most decisively to bring about the most ferocious (in both positive and negative senses) campaign of cult-reform to be found in the Bible. Josiah was not to be deterred! A personal word of exemption from the future cataclysm (which was even more clearly spelled out for Josiah than it had been for Hezekiah) did not stay the hand or stop the voice of this youthful reformer. If anything, I suspect it gave him even more energy and focus to make sure the task was accomplished. No wonder that, in the opinion of the Deuteronomistic Historian, King Josiah is to be ranked "best in show" when it comes to evaluating the various kings of Israel and Judah. And as we soon shall see, the continuing efforts of Josiah will proceed apace, until the task is done.

◆   ## 3. Josiah's religious reforms (23:1-20)

Then the king summoned all the elders of Judah and Jerusalem. [2]And the king went up to the Temple of the LORD with all the people of Judah and Jerusalem, along with the priests and the prophets—all the people from the least to the greatest. There the king read to them the entire Book of the Covenant that had been found in the LORD's Temple. [3]The king took his place of authority beside the pillar and renewed the covenant in the LORD's presence. He pledged to obey the LORD by keeping all his commands, laws, and decrees with all his heart and soul. In this way, he confirmed all the terms of the covenant that were written in the scroll, and all the people pledged themselves to the covenant.

[4]Then the king instructed Hilkiah the high priest and the priests of the second rank and the Temple gatekeepers to remove from the LORD's Temple all the articles that were used to worship Baal, Asherah, and all the powers of the heavens. The king had all these things burned outside Jerusalem on the terraces of the Kidron Valley, and he carried the ashes away to Bethel. [5]He did away with the idolatrous priests, who had been appoint-

ed by the previous kings of Judah, for they had offered sacrifices at the pagan shrines throughout Judah and even in the vicinity of Jerusalem. They had also offered sacrifices to Baal, and to the sun, the moon, the constellations, and to all the powers of the heavens. [6]The king removed the Asherah pole from the LORD's Temple and took it outside Jerusalem to the Kidron Valley, where he burned it. Then he ground the ashes of the pole to dust and threw the dust over the graves of the people. [7]He also tore down the living quarters of the male and female shrine prostitutes that were inside the Temple of the LORD, where the women wove coverings for the Asherah pole.

[8]Josiah brought to Jerusalem all the priests who were living in other towns of Judah. He also defiled the pagan shrines, where they had offered sacrifices—all the way from Geba to Beersheba. He destroyed the shrines at the entrance to the gate of Joshua, the governor of Jerusalem. This gate was located to the left of the city gate as one enters the city. [9]The priests who had served at the pagan shrines were not allowed to serve at* the LORD's altar in Jerusalem, but they were

allowed to eat unleavened bread with the other priests.

[10] Then the king defiled the altar of Topheth in the valley of Ben-Hinnom, so no one could ever again use it to sacrifice a son or daughter in the fire* as an offering to Molech. [11] He removed from the entrance of the LORD's Temple the horse statues that the former kings of Judah had dedicated to the sun. They were near the quarters of Nathan-melech the eunuch, an officer of the court.* The king also burned the chariots dedicated to the sun.

[12] Josiah tore down the altars that the kings of Judah had built on the palace roof above the upper room of Ahaz. The king destroyed the altars that Manasseh had built in the two courtyards of the LORD's Temple. He smashed them to bits* and scattered the pieces in the Kidron Valley. [13] The king also desecrated the pagan shrines east of Jerusalem, to the south of the Mount of Corruption, where King Solomon of Israel had built shrines for Ashtoreth, the detestable goddess of the Sidonians; and for Chemosh, the detestable god of the Moabites; and for Molech,* the vile god of the Ammonites. [14] He smashed the sacred pillars and cut down the Asherah poles. Then he desecrated these places by scattering human bones over them.

[15] The king also tore down the altar at Bethel—the pagan shrine that Jeroboam son of Nebat had made when he caused Israel to sin. He burned down the shrine and ground it to dust, and he burned the Asherah pole. [16] Then Josiah turned around and noticed several tombs in the side of the hill. He ordered that the bones be brought out, and he burned them on the altar at Bethel to desecrate it. (This happened just as the LORD had promised through the man of God when Jeroboam stood beside the altar at the festival.)

Then Josiah turned and looked up at the tomb of the man of God* who had predicted these things. [17] "What is that monument over there?" Josiah asked.

And the people of the town told him, "It is the tomb of the man of God who came from Judah and predicted the very things that you have just done to the altar at Bethel!"

[18] Josiah replied, "Leave it alone. Don't disturb his bones." So they did not burn his bones or those of the old prophet from Samaria.

[19] Then Josiah demolished all the buildings at the pagan shrines in the towns of Samaria, just as he had done at Bethel. They had been built by the various kings of Israel and had made the LORD* very angry. [20] He executed the priests of the pagan shrines on their own altars, and he burned human bones on the altars to desecrate them. Finally, he returned to Jerusalem.

23:9 Hebrew *did not come up to.* 23:10 Or *to make a son or daughter pass through the fire.* 23:11 The meaning of the Hebrew is uncertain. 23:12 Or *He quickly removed them.* 23:13 Hebrew *Milcom,* a variant spelling of Molech. 23:16 As in Greek version; Hebrew lacks *when Jeroboam stood beside the altar at the festival. Then Josiah turned and looked up at the tomb of the man of God.* 23:19 As in Greek and Syriac versions and Latin Vulgate; Hebrew lacks *the Lord.*

NOTES

23:1 Then. As noted in the preceding commentary, Josiah's reaction to the oracle of impending national doom coupled with his own personal exemption was quite different from that of Hezekiah. Rather like Joash, his fatherless counterpart from two centuries earlier, Josiah sought vigorously to renew the covenant (cf. Seow 1999:284-285).

23:2 Book of the Covenant. Apparently this title is analogous to the "Book of the Law" (see the note on 22:8).

23:3 his place of authority beside the pillar. See the first note on 11:14 for a parallel reference from the days of Joash (note that the "people of the land" at that time also demonstrated their public support for the rightful monarch).

renewed the covenant. This is analogous to Jehoida's actions on behalf of Joash in 11:17 (see the note there for details). Sweeney (2007:442), citing Nelson (1981b), compares this action to Joshua's renewal of the covenant in Josh 8:30-35, where Joshua himself read from the Torah the blessings and curses to the people. Japhet (1993:1036-1037) helpfully clarifies that both here in Kings and in the Chronicles parallel (2 Chr 34:31-32), the covenant should be understood as being made "before Yahweh" (not "with Yahweh"); inasmuch as there are two partners in the covenant, they would represent not the people and Yahweh, but the king on the one hand and the people on the other, both pledging themselves to be faithful to Yahweh by keeping faithfully his Torah.

heart and soul. This phrase is akin to the language of Deuteronomy (see the references listed in the second note on 1 Kgs 2:4); also note the fuller phrase ("heart and soul and strength") found in 23:25 (cf. Deut 6:5; these are the only two places where this threefold expression is to be found in the OT). The term usually translated "soul" is *nepesh* [TH5315, ZH5883], a Hebrew word hard to explain with a simple equivalent in English (BDB 659 translates "that which breathes, the breathing substance or being; the inward being"); often *nepesh* is seen as equivalent to "life" or "living being, person" or the like (thus "soul" in that sense, not in the Greek sense of what survives death). The terms *leb* [TH3820, ZH4213] and *lebab* [TH3824, ZH4222]—both "heart"—often denote one's inner nature, i.e., one's mind or will or emotions.

23:4 Baal, Asherah, and all the powers of the heavens. This is a standard listing of the popular non-Yahwistic deities (concerning Baal, see the second note on 1 Kgs 12:28 and the commentary on 1 Kgs 18:41-46; concerning Asherah, see the note on 1 Kgs 14:15; concerning "all the powers of the heavens," see the next verse and the second note on 21:3). It should be noted that all these "articles" were removed from the very Temple of Yahweh. Once again, it should also be noted that Assyria had not insisted on the subjected peoples' worshiping their gods, as long as the suzerainty of Assyria and her gods was not denied (see the first note on 16:10 and, once again, the second note on 21:3 for details). What a devastating picture, therefore, do we find here: rank idolatry in the very center of Jerusalem, the city where Yahweh chose to "place his name" (see the note on 21:4 for further references discussing this crucial Deuteronomic tenet).

on the terraces of the Kidron Valley. The first noun is the somewhat obscure Hebrew term *shademoth* [TH7709, ZH8727], here translated as "terraces" (cf. Cogan and Tadmor [1988:285], who cite Larry Stager's excellent linguistic and architectural study [1982:111-121] of the region in defense of this very probable interpretation). The Kidron Valley is located directly east of Jerusalem (see the second note on 1 Kgs 15:13).

Bethel. It is a bit surprising to find a reference to this notorious northern cult city here (but see Wiseman [1993:301], who suggests that Josiah did seek to expand the borders of Judah during this time of Assyrian weakness). (For the location and significance of this cult city, see the note on 1 Kgs 12:29.) Later on, in 23:15-18, Josiah will notoriously fulfill the prophecy of the anonymous "man of God" of 1 Kgs 13 (see the notes on 1 Kgs 13:1, 13:2) by desecrating Bethel's altar.

23:5 idolatrous priests. This is a good translation of *kemarim* [TH3649, ZH4024], a word which originally meant "priests" in general, but which took on the negative nuance of idolatry or illegitimacy in biblical Hebrew (see Sweeney [2007:447], who further notes the process here of removing priests in outlying areas to aid the centralization of both worship and the collection of revenues in Jerusalem).

pagan shrines. Heb., "high places" (*bamoth* [TH1116, ZH1195]); see the note on 1 Kgs 3:3 for details.

the constellations. A rare word in Hebrew, *mazzaloth* [TH4208, ZH4655]; this is a loanword from Akkadian signifying the fixed locations of the stars in the heavens—hence, probably the ancient equivalent for the signs of the zodiac (cf. Cogan and Tadmor 1988:286).

23:6-7 removed . . . took . . . outside . . . burned . . . ground . . . to dust . . . tore down. Here is a sampling of the forceful verbs used to describe Josiah's thoroughgoing actions of cult cleansing and altar destruction. Other verbs include "defiled" (23:8); "destroyed" (23:12); "smashed . . . to bits" (23:12); "scattered" (23:12); "desecrated" (23:13); "smashed" (23:14); and "demolished" (23:19). This king certainly had his work cut out for him, and he certainly went at it with "all his heart and all his soul."

23:6 Asherah pole. See the note on 1 Kgs 14:15. This particular Asherah pole was set up in the middle of Yahweh's Temple by King Manasseh (see 21:7).

dust. Heb., *'apar* [TH6083, ZH6760]; the actions described here (burning, grinding to dust, throwing the dust over the graves) echo what Moses did to the golden calf in both Exod 32:20 and in Deut 9:21 (cf. Cogan and Tadmor [1988:286], who further note that in the Deuteronomy text, Moses also threw the dust into the valley near the mountain).

23:7 male and female shrine prostitutes. See the note on 1 Kgs 14:24 for this accurate, if somewhat lengthy, translation for the word *qedeshim* [TH6945, ZH7728].

where the women wove coverings for the Asherah pole. The meaning of the Hebrew term translated "coverings" is uncertain; see Cogan and Tadmor (1988:286) for details (cf. Jer 10:9; Ezek 16:16-18 for similar imagery).

23:8 from Geba to Beersheba. Geba is probably Tel el-Ful (Cogan 2001:401-402) or else modern Jaba' (ABD 2.921), either location situated less than 7 mi. [10 km] northeast of Jerusalem; it was a Levitical city in the territory of Benjamin. Geba (along with Mizpah) was mentioned in 1 Kgs 15:22 in reference to King Asa bolstering the northern defenses of Jerusalem to prevent King Baasha of Israel from putting further pressure on the city (Baasha had captured Ramah nearby). In any case, Geba presumably represents the northernmost boundary of seventh-century Judah. Beersheba (see 1 Kgs 19:3), in turn, represents the southernmost significant location in Judah ever since patriarchal times. In the days of Solomon, the expression "from Dan to Beersheba" represented the ideal boundaries of the land (see first note on 1 Kgs 4:25 [5:5]); presumably, the present expression "from Geba to Beersheba" stood as its euphonious seventh-century counterpart.

the gate of Joshua. If Jerusalem is still in view (the Hebrew simply reads "the governor of the city"), the reference here to such a gate is otherwise unknown (cf. Cogan and Tadmor 1988:287). Nevertheless, the present notice does seem to represent the testimony of a contemporary eyewitness; Cogan and Tadmor liken it to a "footnote" to the preceding description of the destroyed "shrines" (*bamoth* [TH1116, ZH1195]). They also suggest the intriguing possibility that this reference is actually to the city of Beersheba (as does Wiseman 1993:302). For the publication of a clay bulla (seal impression) attesting the phrase "governor of the city" (*sar ha'ir* [TH8269/5892, ZH8569/6551]), along with two bearded figures depicted in Assyrian style, see Avigad 1976:178-182, plus plate 33D.

23:9 were not allowed. This is an interpretive translation (cf. NLT mg), but quite probable; Cogan and Tadmor (1988:287) cite Friedman's suggestion that such limitations were akin to those placed upon physically blemished priests as in Lev 21:21-23—no approaching the altar to minister as priests, but food from the (grain) offerings might still be eaten.

23:10 altar of Topheth. This is a reference found only here in Kings, but eight times in Jeremiah (all in chs 7 and 19). "Topheth" probably represents the cultic installation where children were sacrificed and burned in the fire, generally to the god Molech. As both the present reference and the parallels in Jeremiah indicate, it was located at the eastern end of the Hinnom Valley, probably near the spring of En-rogel (cf. the first note on 1 Kgs 1:9). Probably originally pronounced "tephath" ("fireplace" or the like), the Masoretic vocalization "topheth" echoes that of the term "bosheth" or "shame" (cf. Saul's son "Esh-baal" in 1 Chr 8:33, pronounced as "Ish-bosheth" in 2 Sam 2:8 [the term "Baal" later considered a reference to the Canaanite deity, hence, shameful even to pronounce]). For further details, see Thompson 1980:294; cf. Cogan and Tadmor 1988:287-288.

sacrifice a son or daughter in the fire. See the second note on 16:3 for scholarly discussion concerning the probable nature of this horrific practice.

an offering to Molech. See the note on 1 Kgs 11:5; there is the possibility that, at least in certain circles, such a horrendous sacrifice may have even been offered to Yahweh. Cogan and Tadmor (1988:288) list the strong polemics found in Jeremiah and in Ezekiel; perhaps the most haunting of them is Yahweh's total bewilderment at such "offerings": "I have never commanded such a horrible deed; it never even crossed my mind to command such a thing!" (Jer 7:31; cf. Jer 32:35).

23:11 *horse statues . . . dedicated to the sun.* Models of such horse statues, some with solar disks on their foreheads, have been found in Jerusalem and in Hazor (see Wiseman 1993:302-303 for references).

an officer of the court. As noted in the NLT mg, the Hebrew term translated here as "court" (*parwarim* [TH6503A, ZH7247]) is indeed difficult to understand; it appears to come from the Persian language.

23:12 *the upper room of Ahaz.* Cf. the references to King Ahaz's extensive renovations as discussed in the note on 20:11.

two courtyards. Cf. the note on 21:5.

smashed them to bits. This is an uncertain text; the NLT (cf. NRSV, NIV) understands *wayyarats* as from the root *ratsats* [TH7533, ZH8368] (to crush), while Cogan and Tadmor (1988:289) and Sweeney (2007:449) prefer to derive the form from the root *ruts* [TH7323, ZH8132] (to run), hence to do something quickly or hastily, whence Sweeney's "He hurried from there to throw their ashes into the Kidron Valley."

23:13 *Mount of Corruption.* This is the "Mount of Olives" (*har-hammishkhah* [TH4888, ZH5418], "mount of ointment") altered sarcastically to read *har-hammashkhith* [TH4889, ZH5422] ("mount of corruption/destruction"); cf. 1 Kgs 11:7 (in fact, the entirety of 23:13-14 here reflects the listing of Solomon's pagan altars in 1 Kgs 11:5-7; cf. Cogan and Tadmor [1988:289], who attribute that tradition to the same editorial hand as is found here).

23:14 *scattering human bones.* This renders the places ritually impure and unfit for future worship (Sweeney 2007:449); cf. 23:16, 20.

23:15 *the altar at Bethel.* This is a reference to the striking prophecy given back in 1 Kgs 13:1-32 (Josiah is mentioned by name in 13:2).

23:16 *the man of God when Jeroboam . . . tomb of the man of God.* For a defense of the NLT's inclusion here of the longer text (as in LXX; cf. NRSV) as original (cf. NLT mg), see Cogan and Tadmor 1988:289-290. The MT scribe apparently skipped from the first occurrence of the phrase "man of God" to the second, thus omitting all the text in between due to homeoteleuton.

23:18 *from Samaria.* Strictly speaking, the old prophet came from the city of Bethel (see 1 Kgs 13:11); in fact, Samaria (the city) had not yet been built. Probably the reference here is to the kingdom of Israel, which also could now be referred to as "Samaria" (see the next verse).

23:20 *burned human bones.* See the note on 23:14. In summary, as Seow (1999:285) aptly put it, "The narrator makes it clear that Josiah takes no chances and leaves no stone unturned."

COMMENTARY

We finally read the gruesome details of the cult-cleansing itself, some 17 verses filled with death and destruction. Inasmuch as this narrative is clearly written for the Deuteronomistic tradition, it might be usefully compared to other such Deuteronomistic narratives such as those involving "holy war" and the like. There is no avoiding all the bloodthirsty details of such battles (cf., e.g., Josh 6:20-21; 8:24-29; 10:28-42), and there is certainly no holding back on the sordid particulars either there or here. In a style that certainly can be offensive to modern tastes, the narrator takes fierce delight in all this mayhem and destruction (cf. the various verbs of destruction listed in the note on 23:6-7). However, we must not allow such offensive language to deafen us to the underlying message: Yahweh is one (Deut 6:4), and there is therefore only one place where he is properly to be worshiped (Deut 12:4-14; cf. "One Place of Worship" under "Major Themes" in the Introduction). And Yahweh, the self-styled "Jealous One" is very serious about this (cf. the commentary on 1 Kgs 12:25-33). (For a brief discussion of Boyd's thoughts on Yahweh working "incarnationally" in an Israelite culture that celebrates the bloodthirsty narratives of "holy war," as well as narratives of cruelty in the guise of cult-reform such as we find here, see the commentary on 10:18-31.)

In any case, as already noted in the commentary on 22:1-7, nearly the entire account of Josiah's reign can be arranged in a striking palistrophe, as Peter Leithart (2006:268) has pointed out:

> A. Opening: Josiah does not turn to right or left (22:1-2)
>   B. Book of the Torah found (22:3-20)
>   C. Renews covenant according to "book of the covenant" (23:1-3)
>   D. Reforms of Josiah (23:4-20)
>   C'. Passover according to "book of the covenant" (23:21-23)
>   B'. All the words of the Torah (23:24)
> A'. Closing: Josiah turns to Yahweh with heart, soul, strength (23:25)

Thus, Josiah's reform is literarily framed by two ceremonies: the covenant renewal (23:1-3) and the Passover (23:21-23), both said to be held in Josiah's 18th year (see the note on 22:3). And within this palistrophe, there is overall organization to the reform, with focus mostly on Jerusalem and the Temple in 23:4-7, and then moving outward from there to nearby environs in 23:8-14, and then moving on to Bethel, the notorious northern shrine set up three centuries earlier by Jeroboam I (23:15-18, in fulfillment of prophecy given to that tenth-century northern king by the "man of God" from Judah [see the note on 23:15]). Finally, he cleansed the rest of "Samaria" (i.e., the old northern kingdom of Israel, or at least the Assyrian province of that name, which encompassed much of that area [cf. Wiseman 1993:303-304]), destroying the pagan shrines and executing their priests. Thus, Josiah's "reforms" were vigorously undertaken, comprehensive in scope, and devastating in results. And as Leithart (2006:268) puts it, "Josiah reverses the order of Joshua:

Joshua begins in Passover (Josh. 5) and then embarks on a conquest to destroy the shrines of the Canaanites, while Josiah destroys the shrines of Canaanite-Israel and then celebrates Passover."

But why so much death and destruction? Is it really the case that such high-minded ends must be accomplished by such low-minded means? The following are some thoughts concerning this topic. Wiseman, in his Kings commentary (1993:300), first alerted me to an intriguing idea: Josiah was interested in making the Jerusalem Temple more of a "central sanctuary" rather than what it had been since the time of Solomon, a "royal chapel" (see the commentary on 1 Kgs 5:1-18). And this would naturally include fiscal policy, or more specifically, the centralization of the tithing system. In support of this, Wiseman cites the provocative article written some years ago by Claburn entitled "The Fiscal Basis of Josiah's Reforms" (1973:11-22). As the title intimates, Claburn suggests that the Deuteronomic system of tithing (i.e., taxation!) was behind much of King Josiah's reform-minded momentum (cf. Deut 16:16-17). And he then goes on to argue:

> How does an ambitious king most efficiently get his hands on the largest possible proportion of the peasantry's agricultural surplus? . . . If he is smart, he does it not by raising the assessed level of taxes, but by reforming his fiscal system so that he brings into the capital a larger proportion of the taxes already being assessed. He does this by substituting for the semi-independent local dignitaries to whom the peasants had been paying the taxes (but who had been pocketing most of the proceeds locally) a hierarchically organized central internal revenue bureau of paid officials under his direct control. It follows that if the society in which such a fiscal reform is being carried out is still so undifferentiated as to institution and role specialization that the same institutions that have been carrying on other governmental functions have also been serving as the religious organization, altars will probably have to be torn down, pillars dashed in pieces, and sacred poles burned at the sacred places to which the tithes have previously been brought in order to validate and enforce the reform. (Claburn 1973:15-16)

Claburn then explicates the Deuteronomic system of tithing (cf. Deut 14:22-27) to explain how part of the tithe can be used to help with travel expenses, as well as the part the Levites were expected to play in all this. In short, I find this a compelling *addition* to (not *substitution* for) the traditional understanding of the motives behind Josiah's extensive reform efforts.

One may ask if there is any archaeological evidence to support Claburn's hypothesis. Once again, Wiseman provides a clue: the existence of the *lmlk* (meaning "for the king") seal impressions on the handles of clay jars which become widespread around this time (Wiseman [1993:300], citing Na'aman 1979:61-86). Although the dating of these inscribed vessels remains a vexed issue, with the trend now favoring the time of Hezekiah over Josiah (Na'aman 1979:70-86; cf. Lance in ABD 6.184-185; Lipschits 2010:27-28), this may not be as much of an issue as it might at first seem to be, for it is clear that Hezekiah did a fair amount of "cult-cleansing" on his own (cf. the notes on 18:3-4). And the "rosette" stamp impressions do seem to date to Josiah's reign (so Fox 2000:235-242; cf. Cahill [1995:230-252], who, however, prefers the reign of Jehoiakim), again giving economic realia in support of abstract theological concepts such as "revival" and "cult centralization" (cf. Dever 2001:226-227, as also applied in the commentary on 18:1-12), not to mention their attesting the increasing economic *and* theological prominence given to the king and the centralized royal bureaucracy.

In conclusion, as Claburn (1973:14) points out, one effect of centralization was to bring more money and goods to Jerusalem during the pilgrim feasts (cf. Deut 16:16, "gift"); the tithe/tax as paid into a centralized system based in Jerusalem may well be attributable to the reforms. And the benefit to the tithe-payer? Besides the partial use of the tithe for the now necessary travel expenses already mentioned, the "peasant" would naturally come to expect a spectacle worth the trip. And this puts Josiah's Passover (23:21-23) in an entirely new light, for we are told that such a Passover had not been celebrated since before the days of the Judges.

Finally, let us consider the New Testament outworking of this Old Testament inno-vation—consider how important these "pilgrim feasts" had become by the first cen-tury AD. Prominent New Testament events could never have even been conceivable unless the previous Old Testament interest in cult-centralization in the days of Josiah had taken place. Consider the Passover gathering when Jesus was crucified and then resurrected, or perhaps even more dramatically, the following Pentecost (= Feast of Weeks), when Jews gathered from some 15 nations miraculously heard the disciples' testimony about Jesus in their native tongues and then heard Peter's sermon, with the result that some 3,000 were added to the church in one day (Acts 2). Yes, cult-centralization, like the postexilic spread of the synagogue throughout the eastern half of the Mediterranean world, proved foundational for the later propagation of Christianity. Indeed, God sometimes moves in the most mysterious ways!

◆   ## 4. Josiah celebrates Passover (23:21-30)

[21] King Josiah then issued this order to all the people: "You must celebrate the Pass-over to the LORD your God, as required in this Book of the Covenant." [22] There had not been a Passover celebration like that since the time when the judges ruled in Israel, nor throughout all the years of the kings of Israel and Judah. [23] But in the eighteenth year of King Josiah's reign, this Passover was celebrated to the LORD in Jerusalem.

[24] Josiah also got rid of the mediums and psychics, the household gods, the idols,* and every other kind of detestable practice, both in Jerusalem and through-out the land of Judah. He did this in obe-dience to the laws written in the scroll that Hilkiah the priest had found in the LORD's Temple. [25] Never before had there been a king like Josiah, who turned to the LORD with all his heart and soul and strength, obeying all the laws of Moses. And there has never been a king like him since.

[26] Even so, the LORD was very angry with Judah because of all the wicked things Manasseh had done to provoke him. [27] For the LORD said, "I will also banish Judah from my presence just as I have banished Israel. And I will reject my chosen city of Jerusalem and the Temple where my name was to be honored."

[28] The rest of the events in Josiah's reign and all his deeds are recorded in *The Book of the History of the Kings of Judah.*

[29] While Josiah was king, Pharaoh Neco, king of Egypt, went to the Euphrates Riv-er to help the king of Assyria. King Josiah and his army marched out to fight him,* but King Neco* killed him when they met

at Megiddo. ³⁰Josiah's officers took his
body back in a chariot from Megiddo to
Jerusalem and buried him in his own

tomb. Then the people of the land anointed Josiah's son Jehoahaz and made him
the next king.

23:24 The Hebrew term (literally *round things*) probably alludes to dung.   **23:29a** Or *Josiah went out to meet him.*   **23:29b** Hebrew *he.*

NOTES

23:21 *You must celebrate the Passover.* Passover is featured most prominently in Exod 12, but it is also described in Deut 16:1-8. In the Deuteronomistic History, the last and only recorded Passover takes place in the days of Joshua (Josh 5:10-12). It should be noted, however, that 2 Chr 30 does describe at some length a famous Passover previously observed by King Hezekiah, presumably stemming from a historical record independent of Kings (Williamson 1982a:365; Japhet 1993:935).

23:22 *There had not been a Passover celebration like that.* High praise indeed; for some interesting implications stemming from the greatness of this celebration, see the previous commentary section.

23:23 *eighteenth year.* See the note on 22:3 for the significance of this repeated chronological datum.

23:24 *mediums . . . psychics . . . household gods . . . idols.* Again (see second note on 21:6), these practices are clearly forbidden in the Torah. The terms "mediums" and "psychics" here refer to *'oboth* [TH178A, ZH200] and *yidde'onim* [TH3049, ZH3362], respectively, which probably refer to ghosts or spirits from the dead rather than to the mediums or psychics who conjure them up (see Lev 20:27; cf. Cogan and Tadmor 1988:267 and the references cited there). "Household gods" refers to *terapim* [TH8655, ZH9572] (a term used only here in 1–2 Kings, but cf. 1 Sam 19:13, 16, where David's wife Michal [Saul's daughter] places "the teraphim" in David's bed, covered with blankets, so that it appeared he was still sleeping there). McCarter (1980:326) suggests that the term *terapim* may be singular or plural (it appears grammatically to be plural), and that indeed it is best translated "household idols" or the like (cf. Latin *penates*). And the final term used here, "idols," is a reference to the Heb. *gillulim* [TH1544, ZH1658] ("round[ed] things"), a sarcastic term we have seen several times in Kings (cf. NLT mg; also the notes on 17:12; 21:11; the second note on 1 Kgs 15:12).

23:25 *Never before . . . never . . . since.* See the third note on 23:3.

23:26 *the wicked things Manasseh had done.* See the commentary on 21:1-18, and the references cited there. Although most scholars would not consider this section (23:26-27) to be part of the original Josiah tradition, it does accord with Huldah's first oracle of irrevocable destruction (see the note on 22:16 for details).

23:28 *are recorded in* The Book of the History of the Kings of Judah. See "Literary Style" in the Introduction.

23:29 *Pharaoh Neco.* Sometimes labeled "Neco II" (although his grandfather Neco I was only a regional ruler), this pharaoh was the second pharaoh (as usually reckoned) of the 26th (Saite) Dynasty. Neco (sometimes spelled "Necho") ruled over Egypt from 610 to 595 BC, so he was new to the throne when Josiah "met" him at Megiddo (Wiseman 1993:305). But his anti-Babylonian policy was not new, for under Neco's father, Psamtik I (Psammetichus I), the Egyptian army had already marched into Syria in 616 BC to prop up the weakening Assyrian Empire as a counterweight against the newly resurgent Babylonians. Neco, in turn, was able to gain control of northern Syria for several years (c. 609–605 BC), until the Babylonian army under crown prince Nebuchadnezzar attacked the Egyptians at their Syrian base at Carchemish on the Euphrates, forcing them back to Hamath until they eventually withdrew from the land of Syria. By 597 BC Nebuchadnezzar had essentially imposed Babylonian sovereignty over Palestine for good (Roberts 2009:247); essentially, it would not be until the rise of Persia in 539 BC that the Levant would know any other overlord.

marched out to fight him. Lit., "went out to meet him." Some have suggested that this was a summons of Josiah by the pharaoh akin to what the Assyrians had probably done to King Manasseh, as described in 2 Chr 33:11. Most scholars, however, would see Josiah acting on his own initiative and indeed by military means attempting to stop, or at least harass, the pharaoh and his army (this seems clearer in the Chronicler's fuller rendering of the story [2 Chr 35:20-24]). I have argued in the past that Huldah's prophecy of a peaceful death and burial for Josiah (see the note on 22:20) may have given him false bravado in thinking he could stop this powerful force (the strategic location of Megiddo is the logical place to try to do this, to be sure [see next note]). In the Chronicles parallel, Pharaoh Neco is presented as truly speaking the word of God (Elohim) to try to dissuade Josiah from such foolish presumption (2 Chr 35:21-22). But the present text is brief and more enigmatic; as Sweeney (2007:450) points out, "The perfunctory reference to Josiah's death hides more than it reveals." Some scholars have naturally suggested this represents some sort of "conspiracy of silence," but that probably reads too much into the text. Nevertheless, Josiah's tragic death at a relatively young age was surely an embarrassing end to someone so promising—unless this somehow took place according to the will of Yahweh in the sense that Josiah's demise at a young age represents an act of mercy in that he would not see the sad end of his beloved country (cf. Wiseman 1993:299). But even that view reads something into the text, rather than deriving something from the text, which is our first task as exegetes.

Megiddo. This is a strategic mountain pass in Israel where the major seacoast highway (Via Maris), which represents the main route from Egypt to Syria, turns inland from the coastal plain into the Jezreel Valley. This would be a prime location for Josiah, with or without his army, to "meet" Pharaoh Neco (see the previous note).

23:30 buried him in his own tomb. Taking pains to emphasize that at least part of Huldah's prophecy did come true (as a side note, the partial nonfulfillment of Huldah's prophecy should be no cause for alarm, since clearly a person's free will can negate or nullify prophecies [cf. endnote 28 of the Introduction; also the commentary on 20:1-11]). Similarly one can compare 2 Chr 34:26-28 and 35:20-25.

people of the land. Concerning this most important group of landed gentry and the stability they offered time and again to the Davidic dynasty, see the note on 21:24 and the references cited there.

COMMENTARY

In contrast to the preceding sections on King Josiah, the present text moves quite quickly from the sublime to the tragic; as Seow (1999:286) puts it, "The reader of Kings may be forgiven for feeling a little betrayed by the narrator." We have come to expect that predicted history is subject to change (certainly vividly presented as such in the Hezekiah stories of chs 18–20), and the present king, our "hero" Josiah, surely could pull this off as well with regard to the predicted calamity for Judah (22:16-20). So many stirring details—so much effort—yes, so much bloodshed as well. We have no reason to think that Josiah is double-minded in his cult-cleansing endeavors. As for the nagging refrains about the sins of Manasseh (23:26-27; cf. 21:11-16 [plus the upcoming refrain found in 24:2-4]), surely they, as much as the pagan predictions of the Rabshakeh (chs 18–19) and Isaiah's gloomy prophecy of Hezekiah's death (20:1), could be changed by proper Deuteronomistic behavior. But change they will not, and hence this text does poorly if one turns to this Bible narrative as an example for behavioral motivation. But that is not the simple purpose of most of the historical texts found in the Bible (cf. Walton's comments about biblical texts resisting moralization, cited in the commentary on 2:1-18). Still, of all things, cult centralization is one of the most important themes in Deuteronomy and in the Deuteronomistic literature (see "One Place of Worship" under "Major Themes" in the Introduction).

Those who relegate the Bible (especially the OT) to the domain of "fairy tales" will have a problem here. It is too realistic to be placed in such a category. Sometimes the early bird does not get the worm, or as Qoheleth, the writer of Ecclesiastes, puts it, "The fastest runner doesn't always win the race, and the strongest warrior doesn't always win the battle" (Eccl 9:11). Furthermore, Josiah was duly warned by Huldah that the Lord's anger would not be quenched (22:17). That, however, brings up the other issue that strangely dominates the present text: the inaccuracy of Huldah in her other prophecy—the one about Josiah dying in peace (22:20). The present text does not shrink from citing the prophecy as well as noting its nonfulfillment. Naturally, some scholars suggest later interpolations concerning Huldah's words and their nonfulfillment (for a careful study of the implications of such suggestions, see Williamson 1982b:242-248). But that is not the best way to handle the implications of the Josiah material as found in Kings. Cogan and Tadmor (1988:295) argue logically that the very incongruity between Huldah's words and Josiah's actions identify 22:19-20a as part of the original kernel of the prophecy. And 22:20b reprises her first oracle of unrelenting woe (22:16-17). As Cogan and Tadmor conclude, "These words of Huldah remain a striking example of unfulfilled prophecy" (see further the note on 23:30 and the second note on 23:29). Such seeming inconsistencies actually add to, rather than detract from, the authenticity of the biblical text, for no later harmonization of the narrative is to be found here (rather like the various accounts of the resurrection of Jesus—the details vary in each of the accounts).

I would be remiss if I did not conclude this Josiah text with a summary of his uniqueness. Josiah is indeed the hero of the Deuteronomistic editor, and his cult centralization was impressive. But this was not his best accomplishment. Nor was it his institution of "pilgrim festivals," which would later prove to be a boon for both Second Temple Judaism and early Christianity. Nor was it that Josiah was a second, better Hezekiah. No, Leithart (2006:268-269) is on track both when he characterizes Josiah in terms of Nebuchadnezzar, of all people ("What Josiah does throughout this account is curiously similar to what Nebuchadnezzar will soon do in Judah: removing vessels from the Temple, breaking down shrines, and sending people into 'exile.' Reform is a kind of judgment."); and then more profoundly, as the very antithesis of the first Jeroboam (here he cites Nelson 1987:258), "bringing a final end to Jeroboam's liturgical experiments and reuniting the kingdom around a purified worship of Yahweh." Josiah was also a Moses, conforming to the Torah and destroying golden calves. He was a Joshua, not turning to the right or to the left (22:2; cf. the third note on that verse; cf. Josh 1:7; 23:6); in fact, Josiah's Passover was the best one since Joshua's (cf. the note on 23:21). And, last but not least, he was a David (22:2), an entirely worthy successor to the founder of that most important dynasty.

Yet, great as Josiah was, he could not save his nation from destruction. Manasseh could doom the nation, but Josiah could not save it (Hens-Piazza 2006:389). As Seow (1999:287) concludes:

> The most important lesson of all that the passage offers is a negative one. It teaches that human acts of righteousness, even those as thorough and as sincere as Josiah's, are no guarantee of salvation. . . . Josiah initiated an ancient equivalent of a 'back to the Bible' movement, as it were, but the rediscovery of the law does not save. Despite his zealous adherence to 'the book,' there is no salvation for Judah. Salvation, if it comes at all, will be by the grace of God alone, through faith (Eph 2:8).

Sobering words, I submit, for any generation, including our own, which tries so hard to legislate morality. No, the Bible is something quite different from fairy tales, for in the Bible there is no guarantee of living "happily ever after." But our God is a God full of grace. And, if we're faithful, we will indeed live "happily ever after" with him in heaven. Better than any fairy tale!

◆   D. Four Evil Successors to Josiah (2 Kgs 23:31–24:20a)
1. Jehoahaz rules in Judah (23:31-33)

³¹Jehoahaz was twenty-three years old when he became king, and he reigned in Jerusalem three months. His mother was Hamutal, the daughter of Jeremiah from Libnah. ³²He did what was evil in the LORD's sight, just as his ancestors had done. ³³Pharaoh Neco put Jehoahaz in prison at Riblah in the land of Hamath to prevent him from ruling* in Jerusalem. He also demanded that Judah pay 7,500 pounds of silver and 75 pounds of gold* as tribute.

23:33a The meaning of the Hebrew is uncertain.   23:33b Hebrew *100 talents* [3,400 kilograms] *of silver and 1 talent* [34 kilograms] *of gold.*

NOTES

23:31 Jehoahaz. Apparently his original name was "Shallum" (Cogan and Tadmor 1988:303; cf. 1 Chr 3:15; Jer 22:10-12; and for another Shallum, 15:13-15); "Jehoahaz" was his throne name. Akin to the name Ahaz (see the note on 16:1; also see the note on 13:1; a stamp seal attesting the name of this king has been found), "Jehoahaz" probably means "Yahweh has grasped, taken hold of." It should be noted that Jehoahaz was evidently not the firstborn son of Josiah (Jehoiakim, a half brother who succeeded Jehoahaz, was two years older). Malamat (1975:126) suggests that the anti-Egyptian tone of Josiah continued in the brief reign of Jehoahaz, but this policy proved to be "rather premature under the circumstances."

23:32 did what was evil. This is a stereotypical Deuteronomistic evaluation (cf. endnote 2 of the Introduction). But how much "evil" could have taken place in a three-month reign (cf. the note on 21:20)?

23:33 Pharaoh Neco. See the first note on 23:29.

put Jehoahaz in prison at Riblah in the land of Hamath. This site in central Syria will become the infamous location where Nebuchadnezzar, some 20 years later, will pass judgment on Zedekiah for covenant (or treaty) infidelity (25:6). Thus, we find a sad symmetry concerning the fates of these two unfortunate full brothers.

to prevent him from ruling. This is the likely meaning of the Hebrew (cf. Cogan and Tad-mor 1988:303-304).

7,500 pounds of silver and 75 pounds of gold. Lit., 100 talents of silver and a talent of gold (see the second note on 1 Kgs 9:14 for the modern equivalents of the Hebrew talent). Cogan and Tadmor (1988:304) think the number of talents of gold has dropped out of the MT (the Lucianic version of the LXX has "ten" talents, a likely amount—the 100 talents of the LXX seems far too high). In the next section, 23:35 will return to the painful details of paying off this tribute.

COMMENTARY

For the final time we encounter the short, stereotypical notices of some "lesser" kings (see 15:8-31 for earlier parallels in Israel). Historically, these four successors to King Josiah (three of them his sons, and one, Jehoiachin, his grandson) hardly present themselves with distinction, although two of them, Jehoahaz and Jehoiachin, are said to have been on the throne for only three months each (the curious symmetry here is three months, then 11 years, then again three months, then again 11 years). Overall, it is a relatively quick and seemingly relentless plunge downhill to exile. Not that the Judahites were resigned to their fate—quite the contrary. Malamat (1975:125) counts some six changes of Judahite loyalty between Egypt and Babylon in these 20-some years. It will be our melancholy task to document these six shifts in allegiance as the Judahite people and their kings attempt to avoid the inevitable demise of the nation. The first shift is documented in these few verses on Jehoahaz—from Babylon to Egypt.

◆   ## 2. Jehoiakim rules in Judah (23:34–24:7)

³⁴Pharaoh Neco then installed Eliakim, another of Josiah's sons, to reign in place of his father, and he changed Eliakim's name to Jehoiakim. Jehoahaz was taken to Egypt as a prisoner, where he died.

³⁵In order to get the silver and gold demanded as tribute by Pharaoh Neco, Jehoiakim collected a tax from the people of Judah, requiring them to pay in proportion to their wealth.

³⁶Jehoiakim was twenty-five years old when he became king, and he reigned in Jerusalem eleven years. His mother was Zebidah, the daughter of Pedaiah from Rumah. ³⁷He did what was evil in the LORD's sight, just as his ancestors had done.

CHAPTER 24

During Jehoiakim's reign, King Nebuchadnezzar of Babylon invaded the land of Judah. Jehoiakim surrendered and paid him tribute for three years but then rebelled. ²Then the LORD sent bands of Babylonian,* Aramean, Moabite, and Ammonite raiders against Judah to destroy it, just as the LORD had promised through his prophets. ³These disasters happened to Judah because of the LORD's command. He had decided to banish Judah from his presence because of the many sins of Manasseh, ⁴who had filled Jerusalem with innocent blood. The LORD would not forgive this.

⁵The rest of the events in Jehoiakim's reign and all his deeds are recorded in *The Book of the History of the Kings of Judah.* ⁶When Jehoiakim died, his son Jehoiachin became the next king.

⁷The king of Egypt did not venture out of his country after that, for the king of Babylon captured the entire area formerly claimed by Egypt—from the Brook of Egypt to the Euphrates River.

24:2 Or *Chaldean.*

NOTES

23:34 *Eliakim.* With Jehoahaz removed, a half brother of his, Eliakim, is put on the throne by Pharaoh Neco (see the first note on 23:29). "Eliakim" probably means "may El [God] raise up"; the name change to "Jehoiakim" merely changes the theophoric element (the reference to the deity) so it means "may Yahweh raise up" or the like. Cogan and Tadmor (1988:304) suggest that this name change may represent the result of an oath of loyalty sworn to the new overlord, similar to Assyrian practice.

Jehoahaz was taken to Egypt as a prisoner. We now move into a series of similarly dramatic removals from the throne, which will culminate in Jehoiachin's release from prison, which is described at the very end of 2 Kings (25:27) as the note of modest hope that appropriately, if anticlimactically, brings the Deuteronomistic History to its end.

23:35 *collected a tax.* This is perhaps ironic support for the idea of "progressive taxation," or perhaps only blunt realism (only the rich could have any possibility of paying). In any case, once again the "people of the land" were on the hook, this time financially. Here at least there is a sense of bitter poetic justice, for those stalwarts seemed to have a consistently anti-Egyptian bias in their political actions (cf. Sweeney 2007:452). Other ironies include the Menahem-like tenor of Jehoiakim's actions (cf. 15:19-20 for Menahem paying off Tiglath-pileser) and the parallel with good king Hezekiah emptying out Temple and palace treasuries, and even stripping the Temple doorposts, to pay off Sennacherib (18:14-16).

23:37 *did what was evil.* Again, this is the stereotypical Deuteronomistic evaluation (see endnote 2 of the Introduction); this time the condemnation was certainly well earned (see the note on 23:31). The book of Jeremiah also attests that Jehoiakim ended up making a very poor king (cf. Jer 22:13-23; 36:1-32).

24:1 *King Nebuchadnezzar.* This is the second king of the Neo-Babylonian dynasty founded by his father Nabopolassar (620–606 BC); Nebuchadnezzar (sometimes spelled Nebuchadrezzar) reigned for 43 years (605–562 BC)! We first hear of him as crown prince in his victory at the battle of Carchemish (see the first note on 23:29). Soon he would need to return home to assume his father's throne in Babylon, but before that, this energetic king marched west to take tribute from the kings of Syria and Palestine and vanquish the Philistines and destroy Ashkelon. It was about this time that Jehoiakim submitted to Babylon for some three years, as noted in this verse. By the year 600 BC, however, Nebuchadnezzar had suffered severe reverses on the Egyptian border, seemingly prompting Jehoiakim's rebellion (cf. Roberts 2009:246), as well as Nebuchadnezzar's eventual march against Jerusalem in 598 BC, and its capitulation to him in 597 BC (cf. 24:10-17). Jehoiakim had died by this time, with the circumstances of his death remaining most obscure (see Kim 2008b:209; cf. the note on 24:6). Eventually, King Nebuchadnezzar gained the dubious distinction of becoming the one who destroyed the first Temple (see 24:20b–25:21). Jeremiah had termed Nebuchadnezzar "Yahweh's servant" in Jer 27:6. No wonder many in Judah considered this prophet a traitor, or worse!

Jehoiakim surrendered . . . but then rebelled. Here are two more of the six changes of loyalty (the first one, with little choice involved, to be sure) for this final 20-year period of Judahite history.

24:2 *the LORD sent.* Various nations are listed, all sent under the sovereignty of the true God, Yahweh, though one imagines each marched in the name of its national god. For the term "Chaldean" being translated as "Babylonian" (cf. NLT mg), see Cogan and Tadmor 1988:306. Some commentators read the reference to Aram here as a misspelling of Edom (cf. the first note on 16:6 concerning their similarity in Hebrew), but Cogan and Tadmor vehemently disagree. In fact, they suggest that Edom itself may also have been in a state of rebellion (cf. Jer 27).

24:3 *because of the many sins of Manasseh.* Yet again, a major theme of the exilic Deuteronomist (see "The 'Sins of Manasseh'" under "Major Themes" in the Introduction for
details; also see the commentary on 21:1-18).

24:4 *innocent blood.* Obviously the major focus here is on Manasseh, not the king ostensibly discussed. In 21:16, the shedding of "innocent blood" (see the note on that verse
for possible meanings of that expression) is added to the many other sins of Manasseh
discussed throughout the chapter; it seems that both there and here this sin is seen as the
"last straw," causing Yahweh's implacable wrath to remain on Judah.

24:5 *are recorded in* The Book of the History of the Kings of Judah. For the final time
(note that there was no such reference for the reign of Jehoahaz in 23:31-34; nor will there
be for the last two kings of Judah, Jehoiachin and Zedekiah), we find this reference to *The
Book of the History of the Kings of Judah*. On the nature of this source, as well as its significance
in the writing of 1-2 Kings, see "Literary Style" in the Introduction). Wiseman (1993:308)
suggests that these annals ended here, with the siege of the capital city their final entry.

24:6 *When Jehoiakim died.* This is a customary burial formula and offers little about the
circumstances of the death; Jer 22:18-19; 36:30-31 (cf. 2 Chr 36:6) imply that Jehoiakim's
death was hardly peaceful and without incident. Kim (2008b:209) speculates that perhaps
the "people of the land," who would in any case be most pleased to see him gone, commissioned his assassination when they saw Nebuchadnezzar at the very gates of Jerusalem.

24:7 *The king of Egypt did not venture out of his country after that.* See the first note on
23:29 for details.

Brook of Egypt. This is the traditional border between Egypt and Syria-Palestine (see the
first note on 1 Kgs 8:65 for its location and significance).

COMMENTARY

So here are our second and third (of six) policy shifts (see the previous commentary
section for Malamat's depiction of the last days of preexilic Judah); as one might
expect, the results of these shifts proved to be deadly (cf. the notes on 24:1, 6). The
Deuteronomistic presentation concerning Jehoiakim, a crude bully of a king (see Jer
36 for an unforgettable portrayal of this harsh man) is largely formulaic, fixating on
the "sins of Manasseh" as the main cause of the Exile. All we know about Jehoiakim
from these verses is that he was "evil," that he paid the tribute to Pharaoh Neco
largely at the expense of the "people of the land," that his "loyalty" was directed
to Egypt and then to Babylon (to whom he also paid more tribute!), then back
to Egypt, that all this inconsistency evidently caught up with him after 11 years
of tumultuous reign, and that we seem to be spared the details of his death (see
note on 24:6). He was another "placeholder," and also another miserable example
of what a Davidic king (or any leader) should not be like. Thus, the end of Judah
inevitably approaches, ever nearer.

◆   ## 3. Jehoiachin rules in Judah (24:8-17)

[8] Jehoiachin was eighteen years old when
he became king, and he reigned in Jerusalem three months. His mother was
Nehushta, the daughter of Elnathan from
Jerusalem. [9] Jehoiachin did what was evil
in the LORD's sight, just as his father had
done.

[10] During Jehoiachin's reign, the officers

of King Nebuchadnezzar of Babylon came up against Jerusalem and besieged it. ¹¹Nebuchadnezzar himself arrived at the city during the siege. ¹²Then King Jehoiachin, along with the queen mother, his advisers, his commanders, and his officials, surrendered to the Babylonians.

In the eighth year of Nebuchadnezzar's reign, he took Jehoiachin prisoner. ¹³As the LORD had said beforehand, Nebuchadnezzar carried away all the treasures from the LORD's Temple and the royal palace. He stripped away* all the gold objects that King Solomon of Israel had placed in the Temple. ¹⁴King Nebuchadnezzar took all of Jerusalem captive, including all the commanders and the best of the soldiers, craftsmen, and artisans—10,000 in all. Only the poorest people were left in the land.

¹⁵Nebuchadnezzar led King Jehoiachin away as a captive to Babylon, along with the queen mother, his wives and officials, and all Jerusalem's elite. ¹⁶He also exiled 7,000 of the best troops and 1,000 craftsmen and artisans, all of whom were strong and fit for war. ¹⁷Then the king of Babylon installed Mattaniah, Jehoiachin's* uncle, as the next king, and he changed Mattaniah's name to Zedekiah.

24:13 Or He cut apart.   24:17 Hebrew his.

NOTES

24:8 *Jehoiachin*. Also known as "Jeconiah" (1 Chr 3:16-17; Jer 24:1; 27:20) and "Coniah" (Jer 22:24, 28; 37:1), this king only lasted on the throne three months. A son of Jehoiakim, his 37th year of exile (562 BC) represents the last datable event in the books of Kings (see the next note). The name Jehoiachin means, ironically, "may Yahweh establish" (the variant names also contain the same verbal root, *kun* [TH3559, ZH3922]). Kim (2008a:207) notes that in cuneiform records dated to 592 BC, Jehoiachin, "king of Judah," and his five sons are documented as recipients of food rations in Babylon.

24:9 *did what was evil*. This is a stereotypical Deuteronomistic evaluation (see endnote 2 of the Introduction). As with Jehoahaz his uncle, who also lasted only three months on the throne before he was exiled (23:31), surely the evaluation here is more formulaic than historically precise. Remember that Jehoiachin is the only Davidide who is left surviving at the end of 2 Kings (25:27-30)—in exile, to be sure, but nonetheless representing the Davidic hope still alive for all people.

24:10-12 See the summary of Nebuchadnezzar's early military actions in Syria-Palestine found in the first note on 24:1. Inasmuch as there is a new king on the throne, and that he did surrender the city, Nebuchadnezzar's response here is actually rather mild (e.g., he did not level the city, as he does some 11 years later [cf. Kim 2008b:209]). Still, these horrendous events inaugurated the first Judahite exile.

24:12 *In the eighth year of Nebuchadnezzar's reign*. Apparently the writer of this passage was familiar with Babylonian dating practice (he may have been in their employ; cf. Cogan and Tadmor 1988:311); cf. 25:8 (= Jer 52:12); Jer 52:28-30.

24:13 *As the LORD had said beforehand*. Probably, as Cogan and Tadmor (1988:313-314) point out, Isaiah's prophecy (20:16-18) is particularly in view here.

***all the treasures*.** This is obvious hyperbole in light of the extended number of Temple treasures listed in 25:13-17, which were still there for the "main" exilic despoiling of Jerusalem in 586 BC. But surely the present "stripping away" (see the next note) was serious enough. Concerning the possibility of a separate Temple history underlying references such as this, see the note on 12:4.

stripped away. Heb., *wayqatsets* [TH7112, ZH7915], "to cut in pieces"; this verb can also mean "to strip away," as in 16:17; 18:16 (hence the NLT text); but here the NLT mg is probably to be preferred—i.e., the gold objects that Solomon had made were broken up to melt into bullion for easier transport (cf. Cogan and Tadmor 1988:312).

24:14 *all of Jerusalem captive.* This is hyperbolic, for the city may have held 25,000 people or more (cf. Faust 2005:113; also Lipschits 2005:270). But we do find very realistic totals for the various groups of captives in this verse, as well as in 24:16 (cf. Cogan and Tadmor 1988:312 concerning the numerical discrepancies in these verses and their parallels). Na'aman (2007:43) concludes that the main Babylonian deportation from Jerusalem took place at this time.

Only the poorest people. Lit., "the poorest of the people of the land," perhaps a conflation of 25:12 and Jer 52:15 (so Cogan and Tadmor 1988:312); in any case, the aristocratic "people of the land" (cf. 23:30, 35) are not in view here.

24:15 *all Jerusalem's elite.* Thus, in a sense, "all of Jerusalem" was carried off into exile, since most of her leading figures and artisans were now gone. Sweeney (2007:459) notes that they would have been put to work in service to the Babylonian government (cf. Dan 1–6).

24:17 *Jehoiachin's uncle.* He was the half brother of Jehoiachin's father. For details concerning "Mattaniah" or "Zedekiah," see the note on 24:18.

COMMENTARY

Jehoiachin certainly had no occasion to emulate the political fickleness of his father Jehoiakim, for he barely had time to gain the throne in Jerusalem before he surrendered the city to Nebuchadnezzar. But perhaps in a bit of poetic justice, Jehoiachin's fame and reputation eventually flourished as his father's never did, for he did enjoy that famous release from Babylonian prison in his 37th year of exile (see 25:27-30), and he did represent the true king of Judah to the major prophet Ezekiel (who dated his prophecies by his years of imprisonment, not even reckoning Zedekiah as king, but only prince [cf. Ezek 12:10, 12 and mg note on 12:10]), and, most ironically, to the Babylonians (see note on 24:8). Thus, Jehoiachin served historically as only another "placeholder" in the dynasty of David (as king he ruled only most briefly), but in the larger scheme of things he signified much more: For, as has been noted repeatedly, even from the fourth paragraph of the Introduction, he was the one who kept the Davidic hope alive through one of the kingdom of Judah's darkest periods. On a lighter note, he did not have sufficient time on the throne to effect even a single policy shift for his kingdom! (That means the shift back to Babylon, forced by circumstances at the end of his father's reign [shift number four], remained intact for the first nine years of the reign of his successor, his uncle Zedekiah). And finally, it was due to the exile of Jehoiachin and his compatriots that the prophet Jeremiah composed his famous letter from Judah to Babylon, urging them to stay the course for a full 70 years: "'For I know the plans I have for you,' says the LORD. 'They are plans for good and not for disaster, to give you a future and a hope'" (Jer 29:11). This sometimes-misapplied scripture was indeed meant to encourage its hearers, but insofar as they were in exile when many of their compatriots were not. Such was, for some 37 long years, Jehoiachin, deposed "King of Judah."

◆ ## 4. Zedekiah rules in Judah (24:18–20a)

[18] Zedekiah was twenty-one years old when he became king, and he reigned in Jerusalem eleven years. His mother was Hamutal, the daughter of Jeremiah from Libnah. [19] But Zedekiah did what was evil in the LORD's sight, just as Jehoiakim had done. [20] These things happened because of the LORD's anger against the people of Jerusalem and Judah, until he finally banished them from his presence and sent them into exile.

NOTES

24:18 *Zedekiah.* The third son of Josiah to gain the throne, he is commonly reckoned as the last king of Judah (but see the previous commentary section concerning Ezekiel's perspective on the topic). Originally named Mattaniah ("gift of Yahweh"), his name was changed to Zedekiah ("Yahweh is my righteousness/vindication") by Nebuchadnezzar, probably as part of the oath of allegiance to the new suzerain (or overlord). Cogan and Tadmor (1988:312-313) add that the name change is "as though creating a new personality." Zedekiah was the full brother of Jehoahaz (see the note on 23:31), and the sad irony is that both died in exile in the land of their conquerors (Egypt and Babylon, respectively).

24:19 *did what was evil.* For the eighth (or ninth, according to the LXX; see endnote 2 in the Introduction) and final time, we encounter this stereotypical Deuteronomistic formula used for a Davidic king; it is appropriate, if a bit surprising, that Zedekiah is likened to his half-brother Jehoiakim rather than his nephew Jehoiachin in this regard (cf. 23:37; 24:9).

24:20a *These things happened.* In contrast to 24:3, here the onus for the Exile is placed upon the people. Cogan and Tadmor (1988:324) see a frame here with 25:21b, setting off the "chronistic, matter-of-fact report on Zedekiah's last rebellion (24:20b-25:21a)."

COMMENTARY

Finally, we reach the end of the Davidic kings as actual reigning monarchs—representing some 300 years of ups and downs for the little land of Judah. Two final political shifts took place during Zedekiah's reign: He was put on the throne by the Babylonians, rebelled against them in his ninth year (cf. 25:1), and then was forced to bow down to his old nemesis King Nebuchadnezzar, ultimately having his eyes gouged out just after seeing his sons killed (25:6-7). This final, most melancholy "placeholder" with 11 years of reign is reduced to one final flip-flop in allegiance from Babylon to Egypt, and then finally Babylon for the last time. But that is recorded in chapter 25. In the present section, the emphasis falls on Zedekiah being just another Jehoiakim (e.g., the same flip-flopping of allegiances again lead to disaster) and on how Yahweh's anger will now guarantee the banishment of his own people into Babylonian exile.

◆ ## E. The Fall of Jerusalem and Its Aftermath (2 Kgs 24:20b–25:30)
1. The fall of Jerusalem (24:20b–25:7)

Zedekiah rebelled against the king of Babylon.

CHAPTER 25

So on January 15,* during the ninth year of Zedekiah's reign, King Nebuchadnezzar of Babylon led his entire army against Jerusalem. They surrounded the city and built siege ramps against its walls. [2] Jerusalem was kept under siege until the eleventh year of King Zedekiah's reign.

[3] By July 18 in the eleventh year of

Zedekiah's reign,* the famine in the city had become very severe, and the last of the food was entirely gone. ⁴Then a section of the city wall was broken down. Since the city was surrounded by the Babylonians,* the soldiers waited for nightfall and escaped* through the gate between the two walls behind the king's garden. Then they headed toward the Jordan Valley.*

⁵But the Babylonian* troops chased the king and overtook him on the plains of Jericho, for his men had all deserted him and scattered. ⁶They captured the king and took him to the king of Babylon at Riblah, where they pronounced judgment upon Zedekiah. ⁷They made Zedekiah watch as they slaughtered his sons. Then they gouged out Zedekiah's eyes, bound him in bronze chains, and led him away to Babylon.

25:1 Hebrew *on the tenth day of the tenth month*, of the ancient Hebrew lunar calendar. A number of events in 2 Kings can be cross-checked with dates in surviving Babylonian records and related accurately to our modern calendar. This day was January 15, 588 B.C.   25:3 Hebrew *By the ninth day of the [fourth] month* [in the eleventh year of Zedekiah's reign] (compare Jer 39:2; 52:6 and the notes there). This day was July 18, 586 B.C.; also see note on 25:1.   25:4a Or *the Chaldeans;* also in 25:13, 25, 26.   25:4b As in Greek version (see also Jer 39:4; 52:7); Hebrew lacks *escaped.*   25:4c Hebrew *the Arabah.*   25:5 Or *Chaldean;* also in 25:10, 24.

NOTES

24:20b Zedekiah. The NLT (cf. NIV, NRSV), probably correctly (see the note on 24:20a), starts the new section here.

rebelled. Many commentators suggest that renewed interest in Egypt led Zedekiah's advisors to urge him to break his oath of allegiance to Babylon (cf. Jer 27–28; the "triumphal progress" of Psammeticus II (Psamtek II, son of Neco) to "show the flag" in Philistia and in Phoenicia in 592 BC probably helped whet that curiosity (Cogan and Tadmor 1988:322-323; Kitchen 1996:407). Jeremiah himself resolutely counseled again and again against any such rebellion (e.g., in Jer 27:6 he labeled Nebuchadnezzar "Yahweh's servant"). Several times Zedekiah asked Jeremiah for advice (Jer 21:1-10; 37:1-10, 17-21; 38:14-28; cf. Mariottini 2009c:971-972); but the weak-willed king, under much pressure from the court, eventually rejected Jeremiah's unwavering pro-Babylonian perspective and, with a new, more aggressive pharaoh on the throne in 589 BC (Pharaoh Apries, also known as Hophra [cf. Jer 37:5; 44:30], son of Psammeticus), Zedekiah broke his covenant (or treaty) with Nebuchadnezzar and entered into alliance with Egypt, requesting horses and a large army (cf. Ezek 17:15). Nebuchadnezzar in turn marched into Judah, conquered the Judahite cities (except Lachish and Azekah [cf. Jer 34:7; also the so-called "Lachish letters," which almost certainly date from this time, for their text, see e.g. ANET 321]), and put Jerusalem under siege. During a lull in the siege, probably due to the advance of the Egyptian army (reminiscent of Tirhakah's role in Hezekiah's time; see the note on 19:9), Zedekiah and some of the rich people in Judah infamously re-enslaved some Israelites whom they had previously emancipated, presumably to help fight against the Babylonians (cf. Jer 34:8-22). But the Egyptian appearance proved only to delay the inevitable (Jer 37:1-10; cf. ABD 3.286), and by the summer of 586 BC Jerusalem was firmly in Babylonian hands. Thus, in summary, much history has been subsumed under the laconic phrase found here, "Zedekiah rebelled against the king of Babylon."

25:1 January 15. This assumes a date of 586 BC for the actual exile (the "eleventh year" of 25:2). Some scholars still prefer 587 BC, but the NLT does represent the majority consensus (cf. Cogan and Tadmor 1988:317; Barnes 1991:158 note v).

King Nebuchadnezzar. See the first note on 24:1 for details concerning this most significant Babylonian king.

25:3 famine. Sweeney (2007:466) calculates that the city had been under siege some 16 months, which at this point would have represented two lost harvest seasons.

25:4 *a section of the city wall was broken down.* Sweeney (2007:466) points out that it was probably the northern wall that was breached, inasmuch as the ground is more level there and susceptible to sappers (also see the first note on 14:13).

Babylonians. Concerning the translation of "Chaldean" as "Babylonian," see Cogan and Tadmor 1988:306.

between the two walls behind the king's garden. This was apparently a southern escape route near En-rogel Spring (cf. the first note on 1 Kgs 1:9 for its strategic location).

the Jordan Valley. Lit., "the Arabah" (cf. NLT mg); cf. the third note on 14:25. As Sweeney (2007:467) points out, the Deuteronomistic History thus brings Israel's history "full circle," beginning and ending "on the plains of Jericho" (25:5; cf. Josh 2–6; also cf. Joshua's prophecy [Josh 6:26], fulfilled by Hiel of Bethel, who rebuilt the city of Jericho at the cost of two sons [see note on 1 Kgs 16:34]).

25:6 *Riblah.* See the second note on 23:33.

25:6-7 *pronounced judgment . . . gouged out Zedekiah's eyes.* This is not a trial, but an arraignment before a superior, during which the covenant violator is rebuked and faces punishment (Cogan and Tadmor 1988:317-318). A subtle, but perhaps intentional, parallel is to be found with Hiel of Bethel (see the fourth note on 25:4), who also saw two of his children die. Blinding was a common punishment for rebellious slaves in the ancient Near East (Cogan and Tadmor; cf. 1 Sam 11:2, also the longer text in the NLT found after 1 Sam 10:27).

C O M M E N T A R Y

With the death of Zedekiah's sons, it surely seems that the end has come. No more children, no more hope. Still, the Deuteronomistic writer probably understood (and maybe even quietly approved of) the severe "justice" behind Nebuchadnezzar's actions, even if they seem sadistic by modern standards. Alas, how much more sadly literal can it be that the "sins of the fathers are visited upon the sons, to the third and fourth generation of those who hate me" (cf. the commentary on 14:1-22). The brutal truth is that when parents sin, their children often suffer (cf. the popular, sarcastic proverb about "sour grapes" cited by the contemporary prophets Jeremiah [Jer 31:29] and Ezekiel [Ezek 18:2]); how much more is this the case when the parents are in prominent positions of leadership. Thankfully, we now experience the "new covenant" of Jeremiah 31:31-40, where, at least theologically, circumstances have changed significantly (cf. Ezek 18:3-4, "The person who sins is the one who will die").

◆ ## 2. The Temple destroyed (25:8-21)

⁸On August 14 of that year,* which was the nineteenth year of King Nebuchadnezzar's reign, Nebuzaradan, the captain of the guard and an official of the Babylonian king, arrived in Jerusalem. ⁹He burned down the Temple of the LORD, the royal palace, and all the houses of Jerusalem. He destroyed all the important buildings* in the city. ¹⁰Then he supervised the entire Babylonian army as they tore down the walls of Jerusalem on every side. ¹¹Then Nebuzaradan, the captain of the guard, took as exiles the rest of the people who remained in the city, the defectors who had declared their allegiance to the king of Babylon, and the rest of the population. ¹²But the captain of the guard allowed some of the poorest people to stay behind to care for the vineyards and fields.

¹³The Babylonians broke up the bronze pillars in front of the LORD's Temple, the bronze water carts, and the great bronze basin called the Sea, and they carried all the bronze away to Babylon. ¹⁴They also took all the ash buckets, shovels, lamp snuffers, ladles, and all the other bronze articles used for making sacrifices at the Temple. ¹⁵The captain of the guard also took the incense burners and basins, and all the other articles made of pure gold or silver.

¹⁶The weight of the bronze from the two pillars, the Sea, and the water carts was too great to be measured. These things had been made for the LORD's Temple in the days of Solomon. ¹⁷Each of the pillars was 27 feet* tall. The bronze capital on top of each pillar was 7½ feet* high and was decorated with a network of bronze pomegranates all the way around.

¹⁸Nebuzaradan, the captain of the guard, took with him as prisoners Seraiah the high priest, Zephaniah the priest of the second rank, and the three chief gatekeepers. ¹⁹And from among the people still hiding in the city, he took an officer who had been in charge of the Judean army; five of the king's personal advisers; the army commander's chief secretary, who was in charge of recruitment; and sixty other citizens. ²⁰Nebuzaradan, the captain of the guard, took them all to the king of Babylon at Riblah. ²¹And there at Riblah, in the land of Hamath, the king of Babylon had them all put to death. So the people of Judah were sent into exile from their land.

25:8 Hebrew *On the seventh day of the fifth month*, of the ancient Hebrew lunar calendar. This day was August 14, 586 B.C.; also see note on 25:1.   25:9 Or *destroyed the houses of all the important people*.
25:17a Hebrew *18 cubits* [8.1 meters].   25:17b As in parallel texts at 1 Kgs 7:16, 2 Chr 3:15, and Jer 52:22, all of which read *5 cubits* [2.3 meters]; Hebrew reads *3 cubits*, which is 4.5 feet or 1.4 meters.

NOTES

25:8 *August 14.* As noted in the NLT mg, this was the "seventh day of the fifth month" (on the Jewish calendar, the month of Av); concerning the synchronized dating of the 19th year of King Nebuchadnezzar, cf. the note on 24:12. Sweeney (2007:467) gives the rabbinic tradition concerning this process of destruction: Nebuzaradan entered the Temple on the seventh day of Av, set it on fire on the ninth, and the fire burned until the tenth (cf. Jer 52:12). Hence, observant Jews today mourn the destruction of the Temple on the ninth of Av ("Tisha B'Av," falling anywhere from mid-July to mid-August depending on the year).

Nebuzaradan, the captain of the guard. Lit., the "chief butler" or "chief cook" (*rab tab-bakhim* [TH7227B/2876, ZH8042/3184]), but this once again is an archaic title (cf. the "rab-shakeh" of 18:17). As Cogan and Tadmor (1988:318-319) point out, titles of this kind "originated in the circumstances of court service; under special conditions, these trusted individuals were dispatched on missions." In Jer 39:13-14, after the fall of Jerusalem, Nebuzaradan was given the task of overseeing the transfer of the prophet Jeremiah into the custody of Gedaliah (see the note on 25:22 concerning this important Judahite individual).

25:9 *all the important buildings.* The Hebrew here is a bit ambiguous (cf. NLT mg), but this is the more likely translation (cf. Jer 52:13).

25:10 *tore down the walls of Jerusalem on every side.* Sweeney (2007:468) points out that the complete leveling of the walls was unnecessary; destruction of the key gate areas, towers, and, I would add, strategic breaches in the walls themselves, would be sufficient. Many have suggested that these were the walls that Nehemiah later repaired in some 52 days (Neh 1-6), but I suspect, since Nehemiah himself was shocked to hear about the Jerusalem walls' destruction, that it was a recent Persian punitive action that Nehemiah bravely had undone (cf. Williamson 1985:172).

25:11 took as exiles. Many, if not most, of the people of substance were probably already gone (see the first note on 24:14).

25:12 some of the poorest people. This is parallel with 24:14, both linguistically and thematically. In both cases, the "blessing" of being left behind paradoxically falls on those who normally are the least favored in society.

25:13 carried all the bronze away to Babylon. We now return to a section which includes remarkable detail concerning Temple paraphernalia. Perhaps at the risk of dampening the climactic nature of the overall narrative, we read once again in some detail the fate of various Temple appurtenances, whether large (the pillars, the Sea) or small (ash buckets, shovels, ladles, etc.). The closest parallel listing is found in 1 Kgs 7:15-47 for the bronze items, both large and small, and in 1 Kgs 7:48-50 for the articles of gold and silver (cf. 12:13). Once again, all this may derive from a separate Temple history, or at least from Temple records (cf. Wiseman 1993:314; also cf. the note on 12:4, as well as the first note on 16:10).

25:16-17 See the previous note for the parallels to 1 Kgs 7. Possibly these comments stem from a Babylonian count of the booty (cf. Cogan and Tadmor 1988:320), but the close parallels with 1 Kgs 7:41-47 make this less than likely. Mention of the 12 oxen that had served as a foundation for the Sea is lacking here, probably since King Ahaz had removed them, apparently to help pay tribute to the Assyrians (see second note on 16:17). The parallel in Jer 52:20, however, does include the oxen. Thompson (1980:780) thinks they may have been replaced after the time of Ahaz.

25:18 Seraiah the high priest. He is one of only a handful of priests mentioned by name in 1–2 Kings (cf. the first section of the Introduction for details). This Seraiah was the father of Jehozadak, who went into exile (1 Chr 6:14), and whose grandson (or descendant) was Joshua/Jeshua (Hag 1:1), and whose later descendant was none other than Ezra the scribe (Ezra 7:1), the "second Moses" according to the Talmud (b. Sanhedrin 21b-22a).

25:20 at Riblah. See the second note on 23:33.

COMMENTARY

We finally come to the actual destruction of the first Temple and the capital city of Jerusalem. "More attention is paid to the temple than to the city, for it was the symbol of God's presence and glory now departed" (Wiseman 1993:313). Commentators often remark on how objective the tone of the narrative is—especially in light of the horrendous events being described (for emotional accounts of these events, mostly by eyewitnesses, see the book of Lamentations). Sadly, the cautionary prediction given nearly four centuries earlier to King Solomon (1 Kgs 9:6-9; cf. the notes there for details) proved remarkably accurate ("I will make Israel an object of mockery and ridicule among the nations"; 1 Kgs 9:7). Other ties with the Solomonic material include parallel accounts of the various Temple accoutrements and architectural features (cf. the notes on 25:13 and 25:16-17 for specific references).

By now, we are familiar with why these horrible events were allowed to transpire: The people had refused to obey the Torah, especially in regard to the worship of idols and of other gods (cf. 24:20). Of course, the sins of Manasseh were an important issue as well (see the note on 24:3), but that was a moot point in the early sixth century. Admittedly, even the labors of Josiah cited in chapters 22–23 were not able to cancel the Exile, a vivid reminder of how limited our "good deeds" can be in the area of atonement for past sins. But the main point of the present passage is merely to recall, in stunned disbelief, what actually took place, and why. As Lamentations reminds us:

Jerusalem, once so full of people,
    is now deserted.
She who was once great among the nations
    now sits alone like a widow.
Once the queen of all the earth,
    she is now a slave. (Lam 1:1)

How sad it still is to contemplate all the efforts of Solomon and of his successors—now for naught. Of course, Yahweh had warned his people and their leaders,
time and again, that this could happen. But it never did . . . until now.

As a refreshing change of perspective, I want to end this section on a lighter note.
As devotees of a certain Hollywood action film will immediately recall, there is one
Temple object conspicuous by its absence in this extended list of cultic paraphernalia. Of course, I am referring to the Ark of the Covenant. We certainly do not have
the wherewithal to explore this topic here in depth, but I think that it is germane
to the present discussion—at least in the sense that the original audience of this
passage in Kings must have known whither (or at least when) the Ark went missing.
Jeremiah's famous passage (Jer 3:16; cf. the commentary on 1 Kgs 8:1-11) is to the
point: "You will not miss those days [when you possessed the Ark] . . . there will be
no need to rebuild the Ark." Such a sentiment seems to hint that the Ark already was
missing in Jeremiah's day (roughly equal to the time of Josiah, and up to the Exile).
And such Scripture some years ago led the eminent biblical exegete and theologian
Menahem Haran (1963:46-58) to speculate that the infamous "sins of Manasseh"
may have had something to do with its absence. As Haran concluded:

> To sum up: Shishak and Jehoash did no more than empty the Temple treasuries. It was
> Manasseh who set up vessels for Baal and Asherah in the outer sanctum and intro-
> duced the image of Asherah into the inner sanctum of the Temple, and it was probably
> through him that the ark was removed. When Josiah cleansed the Temple, the ark was
> no longer there. Many decades after the "sin of Manasseh," Nebuchadnezzar entered
> the outer sanctum of the Temple and "cut in pieces" its vessels (also plundering the
> Temple treasuries). Thus when the fateful moment of final destruction arrived, eleven
> years after the exile of Jehoiachin, the Temple was already deprived at least of most of
> its inner accessories.

No wonder the Deuteronomistic Historian hated those "sins of Manasseh." (For
a conventional overview of this and other possible scenarios concerning the disappearance of the Ark, see ABD 1.390-391.)

◆   ### 3. Gedaliah governs in Judah (25:22-26)

²²Then King Nebuchadnezzar appointed
Gedaliah son of Ahikam and grandson of
Shaphan as governor over the people he
had left in Judah. ²³When all the army commanders and their men learned that the
king of Babylon had appointed Gedaliah as
governor, they went to see him at Mizpah.

These included Ishmael son of Nethaniah,
Johanan son of Kareah, Seraiah son of Tan-
humeth the Netophathite, Jezaniah* son of
the Maacathite, and all their men.

²⁴Gedaliah vowed to them that the
Babylonian officials meant them no harm.
"Don't be afraid of them. Live in the land

and serve the king of Babylon, and all will go well for you," he promised.

²⁵But in midautumn of that year,* Ishmael son of Nethaniah and grandson of Elishama, who was a member of the royal family, went to Mizpah with ten men and killed Gedaliah. He also killed all the Judeans and Babylonians who were with him at Mizpah.

²⁶Then all the people of Judah, from the least to the greatest, as well as the army commanders, fled in panic to Egypt, for they were afraid of what the Babylonians would do to them.

25:23 As in parallel text at Jer 40:8; Hebrew reads *Jaazaniah*, a variant spelling of Jezaniah.   25:25 Hebrew *in the seventh month*, of the ancient Hebrew lunar calendar. This month occurred within the months of October and November 586 B.C.; also see note on 25:1.

NOTES

25:22 Gedaliah. He was a prominent Judahite from a noble family (son of Ahikam; cf. 22:12) and grandson of Shaphan, the court secretary during the reign of Josiah (cf. 22:3). Gedaliah (meaning "Yahweh is great") was likewise in the king's service, especially if he is to be identified as the person named on a late-seventh-century seal impression found at Lachish ("Belonging to Gedaliah, the Royal Steward" [*lgdlyhw 'shr 'l hbyt*]); cf. Cogan and Tadmor 1988:325; ABD 2.923-924. The present brief report represents an abbreviated account of the extended narrative found in Jer 40:7–41:18.

25:23 at Mizpah. This is probably Tell en-Nasbeh, 8 mi. (13 km) north of the city of Jerusalem, with no destruction level datable to this time (Cogan and Tadmor 1988:326). It was spared by Nebuchadnezzar and able to serve as the provisional capital of the province (cf. Brody 2009). Three centuries earlier, King Asa had fortified Mizpah as a northern defense against attacks on Jerusalem (1 Kgs 15:22).

Ishmael. He was the ringleader (see 25:25; Jer 41:2) of the band of assassins who killed Gedaliah and a number of his supporters. A member of the royal family, Ishmael may have wished to avenge the exile of Zedekiah and the death of his children at the hands of the Babylonians (25:7). Probably a "staunch nationalist" (ABD 3.512), he may have considered Gedaliah not only a collaborator with the enemy but also in essence a usurper of the house of David.

25:24 he promised. The remarkable naivete of Gedaliah is illustrated in more detail in Jer 40:13-16. Josephus (*Antiquities* 10.9.1.155) notes that Gedaliah had a reputation for being both gentle and generous.

25:25 killed. This probably represents a local vendetta against Babylonian collaborators more than a direct challenge to Nebuchadnezzar (Cogan and Tadmor 1988:327), although Jeremiah (Jer 40:14; 41:10) does note the backing of Baalis, king of the Ammonites.

25:26 fled in panic to Egypt. This is an understandable reaction; in 582/581 BC Babylonian reprisals under Nebuzaradan took away another 745 Judahites into exile (as noted in Jer 52:30). Thompson (1980:783) sees this exact figure as being derived from an authentic recording of some kind. After this, Judah eventually became part of the province of Samaria, a most ironic fate since they were the first of God's people to be taken into exile (Wiseman 1993:317).

COMMENTARY

Yet another assassination! We have read of the assassinations of Israelite kings (seven of them; see the commentary on 15:23-26 for details) and a few Judahite kings (four, plus Queen Athaliah; cf. 9:27; 11:16; 12:20; 14:19; 21:23), the gruesome death of Queen Jezebel (9:30-35), and the passing mention of the untimely deaths of Ben-hadad, king of Aram (8:15) and Sennacherib of Assyria (19:37). And here is the murder of a Judahite governor by Judahite royalists. Commentators remark on how objective the tone of this final chapter of 2 Kings is, and that is certainly the case in the present narrative. The book of Jeremiah preserves a longer account of Gedaliah's murder (see the note on 25:22); but even in the present account, enough information is given so as to render a verdict concerning the propriety of the actions, and that verdict seems to be restrained but negative. Why should members of the royal household act this way? Zedekiah deserved the events described in 25:6-7. Jerusalem had been doomed for years. Nebuchadnezzar had appointed a respected member of the Judahite community, and, if perhaps a bit too naive, Gedaliah was a good man. The end result of this cold-blooded assassination was self-defeating: a self-imposed exile in Egypt! As Seow (1999:294) succinctly put it, "The people thus willfully reversed the exodus." The seesaw focus from Egypt to Babylon and then back to Egypt that we have been seeing since the days of Josiah ends here in Egypt. But wait, there is one more scene to be presented—and that, not surprisingly, will take place in Babylon.

◆   ## 4. Hope for Israel's royal line (25:27-30)

27 In the thirty-seventh year of the exile of King Jehoiachin of Judah, Evil-merodach ascended to the Babylonian throne. He was kind to* Jehoiachin and released him* from prison on April 2 of that year.* 28 He spoke kindly to Jehoiachin and gave him a higher place than all the other exiled kings in Babylon. 29 He supplied Jehoiachin with new clothes to replace his prison garb and allowed him to dine in the king's presence for the rest of his life. 30 So the king gave him a regular food allowance as long as he lived.

25:27a Hebrew *He raised the head of.*   25:27b As in some Hebrew manuscripts and Greek and Syriac versions (see also Jer 52:31); Masoretic Text lacks *released him.*   25:27c Hebrew *on the twenty-seventh day of the twelfth month,* of the ancient Hebrew lunar calendar. This day was April 2, 561 B.C.; also see note on 25:1.

NOTES
25:27 *thirty-seventh year.* I have argued elsewhere that this was indeed a significant year (exactly 480 years after the accession of David, as reckoned by antedating; see the commentary for details).

Evil-merodach. Son and successor of Nebuchadnezzar, his Babylonian name was "Amel-Marduk." Harkins (2007) suggests that the Hebrew version of his name ('*ewil merodak* [TH192, ZH213]) contains a pun, with '*ewil* [TH3807, ZH216] meaning "foolish." In any case, he lasted only two years on the throne, being assassinated by his brother-in-law Neriglissar, who in turn reigned for five years.

He was kind to. This is perhaps a too-vague translation of the Hebrew, which reads "he raised the head of" (cf. NLT mg). Elsewhere this idiom denotes "taking note of, paying special attention to" (Gen 40:13, 19, 20; but there the expression can be both positive and negative). In the present passage, the sense may well be "to pardon" or the like (Cogan and Tadmor 1988:328), but the less specific NLT translation well conveys the tenor of the Hebrew.

released him from prison. Most commentators suggest a kind of amnesty given to commemorate Evil-merodach's accession or the like (cf. Cogan and Tadmor 1988:329; Sweeney 2007:469-470). Wiseman (1985:115) notes the later tradition of strong antipathy between Evil-merodach and his father Nebuchadnezzar, the former, at the instigation of Jehoiachin, even removing the latter's corpse from the grave and disposing of it!

25:28 *spoke kindly.* The same idiom is found in 1 Kgs 12:7; there the sense is to speak "appeasing" words (Cogan 2001:348).

gave him a higher place. Lit., "placed his throne above (the thrones of the kings who were with him)"; for the names of some of those "other kings," cf. the "Unger Prism" of Nebuchadnezzar (Cogan and Tadmor 1988:329).

25:29 dine in the king's presence. For Sweeney's comparison with David and Mephibosheth, Saul's grandson, see the references in the next note.

25:30 as long as he lived. See the commentary for the slight variation in the Jeremiah parallel. Note that this is how both the books of Kings and Jeremiah come to an end. For the indication that this is the end of the Davidic dynasty, and also the final outworking of the curse of Elijah, pronounced in the ninth century BC on the descendants of Ahab and Jezebel (so Sweeney 2007:343, 349, 363), see the commentary on 14:1-22.

COMMENTARY

This final section of 2 Kings is probably an appendix to the Deuteronomistic History (Cogan and Tadmor 1988:329-330). Wiseman (1993:308-309, 317) labels it a "second appendix" (the "first appendix" being 24:8–25:26). Many discount its importance for the overall Deuteronomistic History, but I, for one, will not follow in their footsteps.

Young Jehoiachin, ill-starred as king, finally gets (in a sense) his rightful due in this brief but significant section of Scripture. After a 43-year reign, Nebuchadnezzar is finally gone. But Jehoiachin and his children are still around. For whatever reason, Jehoiachin had been put in prison, but then he was released—and not only that, he was given special honor. He was able to retain that honor, evidently, up to the time the books of Kings "went to press" (contrast Jer 52:34, which ends with a reference to the "day of his death"). Thus, a sweet, if quite muted, ending to these books filled with bloodshed, heartache, and tragedy is to be found here.

People who write history obviously cannot make up things, nor do they have much "wiggle room" with how to conclude their story (e.g., the fact that both John Adams and Thomas Jefferson died on the very same day, July 4, 1826, exactly 50 years—to the day—after the ratification of the Declaration of Independence back in 1776, would seem too bizarre for coincidence if it were not so well attested in the historical record). So it is here—at least, that is what I concluded decades ago (for the details, see Barnes 1991:137-149; and for a synopsis, see "Excursus on Chronology" in the Introduction). By ancient rules of reckoning (i.e., antedating), according to the Judahite listing of kings from David to the Exile, Jehoiachin's release from prison took place exactly 480 years after the first crowning of King David on the throne of Judah (to be sure, the actual length of time by modern reckoning was more like 449 years [cf. Barnes 1991:146], but that would not have been evident to the ancient editor). I admit that there is no attestation of any editorial awareness of such a 480-year period of time found anywhere in Kings (although a 480-year period of time between the Exodus and the founding of the first Temple is clearly noted in 1 Kgs 6:1). Nevertheless, in my opinion, it is too remarkable a number to be merely an accident. In any case, in this final appendix to this long and involved history of God's people, we are reminded that one era may be over but another lies ahead. And as I so often have noted throughout this commentary, the Davidic hope still lives! And all peoples on earth will eventually be blessed by that wonderful fact. To God be the glory!

BIBLIOGRAPHY

Ackerman, Susan
2006 Asherah. Pp. 297-299 in *The New Interpreter's Dictionary of the Bible,* vol. 1. Nashville: Abingdon.

Ackroyd, P. R.
1974 An Interpretation of the Babylonian Exile. *Scottish Journal of Theology* 27:329-352.

Aharoni, Yohanan
1974 The Horned Altar of Beer-sheba. *Biblical Archaeologist* 37:2-6.

Ahlström, G. W.
1982 *Royal Administration and National Religion in Ancient Palestine.* Leiden: Brill.

Albright, W. F.
1931 The Discovery of an Aramaic Inscription Relating to King Uzziah. *Bulletin of the American Schools of Oriental Research* 44:8-10.

1944 The Oracles of Balaam. *Journal of Biblical Literature* 63:207-233.

Allen, Leslie C.
1983 *Psalms 101-150.* Word Biblical Commentary 21. Waco: Word.

Andersen, Francis I.
1966 The Socio-juridical Background of the Naboth Incident. *Journal of Biblical Literature* 85:46-57.

Anderson, A. A.
1972 *The Book of Psalms,* vol. 2. New Century Bible Commentary. Grand Rapids: Eerdmans.

1989 *2 Samuel.* Word Biblical Commentary 11. Dallas: Word.

Appler, Deborah A.
2008 Jezebel. Pp. 313-314 in *The New Interpreter's Dictionary of the Bible,* vol. 3. Nashville: Abingdon.

Archer, Gleason L., Jr.
1974 *A Survey of Old Testament Introduction.* Chicago: Moody.

Armerding, Carl Edwin
1975 Were David's Sons Really Priests? Pp. 75-86 in *Current Issues in Biblical and Patristic Interpretation. Studies in Honor of Merrill C. Tenney Presented by His Former Students.* Editor, G. Hawthorne. Grand Rapids: Eerdmans.

Aubet, Maria Eugenia
1993 *The Phoenicians and the West.* Cambridge: Cambridge University Press.

Avigad, Nahman
1976 The Governor of the City. *Israel Exploration Journal* 26:178-182, plate 33D.

Baldwin, Joyce G.
1972 *Haggai, Zechariah, Malachi.* Tyndale Old Testament Commentaries 24. London: InterVarsity.

Baly, Denis
1974 *The Geography of the Bible.* Rev. ed. New York: Harper & Row.

Barnes, William Hamilton
1991 *Studies in the Chronology of the Divided Monarchy of Israel.* Harvard Semitic Monographs 48. Atlanta: Scholars.

1997a *1 & 2 Kings.* Old Testament Study Bible 7. Editor, Stanley L. Horton. Springfield, MO: World Library Press.

1997b Non-synoptic Chronological References in the Books of Chronicles. Pp. 106-131 in *The Chronicler as Historian*. Journal for the Study of the Old Testament Supplement Series 238. Sheffield: Sheffield Academic.

2003 Canaan: Conquest, Covenant Renewal, and Crisis. Pp. 357-407 in *They Spoke from God: A Survey of the Old Testament*. Springfield, MO: Gospel Publishing House.

2009 Tyre. Pp. 693-694 in *The New Interpreter's Dictionary of the Bible*, vol. 5. Nashville: Abingdon.

Beitzel, Barry J.
1985 *The Moody Atlas of Bible Lands*. Chicago: Moody.

Ben-Barak, Zafrira
1991 The Status and Right of the *Gĕbîrâ. Journal of Biblical Literature* 110:23-34.

Bin-Nun, Shoshana R.
1968 Formulas from Royal Records of Israel and of Judah. *Vetus Testamentum* 18:414-432.

Blenkinsopp, Joseph
1983 *A History of Prophecy in Israel*. Philadelphia: Westminster.

2000 *Isaiah 1–39*. Anchor Bible 19. New York: Doubleday.

Boda, Mark J.
2010 *1–2 Chronicles*. Cornerstone Biblical Commentary, vol. 5a. Editor, Philip W. Comfort. Carol Stream, IL: Tyndale House.

Boyd, Greg A.
Forthcoming. *The Crucifixion of the Warrior God: A Cruciform Interpretation of the Old Testament's Violent Portraits of God*. Downers Grove, IL: InterVarsity.

Bright, John
1981 *A History of Israel*. 3rd ed. Philadelphia: Westminster.

Brinkman, J. A.
1964 Merodach-Baladan II. Pp. 6-53 in *Studies Presented to A. Leo Oppenheim, June 7, 1964*. Chicago: Oriental Institute.

Brody, Aaron
2009 Mizpah, Mizpeh. Pp. 116-117 in *The New Interpreter's Dictionary of the Bible*, vol. 4. Nashville: Abingdon.

Broshi, M.
1974 The Expansion of Jerusalem in the Reigns of Hezekiah and Manasseh. *Israel Exploration Journal* 24:21-26.

Brueggemann, Dale
2008 *Numbers* in *Leviticus, Numbers, Deuteronomy*. Cornerstone Biblical Commentary, vol. 2. Editor, Philip W. Comfort. Carol Stream, IL: Tyndale House.

Brueggemann, Walter
1998 *A Commentary on Jeremiah: Exile and Homecoming*. Grand Rapids: Eerdmans.

2000 *1 and 2 Kings*. Macon, GA: Smyth & Helwys.

Cahill, Jane M.
1995 Rosette Stamp Seal Impressions from Ancient Judah. *Israel Exploration Journal* 45:230-252.

Calderone, P. J.
1961 The Rivers of "Maṣor."*Biblica* 42:423-432.

Campbell, Edward F., Jr.
1975 *Ruth*. Anchor Bible 7. Garden City, NY: Doubleday.

Carroll, R. P.
1969 The Elijah-Elisha Sagas: Some Remarks on Prophetic Succession in Ancient Israel. *Vetus Testamentum* 19:400-415.

Cate, Robert L.
1994 *An Introduction to the Historical Books of the Old Testament*. Nashville: Broadman & Holman.

Childs, Brevard S.
1963 A Study of the Formula, Until This Day. *Journal of Biblical Literature* 82:279-292.

1967 *Isaiah and the Assyrian Crisis*. London: SCM.

1974 *The Book of Exodus*. The Old Testament Library. Philadelphia: Westminster.

1979 *Introduction to the Old Testament as Scripture.* Philadelphia: Fortress.

1980 On Reading the Elijah Narratives. *Interpretation* 34:128-137.

2001 *Isaiah.* Louisville: Westminster/John Knox.

Christensen, Duane L.
2002 *Deuteronomy 21:10–34:12.* Word Biblical Commentary 6B. Nashville: Thomas Nelson.

Claburn, W. Eugene
1973 The Fiscal Basis of Josiah's Reforms. *Journal of Biblical Literature* 92:11-22.

Clifford, Richard J.
1980 Psalm 89: A Lament over the Davidic Ruler's Continued Failure. *Harvard Theological Review* 73:35-47.

Cogan, Mordechai
1968 A Technical Term for Exposure. *Journal of Near Eastern Studies* 27:133-135.

1974 *Imperialism and Religion: Assyria, Judah and Israel in the Eighth and Seventh Centuries B.C.E.* Missoula, MT: Scholars.

1978 Israel in Exile—The View of a Josianic Historian. *Journal of Biblical Literature* 97:40-44.

1983 "Ripping Open Pregnant Women" in Light of an Assyrian Analogue. *Journal of the American Oriental Society* 103:755-757.

2001 *I Kings.* Anchor Bible 10. New York: Doubleday.

2008 *The Raging Torrent: Historical Inscriptions from Assyria and Babylonia Relating to Ancient Israel.* Jerusalem: Carta.

Cogan, Mordechai, and Hayim Tadmor
1988 *II Kings.* Anchor Bible 11. New York: Doubleday.

Cohn, Robert L.
1983 Form and Perspective in 2 Kings V. *Vetus Testamentum* 33:171-184.

Coogan, Michael D.
2009 Warrior, Divine. Pp. 815-816 in *The New Interpreter's Dictionary of the Bible,* vol. 5. Nashville: Abingdon.

Cross, Frank Moore, Jr.
1964 The History of the Biblical Text in the Light of Discoveries in the Judean Desert. *Harvard Theological Review* 57:281-299.

1972 An Interpretation of the Nora Stone. *Bulletin of the American Schools of Oriental Research* 208:13-19.

1973 *Canaanite Myth and Hebrew Epic.* Cambridge, MA: Harvard University Press.

1998 *From Epic to Canon.* Baltimore: Johns Hopkins University Press.

Dahood, Mitchell
1970 *Psalms III.* Anchor Bible 17A. Garden City, NY: Doubleday.

Davies, Graham I.
1986 *Megiddo.* Grand Rapids: Eerdmans.

Dearman, J. Andrew
1990 My Servants the Scribes: Composition and Context in Jeremiah 36. *Journal of Biblical Literature* 109:403-421.

Deller, K.
1965 Review of Roland De Vaux's *Les sacrifices de l'Ancien Testament. Orientalia* 34:382-386.

Dever, William G.
2001 *What Did the Biblical Writers Know and When Did They Know It?* Grand Rapids: Eerdmans.

DeVries, Simon J.
1978 *Prophet against Prophet.* Grand Rapids: Eerdmans.

1985 *1 Kings.* Word Biblical Commentary 12. Waco: Word.

Dillard, Raymond B.
1999 *Faith in the Face of Apostasy.* Phillipsburg, NJ: P & R.

Ehrlich, Carl S.
2007 Gath. Pp. 524-525 in *The New Interpreter's Dictionary of the Bible,* vol. 2. Nashville: Abingdon.

Eichrodt, Walther
1961 *Theology of the Old Testament,* vol. 1. Translator, J. A. Baker. Philadelphia: Westminster.

1967 *Theology of the Old Testament,* vol. 2. Translator, J. A. Baker. Philadelphia: Westminster.

Faust, Avraham
2005 The Settlement of Jerusalem's Western Hill and the City's Status in Iron Age II Revisited. *Zeitschrift des Deutschen Palästina-Vereins* 121:97-118.

Fox, Nili Sacher
2000 *In the Service of the King: Officialdom in Ancient Israel and Judah.* Cincinnati: Hebrew Union College Press.

Freedman, David Noel
1997 The Law and the Prophets. Pp. 139-151 in *Divine Commitment and Human Obligation.* Grand Rapids: Eerdmans.

Frick, Frank S.
1971 The Rechabites Reconsidered. *Journal of Biblical Literature* 90:279-287.

Friedman, Richard Elliott
1981 From Egypt to Egypt: Dtr1 and Dtr2. Pp. 167-192 in *Traditions in Transformation.* Winona Lake, IN: Eisenbrauns.

1997 *Who Wrote the Bible?* 2nd ed. New York: HarperSanFrancisco.

1998 *The Hidden Book in the Bible.* San Francisco: HarperSanFrancisco.

Fritz, Volkmar
2003 *1 & 2 Kings.* Minneapolis: Fortress.

Geller, M. J.
1976 A New Translation for 2 Kings XV 25. *Vetus Testamentum* 26:374-377.

Geoghegan, Jeffrey C.
2010 The Redaction of Kings and Priestly Authority in Jerusalem. Pp. 109-118, 194-197 in *Soundings in Kings.* Minneapolis: Fortress.

Glueck, Nelson
1943 Ramoth-gilead. *Bulletin of the American Schools of Oriental Research* 92:10-16.

Glueck, Nelson, and Gary D. Pratico
1993 Kheleifeh, Tell el. Pp. 867-870 in *The New Encyclopedia of Archaeological Excavations in the Holy Land,* vol. 3. Editor, E. Stern. Jerusalem: Carta.

Gooding, David Willoughby
1964 Ahab according to the Septuagint. *Zeitschrift für die alttestamentliche Wissenschaft* 76:269-280.

1965a Pedantic Timetabling in 3rd Book of Reigns. *Vetus Testamentum* 15:153-166.

1965b The Septuagint's Version of Solomon's Misconduct. *Vetus Testamentum* 15:325-335.

1965c An Impossible Shrine. *Vetus Testamentum* 15:405-420.

1967a Temple Specifications: A Dispute in Logical Arrangement between the MT and the LXX. *Vetus Testamentum* 17:143-172.

1967b The Septuagint's Rival Version of Jeroboam's Rise to Power. *Vetus Testamentum* 17:173-189.

1969 Text-sequence and Translation-revision in 3 Reigns 9:10-10:33. *Vetus Testamentum* 19:448-463.

1970 Review of *Chronology and Recensional Development in the Greek Text of Kings* by James Donald Shenkel. *Journal of Theological Studies* 21:118-131.

1976 *Relics of Ancient Exegesis: A Study of the Miscellanies in 3 Reigns 2.* London: Cambridge University Press.

Gray, John
1970 *I and II Kings.* 2nd ed. The Old Testament Library. Philadelphia: Westminster.

Green, Alberto R. W.
1975 *The Role of Human Sacrifice in the Ancient Near East.* Missoula, MT: Scholars.

Greenberg, Moshe
1983 *Ezekiel 1-20.* Anchor Bible 22. Garden City, NY: Doubleday.

Halpern, Baruch
1981 The Uneasy Compromise: Israel between League and Monarchy. Pp. 59-96 in *Traditions in Transformation.* Winona Lake, IN: Eisenbrauns.

1988 *The First Historians.* San Francisco: Harper & Row.

Halpern, Baruch, and David S. Vanderhooft
1991 The Editions of Kings in the 7th-6th Centuries B.C.E. *Hebrew Union College Annual* 62:179-244.

Hamilton, Mark W.
2009 Solomon. Pp. 317-326 in *The New Interpreter's Dictionary of the Bible*, vol. 5. Nashville: Abingdon.

Hanson, Paul D.
1968 The Song of Heshbon and David's "Nîr." *Harvard Theological Review* 61:297-320.

Haran, Menahem
1963 The Disappearance of the Ark. *Israel Exploration Journal* 13:46-58.
1967 The Rise and Decline of the Empire of Jeroboam Ben Joash. *Vetus Testamentum* 17:266-335.
1978 *Temples and Temple Service in Ancient Israel*. Oxford: Clarendon.

Harkins, R. Justin
2007 Evil-Merodach. P. 361 in *The New Interpreter's Dictionary of the Bible*, vol. 2. Nashville: Abingdon.

Harrison, R. K.
1969 *Introduction to the Old Testament*. Grand Rapids: Eerdmans.
1970 *Old Testament Times*. Grand Rapids: Eerdmans.
1980 *Leviticus*. Tyndale Old Testament Commentaries 3. Downers Grove, IL: InterVarsity.

Hart, Stephen
1986 Sela': The Rock of Edom? *Palestine Exploration Quarterly* 118:91-95.

Hendel, Ronald
2008 *Leitwort* Style and Literary Structure in the J Primeval Narrative. Pp. 93-109 in *Sacred History, Sacred Literature: Essays on Ancient Israel, the Bible, and Religion in Honor of R. E. Friedman on His Sixtieth Birthday*. Editor, S. Dolansky. Winona Lake, IN: Eisenbrauns.

Hens-Piazza, Gina
2006 *1—2 Kings*. Abingdon Old Testament Commentaries. Nashville: Abingdon.

Hestrin, Ruth, and Michael Dayagi
1974 A Seal Impression of a Servant of King Hezekiah. *Israel Exploration Journal* 24:27-29, plates 2B and 2C.

Higginbotham, Carolyn
2007 Egypt. Pp. 206-226 in *The New Interpreter's Dictionary of the Bible*, vol. 2. Nashville: Abingdon.
2009 Neco. P. 247 in *The New Interpreter's Dictionary of the Bible*, vol. 4. Nashville: Abingdon.

Hobbs, T. R.
1985 *2 Kings*. Word Biblical Commentary 13. Waco: Word.

Holladay, John S.
2009 How Much Is That in . . .? Monetization, Money, Royal States, and Empires. Pp. 207-222 in *Exploring the Longue Durée: Essays in Honor of Lawrence E. Stager*. Winona Lake, IN: Eisenbrauns.

Howard, David M., Jr.
1993 *An Introduction to the Old Testament Historical Books*. Chicago: Moody.

Hurowitz, Victor
1986 Another Fiscal Practice in the Ancient Near East: 2 Kings 12:5-17 and a Letter to Esarhaddon (*LAS* 277). *Journal of Near Eastern Studies* 45:289-294.
1992 *I Have Built You an Exalted House*. Journal for the Study of the Old Testament Supplement Series 115. Sheffield: Sheffield Academic.

Japhet, Sara
1993 *I and II Chronicles*. Louisville: Westminster/John Knox.

Johnston, Philip S.
2005 Sheol. P. 227 in *The New Interpreter's Dictionary of the Bible*, vol. 5. Nashville: Abingdon.

Jones, Brian C.
2009 Sela. P. 157 in *The New Interpreter's Dictionary of the Bible*, vol. 5. Nashville: Abingdon.

Jones, Gwilym H.
1984 *1 and 2 Kings*. 2 vols. New Century Bible Commentary. Grand Rapids: Eerdmans.

Kahn, Dan'el
2001 The Inscription of Sargon II at Tang-i Var and the Chronology of Dynasty 25. *Orientalia* 70:1-18.

Kaiser, W.
1974 The Blessing of David: Humanity's Charter. Pp. 298-318 in *The Law and the Prophets*. Editor, J. H. Skilton. Philadelphia: Presbyterian & Reformed.
1978 *Toward an Old Testament Theology*. Grand Rapids: Zondervan.

Katzenstein, H. Jacob
1955 Who Were the Parents of Athaliah? *Israel Exploration Journal* 5:194–197.
1997 *The History of Tyre.* 2nd ed. Beer Sheva, Israel: Ben-Gurion.

Kelle, Brad E.
2006 Ben-Hadad. Pp. 426–428 in *The New Interpreter's Dictionary of the Bible,* vol. 1. Nashville: Abingdon.

Kim, Uriah
2006 Ashurbanipal, Assurbanipal. P. 302 in *The New Interpreter's Dictionary of the Bible,* vol. 1. Nashville: Abingdon.
2008a Jehoiachin. Pp. 207–208 in *The New Interpreter's Dictionary of the Bible,* vol. 3. Nashville: Abingdon.
2008b Jehoiakim. Pp. 208–209 in *The New Interpreter's Dictionary of the Bible,* vol. 3. Nashville: Abingdon.

Kitchen, K. A.
1966 *Ancient Orient and Old Testament.* Downers Grove, IL: InterVarsity.
1977 *The Bible in Its World.* Downers Grove, IL: InterVarsity.
1989 Two Notes on the Subsidiary Rooms of Solomon's Temple. *Eretz Israel* 20:107*–112*.
1996 *The Third Intermediate Period in Egypt (1100–650 B.C.).* 2nd ed. Oxford: Aris & Phillips.
1997 Sheba and Arabia. Pp. 126–153 in *The Age of Solomon.* Leiden: Brill.
2003 *On the Reliability of the Old Testament.* Grand Rapids: Eerdmans.

Kletter, Raz
1991 The Inscribed Weights of the Kingdom of Judah. *Tel Aviv* 18:121–163.
1998 *Economic Keystones: The Weight System of the Kingdom of Judah.* Journal for the Study of the Old Testament Supplement Series 276. Sheffield: Sheffield Academic.
2009 Weights and Measures. Pp. 831–841 in *The New Interpreter's Dictionary of the Bible,* vol. 5. Nashville: Abingdon.

Knoppers, Gary N.
1997 The Vanishing Solomon. *Journal of Biblical Literature* 116:19–44.

Knudtzon, J. A.
1910 *Die El-Amarna-Tafeln.* Vorderasiatische Bibliothek. Leipzig: Hinrichs.

Kuan, Jeffrey Kah–Jin
2007 Hezekiah. Pp. 818–821 in *The New Interpreter's Dictionary of the Bible,* vol. 2. Nashville: Abingdon.

Kugel, James L.
1981 *The Idea of Biblical Poetry.* New Haven, CT: Yale University Press.

Labuschagne, C. J.
1965 Did Elisha Deliberately Lie? A Note on II Kings 8:10. *Zeitschrift für die alttestamentliche Wissenschaft* 77:327–328.

Laffey, Alice L.
1989 1 and 2 Kings. Pp. 296–320 in *The Collegeville Bible Commentary.* Collegeville, MN: Liturgical.

Lambdin, Thomas O.
1971 *Introduction to Biblical Hebrew.* New York: Charles Scribner's Sons.

Lawlor, John I.
2009 Zair. P. 954 in *The New Interpreter's Dictionary of the Bible,* vol. 5. Nashville: Abingdon.

Leithart, Peter J.
2005 Counterfeit Davids: Davidic Restoration and the Architecture of 1–2 Kings. *Tyndale Bulletin* 56:2:19–33.
2006 *1 & 2 Kings.* Brazos Theological Commentary on the Bible. Grand Rapids: Baker.

Leuchter, Mark
2006 *Josiah's Reform and Jeremiah's Scroll: Historical Calamity and Prophetic Response.* Hebrew Bible Monographs 6. Sheffield: Sheffield Phoenix.

Lewis, C. S.
1966 *Letters of C. S. Lewis.* Editor, W. H. Lewis. New York: Harcourt Brace Jovanovich.

Lewis, Theodore J.
1998 Divine Images and Aniconism in Ancient Israel. *Journal of the American Oriental Society* 118:36–53.

Linville, James
1997 Rethinking the "Exilic" Book of Kings. *Journal for the Study of the Old Testament* 75:21–42.

Lipiński, E.
1988 Royal and State Scribes in Ancient Jerusalem. Pp. 157-164 in *Congress Volume: Jerusalem, 1986.*
    Supplements to Vetus Testamentum 40. Leiden: Brill.

Lipschits, Oded
2005 *The Fall and Rise of Jerusalem.* Winona Lake, IN: Eisenbrauns.

Lipschits, Oded, et al.
2010 Royal Judahite Jar Handles: Reconsidering the Chronology of the *lmlk* Stamp Impressions.
    Tel Aviv 37:3-32.

Long, Burke O.
1984 *1 Kings.* Forms of the Old Testament Literature, vol. 9. Grand Rapids: Eerdmans.

1991 *2 Kings.* Forms of the Old Testament Literature, vol. 10. Grand Rapids: Eerdmans.

Longman, Tremper, III
2006 *Song of Songs* in *Job, Ecclesiastes, Song of Songs.* Cornerstone Biblical Commentary, vol. 6.
    Editor, Philip W. Comfort. Carol Stream, IL: Tyndale House.

Longman, Tremper, III, and Daniel G. Reid
1995 *God Is a Warrior.* Grand Rapids: Zondervan.

Lundbom, Jack R.
1986 Baruch, Seraiah, and Expanded Colophons in the Book of Jeremiah. *Journal for the Study of the
    Old Testament* 36:89-114.

1999 *Jeremiah 1–20.* Anchor Bible 21A. New York: Doubleday.

Machinist, Peter
1983 Assyria and Its Image in the First Isaiah. *Journal of the American Oriental Society* 103:719-737.

Malamat, Abraham
1975 The Twilight of Judah: In the Egyptian-Babylonian Maelstrom. Pp. 123-145 in *Congress Volume:
    Edinburgh 1974.* Supplements to Vetus Testamentum 28. Leiden: Brill.

Mariottini, Claude
2009a Menahem. Pp. 40-41 in *The New Interpreter's Dictionary of the Bible,* vol. 4. Nashville: Abingdon.

2009b Pekah. Pp. 426-427 in *The New Interpreter's Dictionary of the Bible,* vol. 4. Nashville: Abingdon.

2009c Zedekiah. Pp. 971-973 in *The New Interpreter's Dictionary of the Bible,* vol. 5. Nashville: Abingdon.

Mastin, B. A.
1979 Was the *Šālîš* the Third Man in the Chariot? Pp. 125-154 in *Studies in the Historical Books of the
    Old Testament.* Supplements to Vetus Testamentum 30. Leiden: Brill.

McCane, Byron
2006 Burial. Pp. 509-510 in *The New Interpreter's Dictionary of the Bible,* vol. 1. Nashville: Abingdon.

McCarter, P. Kyle, Jr.
1980 *I Samuel.* Anchor Bible 8. Garden City, NY: Doubleday.

1001 *II Samuel.* Anchor Bible 9. Garden City, NY: Doubleday.

McComiskey, Thomas E.
1992 Hosea. Pp. 1-237 in *The Minor Prophets,* vol. 1. Grand Rapids: Baker.

McKenzie, Steven L.
1984 *The Chronicler's Use of the Deuteronomistic History.* Harvard Semitic Monographs 33. Atlanta:
    Scholars.

1991 *The Trouble with Kings.* Supplements to Vetus Testamentum 42. Leiden: Brill.

2008 Kings, First and Second Books of. Pp. 523-532 in *The New Interpreter's Dictionary of the Bible,* vol. 3.
    Nashville: Abingdon.

2009 Uzziah. Pp. 722-724 in *The New Interpreter's Dictionary of the Bible,* vol. 5. Nashville: Abingdon.

McMurray, Heather R.
2006 Amon. P. 133 in *The New Interpreter's Dictionary of the Bible,* vol. 1. Nashville: Abingdon.

Mettinger, Tryggve N. D.
1995 *No Graven Image? Israelite Aniconism in Its Ancient Near Eastern Context.* Stockholm:
    Almqvist & Wiksell.

Meyers, Carol
1998 Kinship and Kingship: The Early Monarchy. Pp. 221-271 in *The Oxford History of the Biblical World.*
    New York: Oxford University Press.

Meyers, Carol L., and Eric M. Meyers
1993 *Zechariah 9–14.* Anchor Bible 25C. New York: Doubleday.

Millard, Alan
1989 The Doorways of Solomon's Temple. *Eretz Israel* 20:134*-139*.

1997 King Solomon in His Ancient Context. Pp. 30-53 in *The Age of Solomon.* Leiden: Brill.

Montgomery, James A.
1951 *A Critical and Exegetical Commentary on the Books of Kings.* International Critical Commentary. Edinburgh: T&T Clark.

Moore, Carey A.
1971 *Esther.* Anchor Bible 7B. Garden City, NY: Doubleday.

Moran, William L.
1992 *The Amarna Letters.* Baltimore: Johns Hopkins University Press.

Morkot, Robert G.
2000 *The Black Pharaohs: Egypt's Nubian Rulers.* London: Rubicon.

Mulder, Martin J.
1998 *1 Kings.* Historical Commentary on the Old Testament. Leuven, Belgium: Peeters.

Na'aman, Nadav
1979 Sennacherib's Campaign to Judah and the Date of the *LMLK* Stamps. *Vetus Testamentum* 29:61-86.

1993 Azariah of Judah and Jeroboam II of Israel. *Vetus Testamentum* 43:227-234.

2007 When and How Did Jerusalem Become a Great City? The Rise of Jerusalem as Judah's Premier City in the Eighth–Seventh Centuries B.C.E. *Bulletin of the American Schools of Oriental Research* 347:21-56.

Nelson, Richard D.
1981a *The Double Redaction of the Deuteronomistic History.* Journal for the Study of the Old Testament Supplement Series 18. Sheffield: Journal for the Study of the Old Testament Press.

1981b Josiah in the Book of Joshua. *Journal of Biblical Literature* 100:531-540.

1987 *First and Second Kings.* Interpretation. Atlanta: John Knox.

Nicholson, E. W.
1967 *Deuteronomy and Tradition.* Philadelphia: Fortress.

Noth, Martin
1981 *The Deuteronomistic History.* Journal for the Study of the Old Testament Supplement Series 15. Sheffield: Journal for the Study of the Old Testament Press.

Oates, David
1963 The Excavations at Nimrud (Kalḫu), 1962. *Iraq* 25:6-37.

Oded, B.
1972 The Historical Background of the Syro-Ephraimite War Reconsidered. *The Catholic Biblical Quarterly* 34:153-165.

Olyan, Saul
1984 *Hăšālôm*: Some Literary Considerations of 2 Kings 9. *The Catholic Biblical Quarterly* 46:652-668.

Oswalt, John N.
1986 *The Book of Isaiah, Chapters 1–39.* Grand Rapids: Eerdmans.

Page, Stephanie
1968 A Stela of Adad-nirari III and Nergal-ereš from Tell al Rimah. *Iraq* 30:139-153.

Paul, Shalom M.
1969 Sargon's Administrative Diction in II Kings 17:27. *Journal of Biblical Literature* 88:73-74.

Peckham, Brian
1985 *The Composition of the Deuteronomistic History.* Harvard Semitic Monographs 35. Atlanta: Scholars.

Penner, Ken M.
2009 Nimshi. P. 275 in *The New Interpreter's Dictionary of the Bible,* vol. 4. Nashville: Abingdon.

Person, Raymond F., Jr.
1993 *Second Zechariah and the Deuteronomic School.* Journal for the Study of the Old Testament Supplement Series 167. Sheffield: Journal for the Study of the Old Testament Press.

2002 *The Deuteronomic School: History, Social Setting, and Literature.* Studies in Biblical Literature 2. Atlanta: Society of Biblical Literature.

Pitard, Wayne T.
1987 *Ancient Damascus*. Winona Lake, IN: Eisenbrauns.

Pratico, Gary D.
1985 Nelson Glueck's 1938–1940 Excavations at Tell el-Kheleifeh: A Reappraisal. *Bulletin of the American Schools of Oriental Research* 259:1-32.

Pritchard, James B.
1969 *Supplementary Texts and Pictures*. Princeton: Princeton University Press.

Propp, William C.
2006 *Exodus 19–40*. Anchor Bible 2A. New York: Doubleday.

Provan, Iain
1995 *1 and 2 Kings*. New International Biblical Commentary. Peabody, MA: Hendrickson.

Rad, Gerhard von
1953 *Studies in Deuteronomy*. London: SCM.

1962 *Old Testament Theology*, vol. 1. New York: Harper & Row.

1965 *Old Testament Theology*, vol. 2. New York: Harper & Row.

Rahlfs, Alfred
1935 *Septuaginta: id est Vetus Testamentum graece iuxta LXX interpretes*. 2 vols. Stuttgart: Deutsche Bibelstiftung.

Ramm, Bernard
1954 *The Christian View of Science and Scripture*. Grand Rapids: Eerdmans.

Redford, Donald B.
1992 *Egypt, Canaan, and Israel in Ancient Times*. Princeton: Princeton University Press.

Rendsburg, Gary A.
2002 *Israelian Hebrew in the Book of Kings*. Occasional Publications of the Department of Near Eastern Studies and the Program of Jewish Studies, Cornell University 5. Bethesda, MD: CDL.

Roberts, J. J. M.
2009 Nebuchadnezzar, Nebuchadrezzar. Pp. 245-247 in *The New Interpreter's Dictionary of the Bible*, vol. 4. Nashville: Abingdon.

Robinson, H. Wheeler
1946 *Inspiration and Revelation in the Old Testament*. Oxford: Clarendon.

Rowley, H. H.
1962 Hezekiah's Reform and Rebellion. *Bulletin of the John Rylands Library* 44:395-431.

1963 *From Moses to Qumran: Studies in the Old Testament*. New York: Association Press.

Scott, R. B. Y.
1965 *Proverbs, Ecclesiastes*. Anchor Bible 18. Garden City, NY: Doubleday.

Scurlock, Joann
2009 Nisroch. P. 277 in *The New Interpreter's Dictionary of the Bible*, vol. 4. Nashville: Abingdon.

Segal, Alan F.
2006 Afterlife. Pp. 65-68 in *The New Interpreter's Dictionary of the Bible*, vol. 1. Nashville: Abingdon.

Seow, Choon-Leong
1999 The First and Second Books of Kings. Pp. 3-295 in *The New Interpreter's Bible*, vol. 3. Nashville: Abingdon.

Shenkel, James Donald
1968 *Chronology and Recensional Development in the Greek Text of Kings*. Harvard Semitic Monographs 1. Cambridge, MA: Harvard University Press.

Shiloh, Yigal
1977 The Proto-Aeolic Capital—the Israelite "Timorah" (Palmette) Capital. *Palestine Exploration Quarterly* 109:39-52.

Smith, Mark S.
1990 *The Early History of God*. San Francisco: Harper & Row.

1991 *The Origins and Development of the Waw-consecutive: Northwest Semitic Evidence from Ugarit to Qumran*. Harvard Semitic Studies 39. Atlanta: Scholars.

Solomon, Ann M. Vater
1985 Fable and Jehoash's Fable of the Thistle and the Cedar. Pp. 114-132, 150-153 in *Saga, Legend, Tale, Novella, Fable.* Journal for the Study of the Old Testament Supplement Series 35. Sheffield: Journal for the Study of the Old Testament Press.

Solvang, Elna K.
2006 Bathsheba. Pp. 409-410 in *The New Interpreter's Dictionary of the Bible,* vol. 1. Nashville: Abingdon.

Spalinger, Anthony
1973 The Year 712 B.C. and Its Implications for Egyptian History. *Journal of the American Research Center in Egypt* 10:95-101.

1978 The Foreign Policy of Egypt Preceding the Assyrian Conquest. *Chronique d'Égypt* 53:22-47.

Speiser, E. A.
1964 *Genesis.* Anchor Bible 1. New York: Doubleday.

Stager, Lawrence E.
1982 The Archaeology of the East Slope of Jerusalem and the Terraces of the Kidron. *Journal of Near Eastern Studies* 41:111-121.

Stith, D. Matthew
2008 Jehu. Pp. 212-214 in *The New Interpreter's Dictionary of the Bible,* vol. 3. Nashville: Abingdon.

Stuart, Douglas
1984 *Old Testament Exegesis.* 2nd ed. Philadelphia: Westminster.

1987 *Hosea-Jonah.* Word Biblical Commentary 31. Waco: Word.

Sukenik, E. L.
1931 Funerary Tablet of Uzziah, King of Judah. *Palestine Exploration Quarterly* 63:217-220, plates I and II.

Sweeney, Marvin
2001 *King Josiah of Judah: The Lost Messiah of Israel.* Oxford: Oxford University Press.

2007 *I & II Kings.* The Old Testament Library. Louisville: Westminster John Knox.

Swete, Henry Barclay
1914 *An Introduction to the Old Testament in Greek.* Cambridge: Cambridge University Press.

Tadmor, H.
1979 The Chronology of the First Temple Period: A Presentation and Evaluation of the Sources. Pp. 44-60, 318-320 in *The World History of the Jewish People, First Series: Ancient Times. Vol. 4, Part 1: The Age of the Monarchies: Political History.* Editor, Abraham Malamat. Jerusalem: Massada.

Tawil, Hayim
1982 The Historicity of 2 Kings 19:24 (= Isaiah 37:25): The Problem of *Ye'ōrê Māṣôr. Journal of Near Eastern Studies* 41:195-206.

Tetley, M. Christine
2005 *The Reconstructed Chronology of the Divided Kingdom.* Winona Lake, IN: Eisenbrauns.

Thiele, Edwin R.
1951 *The Mysterious Numbers of the Hebrew Kings.* 1st ed. Chicago: University of Chicago Press.

1974 Coregencies and Overlapping Reigns among the Hebrew Kings. *Journal of Biblical Literature* 93:174-200.

1983 *The Mysterious Numbers of the Hebrew Kings.* 3rd ed. Grand Rapids: Zondervan.

Thompson, J. A.
1980 *The Book of Jeremiah.* New International Commentary on the Old Testament. Grand Rapids: Eerdmans.

Tigay, Jeffrey H.
1996 *Deuteronomy.* The JPS Torah Commentary. Philadelphia: JPS.

Toorn, Karel van der
2006 Baal. Pp. 367-369 in *The New Interpreter's Dictionary of the Bible,* vol. 1. Nashville: Abingdon.

Ullendorff, Edward
1963 The Queen of Sheba. *Bulletin of the John Rylands Library* 45:486-504.

Ussishkin, David
1979 The "Camp of the Assyrians" in Jerusalem. *Israel Exploration Journal* 29:137-142.

2008 Lachish. Pp. 555-562 in *The New Interpreter's Dictionary of the Bible,* vol. 3. Nashville: Abingdon.

Vannoy, J. Robert
2009 *1–2 Samuel.* Cornerstone Biblical Commentary, vol. 4a. Editor, Philip W. Comfort. Carol Stream, IL: Tyndale House.

Vaux, Roland de
1965 *Ancient Israel.* New York: McGraw-Hill.

Viviano, Pauline A.
1987 2 Kings 17: A Rhetorical and Form-critical Analysis. *The Catholic Biblical Quarterly* 49:548-559.

Wallace, H. N.
1986 The Oracles against the Israelite Dynasties in 1 and 2 Kings. *Biblica* 67:21-40.

Walsh, Jerome T.
1996 *1 Kings.* Berit Olam. Collegeville, MN: Liturgical.

Waltke, Bruce K., and M. O'Connor
1990 *An Introduction to Biblical Hebrew Syntax.* Winona Lake, IN: Eisenbrauns.

Walton, John H.
2001 *Genesis.* The NIV Application Commentary. Grand Rapids: Zondervan.

Weinfeld, Moshe
1972 *Deuteronomy and the Deuteronomic School.* Oxford: Clarendon.

Wenham, Gordon
1994 *Genesis 16–50.* Word Biblical Commentary 2. Dallas: Word.

Williamson, H. G. M.
1982a *1 and 2 Chronicles.* New Century Bible Commentary. Grand Rapids: Eerdmans.

1982b The Death of Josiah and the Continuing Development of the Deuteronomic History. *Vetus Testamentum* 32:242-248.

1985 *Ezra, Nehemiah.* Word Biblical Commentary 16. Waco: Word.

1996 Hezekiah and the Temple. Pp. 47-52 in *Texts, Temples, and Traditions: A Tribute to Menahem Haran.* Winona Lake, IN: Eisenbrauns.

Wilson, Robert R.
1980 *Prophecy and Society in Ancient Israel.* Philadelphia: Fortress.

Wiseman, Donald J.
1982 "Is It Peace?"—Covenant and Diplomacy. *Vetus Testamentum* 32:311-326.

1985 *Nebuchadrezzar and Babylon.* Oxford: Oxford University Press.

1993 *1 & 2 Kings.* Tyndale Old Testament Commentaries 9. Downers Grove, IL: InterVarsity.

Wolff, Hans Walter
1975 The Kerygma of the Deuteronomic Historical Work. Ch. 5 (pp. 83-100, 141-143) in *The Vitality of Old Testament Traditions* by Walter Brueggemann and Hans Walter Wolff. Atlanta: John Knox.

1977 *Joel and Amos.* Hermeneia. Philadelphia: Fortress.

Würthwein, Ernst
1984 *Die Bücher der Könige: 1.Kön. 17 2.Kön. 25.* Göttingen: Vandenhoeck & Ruprecht.

Yadin, Yigael
1978 The "House of Ba'al" of Ahab and Jezebel in Samaria, and That of Athaliah in Judah. Pp. 127-135 in *Archaeology in the Levant.* Warminster, England: Aris & Phillips.

Yeivin, S.
1974 'Ēdūth. *Israel Exploration Journal* 24:17-20.

Younger, K. Lawson, Jr.
2007a Esarhaddon. Pp. 289-290 in *The New Interpreter's Dictionary of the Bible*, vol. 2. Nashville: Abingdon.

2007b Hoshea. Pp. 900-901 in *The New Interpreter's Dictionary of the Bible*, vol. 2. Nashville: Abingdon.

2009a Sargon. Pp. 110-111 in *The New Interpreter's Dictionary of the Bible*, vol. 5. Nashville: Abingdon.

2009b Sennacherib. Pp. 167-169 in *The New Interpreter's Dictionary of the Bible*, vol. 5. Nashville: Abingdon.

Zohary, Michael
1982 *Plants of the Bible.* Cambridge: Cambridge University Press.

Zuidhof, Albert
1982 King Solomon's Molten Sea and (π). *Biblical Archaeologist* 45:179-184.